THE WORLD of MUSICAL COMEDY

*42nd Street*Photo by Martha Swope

STANLEY GREEN

THE WORLD of MUSICAL COMEDY

The story of the American musical stage as told through the careers of its foremost composers and lyricists

FOURTH EDITION, REVISED AND ENLARGED

DA CAPO PRESS

Library of Congress Cataloging in Publication Data

Green, Stanley
    The world of musical comedy.

    (A Da Capo paperback)
    Reprint. Originally published: San Diego: A. S. Barnes,
1980.
    "Supplemented with author corrections"—P.
    Includes bibliographical references and index.
    1. Musical revue, comedy, etc.—United States.
2. Composers—United States. 3. Librettists—United
States. I. Title.
ML1711.G74   1984   782.81′0973   83-26340
ISBN 0-306-80207-4 (pbk.)

This Da Capo Press paperback edition of *The World of Musical Comedy*
is an unabridged republication of the fourth edition published in
San Diego in 1980, here supplemented with author corrections.
It is reprinted by arrangement with A. S. Barnes & Co., Inc.

7 8 9 10

Published by Da Capo Press, Inc.

A member of the Perseus Books Group

For my mother and father,
who first introduced me to
the world of musical comedy

CONTENTS

FOREWORD

To The First Edition

by Deems Taylor

STRICTLY SPEAKING, a book such as this one—like the guest of honor at a banquet—needs no introduction. Today, the American musical is admittedly without an equal anywhere in the world, although as recently as during the Gay Nineties it was the Viennese operetta that ruled the entertainment world. The evolution of this strictly American art form has taken place within the space of one lifetime—mine.

I witnessed many of the events chronicled in this book and knew many of the men who made these events possible. Victor Herbert encouraged me to study music and become a composer when he heard a college show that I had written; my first professional work was a show that was actually produced on Broadway by Charles Dillingham; I distinguished myself by delivering a tribute to the music of Jerome Kern over C.B.S. in 1941 in which I stated that I had long been a devoted "Fern can"; and not too long ago I wrote one of the ever-growing lists of biographies of Richard Rodgers and Oscar Hammerstein II. Under these circumstances, I will have to leave the facts, biographical sketches, and critical esti-

mates to the book itself and make this foreword a completely personal one.

One thing I will say before I dive into my memories, and that is that the people you are going to read about are musicians and deserve to be taken seriously as artists. The creators of musical comedy in America are a body of men (and some women) who have consistently refused to do less than the best that was in them. Anyone who works in a popular medium is constantly faced with pressures from his investors not to experiment, not to innovate; to write down, to compromise, and to be safe. If the creators of musical comedy had allowed themselves to have this sort of view of what would be successful, there would be no American musicals today—we would still be listening to Viennese operettas.

I remember an evening after World War I when I was one of a group of delighted guests at a party given by Neysa McMein, the illustrator. The reason for our delight was another guest, a young man who enjoyed the double distinction of having written some Yale football songs and of having actually joined the Foreign Legion. He played and sang some of his latest songs (one, I remember, was entitled "The Bandit Band") which received loud acclaim. We agreed that they were tuneful and absolutely charming. But many of us, myself among them, also agreed that his tunes were far too tricky and his lyrics much too sophisticated ever to have any popular success. The young guest of honor denied both accusations, and he was right. His name was Cole Porter.

There was an afternoon in the thirties when I was equally dubious and equally wrong. George Gershwin had telephoned to suggest that we have lunch together and then go to the ball game. During lunch he remarked that he was just finishing an opera about Negro life in the South.

"A *what*?" I said.

"You heard me."

So back to his house we went, and he played me all four hours of the score of *Porgy and Bess*. He was right. It *was* an opera—and we never did get to the ball game.

My acquaintance with musical comedy began long, long ago, when I used to spend part of my summer vacations with my Philadelphia cousins. Among the season's attractions were the concerts in Willow Grove Park given by Victor Herbert and his orchestra. There were four of these every day, two in the afternoon and two in the evening.

One cousin and myself were Herbert idolaters, and we wanted to hear all four concerts. But the question of money reared its ugly head. Each of us was given fifty cents to cover all expenses. Trolley car fare to Willow Grove and return was thirty cents. Admission to the park was another fifteen. This left us exactly five cents for dinner, if we wanted to stay for the evening. We did, naturally, so eventually we solved the problem. We would each buy five cents' worth of the cheapest and most villainous candy we could find. This, when eaten, would render the thought of any dinner abhorrent,

whereat (slightly green but smiling bravely) we would happily sit through the two evening concerts, hearing excerpts from such Herbert scores as *The Wizard of the Nile*, *The Idol's Eye*, and his latest, *Babes in Toyland*.

Incidentally, in after years, Victor Herbert told me that if it were physically possible, he made it a point to compose at least one tune every day. I doubt if any other composer has ever equalled that record.

One important event that this book neglects to mention is the production in 1911 of a musical comedy called *The Echo*, for which I wrote the original score. In those bad old days, it was the custom for numbers to be interpolated in musical productions at the producer's whim. *The Echo* was produced by Charles Dillingham, who promptly proceeded to hire all the dancers in the world to perform in it, all of whom brought their own music. To liven up the proceedings further, Mr. Dillingham commissioned several young song writers to write individual songs which were then scattered through the production. By the time the show opened, only three of my original numbers were left in the score (although an over-optimistic publisher had already published four).

One of the young writers who had a song in *The Echo* was Jerome Kern, who was to become one of my closest friends. On opening night, legend has it, Kern was standing nervously at the back of the theatre, where he was seen by Bruce Edwards, Dillingham's manager.

"I hope your show goes well tonight, old man," Bruce said kindly to Kern.

Fourteen men said, "Thanks."

Shortly before his death in 1945, Jerry Kern came East for the rehearsals of the revival of *Show Boat*. While he was there, he was able to attend the formal meeting of the National Institute of Arts and Letters at which he was made officially a member, and thereby became the second popular composer ever to be elected to that honorary body. The only musical comedy composer to gain that honor before him was Victor Herbert, and there has been only one since—Richard Rodgers.

But popular composers have had their fans among so-called "serious" musicians nonetheless. One of the most ardent admirers of Vincent Youmans' music was Sergei Rachmaninoff, who never tired of playing his scores. You don't have to be told that Youmans was an equally ardent admirer of Rachmaninoff's music!

He was a passionate devotee of orchestral music, and the larger the orchestra the better. He thought nothing of hiring forty musicians for one of his revues (the usual allotment is twenty-eight). On the other hand, he was deeply suspicious of librettists and lyric writers—doubtless because he had suffered so much at the hands of hack collaborators. All this led to his last folly, a revue without a book. It was a potpourri of songs, (concert) dances, and pantomimes. I played a part in it, to the extent that a four-foot dummy of myself lolled against the proscenium arch doing a sort of narration job (he finally did consent to have a book, and a holy terror it was, too).

I went down to Baltimore to attend the matinee following the opening, and arrived at the theater about halfway through the performance. The book, I discovered, had been junked overnight, but what was left was pretty awful. People were stumping indignantly up the aisles, on their way to demand their money back, to all of which Youmans paid not the slightest attention. I caught his eye, and he beckoned me to stand beside him. He was radiant. "You hear that?" he murmured. "Fifty men in the orchestra pit!"

That disaster cost his backers one hundred and ninety thousand dollars.

The ranks are thinning. Of the composers who flourished during the tens-twenties-thirties-forties, very few are left. Most of them died at ages that we would consider merely middle-aged. Of the great ones, the most untimely departure was that of George Gershwin, who died at thirty-eight. Vincent Youmans died at forty-seven, Jerome Kern at sixty, and Victor Herbert and Oscar Hammerstein II at sixty-five. As this book goes to press (1960), perhaps the oldest survivor of the formative years of musical comedy is Rudolf Friml, at eighty-one.

Friml, by the way, has a system of composing that is, I think, unique. As he described it to me, he first turns on a tape recorder; then, going to the piano, he improvises for an hour. After this he listens to the playback and jots down whatever tunes he might be able to use.

Another system of composing is attributed to Irving Berlin. He is so unbelievably prolific, both as to words and music, that a rumor was started in Tin Pan Alley by jealous composers to the effect that Berlin's songs are all written by "a little colored boy" who plays them to him. I didn't know that Irving knew this story until one day, several years ago, when I was going through the MGM studios with him. As we entered his office he waved a careless hand toward an ancient upright piano that huddled in one corner, observing, "That's where the little colored boy lives."

Irving Berlin is a man whose achievement is solidly based on an appraisal of what he does and does not know. He is anything but conceited. One of the eagerly awaited events in the musical New York of the twenties was Walter Damrosch's annual New Year's Day party, to which one and all flocked, there to imbibe wassail and other beverages. You rang the bell of the Damrosch home, the front door opened a crack, revealing a hand holding a glass, and a voice said, "Drink this." You did, the door opened, you entered, and you spent a happy afternoon. It was not, incidentally, a rowdy afternoon.

At one of these, Berlin was among the guests. I heard Damrosch say, "Irving, with your talent you ought to study music seriously."

"Doctor Damrosch," said the composer, "I have a very slender talent; and if I were to study music I might end up by despising my own stuff."

"You are quite right," said Damrosch.

I have written so much about Richard Rodgers that there is little left for me to say here about him, except that he is a dear friend. But I can't write about musical comedy without at least mentioning one of our contemporary giants. Rodgers is a compartmentalist. When he is working on a show, he works literally day and night. But otherwise, he doesn't go near the piano, and never whiles away an evening playing for friends. (In this respect he is totally unlike George Gershwin, about whom Oscar Levant once said, "An evening with Gershwin is a Gershwin evening.")

It has been a privilege for me to know, and sometimes to work with, all these men. After all, there have only been three forms of musical stage entertainment in the history of Western culture that in their day have been huge money-makers and also perfected art forms. These three are Italian grand opera, the Viennese operetta, and the American musical comedy. We can be proud that one of these belongs to us.

PREFACE

THIS IS THE FOURTH expanded and revised edition of a book that was first published in 1960. Though there are certain changes in the early part of the text, the main alterations involve chapters 22 to 31. Here the reader will find seven chapters devoted to eleven writers whose output and influence now deserve greater attention than had previously been warranted, as well as three chapters covering twenty-one others, primarily those who have emerged since the last edition was published. In addition, the Appendix has been extensively rewritten, not only to accommodate new entries but also to include the latest available recordings of all the scores.

The World of Musical Comedy covers the vast, vaguely defined area between opera and vaudeville and, at times, incorporates elements of both. "Musical comedy" is, of course, a generic term that refers to the various forms of entertainment included under the more formal designation of "American musical theatre." It covers operetta, comic opera, musical play (now frequently merely called "musical"), musical comedy itself, revue, and, in the past, spectacle or ex-

travaganza. These forms are difficult to define precisely, as they usually overlap. However, in general, the terms operetta, comic opera, and musical play denote a greater dependence on music in the telling of a story than does musical comedy. Revue and spectacle are closest to vaudeville, as they usually consist of unrelated songs, dances, and sketches.

The growth of the American musical theatre has been in the development of all its component parts. No show can succeed today on the quality of its music and lyrics alone; they must be part of the overall fabric of the production. And that fabric is made up of all the theatrical arts that have evolved through the years.

Because music is the one essential ingredient of this form of entertainment, I have chosen to tell the story of *The World of Musical Comedy* through the lives and careers of its most significant composers and lyricists. Of all the arts that are mobilized in this field, music has the most consistency. A good song is a good song whether it was written in 1900 or yesterday, since it has the power to affect people's emotions long after the particular work for which it was composed has been forgotten. Indeed, it is because of their music that shows first presented during the early years of this century can still be revived; even the most recent attractions are known to people throughout the world primarily through the appeal of their songs.

The cooperation of many people in the preparation of all editions of *The World of Musical Comedy* has been both heartening and indispensable. I am especially indebted to four alert and knowledgeable individuals, the late Charles Gaynor, Irma Hunt, Frank Jacobs, and Alfred Simon, for their painstaking reading of the original manuscript. In addition to the writers discussed in the book who responded readily to my requests for information, assistance has been given by Edward N. Waters, Helmy Kresa, Hilda Schneider, Tom Weatherly, Irving Brown, Edward Cole, the late Richard Maney, Dan Langan, Chester Kopaz, Liz Dribben, Ken Harper, and James J. Fuld. The staff of the Theatre Collection of the New York Public Library, particularly Paul Myers and William Anderson, was also most cooperative.

For help in obtaining photographs, my appreciation goes to Richard Frohlich of ASCAP, Russell Sanjek of BMI, the CBS Press Department, the Lynn Farnol Group, Edward Jablonski, Grace McCabe, John Springer, the late Jay Culver of Culver Pictures, Harry Collins of Brown Brothers, Otis Guernsey Jr., Vivien Friedman of Chappell Music, Capitol Records, David Powers, Louis Botto, Joshua Ellis, Henry Lehrman, Sol Jacobson, Lewis Harmon, Mary Bryant, Bob Ullman, Merle Debuskey, Bill Schelble, Sandy Manley, Betty Lee Hunt, Bill Evans, and Robert Ganshaw.

Most important, to my wife, Kay, my gratitude is boundless.

STANLEY GREEN

THE WORLD of MUSICAL COMEDY

CHAPTER ONE

PROLOGUE

ALTHOUGH THERE WERE many earlier examples of dramas interspersed with music and dancing, *The Black Crook*, in 1866, was the first truly successful venture in America to combine the two forms of entertainment. The distinction, however, was achieved somewhat by accident. A French ballet company had been signed to appear at the Academy of Music in New York City, but, before it arrived, the theatre burned down. At about the same time, *The Black Crook*, an incredibly ridiculous melodrama loosely based on the *Faust* legend, was being prepared for presentation at Niblo's Garden. As the play seemed to have little chance of succeeding without some added attraction to lure the public, the producer hired the ballet company to perform in those sequences that could utilize the services of dancing demons and spirits. The grafting may have been crude (the opening night performance lasted from 7:45 P.M. to 1:15 A.M.), but the sight of one hundred bare-limbed dancers proved to be irresistible to post-Civil War audiences. *The Black Crook* ran for sixteen months, was revived almost continually, and toured the United States for more than forty years.

Such a phenomenal success encouraged others to present similar attractions. These early attempts, however, bore little resemblance to the musical theatre as we know it today; musical interludes were either forcibly inserted into dramatic sequences or performed between scenes. Moreover, the music was usually gathered from many different sources, though *Evangeline*, in 1874, did have all of its songs composed by one man, Edward E. Rice. Many of the productions of the late 1800's relied heavily on spectacular scenic effects. The leaders in this field were the Kiralfy brothers, whose *Around the World in Eighty Days* and *Excelsior* became successful because of their dazzling settings rather than the attractiveness of their melodies. *Excelsior*, presented in 1883, was the first production to feature electric lighting, an innovation that required the personal supervision of Thomas A. Edison.

During this period, many European operettas were being imported and found a large following. At the same time, however, American writers were beginning to find new and native models for characters in their plots. In 1879, Ned Harrigan and Tony Hart introduced recent immigrant types in their series of shows about the rowdy Mulligan Guards. Soon afterward, Charles Hoyt discovered the great appeal of various regional characters. Hoyt's biggest success, *A Trip to China-town*, featured three remarkably durable songs: "The Bowery," with music by Percy Gaunt, "Reuben and Cynthia," which Gaunt and Hoyt adapted from the previously written "Reuben and Rachel," and the interpolated "After the Ball," by Charles K. Harris.

Away from the "legitimate theatre," Tony Pastor's Music Hall, which had opened on the Bowery during the Civil War, was the nation's leading variety theatre when it moved uptown to 14th Street in 1881. Pastor's type of entertainment soon led to vaudeville and, eventually, the Broadway revue.

The twentieth century began with Victor Herbert and George M. Cohan as the leading American figures in the musical theatre. In the second decade, despite many foreign operettas imported after the success of Franz Lehár's *The Merry Widow*, Guy Bolton, P. G. Wodehouse, and Jerome Kern achieved a wide following with their intimate, well-constructed Princess Theatre musicals.

The 1920's introduced such major talents as George and Ira Gershwin, Oscar Hammerstein II, Vincent Youmans, Rodgers and Hart, and Cole Porter. Nevertheless, it was not a period distinguished by many changes in the *structure* of the musical comedy theatre. Of all the musicals written and produced during that decade, only *Show Boat* was able to offer an adult libretto combined with superior music and lyrics.

The Thirties were years of experimentation. *Strike Up the Band* introduced political satire. In Kern's and Otto Harbach's straightforward love story, *The Cat and the Fiddle*, the music and plot were indispensable to each other. The

following year, Kern and Hammerstein accomplished the same thing with *Music in the Air*. The "folk-opera" *Porgy and Bess* was the most ambitious creation of the decade; it still remains the most universally acclaimed operatic work by an American composer. The plot of *On Your Toes* was the first to have integrated ballet sequences. *Knickerbocker Holiday* made a genuine attempt to fuse a philosophical book with songs pertinent to the play's action.

The librettos of the Forties continued to show maturity. *Cabin in the Sky* made imaginative use of Negro folklore. *Lady in the Dark* probed the subconscious with more daring than was customary even in the nonmusical theatre. An unsavory character was the hero of *Pal Joey*. The most impressive work of the decade was *Oklahoma!*, the first Rodgers and Hammerstein collaboration, which artfully blended libretto, score, and dances. Its tremendous success encouraged other writers to risk unusual themes. *Bloomer Girl* was concerned with equal rights during the Civil War period. *Street Scene* took a compassionate view of the inhabitants of a New York tenement. *Finian's Rainbow* blended Irish whimsy with the sad plight of southern sharecroppers. *Brigadoon* related a tender, evocative Scottish legend. Even the writers of more traditional musical comedies kept up with the trend. Irving Berlin's *Annie Get Your Gun* and Cole Porter's *Kiss Me, Kate* were entertaining, adult stories with music and lyrics that perfectly complemented their subject matter. The decade ended with *South Pacific*, among the most universally popular of all Rodgers and Hammerstein's works.

In the Fifties and Sixties, there was an even greater dependence on themes of substance. Marcel Pagnol, Sidney Howard, John Steinbeck, Bernard Shaw, Voltaire, Eugene O'Neill (twice), Jane Austen, Edmond Rostand, T. H. White, Thornton Wilder, Sholom Aleichem, Clifford Odets, Cervantes, and Christopher Isherwood all turned up as progenitors of some of the decades' more ambitious musicals. This was the period that also saw the emergence of the director-librettist and the director-choreographer. George Abbott* and Joshua Logan had been writing and staging musicals for many years, but it was not until the Fifties that they became such dominant double-duty talents. Abbott's dual contributions to *The Pajama Game, Damn Yankees, New Girl in Town* and *Fiorello!*, and Logan's to *South Pacific, Wish You Were Here* and *Fanny* all helped achieve the goal of unified productions. Certainly the same is true of director-librettist Abe Burrows, whose biggest successes in the two areas have been *Can-Can* and *How to Succeed in Business Without Really Trying*. And while they received no credit for writing, both George S. Kaufman, director of *Guys and Dolls*, and Moss Hart, director of *My Fair Lady* and *Camelot*, could call upon their respective experience as seasoned librettists to add greater theatrical perspective to their work.

George Balanchine and Agnes de Mille were the first modern choreographers to stage entire productions. The trend continues strongly today, based largely upon the assumption that directors schooled in the dance are better equipped to endow a production with a more pronounced homogeneity of style. Among the most successful director-choreographers have been Jerome Robbins (*Bells are Ringing, West Side Story, Gypsy, Fiddler on the Roof*), Michael

Kidd (*Li'l Abner, The Rothschilds*), Bob Fosse (*Sweet Charity, Pippin, Chicago*), Gower Champion (*Bye Bye Birdie, Carnival, Hello, Dolly!, 42nd Street*), Joe Layton (*No Strings, Barnum*), Ron Field (*Applause*), and Michael Bennett (*Follies, A Chorus Line, Ballroom*). In another area of dual responsibility, that of producer-director, those most prominent have been Harold Prince, with *She Loves Me, Cabaret, Company*, and *A Little Night Music*, and Philip Rose, with *Purlie* and *Shenandoah*.

The importance of the relationship between story and song and dance has helped bring about the decline of the once high-riding revue. George Lederer offered the first program of disconnected songs, dances and satirical sketches in 1894. He called his entertainment *The Passing Show*, a title later appropriated by the Shubert brothers for their own series of revues. Florenz Ziegfeld opened the first of his twenty-one annual *Follies* in 1907, and other impressarios were quick to copy the yearly pattern. In the early Twenties, the *Greenwich Village Follies*, Raymond Hitchcock's *Hitchy-Koo* revues, and *George White's Scandals* were popular annual enterprises. They were soon joined by such other periodic pleasures as Irving Berlin's *Music Box Revues*, *Earl Carroll's Vanities*, and the *Grand Street Follies*. By the Thirties, only Ziegfeld, White, and Carroll were offering entertainments of this kind, and then only sporadically.

What the Thirties gave us was a sleeker, more sophisticated revue, with Howard Dietz and Arthur Schwartz setting both the pace and the pattern with *Three's a Crowd, The Band Wagon* and *Flying Colors*. Light-hearted up-to-the-minute satire, led by the Irving Berlin-Moss Hart "newspaper" revue, *As Thousands Cheer*, soon made way for a more socially conscious, if equally entertaining form, best exemplified by Harold Rome's *Pins and Needles*. (At the other extreme were the anything-for-a-laugh

*The important part George Abbott has played in the careers of young writers for the musical stage has earned him the title of "apprentice's sorcerer." Since 1941, he has been the director and frequently the author of the first—or first successful—musicals by the following composers and lyricists: Hugh Martin and Ralph Blane (*Best Foot Forward*); Leonard Bernstein, Betty Comden and Adolph Green (*On the Town*); Jule Styne and Sammy Cahn (*High Button Shoes*); Frank Loesser (*Where's Charley?*); Richard Adler and Jerry Ross (*The Pajama Game*); Bob Merrill (*New Girl in Town*); Mary Rodgers and Marshall Barer (*Once Upon a Mattress*); and Jerry Bock and Sheldon Harnick (*Fiorello!*).

slapstick variety shows such as Olsen and Johnson's *Hellzapoppin* and *The Streets of Paris*.) The last successful year for the conventional revue was 1948, with *Make Mine Manhattan* (Richard Lewine-Arnold Horwitt), *Inside U.S.A.* (Dietz-Schwartz) and *Lend an Ear* (Charles Gaynor). It was no coincidence that 1948 was also the first big year that television began keeping entertainment seekers glued to their home screens. Since variety-type musical shows were then the most popular form of video diversion, it became increasingly important for stage musicals to engage an audience in a coherent story—or at least project a unified theme—in order to lure people away from their living room box. Thus, from an average of fourteen revues offered each season during the Twenties, seven during the Thirties and six during the Forties, there were only three per season in the Fifties and virtually none at all since then.

But wait. The revue *concept* still manages to attract theatregoers to Broadway, but now it must be decked up in a variety of disguises. Certain "theme" musicals of today—*Hair, Company, A Chorus Line, Runaways* come to mind—have taken over the more episodic revue style with its sketches, songs and dances and have given it a fresh and modern application. *Dancin'*, which is nothing else but, successfully limits itself to just one of these ingredients for an entire evening. Then there are the "retrospective" shows, little more than cabaret entertainments, in which anywhere from two to a dozen singers and possibly a *conferencier* traverse the catalogue of an eminent songwriter or team. Their natural habitat has been off Broadway (where thrived Ben Bagley's *Decline and Fall of the Entire World as Seen Through the Eyes of Cole Porter*; *Jacques Brel Is Alive and Well and Living in Paris*; and *Oh, Coward!*), but others, such as *Side by Side by Sondheim* (from London) and *Ain't Misbehavin'* (celebrating Fats Waller)

have also prospered handsomely on Broadway.

Ever since the Thirties, the primary concern of the musical theatre has been to utilize song and dance integrally within the context of a story. Musical numbers can be integrated in three general ways: by creating the proper mood, by revealing character, and by advancing the plot. "Summer Time" from *Porgy and Bess*, "Oh, What a Beautiful Mornin'" from *Oklahoma!*, and "Tradition" from *Fiddler on the Roof* are used mainly for atmosphere, to put the audience in the right frame of mind for the story to follow. Billy Bigelow's "Soliloquy," Don Quixote's "The Impossible Dream," Charity's "Where Am I Going?," and Phyllis Stone's "Could I Leave You?" (from *Follies*) tell us something about the characters and the way they think and feel. "Something Wonderful" in *The King and I*, "The Rain in Spain" in *My Fair Lady*, and "Ice Cream" in *She Loves Me* all come at climactic moments replacing dialogue or action to heighten the dramatic impact. At times a theatre song can serve more than one function. "I've Grown Accustomed to Her Face," for example, not only reveals Henry Higgins' changing attitude toward Eliza but also bridges the action to the final scene.

No matter how tightly constructed a musical may be, however, there is always room enough for at least one number— "Hello, Dolly!" in *Hello, Dolly!*, "Shipoopi" in *The Music Man*, or "N.Y.C." in *Annie*—that is inserted solely as an applause-catching specialty with scant relationship to the plot. Frequently, too, writers can overcome the problem of getting people to break out into song in the midst of a story by dealing with theatrical themes and creating a show within a show—as in *The Cat and the Fiddle, Pal Joey, Gypsy, Funny Girl*, and *Cabaret*. Or by having the entire structure of the musical become an audition for a show, as in *A Chorus Line*.

In achieving a skillful blend of song and story, the modern musical makes use of all the available arts of stagecraft. Curiously, no matter how advanced these arts have become and how well they have been coordinated, the plots of our musicals are still frequently well-tested variations on well-tested formulas, usually adaptations of plays, novels, or films. The most persistent theme has been the Pygmalion legend, or its almost indistinguishable parallel, the Cinderella story. The process through which a poor or unattractive girl is transformed into a glamorous star or radiant beauty and wins the man of her dreams has always been a happy wish-fulfillment with which audiences readily empathize. Variations on the theme have been found in *Mlle. Modiste* (1905), Parisian hat-shop employee to prima donna; *The Firefly* (1912), Italian street singer to prima donna; *Irene* (1919), upholsterer's assistant to society belle; *Sally* (1920), dishwasher to Ziegfeld star; *Peggy-Ann* (1926), small-town drudge to dreamed-of adventuress; *Lady in the Dark* (1941), austere career woman to imagined femme fatale; *Annie Get Your Gun* (1946), illiterate hillbilly to world-famous sharpshooter; *Silk Stockings* (1955), drab Communist to vivacious beauty; *My Fair Lady* (1956), cockney flower seller to belle of the ball; *Gypsy* (1959), talentless vaudeville trouper to burlesque headliner; *Funny Girl* (1964), ugly duckling to Ziegfeld star; *Annie* (1977), orphan to heiress.

Early in December 1979, *Grease* (which closed four months later) slid past long-run record holder *Fiddler on the Roof* to become the longest running production in Broadway history. Before *Oklahoma!* (the longevity champion between July 1946 and July 1961), only two musicals, *Pins and Needles* and *Hellzapoppin*, had run over 800 performances; since *Oklahoma!*, there have been more than forty. In the days of Victor Herbert and George M. Cohan, a Broadway run may have indicated a certain prestige but a show had to do well on the road to succeed financially. The Depression of the Thirties, plus the attraction of inexpensive screen entertainment, greatly reduced the number of touring companies, while improved means of transportation enabled more people to travel to New York to see the productions on Broadway. In recent years, high operating costs have made it essential for shows to remain in New York longer in order to realize a profit.

Certainly, too, musicals today, despite their steep ticket prices, attract a wider audience than the Manhattan-based "carriage trade" that once constituted the bulk of theatregoers. This is, of course, due to their ever-broadening appeal; from the days of *Oklahoma!* and the end of World War II, shows have sought out new audiences—the black, the middle class, the young—that had been largely overlooked when the Broadway musical was earning its reputation for urbanity and sophistication.

Then there is the impact of original-cast recordings. Despite mounting costs, almost all musicals that open on Broadway—and even some that don't—are preserved on records, since it is widely held that hearing songs exactly the way they are performed in the theatre contributes to a desire to see the actual performance. Decca (now MCA) made the first complete original-cast album in 1943 when it recorded the *Oklahoma!* score. For a while, record companies were keenly competitive about securing cast-album rights; even though the aggressiveness has considerably abated the labels still enjoy the prestige and "glamour" of being associated with a hit musical. But there's more to it than that. Because of rapidly diminishing production costs, an original-cast LP can make a greater profit than that realized from box office ticket sales. In 1956, the Columbia Broadcasting System was the sole investor in *My Fair Lady*, thus insuring that Columbia Records, a division of CBS, would get the recording rights. The gamble paid off handsomely: *My Fair Lady* became the largest selling cast album of all time.

Two recent developments bearing on the current musical-theatre scene have been the escalation of ticket prices and the amplification of voices. Top prices for musicals were $1.50 from the late 1880s to the end of the first World War. By the end of the Twenties it was up to $7.70, then down again to $4.40 and $3.85 during the Depression years. Since the Forties, Saturday night orchestra seats have risen from $4.40 for *Oklahoma!*, to $8.05 for *My Fair Lady*, to $9.40 for *Fiddler on the Roof*, to $15 for *Promises, Promises*, to $17.50 for *Chicago*, to $22.50 for *On the Twentieth Century*, to $30 for *Camelot*—and that still may not be the end. Of course, production costs have skyrocketed (*Oklahoma!* was brought in for $80,000, *Ballroom* for over two million), but what gives many cause for alarm is that the cheapest seats—those in the very last row of the balcony—were costing as high as $16 by the middle of 1980. At this writing, the show with the distinction of having the highest-lowest ticket price is *Dancin'*, which, when it opened in March 1978, had priced its *most* expensive weeknight seats at the same figure of $17.50 that only nine months later it would be charging for its *least* expensive Saturday-night seats. Whatever the reasons, musicals may soon be in danger of pricing themselves beyond the reach of all but the expense account set.

As for the theatre's current mania for sonic boosting, many people are simply turned off whenever the microphones are turned on. Using a rationale of dubious authenticity that today's audiences are accustomed to amplified sound, pro-

ducers have strapped body mikes to their actors and installed all sorts of expensive electronic equipment to make sure that voices and musical instruments create an unnatural, unnecessary, and unnerving barrier between performer and audience. While this practice has been defended on the grounds that those in the upper reaches of the balcony need no longer strain their ears, one wonders why the amplification cannot be limited to this specific area, a custom that is followed in many large European houses.

In recent years various terms have been applied to new developments in the musical theatre. For awhile everyone seemed concerned about the "integrated" musical, which aimed for story, song and dance to flow not only harmoniously but seamlessly. More recently, there has been emphasis on the "concept" musical, in which a particular staging device takes precedence over the narrative to achieve the desired effect. And, as we have seen, some musicals don't even need a narrative at all.

It's been demonstrated often enough in the past, but it's always wise to bear in mind that the musical theatre is never fettered by theme, approach, device, subject matter, or trend. As Richard Rodgers wrote in his autobiography, *Musical Stages*, "I am often asked where I think the musical theatre is heading. It's one question I try to dodge because I don't think it's heading anywhere until it's already been there. One night a show opens and suddenly there's a whole new concept. But it isn't the result of a trend; it's because one, two, three, or more people sat down and sweated over an idea that somehow clicked and broke loose. It can be about anything and take off in any direction, and when it works, there's your present and your future."

Barnum *(1980).*
Jim Dale, in the title role, sings "Out There" as he walks the tightrope to Jenny Lind at the end of Act I. (Costumes by Theoni V. Aldredge. Setting by David Mitchell.)

Victor Herbert.

CHAPTER TWO

VICTOR HERBERT

THE EMERGENCE OF Victor Herbert as the first important composer of the American musical stage could not have been anticipated from his background. He was born in Dublin, educated in Germany, performed in symphony orchestras throughout Europe, and did not arrive in the United States until he was twenty-seven. Moreover, his coming to this country had nothing to do with writing musical comedies and operettas. He came here to play the cello in the orchestra of the Metropolitan Opera Company, and his Broadway career did not begin until eight years later.

Born on February 1, 1859, Victor Herbert was the son of Edward and Fanny Lover Herbert. His father died when Victor was a child of two; and during his youth, he was strongly influenced by his maternal grandfather, Samuel Lover, the celebrated Irish artist-novelist-poet-composer.

After his mother's remarriage to a German physician, the boy was taken to live in Stuttgart. Although he was expected to follow in his stepfather's career, he was far more attracted to music than to medicine, and at fifteen began to study the cello. Herbert subsequently joined touring orchestras as a member of the string section and as a soloist. In Vienna, he played for a year in the orchestra of Johann Strauss's brother, Eduard, where he quickly acquired the difficult knack of conducting Viennese waltzes with the proper authority and lilt. During his five years with the Court Orchestra of Stuttgart, Herbert studied composition under Max Seifriz, a highly regarded conductor and composer. His first work, the *Suite for Cello and Orchestra*, was published at that time.

When Herbert was twenty-six, he met Therese Förster, a young soprano who had recently become a member of the Royal Opera at Stuttgart. They soon fell in love and made plans to marry—plans that were suddenly accelerated by an unusual stroke of good luck.

The Metropolitan Opera Company of New York, having completed its first season of German operas, was anxious to recruit new singers for its Wagnerian repertory. Frank Damrosch, one of the Metropolitan's scouts, journeyed to Stuttgart to audition a young tenor. The tenor failed to impress him, but while there Damrosch decided to listen to some other singers. Fraulein Förster pleased him so much that he promptly offered her a contract. Although she was elated with the offer, she insisted, with the blind confidence of youth, that her fiancé would also have to be hired. Damrosch was a bit skeptical, but when he heard Herbert play, he signed another contract. Therese Förster and Victor Herbert were married in Vienna, and spent their honeymoon on a steamer bound for New York.

Therese sang at the Metropolitan for only one season; from then on she was content to remain in the background. For Herbert's appearances as a soloist with Theodore Thomas's and Antol Seidl's orchestras were becoming important events in the musical life of New York, and he was rapidly being recognized as one of the country's leading cellists. In addition, he was winning a limited fame as a composer of concert music and as a conductor. However, such accomplishments gave him only partial satisfaction. Herbert was a warm, gregarious, fun-loving

Victor Herbert upon his arrival in New York at the age of 27.

man who enjoyed all the popular amusements of the day—bands, parades, operettas, musical comedies—and he was extremely anxious to move to the top of this world. "Is it a crime to be popular?" he once asked. "I believe that which is not popular is not of much benefit to the world."

It was, therefore, natural that when he was offered the post of director of the 22nd New York National Guard Band (succeeding the famous Patrick Gilmore), he was delighted to accept. Such a position would not only relieve him of the monotony of playing in an orchestra, but it would also give him time to compose and perform music that could win him wider popular acclaim than he could ever receive from opera and concert audiences.

Although Herbert enjoyed his work as bandmaster, he knew that only the musical stage could give him the perfect outlet for his composing gifts. When he first began to give serious thought to working in the popular theatre, Herbert wanted to write for a kind of "folk theatre" he equated with the earthy entertainments of Harrigan and Hart. Though his Irish heritage made this ambition understandable, he soon realized that by training and temperament he was far better suited to follow the tradition of the middle European operetta.

According to Edward N. Waters, Herbert's biographer, the composer's first comic opera was *La Vivandière*, written in 1893 especially for Lillian Russell. Little is known about it, however, because it was never produced. The following year, Herbert wrote *Prince Ananias* for The Bostonians, a well-known touring company. They opened it in New York on November 20, 1894. The score for the new work was attractive, but it was hampered by an unusually dull and awkward libretto. Nevertheless, and in spite of a lukewarm reception, the operetta remained in the company's repertory for about two years.

Herbert's second production, *The Wizard of the Nile*, in 1895, began his frequent association with librettist Harry B. Smith and established him as one of the leading light opera composers in the country. Smith wrote the book as a vehicle for Frank Daniels, a popular comedian who had won fame for his performances in Charles Hoyt's musical farces. Herbert completed the delightful Near Eastern-flavored score within a month. In addition to the song "Star Light, Star Bright," the show is best remembered today for a recurring line, "Am I a wiz?" which soon became a popular slang expression.

Having supplied Daniels with a notable Broadway debut set in Egypt, Herbert and Smith created other musicals for him with equally exotic locales—India for *The Idol's Eye*, Afghanistan for *The Ameer*, Persia for *The Tattooed Man*. None of these repeated the triumph of *The Wizard of the Nile*, though *The Idol's Eye* did give Daniels a particularly clever number about the contented wife of "The Tattooed Man" of the circus:

"Oh, why should I go abroad," she said,
"To Germany, France or Rome?
    When so fine a collection
    Awaits my inspection
In our happy little home."

In this exciting world of nerve-racking deadlines, frantic opening nights, and temperamental stars, Victor Herbert was able to find the stimulus for his most enduring compositions. He was a desperately hard worker; he loved the challenge that each new contract presented; and he enjoyed the money his work brought him.

Aside from the pleasure he found in composing, his favorite pastime was eating and drinking the best food and wine. Indeed, as his publisher, Isidore Witmark, once related, Herbert had an ingenious way of combining his work with his fondness for drink. In the season of 1899–1900, he composed the scores for four operettas almost simultaneously, while imbibing an appropriate wine for each one to get him in the proper mood. For *Cyrano de Bergerac*, which had a French locale, he drank claret and burgundy; for *The Singing Girl*, with its Austrian setting, Rhine wine and moselle; for the Afghan-flavored *Ameer*, some special "hard stuff"; for *The Viceroy*, an operetta laid in Venice, there was chianti. All these wines were kept on ice in a washtub in his studio because Herbert jumped from one score to another as it pleased him, rather than composing one at a time.

During his career, Victor Herbert helped establish the fame of three sopranos of unusual ability—Alice Nielsen, Fritzi Scheff, and Emma Trentini. The magic worked both ways. Herbert seemed to compose his best music when he worked with, and for, an outstanding singer. Even though *The Serenade*, Herbert's first truly distinguished score, was commissioned for The Bostonians in 1897, and was not created especially for Miss Nielsen, the leading role was given to her at the composer's insistence. Only twenty years old at the time, the soprano left the company the following year to form her own Alice Nielsen Comic Opera Company. Herbert and Smith then supplied her with a second substantial hit, *The Fortune Teller*, in which Eugene Cowles sang the comforting lullaby, "Gypsy Love Song" ("Slumber on, my little gypsy sweetheart"). Miss Nielsen offered the amusing "Always Do as People Say You Should," and the spirit of comic-opera gypsies was tempestuously conveyed in "Romany Life."

Despite his heavy schedule of theatre work, soon after the opening of *The Fortune Teller* Herbert became musical director of the Pittsburgh Symphony Orchestra. That Leonard Bernstein could be both the conductor of the New York Philharmonic and also the composer of musical comedy scores is accepted today as proof of his great and

Culver Pictures, Inc.

The Fortune Teller (1898).
A dramatic moment during
the operetta. Alice Nielsen, the
star, is the one in the officer's
uniform about to draw her
sword.

Herbert quickly sued *The Musical Courier* for libel. Expert testimony was offered on both sides as to what, if any, plagiarism had taken place. The trial was a sensation, and when all the bombast and rhetoric had spent itself, Herbert was awarded damages by the court.

After devoting about three years almost exclusively to the Pittsburgh Symphony, Herbert returned to Broadway in 1903. Fred Hamlin and Julian Mitchell, who had produced the highly successful *Wizard of Oz* by A. Baldwin Sloane and L. Frank Baum, commissioned him and Glen MacDonough to write a sequel. The new work was *Babes in Toyland*. Although it lacked the sturdiness of its predecessor's libretto, *Toyland* had a score of such appeal that it gave the play a lyricism the other production lacked. In fact, whenever it is revived today, the original score is always performed, whereas *The Wizard of Oz* inevitably substitutes the songs written for the 1939 movie version by Harold Arlen and E. Y. Harburg. Among the pieces that still give *Babes in Toyland* its continued charm are "March of the Toys," "Toyland," and the disarming "I Can't Do the Sum," which is performed to the accompaniment of chalk tapping on slates.

In 1950, Irving Berlin's *Call Me Madam* was concerned with the misadventures of a lady ambassador to the court of a mythical country called Lichtenburg; in 1904, Victor Herbert's *It Happened in Nordland* was concerned with the misadventures of a lady ambassador to the court of a mythical country called Nordland. But there the similarity ended. The Herbert work, written with Glen MacDonough, was a rather meandering though commercially successful vehicle for two popular entertainers, Marie Cahill (as Ambassador Katherine Peepfogle) and Lew Fields (as her long-lost brother, Hubert).

Both Fields, who was appearing for the first time without Joe Weber, his regular partner, and Miss Cahill were con-

varied talents. At the turn of the century, however, Herbert's dual occupation subjected him to a violent attack by Marc Blumenberg, editor of *The Musical Courier*. One particularly strong editorial boldly stated: ". . . this paper . . . long since declared not only that *The Fortune Teller* has no merit whatever, but that all of Victor Herbert's 'written-to-order' comic operas were pure and simple plagiarisms . . . Everything written by Herbert is copied; there is not one original strain in anything he has done . . . How Pittsburgh intelligence could ever select this clever bandmaster as its symphony director passes comprehension, unless indeed the people there never really appreciated the true significance of the artistic movement a permanent symphony orchestra represents . . . The great symphony conductors are not drafted from the ranks of the composers of the shoddy American farce operas, alias leg shows, nor are they taken from the leaders of the parading military bands. . . ."

Babes in Toyland *(1903).*
William Norris and Mabel
Barrison lead the children of
Toyland in singing "I Can't
Do the Sum." (Setting by
John Young.)

N.Y. Public Library

It Happened in Nordland
(1904).
The American ambassadress to
Nordland, Katherine
Peepfogle, is deaf to the
entreaties of her long-lost
brother, Hubert. Marie Cahill
and Lew Fields were the stars.
(Setting by John Young.)

Culver Pictures, Inc.

tinually adding lines and changing "business." Herbert was particularly irritated with his female star, who went so far as to interpolate some of her own specialty numbers. The situation between star and composer became so strained that she refused to tour in the show. When *It Happened in Nordland* returned to New York, the part of the ambassadress was played by the equally undisciplined Blanche Ring, who quit after she too encountered difficulty when she insisted on adding special material. Finally, the role of Katherine Peepfogle was given to Pauline Frederick, a young actress in the company who subsequently won success in many dramatic roles on Broadway.

The score of *It Happened in Nordland* had many charming numbers, with "Absinthe Frappe" the biggest hit. "Al

Fresco," originally a piano piece Herbert had written under the name of Frank Roland to test its popularity, was performed at the beginning of the second act to provide an appropriate musical setting for a gay carnival scene. Four years later, Herbert again wrote a score for a Lew Fields musical, *Old Dutch*, though it is mostly remembered today for the scene-stealing debut of a nine-year-old actress named Helen Hayes.

Writing sequels to long-running musicals and vehicles for popular entertainers was profitable, but Herbert was anxious to compose again for a truly gifted prima donna. Alice Nielsen had deserted comic opera for grand opera (only to return briefly in 1917 in Rudolf Friml's *Kitty Darlin'*), but producer Charles Dillingham had lured the vivacious, Viennese-born Fritzi Scheff from grand opera to comic opera. Although *Babette*, the first operetta Herbert composed for her, was a failure, the composer, in 1905, joined librettist Henry Martyn Blossom, Jr., to create her greatest success, *Mlle. Modiste*. In story and dialogue, the musical was far more adult than anything Herbert had previously done.

"Kiss Me Again," Herbert's most universally popular piece, was introduced in *Mlle. Modiste*. At first, Miss Scheff did not want to sing it because she felt it was too low for her voice. Blossom and Dillingham agreed with the prima donna and recommended that Herbert drop it from the score. The composer, however, was adamant, and the song remained in the show. "Kiss Me Again" was not originally sung as the sincere ballad it is accepted as today. Playing the role of Fifi, a stage-struck employee of a Paris hat shop, Fritzi Scheff offered it as part of a lengthy routine called "If I Were on the Stage." In it she attempted three different types of songs that might be suitable for her theatrical debut. As a country maid, she performed a gavotte, and as a French lady of history, a polonaise. Then, to introduce the third song,

Old Dutch (1909).
Though her part was small, this nine-year-old actress made an auspicious New York debut. As the critic of the New York Herald *wrote: "Miss Helen Hayes, a wee miss, won the favor of the audience by a bit of acting that was refreshing."*

Culver Pictures, Inc.

Mlle. Modiste (1905).
True love conquers in the final
scene at the charity bazaar.
Fifi (Fritzi Scheff) is at last
welcomed into the family of
her beloved, Capt. Etienne de
Bouvray (Walter Percival), by
his uncle, the Comte de St.
Mar (William Pruette).
Claude Gillingwater stands
between Pruette and Miss
Scheff. (Setting by Homer
Emens.)

she sang:

But best of all the parts I'd play,
If I would only have my way,
Would be a strong romantic role;
Emotional and full of soul.
And I believe for such a thing
A dreamy sensuous waltz I'd sing . . .

and immediately glided into "Sweet summer breeze, whispering trees . . ."

Herbert wrote two other operettas for Fritzi Scheff, *The Prima Donna* and *The Duchess*, but neither matched the triumph of *Mlle. Modiste.*

Much as he might have liked to write exclusively for gifted singers, Herbert could never bring himself to refuse a potentially commercial success. Therefore, in 1906, he readily agreed to collaborate with Henry Blossom on *The Red Mill*, a musical tailored to fit the talents of comedians Dave Montgomery and Fred Stone. The team had scored a great success three years earlier as the Tin Woodman and the Scarecrow in *The Wizard of Oz*, and the new vehicle turned out to be equally popular even though the stars managed to turn the show into more of a rowdy variety act than a book musical. Its run of 274 performances was the longest of any Herbert work performed during his lifetime.

The score, possibly Herbert's most deliberately commercial one, was as responsible as the stars for the show's great appeal. (Another factor that helped *The Red Mill* succeed was that it had the first moving electric sign ever erected on Broadway.) Included in its succession of attractive melodies were the delicate "Moonbeams"; the piquant hymn to self-satisfaction, "When You're Pretty and the World Is Fair" ("Why be bothered by a thought or care?"); the strutting march, "Every Day Is Ladies' Day with Me"; and "In Old New York," a rollicking paean to the city where "the peach crop's always fine."

Like *The Fortune Teller* and *Mlle. Modiste, Naughty Marietta* was created for a particular prima donna. This was the diminutive Emma Trentini who, with her rotund leading man, Orville Harrold, had been one of the featured singers of Oscar Hammerstein's Manhattan Opera Company. Mounting debts had forced the colorful Hammerstein to return to the world of lighter entertainment and in 1910 he produced *Naughty Marietta* with all the care that he customarily lavished on grand opera.

Herbert's score was equal to the high standards of performance and production. It captured the flavor of old New Orleans so fully that Earl Derr Biggers, then a critic for the Boston *Traveler*, was inspired to write: "The warmth of 'Little Paris' must have been in Mr. Herbert's very blood when he did the score of this piece. Pirates, belles, knights resplendent in haberdashery, roses, convent walls must have danced before his eyes. (Is it proper for a convent wall to dance?) No matter. Romance was in the soul of Mr. Herbert."

The romance in Mr. Herbert's soul has proven to be extremely durable. The buoyant coloratura classic "Italian Street Song" ("Zing, zing, zi-zi-zi-zi-zi-zi ZING BOOM AY!"); the sweeping confession, "I'm Falling in Love with Someone"; the magnolia-drenched " 'Neath the Southern Moon"; the heroic "Tramp, Tramp, Tramp"; the intense, expansive "Ah, Sweet Mystery of Life"—all these were part of a score that, along with Sigmund Romberg's *The Desert Song*, has epitomized the word "operetta" to more people than any other American work.

Soon after the première of *Naughty Marietta*, a young actress named Christie MacDonald won acclaim in *The Spring Maid*, written by Heinrich Reinhardt and the Smith brothers, Harry Bache and Robert Bache. Just three years later, the brothers and Fred De Gresac (a young woman whose real first name was Frederique) collaborated with Victor Herbert to create the delightful *Sweethearts* for Miss MacDonald.

The new work was one of those throughout the history of the musical stage that takes place in a mythical kingdom (in this case, Zilania). Many of the songs are fondly remembered today—the fervent, but impractical title piece, "Sweethearts" ("can live on love alone"), "Game of Love," "Angelus" (developed from the ringing of the actual Angelus), and the bouncy tale of a foiled elopement, "Jeannette and Her Little Wooden Shoes":

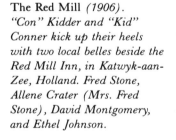

The Red Mill (1906). "Con" Kidder and "Kid" Conner kick up their heels with two local belles beside the Red Mill Inn, in Katwyk-aan-Zee, Holland. Fred Stone, Allene Crater (Mrs. Fred Stone), David Montgomery, and Ethel Johnson.

Culver Pictures, Inc.

Culver Pictures, Inc.

Naughty Marietta (1910).
Orville Harrold, as Capt.
Richard Warrington, and
Emma Trentini, as Marietta
d'Altena, indulge in some
coquettish finger holding.

Clip-clop-clop,
Clip-clop-clop,
Over the tiles—
    Her feet
        were petite,
But you heard her for miles.*

With a modernized book, *Sweethearts* was successfully revived on Broadway in 1947 with Bobby Clark as the star.

Sweethearts was also important in establishing the authority of the American Society of Composers, Authors and Publishers (ASCAP). Herbert, along with composers Silvio Hein, Gustave Kerker, Raymond Hubbell, and Louis Hirsch, librettist Glen MacDonough, publishers George Maxwell and Jay Witmark, and attorney Nathan Burkan, had organized the society in 1914 to ensure that its members would receive whatever royalties were due from public performances of their music. The Society's first test case came the following year when Herbert brought suit against Shanley's Restaurant because its orchestra had played the song "Sweethearts" without authorization. After hearing both sides, Judge Learned Hand ruled against the composer. Herbert appealed to the Circuit Court of Appeals, where the verdict again went against him. Finally the U.S. Supreme Court ruled in favor of Herbert's position, in a decision written by Justice Oliver Wendell Holmes. The power of ASCAP was at last recognized!

The rest of Victor Herbert's career never achieved the heights he reached in his earlier works. Between *The Madcap Duchess* (1913) and the posthumously produced *The Dream Girl* eleven years later, the composer wrote twelve complete scores, plus many songs interpolated in book musicals and revues. Though some of the shows attained respectable runs, they are chiefly remembered because of one or two arias from

*From *Sweethearts* (Music by Victor Herbert, Lyrics by Robert B. Smith). Copyright 1913, 1940 by G. Schirmer. Reprinted by permission.

Culver Pictures, Inc.

Sweethearts *(1913)*.
The ardent Prinz Franz of Zilania (Thomas Conkey) woos the demure Sylvia (Christie MacDonald) not knowing that she is really a princess.

each—"I Might Be Your Once-in-a-While" from *Angel Face*, "When You're Away" from *The Only Girl*, "Neapolitan Love Song" from *The Princess Pat*, "Thine Alone" and the incongruously titled "Free Trade and a Misty Moon" from *Eileen*, and "A Kiss in the Dark" from *Orange Blossoms*.

Herbert died of a heart attack on May 26, 1924, at the age of sixty-five. None of his contemporaries, and few who succeeded him, achieved as complete a mastery of the art of composing music for the theatre. When he began to compose for the Broadway stage, the most accomplished writers were John Philip Sousa, Reginald DeKoven, and Gustave Kerker. Herbert was unquestionably their superior in melodic inspiration and versatility, yet the musical theater that he represented was not really any more advanced than theirs. His chief historical impact was that during the first two decades of the century he stood alone in raising the standards of theatre music and orchestrations. No matter how pressed he was, Herbert always turned out work that revealed great care in both composition and in the way in which the theatre orchestra might best enhance the effectiveness of a score. "Some composers think in terms of the piano," he once said, "but I pay little attention to it. I consider all the resources of orchestra and voice given me to work with. If I did not work out my own orchestrations, it would be as if a painter conceived the idea of a picture and then had someone else paint it."

Victor Herbert was part of the Old World school of sentimental ballads, swirling waltzes, and spirited marches. Within this traditional form, however, he created a richly melodious musical theatre that was so well attuned to the New World that he became the dominant composer of the early days of the American musical theatre.

Courtesy ASCAP

On April 16, 1916, some members of the recently formed American Society of Composers, Authors, and Publishers took part in an Actor's Fund Benefit at the Century Theatre in New York City. Seated at the piano is Oscar Hammerstein I, producer of Naughty Marietta. *Standing behind him are Jerome Kern, Louis A. Hirsch, A. Baldwin Sloane, Rudolf Friml, Alfred Robyn, Gustave Kerker, Hugo Felix, John Philip Sousa, Leslie Stuart, Raymond Hubbell, John Golden, Silvio Hein, and Irving Berlin.*

Courtesy ASCAP

Seven years later, a similar group met for a similar purpose. Standing behind Victor Herbert are Gustave Kerker, Raymond Hubbell, Harry Tierney, Louis A. Hirsch, Rudolf Friml, Robert Hood Bowers, Silvio Hein, A. Baldwin Sloane, and Irving Berlin.

George M. Cohan.

CHAPTER THREE

GEORGE M. COHAN

VICTOR HERBERT AND GEORGE M. COHAN were the two most important creative figures of the American musical stage during the first decade of the twentieth century. Apart from this, and the coincidence that both were of Irish descent, each man epitomized an entirely disparate form of musical theatre. Herbert, the thoroughly trained musician, sought to perpetuate the traditions of the Viennese operetta; Cohan, the untrained song-and-dance man, tried to break away from anything that suggested the Old World. For Herbert, the Broadway stage was something of a step downward from the elevated world of opera and the concert hall; for Cohan, it was a definite step upward from the world of vaudeville of which he had been a part since birth. Herbert felt that the music and the orchestrations and the singers were the most important elements, but Cohan, who created most of his tunes from four chords he could play on only the black keys of a piano, believed that the essential ingredient of a musical show was "Speed! Speed! And lots of it! That's the idea of the thing. Perpetual motion!"

In a larger sense, both men were sym-bols of the changes taking place in the age in which they lived. The portly, elegant, mustachioed Victor Herbert was a genuine Victorian figure whose carriage-trade entertainments kept alive the spirit of an earlier day which many people were reluctant to give up, whereas the brash, fast-talking George M. Cohan spoke and sang directly to a new world and to a new century. "Never was a plant more indigenous to a particular part of the earth than was George M. Cohan to the United States of his day," Oscar Hammerstein II once wrote in the New York *Times*. "The whole nation was confident of its superiority, its moral virtue, its happy isolation from the intrigues of the 'old country,' from which many of our fathers and grandfathers had migrated."

While these attitudes shone through most of Cohan's works, the character he himself usually portrayed was not a loud-mouthed braggart. Compared to the exaggerated antics of some of the comedians for whom Victor Herbert wrote—Frank Daniels (with his trick eyebrows), Francis Wilson, Montgomery and Stone—Cohan's characterizations were models of subtlety, frequently in contrast

N.Y. Public Library

The Four Cohans—Jerry, Nellie, Josie, and George.

to the razzle-dazzle of his own entertainments. Strutting, prancing, talking a song out of the corner of his mouth in a deep nasal twang, he was the personification of the debonair man of affairs with whom audiences were happy to identify themselves.

As Cohan was the star-composer-lyricist-librettist-director-producer of most of his shows, the public image of the man was taken from his stage roles. And Cohan was delighted to encourage the impression that he was indeed the living incarnation of George Washington, Jr., The Yankee Doodle Boy, The Yankee Prince, The Little Millionaire, The Man Who Owns Broadway, and The Song and Dance Man. Conversely, many of Cohan's stage characters were based on actual people he had met or read about. In *The Governor's Son* and *Running for Office*, Cohan depicted Tammany politicians he became acquainted with at the chowder outings of Big Tim Sullivan, one of the local bosses. For his first hit, *Little Johnny Jones*, he modeled the title part to fit Tod Sloan, a famous American jockey, and for the other main character, "The Unknown," he took as his inspiration the personality of Big Tom Foley, a former New York sheriff. Kid Burns of

Forty-Five Minutes from Broadway was copied directly from an ex-prizefighter whose name was really Kid Burns.

In his song, "The Yankee Doodle Boy," Cohan said that he was "born on the Fourth of July." Though his birth certificate gave the date as the third of July, 1878, Cohan's biographer, John McCabe, has offered convincing proof that the song lyric was correct. The place was Providence, Rhode Island. His parents, Jeremiah (known as "Jerry") and Helen (known as "Nellie") were vaudeville performers; George first appeared in front of the footlights as an infant, when he was carried on stage during a scene in one of his father's skits, *The Two Dans*. At eight, he played the violin in the pit orchestra; the following year he spoke his first lines on the stage. He later starred as *Peck's Bad Boy*, a part for which the pugnacious youth was exceptionally well qualified. Soon he began to write material for his family's act, The Four Cohans, which consisted of himself, his parents, and his sister, Josephine.

Cohan's first song was published when he was sixteen. It was called "Why Did Nellie Leave Her Home?" (the girl was named after his mother), but the pleasures of its publication were greatly lessened when the young composer discovered that another writer, Walter Ford, had been called in to rewrite the lyrics. From then on, however, he wrote all of his own music and words. Some of his early successes were "Hot Tamale Alley" (a favorite of vaudeville star, May Irwin), "Venus, My Shining Love," and "I Guess I'll Have to Telegraph My Baby" ("I need the money bad, 'deed I do").

As a vaudeville act, The Four Cohans had become one of the nation's leading attractions by the turn of the century. In addition to writing all their material, George was also the business manager. He was able to demand the unusually high sum of $1,000 per week for the act in addition to specifying billing, routes, and lengths of engagements. But the uncertainties and discomforts of trouping all over the country made Cohan long for the prestige of appearing on Broadway, not as part of a variety program, but in his own musical comedy. To gain this end, he made a deal with Louis Behman of the Hyde and Behman vaudeville circuit, to have The Four Cohans tour for one season, after which they would star in a musical comedy on Broadway to be produced by Behman. Cohan had already written his Broadway script, based on his own vaudeville sketch, *The Governor's Son*. So it was that the Four Cohans (with the addition of George's new wife, Ethel Levey) toured the country, and the following season, on February 25, 1901, New Yorkers saw the first musical written and directed by George M. Cohan.

The Governor's Son had a less-than-brilliant debut. The company, unaccustomed to a New York first-night audience, showed signs of nervousness. The pacing lacked spirit and spark. To make things worse, Cohan sprained his ankle in the first scene and had to limp through the rest of the performance. In spite of the discouraging critical verdict, the twenty-two-year-old author would not accept defeat. He closed the show after a month and took it on the road for a profitable tour. The following year, Cohan tried Broadway again with *Running for Office*, another expanded vaudeville sketch. Again he found New York audiences cool to his efforts.

This show also did well on the road, but it meant little to Cohan; Broadway, as he said, was "the only bell I wanted to ring." So determined was he to win recognition in the legitimate theatre that he formed a partnership in order to have someone handle the business end while he devoted his time to improving his writing. Through a mutual friend, he met Sam H. Harris, a one-time manager of boxer Terry McGovern, who had had some experience producing melodramas

on the Bowery with Al Woods and Paddy Sullivan. After a Sunday ride on a ferryboat, Cohan and Harris shook hands on a business partnership that was to last for fifteen years. (They were also related through marriage. Following his divorce from Ethel Levey in 1907, Cohan married Agnes Nolan, a dancer; two years later, Harris married her sister, Alice.)

Cohan's first Broadway success came in 1904; *Little Johnny Jones* followed the pattern of his first two musicals by opening to generally unfavorable reviews and an apathetic public. The company beat a fast retreat to the road. With Harris now taking care of the business details, however, Cohan could do considerable rewriting while the show was touring.

Little Johnny Jones *(1904).*
Johnny Jones, an American
jockey in England, is slightly
taken aback by the antics of
his girl friend, Goldie Gates.
George M. Cohan, Donald
Brian, and Ethel Levey.

Brown Bros.

Forty-Five Minutes from Broadway *(1906).*
The final scene in the play in which Mary (Fay Templeton) proves her love for Kid Burns (Victor Moore) by tearing up the will that would have made her rich.

When he bravely brought it back to New York the same season, it suddenly caught on and ran for a respectable three and a half months.

The naïve, patriotic sentimentality of *Little Johnny Jones,* combined with its headlong pace, caught the spirit of a country just beginning to emerge as a world power. Cohan's story of an American jockey wrongly accused of throwing a race in England served as a perfect vehicle for him to project his magnetic personality and to express such honest, direct emotions as the exultant "Yankee Doodle Boy" and "Give My Regards to Broadway." The tunes were meant to be whistled; the lyrics came from the heart. New York, as well as the entire country, soon responded to the electricity of George M. Cohan.

Everything that Cohan had written before 1906 had featured only himself, his family, and the American flag. It was, therefore, an irresistible challenge when producer A. L. (Abraham Lincoln)

Erlanger approached him with the idea of writing a vehicle for Fay Templeton, a popular singer and comedienne who had won fame at the Weber and Fields Music Hall. "Think you could write a play without a flag?" Erlanger asked Cohan. Cohan's reply was typically flippant: "I could write a play without anything but a pencil."

Cohan and his pencil created *Forty-Five Minutes from Broadway,* an even bigger hit than *Little Johnny Jones.* Opening on January 1, 1906 (one week after Victor Herbert's *Mlle. Modiste*), it was a well-constructed amalgam of melodrama and songs, among which were "Mary's a Grand Old Name" and "So Long, Mary." The title number, an amusing piece extolling the virtues of country life in New Rochelle, called the natives "Reubens" and noted their "whiskers like hay." These aspersions caused the local Chamber of Commerce to issue a proclamation urging the townspeople to boycott the show, thus giving Cohan some gratuitous publicity. Although Miss Templeton was the star, a young actor named Victor Moore, who had never appeared in a musical comedy before, gave an equally impressive performance as the "square-sporting man," Kid Burns. (When *Forty-Five Minutes from Broadway* was revived in 1912, Cohan himself took the part.)

With *George Washington, Jr.,* Cohan returned to his family and the flag. In spite of its preposterous story, which dealt with a rich young man so incensed over his father's Anglomania that he adopted the name of the father of his country, the show succeeded chiefly because of the great appeal of Cohan and his songs. "I was born in Virgin-YUH! That's the state sure to win YUH!," sang Ethel Levey to the second balcony. With his head cocked to one side, Cohan delivered the irresistible "You're a Grand Old Flag." (Ironically, the song was originally called "You're a Grand Old Rag," but the protests of patriotic organizations forced the Yankee Doodle Boy to substitute "flag" for the affectionate term "rag.")

The originality and freshness soon ran out of George M. Cohan's musicals, even though they still found a wide audience. In 1907, Cohan offered a revised version of *Running for Office* called *The Honeymooners*, and he wrote *The Talk of New York* so that Victor Moore might again portray the popular character of Kid Burns. (The song hits were "When We Are M-A-Double R-I-E-D" and "When a Fellow's on the Level with a Girl That's on the Square.") *Fifty Miles from Boston* in 1908 (in which "Harrigan" was first sung) merely put the familiar Cohan characters into a new New Rochelle setting—this time North Brookfield, Massachusetts, where the author spent his summers.*

Josie Cohan, who had left the act before *Little Johnny Jones*, was reunited with her family for *The Yankee Prince* in 1908, an occasion that inspired the star to bill himself as "George M. Cohan and his Royal Family." The customary chauvinism of Cohan's plots was here expanded to include a firm stand against the then-current practice of rich American families marrying off their daughters to titled foreigners. Cohan's feelings on the subject were expressed in the song, "I'm to Marry a Nobleman" ("Quite a dutiful girl am I, Going to marry an earl am I"). Two and one-half years later Jerry and Nellie Cohan made their final appearances on the stage in George's *The Little Millionaire*.

The trend toward revues accelerated in the mid-1910's. In an attempt to keep up with the change, Cohan presented *Hello, Broadway!*, "A Musical Crazy Quilt Patched and Threaded Together with

George Washington, Jr.   N.Y. Public Library
(1906).
George M. Cohan, in the title role, spurns the hand of his father, played by Jerry Cohan. (Setting by John Young.)

---

*It was during the tryout of *Fifty Miles from Boston* that Donald Brian, the leading man, received an offer to co-star in another musical then in rehearsal. Cohan agreed to release him from his contract and, as Prince Danilo in Lehár's *The Merry Widow*, the young tenor became one of the first matinee idols of the musical theatre.

Words and Music and Staged by George M. Cohan." There were also two editions of *The Cohan Revue.* Irving Berlin contributed half the score to the second one, which was described by its baseball-loving author as "A Hit and Run Play Batted out by George M. Cohan." These shows presented broad travesties on current theatrical attractions very much in the spirit of the old Weber and Fields burlesques. They always had at least one character who visited various places and entertainments to give them some semblance of a theme. In *Hello, Broadway!*, for example, Cohan (co-starring with William Collier) played "George Babbit, the Millionaire Kid," whose tour of New York took him to see such attractions as Louise Dresser as "Patsy Pygmalion, a Flower Girl" in a lampoon of the latest

Bernard Shaw comedy, and Peggy Wood impersonating Elsie Ferguson in the dramatic play, *Outcast.* Miss Wood recalls that she was also in the finale, "draped in a costume of white satin decorated with red beads embroidered in stripes, a blue bodice with silver stars, and a spiked crown. I leave it to you what I was as."

Even though younger musical talents, such as Jerome Kern and Irving Berlin, were soon surpassing Cohan in the freshness, skill, and variety of their work, Cohan continued to be active in all phases of the theatre. Yet his most famous World War I song, "Over There," had nothing to do with show business. Skillfully built on the repetition of three bugle call notes and catchy enough to be whistled even after being heard but once, the song became the most popular musical expression of the war. Cohan later wrote a sequel to it which enjoyed a brief vogue. It was called "When You Come Back, and You Will Come Back" ("There's a whole world waiting for you").

One of Cohan's great skills was that of play doctor. In 1919, when an old-fashioned cloak-and-dagger operetta called *The Royal Vagabond* was floundering during its out-of-town tryout, Cohan rewrote and restaged it, and turned it into a hit as a "Cohanized Opera Comique." During the run of this show, the famous strike of Actors' Equity was called to compel producers to recognize the recently formed union. Even though Cohan was both an actor and a producer, his loyalties were entirely on the side of management, and he did everything he could to crush the eventually victorious union. For the rest of his career, Cohan steadfastly refused to join Equity and always had to receive special permission to perform.

The irony of this dispute is that throughout the rest of his life Cohan won far greater fame as an actor than as a writer or producer. Indeed, his two most distinguished performances, Nat Miller in Eugene O'Neill's *Ah, Wilderness!* (1934), and President Roosevelt in *I'd Rather Be Right* (1937), were in plays written and produced by others. Although Cohan had already presented two musicals not written by himself (*Mary* and *The O'Brien Girl*, both by Louis Hirsch, Otto Harbach, and Frank Mandel), his impersonation of F.D.R was his only appearance in a musical created by other talents. It was no secret that while he was happy to be reunited with the producer, Sam Harris, he felt uncomfortable singing the songs Rodgers and Hart had written for him.

George M. Cohan died on November 4, 1942, at the age of sixty-four. As a creative force in the molding of the American musical theatre, however, his influence had ended many years before. His

Photo by Alfredo Valente

I'd Rather Be Right (1937).
George M. Cohan, as Franklin D. Roosevelt, delivers a radio speech in front of a portable fireplace.

George M! *(1968).*
Joel Grey (as George M.)
strutting through "I'm a
Yankee Doodle Dandy" in a
scene from Little Johnny
Jones. *(Costumes by Freddy*
Wittop; setting by Tom John.)

entire appeal as a writer was based on his youthful verve, his breeziness, and his popular flag waving. No matter what he wrote during his later life (his last musical, *Billie*, was produced in 1928), Cohan never progressed beyond the simple entertainments he had created early in the first decade of the century.

Victor Herbert and George M. Cohan were separate and distinct, yet typical, products of their time. They set the pattern for the two different kinds of musicals that were to flourish in the Twenties, the romantic operettas and the fast-moving musical comedies. Even today, we still see their influence at work. *My Fair Lady* may display a dramatic and musical cohesion undreamed of by Herbert, but it does follow in the stunningly theatrical tradition that he represented. As for Cohan, surely the pace of a George Abbott show or the atmosphere and characters of *The Music Man* attest to the continued appeal of his brand of musical comedy. What's more, in 1968 theatregoers were flocking to a high-powered musical based on the life of Cohan himself. In addition to some thirty Cohan songs, *George M!* offered Joel Grey strutting through the title role with breezy, flag-waving assurance. Proof indeed that Broadway still has a soft spot for the kind of theatre that first burst upon the scene in the dynamic, sentimental, corny, song-and-dance shows created by George M. Cohan.

Rudolf Friml.

CHAPTER FOUR

RUDOLF FRIML
OTTO HARBACH

DESPITE THE MOVEMENT toward a genuinely native musical theatre that George M. Cohan started, there has always been a large audience for the sentimental and romantic operettas that are more a part of the Old World than the New. Victor Herbert's mantle as the leading composer of operetta in America fell on the shoulders of Rudolf Friml and Sigmund Romberg. Both Friml and Romberg were of European birth, both were thoroughly schooled in classical music, and both settled in New York in the early 1900's. Friml, the older, had his last success in 1928 with *The Three Musketeers*; Romberg, as if to confuse those who like theatrical trends to be neatly defined, had one of his greatest hits, *Up in Central Park*, as late as 1945. But the period during which both men scored their greatest triumphs was roughly from the outbreak of the First World War to the Wall Street Crash. Between them, Friml and Romberg perpetuated a musical theatre that was colorful, nostalgic, and melodious—surely as soothing to the tired businessman as a leg show.

Rudolf Friml won fame far quicker than did Sigmund Romberg, although only a year separated their initial contributions to the theatre. In 1912, Friml was suddenly called upon to substitute for Victor Herbert as composer of *The Firefly*—a task for which he seemed to have had little training or inclination. He was born in Prague, Bohemia (now Czechoslovakia), on December 7, 1879. At ten, he composed a barcarolle. Four years later, he enrolled in the Prague Conservatory of Music, where he studied composition under Antonin Dvorák. He was such an excellent student that he completed a six-year course in three years. After graduation, Friml went on a concert tour of Europe with a fellow student, the violinist Jan Kubelik; in 1901, they gave their first recital in the United States. Three years later, Friml performed his own composition, the *Piano Concerto in B-Major*, at Carnegie Hall, with Walter Damrosch conducting the New York Symphony. The response to his work was so favorable and his future seemed so assured that the young composer decided to remain in the United States.

In March 1912, a newspaper item announced that Emma Trentini, then starring in *Naughty Marietta*, would next

The Firefly *(1912).*
A scene in the first act in which Emma Trentini (supposedly disguised as a cabin boy) exchanges harsh words with Audrey Maple. Looking on are Roy Atwell, Katherine Stewart, Ruby Norton, and Craig Campbell (Costumes by W. Matthews.)

Culver Pictures, Inc.

appear in a new work by Victor Herbert and librettist Otto Abels Hauerbach (since changed to "Harbach"), under the sponsorship of Oscar Hammerstein's son, Arthur. But these plans collapsed the following month. At a special performance of *Naughty Marietta* conducted by Herbert himself, Miss Trentini publicly insulted the composer by refusing to sing an encore of his "Italian Street Song," despite the demands of the audience. Herbert, in a rage, stormed from the orchestra pit, handed the baton to William Axt. the regular conductor, and refused to have anything further to do with the temperamental actress or her next vehicle.

A near-frantic search was then begun to find a suitable replacement for Herbert to compose the score of the forthcoming musical. Because none of the prominent song writers of the day could match Herbert's skill at writing operetta, Hammerstein felt that an unknown composer, one with a thorough background in the classics, would be best suited to take over the assignment. Friml, who had not achieved the stature he had hoped for in the world of concert music, had become interested

in composing for the stage. When he heard about the search for someone to do the *Firefly* score, he felt that this might be his big chance. At the urging of Rudolph Schirmer, his publisher, and also of Max Dreyfus of Harms, Inc., Arthur Hammerstein agreed to let the thirty-three-year-old composer take over the assignment. Friml completed the score for *The Firefly* within a month, Signorina Trentini had a second hit in a row, and from then until 1934, the serious, classics-trained composer and pianist devoted himself almost exclusively to the world of Broadway musicals.

The story of *The Firefly* was constructed along familiar Cinderella lines: an Italian street singer disguises herself as a cabin boy to be near the yachtsman she loves, and somehow ends up a prima donna. Though the plot was serviceable, the music and the singing were unquestionably the chief attractions. Critic H. T. Parker, writing in the Boston *Transcript,* observed: "Mr. Friml writes for an orchestra like a musician, setting it to warm, songful, rhythmic and well-colored accompaniments and not like a Broadway jingler picking out his 'toons' with one finger on the piano and leaving the rest to an assistant and the drum sticks."

Among the best of Friml's melodies are "Giannina Mia" (another Italian street song for the diva), "Love Is Like a Firefly," "When a Maid Comes Knocking at Your Heart," and the swooping waltz, "Sympathy." ("The Donkey Serenade," without which no revival of *The Firefly* would dare be presented, was created for the 1937 film version of the operetta from a piano piece originally called "Chanson.") It should be noted, incidentally, that Emma Trentini's relationship with Rudolf Friml was far more amicable than it had been with Victor Herbert. When Friml's wife divorced him in 1915, she named the singer as corespondent.

With his first attempts for the theatre an immediate success, Friml gladly signed a contract to create additional scores for Arthur Hammerstein. His next three, *High Jinks*, *Katinka*, and *You're In Love*, were notable hits during the mid-1910's. *High Jinks* (the title referred to a perfume that was sprayed on the audience) contained the waltz "Love's Own Kiss," the slyly amusing "Not Now But Later," and the insinuating piece piece of nonsense:

Something seems tingle—
    ingle—
        ingle—
            ingle—
                ingle-ing
So queer,
Here in your ear,
Nearer and near . . .*

The quasi-oriental "Allah's Holiday" came from *Katinka*, as did "Rackety-Coo" (which had a flock of trained pigeons accompanying the singing), and the inevitable grandiose waltz (with a

Culver Pictures, Inc.

Sometime *(1918)*.
Ed Wynn, as Loney Bright, is slightly dazed by the charms of Argentine dancer Mildred LeGue.

*From *High Jinks* (Music by Rudolf Friml, Lyrics by Otto Harbach). Copyright 1913, 1941 by G. Schirmer. Reprinted by permission.

Otto Harbach.

particularly grandiose title), " 'Tis the End, So Farewell." *You're in Love*, in 1917, had the distinction of being the first Broadway musical to employ a young Columbia University graduate, Oscar Hammerstein II, here serving as an assistant stage manager for his uncle's production.

Broadway continued to provide Friml with commercial successes, though many of his assignments during the late 1910's and early 1920's were for inferior works. Moreover, their post-war stories and settings found the composer straining to create rhythms and melodies that were contrary to his natural musical inclination. Four of his shows achieved respectable runs during this period—*Sometime* (sometimes written *Some Time*) starring Ed Wynn, with Francine Larrimore and Mae West; *Tumble In*, described as "A Comic Rhapsody in Two Raps and Four Taps"; *The Little Whopper*, featuring Vivienne Segal and David Torrence; and *The Blue Kitten*, with Joseph Cawthorn.

With the exception of *Sometime*, all of these Friml musicals were written in collaboration with lyricist-librettist Otto Harbach, with whom the composer allied himself for a total of eleven stage productions. Harbach, the son of a Danish immigrant, was born in Salt Lake City, Utah, on August 18, 1873. After earning his M.A. at Knox College in Galesburg, Illinois, he spent six years as a professor of English at Whitman College, in Walla Walla, Washington. At 29, he gave up the post to study for his Ph.D. at Columbia University. Once in New York, however, he found that teaching no longer interested him. His first job in the city was as a reporter for a short-lived newspaper; then, for a while, he became a copywriter at the George Batten advertising firm. Broadway, however, was becoming the strongest magnet. Harbach's first collaborator was composer Karl Hoschna, with whom he wrote two immensely successful musicals, *Three Twins* ("Cuddle Up a Little Closer, Lovey

Mine" came out of this one) and *Madame Sherry* ("Every Little Movement Has a Meaning All Its Own"). Within a few years, Harbach was among the most prolific writers for the stage; by the time his career was over his output, either as librettist and/or lyricist or co-librettist and/or co-lyricist, totalled 43 musical productions. Of these, ten were written in partnership with Oscar Hammerstein II, whom he had met through the younger man's Uncle Arthur.

In addition to Hoschna and Friml, other composers who worked with Harbach were Louis Hirsch (*Going Up, Mary, The O'Brien Girl*), Vincent Youmans (*Wildflower, No, No, Nanette*), Jerome Kern (*Sunny, Criss-Cross, The Cat and the Fiddle, Roberta*), George Gershwin (*Song of the Flame*), and Sigmund Romberg (*The Desert Song*). From 1950 to 1953, Harbach served as president of the American Society of Composers, Authors and Publishers. He died in New York on January 24, 1963, at the age of 89. Paying tribute to Harbach's accomplishments, Tom Prideaux wrote in *Life*: "His words and the music were as happily mated as the lovers he wrote about."

Friml and Harbach wrote most of their early shows for Arthur Hammerstein, whose love of spectacular stage effects led to the creation of the greatest success ever scored by the three men. Early in 1924, someone had told the producer about an ice carnival held every year in Quebec which was culminated in the melting down of a huge ice palace. This struck Hammerstein as a great idea for the theatre—even though he had neither the story to go with it nor did he have any idea how the spectacle could be accomplished on stage. He quickly dispatched Harbach and nephew Oscar Hammerstein to Canada to research the project. When they arrived they found that no one had ever heard of such a celebration. Even this news did not discourage the elder Hammerstein. So

Rose-Marie *(1924).*
The ladies of the ensemble as
they performed the "Totem
Tom-Tom" dance. "One of the
most effective chorus numbers
we have ever seen," wrote
Robert Benchley in Life.
(Costumes by Charles
LeMaire.)

determined was he to have his next musical with a Canadian locale that he told the writers to forget about the ice carnival and the ice palace and to make up their own story. He then hired Friml and Herbert Stothart to compose the score, signed Mary Ellis, Dennis King, and William Kent for the leads, and, in September 1924, unveiled one of the decade's most enduring musicals, *Rose-Marie.*

In addition to being the first (and only) stage musical to have the Canadian Rockies as a setting, *Rose-Marie* was a pioneering effort in its use of a murder as an important part of the story and in its attempts to integrate the music with the plot. In fact, instead of listing the individual songs, the printed program carried the following message: "The musical numbers of this play are such an integral part of the action that we do not think we should list them as separate episodes. The songs which stand out, independent of their dramatic association, are 'Rose-Marie,' 'Indian Love Call,' 'Totem Tom-Tom,' and 'Why Shouldn't We?' in the

first act, and 'The Door of My Dreams' in the second act." The need for such a note may seem pretentious and misleading today, as the play did contain many specialty numbers. Nevertheless, there was such an undeniably conscientious attempt to fit songs intelligently within the framework of a plot that Arthur Hornblow of *Theatre Magazine* considered it "head, shoulders, and waist above the customary dribble about Prohibition and Brooklyn."

A year after appearing in *Rose-Marie,* Dennis King starred in another outstanding Friml operetta, *The Vagabond King.* Faced with the competition of *No, No, Nanette, Dearest Enemy,* and *Sunny* all opening within the same seven-day period, *The Vagabond King* was still capable of achieving an impressive run of over 500 performances. Adapted by Brian Hooker and W. H. Post from Justin McCarthy's *If I Were King,* the story had a fanciful tale of how poet François Villon became king of France for a day. Its melodies, rich in emotion and spirit,

Culver Pictures, Inc.

Rose-Marie *(1924).*
According to Arthur
Hornblow of Theatre
magazine, *"Mary Ellis*
establishes herself as the peer
of any musical show star in
this country." This is the way
she looked in the wedding
scene. (Costume by Charles
LeMaire.)

*The Vagabond King (1925).
Dennis King, as Francois
Villon, about to lead the
"rabble of low degree."
(Costume by James
Reynolds.)*

included "Only a Rose" ("I gi-i-i-ve you"), "Waltz Huguette," "Some Day," and the earthy, stirring call to arms, "The Song of the Vagabonds":

Onward! Onward! Swords against the
    foe! Forward! Forward! The lily ban-
    ners go!*

Friml's last success, *The Three Mus-keteers*, was presented by Florenz Ziegfeld in 1928. For the third time, Dennis King was the dashing hero of a Friml operetta, this time appearing as D'Artagnan opposite Vivienne Segal as Lady Constance. The production's extreme length (its opening-night performance continued past midnight) prompted Alexander Woollcott's famous comment, "I did greatly enjoy the first few years of Act I." Apparently this did not disturb greedier playgoers who kept the operetta running almost a year.

Although Friml "poured melody out of his sleeve" (in Otto Harbach's phrase), after the Twenties he seemed unable either to keep up with musical and theatrical changes, or to create anything in his accustomed style that could attract the wide and loyal following he once had. There was little appeal in either *Luana* or *Music Hath Charms*; the quickly accelerating changes within the world of musical comedy during the early Thirties had made it imperative for a new work to offer more than soaring, melodic arias. Friml was aware of the change, yet he realized that the modern sophisticated musicals born of the Depression years were not for him. "When I write music for the theatre," he once told an interviewer in the mid-Thirties, "I like books with charm to them. And charm suggests the old things—the finest things that were done long ago. I like a full-bodied libretto with luscious melody, rousing choruses, and romantic passions."

Rudolf Friml, who died in Hollywood, California, November 12, 1972, at the

The Three Musketeers
(1928).
*Athos (Douglass Dumbrille),
Aramis (Joseph Macaulay),
and Porthos (Detmar Poppen)
cross swords with the dashing
D'Artagnan (Dennis King).
Mr. King, according to Percy
Hammond, had "the voice of a
canary, the grace of a swallow,
and the valor of an eagle."
(Costumes by John Harkrider;
setting by Joseph Urban.)*

Culver Pictures, Inc.

age of 92, was probably the least assimilated composer of the American musical theatre. His European background, his classical training, and his basically Old World outlook combined to give most of his scores—even his earliest ones—a fundamentally old-fashioned quality. That they continue to have great appeal, however, there is no doubt. Though most of the musical comedies of the Twenties and Thirties can no longer be performed as originally written, the rich, emotional music of Rudolf Friml continues to provide occasions of melodic pleasure whenever his operettas are revived. Like Sigmund Romberg, he is a composer whose melodies are best appreciated when heard far from the rush of Broadway, preferably in open-air theatres on balmy, romantic summer evenings.

Sigmund Romberg.

CHAPTER FIVE

SIGMUND ROMBERG

ALTHOUGH BOTH SIGMUND ROMBERG AND RUDOLF FRIML won fame through their series of operettas, the former was a far more prolific and versatile composer. His debut in the musical theatre may have been less auspicious, but he was able to maintain his position there for a much longer period. In fact, no other theatre composer has ever matched Romberg's output: from *The Whirl of the World* in 1914 to the posthumously produced *The Girl in Pink Tights* forty years later, he was the composer of up to sixty musicals. These included operettas, musical comedies, spectacles, and revues, all in such profusion that their names are easily confused—*Maytime* and *May Wine*, *Blossom Time* and *Cherry Blossoms*; *The Whirl of the World* and *A World of Pleasure*; *Dancing Around* and *The Dancing Girl*; *The Magic Melody*, *Forbidden Melody*, and just plain *Melody*.

Sigmund Romberg was born in Nagy Kaniza, Hungary, on July 29, 1887. His first composition, "The Red Cross March," was written while he was still in elementary school. Although his early fondness for music greatly pleased his parents, they did not want him to become a musician, and so sent him off to Vienna to study engineering. There, away from the stern glances of his parents, he gave only part of his time to academic studies, putting much of his energy toward the study of composition and harmony under Victor Heuberger.

Romberg was interested in almost every kind of music, but became increasingly devoted to operettas. He spent many evenings at the local theatres, viewing the creations of Johann Strauss, Oscar Straus, Franz Lehár, and other prominent Viennese composers. In a vain attempt to dissuade him from following a musical career, Romberg's parents permitted him to take a trip to England and to the United States, hoping that this would give him sufficient time and "maturity" to become convinced of the wisdom of continuing his engineering studies. After two weeks in London, the twenty-two-year-old traveler sailed for New York. On his arrival, he immediately became caught up in the excitement and vitality of the city. Because the money his parents had given him was almost gone, Romberg took a job as a worker in a pencil factory at seven dollars a week. Soon he secured a more suitable position as a pianist in a small East Side café; later, he was hired by a larger restaurant. Determined to remain in New York, Romberg advised his parents that he would not return to Hungary and that he intended to become an American citizen.

He now had a new ambition—he wanted to compose popular songs. The ragtime craze, sparked by Irving Berlin's "Alexander's Ragtime Band," had made revolutionary changes in the kind of music performed in restaurants. As conductor of the orchestra at Bustanoby's, a popular eating place, Romberg was persuaded by music publisher Edward Marks to try to write a turkey trot in the style of a popular French tune, "Très Moutarde." Romberg deliberately copied its rhythm for his first two published songs, "Some Smoke" and "Leg of Mutton"—even adding alternate French titles, "De la Fumée" and "Le Gigot," to emphasize the relationship. They became instantly popular with the restaurant's

The Passing Show of 1915.
The fourth edition of the Shuberts' annual revue featured Willie Howard as Charlie Chaplin and Marilyn Miller as Mary Pickford.

Culver Pictures, Inc.

patrons, as did another early effort, a waltz called "The Poem" ("Le Poème").

The first two numbers attracted the attention of J. J. Shubert, a steady customer at Bustanoby's. J. J. and his brother, Lee, were successful Broadway producers and theatre owners whose large organization turned out both dramatic and musical attractions with almost assembly-line precision. The brothers had built the Winter Garden Theatre as a showcase for a series of lavish musicals to be offered on a well-regulated time table—a different spectacle for the fall and spring, plus an annual revue called *The Passing Show* during the summer. Louis Achille Hirsch and Jean Schwartz had collaborated with librettist-sketchwriter-lyricist Harold Atteridge on most of the Winter Garden shows, and Hirsch was to be the composer for the next offering, *The Whirl of the World*, scheduled to open in January, 1914. But just as an argument between Victor Herbert and Emma Trentini had brought about Rudolf Friml's first Broadway score, so a disagreement between Hirsch and J. J. Shubert was responsible for winning Romberg his first assignment. However, the two commissions were completely dissimilar.

Shubert wanted Romberg to provide innocuous, pleasant tunes for his extravaganza. Never, under any circumstances, was the music to detract from the scenic splendor, the antics of the comedians, or the bevy of girls, girls, girls. Indeed, in a brochure heralding the pleasures of *The Whirl of the World*, the entertainment was enticingly described as "An Isle of Gorgeousness, Fun and Music, Entirely Surrounded by Girls. Wherever You Look—Just Girls. Whenever You Look —Just Girls." Although this advertisement named the leading members of the cast (Lillian Lorraine, Bernard Granville, Eugene and Willie Howard, Walter C. Kelly, Rozsika Dolly), there was no mention at all of the composer. Moreover, the critics paid scant attention to the music. So overcome by the isle of gorgeousness was Alan Dale of the *American* that he devoted part of his review to the mock warning: "Oh, mothers of lads, send your susceptible ones to *The Philanderer*—or, er, Forbes-Robertson, but keep them, aye, keep them from the Winter Garden!"

Romberg was young and ambitious, and though the score brought little fame or satisfaction, he became convinced that the best way for him to succeed was to accept Shubert's offer to become a staff composer. The work would be steady, he would be paid well, and he was confident that some day he would have the opportunity to show his talent.

With Atteridge as collaborator, the new cog in the Shubert theatrical wheel ground out a lengthy procession of songs for revues and spectacles, most of which have long been forgotten. But there were the occasionally compensating pleasures of working with talented performers. Marilyn Miller returned from the Lotus Club in London to make her Broadway debut singing Romberg's "Omar Khayyam" in *The Passing Show of 1914*. Al Jolson, who had attracted much notice in *Vera Violetta* in 1911, became a star in *Dancing Around*, though many of his specialty numbers were written by other composers.

Romberg also received assignments to add music to European importations. One of these was *The Blue Paradise*, produced in 1915. Based on a Viennese operetta for which Edmund Eysler had created the original score, it was a tender, nostalgic musical about a fleeting romance at an inn called The Blue Paradise. For the important scene in which the young girl must say a final goodbye to her lover, the composer wrote the touching waltz, "Auf Wiedersehn," which became his first successful song. (The words were by Herbert Reynolds, who had been the lyricist for Jerome Kern's first big hit, "They Didn't Believe Me," the previous year.)

The Blue Paradise was also responsible for beginning a notable theatrical ca-

N.Y. Public Library

reer. After the leading soprano had proved unsatisfactory during the tryout, a search was made to find a suitable replacement. Because none of the professional singers auditioned seemed right for the part of the innocent and unspoiled heroine, the Shuberts decided to take a chance on an eighteen-year-old vocal student at the Curtis Institute of Music in Philadelphia. The girl was Vivienne Segal, who managed to give a memorable opening-night performance after only four days of rehearsing.

From *The Whirl of the World* to *The Passing Show of 1917*, Sigmund Romberg worked on fourteen musicals—all within twenty-six months! There was nothing about these entertainments to inspire a composer of Romberg's temperament; his melodies served the purpose for which they were written and little more. However, his next assignment, *Maytime*, made him optimistic that, at last, his hack-writing days would be over. Adapted by Rida Johnson Young from a Viennese operetta, it starred Peggy Wood and Charles Purcell in just the kind of sentimental, bittersweet romance that the composer loved, and for

The Blue Paradise (1915). Ted Lorraine and Vivienne Segal seem to be powerless to keep Teddy Webb from choking on a loaf of bread.

which he would create his most endearing music. Heralded in advertisements as "Fragrant as Flowers in May," *Maytime* was brimming full of melodic warmth, with the touching waltz "Will You Remember?" and the expressive "Road to Paradise" as its most lasting songs. The musical became Broadway's most popular attraction during the World War I years, running almost 500 performances. During the run, John Charles Thomas, later to become a leading tenor at the Met, succeeded Purcell.

The image of the new Romberg, however, could not replace the old. Shubert made him follow *Maytime* with such transient diversions as *Doing Our Bit* (with Ed Wynn, Frank Tinney, and the Duncan Sisters); *Over the Top* (the first New York musical to feature two youngsters from Nebraska, Fred and Adele Astaire); *Sinbad* (Romberg's third show for Al Jolson, but again full of interpolated numbers); and two more of the inevitable *Passing Shows* (these featuring the Astaires, Willie and Eugene Howard, Nita

Maytime (1917).
Young Ottillie Van Zandt and Richard Wayne are a rich girl and a poor boy who have fallen in love. Peggy Wood played Ottillie and Charles Purcell was Richard. According to Miss Wood, Maytime *was the show the boys all asked to see before they went overseas.*

Naldi, Charles Winninger, and James Barton).

Enough, this time, was enough. Critics were beginning to look upon *Maytime* as an accident, and the name Sigmund Romberg was again becoming a synonym for Shubert hack. As soon as he had finished his assignment for *The Passing Show of 1919*, Romberg broke with the producers to form his own producing organization with Max R. Wilner. Although they had ambitious plans, neither of their productions, *The Magic Melody* and *Love Birds*, was successful. When the partnership was dissolved after only two years, the composer reluctantly went back to his former employers. (During this period of independence, Romberg also contributed eight songs to Lew Fields's *Poor Little Ritz Girl*, which had originally been intended as the sole product of a new song-writing team, Richard Rodgers and Lorenz Hart.)

Upon his return, Romberg was given an assignment that J. J. Shubert was sure would please him. Dorothy Donnelly had adapted *Blossom Time* from a Viennese operetta, *Das Dreimäderlhaus*, for which Heinrich Berté had rearranged well-known themes by Franz Schubert into appropriate vocal arias. Convinced that Romberg could do a better job of organizing the songs than Berté had done, Shubert wanted the composer to scrap the previous arrangements and to create his own. Although the idea of tampering with another composer's works did not appeal to Romberg, he was greatly in need of money and reluctantly accepted the commission.

The plot of *Blossom Time*, accurately described by Romberg's biographer, Elliott Arnold, as "the old *Cyrano de Bergerac* story played somewhat in reverse," was a fictitious piece about Franz Schubert's unrequited love for a girl named Mitzi. In spite of its high sugar content, the operetta became a favorite of both critics and public. Even the usually acerbic George S. Kaufman, then a re-

Culver Pictures, Inc.

Brown Bros.

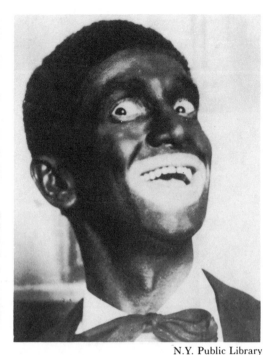

N.Y. Public Library

Blossom Time *(1921).*
Olga Cook (as Mitzi) listens
as Bertram Peacock (as Franz
Schubert) plays his "Song of
Love."

Bombo *(1921).*
Romberg was the nominal
composer of this Al Jolson hit,
but other writers were called
in to contribute such songs as
"Toot Toot Tootsie," "April
Showers," and "My Mammy."

viewer for the *Times*, wrote of the "songs of passionate longing that illuminate *Blossom Time* like pictures in a Christmas book." Four road companies set out soon after it opened on September 29, 1921, thereby beginning the celebrated cross-country association of Schubert and Shubert.

Despite Romberg's preference for tender romances, the Shubert brothers' formula of musical creation could not be altered to suit one composer. The week after *Blossom Time* opened on Broadway, *Bombo*, another Romberg vehicle for Jolson, had its première. Indeed, it was not until three years had elapsed (and ten musicals had expired) that Shubert again offered the composer a score worthy of his ability. Billed as "A Stupendous Musical Production," *The Student Prince in Heidelberg* was in the direct line of *The Blue Paradise* and *Maytime*, as it told of the fleeting love affair between Prince Karl (Howard Marsh) and a waitress named Kathy (Ilse Marvenga) in the university city of Heidelberg. The story provided the composer with inspiration for some of his most dulcet melodies and robust rhythms—"Golden Days," "To the Inn

We're Marching," "The Drinking Song" (a great favorite with Prohibition audiences), "Deep in My Heart, Dear," and "Serenade." With a total of 608 performances in New York, *The Student Prince* had the longest run of any Romberg operetta.

It had taken almost eleven years, but Sigmund Romberg had finally achieved the eminence of a composer who could choose his own assignments—and producers. For Ziegfeld he did the successful *Louie the 14th* (referring to a waiter named Louie, played by Leon Errol, who was hired as the fourteenth guest at a dinner party), and for the new producing team of Laurence Schwab and Frank Mandel, he created the music for that exotic saga of burning dunes and lofty tunes, *The Desert Song*. Originally known as *Lady Fair*, this production marked the composer's first association with Otto Harbach and Oscar Hammerstein II, who supplied the lyrics and collaborated on the book with Mandel. Its cast was headed by Robert Halliday and Vivienne Segal (as in *The Blue Paradise*, she had been called in just before the opening to replace another actress), with Eddie Buzzell as the leading comic.

The Student Prince in
Heidelberg (1924).
*Peeking out from behind the
roses are the romantic duo,
Prince Karl (Howard Marsh)
and Kathy (Ilse Marvenga).*

The Desert Song (1926).
*A moment of high drama in
French Morocco, as Margot
Bonvalet (Vivienne Segal)
pleads with Gen. Birabeau
(Edmond Elton) to spare the
life of the Red Shadow
(Robert Halliday). Also
deeply concerned is the native
girl, Azuri (Pearl Regay).
(Costumes by Vyvyan Donner
and Mark Mooring; setting by
Woodman Thompson.)*

N.Y. Public Library

Brown Bros.

The score, still a great favorite, contained the smoldering title song, the muscular "Riff Song," the ardent "One Alone," and the slightly out-of-place tribute to the Elinor Glyn-Clara Bow influence, simply called "It."

The remarkable durability of *The Desert Song* has made most people forget that it received a mixed critical reception when it opened in 1926, and that a full month elapsed before it caught on with the public. The sheik plot was so old fashioned that Richard Watts, Jr., began his *Herald Tribune* review with: "The question of how simple-minded the book of a musical comedy can be was debated last night, and the verdict arrived at was 'no end.'" But the songs, combined with an enticing locale that has always conjured up an atmosphere of mystery and grand passion, still make *The Desert Song* one of the small group of musicals that summer-theatre managers can usually depend on to play to packed houses.

The Shubert brothers induced Romberg back to write for a few moderately popular attractions, and one, *My Maryland* (based on Clyde Fitch's *Barbara Frietchie*), that was a decided hit. With many producers now bidding for his services, the composer agreed to undertake two commissions at almost the same time: Schwab and Mandel signed him to compose the music for *The New Moon*, and Ziegfeld hired him for *Rosalie*.

Because of the problem created by writing two scores almost simultaneously, Romberg insisted that George Gershwin be called in to share the work on *Rosalie*. The results may have been musically anachronistic, but Marilyn Miller and Jack Donahue helped make the up-to-date operetta a huge success. (The story was particularly timely, inspired as it was by the recent well-publicized visit to New York of Queen Marie of Rumania and her daughter, Princess Ileana. Also, one of the leading characters was modeled after Lindbergh.)

The New Moon could have used all of Romberg's time. With a book written by Hammerstein, Mandel, and Schwab, the show was such a disaster when it opened in Philadelphia in December, 1927, that it was quickly withdrawn for repairs. The libretto was completely rewritten, an almost entirely new score was composed, and major replacements were made in the cast. What should have been titled *The New New Moon* reopened eight months later in Cleveland. This time all went well, and it soon began a highly profitable New York engagement. Starring Robert Halliday and Evelyn Herbert, the musical was very much in the accepted tradition of Graustarkian operetta, even though its adventuresome tale was based on an actual historical occurrence. As for the performances, according to Robert Benchley, "We haven't seen such refayned acting since the days when the Mysterious Stranger with the white plume turned out to be Prince Boris in disguise. And *then* what merry-making at the inn there was! A toast, a toast to Prince Boris!"

The score of *The New Moon* contained more hits than any other Romberg musical—"One Kiss" (echoing Vincent Youmans' "No, No, Nanette"), "Wanting You," "Stouthearted Men," "Lover, Come Back to Me" (described by critic Percy Hammond as "A hot torch psalm"), and "Softly, As in a Morning Sunrise" (which has prompted some unromantic souls to question if there is any other kind).

In addition to many motion picture assignments in the 1930's, Romberg continued to compose for the theatre, though with lessened activity and success. The moderately popular *May Wine*, written with Frank Mandel and Oscar Hammerstein II, was somewhat daring because it dealt with psychoanalysis and because it also eliminated the customary chorus line. Nevertheless, the story was still so basically time-worn that George

Culver Pictures, Inc.

Rosalie (1928).
Jack Donahue, George Gershwin, Sigmund Romberg, Marilyn Miller, and Florenz Ziegfeld backstage during a rehearsal.

John Springer Collection

The New Moon *(1928).*
Robert Halliday, Evelyn Herbert, and William O'Neal find happiness on a peaceful island after arriving on the good ship New Moon.
(Costumes by Charles LeMaire.)

Up in Central Park (1945).
Helen Tamiris' "Skating
Ballet" was in the manner of
an animated Currier and Ives
print. (Costumes by Grace
Houston and Ernest Schraps;
setting by Howard Bay.)

Photo by Lucas-Pritchard

Jean Nathan dismissed it as "a musical mothball laid scenically in Vienna and critically in Cain's."

Like Friml, Romberg cared little about keeping up with musical trends. For a while, when it seemed that audiences no longer appreciated his type of musical theatre, he abandoned composing to form an orchestra. It toured successfully during the early Forties, giving concerts devoted to semiclassical music, with an emphasis on Romberg's own compositions.

Romberg returned to Broadway in 1945 with *Up in Central Park*. The previous year, producer Michael Todd had read a book about the corrupt political leader, Boss Tweed, and his gang. This gave him an idea for a musical of old New York that would contrast the machinations of Tweed and Tammany Hall with the simple pastoral pleasures of Central Park. When Todd approached Herbert and Dorothy Fields to write the book, they immediately thought of Romberg for the music. The opportunity to create another period score proved irre-

sistible, and he readily agreed to compose the music, with Miss Fields supplying the lyrics. Their songs succeeded admirably in capturing the nostalgic, Currier and Ives atmosphere of the production, most notably in "The Big Back Yard," "Carousel in the Park," "April Snow," and "Close as Pages in a Book." The libretto may have been moldy, but wartime audiences found in the musical enough of the romantic charm of a bygone day to make it one of Romberg's longest-running hits.

The composer's last two theatrical ventures were also set in New York in the nineteenth century. Neither one, however, did well at the box office. *My Romance*, adapted from Edward Sheldon's play, *Romance*, was Romberg's first Shubert production in eighteen years. Other than making a star of Anne Jeffreys, however, it offered little that was noteworthy.

On November 10, 1951, at the age of sixty-four, Romberg died of a cerebral hemorrhage. The show he was working on at the time, *The Girl in Pink Tights*, was produced two and a half years later, with a score completed by Don Walker. Its historically inaccurate account of the first American musical comedy hit, *The Black Crook*, may have been fairly dull, but it did serve well enough to display the ample talents of Jeanmaire, the dynamic French dancer, making her first appearance in a Broadway musical.

Once when he was asked about musical trends, Sigmund Romberg replied, "I don't care what the form is. But a melody is still a melody. Nothing succeeds like a popular tune—a romantic tune. Romantic music will never die because deep at the roots of all people is the theme of love." Today, we might add to the Romberg observation that nothing succeeds like a Romberg operetta—particularly in the summertime. Whether they are presented in the open or under a tent; whether with amateurs, semiprofessionals, or all-Equity casts, the hardiest, most perennial summer-theatre attractions are the melodious, old-fashioned, but enduring works overflowing with sentiment, charm, and romance. Indeed, as the Jerry Bock-Sheldon Harnick song, "Summer Is," so delightfully tells us:

> Winter is gloves and homburg,
> Winter is cold cement;
> Summer is Sigmund Romberg
> In a music tent.*

*Reprinted by permission of Valando Music Corp.

Jerome Kern.

CHAPTER SIX

JEROME KERN

FRANZ LEHAR's *The Merry Widow* swirled into New York at the New Amsterdam Theatre on October 21, 1907. Not only did it become the supreme musical attraction of the period, but it also inaugurated Broadway's greatest influx of European-originated or European-inspired operettas. Thereafter, for almost a decade, anything that had been shown on the banks of the Thames, the Seine, or, even better, the Danube, was imported by hopeful producers anxious to duplicate the success of the Lehár work. Of course, American writers were also creating musical entertainments. But apart from the George M. Cohan shows and the elaborate Ziegfeld and Shubert revues, the strains of the waltz heard in the Kingdom of Graustark set the musical pattern on Broadway for at least ten years.

This pattern may be detected merely from the titles of some of the leading importations. After *The Merry Widow* came *The Gay Hussars* by Emmerich Kalman, followed by Oscar Straus's *The Chocolate Soldier* and Lehár's *The Count of Luxembourg*. Female royalty of the day included *The Dollar Princess, The*

Slim Princess, The Balkan Princess, and *The Merry Countess* (which was just another name for Johann Strauss's *Die Fledermaus*). Ladies of less noble birth were ardently serenaded in *The Spring Maid, The Pink Lady, The Quaker Girl, The Doll Girl*, and even *The Peasant Girl*. Broadway also had a *Sunshine Girl* by Paul Rubens and a *Midnight Girl* by Jean Briquet, while *The Girl from Montmartre, The Maid of Athens*, and *The Girl from Brazil* used titles designed to emphasize the exotic nature of their respective locales.

Although such a grand parade of grand operettas did occasionally provide evenings that were entertaining, these productions usually proved to be just too heavy, in their original form, for American audiences, and it was often necessary to call in an American composer—or, at least, one familiar with American audiences—to provide some light, bright tunes to make them more palatable. The man most often chosen for this musical grafting was a young, studious-looking song-writer named Jerome Kern. Kern had the knack of injecting a new lilt into the most soporific operettas; frequently, his would be the only songs in the scores to achieve any kind of popularity with sheet-music and record buyers.

These assignments gave Kern steady work for over ten years. Yet he was well aware that there was something wrong with a musical theatre that made such interpolations necessary, and he was determined that some day he would do what he could to rid the stage of patch-work scores and the artificial extravaganzas for which they were assembled. The Princess Theatre musicals in the mid-1910's gave him his long-desired opportunity. They were fresh, intimate, well-integrated shows, full of youth and melody, and they served better than anything else to establish Kern's reputation as a composer.

Perhaps more important than their popular acceptance, Kern's songs and musicals had an incalculable influence on future theatre composers. In 1914, a sixteen-year-old boy named George Gershwin attended his aunt's wedding at the Grand Central Hotel. After listening to the orchestra play Kern's "You're Here and I'm Here" from *The Laughing Husband*, he became so impressed with the number that he resolved to try to emulate the composer's invigorating style. Two years later, Richard Rodgers, then fourteen, saw Jerome Kern's musical, *Very Good Eddie*, almost a dozen times at the Standard Theatre at Broadway and 90th Street in order to absorb what he could of its sparkling and original music.

Years later, in recalling those days, Rodgers wrote in the New York *Times*: "Kern was typical of what was, and still is, good in our general maturity in this country in that he had his musical roots in the fertile middle European and English school of operetta writing, and amalgamated it with everything that was fresh in the American scene to give us something wonderfully new and clear in music writing."

Jerome David Kern was born in New York, on January 27, 1885. His father, Henry Kern, owned a street sprinkling concession in Manhattan; his mother, Fanny, was a gifted pianist and Jerome's first teacher. Soon after his son was born, the elder Kern sold his business to work in a department store in Newark, New Jersey, where "Romie" Kern attended grammar and high school. Because of his interest in music, he soon became proficient at the organ, and also composed songs for the school plays. In spite of this interest, however, his father insisted that he join him in the family business. One of his first assignments was to buy two pianos from a dealer in New York. The man proved to be so persuasive that the seventeen-year-old buyer was talked into purchasing *two hundred* pianos. This experience convinced Kern's enraged father that his son was no businessman (though he eventually sold all two hundred at a profit) and he gave in to his wife's and his son's entreaties: Jerome could go to music school.

At the New York College of Music, Kern studied piano and harmony for about a year. He then persuaded his father to let him go to Europe for further studies in theory and composition. After spending some time on the Continent, he went to London, where he was able to secure song-writing jobs with various producers. The tasks were menial, but they did give him good experience. In those days, English audiences always arrived fashionably late to the theater; to accommodate this custom, unrelated songs were usually interpolated at the start of the shows to fill in the time while people were being seated. Kern created many such numbers, few of which received any notice.

Kern returned to New York early in 1904 determined to find a place in the world of musical comedy. His work in London, unimportant though it was, had convinced him that only in the theatre could he write the kind of music for which he was best suited and which gave him the greatest personal satisfaction. With this goal in mind, he planned his career with considerable foresight. Following a brief period as a song-plugger for the Lyceum Publishing Company (which had published his first piece, "At the Casino," even before he entered the New York College of Music), he was hired by Max Dreyfus of T. B. Harms as a salesman. Since Harms was a leading publisher of theatre scores, this enabled Kern to become friendly with many of the people associated with the musical theatre. He quickly convinced them of his talents as a pianist, and whenever the need arose for someone to serve as a rehearsal pianist, it was Jerome Kern who was most frequently in demand. Once hired, he would take every opportunity he could—usually during the lunch period or during rehearsal breaks—to play his own compositions. These tunes often sounded much fresher than anything in the original score—particularly after weeks of rehearsing the same numbers—and presently a song or two by Jerome Kern would be added to the production.

Kern's first important assignment came in 1904 when he revised the score of an English show, *Mr. Wix of Wickham*, to fit the special talents of Julian Eltinge, the celebrated female impersonator, who was making his first appearance in a musical comedy. The composer's efforts won the critical ap-

probation of the *American's* Alan Dale: "Its music by Jerome D. Kern towers in such an Eiffel way above the average hurdy-gurdy, penny-in-the-slot primitive accompaniment to the musical show that criticism is disarmed."

The next year, Kern had his first song hit, "How'd You Like to Spoon with Me?", set to a lyric by Edward Laska. Included in another English import, *The Earl and the Girl*, the fetching invitation was accompanied by a bevy of six young ladies, all dressed in organdy, who sat on flower-bedecked swings that swung over the audience.

Between *The Earl and the Girl* in 1905 and *The Red Petticoat*, Kern's first complete score five years later, the composer had songs interpolated in *The Catch of the Season*, *The Rich Mr. Hoggenheimer*, *The Dairy Maids*, *Fascinating Flora*, *Fluffy Ruffles*, *The Dollar Princess*, *The Gay Hussars*, *The Kiss Waltz*, and at least a dozen others. He was also co-composer of *The King of Cadonia* and *La Belle Paree*. The latter ("A Cook's Tour through Vaudeville with a Parisian Landscape"), was part of the program offered as the initial attraction of the Winter Garden Theatre. Making his Broadway debut in the show was Al Jolson, who played Erastus Sparkler, "a

La Belle Paree (1911). This "Jumble of Jollity" was the featured attraction of the first program at the Winter Garden. Among the identifiable members of the cast are Kitty Gordon (third from left), Mitzi Hajos (fifth from left), and Stella Mayhew and Al Jolson (sixth and seventh from right). It was Jolson's first appearance in a Broadway show.

Culver Pictures, Inc.

colored aristocrat of San Juan Hill, cutting a wide swath in Paris." *La Belle Paree* was one of the few productions Kern was associated with at the time that did not owe its origin to a work created in Europe.

The Red Petticoat was another all-American product. Adapted by Rida Johnson Young from her play *Next!*, the musical dealt with the adventures of a lady barber, Sophie Brush (played by Helen Lowell), in the silver-mining town of Lost River, Nevada. The lode was not a rich one, for the musical only ran for two months, but it did have the distinction of being the first musical comedy western.

Even after *The Red Petticoat*, Kern continued to supply additional songs for imported shows. Such an assignment was the somewhat misleadingly titled *The Girl from Utah*, an English musical with an English setting about a girl *from* Utah. Although the show had been a hit in London, producer Charles Frohman left nothing to chance. He hired Donald Brian, Julia Sanderson, and Joseph Cawthorn for the leads and commis-

sioned Jerome Kern and Harry B. Smith to provide at least five new numbers. One of the additional songs, the soft, lovely "They Didn't Believe Me," was a contribution of Kern and M. E. (Michael Elder) Rourke, who had just begun to write lyrics under the pen name of Herbert Reynolds. As sung by Miss Sanderson and Mr. Brian, it not only became the outstanding song in the show, but it established Jerome Kern as one of the leading musical talents in the theatre.

His next endeavor, *90 in the Shade*, was a quick failure. Nevertheless, it served to begin his association with an English-born librettist, Guy Reginald Bolton. About this time (1915), F. Ray Comstock was having difficulties in presenting suitable attractions at his 299-seat Princess Theatre. He mentioned his problem to Elisabeth Marbury, a well-known literary agent, who came up with an idea: why not put on a series of musicals? "Everyone seems to be reforming the drama," she told him. "Various societies are doing their best to elevate it. It seems to me that now is the time for someone to do the same thing for musical comedy." Comstock agreed to give the plan a trial. He also made Bessie Marbury his co-producer and, at her suggestion, hired Guy Bolton and Jerome Kern to supply the librettos and music.

The Princess Theatre musicals gave the thirty-year-old composer the chance he had been waiting for. The new shows would have modern stories dealing with people caught in comic but believable situations, uncluttered by massed choruses or spectacular scenery. The casts would be limited to about thirty, the orchestra would consist of eleven pieces, and there would be only two sets in each production. But most important to Kern was that he could at last create songs that would be introduced logically and meaningfully into the action of the play without the usual lengthy and obvious song cues.

The project was undeniably risky. Broadway audiences seemed to be satis-

The Girl From Utah *(1914).*
Joseph Cawthorn, Julia Sanderson, and Donald Brian.

Culver Pictures, Inc.

fied with the elaborate costume musicals that were still the biggest drawing card in the musical theatre. Also, many theatre people doubted that such an adventurous scheme could attract customers to the tiny playhouse. Indeed, the first of the Princess Theatre series, *Nobody Home*, was a compromise between new and old. It was based on Paul Rubens' English musical, *Mr. Popple of Ippleton*, and even contained a few interpolated songs. However, Kern and Bolton (aided by at least three other lyricists) managed to turn it into what the ads called "a zippy, fox trotty musical treat," and its run of four months was decidedly encouraging. (It later toured with Fanny Brice succeeding Adele Rowland in the leading feminine role.)

By December, 1915, when they offered the second attraction, *Very Good Eddie*, Kern and his associates had perfected the new technique to such a degree that the show was an instant hit. The original libretto by Philip Bartholomae and Guy Bolton may not have been marked by any literary distinction, but it told a credible, human story about two average honeymooning couples and the comic situations that arise when they become uncoupled on a Hudson River steamboat. As Bolton wrote in his book *Bring on the Girls!*: "It was the first of its kind to rely on situation and character laughs instead of using clowning and Weberfieldian crosstalk with which the large-scale musical filled in between the romantic scenes."*

In addition, *Very Good Eddie* had a particularly winning score which included "Some Sort of Somebody" (the lyric was by Elsie Janis, who had previously introduced it in *Miss Information*); Ernest Truex's "Thirteen Collar," and the plaintive "Babes in the Wood." The show played one year in New York. Sixty years later, the Goodspeed Opera mounted a tasty Broadway revival that ran the season.

*From *Bring on the Girls!* by P. G. Wodehouse and Guy Bolton. New York: Simon and Schuster, Inc.

Culver Pictures, Inc.

Very Good Eddie *(1915). Eddie (Ernest Truex) finds himself in the embarrassing situation of going on a honeymoon with another man's bride. The equally embarrassed lady is Alice Dovey.*

At the opening night of *Very Good Eddie*, Kern met an old friend, P. G. (Pelham Granville) Wodehouse, with whom he had once collaborated on some songs for a London musical, *The Beauty of Bath*. Kern introduced Bolton to Wodehouse, the three had supper together, and before the evening ended they had agreed to form a partnership with Bolton and Wodehouse collaborating on the librettos and Wodehouse writing the lyrics to Kern's compositions.

The new team lost little time. During 1917, Bolton, Wodehouse, and Kern collaborated on four musicals—*Have a Heart, Oh, Boy!, Leave It to Jane*, and *Miss 1917* (an unsuccessful revue with music also by Victor Herbert). *Have a Heart* was originally intended to follow *Very Good Eddie* at the Princess. Unknown to Kern and Bolton, however, Wodehouse had already promised the musical to Col. Henry W. Savage, the producer of *The Merry Widow*. Billed as "An Up-to-Date Musical Comedy," *Have a Heart* had some attractive melodies ("And I Am All Alone," "The Road That Lies

Before"), and an amusing title song which revealed the deep concern felt by a remarkably solicitous department-store owner for the welfare of his employees.

Kern and Bolton (plus Wodehouse) returned to the Princess Theatre shortly thereafter for their greatest triumph, *Oh, Boy!* According to Bolton's claim at the time, the musical was one in which "every song and lyric contributed to the action. The humor was based on situation, not interjected by the comedians." Recruited for its cast were Marion Davies and Justine Johnstone, two of Ziegfeld's most celebrated showgirls, who had small but decorative roles in support of the principals, Anna Wheaton, Tom Powers, Marie Carroll, Hal Forde, and Edna May Oliver. The sprightly "Till the Clouds Roll By" was the most popular song.

Although it was not presented at the Princess Theatre, *Leave It to Jane* was created for the Princess Theatre management, and everyone concerned made sure that it adhered to the prescribed rules of integration and intimacy. As one of the earliest musicals to use a college campus for a setting, it gave the composer and lyricist the opportunity to write songs

dealing with such historical and literary subjects as "Sir Galahad," "Cleopatterer," and the legend of the Lorelei in the willowy "Siren's Song." More modern sentiments were expressed in the go-getter's anthem, "Just You Watch My Step," while the entire company energetically joined in the advice to leave it to Jane, Jane, Jane. The show was so coherent and logical in its libretto, lyrics, and music that Alan Dale was moved to comment in the New York *American*: "No more are we asked to laugh at the bottle-nosed comedian as he falls down stairs; no longer is the heroine a lovely princess masquerading as the serving maid, and no more is the scene Ruritania or Monte Carlo. Today is rationally American, and the musical show has taken on a new lease of life."

The second and last musical by Bolton, Wodehouse, and Kern to play the Princess was the exclamatory successor to *Oh, Boy!*, called *Oh, Lady! Lady!!* The plot of the new work was concerned with pre- and post-marital complications on Long Island and in Greenwich Village, and its cohesion between song and story was equal to that achieved in its predecessor. Seldom before had Kern's music or

Oh Boy! (1917).
Tom Powers and Marie Carroll are the ones in the center being joined in matrimony by a justice of the peace. To their left are Hal Forde and Anna Wheaton. Edna May Oliver is second from the right. Justine Johnstone (far left) and Marion Davies (third from left) were recent graduates of the Ziegfeld Follies.

Culver Pictures, Inc.

Wodehouse's lyrics been more delectable. In "Before I Met You," both Vivienne Segal and Carl Randall, in the leading roles, admitted to previous loves—she had had a crush on John Drew when she was nine and he had been enamored of Lillian Russell when he was fourteen. "Not Yet" was an amusingly coquettish postponement of marriage, and in "Greenwich Village" Broadway had its first musical description of New York's Latin Quarter.

One song sung by Miss Segal during the tryout was dropped from the score before the New York première. It was a torch ballad in which the singer, after dreaming of her ideal man in the verse, then admitted:

Along came Bill
Who's quite the opposite
Of all the men
In story books.
In grace and looks
I know that Apollo
Would beat him all hollow . . .*

This lyric, however, did not accurately describe the talented and handsome Carl Randall (who played the part of Willoughby Finch). Therefore, another song, "Do Look at Him," in which Bill did live up to the man of Miss Segal's dreams, had to be substituted. Three years later, attempts were made to fit "Bill" into *Sally*, but Marilyn Miller's voice was too small to make it effective. In fact, it was not until 1927, when a tearful lament was needed for Helen Morgan in a cabaret scene in *Show Boat*, that the song was revived (and revised) and at last heard on a New York stage.

The Princess Theatre shows of Guy Bolton, P. G. Wodehouse, and Jerome Kern were the first real advancements in the development of a truly native musical theatre—despite the fact that two of the members of the trio were born in En-

*Copyright © 1918 by T. B. Harms Company, New York. Copyright renewed.

Courtesy Helen Rich

N.Y. Public Library

Leave It to Jane *(1917).*
Posing on the campus of good old Atwater College are Arlene Chase, Oscar Shaw, Helen Rich, Olin Howland, Tess Mayer, and Ruloff Cuttin.

Oh, Lady! Lady!! *(1918).*
The happy newlyweds, Mollie (Vivienne Segal) and Willoughby Finch (Carl Randall). (Setting by Clifford Pember.)

N.Y. Public Library

Morris Gest (coproducer of Leave It to Jane)*, P. G. Wodehouse, Guy Bolton, F. Ray Comstock, and Jerome Kern.*

gland! Not only did their musicals point up the excesses of many of the contemporary extravaganzas and operettas, but they also made the formulas of George M. Cohan seem crude and obvious. Today, this "integration" might appear somewhat awkward to modern audiences, but it is important to point out that all the Princess Theatre musicals were conscientious efforts to break away from the conventions of the theatre at that time and to establish a genuinely new form of musical comedy. Kern said, "It is my opinion that the musical numbers should carry the action of the play and should be representative of the personalities of the characters who sing them. Songs must be suited to the action and the mood of the play." That view was expressed in 1917.*

Jerome Kern was undeniably sincere in his aims for the musical comedy theatre, but he had little opportunity to put them into practice when he again began to write for the regular Broadway stage. His successes at the Princess had given him prestige equal to any other theatre

*Four more Princess Theatre shows followed *Oh, Lady! Lady!!*, though none was successful. The theatre itself attracted little notice until 1937 when the International Ladies Garment Workers Union bought it, renamed it the Labor Stage, and presented a modest revue of its own titled *Pins and Needles*.

composer, yet when Henry Savage, or Charles Dillingham, or Florenz Ziegfeld wanted him for a lavish new production, he found that they cared little for his theories of how musicals should be constructed. They wanted love songs, specialty songs, chorus songs, and, above all, hit songs, and whether a song fitted a situation in a story meant little to them. Kern had no other choice than to go along with what they wanted—if he wanted to stay active in the Broadway theatre. Therefore, it was not until he wrote *Show Boat* in 1927 that the composer again contributed anything notable to the form of musical comedy. His biggest hits of the first half of the Twenties were two conventionally ornate star vehicles with almost indistinguishable titles, *Sally* (1920) and *Sunny* (1925).

Ziegfeld planned *Sally* with meticulous care. It was to be the first starring appearance in a book musical of the delightful Marilyn (then spelled "Marilynn") Miller. To give her the strongest possible support, the producer signed two expert comedians, Leon Errol and Walter Catlett, for important roles. Originally, it was to have been another Bolton, Wodehouse, and Kern collaboration, but as Wodehouse was in London writing a novel, most of the lyrics were written by a fellow Englishman, Clifford Grey. The book, a durable Cinderella fable about a poor slavey who becomes a *Ziegfeld Follies* star, was patterned along lines similar to a recent hit called *Irene*. (Indeed, *Sally* was also related to two other shows that followed it: *Mary* and the all-inclusive *Sally, Irene and Mary*.)

Though the eminent Victor Herbert was called upon to provide a "Butterfly Ballet" for the finale, it was Jerome Kern whom Alexander Woollcott was now referring to as "that fount of melody." Three of Kern's songs for *Sally* were originally intended for two unproduced musicals—from *The Little Thing*, he took "The Church 'round the Corner" (lyric by Wodehouse), and from *Brewster's Millions*, he added the airy "Whip-poor-will" and the poignant "Look for the Silver Lining" (both lyrics by George Gard "Bud" DeSylva). The New York run of *Sally* was 570 performances, just two less than the initial run of *Show Boat*.

Sunny, which opened five years after *Sally*, made every effort to capitalize on the fame of its predecessor. Produced by Charles Dillingham, its "box-office" cast was headed by Marilyn Miller (again in the title role), Jack Donahue, Clifton Webb, Mary Hay (who had also been in *Sally*), Joseph Cawthorn, Cliff "Ukulele Ike" Edwards (succeeded during most of the run by Borrah Minevitch), Pert Kelton, and George Olsen and his Orchestra. It also marked the first association between Jerome Kern and the team of Otto Harbach and Oscar Hammerstein II. As in *Sally*, there was little attempt to tell a coherent tale in dialogue and songs ("Our job was to tell a story with a cast that had been assembled as if for a revue," recalled Hammerstein). But the performances were excellent, the James Reynolds settings and costumes were sumptuous, and the songs, especially the still-popular "Who?," were whistled and hummed as soon as they were heard. Among them were the title number (with its nonconformist advice, "Never comb your hair, Suuuunny!"); the consoling duet, "Two Little Bluebirds"; "D'Ye Love Me?"; and the joyfully expectant "When We Get Our Divorce."

Secure in his fame and prestige, Kern was anxious to try something more daring than the frothy entertainments he was regularly called upon to turn out. The breezy intimacy of the Princess shows had given way to opulent star-studded attractions, as inane in their way as the turgid operettas for which he had once supplied additional songs. Both Kern and Hammerstein discussed the matter often, and they finally agreed to

Brown Bros.

undertake an adult musical together if either one ever found a good enough story.

Relaxing one evening, Kern began to read a new novel by Edna Ferber called *Show Boat*. Even before he had finished it, he knew that here, at last, was the perfect work to transform into a musical. Not only did it have a great title, but it also had a romantic, yet credible story, colorful characters, and nostalgic locales. Hammerstein, also excited about its possibilities, promptly agreed to do the adaptation and the lyrics.

Many old pros in the theatre thought the scheme was impractical. *Show Boat* shattered too many musical comedy conventions and taboos. It dealt with two unhappy marriages. It showed the harsh life of southern Negroes. Part of its dramatic conflict resulted from the delicate subject of miscegenation. The biggest surprise of the year came when Florenz Ziegfeld agreed to produce it. Perhaps

Sally *(1920)*.
Walter Catlett obviously feels he can make a glamorous star of Marilyn Miller, the poor dishwasher of the Alley Inn. Mary Hay, however, seems momentarily distracted. (Setting by Joseph Urban.)

Brown Bros.

the Great Glorifier had some notion about glorifying the American Negro, but he soon realized that in this production the authors would need a free hand in most artistic matters.

Show Boat broke with tradition right from the start. In the first scene on the Natchez levee, there were no rows of leggy young ladies all chirping in unison about how it feels just dandy to be with Cap'n Andy. The writers took the bold step of opening the play with a group of colored dock workers lamenting the drudgery of lifting the back-breaking bales of cotton. When the ladies of the town arrived with their beaux to welcome the showboat troupe, both whites and Negroes sang about the "cotton blossom"—the townspeople referring to the name of the ship and the stevedores still concerned only with the weight of the cotton bales. Other numbers were equally valid with regard to character and to mood. "Make Believe"—which

came right after the self-doubting "Where's the Mate for Me?", sung by the gambler, Gaylord Ravenal—was a sentiment both Ravenal and Magnolia Hawks could express naturally upon first meeting. Later, the expansive "You Are Love" revealed their more mature emotions. To provide a unifying theme for the somewhat sprawling plot, "Ol' Man River" was sung by a Negro dock worker to convey the hopelessness he felt in contrast to the might and indifference of the Mississippi River.

For the tragic mulatto, Julie LaVerne, there were two songs to reveal her deep attachment to her worthless man— "Can't Help Lovin' Dat Man" and "Bill," the song that had been discarded from *Oh, Lady! Lady!!* Ravenal's "Till Good Luck Comes My Way" was a swaggering piece in which Kern skillfully repeated four bars from "Make Believe" in order to point up Magnolia's hold on the outwardly indifferent gambler. The comic dancers, Frank and Ellie, had an amusing duet in "I Might Fall Back on You," and Ellie, as a solo, did the mocking lament, "Life upon the Wicked Stage."

Ziegfeld wanted to make *Show Boat* the initial attraction at his newly constructed Ziegfeld Theatre, with Elizabeth Hines, Guy Robertson, and Paul Robeson signed for the leading parts. Production delays, however, forced him to substitute *Rio Rita* (score by Harry Tierney and Joseph McCarthy) as the Ziegfeld Theatre's first tenant in February, 1927.*

Heralded as "An All-American Musical Comedy," *Show Boat* began its tryout tour in Washington, D.C., with a cast headed by Charles Winninger (Cap'n Andy), Norma Terris (Magnolia), Howard Marsh (Ravenal), Jules Bledsoe (Joe), Helen Morgan (Julie), and the team of Sammy White and Eva Puck as

*The producer's cancellation of the *Show Boat* contracts provoked a $55,000 law suit by Miss Hines. She later settled for $12,000.

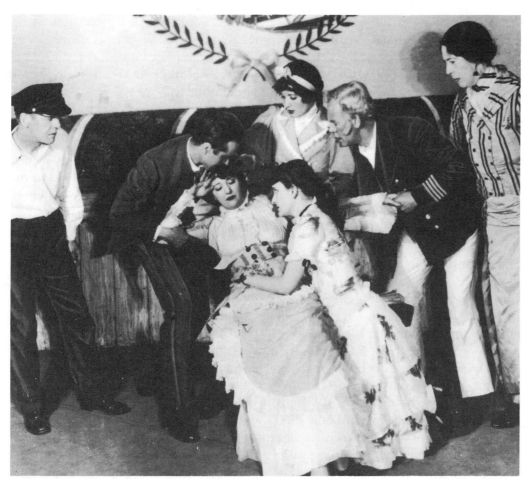

Show Boat *(1927)*.
The dramatic scene in which Julie, the mulatto entertainer of the "Cotton Blossom," faints after her white husband, Steve Baker, has sucked the blood from one of her fingers. Francis X. Mahoney as Rubber Face, Charles Ellis as Steve, Helen Morgan as Julie, Norma Terris as Magnolia, Eva Puck as Ellie, Charles Winninger as Cap'n Andy, and Edna May Oliver as Parthy. (Costumes by John Harkrider; setting by Joseph Urban.)

Brown Bros.

Cap'n Andy quiets the crowd during a performance of "The Parson's Bride," after a backwoodsman, in the box directly above his head, has threatened to shoot the villain in the play. Charles Winninger as Cap'n Andy.

Culver Pictures, Inc.

Frank and Ellie. At its first public performance, the show ran an hour and a half overtime. This caused the deletion of seven songs, including "Mis'ry's Comin' 'Round," parts of which still remain in the score as background themes. "Why Do I Love You?," the third major love duet, was added in Philadelphia.

Show Boat arrived at the Ziegfeld Theatre on December 27, 1927, preceded by the largest advance ticket sale up to that time. It became such a substantial hit that, within a year after its opening, the producer made plans to assemble another company to run concurrently in New York, with Raymond Hitchcock as Cap'n Andy, Libby Holman as Julie, and Paul Robeson as Joe. These plans, however, never materialized. At the completion of its run, *Show Boat* toured for seven months with its original cast, except that Miss Terris was succeeded by her understudy, Irene Dunne.

Ziegfeld revived the musical only three years after its first New York engagement. Apart from the replacements of Dennis King for Howard Marsh and Paul Robeson for Jules Bledsoe, the featured performers were the same as in the original company. A second major revival in 1946 ran for a year at the Ziegfeld Theatre. Its cast was headed by Ralph Dumke, Jan Clayton, Carol Bruce, Kenneth Spencer, and Buddy Ebsen.

Of all his musicals, *Show Boat* is undeniably Jerome Kern's most impressive work. It remains as warm and colorful to today's audiences as it was to those of thirty years ago. Its magnificent score is such an essential part of the story that even the time-worn sequences still have the power to move audiences. By at least attempting to deal with the serious aspects of society, Kern and Hammerstein broadened the scope of subject matter and treatment in the musical theatre and thus laid the foundation for *Porgy and Bess, South Pacific,* and other serious musical plays. In his review of *Show Boat* in *McCalls*, Stark Young accurately predicted: "Some of its best numbers are

so successful in their combination of the theatrical elements, music, acting, scene, as to suggest openings for the development not of mere musical comedy, but of popular opera."

The great success scored by Helen Morgan in *Show Boat* prompted Kern and Hammerstein to write a musical specifically for her, *Sweet Adeline,* which was frankly designed to capitalize on the singer's great popularity. Nevertheless, with a score that included such pieces as "Why Was I Born?" and "Don't Ever Leave Me," the authors made effective use of music to enhance the sweet, delicate, turn-of-the-century atmosphere of the story.

During the early Thirties, the musical theatre offered many sophisticated and satirical works that reflected the mood of a country going through a depression. This was not the theatre of Jerome Kern. In his musicals he tried to capture a quality of timelessness that would have no relation either to the artificial operettas of the past or to the glossy smartness of most contemporary productions. Particularly with *The Cat and the Fiddle* (written with Otto Harbach) and *Music in the Air* (written with Oscar Hammerstein), Kern shut out the world around him and replaced it with a very personal theatrical world of his own. Both of these musicals were set in modern Europe (but contained no political implications), both were concerned with backstage romances, and both depended completely on music to tell their stories. Each work even avoided a conventional designation—*The Cat and the Fiddle* was billed as "A Musical Love Story," while *Music in the Air* was "A Musical Adventure."

"Broadway has not heard lovelier music in all its life," was the glowing verdict of the *American's* critic, Gilbert Gabriel, in his review of *The Cat and the Fiddle.* As for the spell cast by *Music in the Air,* it was potent enough to have Alexander Woollcott hail it as "that endearing refuge, that gracious shelter from a troubled

N.Y. Public Library

Photo by Vandamm

The Cat and the Fiddle
(1931).
Georges Metaxa and Bettina
Hall are serenaded by George
Meader singing "The Night
Was Made for Love." (Setting
by Henry Dreyfuss.)

Music in the Air (1932).
Following their adventures in
the sophisticated theatrical
world of Munich, Karl and
Sieglinde return to their
simple life in Edendorf, in the
Bavarian mountains. Reinald
Werrenrath as Cornelius, Al
Shean as Dr. Lessing, Mary
McQuade as Tila, Katherine
Carrington as Sieglinde, and
Walter Slezak as Karl.
(Costumes by John Harkrider;
setting by Joseph Urban.)

Music in the Air (1932).
Oscar Hammerstein II and
Jerome Kern photographed in
the orchestra pit of the Alvin
Theatre during a rehearsal.

Photo by Vandamm

Roberta *(1933).*
Bob Hope has difficulty
tearing Ray Middleton away
from Lyda Roberti and Sydney
Greenstreet. (Costumes by
Kiviette; setting by Clark
Robinson.)

Photo by Vandamm

world . . . so drenched in melody that it is an unfailing delight." Both productions—particularly *The Cat and the Fiddle*—were burdened by a stodgy plot, but the songs and the adroit way in which they contributed to the action brought a quality of lyricism to the Broadway theatre that no other musical of the period could match. Among the melodies of *The Cat and the Fiddle* were "The Night Was Made for Love," "She Didn't Say, 'Yes,'" "Try to Forget," "One Moment Alone," and "I Watch the Love Parade." From *Music in the Air* have come "I've Told Every Little Star," "And Love Was

Born," "The Song Is You," and "In Egern on the Tegern See."

Although Kern and Harbach's *Roberta* attempted to follow the pattern of *The Cat and the Fiddle* and *Music in the Air*, it was far too dependent on the stock formulas of musical comedy. The show was a commercial success, however, partly due to its now famous cast (Tamara, Ray Middleton, Bob Hope, Sydney Greenstreet, Fay Templeton, and George Murphy, plus Fred MacMurray as a member of a vocal and instrumental group known as the California Collegians), and partly due to its many attractive Jerome Kern melodies. One of them, "Smoke Gets in Your Eyes," ranks among the composer's most inspired creations, but some found its beauties hard to detect upon first hearing. In his review in the *World-Telegram*, critic Robert Garland complained: "There's no tune you can whistle when you leave the theatre. I tried to pucker on the one about smoke getting in your eyes, but it turned out to be 'The Last Roundup' before I reached the sidewalk."

From 1934 on, Jerome Kern made his permanent home in California, where he composed many songs for the films. He returned to New York twice for theatre assignments. In 1939, he collaborated with Oscar Hammerstein II on *Very Warm for May*, a commercial failure in spite of a frequently witty book and a score that contained the classic "All the Things You Are."

Six years later Kern returned to New York. He planned to produce a revival of *Show Boat* with Hammerstein, and he was also preparing a score for a musical sponsored by Rodgers and Hammerstein based on the life of Annie Oakley. A few days after his arrival in the city he suffered a fatal heart attack. He died on November 11, 1945, at the age of sixty.

Jerome Kern was the first real pioneer in the creation of a genuinely native musical theatre, the "daddy of modern musical comedy music," as Arthur Schwartz once called him. Apart from his unrivaled gifts as a melodist, he was a brilliant creator of purely functional theatrical music. It was in the application of this ability that he had such a profound influence on the structure of the American musical stage. Frequently dogmatic about the manner in which his songs were to be performed, he was nonetheless the first major composer to become actively interested in raising the level of musical comedy librettos and lyrics.

Photo by Lucas-Monroe

Very Warm for May *(1939)*.
Robert Shackleton, Richard Quine, Grace McDonald, and Eve Arden in an amorous predicament. (Costumes and setting by Vincente Minnelli.)

Irving Berlin.

CHAPTER SEVEN

IRVING BERLIN

BOTH TIN PAN ALLEY and the Broadway musical theatre are ostensibly concerned with popular music, but the attitudes and approaches of song-writers in both localities are almost entirely different. Tin Pan Alley writers are only interested in creating hit songs with the widest possible appeal to the record and sheet-music buying public. Composers and lyricist for the theatre, however, are interested in the finer points; how songs fit characters and situation in the story, and how they are sung and performed. That many show tunes become individual hits is proof of their power to surmount the manu theatrical elements— settings, costumes, dancing, singing, plot—that are also vying for the audience's attention.

Geographically, Tin Pan Alley is just around the corner from Shubert Alley, but only a surprisingly few writers have managed to turn that corner successfully. The prolific Walter Donaldson wrote two scores in the Twenties, the flop *Sweetheart Time* and the hit *Whoopee* (written with the equally prolific lyricist, Gus Kahn). In later years, such Brill

Building alumni as Bob Merrill ("Doggie in the Window"), Ervin Drake ("I Believe"), and John Kander and Fred Ebb ("My Coloring Book") have enjoyed success in the musical theatre. Conversely, theatre writers occasionally take a stab at writing strictly commercial pieces. Such standards as the Gershwin brothers' "The Man I Love," Rodgers and Hart's "Blue Moon," and Kern and Hammerstein's "The Last Time I Saw Paris" achieved popularity unaided by their introduction in a play or a movie.

Irving Berlin is unique among his colleagues. He has lived and thrived in both worlds. Some of his most enduring songs were first heard across the footlights, but just as many were composed with no other purpose than to strike a responsive chord in as many people as possible. Not only has Berlin thrived, he has been a leader in both areas. A creator of music and lyrics for over half a century, he has written songs that have become so much a part of our lives that it is a bit difficult to think of him as once having been the most daring and influential innovator in the field of popular music.

Berlin popularized ragtime with "Alexander's Ragtime Band," thereby starting the dance craze and paving the way for the popular acceptance of jazz. He introduced ragtime into the theatre with *Watch Your Step*, and later wrote the music for four *Music Box Revues*, probably the most tasteful, melodious series ever offered. In the Thirties, he kept up with the times by contributing to the politically satirical musicals born of the depression years. Then, in 1946, after forty years as a song-writer, Berlin was able to achieve his greatest theatrical success, *Annie Get Your Gun*.

As a creator of popular songs, Irving Berlin has the wonderful ability to communicate his own emotions in words and music. Frequently working with a title idea or an accidental phrase, he has developed many of his most famous songs from everyday expressions that are instantly understood and appreciated. Four of his ballads, "All Alone," "What'll I Do?," "Always," and "Remember," are considered today as the apotheosis of the romantic waltz. Yet each one begins with an almost conversational phrase ("All alone, I'm so all alone . . ."; "What'll I do . . ."; "I'll be loving you, always . . ."; "Remember the night . . .") and then goes on to unexpected musical and lyrical ideas. Berlin himself has said, "There's no such thing as a new melody. Our work is to connect the old phrases in a new way, so that they will sound like a new tune. Do you know that the public, when it hears a new song, anticipates the next line? Well, the writers who do *not* give them something they are expecting are those who are successful."

Famous for the apparent simplicity of many of his songs, Berlin has also created melodies and lyrics of remarkable ingenuity. Of these, "Lazy," composed in 1924, is a notable example. Its melodic line, which switches every four or eight bars without repeating a previous musical phrase, is so artfully constructed that the singer is made to sound as if he is actually getting lazier and lazier. Moreover, it was mated to a lyric abounding in such intricate rhyming as:

> I wanna peep through the deep
> Tangled wildwood
> Counting sheep till I sleep
> Like a child would.
> With a great big valise-full
> Of books to read where it's peaceful,
> While I'm killing time
> Being lazy.*

Irving Berlin was born in the little Russian town of Temun (he himself is not sure of the exact spelling) on May 11, 1888, the youngest of eight children of Cantor Moses and Leah Baline. His real first name is Israel. At the age of two, he was taken by his family to the United States in their escape from the anti-Semitic raids of the Cossacks. Along with many other immigrant families, the Balines went to live on the lower East Side of New York. As Berlin recalls, "There were ten of us in four rooms, and in the summer some of us slept on the fire escape or on the roof. I was a boy with poor parents, but I didn't starve; I wasn't cold or hungry. There was always bread and butter and hot tea. I guess I never felt poverty because I'd never known anything else."

Irving was eight when his father died. Just six years later, to avoid being a burden to his mother, he ran away from home. To a runaway boy, the Bowery was the only place to go. There Berlin earned pennies by favoring saloon patrons with his vocal renditions of the tearful ballads of the day. One evening he discovered an abandoned upright piano in the back room of a saloon, and he would return there night after night to try to pick out tunes on the worn keyboard. This was as far as his musical ed-

*Copyright 1924 Irving Berlin. Copyright renewed. Reprinted by permission of Irving Berlin Music Corporation.

ucation ever went; he still can play only in the key of F sharp.

In the early years of the century, it was not particularly difficult to get a part in the chorus of a touring musical show. Berlin was only fourteen when he was seen briefly in Edward E. Rice's production, *The Show Girl*. The show eventually reached Broadway, but Berlin was left stranded in Binghamton.

Despite reverses, Berlin became convinced that his future lay in the field of music. He next got a job as a song plugger for Harry Von Tilzer, a leading composer and publisher. One of Von Tilzer's songs was then being introduced by Buster Keaton and his family at Tony Pastor's Music Hall. Berlin's job was simple. After the song was sung, he would rise from his seat in the balcony— as if spontaneously inspired—to reprise the refrain of the song. For this he received five dollars a week.

Berlin soon acquired a steadier position as a singing waiter at the fashionably named Pelham Café in Chinatown. It was while working there that the young minstrel wrote his first lyric. The song was "Marie from Sunny Italy," and the music was created by "Nick" Nicholson, the pianist at the café. It came to be written because Nicholson and the proprietor, Mike Salter, became irritated when they discovered that two waiters at a rival tavern had already written a song and had had it published. As Berlin was already known for his parodies of popular songs, Nicholson asked him to write the words for the new piece. They even found a publisher, Joseph W. Stern and Company (which later published Romberg's first compositions), but all "Marie from Sunny Italy" ever netted the neophyte lyricist was thirty-seven cents. The song, however, started both a career and a new name: "I. Berlin" was the way he was credited on the sheet music.

Undaunted by the meager returns from his first effort, Berlin tried writing other songs, this time creating both the words and the music. His initial attempts resulted in "The Best of Friends Must Part," "Queenie, My Own," and "Dorando." The last song (an Italian dialect number about a famous marathon runner) was the one that really started Berlin's career as a full-time song-writer. It had been commissioned by a vaudeville performer who never returned to claim it or to pay the promised ten dollars. Unwilling to let his efforts go unrewarded, young Berlin bravely took the manuscript to Ted Snyder, a composer and publisher. To Berlin's surprise, Snyder liked the lyric so much that he offered twenty-five dollars for both the words and the music. There was just one difficulty—Berlin had written only the words. Putting on a bold front, he nervously improvised a hesitant melody while an arranger took down the notes. Fortunately, he got away with the ruse

Courtesy Irving Berlin

Irving Berlin working for Ted Snyder as a $25 a week composer.

and the song was published. It even sold copies. Even more successful was "Sadie Salome, Go Home," an operatic parody, which prompted Snyder to hire Berlin as a staff lyricist at twenty-five dollars a week, plus royalties. As Alexander Woollcott, Berlin's biographer, wrote, "He had turned a corner and found himself in Tin Pan Alley."

Berlin worked hard, even painfully, on his songs. His ambition was to write the music as well as the words, and in order to show Snyder that he could do both, the young man would return to the office every morning at two and work until dawn. He turned out songs in such profusion—with an impressive amount of hits—that Snyder took him in as a partner. The two men also appeared together in a revue, *Up and Down Broadway*, in which they were attired as tennis playing men-about-town and sang a medley of their creations.

In 1911, Berlin, as a successful music publisher and writer of more than fifty songs, was elected to membership in the exclusive theatrical club, The Friars. The club was then preparing its first annual *Friars' Frolics* revue. Berlin was going to appear in it with his idol, George M. Cohan, and he was anxious to introduce a new song in honor of the occasion. He had already published a song called "Alexander and his Clarinet"; although it did not do very well, Berlin felt that the lyric could still be salvaged if combined with a stronger melody. He tried it out with an untitled instrumental piece he had composed, and found that with certain changes in the words it not only could be made to fit but that it also had a particularly infectious quality. He called it "Alexander's Ragtime Band." Encouraged by its reception in the *Friars' Frolics*, Berlin submitted it to the management of the *Folies Bergère*, a vaudeville show, which promptly rejected it. "Alexander" finally found a home on Broadway—if only tem-porarily—as part of the musical accompaniment at the Columbia Burlesque House.

The first real response to "Alexander's Ragtime Band" came when it was trumpeted out by the dynamic Emma Carus during a vaudeville engagement in Chicago. Audiences quickly responded to the compelling invitation to "Come on an' hear! Come on an' hear!" and before long the entire nation was singing it and dancing to it. Technically, except in a few places, the song is not authentic ragtime. But Berlin, who had tried to popularize the "ragged meter" before, felt that it would be uncommercial at the time and so used a melody that combined a march rhythm, simulated bugle calls, and a deliberately borrowed line from Stephen Foster's "Old Folks at Home." To the public, however, the song was different enough and exciting enough to be accepted as something brand new. Tin Pan Alley had safely broken with the past, ragtime ballroom dancing (with its menagerie of Turkey Trots, Bunny Hugs, and Grizzly Bears) became the latest dance craze, and at twenty-three, Irving Berlin was the most successful songwriter in the United States.

Just as Berlin was beginning to enjoy his sudden eminence, his young bride, the former Dorothy Goetz (sister of songwriter and producer E. Ray Goetz) died after contracting typhoid fever on their wedding trip to Cuba. This tragedy inspired his first real ballad, "When I Lost You," a marked departure from the earlier comic dialect numbers he had written to cover his lack of grammatical assurance.

Although many of Berlin's early creations had been added to musical comedies and revues, it was not until 1914 that he was given the opportunity to compose an entire score. At the urging of producer Charles Dillingham, Berlin wrote the songs for *Watch Your Step*, "A Syncopated Musical Show" designed specifically to show off the dancing skills of

Vernon and Irene Castle. The program credited "plot, if any" to the ubiquitous Harry B. Smith, though the show was basically a revue. Smith, who had served as lyricist for many of the theatre's greatest composers, admired Berlin's facility with rhymes, particularly one in the song of the matinee idol, "They Always Follow Me Around":

> The matinee I play on Wednesday
> Is what I've nicknamed my old hen's day.*

The number that has remained the most popular is "Play a Simple Melody," in which a counter melody is ingeniously used to comment musically and verbally on the old-fashioned sentiments of the main theme. But there was such a native vitality and freshness about the entire score that the anonymous critic of *Theatre Magazine* summed up his appraisal of the music by stating unequivocally, if ungeographically, "Berlin is now a part of America."

Other musicals followed in rapid succession. Among them were *Stop! Look! Listen!*, *The Century Girl* (with songs also by Victor Herbert), and *Dance and Grow Thin*, one of the then-fashionable midnight revues that entertained theatregoing insomniacs.

During the First World War, Sgt. Irving Berlin received a special commission to write the songs for *Yip, Yip, Yaphank*, "A Musical 'Mess' Cooked Up by the Boys of Camp Upton." George M. Cohan may have conveyed the spirit of aggressive patriotism in his rousing "Over There," but it was Berlin who caught the more human emotions of the lowly soldier in such poignant pieces as "Oh, How I Hate to Get Up In the Morning" and "Kitchen Police," the latter with its mocking, mournful lines:

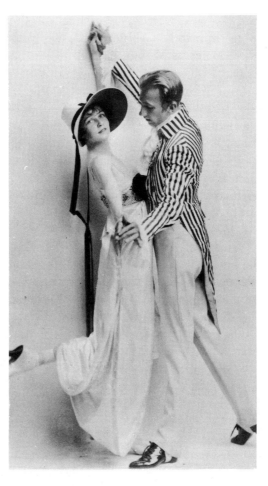

Watch Your Step *(1914)*.
The Castle Walk as performed by Vernon and Irene Castle.

Brown Bros.

> Against my wishes
> I wash the dishes
> To make
>   this
>   wide
>   world
> Safe for democracy*

The highlight of the minstrel show that opened the first act of *Yip, Yip, Yaphank* was the joyous cakewalk, "Mandy," also used by Berlin in the *Ziegfeld Follies* the following year. In the new production, it became the first act finale, and it brought down the curtain on a strutting spectacle featuring Van and Schenck, Marilyn Miller as the famous minstrel, George Primrose, and Ray Dooley as Mandy.†

The *Follies of 1919* contained other delightful Irving Berlin songs—"A Pretty Girl Is Like a Melody" (which became the unofficial theme song of *all* the *Follies*); "You'd Be Surprised" (a wide-eyed piece of suggestiveness sung by Eddie Cantor); and an anti-Prohibition Bert Williams specialty, "You Cannot Make Your Shimmy Shake on Tea," co-authored with Rennold Wolf.

When he was still in uniform, Berlin once made a casual suggestion to Sam Harris that led to one of his most ambitious and successful ventures. Meeting the Broadway producer at the Friars Club one day, he remarked, "Sam, if you ever build a theatre just for musicals, why not call it the Music Box?" Several weeks later, Harris telephoned Berlin.

Music Box Revue of 1921.
Irving Berlin as he appeared in the next-to-closing spot with the young ladies known as the Eight Notes. The eighth note (extreme right) is Miriam Hopkins.

†Another song first intended for *Yip, Yip, Yaphank* was never used because its author felt that it was too full of patriotic zeal to fit comfortably into the revue's light-hearted format. This was "God Bless America," which remained unpublished until twenty years later when it was introduced by Kate Smith at an Armistice Day celebration.

"Remember that Music Box idea of yours? Well, I've just bought a piece of land on the Astor property on West 45th Street. You can have your Music Box whenever you want it."

In association with film producer Joseph Schenck, Harris and Berlin built the intimate, elegantly appointed Music Box as the only theatre ever intended to display the musical creations of just one composer in a series of annual revues. The *Music Box Revues* were as lavish as anything Ziegfeld put on, but they showed decidedly more imagination in stagecraft and in settings. Writing of the second edition, critic Alexander Woollcott commented that for a while it looked as if none of the players "would be permitted to resort to any such routine and hackneyed entrance as merely walking on the stage. No, they emerge from tree trunks and bird cages, spring up out of trap doors and lightly swing down from high trapezes. When this is not possible they walk groggily down interminable staircases of black velvet, managing the perilous descent as nonchalantly as possible under the circumstances of having to carry with them gowns of silver sequins weighing about a ton each."

In addition to their technical innovations, the *Music Box Revues* were so distinguished by the quality of their humor and their music that people eagerly parted with the unusually high price of $5.50 per ticket in order to experience the myriad pleasures of sight and sound (and in two editions, even smell) that were assembled under the guidance of director Hassard Short.

At a cost of $947,000 for the theatre (including the land) and almost $188,000 for the first *Music Box Revue*, both were officially opened on September 22, 1921. Customers came to see the theatre and the revue in such numbers that construction and production expenses were paid back before a year had gone by. Among the musical attractions of this edition were the Brox Sisters tearing through the

Courtesy Irving Berlin

masterful rag, "Everybody Step"; Sam
Bernard commenting wryly on dance-
floor gyrations in "They Call It Dancing" ("A man can squeeze all the she's/
With his arms and his knees"*); and
Paul Frawley and Wilda Bennett singing
the graceful theme song, "Say It with
Music." Unlike "A Pretty Girl Is Like a
Melody," which developed into the anthem of the *Ziegfeld Follies* almost accidentally, "Say It with Music" was
composed especially to be the official
song of all the *Music Box Revues*. However, this "molten masterpiece" (in Percy
Hammond's phrase) was completed long
before the theatre itself was finished, and
Berlin, still the irrepressible song-plugger, could not wait until the première to

Music Box Revue of 1924.
*Bobby Clark and Fanny Brice
in the sketch, "Adam and
Eve," by Bert Kalmar and
Harry Ruby. Note Miss
Brice's snake headdress.
(Costumes by James
Reynolds.)*

Culver Pictures, Inc.

Ziegfeld Follies of 1927.
*Backstage shot of Eddie
Cantor, Florenz Ziegfeld,
Irving Berlin, and dance
director Sammy Lee
surrounded by the ladies of the
chorus.*

hear it played by an orchestra. One night he gave the manuscript to the band leader at the Sixty Club to play just once. But the customers kept demanding it again and again, and "Say It with Music" was whistled and sung by New Yorkers for months before its official introduction.

Other *Music Box Revues* were also filled with musical riches. The lilting jewel, "Lady of the Evening," was in the second edition, in which it was sung by John Steel who stood alone on the stage in front of a simple rooftop background. In the same show, Grace La Rue, wearing a dress with a hoop skirt that filled almost the entire stage, yearned tenderly for "those dear old Crinoline Days," while Charlotte Greenwood revealed the plight of a long-legged girl in "I'm Looking for a Daddy Long Legs." The first-act finale, depicting Satan's Palace, had the McCarthy Sisters leading the cast through the fiery "Pack Up Your Sins and Go to the Devil."

The third *Music Box Revue* added Grace Moore to the roster to sing "An Orange Grove in California" with John Steel, against a setting of orange trees which sprayed the audience with orange-scented perfume. "What'll I Do?," also sung by Miss Moore and Mr. Steel, was added during the run of the show. "Learn to Do the Strut," led by the Brox Sisters, had the full company dancing on a raised stage that was slanted down to the footlights. The 1923 *Music Box Revue* was also responsible for the professional acting debut of Robert Benchley, then the drama critic for the old *Life*. Benchley had appeared with a number of other literary celebrities in an amateur revue called *No, Sirree!* at the Hotel Algonquin. His routine was a parody of all the dull treasurers' reports he had ever heard, and it was so funny that Berlin and Harris, who were at the perfor-

*Copyright © 1921 Irving Berlin. Copyright renewed. Reprinted by permission of Irving Berlin Music Corporation.

mance, asked him to do the act in their next revue. Because he did not feel that a drama critic should also be a professional entertainer, Benchley demanded what he considered the outlandish fee of $500 a week. When Harris agreed to the figure, the humorist reluctantly gave in. His bumbling "Treasurer's Report" has since become a classic.

"All Alone" was interpolated briefly in the fourth and final *Music Box Revue*. Grace Moore and Oscar Shaw sang it to each other via illuminated telephones as they stood on opposite sides of a bare, darkened stage. Others present were Fanny Brice to wail the song of the immigrant, "Don't Send Me Back to Petrograd," and to confess, with appropriate relish, "I Want to Be a Ballet Dancer"; Clark and McCullough to tell the sibilant tale of "A Couple of Senseless Censors"; and Grace Moore to sing the romantic "Tell Her in the Springtime," accompanied by more perfume spraying.

Although they were still popular, four *Music Box Revues* were apparently the limit for the series. Ideas no longer seemed quite so fresh or daring, even with John Murray Anderson of the *Greenwich Village Follies* succeeding Hassard Short as director of the last edition. (It was an even exchange, as Short then replaced Anderson for the 1925 *Follies*.) Berlin, convinced that he needed a change, agreed to supply the songs for the Marx Brothers' *The Cocoanuts*, one of his lesser efforts.

Grace Moore once wrote that whenever she sang a romantic ballad in one of the *Music Box Revues* she always felt as if she were a singing telegram. For it was about that time that Irving Berlin had met and fallen in love with Ellin Mackay, daughter of the socially prominent president of Postal Telegraph, Clarence Mackay. In spite of the opposition of Ellin's father, she and Berlin were married after one of the most widely reported courtships of the Twenties.

Face the Music *(1932).*
Mary Boland, as Mrs. Martin
Van Buren Meshbesher, is
perched atop the elephant for
the grand finale. (Costumes by
Kiviette; setting by Albert
Johnson.)

Photo by Vandamm

As Thousands Cheer *(1933).*
Marilyn Miller, Clifton Webb,
and Helen Broderick about to
stroll down Fifth Avenue in
the Easter Parade of 1883.
(Costumes by Irene Sharaff.)

Photo by Vandamm

Photo by Vandamm

As Thousands Cheer *(1933).*
Ethel Waters sings "Supper
Time."

In the early Thirties, the elaborate revues and musical comedies were rapidly becoming out of date; the unhappy state of the United States had provoked a deeper social awareness in the theatre of Broadway, even in its most customarily frivolous branch. Not that musicals could not and should not be lighthearted and entertaining, but song-and-dance attractions, just like every other aspect of American life, reflected the times. The Gershwin brothers with Morrie Ryskind and George S. Kaufman had inaugurated the era of adult, satirical musicals when they wrote *Strike Up the Band* and *Of Thee I Sing*. Berlin, along with librettist Moss Hart, was quick to move along in the new direction with *Face the Music* in 1932 and *As Thousands Cheer* in 1933.

Both Berlin shows were daring. *Face the Music* dealt with the general theme of the depression and the specific theme of police and political corruption. It also managed to aim some of its darts at the more vulgar and elaborate forms of musical shows. Although Irving Berlin is not generally thought of as a lyricist in the socially conscious vein of E. Y. Harburg or Harold Rome, he easily adapted himself to the demands of the script. However, while his lyrics contained topical references and comments, he never forgot that he was still writing songs for a gay musical comedy. Thus we find him either cheerfully optimistic about the economic situation in "Let's Have Another Cup o' Coffee," or bravely indifferent in "I Say It's Spinach" ("And the hell with it"), or completely in a melodious world of his own in "Soft Lights and Sweet Music."

As Thousands Cheer had a strikingly original format: the entire revue was created out of sections of a daily newspaper, with individual scenes depicting news events, the funnies, the lonelyhearts column, the society page, and other features. Real names of famous people were used, so that in one evening an audience might see Prince Mdivani (Clifton Webb) wooing Barbara Hutton (Marilyn Miller) with "How's chances, for one of those glances . . ."; or Aimee Semple MacPherson (Helen Broderick) trying to get Mahatma Gandhi (Mr. Webb) to end his hunger strike; or John D. Rockefeller (Mr. Webb) going after his children with a carving knife after they have made him a present of Rockefeller Center on his ninety-fourth birthday; or Josephine Baker (Ethel Waters) admitting that, in spite of her fancy French chateau, she still had "Harlem on My Mind."

Miss Waters made even more lasting impressions with her interpretations of two other headlines. "HEAT WAVE HITS NEW YORK" offered her as a highly animated weather report, relating the sizzling tale of the lady from Martinique who started the heat wave by making her seat wave; "UNKNOWN NEGRO LYNCHED BY FRENZIED MOB" showed her as the man's widow who wonders aloud as she sets the table how she will be able to tell her children that their father "ain't comin' home no more." Before the show opened in Philadelphia to begin its tryout tour, there were many who felt that such a threnody had no place in a lavish revue. Both Berlin and producer Sam Harris were adamant; the number stayed in and became one of the most moving pieces ever sung in the theater. "If one song can tell the whole tragic history of a race," she wrote in her autobiography, *His Eye Is on the Sparrow*, " 'Supper Time' was that song."*

For the first-act finale, Berlin went back to a tune he had composed sixteen years before under the title, "Smile and Show Your Dimple." The scene in *As Thousands Cheer* was the rotogravure section showing an old-fashioned Easter Parade on Fifth Avenue. And leading the

*From *His Eye Is On the Sparrow* by Ethel Waters and Charles Samuels. Garden City, N.Y.: Doubleday & Company; 1951.

Photo by Fred Fehl

Louisiana Purchase *(1940). Victor Moore as the investigating Sen. Oliver P. Loganberry looks the other way as a disguised political agent (William Gaxton) sets the table for his rendezvous with Vera Zorina. Critic John Anderson uncompromisingly labeled Mr. Moore "the most endearing comedian on our stage." (Costumes and setting by Tom Lee.)*

grand parade was the debonair Clifton Webb serenading the lovely Marilyn Miller with the old melody set to a new lyric, "In your Easter bonnet. . . ."

Eight years later (after writing three film scores for Fred Astaire and Ginger Rogers), Irving Berlin returned to Broadway—and another musical about politics. Unfortunately, the satire of *Louisiana Purchase* was not very barbed, even though the show dealt with such a likely subject as the attempts of a Huey Long henchman (William Gaxton) to blackmail an investigating senator (Victor Moore) by getting him involved with three attractive ladies (Vera Zorina, Carol Bruce, and Irene Bordoni). Berlin's output was up to his best—two appealing ballads, "It's a Lovely Day Tomorrow" and "You're Lonely and I'm Lonely"; Moore's plaintive "What Chance Have I?"; the spiritual-derived "Lord Done Fixed Up My Soul"; and the amorously tenacious "You Can't Brush Me Off."

Except for the brilliant World War II all-soldier show, *This Is the Army* (with

Courtesy Irving Berlin

This Is the Army *(1942)*.
Irving Berlin, once again in
his World War I uniform, is
about to break out into "Oh,
How I Hate to Get Up in the
Morning."

the composer back in uniform to bleat again, "Oh, How I Hate to Get Up in the Morning"), a number of years elapsed before Berlin wrote his next show. During that time, the musical theatre, like almost everything else in the world, was going through important changes. The emergence of Rodgers and Hammerstein had placed greater emphasis on the book value of musicals, and composers were forced to become more concerned with the way their songs were integrated with the librettos.

Annie Get Your Gun presented a challenge to Irving Berlin for two reasons: it was being produced by Rodgers and Hammerstein themselves, and he had been asked to take over the assignment only after the death of Jerome Kern, the original composer. When he was first approached in the fall of 1945, Berlin frankly admitted to Hammerstein that he just did not think he was capable of such a task. Hammerstein's insistence that he was the only one who could do the score made the composer reconsider, and he agreed to go away to Atlantic City for a week to think over the proposition. Not only did he think, he worked, composing songs such as "Doin' What Comes Natur'lly," "There's No Business like Show Business," and "They Say It's Wonderful."

Still uncertain, Berlin returned to New York. He told Rodgers and Hammerstein that he had written a few songs and wanted to audition for them. Once the songs were heard, of course, Berlin easily demonstrated to the producers' satisfaction—if not to his own—that he was still a master at writing musical comedy numbers. Moreover, these were songs that fitted logically into the story and perfectly suited the characters for whom they were intended. Berlin was also able to create something of a new stage personality for Ethel Merman, the star of the show. Before she played Annie, Miss Merman had always had to have some comic angle injected into her love songs, because composers and lyricists felt that

Annie Get Your Gun (1946). *Wrote Wolcott Gibbs: "Ethel Merman, whose voice might easily have tumbled the walls of Jericho, has some songs that will probably do the same thing for the Imperial Theatre." Here she is seen trumpeting "You Can't Get a Man with a Gun." (Costume by Lucinda Ballard.)*

the usual Merman characterization of a brassy but big-hearted dame would not be believable in a sincere romantic expression. Berlin gave her such straight ballads as "They Say It's Wonderful" and "I Got Lost in His Arms" to help reveal the genuine warmth and femininity of the character. Even the exuberant pieces, "You Can't Get a Man with a Gun," "Doin' What Comes Natur'lly," and "I Got the Sun in the Morning," were still part of the personality of the determined but womanly sharpshooter. As Merman herself admits, "Irving Berlin made a lady out of me."

Although *Annie Get Your Gun* produced the unofficial anthem of the theatre, "There's No Business Like Show Business," the song was almost thrown out of the score because Berlin mistakenly thought Rodgers did not like it. While he himself continually has such doubts about his work, Berlin is convinced that the opinion of the public is never wrong. As Howard Dietz has written, "He does not care to be considered witty or brilliant or artistic. He wants to be a hit." Surely, the musical's Broadway run of 1,147 performances gave Berlin exactly what he wanted, and was more responsible than anything else for wiping out the feeling of uncertainty that he felt when he first undertook the assignment. (Once, when a friend described *Annie Get Your Gun* as old-fashioned, Berlin replied, "Yes, a good old-fashioned smash!")

Three years after *Annie Get Your Gun*, Berlin had a fair success in *Miss Liberty*, on which he collaborated with Robert E. Sherwood (book) and Moss Hart (direction). The tale of the search for the model who posed for the Statue of Liberty is best remembered for the composer's moving musical setting to Emma Lazarus' poem, "Give Me Your Tired, Your Poor" (which is inscribed on the base of the statue), and the sight of the seventy-one-year-old Ethel Griffies kicking up her heels and croaking "Only for Americans."

Call Me Madam, another vehicle for Ethel Merman, brought Irving Berlin back to Broadway in 1950. Inspired by the appointment of Washington party-giver Perle Mesta as President Truman's ambassador to Luxembourg, Howard Lindsay and Russel Crouse created a harmless spoof that offended no one. Even Harry Truman, in the person of former musical comedy juvenile Irving Fisher, nightly took a curtain call with Miss Merman. The song that has lingered the longest from the score is "You're Just in Love," with its down-to-earth counter melody commenting sympathetically on the starry-eyed emotions

Annie Get Your Gun (1946). The final tableau. Ray Middleton as Frank Butler and Ethel Merman as Annie Oakley are in the center, flanked by William O'Neal as Buffalo Bill and George Lipton as Pawnee Bill. (Costumes by Lucinda Ballard; setting by Jo Mielziner)

Courtesy Irving Berlin

Call Me Madam *(1950).*
Backstage shot of Raoul Pène
DuBois (settings and
costumes), Leland Hayward
(producer), Jerome Robbins
(choreographer), Howard
Lindsay (colibrettist), Russel
Crouse (colibrettist), Ethel
Merman, Paul Lukas, Irving
Berlin, and, kneeling, George
Abbott (director).

Photo by Friedman-Abeles

*Annie Get Your Gun (1966).
On the occasion of the
twentieth anniversary revival
at Lincoln Center: producer
Richard Rodgers, star Ethel
Merman, co-librettist Dorothy
Fields, composer-lyricist
Irving Berlin.*

Mr. President *(1962).
President Robert Ryan and
First Lady Nanette Fabray get
away from the cares of the day
"In Our Hideaway."*

Photo by Friedman-Abeles

of the main theme. "They Like Ike," a relatively nonpartisan specialty number, soon became both a campaign song and a much-chanted slogan merely by changing the pronoun to the first person.

Twelve years later, Irving Berlin bounced back into the theatre—and back into politics. The vehicle, *Mr. President*, was again written with the usually dependable Lindsay and Crouse. This time, however, they failed to come up with much that was original or pointed about the political scene, and Berlin's generous score—19 numbers!—was still not enough to compensate. The best of them were Nanette Fabray's rousing affirmation, "They Love Me," and the pounding chorale, "Glad to Be Home Again." Despite a near-record advance ticket sale of more than $2,650,000, *Mr. President* remained in office a little over seven months and left with a deficit of $100,000.

Irving Berlin has been called the "Last of the Troubadours." It is an accurate title. The troubadours of the Middle Ages may not have been trained musicians, but they did have the rare faculty of being able to communicate their sentiments and their songs to vast numbers of people. Possibly no other song-writer in history has had this gift to such an extent as Irving Berlin. Whether he is writing about a soldier who hates to get up in the morning, a lonely lover who waits by the telephone, the thrills of taking a bow on the stage, the simple joys of getting out on a dance floor, or any of the hundreds of other human emotions, and thoughts, and experiences he has written about, Irving Berlin knows how to express feelings in such a way that they are universally shared.

Jerome Kern's succinct tribute to Berlin's ability to embody a nation's music is justly famous: "Irving Berlin has no *place* in American music. He *is* American music," was the way he once ended a letter to Alexander Woollcott, when Woollcott was preparing a biography of the composer. Preceding this, Kern summed up beautifully the ways in which Berlin's music epitomized the average American: "Both the typical Yankee and the Berlin tune have humor, originality, pace, and popularity; both are wide-awake, and both are sometimes a little loud—but what might unsympathetically be mistaken for brass, is really gold ... He doesn't attempt to stuff the public's ears with pseudo-original, ultra-modernism, but he honestly absorbs the vibrations emanating from the people, manners and life of his time, and in turn, gives these impressions back to the world—simplified—clarified—glorified."

Ira and George Gershwin.

CHAPTER EIGHT

GEORGE and IRA GERSHWIN

THE DEATH OF George Gershwin on July 11, 1937, was a stunning, almost unbelievable event. At the age of thirty-eight, at the height of his creative powers, he died in Hollywood of a brain tumor—a tragedy made all the sadder by the lingering doubts of many that if a certain brain specialist had been located in time, Gershwin's life might have been saved. The consolation that he is kept alive through the continuous performing of his music is always tempered by speculation as to what he might have gone on to achieve. Oscar Levant wrote in *A Smattering of Ignorance*: "No quantity of music could compensate for the loss of his corporeal presence, the cessation of his creative being—especially when we could have had both."* Vernon Duke, in his autobiography, *Passport to Paris*, echoed the sentiment: "Death can be kind and it can be just; but it had no business taking our George, who was in the full flower of his fine youth and who was unquestionably doing his best work."†

*From *A Smattering of Ignorance* by Oscar Levant. Garden City, N.Y.: Doubleday and Company.
† From *Passport to Paris* by Vernon Duke. Boston: Little, Brown and Company.

The frustration that many felt was understandable. For, in many ways, Gershwin represented the exciting, daring, adventuresome spirit of American youth itself. Not only did he capture the pulse of the people, but, as Arthur Schwartz has commented, "he quickened it." To his friends and co-composers, he was an acknowledged leader—warm, understanding, and just as eager to praise someone else's music as he was to delight in his own. Indeed, this feeling about his own music, which led many to think of him as conceited, was nothing more than an almost detached and honest appreciation of his own worth, and he showed equal enthusiasm for the songs of Irving Berlin, Jerome Kern, and others. It was Gershwin who helped Vincent Youmans get his first assignment on Broadway, and composers such as Arthur Schwartz, Vernon Duke, and Harold Arlen have attested to Gershwin's encouragement and help. The people who knew George Gershwin only through his music felt his death almost as keenly as did his friends. Even though audiences may not have been fully conscious of it, the personality of Gershwin and of his music was the same. According to Arlen, "He bubbles just as much as his music does. That is why I believe that anyone who knows George's work, knows George. The humor, the satire, the playfulness of most of his melodic phrases were the natural expression of the man."

In a literal sense, Gershwin and his songs were seldom parted during the composer's life. He was an expert pianist with an almost compulsive urge to play his own music. People gave parties for him because they knew he would be delighted to spend the entire evening entertaining them at the piano. Frequently, Gershwin became so excited about a new score that he would play the songs in public well in advance of the première of the show for which they were intended. "George's music gets around so much before an opening," George S. Kaufman once remarked dryly, "that the first night audience thinks it's at a revival."

Gershwin had the remarkable ability of projecting his own magnetism through the bright, athletic rhythms of his songs. He was also the first—and, at this writing, the only—song-writer who started out in Tin Pan Alley ever to be accepted with equal honors as a composer of concert and opera music. Herbert, Friml, Duke, Weill, and Bernstein all came to Broadway after years of training and experience as "classical" musicians and composers; Gershwin's apprenticeship as a "classical" musician and composer was spent as a song-plugger, vaudeville accompanist, rehearsal pianist, and the creator of the music for *George White's Scandals*. Today, his greatness rests not only on his succession of outstanding show tunes, but also on such works as the *Rhapsody in Blue*, the *Piano Concerto in F*, *An American in Paris*, and *Porgy and Bess*. None of the other composers discussed in this book—no matter what their backgrounds—ever mastered as many forms of musical expression as did George Gershwin. And he did it in less than twenty years.

Gershwin was born in Brooklyn on September 26, 1898. His parents were

Morris and Rose Gershvin, who later substituted the more Americanized *w* for the *v*. George was the second of four children; his older brother, Ira, was born on December 6, 1896. Their father was constantly becoming involved in a variety of business activities (turkish baths, bakeries, restaurants, etc.) that required the family to move from one neighborhood to another almost yearly. While they were living on the lower East Side of Manhattan, Mrs. Gershwin bought a piano. She wanted Ira to take lessons, but when George showed the greater musical aptitude, he was substituted for his reluctant brother. George's first important teacher was Charles Hambitzer, who later brought him to Edward Kilenyi for instructions in theory.

Music quickly became Gershwin's life. He left the High School of Commerce to take a job as a pianist for the Jerome H. Remick Music Publishing Company; at fifteen, he was the youngest pounder in Tin Pan Alley. His first attempts at composing, "Since I Found You," and "Ragging the Traumerei," went unpublished, although he did manage to sell his third effort to publisher Harry Von Tilzer for five dollars. Murray Roth's lyric was almost self-contained in the title—"When You Want 'Em, You Can't Have 'Em; When You Have 'Em, You Don't Want 'Em." It referred, of course, to man's ambivalent attitude toward women.

At the beginning of Gershwin's career, his two idols were Irving Berlin and Jerome Kern. ("Many things I wrote at this period sounded as though Kern had written them himself," he later admitted.) He not only admired Kern's songs, he also admired Kern's success in getting his early works interpolated in musicals. Trying to emulate this success, Gershwin quit his job at Remick's to become a vaudeville accompanist. Then when he heard of an opening for a rehearsal pianist for a musical (with a score provided by both Jerome Kern and Victor Herbert), he applied for the job and was hired. Though the show itself, *Miss*

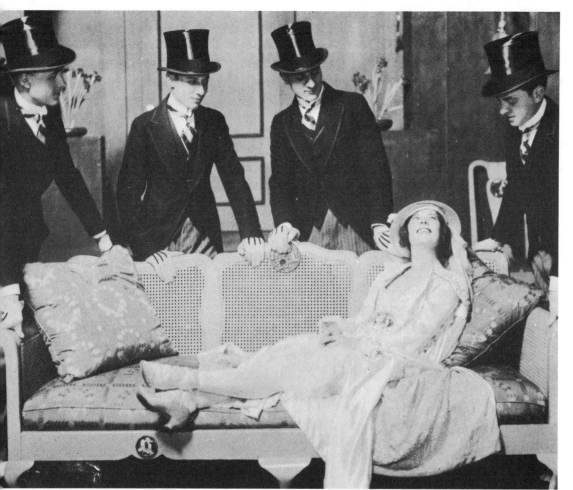

Culver Pictures, Inc.

La La Lucille *(1919).*
The first Broadway musical
for which Gershwin wrote the
entire score. The scene shows
Marjorie Bentley surrounded
by four dapper gentlemen of
the chorus.

1917, lasted only forty-eight performances, the job proved to be an important step in the fledgling composer's
career. The revue was housed at the
Century Theatre, where, as a possible
impetus to business, a series of Sunday
evening variety "concerts" was presented. Gershwin, who had been hired to
play at these performances, persuaded
Vivienne Segal to introduce two of his
songs, "You-oo Just You," a romantic
ballad of Old Dixie, and "There's More
to the Kiss Than the X-X-X," which
made use of the simulated sounds of a
kiss as part of the lyric. Someone brought
the songs to the attention of publisher
Max Dreyfus who thought so highly of
them that he engaged Gershwin, not as a
lowly song plugger or salesman, but as a
regular staff composer.

In 1918, George and Ira wrote their
first professional song together, "The
Real American Folk Song" ("Is a rag—a
mental jag"). Nora Bayes sang it in
Ladies First. The same year, Dreyfus
recommended George Gershwin to a
producer who was planning a revue starring Joe Cook. The show was called
Half-Past Eight, with Gershwin contributing five songs. The attraction turned
out to be so poor that it never got any
closer to New York than Syracuse.

A more significant advancement occurred a few months later. Alex A.
Aarons, a musician and incipient producer, had become fascinated by the
many original touches Gershwin put into
his music. Soon the two men began making plans for the show that was to mark
their mutual debuts on Broadway, *La La
Lucille* ("The New Up-to-the-Minute
Musical Comedy of Class and Distinction"). Though it was initially presented
by Alex's father, Alfred E. Aarons,

within a few weeks the names of Alex A. Aarons and George B. Seitz appeared on the program as co-sponsors.

La La Lucille, a moderately amusing bedroom farce, served well enough as a showcase for the talents of the twenty-year-old composer, and it had a respectable run. Appraising its score, Heywood Broun wrote in the *Tribune*: "The music is spirited rather than melodious. 'Tee-Oodle-Um-Bum-Bo' was the song most appreciated by the first-night audience. This may furnish some clue to the nature of the lyrics." "Personally," countered Alan Dale of the *American*, "I prefer 'Tee-Oodle-Um-Bum-Bo' to bed, bath, or plot. In the favorite parlance of the theatre, it has 'ginger.' "

The "ginger" of "Tee-Oodle-Um-Bum-Bo" was rather bland compared to the ingredients found in "Swanee," Gershwin's first really big hit, which he wrote with Irving Caesar. "At that time," Caesar recalls, "there was a raging one-step sensation, 'Hindustan.' I said to George that we ought to write a one-step and give it an American flavor." The two men discussed the idea at dinner, took a bus ride up to Gershwin's home on Washington Heights, and completed the entire song in about fifteen minutes. "Swanee" attracted little notice when it was first introduced in 1919 in a revue at the newly constructed Capitol Theatre at Broadway and 50th Street. However, Al Jolson, who was then touring in his Winter Garden hit, *Sinbad*, liked it so much that he reintroduced it in his own show. There was no doubt that Jolson's spirited delivery made the difference; before long, "Swanee" became the biggest hit in the country.

The composer's reputation as a result of "Swanee" made it easy for him to convince George White that he should be given the commission to supply songs for the next edition of the *George White's Scandals*. White had begun his series of annual revues the previous year; they were youthful, fast-moving affairs, and

the driving excitement of Gershwin's songs made him well-suited to provide the proper kind of music. While his output covered five successive editions, from 1920 to 1924, few of these songs are known today. Only the gracefully flowing "Drifting Along with the Tide" and the pseudo-tropical "South Sea Isles" have survived the first two editions—and even they are rarely performed. However, the 1922 *Scandals* did have the remarkably constructed "Stairway to Paradise" (revised from an earlier song, "New Step Every Day") for an elaborate first-act finale in which the entire company joined in the ascent. Otherwise, there were such undistinguished items as "I Found a Four-Leaf Clover" ("And the next day I found you") and "Cinderelatives," a serenade to the rags-to-riches heroines of such recent Broadway musicals as *Irene*, *Sally*, *The Love Nest*, *The O'Brien Girl*, and *Good Morning Dearie*.

The most unusual item of the 1922 *Scandals* was a twenty-minute "jazz opera" by Gershwin and B. G. DeSylva called *Blue Monday*. While it was a tentative step in the direction that the composer was later to follow in *Porgy and Bess*, it proved so out of place in its scandalous surroundings that it was cut from the show after the opening-night performance. As in Gershwin's later folk opera, the work dealt with the theme of infidelity among Negroes, although in the custom of the day, white members of the cast appeared in blackface.

The critics were a little confused by *Blue Monday*. Kenneth Macgowan of the *Globe* called it "a very painful and long-drawn incident, a sort of ragtime opera, that drags the tedious 'Mammy' motif to unbearable lengths"; Charles Pike Sawyer of the *Post* was of the opinion that, "from an artistic point of view, it was the best number in the show"; the unspecified critic of the *Telegram* (who must have been at a different theatre) referred to it as "a delicious bit of musical fun"; Charles Darnton of the *Evening*

World hit the hardest with "the most dismal, stupid, and incredible blackface sketch that has probably ever been perpetrated"; while the *Sun's* Stephen Rathbun summed up his verdict with, "It's not successful from any angle—comedy, burlesque, opera or tragedy."

Admittedly, Gershwin had much to learn before he could master the operatic form. Yet, in spite of its apparent defects, *Blue Monday* (later retitled *135th Street*) did have some moving themes. Of these, "Blue Monday Blues" still remains a haunting, expressive piece that conveys so well the feeling of frustration and hopelessness on a day when everything goes wrong.

The year 1924 was a memorable one for Gershwin; he began his career as a composer and performer of concert music, and he wrote his first Broadway musical comedy in collaboration with his brother, Ira. The first important event took place at Aeolian Hall in February. Paul Whiteman, who had been featured with his orchestra in the *Scandals of 1922*, was one of the few who had always had a fondness for *Blue Monday*. While working on the show, Whiteman told Gershwin about an idea he had for a concert devoted to American music. Would George be able to contribute a serious composition for the occasion? The result was the *Rhapsody in Blue*, which Gershwin himself performed with Whiteman's augmented "Palais Royal Orchestra." The enthusiastic reception to the *Rhapsody* (which had been given the choice "next-to-closing" spot on the program) presaged the eminence Gershwin would later attain as both a "serious" composer and performer.

Lady, Be Good!, which opened in December, was Gershwin's second major musical event of the year. Not only was it the first success on which he and Ira collaborated (*A Dangerous Maid* had failed on the road in 1921), but it also inaugurated a series of seven musicals they were to write for a producing firm Alex Aarons had recently organized with a former actor, Vinton Freedley. Excluding the unsuccessful *Tell Me More!*, which was produced by Aarons alone, the seven productions were: *Lady, Be Good!* (Fred and Adele Astaire); *Tip-Toes* (Queenie Smith, Allen Kearns, Jeanette MacDonald); *Oh, Kay!* (Gertrude Lawrence, Oscar Shaw, Victor Moore); *Funny Face* (the Astaires, Victor Moore); *Treasure Girl* (Gertrude Lawrence, Clifton Webb); *Girl Crazy* (Willie Howard, Ginger Rogers, Ethel Merman); and *Pardon My English* (Jack Pearl, Lyda Roberti). Of these, only *Treasure Girl* and *Pardon My English* were failures. Indeed, the last production was such a fiasco that it was one of the direct causes of the termination of the ten-year Aarons and Freedley partnership.

At first, it was the producers' intention to have these shows follow the bright, witty pattern of the old Princess Theatre attractions, only, according to Guy Bolton, on a larger scale. (Bolton was co-librettist on four of the musicals, and was joined on *Oh, Kay!* by his Princess Theatre collaborator, P. G. Wodehouse.) Despite these intentions, the shows soon became star vehicles rather than closely coordinated book-and-music shows. But in choosing a composer like Gershwin, Aarons and Freedley were motivated by the same considerations that had prompted F. Ray Comstock and Elisabeth Marbury to choose Jerome Kern—he was the freshest, most original composer of theatre music on Broadway. Though he was again following in the pattern of his first idol, Kern, Gershwin could no longer be accused of imitating him. His own sparkling music had already established its individuality; the Aarons-Freedley succession of hits merely provided him with greater opportunities to develop his skills. For although these shows pioneered no new theatrical ground, they did feature a number of outstanding performers who inspired the composer to produce some of his most enduring music.

Lady, Be Good! *(1924).*
Adele and Fred Astaire
perform their famous run-
around step to "Swiss Miss."

Brown Bros.

Lady, Be Good! gave Fred and Adele Astaire their second Broadway triumph. They had just returned from England where they had captivated audiences in Alex Aarons' production of *Stop Flirting* (called *For Goodness Sake* in New York). With the Gershwins' help they scored an even greater success in the new musical. *Lady, Be Good!* had a whole hopper of engaging tunes—the wistful "So Am I"; "Fascinating Rhythm"; the lonely, light-hearted plea, "Oh, Lady, Be Good!"; and the ragtime lament of the ardent suitor, " 'The Half Of It, Dearie' Blues."

One of the scenes early in the first act of *Lady, Be Good!* has always been considered as something of a classic in the field of pure mid-Twenties musical comedy. As the curtain rises, Fred and Adele, as brother and sister, have just been evicted from their apartment. Surrounded by their furniture, they try to cheer each other up by arranging the tables and chairs as if they were in their own home. Adele even hangs up a GOD BLESS OUR HOME sign on the nearest lamppost. When it begins to rain, Fred and Adele duck under a huge umbrella and break out into a consoling song-and-dance duet, "Hang On to Me."

"The Man I Love," one of the composer's most popular songs, had been intended for *Lady, Be Good!*, but it was dropped before the show reached New York. It fared no better three years later, when it was added to the first version of *Strike Up the Band*; then the musical itself closed on the road. The following year, after an attempt to fit "The Man I Love" into *Rosalie*, the song was dropped again. That it was never sung on Broadway did not disturb Gershwin. "The song is not a production number," he once explained. "It allows little or no action while it is being sung. It lacks a soothing, seducing rhythm; instead, it has a certain slow lilt that disturbs the audience instead of lulling it into acceptance. Then, too, there is the melody, which is not easy to catch; it presents too many chromatic pitfalls." Pitfalls or not,

"The Man I Love" did manage to succeed on its own, unaided by a theatrical presentation.

Tell Me More!, which opened in April, 1925, was unsuccessful. But it did have one distinction: during its tryout tour it was known as *My Fair Lady*. This was also the name of one of the songs, with the musical derivation of its title line stemming from "London Bridge Is Falling Down."

The same year, Aarons and Freedley offered a more profitable Gershwin attraction called *Tip-Toes.* "Looking For a Boy," "Sweet and Low-Down" (sung to the accompaniment of a group of kazoo trumpets), and "That Certain Feeling" were some of its musical pleasures. In his book *Lyrics on Several Occasions*, Ira Gershwin claims that *Tip-Toes* had the first score in which he noticed any development in his skills as a lyricist. He was particularly pleased with "These Charming People," which he felt was at last equal to the kind of witty lyrics that P. G. Wodehouse had created for the Princess Theatre shows.

The gay, modern pattern of musical comedy was scrupulously adhered to in a tale of rum-running and Long Island society called *Oh, Kay!* For their star, Aarons and Freedley were able to secure Gertrude Lawrence, then very much in demand as a result of her success in the imported *Charlot's Revues*. Her reason for choosing *Oh, Kay!* as her first American musical was simple: "George Gershwin was writing the music especially for me."

After its opening on November 8, 1926, the score of the Gershwin-Gershwin-Bolton-Wodehouse musical prompted critic Percy Hammond to dub the composer as the "premier music-master," and to reveal how "all of us simply floated away on the canoodling notes of 'Maybe,' and were brought back to Broadway by such flesh and bony anthems as 'Fidgety Feet' and 'Clap Yo' Hands.'" As for "Someone to Watch Over Me," Hammond testified that Gershwin had

Tip-Toes *(1925).*   Brown Bros.
The distracted lady about to have her pocked picked is Jeanette MacDonald. The pranksters are Allen Kearns and Robert Halliday.

Photo by Vandamm

"wrung the withers of even the most hard-hearted of those present."

After creating another sensation in England in *Lady, Be Good!*, the Astaires returned to Broadway in *Funny Face.* Although its book was initially to have been the product of Fred Thompson and Robert Benchley, the humorist withdrew during its hectic out-of-town tryout and was succeeded by Paul Gerard Smith. Almost to everyone's surprise, when the show opened in November, 1927, at the newly built Alvin Theatre ("Al" for Alex Aarons, "vin" for Vinton Freedley), it turned out to be an unqualified smash. The combination of the singing and the dancing of Fred and Adele and the songs of George and Ira again proved irresistible, particularly in such numbers as "He Loves and She Loves," "High Hat," "My One and Only," "Funny Face" (a forerunner of Rodgers and Hart's "My Funny Valentine" as a paean to physical plainness), and the

brilliant compilation of conversational cliches, "The Babbitt and the Bromide," during which the Astaires performed their celebrated "run-around" dance.

Apparently, neither the presence of Gertrude Lawrence nor the Gershwin songs could help *Treasure Girl.* It lasted only two months, in spite of a score that included "I've Got a Crush on You," "Where's the Boy?," "Oh, So Nice," "Feeling I'm Falling," and "I Don't Think I'll Fall in Love Today" (which dared to rhyme the seven syllable word "incompatibility" with "A B C").

Aarons and Freedley and the Gershwin brothers came back successfully in 1930 with *Girl Crazy.* Perhaps its simple-minded story was already old-fashioned (the Gershwins' *Strike Up the Band* had opened earlier that year), but there were enough other attractions to compensate for the book. In a part originally intended for Bert Lahr, Willie Howard gave an immensely comic performance as a New York taxi driver who takes a fare to Custerville, Arizona, and ends up as the sheriff. The leading female character was played by a nineteen-year-old dancer named Ginger Rogers, who had already attracted notice in *Top Speed* and in the film *Young Man of Manhattan.* She was given the romantic songs ("But Not for Me" and "Embraceable You") which were suitable for her small but attractive voice. The more raucous, direct numbers, however, needed someone who could really belt them out. Freedley found the girl he wanted at the Brooklyn Paramount where, for the first time, Ethel Zimmermann from Astoria, Long Island, was singing professionally as Ethel Merman. At the opening night of *Girl Crazy* it was she who scored the greatest personal triumph with her delivery of "Sam and Delilah," "Boy! What Love Has Done to Me!", and "I Got Rhythm." During the last number, as *Newsweek* magazine once noted, Miss Merman made history by holding one note for the full second chorus in defiance of the second law of thermodynamics, i.e., all forces must eventually come to rest.

But for a world going through the Depression, the completely meaningless, anything-for-a-laugh musical was rapidly losing its flavor and, beginning with *Strike Up the Band*, the Gershwin brothers and their collaborators were in the forefront of the change. *Strike Up the Band* was originally to have been presented in 1927, but the anti-war sentiments of the George S. Kaufman book were so uncompromising—even to the ending in which the United States is seen preparing for war with the Soviet Union—that it folded on the road. Morrie Ryskind's revised script three years later blunted the edge somewhat by having the action take place in a dream, changing the enemy to Switzerland, and giving the leads to two zany comics, Bobby Clark and Paul McCullough. Nevertheless, *Strike Up the Band* was a bold innovation in the musical theatre, capable of inspiring William Bolitho to comment in the *World*: "I don't remember ever before in a musical comedy having noticed or understood what it was all about. Here all is not only clear but really startling. Of all things in the world, here is a bitter, rather good satirical attack on war, genuine propaganda at times, sung and danced on Broadway to standing room only."

"I've Got a Crush on You" was salvaged from the unsuccessful *Treasure Girl*, while others in the amorous spirit were the mellifluous "Soon" and the bashful lover's stammering proposal, "I Mean to Say." Most of the numbers, however, were used to fill a more important need—commenting satirically upon developments in the plot and upon the characters. "The Unofficial Spokesman," inspired by the career of President Wilson's adviser, Colonel House, gave advice on how to reach the top in politics (keep your mouth shut), and "A Typical Self-Made Man" detailed the steps that must

Culver Pictures, Inc.

Photo by Vandamm

Funny Face *(1927)*. *The ladies Fred Astaire is pointing to are Betty Compton, Adele Astaire, and Gertrude McDonald.*

Strike Up the Band *(1930)*. *Paul McCullough and Bobby Clark.*

Girl Crazy *(1930)*.
Ethel Merman as Kate Fothergill. Miss Merman, according to Time *magazine, "approaches sex in song with the cold fury of a philosopher. She aims at a point slightly above the entrails, but she knocks you out just the same."*

Of Thee I Sing *(1931)*.
Lyricist Ira Gershwin, composer George Gershwin, colibrettists George S. Kaufman and Morrie Ryskind.

Culver Pictures, Inc.

Courtesy Ira Gershwin

be taken for the go-getter in business. The mocking title song (which, ironically, has since become accepted as a sincerely patriotic march) set the tone of the entire show both in words and music.

Strike Up the Band was a satirical musical comedy. *Of Thee I Sing* was more in the style of a Gilbert and Sullivan satirical comic opera. Produced by Sam H. Harris, it united for the first time the comedy team of William Gaxton and Victor Moore as the immortal John P. Wintergreen and Alexander Throttlebottom, candidates, respectively, for President and Vice President of the United States. The script by Kaufman (he also directed) and Ryskind was careful to aim its darts not at individuals but at various aspects of society—political conventions, the Congress, the Supreme Court, bathing beauty contests, even motherhood. Yet, it was all done so artfully and entertainingly that there was never a hint of viciousness or preaching.

In 1932, *Of Thee I Sing* received the Pulitzer Prize for drama. Although this was the first time that the writers of a musical comedy were so honored, the judges refused to include the name of George Gershwin in its citation on the strict technicality that he had not contributed to the actual story. The fact was, of course, that the entire production was built on the music, either in its satirical commentary or in its dramatic use to propel and develop the action of the play.

The proper mood is set immediately. When the curtain rises the stage is full of a group of noisy campaigners and voters marching up and down and singing the stirring "Wintergreen for President" while waving banners with such slogans as "TURN THE REFORMERS OUT," "VOTE FOR PROSPERITY AND SEE WHAT YOU GET," and "WINTERGREEN—THE FLAVOR LASTS." The music itself, Oscar Levant once observed, contains "an actual feeling of social comment," particu-

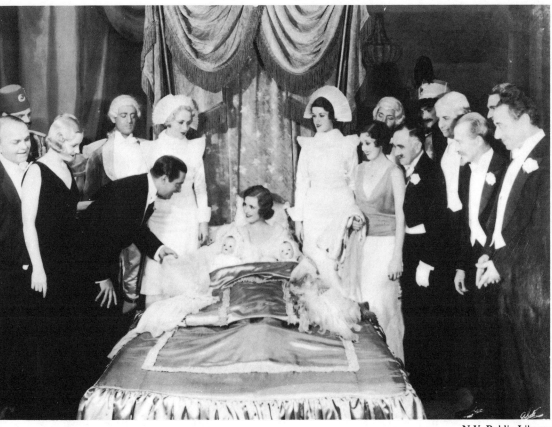

Of Thee I Sing *(1931).*
The final scene in the musical.
The proud parents of twins
are President John P.
Wintergreen (William
Gaxton) and Mary Turner
Wintergreen (Lois Moran).
Vice President Alexander
Throttlebottom (Victor
Moore) beams approvingly, at
the far left. (Setting by Jo
Mielziner.)

N.Y. Public Library

larly with the intermingling of various airs including "Tammany," "The Sidewalks of New York," and "Hail, Hail, the Gang's All Here."

The song, "Of Thee I Sing," in which the word "baby" is irreverently added to the familiar line from "America," is another example of the deftness of the Gershwin brothers' touch. But, more than consisting of mere touches, the music for *Of Thee I Sing* was employed throughout in what was unquestionably the most closely integrated manner of any Broadway show to that time. Almost all of the Atlantic City bathing-beauty pageant episode was set to music, carrying the action from the selection of Diana Devereaux as queen to the conclusion, in which Wintergreen refuses to marry her because she cannot bake corn muffins. The last scenes of the play, with their profusion of political, judicial, diplomatic, amorous, and natal complications, were sung in a series of arias, choruses,

and recitatives. Indeed, almost everything about *Of Thee I Sing* was created with a skill that had rarely been equaled in the musical comedy theatre.

Sequels seldom succeed. In 1933, *Let 'Em Eat Cake*, the successor to *Of Thee I Sing*, adhered faithfully to the rule. With the same producer, librettists, director, and stars, the new work was more astringent, more cutting than the first. An almost grim mood penetrated its discordant, contrapuntal score. Indeed, even the single love song "Mine" used a chorus to interject a sarcastic commentary during Wintergreen's serenading of Mary Turner. In spite of its failure at the box office, however, Gershwin still felt that *Let 'Em Eat Cake* was his best work to that date, calling it "the composer's claim to legitimacy."

Ever since a particularly trying day in 1926 when nothing seemed to go right at a rehearsal of *Oh, Kay!*, George Gershwin's ambition had been to compose an

Culver Pictures, Inc.

Let 'Em Eat Cake (1933). John P. Wintergreen (William Gaxton) establishes a dictatorship of the proletariat and sings "Let 'Em Eat Cake" as the first act finale. Joining him on the White House portico are the faithful Mary (Lois Moran) and Alexander Throttlebottom (Victor Moore). (Setting by Albert Johnson.)

opera based on DuBose Heyward's short novel, *Porgy*. After returning home that day, he picked up the book hoping that it would lull him to sleep. He read it straight through, however, and became so excited about its possibilities for the theatre that, at four in the morning, he scribbled a letter to Heyward expressing his interest in transforming the novel into an opera. To his surprise, Gershwin soon learned that Dorothy Heyward, the author's wife, had already begun to dramatize his story of the lame beggar of Catfish Row. But this did not really matter; Gershwin, with a remarkable cool personal insight, knew that it would take him years of study before he would have sufficient command of his medium to undertake such an ambitious project. DuBose Heyward collaborated with his wife on the play, the Theatre Guild produced it in 1927, and *Porgy* became one of the dramatic hits of the Broadway season.

Its success only fortified Gershwin's conviction that he must, someday, create an opera out of *Porgy*. In fact, the composer made no secret of this conviction even when the play opened. Critic Gilbert Gabriel of the *Sun*, who was one of the few who did not like the play, prophetically summed up his observations with: "It seems all bits, and nothing but. Or else nothing but the beginnings of the opera George Gershwin hopes to make of it."

In 1932, the Gershwin-Heyward correspondence began again. Although the composer was still interested in *Porgy*, he advised Heyward that there would have to be further delays because of his commitments to write the music for *Pardon My English* and *Let 'Em Eat Cake*. Heyward was particularly disappointed by this news; he had hoped that Gershwin's proposed operatic version of *Porgy* would bring a reverse in the financial difficulties he was having at the time. The Theatre Guild had already approached him with the tempting idea of letting Jerome Kern and Oscar Hammerstein II make a musical of the story with Al Jolson in the title role. Heyward, however, agreed to wait for Gershwin when the composer gave his assurance that he would definitely begin the opera once *Let 'Em Eat Cake* had opened on Broadway. Five days after the première, contracts were signed with the Theatre Guild; shortly thereafter, the actual writing of *Porgy and Bess* was begun.

Most of the collaboration between November, 1933, and July of the following year was done by mail, as Heyward preferred writing in the South and Gershwin was kept in New York by a radio contract. Their postal teamwork was arranged so that scenes and lyrics would be written first, and then mailed north to Gershwin to supply the appropriate music. A few months after the project had started, Ira Gershwin joined the collaboration as co-lyricist and general liaison man. (Heyward once wrote how, upon receiving the scenes, "the brothers Gershwin, after their extraordinary fashion, would get at the piano, pound, wrangle, swear, burst into weird snatches of song, and eventually emerge with a polished lyric.")

Including visits to Charleston, South Carolina, where the Heywards lived, Gershwin worked on the score for eleven months. Nine more were devoted to orchestrations. During its creation, the opera was called *Porgy*, but to avoid confusion with the original play—and to

Photo by Vandamm

Porgy and Bess *(1935)*. *The citizens of Catfish Row are about to go off on a picnic on Kittiwah Island. Sportin' Life (John W. Bubbles) stands on a table at the left; Porgy (Todd Duncan) and Bess (Anne Brown) are seated on the steps at the right. (Setting by Sergei Soudekine.)*

give it a more "operatic" flavor—the name was changed to *Porgy and Bess*. Rouben Mamoulian (who had also directed the nonoperatic *Porgy*) staged the new work, and the cast, consisting mostly of unknown singers and actors, was headed by Todd Duncan (Porgy), Anne Brown (Bess), and John W. Bubbles (Sportin' Life). Alexander Smallens conducted the forty-two-piece orchestra. Billed as "An American Folk-Opera," *Porgy and Bess* opened at the Alvin Theatre on October 10, 1935.

Convinced that *Porgy and Bess* was worthy of both dramatic and musical appraisal, the larger daily newspapers sent both drama and music critics to the première, and then ran their reviews in adjoining columns. There were wide differences of opinion with both groups, although, in general, the drama reviewers liked it better than the music critics. Burns Mantle (*News*) gave it his highest rating of four stars; Brooks Atkinson (*Times*) wrote: "The story gained by its musical investiture"; John

Mason Brown (*Post*): "A memorable production"; Robert Garland (*World-Telegram*): "A modern masterpiece." There were also varying degrees of approval from Richard Watts, Jr., (*Herald Tribune*), Gilbert Gabriel (*American*), and Walter Winchell (*Mirror*). Among those who disapproved were John Anderson of the *Journal*, who felt that it was too long; George Jean Nathan of *Life* ("indeterminate, wobbly, and frequently dull"); Stark Young of the *New Republic* ("curiously monotonous"), and Joseph Wood Krutch of *The Nation* ("I never felt myself profoundly interested or deeply moved").

The music critics seemed to have had some difficulty in trying to determine what *Porgy and Bess* really was. Samuel Chotzinoff (*Post*) called it a "hybrid"; Robert A. Simon (*The New Yorker*): "forceful and often brilliant"; Leonard Liebling (*American*): "the first authentic American opera"; Winthrop Sargeant: "no advance in American operatic composition"; Pitts Sanborn (*World-Tele-*

Photo by Vandamm

Porgy and Bess *(1935)*.
The picnic at Kittiwah Island.
John W. Bubbles, as Sportin'
Life, sings "It Ain't
Necessarily So." (Setting by
Sergei Soudekine.)

gram): "an unquestionable advance in Gershwin's art"; Paul Rosenfeld: "the score sustains no mood"; Marcia Davenport (*Stage*): "qualities of conviction and genuineness and importance"; Virgil Thomson (*Modern Music*): "falsely conceived and rather clumsily executed, but it is an important work"; Olin Downes (*Times*): "much to recommend it even though it does not utilize all the resources of the operatic composer."

Whether *Porgy and Bess* is really an opera is still being debated; that it is surely one of the most fully realized musical plays of the American theatre there is no doubt. By combining elements of the Broadway stage that he knew so well with the more challenging features of opera with which he was less familiar, Gershwin created a theatrical and musical entity that still stands as a drama of towering emotional power and vitality. More than any other work, it is most universally accepted as a genuine American opera.

Although its initial presentation lasted a mere 124 performances in New York (remarkable for a new opera but a flop according to Broadway standards), the subsequent major revivals of *Porgy and Bess* in 1942 (Cheryl Crawford production), in 1953 (as part of the Blevins Davis-Robert Breen international tour), and in 1976 (Houston Opera version with Clamma Dale) have raised the total number of its Broadway performances to 837.

What would George Gershwin have accomplished had he not died in 1937? His entire career had been the most steady, step-by-step advance of any theatre composer. There was some overlapping, but it is remarkable that his rise was so chronologically systematic—from revues (1920–1924), to musical comedies (1924–1930), to satirical comic operas (1931–1933), to an American folk-opera (1935). This continual striving after new means of expression certainly would have continued. In their book *The Gershwin Years*, Edward Jablonski and Lawrence D. Stewart reveal that before he died, the composer was planning a film ballet for George Balanchine, a symphony, and a concert tour of Europe. For the theatre he was considering three proposals: a musical cavalcade of American history for the Theatre Guild; a musical about the writing of a musical, with a book by George S. Kaufman and Moss Hart; and an opera with a libretto by Lynn Riggs. Nor had he forgotten DuBose Heyward. According to Frank Durham, the novelist's biographer, Gershwin wrote to his *Porgy and Bess* collaborator just six months before his death to discuss the possibilities of adapting Heyward's book *Star-Spangled Virgin* for the musical stage.

No matter what Gershwin would have chosen to do, however, this much is certain: it would have revealed yet another facet of the inquisitive nature and creativity that distinguished both the man and the musician.

Vincent Youmans.

CHAPTER NINE

VINCENT YOUMANS

IF EVER A PERIOD of musical comedy belonged to its composers and lyricists it was the decade between 1920 and 1930. The war had succeeded in doing what Cohan, and later Kern and Berlin, had been trying to do since the turn of the century—it cut to a minimum the influx of European operettas, thus enabling the works of a rising generation of American writers to be heard. "Back in those days," Douglas Watt once wrote in *The New Yorker*, "a sense of gaiety predominated among songwriters, but there was also a sense of pride—pride in the stimulating little island called Manhattan, pride in breaking away from European-influenced operettas, and, most of all, pride in their own audacity, for almost all of them were young men."

The twenty-year-old George Gershwin had led the way in 1919 with *La La Lucille*. Oscar Hammerstein II was twenty-four when he wrote the book and lyrics for his first musical, *Always You*, the following year. A few months later, Richard Rodgers, then all of eighteen, and Lorenz Hart, then twenty-five, were represented by their first show, *Poor Little Ritz Girl*. When he was twenty-two,

Vincent Youmans composed the music for his initial entry, *Two Little Girls in Blue*, with lyrics by the twenty-four-year-old Ira Gershwin. Cole Porter, though he had written two scores before the Twenties, came back from Europe at the age of thirty-one to do *The Greenwich Village Follies of 1924*. The same year, Howard Dietz was twenty-eight when he wrote the words to Jerome Kern's music for *Dear Sir*; two years later, his future partner, Arthur Schwartz, contributed his first numbers to *The Grand Street Follies* when he was twenty-five.

Of all the young composers, however, none was more the product of, or is more directly associated with, the Broadway musical theatre of the 1920's than Vincent Youmans. All his successful stage productions were presented during that period, including three, *Wildflower, No, No, Nanette*, and *Hit the Deck*, that were among the biggest hits of the decade.

Youmans' career has always been somewhat overshadowed by that of the more prolific George Gershwin. Indeed, there are several striking, if superficial, parallels in their lives and works. You-

Culver Pictures, Inc.

Two Little Girls in Blue
(1921).
Madeline and Marion
Fairbanks (as Dolly and Polly
Sartoris) have many shipboard
adventures on their way to
India to claim an inheritance.
It was the first Broadway
musical for both Vincent
Youmans and Ira Gershwin.

mans was born on September 27, 1898, just one day after Gershwin. Both worked for Max Dreyfus when they were young, and both were given their first Broadway assignments by Alex Aarons. The Youmans show, *Two Little Girls in Blue*, even had a book written by Fred Jackson, the author of Gershwin's *La La Lucille*, and the lyricist was George's brother, Ira. Toward the end of the 1920's, Gershwin and Youmans attempted to broaden the scope of the musical theatre, though only Gershwin was able to succeed in his more adventuresome undertakings. And, of course, the tragedy of the two composers is that their careers came to an end when they were both young—Gershwin died at thirty-eight and Youmans was forced into retirement because of tuberculosis when he was thirty-five.

The personalities of the men, however, were entirely different. Gershwin was gregarious, warmhearted, vibrant, while Youmans was a genuinely shy person whose constant illnesses were partly responsible for making him seem cold and

aloof. In their careers, Gershwin was surely the more fortunate of the two in having such a close working arrangement with his brother; Youmans seldom was able to find a lyricist worthy of his music, and, in fact, seldom worked with the same one twice. But perhaps the most unfortunate aspect of Youmans' life was that he had to stop working when he was so young; Gershwin, at least, was spared the mental and physical strain of a prolonged invalidism.

Vincent Millie Youmans (he was the third in his family with that name) was born in New York. His father was a prosperous maker of men's hats, and his mother, Lucy (Gibson) Youmans, came from a socially prominent family. At the age of four, young Vincent could play chords on the piano; soon afterward, encouraged by his mother, he began to take lessons. Although he first wanted to become an engineer, he took his father's advice and got a job with a Wall Street brokerage firm. After enlisting in the Navy at the outbreak of the war, Youmans was assigned to the Great Lakes Naval Training Station, where he began to compose songs and produce shows for his fellow servicemen.

This experience changed his mind about his future career; upon his return to civilian life, he was determined to become a song-writer. To achieve this aim, he followed the familiar path of song-plugger (for Max Dreyfus) and rehearsal pianist (mostly for Victor Herbert operettas). In 1920, inspired by the motion picture *The Country Cousin*, Youmans wrote his first published song and gave it the same title. Alfred Bryan, the veteran lyricist, wrote the words.

Youmans and Gershwin first met and became good friends when they were both working for Harms. Gershwin, highly appreciative of Youmans' talent, played a number of his friend's songs to convince producer Alex Aarons that he should hire Youmans for his next musical, *Two Little Girls in Blue*. Aarons was impressed, and Youmans got the job as

*Wildflower (1923).
Edith Day as the strong-willed
Nina Benedetto, who can
inherit her grandfather's
millions only by keeping her
temper under control for six
months. (Costume by Charles
LeMaire; setting by Frank E.
Gates and E. A. Morange.)*

co-composer with Paul Lannin, with lyrics supplied by Ira Gershwin (then modestly known by the pesudonym Arthur Francis).

Just before rehearsals began, Aarons sold the musical to A. L. Erlanger for $100,000. The composer and lyricist were retained but Ned Wayburn, Erlanger's director, warned Youmans and Ira Gershwin to stay away from rehearsals lest the producer become panicky over their youthful appearances. Erlanger really had no cause to worry. *Two Little Girls in Blue*, which opened in May, 1921, had a respectable run of 135 performances and produced three songs ("Who's Who with You," "Dolly," and "Oh, Me! Oh, My!") that sold a good many reams of sheet music.

Youmans' second musical, *Wildflower*, was one of the biggest successes of the Twenties. Responsible for its plot and

lyrics were Otto Harbach and Oscar Hammerstein II, who had been brought together in 1920 by producer Arthur Hammerstein. Harbach, the older of the two, had already written such hits as *Three Twins*, *Madame Sherry*, and *The Firefly*, and the producer felt that he would be of great help to his young nephew, then begining to write for the theatre. The year that they met, Harbach and Hammerstein collaborated on the successful *Tickle Me* (for Frank Tinney) and the unsuccessful *Jimmie*, both with music by Herbert Stothart. In 1923, the trio of Harbach, Hammerstein, and Stothart—augmented by Vincent Youmans—was reunited by Arthur Hammerstein for *Wildflower*.

Wildflower gave Edith Day her biggest success since Harry Tierney's and Joseph McCarthy's *Irene*. The score contained many delightful numbers,

No, No, Nanette (1925).
Louise Groody & Charles
Winninger sing "I Want to Be
Happy."

Brown Bros.

among them the ever-recurrent "Bam-balina," which told of an eccentric old fiddler at a country fair who liked to stop playing in the middle of a number just to embarrass the dancers. The critics were far from happy about the story. The *News's* Burns Mantle dismissed it as "one of those 'here come the girls and boys now' operettas," though Robert Benchley of *Life*, while conceding that the book was weak, concluded his review on a philosophical note: "If you're going in for books, you might as well stay home and tell stories every evening."

In spite of its shorter Broadway run, *No, No, Nanette* had a far more impressive history than *Wildflower*. Indeed, if we consider its worldwide reception and its numerous touring companies, *No, No, Nanette* was probably the biggest international hit of any of the conventional musical comedies of the decade. Without being pioneering or even particularly original, it was nonetheless a skillful combination of many of the stock farce elements then so common in musical

comedy—the philandering husband, the domineering wife, the innocent ingenue, and the amorous complications resulting from mistaken identity.

At first, *No, No, Nanette* showed all the symptoms of pre-Broadway egg-laying. Immediately following the coolly received opening performance in Detroit, in April, 1924, producer H. H. Frazee made some drastic changes: he took over as director, made librettists Frank Mandel and Otto Harbach rewrite the script, and threw out five songs. After frantic effort, Youmans and lyricist Irving Caesar produced four new numbers, including two, "I Want to Be Happy" and "Tea for Two," that became the hits of the show.

Frazee continued making changes even after the show opened in Chicago. In June, he replaced almost all of the original leads, with the two most important roles, the negatively admonished heroine and the playboy husband, taken over by Louise Groody and Charles Winninger. The musical quickly became such a hit that the producer kept it in Chicago for almost a year. Even before this company was to arrive in New York, Frazee took the unprecedented step of sending out three other companies to tour the United States, and of allowing the musical to be presented in London and other foreign localities. When, on September 16, 1925, *No, No, Nanette* at last opened in New York at the Globe Theatre (now the Lunt-Fontanne), it settled down to a respectable run of 321 performances. (Youmans always maintained that it could have run much longer if it had not toured so extensively both before and during the Broadway engagement.)

The music and lyrics of *No, No, Nanette* are full of the irresistibly buoyant spirit of the Twenties. Indeed, the words occasionally seem to be unconsciously parodying the entire era. When the curtain rises on the first scene (the reception room in the home of wealthy

Jimmy Smith), a covey of boys and girls are seen as they arrive to call on Nanette, Jimmy's ward. While waiting for her, they prance merrily down to the footlights to reveal gleefully in song that they are all "flippant and fly and free," and that they only have time for "petting parties with the smarties." Much of the period flavor is also captured in "You Can Dance with Any Girl at All," "Too Many Rings Around Rosie" ("Will Never Get Rosie a Ring!"), and the sparkling title song (whose melody Youmans appropriated from his own "My Boy and I," heard briefly in *Mary Jane McKane*).*

By 1927, although his output was limited by ill health, Youmans had become recognized as one of the leading composers of the theatre. Yet he was seldom satisfied with the way his songs were sung or performed. His first seven scores had been created with at least nine lyricists for six different producers, and his relationship was not close with any of them. He knew that he would always have to depend on others for lyrics, but there was nothing to prevent him from becoming his own producer. Therefore, at twenty-eight, Youmans formed a partnership with Lew Fields (who withdrew shortly after the opening) to present *Hit the Deck*, "A Nautical Musical Comedy" written by Fields's son, Herbert. "For the first time in my life," Youmans said at that time, "I am able to select my own singers and my own cast to interpret my music and to play the parts as I would like to have them played. For the past six or seven years, I have been completely at the mercy of the managers and of the actors."

Hit the Deck, with a cast headed by Louise Groody, Charles King, and Stella

*Two years after *No, No, Nanette* opened in New York, producer Frazee presented an alliterative sequel, the short-lived *Yes, Yes, Yvette*, with lyrics by Caesar and music by Phil Charig and Ben Jerome. In 1971, a handsomely mounted production of *No, No, Nanette* was so successfully revived that it sparked the nostalgia craze. Ruby Keeler, after a Broadway absence of forty-one years, headed the cast.

Brown Bros.

Mayhew, became Youmans' third big hit of the Twenties. To critic Percy Hammond, though he allowed that it did contain a "few fleshly jots and tittles," the show was "clean, pretty, bright, and happy," with "quantities of jolly dancing, three good songs, and romance teeming with badinage and bon mots." Its story was also considered stronger than most musical comedies of the day as it was based on a popular play, *Shore Leave*, which had been shown on Broadway five years before.

Two of the "three good songs" mentioned by Hammond were undoubtedly "Sometimes I'm Happy" and "Hallelujah!" Coincidentally, both had melodies that were not specifically created for *Hit the Deck*. "Hallelujah!", the first song Youmans had ever written, was composed during the First World War at Great Lakes. Somewhat timidly, he

Hit the Deck *(1927).* "Bilge" Smith *(Charles King)* surrounded by the admiring ladies of the ensemble. *(Costumes by Mark Mooring; setting by Ward and Harvey.)*

Rainbow *(1928).*
Libby Holman, as Lotta, about
to sing the torch song, "I Want
a Man." (Costume by Charles
LeMaire.)

showed the manuscript to "Red" Carney, the bandmaster of his group, who thought the piece had merit. According to Youmans, Carney was the first man ever to encourage him to become a composer, though, paradoxically, Carney never played the number.

"Sometimes I'm Happy" had been known as "Come on and Pet Me" when Oscar Hammerstein II and William Cary Duncan first put words to it for the 1923 musical *Mary Jane McKane*. However, it was cut before the show reached New York. In 1925, with a new lyric by Irving Caesar and Clifford Grey, "Sometimes I'm Happy" was added to the score of *A Night Out*. This time it was the show itself that did not reach New York. Youmans had faith that the song would eventually become a hit, and he made sure that a suitable place was found for it in *Hit the Deck*.

Vincent Youmans never again had a theatrical hit for which he composed the entire score. Because of failing health, he agreed to relinquish his producing activities temporarily to write the songs for Philip Goodman's production of *Rainbow*. The prospects of the show were decidedly favorable: the libretto, by Laurence Stallings and Oscar Hammerstein II, was an especially strong one, and Hammerstein's lyrics and Youmans' music were combined into a surging, dramatic score. Set in 1849 during the California gold rush, the story told of a young scout at Fort Independence, Missouri, who kills an officer in self-defense, joins a wagon train heading West, and eventually wins both a pardon and the colonel's daughter. With its realistic situations, lusty dialogue, three-dimensional characters, and intelligent use of music, *Rainbow* was in the grand tradition of *Show Boat*, with which it was favorably compared.

Unfortunately, when presented on the stage, the production lacked pace, and almost everything went wrong with it during its première on November 21, 1928.

The first-act curtain didn't fall until ten minutes to eleven, a mule misbehaved on stage, the backdrops twitched and shook throughout the entire evening, and, as Gilbert Gabriel wrote, "One intermission was so long and lapsy that the orchestra played everything but 'Dixie' to fill it up." Moreover, as a result of a disagreement between Youmans and the producer, the single love duet, "Who Am I That You Should Care for Me?" (lyric by Gus Kahn), had been removed during the tryout, leaving the score with stirring marches, torch songs, comic numbers, but not one real ballad. Most of the critics, fortunately, overlooked its faults to comment enthusiastically about the daring and originality of the work. The cast included Allan Prior, Charles Ruggles, Louise Brown, Mae Barnes, and the torrid Libby Holman, who achieved her first notice on Broadway by intoning the languorous "I Want a Man." The show never recovered from its opening-night problems, and lasted only thirty performances.

After his disappointment with *Rainbow*, Youmans again tried to be his own producer. He bought the Cosmopolitan Theatre at Columbus Circle, renamed it the "Youmans' Cosmopolitan," and set about preparing *Great Day!*, with "characters and locale of the story conceived by Vincent Youmans." But nothing went the way he wanted it. During the four months of tryouts before its October, 1929, opening in New York, writers, directors, actors, and even the costume designer quit or were fired. Moreover, of its ten original songs, only "Happy Because I'm in Love," "More Than You Know," "Without a Song," and "Great Day" were in the show by the time it had its Broadway première. (Among the casualties was Harold Arlen, who played the part of the piano player in the scene in the Hot Ace Dance Hall, and sang a song called "Doo-Dah-Dey.") *Great Day!* lasted six performances longer than *Rainbow*.

Youmans' misfortunes continued. In 1930, Ziegfeld wanted him for a production that appeared to be a certain hit: the combined talents of Marilyn Miller and Fred and Adele Astaire in a story based on an idea by Noël Coward. The show was called *Smiles*, though few were seen during either its preparation or its presentation. From the start, Youmans had difficulties with both Ziegfeld (who added Walter Donaldson's "You're Driving Me Crazy" and "Keep Smiling and Carry On" during the brief New York run), and Marilyn Miller (who sang a special lyric, "What Can I Say?" to the tune of "Time on My Hands," the hit song of the show). On the bright side there was a dance routine to "Say, Young Man of Manhattan," in which Fred Astaire, in top hat and tails, danced around chorus boys in similar attire and shot them down with his cane. The idea was later used in the film *Top Hat*, with which it has since become identified.

Through the Years, based on *Smilin' Through*, was another ambitious musical and another flop. Youmans produced it himself, gave it a painstaking production (including a forty-five piece orchestra), but the story was heavy and old-fashioned. The title song was always the composer's favorite.

Take a Chance *(1932).*
One of the musical numbers in a Broadway-bound revue called Humpty Dumpty *was "Eadie Was a Lady," sung by Ethel Merman. "She sings it," wrote Percy Hammond, "in an anteprohibition New Orleans supper club, where, surrounded by chorus girls disguised as amorous sailors from the U.S. battleship* Tampico, *she mourns the death of Eadie, a sister in sin. Ere she is through with the jocular threnody her audience is clapping its hands and waving its handkerchiefs in deserved approval."*
(Costumes by Kiviette and Charles LeMaire; setting by Cleon Throckmorton.)

N.Y. Public Library

In 1932, Youmans was called in to bolster the score of a musical called *Humpty Dumpty*, then floundering in its pre-Broadway tryout. Renamed *Take a Chance*, its original score by Richard A. Whiting, Herb Brown Nacio (better known as Nacio Herb Brown), and B. G. DeSylva was then augmented by seven songs by Youmans, two of which were dropped before New York. The show was one of Ethel Merman's early triumphs, with the final curtain delayed almost every evening by her exciting delivery of such show-stopping numbers as the Whiting-DeSylvia-Nacio "Eadie Was a Lady" (with additional lyrics by Roger Edens), and the Youmans-DeSylva optimistic, revivalistic "Rise 'n Shine." Other Youmans efforts included the schizophrenic dilemma of "pop" singers, "Should I Be Sweet?" ("... or hot? It's up to yooooou!"), and two attractive duets, "So Do I" and "Oh, How I Long to Belong to You," both sung by June Knight and Jack Whiting.

In all, the Vincent Youmans catalogue consists of less than one hundred songs, published within a thirteen-year period. But in this group are some of the most continually performed "standards" of popular music. Because his more ambitious works such as *Rainbow, Great Day!*, and *Through the Years* failed to win popular support, Youmans has become far better remembered for the quality of his music than for his innovations in the musical theatre. His intriguing harmonies and syncopations combined with a disarming economy of notes have become something of a trademark, as have such spiritual-inspired, emotionally compelling pieces as "Hallelujah!," "Great Day," and "Rise 'n Shine." But Youmans, who died on April 5, 1946, at the age of forty-seven, could also create songs that overflowed with rich melody and sentiment, distinguished by his total mastery of the composer's craft.

Lorenz Hart and Richard Rodgers.

CHAPTER TEN

RICHARD RODGERS
and LORENZ HART

APART FROM THOSE men who not only create music but also write their own lyrics, the theatre composer, as a rule, has outshone the lyricist. In the early days of the twentieth century, words of popular songs were usually so uninspired that the reputations of Victor Herbert, Sigmund Romberg, and others were far greater than those of their lesser endowed collaborators. Even more modern song-writers, such as Kern or Youmans, were better known than most of the writers who joined words to their melodies. Although the Gershwin brothers were a closely welded team, the billings usually listed "Music by George Gershwin" ahead of all other credits, and, in some cases, in larger letters than those allotted to Ira. The first composer-lyricist team to create musicals for which each man received equal recognition was that of Rodgers and Hart.

For the first 40 years of his career, Richard Rodgers had only two partners, Lorenz Hart and Oscar Hammerstein II. In each case the partnership was entirely equal. No one ever referred to a "Richard Rodgers musical"; it was always "Rodgers and Hart" or "Rodgers and Hammerstein." This "collaborative fidelity of Rodgers," Hammerstein once wrote, "is significant, I think, because it illustrates a sense of pattern and constructive purpose which never leaves him. This is not just professional habit, but a view of life."*

It also illustrates why a song by Rodgers, whether its lyric was written by Hart or Hammerstein, seems to have been the product of just one man. There is always the effect of not only a singleness of expression but of a singlemindedness as well. For to fuse lyrics with music so that each seems to belong totally and indivisibly with the other, both composer and lyricist must yield a little so that neither element in the song is given sustained prominence. It is this ability to compromise that has marked the most successful song-writing teams. That Rodgers has been able to achieve a close unity with two such disparate lyricists as Hart and Hammerstein, and to produce brilliant music with both, is a mark of his dedication and his uniqueness.

*From *The Rodgers and Hart Song Book*, with Foreword by Oscar Hammerstein II. New York: Simon and Schuster, Inc., 1951.

Richard Charles Rodgers was born on June 28, 1902, near Arverne, Long Island, where his parents, William and Mamie Rodgers, were spending the summer. His mother was a fine pianist and his father, a doctor, was a good baritone. They frequently held family concerts in their New York apartment of all the latest musical comedy and operetta successes. By the time Dick was four, he could pick out melodies on the piano; at six, he was able to play with both hands. From an early age he was enchanted by the theatre, particularly the musical theatre. When he was in his teens, Saturday afternoon would find him at the matinée of a musical; if it were by Jerome Kern, he would see it over and over again. As he once told Arnold Michaelis in a recorded interview, "If you were at all sensitive to music, Kern had to be your idol. You had to worship Kern."

It was at a summer camp in Maine, Camp Wigwam (later to be attended by Frank Loesser), that the fourteen-year-old Richard Rodgers wrote his first song, the words and music to "Campfire Days." The same year he multigraphed and distributed his first copyrighted song, "Auto Show Girl," with a lyric by David Dyrenforth.

Unlike most song-writers, Rodgers was fortunate in having a father who encouraged and helped him in his musical interests. Dick's older brother, Mortimer, however, was responsible for giving him his first chance to write for the theatre. Mortimer belonged to a social group known as the Akron Club. In 1917, when the club decided to put on an original musical comedy for the benefit of the New York *Sun* Tobacco Fund for servicemen, he managed to convince his fellow members that his fifteen-year-old brother should be allowed to write the songs. Called *One Minute Please*, the show was presented at the Grand Ballroom of the Plaza Hotel. Among the numbers were such intriguingly titled compositions as "When They Rub Noses in Alaska," "I'm a Vampire," and "At the Movies" ("If your sweetie should prove fickle, You can love her for a nickel").

Rodgers' score was so well received that the following year he was asked to contribute the music and lyrics for the second Akron show, *Up Stage and Down*. With his father assisting him on some of the melodies, and his brother helping out with the lyrics, Rodgers contributed sixteen numbers to the show. Five of them were considered good enough to be published, but the young composer did not have to find a receptive music company. His father gave him the money and he published the songs himself.

When Rodgers was only seventeen, the first Rodgers and Hart song was sung in a Broadway musical. The two young men had been brought together the previous year by a mutual friend, Philip Leavitt, who felt that they would make a good song-writing team.

Lorenz Milton Hart was born May 2, 1895, in New York City. His parents were Max and Frieda Hart, and, on his father's side, Larry descended from Heinrich Heine, the German poet. He was an inveterate reader with a great interest in both classical literature and the classical theatre. Hart was only seven when he saw his first play; from then on, he attended the theatre as regularly as he could. At Columbia University, he was active in the Varsity Shows, but he left Morningside Heights after three years to work for the Shubert brothers as a play translator. In recalling his first meeting with Hart, Rodgers once wrote in *Theatre Arts Monthly*: "He was violent on the subject of rhyming in songs, feeling that the public was capable of understanding better things than the current mono-syllabic juxtaposition of 'slush' and 'mush.' It made great good sense, and I was enchanted by this little man and his ideas. Neither of us mentioned it, but we evidently knew we'd work together, and I left Hart's house having acquired in one

Culver Pictures, Inc.

Poor Little Ritz Girl *(1920).*
Lulu McConnell, of the Poor
Little Ritz Girl *company, does*
some heavy emoting for the
benefit of stage manager Grant
Simpson. Aileen Poe, another
member of the cast, looks
rather disdainfully at the
performance.

afternoon a career, a partner, a best friend and a source of permanent irritation."

The new partners began to work together almost immediately. Leavitt, the man who had introduced them, was a neighbor and a good friend of Lew Fields, the famous comedian and producer, and in the summer of 1919, he arranged an audition for the new team to be held at Fields's Far Rockaway home. "In those days," Rodgers recalled, "all a show tune needed to be acceptable was attractiveness and a potential hit quality." Thus, after listening to all the material, Fields promptly decided to add one song, "Any Old Place with You," to the score of *A Lonely Romeo*, a musical in which he was then appearing on Broadway. The number was fitted into the show rather handily, and it became the first published song by Rodgers and Hart. "Any Old Place with You" remains an enjoyable, bouncy piece with a clever lyric that makes use of the names of geographic locations ("I'll go to hell for ya—or Philadelphia!") to create a series of original and unexpected rhymes.

Rodgers entered Columbia University in the fall of 1919. When Deems Taylor once asked him why he chose Columbia, his answer was simple: the Varsity Show. He was there only a few months when he and Hart wrote the score for a musical, *Fly with Me*, which was accepted by the Varsity Show committee. Oscar Hammerstein II, a member of the committee, even collaborated with Rodgers on one song, "There's Always Room for One More." *Fly with Me* was a satire on undergraduate life on an island ruled by the Soviets. It was greeted so enthusiastically that S. Jay Kaufman of the *Globe* wrote of the young composer: "Several of his tunes were capital. We have not heard of Mr. Rodgers before. We have a suspicion we will hear of him again."

Another member of the audience who was impressed was Lew Fields. Once again he made a quick decision: he would use some of the songs in his next musical comedy, *Poor Little Ritz Girl*. This, of course, was exciting news to Rodgers and Hart. In addition to three songs from *Fly with Me* ("Don't Love Me Like

Othello," "Peek in Pekin," and "Dreaming True," which became, respectively, "You Can't Fool Your Dreams," "Love's Intense in Tents," and "Love Will Call"), the team turned out twelve new songs for the production. That was as far as their association with *Poor Little Ritz Girl* went. Fields bought the songs outright, and never felt it necessary to consult such inexperienced talent during the show's preparation. Consequently, Rodgers and Hart were not advised of the producer's decision to cut eight of their numbers right after the Boston tryout, replacing them with eight by the more experienced Sigmund Romberg and Alex Gerber. Perhaps Fields had become nervous about entrusting an entire score to an eighteen-year-old college freshman and his twenty-five-year-old partner. Whatever the reason, the first the partners knew about the change was when they arrived at the Central Theatre for the première on July 27, 1920.

Poor Little Ritz Girl was a lightweight comedy of mistaken identity, using the musical-show-within-a-musical-show technique to present many of the songs. In spite of their decimated contribution, Rodgers and Hart did succeed in gaining some recognition. Kenneth Macgowan of the *Globe* liked Rodgers' "hard, brisk tunes," and Heywood Broun of the *Tribune* commented that "the neglected lyric also gets more of its due than usual, for 'Mary, Queen of Scots' seems to us the most rollicking ballad we have heard in a twelvemonth. It is perhaps fitting to mention that Richard C. Rodgers composed the music for this ditty as well as that for another excellent song, 'What Happened Nobody Knows.' The more serious songs are from Sigmund Romberg, and they are pleasing, but hardly as striking as the lighter numbers."

Such favorable comments, however, made little impression on Broadway producers who were reluctant to take a chance on two brash young men and

their unorthodox approach to songs. Rodgers reluctantly returned to Columbia and, with Hart, wrote the next Varsity Show, *You'll Never Know* (which included two songs, "Will You Forgive Me?" and "Let Me Drink in Your Eyes," that had been written for *Poor Little Ritz Girl* but were never used). Oscar Hammerstein II directed the show. After his second year at Columbia, Rodgers left to enroll in the nearby Institute of Musical Art (now the Juilliard School of Music). During his two years there, he found time to continue writing musicals with Hart for the Akron Club and almost any other social group that asked him. In many of these undertakings, the partners were joined by Lew Fields's son, Herbert, as either book director or dance director.

In 1924, under the perhaps protective *nom de drame* of "Herbert Richard Lorenz," Fields, Rodgers, and Hart collaborated on a comedy for Lew Fields called *The Melody Man*. Though it was about the music-publishing business and included two songs ("I'd Like to Poison Ivy" and "Moonlight Mama"), the play was not really a musical. Nor was it a hit. But it did accomplish two things: it helped to launch the career of a young actor named Fredric March, and it inaugurated the most successful musical comedy-writing trio since Bolton, Wodehouse, and Kern.

Just before the beginning of the long string of Fields, Rodgers, and Hart book musicals, the trio was associated in the production of a now-legendary revue of the mid-Twenties, *The Garrick Gaieties*. Fields's position as dance director, however, made the show a far less important assignment for him than it was for Rodgers and Hart.

The Garrick Gaieties provided the song-writers with the opportunity they badly needed. Rodgers and Hart had started auspiciously enough with *Poor Little Ritz Girl* in 1920. Yet for five years they had been unable to interest producers or music publishers; except for *The Melody Man*, they had had to devote their energies exclusively to creating amateur shows. Benjamin Kaye, a lawyer and close friend of the Rodgers family, was anxious to do what he could to help the young composer. A sometimes writer himself (he had once written the words to a Rodgers song, "Prisms, Plums and Prunes," which was in the Akron Club show *Up Stage and Down*), Kaye was helping to organize an intimate revue with a group of young actors who had appeared in Theatre Guild plays, and it was their hope that the Theatre Guild itself might sponsor the entertainment. The Guild had just built the Guild Theatre (now the ANTA), but had run short of the money needed to buy new tapestries. The revue would serve a double purpose: it would give young talent a chance to be seen, and it would raise the necessary amount for the tapestries.

At Kaye's suggestion, Rodgers was chosen as composer; at Rodgers' insistence, Hart was chosen as lyricist. Lawrence Langner and Theresa Helburn, the managers of the Guild, agreed to sponsor the show and to allow it to be shown for two Sunday performances at the Garrick Theatre. With a top price of $2.20 a ticket, *The Garrick Gaieties* featured a cast of unknown performers including Sterling Holloway, Elisabeth (Libby) Holman (in her first Broadway appearance), Edith Meiser, Romney Brent, Philip Loeb (who also directed), Lee Strasberg, and Sanford Meisner. Harold Clurman was the stage manager, and Rodgers himself conducted the tiny pit orchestra. Although it had been planned to show *The Garrick Gaieties* only on Sunday, May 17, 1925, the demand for tickets was so great that six extra performances were given. When the demand continued unabated, the show settled down for a six-month run.

The Garrick Gaieties followed the pat-

Photo by Vandamm

The Garrick Gaieties (1925). Philip Loeb and Sterling Holloway, who were in the original 1925 production, were joined by Neal Caldwell when "The Three Musketeers" was revived for the 1930 edition of The Gaieties. (Costumes by Kate Drain Lawson.)

tern set by the *Greenwich Village Follies* and *The Grand Street Follies*. It was a fresh, youthful, impudent, seemingly spontaneous revue with some of its satirical barbs aimed at the Theatre Guild itself and its fondness for heavy dramatic productions. There was in both the first and the second *Gaieties* (the second was given in 1926) such a high level of wit and melody that they have since become landmarks in the history of the revue. (Wells Root of the *World*, who attended that first Sunday performance, predicted with some accuracy that its program "will be dug up from nowhere in ten years and conned with reminiscent chuckles.")

"Manhattan," an almost wistfully bucolic tune combined with a bright, intricately rhymed lyric, was the hit of the 1925 edition, though "Sentimental Me," in which the excessively ardent emotions of popular love ballads were parodied, was also outstanding. In the 1926 *Gaieties*, the most popular item was "Mountain Greenery," a brisk number that was something of a companion piece to "Manhattan" as it sang the praises of vacations in the country. Each edition also contained a lengthy musical production as the first-act finale. In the first *Gaieties*, *The Joy Spreader* was an attempt at a jazz opera, with the inspiration for its book credited to Gilbert Seldes, "who is therefore primarily responsible for this outrage." The second *Gaieties* included a devastating lampoon of operettas called *Rose of Arizona*. As the title indicates, one of the main targets was *Rose-Marie*, with the setting changed from the Canadian Rockies to the Mexico–Arizona border. The Rodgers and Hart work had a chorus line of muscular soldiers, eight chorus girls depicting different flowers, and a group of songs all obviously plagiarized from well-known tunes ("It May Rain When the Sun Stops Shining" was an especially bright takeoff on "Till the Clouds Roll By.")*

Although most of the critics hailed the two revues, there seems to have been a slight preference for the first one. Robert Benchley felt that "Rodgers and Hart's music and lyrics, together with the burlesque sketches and the playing of half-a-dozen hitherto unknown youngsters, should be a standing taunt and source of chagrin to those uptown revue managers who keep putting on the same old thing each year." On viewing the second *Gaieties*, Percy Hammond commented, "Last year it seemed to be saying 'Ain't I Cute, I'm only six'; which it was. But this time it is a wise and flippant ingenue, well versed in the ways of the world, though a bit awkward in pursuing them."†

Between the 1925 and 1926 *Garrick Gaieties*, two Fields, Rodgers, and Hart book musicals, *Dearest Enemy* and *The Girl Friend*, were shown in New York. *Dearest Enemy*, which was written even before the first *Gaieties*, was variously described as an "operetta with more than a chance flavor of Gilbert and Sullivan" (*Times*); "something very akin to a genuine comic opera" (Arthur Hornblow, *Theatre* magazine); and "a baby grand opera" (Percy Hammond, *Herald Tribune*). The trio had originally taken the manuscript to Lew Fields, but he had feared that its story of how Mrs. Robert Murray (of Manhattan's Murray Hill) detained General Howe during the American Revolution would not be commercial. The musical was eventually sponsored by the husband of Helen Ford, the star of the show.

Rose of Arizona, apparently, was the grandmother of *Little Mary Sunshine*, Rick Besoyan's clever spoof of the same type of musical theatre, produced over thirty years later.

†In 1930, a third *Garrick Gaieties*, with songs by many different writers, was presented by the Theatre Guild. Although some of the members of the original company were present, and many of the original Rodgers and Hart songs were used, it was far less successful than its predecessors. The cast included Albert Carroll, Edith Meiser, Philip Loeb, Sterling Holloway, Imogene Coca, and, making her musical comedy debut, Rosalind Russell.

There was a well-sustained attempt to fit the music into both the story and the period. The ballads, "Here in My Arms," "Bye and Bye," and "Here's a Kiss," were dainty, charming pieces, while the comic numbers, among them "Old Enough to Love" (a gayer approach to mature love than Kurt Weill's "September Song") and "War Is War," were both funny and appropriate. "Sweet Peter" went back to an even earlier New York as it told how the boom-boom-boom of Peter Stuyvesant's wooden leg always alerted his wife when he came home drunk. In summing up his opinion of *Dearest Enemy*, Frank Vreeland of the *Telegram* wrote: "We have a glimmering notion that someday they [Fields, Rodgers, and Hart] will form the American counterpart of the once great triumvirate of Bolton, Wodehouse, and Kern."

The new triumvirate's next show, *The Girl Friend*, was indeed in the spirit of the bright, up-to-date productions once offered at the Princess Theatre. Presented by Lew Fields, with Sammy White and Eva Puck in the leads, the musical won critical and popular favor. Its book, according to Abel Green of *Va-*

riety, "is the best libretto Fields has contributed so far and is only parred by the songs with ultra-smart lyrics and oddly rhythmed and fetching tunes." Among them were the classic of city-life contentment, "The Blue Room," and the jagged ode to "The Girl Friend."

"From the beginning," wrote an unspecified *Times* critic in his review of *Peggy-Ann*, "Fields, Rodgers, and Hart have brought freshness and ideas to the musical comedy field, and in their new piece they travel a little further along their road." The show, which opened in December, 1926, was daring in almost every respect but its title. Roughly based on a 1910 Marie Dressler musical called *Tillie's Nightmare*, the entire story was a dream, with the exception of a prologue and an epilogue. Many of the conventions of musical comedy were both shattered and satirized as the slightly Freudian saga took the heroine (Helen Ford) from her home in Glens Falls, New York, to New York City's Fifth Avenue, out to sea in a yacht and then a raft, and finally to a Havana race track. There was no opening chorus, nor were there any songs at all for the first fifteen

Culver Pictures, Inc.

Photo by Vandamm

Dearest Enemy *(1925). Charles Purcell, as Capt. Sir John Copeland, is temporarily at the mercy of Helen Ford, as patriotic Betsy Burke, in this tale of the American Revolution. (Costumes by James Reynolds; setting by Clark Robinson.)*

A Connecticut Yankee *(1927). "That irrepressible young trinity" (as Gilbert Gabriel called them), Herbert Fields, Richard Rodgers, and Lorenz Hart, photographed backstage at the Vanderbilt Theatre.*

A Connecticut Yankee *(1927).*
Queen Morgan Le Fay (Nana
Bryant) seems to have
hypnotized the Yankee
(William Gaxton). (Costumes
by John Hawkins, Jr.)

Photo by Vandamm

minutes. When the dancing girls did arrive, they were used functionally within the plot rather than as unrelated ornaments. The ending, when Peggy-Ann finally awoke from her three-hour dream, was actually performed in semi-darkness.

That such an adult and original work could succeed commercially in the mid-Twenties so encouraged its trio of writers that they followed it with another dream fantasy. Early in 1921, Fields, Rodgers, and Hart had taken a six-month option on Mark Twain's *A Connecticut Yankee in King Arthur's Court*, but they were unable to interest a producer. Six years later, they had little difficulty in getting Lew Fields and Lyle D. Andrews, the co-producers of *Peggy-Ann*, to sponsor it as the next attraction at the Vanderbilt Theatre. In inventiveness and wit it may have been a less-inspired offering than its predecessor, but *A Connecticut Yankee* nevertheless attracted audiences in such throngs that it became the first Rodgers and Hart musical to run over 400 performances. The music and lyrics were an important factor in its popularity. "My Heart Stood Still" (originally sung earlier in the year by Jessie Matthews and Richard Dolman in a London revue, *One*

Dam Thing After Another) was a warm, rich melody wedded to an uncommonly expressive lyric, made all the more effective by Hart's use of simple monosyllabic words. Another hit of the score, "Thou Swell," revealed the lyricist in a more characteristic vein as he mixed old English and new American.

In 1943, after Rodgers and Hammerstein had begun their collaboration with *Oklahoma!*, Rodgers himself produced an up-dated version of *A Connecticut Yankee*. This time, the Yankee was a lieutenant in the Navy and the girl a corporal in the W.A.C. Another change enlarged the relatively minor character of Queen Morgan Le Fay to fit the major talents of Vivienne Segal. It was in this production that she introduced the hilariously macabre inventory, "To Keep My Love Alive," which, in Rodgers's words, showed "the inability on Larry's part to succumb to a cliché or to rhyme any way but brilliantly."

Rodgers and Hart had three shows on Broadway in 1928, *She's My Baby*, *Present Arms*, and *Chee-Chee*. Following the quick failure of *She's My Baby* (in spite of the efforts of Beatrice Lillie, Clifton Webb, and Irene Dunne), the composer and lyricist went back to the Fields family for their next musical. Herbert Fields, having recently written a libretto about the Navy in *Hit the Deck*, now turned his attention to the Marines in *Present Arms*. This, too, became a well-attended attraction, with critics comparing it to both *Hit the Deck* and the DeSylva-Brown-Henderson musical *Good News*. The songs, happily, were pure Rodgers and Hart—among them the unregretful "You Took Advantage of Me."

Chee-Chee, also with a book by Herbert Fields, was an ambitious work that tried to make all the songs adhere firmly to the story line. Rodgers and Hart had been anxious to write this kind of show for a long time. As Hart described it before the opening, it would be "a new form of musical show," in which "the songs are going to be a definite part of the progress of the piece, not extraneous interludes without rhyme or reason." Even its program note—similar to that of *Rose-Marie*—contained the following information: "The musical numbers, some of them very short, are so interwoven with the story that it would be confusing for audiences to peruse a complete list." Only six, including "Moon of My Delight" and "I Must Love You," were then specified by title. Everything, in fact, seemed promising about *Chee-Chee* except a plot that related the fairly indelicate account of how the son of the Grand Eunuch of old China avoided inheriting his father's exalted position. The show lasted thirty-one performances.

The quick failure of *Chee-Chee* ended Rodgers and Hart's association with Lew Fields and temporarily halted their collaboration with Herbert Fields. It also made them a little cautious. *Spring Is Here* and *Heads Up!*, their next two shows, were formula entertainments, both produced by Alex A. Aarons and Vinton Freedley. *Spring Is Here* did have "With a Song in My Heart" (though it had to be sung by the "other man," John Hundley, because the star, Glenn Hunter, could not sing); *Heads Up!* offered the gently lapping "Ship without a Sail." This was also the first Broadway musical to provide a young dancer named Ray Bolger with sufficient opportunity to demonstrate his remarkable talent.

Nor was there anything outstanding about *Simple Simon*, a lavish Ziegfeld production of 1930 in which Ed Wynn starred. Of the Rodgers and Hart songs, the maudlin "Ten Cents a Dance" has become the most popular. It was introduced by Ruth Etting, who had succeeded Lee Morse only twenty-four hours before the New York opening. During the tryout, Ziegfeld insisted that one song, "Dancing on the Ceiling," would have to be cut. Luckily, Rodgers

and Hart were able to salvage it for Jessie Matthews to sing in a London musical, *Ever Green*.

America's Sweetheart, in 1931, was the last original musical comedy written by Fields, Rodgers, and Hart. As the Mary Pickford allusion in the title suggests, it was a satire on Hollywood, where the trio had just spent some time working on a film called *The Hot Heiress*. For the leading female role of an aspiring movie actress, the authors chose an unknown singer, Harriette Lake, whom they had seen in a brief part in *Smiles* during its Boston tryout. Described by *Time* as "a lovely synthesis, one part Ginger Rogers, one part Ethel Merman," Miss Lake soon emerged with a definite personality of her own under the name of Ann Sothern.

In general, although Dorothy Parker commented in *The New Yorker* that Hart's rhymes were "less internal than colonic," greater praise was bestowed on the score than on the script. According to Brooks Atkinson, there was "a rush about the music and a mocking touch in the lyrics that make the score more deftly satirical than the production."

Despite the attitude they had shown toward the movie industry in *America's Sweetheart*, Rodgers and Hart spent the next three and one-half years in Hollywood. Upon their return to New York in 1935, their first assignment was to create the songs for Billy Rose's mammoth *Jumbo*, the final production to play at the Hippodrome Theatre. With John Murray Anderson as over-all director and George Abbott staging the book (his first musical), *Jumbo* was, according to Percy Hammond, "a sane and exciting compound of opera, animal show, folk drama, harlequinade, carnival, circus, extravaganza, and spectacle." Jimmy Durante headed the cast of ninety humans and almost as many animals.

The myriad problems of such a huge undertaking—financial as well as creative—compelled Billy Rose to delay the

Simple Simon *(1930).*
Ed Wynn comes to the rescue
of Cinderella in this musical
Mother Goose fantasy. "Wynn
has never seemed so
indisputably great," wrote
Brooks Atkinson.

Culver Pictures, Inc.

America's Sweetheart *(1931).*
Rodgers and Hart's musical
about the movies had Jack
Whiting and Harriette Lake
(better known as Ann
Sothern) as two ambitious
young actors. In this scene,
Miss Lake is obviously not
amused at Mr. Whiting's gift
of a success horseshoe
consisting of fruits and
vegetables. (Costumes by
Charles LeMaire; setting by
Donald Oenslager.)

Brown Bros.

Jumbo *(1935).*
The "Circus Wedding" finale
with Donald Novis and Gloria
Grafton as the groom and
bride. (Costumes by Raoul
Pène du Bois; production
designed by Albert Johnson.)

On Your Toes *(1936).*
George Balanchine's Slaughter
on Tenth Avenue *ballet.*
Tamara Geva as the Strip-
Tease Girl, George Church the
Big Boss, and Ray Bolger the
Hoofer. (Costumes by Irene
Sharaff; setting by Jo
Mielziner.)

Babes in Arms *(1937).*
Aljan de Loville, as a French
pilot, makes a forced landing
in the midst of Mitzi Green,
Rolly Pickert, Alfred Drake,
Ray Heatherton, and Wynn
Murray. (Costumes by Helene
Pons; setting by Raymond
Sovey.)

Photo by Lucas-Pritchard

première for almost three months beyond its scheduled date. Surprisingly, after it did open, Broadway customers kept it running for only five months. After closing in New York, it reopened at the Dallas Exposition with Eddie Foy, Jr., in the Durante part. But eventually, as a headline in *Variety* sadly revealed: "'JUMBO' DISINTEGRATES INTO 50-CENT CIRCUS; TEXAS DATE ANOTHER FLOP, RAN SHOW $30,000 FURTHER INTO RED."

Although they were always anxious to explore novel ideas for the musical stage, Rodgers and Hart were never completely successful in contributing to the structure of the musical theatre until *On Your Toes* in 1936. This time the partners decided to write the book themselves, which they did in collaboration with George Abbott. Thus, they were able to create a strikingly unified production that not only offered a coherent story but also utilized dancing as an integral part of the action. For the important post of dance director, they secured George Balanchine, the ballet choreographer, whose only previous Broadway experience had been in staging some of the dances for the *Ziegfeld Follies of 1936.* The most memorable sequence in *On Your Toes* was the *Slaugh-*

ter on Tenth Avenue ballet, in which Balanchine's choreography, the dancing of Ray Bolger and Tamara Geva, the sleazy excitement of Rodgers' music, and the ballet's dramatic importance all combined to lift *On Your Toes* to a position as one of the supreme theatrical achievements of the mid-Thirties.

The producer of *On Your Toes* was Dwight Deere Wiman. For the next two years he followed it with annual spring musicals bearing the credits, "Book, music, and lyrics by Rodgers and Hart," and "Choreography by George Balanchine." In 1937, their combined efforts created *Babes in Arms*; in 1938, it was *I Married an Angel.*

Babes in Arms was full of *Garrick Gaieties* youthfulness, with a cast headed by such youngsters as Mitzi Green, Ray Heatherton, the Nicholas Brothers, Wynn Murray, and, in minor roles, Alfred Drake and Dan Dailey. More important, it was another serious attempt to make each song serve a purpose in the story, which, conveniently, was concerned with young people putting on an amateur musical. Seldom has one show produced so many enduring hits—the saga of the vocal phenomenon known as "Johnny One Note"; the almost psychological "Where or When"; "My Funny Valentine," in which the warmth of the music conveys so perfectly the true intent of the slightly exaggerated lyric; the duet, "I Wish I Were in Love Again," with its unusual combination of disillusionment and ebullience; and the brazen confession of the nonconformist, "The Lady Is a Tramp."

John Anderson in the *Journal-American* hailed *I Married an Angel* as "a winged wonderwork from the musical heavens of Rodgers and Hart," an appraisal that may have been only slightly excessive. The story, which Rodgers and Hart had originally adapted for the movies in collaboration with Moss Hart, was an imaginative tale of a Budapest banker (Dennis King) who vows that he

I Married an Angel *(1938).*
Walter Slezak and Dennis
King. (Costumes by John
Hambleton; setting by Jo
Mielziner.)

"Beauty is truth, truth beauty
/ Gabriel blow your root-toot-
tooty," sing Vera Zorina and
fellow angels in "Angel
without Wings."

will marry only an angel, and the awkward situations that arise when a real angel (Vera Zorina) actually becomes his bride. The cast was particularly notable. Both King and Walter Slezak had recently distinguished themselves in straight dramas. After an eight-year self-imposed exile from the musical stage, Vivienne Segal returned to Broadway in the kind of light comedy part she had been trying to get ever since *The Three Musketeers*, her last musical, in which she had also appeared opposite Dennis King. Vera Zorina, who had scored a hit in the Tamara Geva role in the London production of *On Your Toes*, gave her most fondly remembered performance as the lovely angel-bride.

I Married an Angel, the first musical to be directed by Joshua Logan, also benefited from Jo Mielziner's decor, which incorporated treadmills and a curtain that functioned like a huge Venetian blind.

The score offered such glittering Rodgers and Hart gems as "Did You Ever Get Stung?" ("Where the doctor can't help you"), "I Married an Angel," "I'll Tell the Man in the Street," "A Twinkle in Your Eye," and the poignant "Spring Is Here," in which the beauties of spring are found to have little appeal when one is unloved. However, the undisputed show-stopper was the audacious travesty of every Roxy and Radio City Music Hall stage spectacle, "At the Roxy Music Hall" ("It's a Wonderland where everyone is Alice/Where the ladies' room is bigger than a palace."*)

Between *Babes in Arms* and *I Married an Angel*, Rodgers and Hart and librettists George S. Kaufman and Moss Hart collaborated on a musical social satire, *I'd Rather Be Right*. Following the precedent set by Moss Hart's and Irving

---

*Copyright © 1938 Robbins Music Corporation. Used by special permission.

Berlin's *As Thousands Cheer*, actual living people were portrayed. Instead of offering impersonations in a number of blackout sketches, however, *I'd Rather Be Right* was a regular book musical with President Franklin D. Roosevelt as the leading character. Portraying the role was the semiretired, but still agile, George M. Cohan.

Because of the news value of such a production, newspapers and news magazines treated the preparation of *I'd Rather Be Right* as a major event. There were headlines when, during the Boston tryout, Cohan refused to sing an uncomplimentary line about his friend, Al Smith, in the song, "Off the Record." There were more headlines when Noël Coward was called in to help rewrite and restage some of the material. There were still more headlines concerning the friction between Cohan and Rodgers and Hart, whom the star disparagingly referred to as "Gilbert and Sullivan." Even the New York *Times* devoted an editorial to "Spoofing the Great" (they were for it). All these helped give the show a record advance sale of $300,000. ("Why the idea of calling George M. Cohan Franklin D. Roosevelt should have engendered so intense an interest I cannot figure out," wrote George Jean Nathan in *Newsweek*, "unless it was because Franklin D. Roosevelt, on the other hand, has been called everything under the sun but George M. Cohan.")

Almost inevitably, when *I'd Rather Be Right* at last arrived at the Alvin Theatre in New York on November 2, 1937, there were some who felt disappointed. Richard Lockridge, whose review was carried on page one of the *Sun* and contained almost every punch line in the show, commented that it was not always brilliant satire. In comparing it with *Of Thee I Sing*, which almost everyone did, the general feeling was that Gershwin, Gershwin, Kaufman, and Ryskind were more skillful than Rodgers, Kaufman, and the *Zwei Herzen* (as John Mason Brown referred to the unrelated Moss and Lorenz). George M. Cohan, however, scored a great personal triumph that might well have elected *him* President, and audiences were made acutely aware that nowhere else in the world could so outspoken a production be shown.

The score for *I'd Rather Be Right* was written in just three weeks. It contained only one moderately popular song, "Have You Met Miss Jones?"; the rest of the numbers being too satirical and too close to the theme for any of them to catch on.

After their three-in-a-row springtime musicals for Dwight Deere Wiman, Rodgers and Hart evened their seasonal average by writing three successive fall shows for producer-director George Abbott—*The Boys from Syracuse* (libretto by Abbott) in 1938, *Too Many Girls* in 1939, and *Pal Joey* in 1940. The first of these, an uninhibited fast-moving adaption of Shakespeare's *The Comedy of Errors*, so impressed Richard Watts, Jr., of the *Herald Tribune*, that he wrote: "If you have been wondering all these years just what was wrong with *The Comedy of Errors*, is it now possible to tell you. It has been waiting for a score by Rodgers and Hart and direction by George Abbott."

The long-awaited score still remains one of the team's finest, highlighted by "This Can't Be Love," "You Have Cast Your Shadow on the Sea," "Falling in Love with Love," the show-stopping "Sing for Your Supper," and the romantic tribute to the winter solstice, "The Shortest Day of the Year." The two Dromios were played by Jimmy Savo and Teddy Hart (Larry's brother), and their masters were Eddie Albert and Ronald Graham.

Too Many Girls had a collegiate setting (Pottawatomie College, Stop Gap, New Mexico) and a sterling football backfield

Photo by Alfredo Valente

Photo by Vandamm

I'd Rather Be Right *(1937).*
Gathered around the piano in Sam Harris' office are producer Harris, lyricist Lorenz Hart, composer Richard Rodgers, colibrettists Moss Hart and George S. Kaufman, and star George M. Cohan.

The Boys from Syracuse *(1938).*
Marcy Westcott, Wynn Murray and Muriel Angelus stopping the show with "Sing for Your Supper." (Costumes by Irene Sharaff.)

Photo by Hermann-Pix

Too Many Girls *(1939).*
Desi Arnaz, as the football
hero of Pottawatomie College,
leads the students in the torrid
"Spic and Spanish" number.
On the right is an equally
animated Diosa Costello, and
behind them is Van Johnson.
(Costumes by Raoul Pène du
Bois.)

in Hal LeRoy, Eddie Bracken, Desi Arnaz, and Richard Kollmar, cheered on by coeds Marcy Westcott, Mary Jane Walsh, and Diosa Costello. One of the energetic undergraduates was Van Johnson, who later succeeded Kollmar for the tour. The production had so much vitality and so many fine Rodgers and Hart songs that few were troubled by its old-fashioned book or the awkward way some of the numbers were incorporated into it.

The idea of fashioning a musical out of a series of short stories about a conniving hoofer named Joey Evans was first suggested by the author himself, John O'Hara, in a letter to Rodgers. It took Rodgers and Hart only five minutes to decide to do it, and they promptly notified O'Hara that they would be glad to write the songs if he supplied the book. For the leading part, Rodgers chose a young actor named Gene Kelly, whom he had seen in a dancing role in William Saroyan's *The Time of Your Life.* As his middle-aged, worldly patroness there could be no other actress than Vivienne

Segal, who had recently demonstrated her gifts as a brittle comedienne in *I Married an Angel.*

In many ways, *Pal Joey* was the pinnacle of the Rodgers and Hart collaboration. The score was purposely unsentimental and sardonic, allowing only one love song, "I Could Write a Book," and even that was an insincere expression. Throughout, there was a cohesion of mood between music and plot that was remarkable, though not all the songs were used to advance the action. Some of the best ("Happy Hunting Horn," "The Flower Garden Of My Heart," "That Terrific Rainbow") were part of a nightclub floor show; "Zip" was an out-of-nowhere, in-front-of-the-curtain routine; "Do It the Hard Way" was a specialty number for tumbler Jack Durant. Others, however, such as "(In Our Little) Den of Iniquity," "Bewitched, Bothered, and Bewildered," and "Take Him," were all intelligently introduced as part of the story. In whatever manner they were performed, however, all the songs shed light on the smoky individuals who sang them and about whom they were sung.

Peopled by characters who were either unattractive or just stupid, *Pal Joey* was too far from musical comedy orthodoxy for many of the patrons and some of the critics. "Although it is expertly done, can you draw sweet water from a foul well?" asked Brooks Atkinson. To Wolcott Gibbs, however, it was that rarity, "A song-and-dance production with living, three-dimensional figures, talking and behaving like human beings."

Pal Joey may well have been ahead of its time. When it was revived in 1952 by Jule Styne and Leonard Key, it met with much greater success. "While Joey himself may have been fairly adolescent in his thinking and his morality," Rodgers observed shortly before the second opening, "the show bearing his name certainly wore long pants, and in many respects forced the entire musical comedy theatre to wear long pants for the first

Photo by Vandamm

Pal Joey *(1940).*
Joey's dream of the Chez Joey
night club at the end of the
first act. Gene Kelly and
Vivienne Segal are in the
center. Van Johnson is at the
extreme right. (Costumes by
John Koenig; setting by Jo
Mielziner.)

time." With Vivienne Segal in her original role, with Joey played by Harold Lang (understudied by Bob Fosse), and with hardly a line changed, the musical had the longest run (542 performances) of any Rodgers and Hart production. The once divided critics were now almost unanimous in their praise. Words like "masterpiece" and "classic" were in their reviews, and some compared it to the Kurt Weill-Bert Brecht *Die Dreigroschenoper.* Even Brooks Atkinson could now feel that "it renews confidence in the professionalism of the theatre," while a slightly gloating Wolcott Gibbs noticed that "standards apparently have changed, because up to now I have met nobody who found anything embarrassing in the goings on."

The April before the first *Pal Joey* opened, Dwight Deere Wiman tried to revive his streak of spring musical successes with Rodgers and Hart's *Higher and Higher,* but it was a failure. The producer was more fortunate in the summer of 1942 when he joined Rodgers (in association with Richard Kollmar) to

present *By Jupiter.* Starring the nimble Ray Bolger, it was a formula Rodgers and Hart show full of what the customers could easily appreciate as pre-World War II glamour, and it became one of the team's most profitable undertakings.

The partnership of Rodgers and Hart, however, was all but finished. Hart, a brilliant, unstable man given to mysterious disappearances for weeks at a time, was becoming extremely difficult for Rodgers to work with. In 1941, the composer had secretly aligned himself with George Abbott as co-producer of *Best Foot Forward* (score by Hugh Martin and Ralph Blane), and early in September of that year had discussed with his old friend, Oscar Hammerstein II, the possibility of a partnership if the time ever came when Hart could no longer continue. When Theresa Helburn of the Theatre Guild approached Rodgers with the idea of adapting Lynn Riggs's play, *Green Grow the Lilacs,* into a musical, he immediately became enthusiastic about the project. Hart demurred. He didn't feel well, it wasn't their kind of

Photo by Eileen Darby—Graphic House

Pal Joey (1952).
Vivienne Segal recreates her
original role of Vera Simpson,
and Harold Lang is the new
Joey Evans. Here they sing
("In Our Little Den) of
Iniquity." (Costumes by Miles
White; setting by Oliver
Smith.)

show, and if Rodgers really wanted to do the show, why didn't he choose another lyricist. It was then that Rodgers and Hammerstein agreed to work together on the play that eventually became *Oklahoma!* Hammerstein, in fact, had long wanted to make a musical out of *Green Grows the Lilacs*, and had even tried unsuccessfully to interest Jerome Kern in collaborating on it.

The last show Lorenz Hart worked on was the 1943 production of *A Connecticut Yankee*. Throughout the opening-night performance, Hart remained in the rear of the theatre, walking back and forth and muttering to himself. When Rodgers looked for him after the final curtain, he was nowhere to be found. Two days were spent in frantic efforts to locate him. When he was finally found unconscious in a hotel room, Hart was immediately rushed to Doctors Hospital, suffering from acute pneumonia. Rodgers and his wife were with him almost constantly for three days, but he never regained consciousness. On November 22nd, in the midst of an air-raid-drill blackout, Lorenz Hart died. He was forty-eight years old.

The collaboration between Rodgers and Hart was a unique one in many ways. Aside from its productivity and longevity, it was a near-perfect combination of frequently sharp, sophisticated lyrics set to music that was just as frequently warm and lyrical. The remarkable thing, of course, is how well each man complimented the other's style, adding something both inseparable from, and indispensable to, the total effect. (The Rodgers and Hart technique, incidentally, was somewhat opposite from

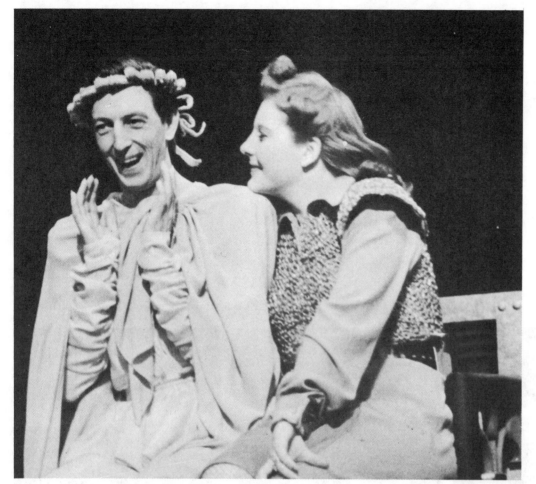

Photo by Richard Tucker

By Jupiter *(1942).*
Ray Bolger as Sapiens and
Benay Venuta as Hippolyta in
a musical remake of Julian
Thompson's The Warrior's
Husband. *(Costumes by Irene*
Sharaff.)

that of the Gershwin brothers. George's hard-driving, jagged rhythms were often smoothed down by what Vernon Duke has called the "lazy, good-natured, placidly *gemutlich* fun with words that was Ira's characteristic.")

Freshness, charm, and daring, coupled with an unquenchable spirit of youthfulness, were present in almost everything that Rodgers and Hart wrote. The methodical, outwardly calm composer and his excitable, cigar-chewing partner were continually seeking new ideas in songs and in stories, and the range of subject matter in their musicals attests to their inquisitive, experimental nature. *Time* magazine wrote, in 1938: "As Rodgers and Hart see it, what was killing musi-comedy was its sameness, its tameness, its eternal rhyming of June with moon. They decided it was not enough to be just good at the job; they had to be constantly different also. The one possible formula was: *Don't have a formula*; the one rule for success: *Don't follow it up.*"

*B. G. DeSylva, Lew Brown
and Ray Henderson.*

Photo by Max Mun Autrey. Courtesy Ray Henderson

CHAPTER ELEVEN

B. G. DeSYLVA
LEW BROWN
and RAY HENDERSON

FROM THE STANDPOINT OF PRODUCTIVITY—at least—there has never been, nor will there ever be again, a period like the Twenties. At no time during the decade did the number of new Broadway musicals, both book shows and revues, drop below thirty-seven per season. During two seasons, 1920–21 and 1927–28, the figure reached the staggering total of forty-eight! Reasons for this musical plethora along Broadway are easy to find: costs were relatively low and, except for night clubs and vaudeville, there just was no competition from any other media offering light theatrical entertainment embellished by songs.

Such multiplicity of attractions naturally required a corresponding multiplicity of composers and lyricists. Operetta was special. That was still primarily for the European-trained, classically oriented. But musical comedy and revue required writers who were not only versatile but adept at creating self-sustaining songs, songs that could tell their stories and express their emotions succinctly and completely, with only a nodding relationship to the stories to which they were affixed. Apart from their quality, musical numbers stood out because they literally stood out; they were spotlighted and illuminated as soon as the boy tossed a line at the girl that set up the song cue.

In musical construction and in lyrical expression many of the songs for the average musical of the Twenties were undeniably period pieces. They sighed and they bubbled with the innocence of the decade. They were created solely for the entertainments of their time and they reflected it. Yet while that time has long since faded, the songs of the decade continue to exert an emotional hold on the listener. They transport us, as no play or costumed operetta could, into a more naive but unquestionably happier period of our national life.

There were hundreds of writers then, pouring out song after song, and meeting almost any requirement of the usually patchquilt productions then being offered. Harry Tierney and Joe McCarthy emphasized sweet romance in *Irene*, knockabout comedy in the Eddie Cantor vehicle, *Kid Boots*, and south-of-the-border spectacle in *Rio Rita*. Harry Ruby and Bert Kalmar kept things light and lively in such farcical diversions as *The Ramblers* (for Clark and Mc-

Cullough), *The Five O'Clock Girl, Good Boy*, and the Marx Brothers' *Animal Crackers*.

But among the creators of hummable, durable "period" songs, no team ever enjoyed the success of B. G. ("Buddy") DeSylva, Lew Brown and Ray Henderson. It was their special knack to take an up-to-date topic—be it college life or country club life or aviation or whatever—and deck it out with a serviceable book, some bright numbers for raucously funny clowns like Bert Lahr or personality boys like Harry Richman, and then tie the whole bundle together into an uptempoed, youthful, gag-filled package. The songs could be whistled by anyone and their lyrics—beginning with a catch phrase like "You're the cream in my coffee" or "Button up your overcoat"—were hard to forget. The credit line, "Songs by DeSylva, Brown and Henderson," was enough to stamp the entertainment with the writers' own particularly well-meshed personalities; to this day, it still symbolizes a body of works that was especially endemic both to period and locale.

Although their creativity frequently overlapped and specific credits for lyrics or music were seldom listed, in general DeSylva and Brown worked on the words and Henderson on the music. Taking them in the order of their billing, B. G. DeSylva—known as "Bud" or "Buddy" but christened "George Gard"—was born in New York on January 27, 1895. His father, an actor-turned-lawyer, moved the family to Los Angeles when young Buddy was two. At four the precocious youngster appeared in a local benefit show billed as "Baby Gard," and was even offered a contract to tour the B. F. Keith vaudeville circuit. Mother wouldn't hear of it, however, and Buddy remained home to attend the local high school and, briefly, the University of Southern California. The summer following his sophomore year, he joined three classmates as singing and ukulele-

strumming "Hawaiians" at a nearby country club. He had also begun making up songs which he sang for the club's members and their guests, including, one night, Al Jolson. Ever on the lookout for new material, Jolson particularly liked one DeSylva song, " 'N Everything," bought a half interest in it, and sang it in *Sinbad* later that year. That was all the impetus DeSylva needed; he promptly came east to see if he could make a full-time career of song writing. Six months later he received his first royalty check—$16,000.

DeSylva needed no further convincing. He signed with the Remick Publishing Company, and began turning out even bigger hits for Jolson—"Avalon" written with Vincent Rose, "April Showers" with Louis Silvers, "California, Here I Come" with Joe Meyer. In 1919, when he was twenty-four, DeSylva joined with a twenty-year-old piano-pounder named George Gershwin to write his—and Gershwin's—first Broadway score, *La La Lucille*. Other distinguished collaborations soon followed. With Jerome Kern, DeSylva wrote "Look for the Silver Lining," the song hit from *Sally*, and, with Victor Herbert, the score for *Orange Blossoms* (including "A Kiss in the Dark"). The team of DeSylva and Gershwin was reunited for the *George White's Scandals* of 1922, which they followed with two other annual editions (among their songs: "I'll Build a Stairway to Paradise" and "Somebody Loves Me"). When Gershwin gave up composing music for the George White extravaganzas to concentrate on writing for book shows, the producer decided to replace him with a promising young Tin Pan Alley composer named Ray Henderson. But Henderson, who had been writing on and off with lyricist Lew Brown, was anxious to establish a steady partnership with Brown. This put White in an awkward position since he had already signed DeSylva for the next edition of his

Culver Pictures, Inc.

Sinbad *(1918).*
Sinbad (Forrest Huff)
discovers Inbad (Al Jolson)
prowling about the harem.
Jolson sang DeSylva's first hit,
" 'N Everything," in this show.

Scandals. His solution: why don't the three try to work together? They did, found that their talents meshed, and thus began a song-writing triumvirate that was to last until 1931.

Lew Brown had been the first of the trio to meet with success. Born in Odessa, Russia, on December 10, 1893, he was brought to the United States by his immigrant parents when he was five. At sixteen, while serving as a lifeguard at a Rockaway beach, he began jotting down parodies of popular songs of the day. Then he tried a few original lyrics and, at the urging of friends, showed them to veteran composer Albert Von Tilzer. Von Tilzer liked Brown's lyrics, and the two began a fruitful collaboration. At nineteen, Lew Brown had had his first success with Von Tilzer, "I'm the Lonesomest Gal in Town," which the team soon followed up with "Give Me the Moonlight, Give Me the Girl," "I

May Be Gone for a Long, Long Time" (Grace LaRue introduced it in *Hitchy-Koo, 1917*), and "I Used to Love You but It's All Over Now."

In 1922, publisher Louis Bernstein, of Shapiro-Bernstein, spotted Brown as the perfect partner for a young composer he had under contract named Ray Henderson. The first Brown and Henderson song, "Georgette," did pretty well and was interpolated in the *Greenwich Village Follies.* Henderson, who was born in Buffalo, N.Y., on December 1, 1896, was taught piano by his mother even before he went to grammar school. After studying at the Chicago Conservatory, he joined local dance bands as a pianist. From Chicago, he went to New York where he climbed the musical ladder from song-plugger, to arranger-pianist, to composer. During the early Twenties, Henderson's gifts became recognized with such efforts as "That Old Gang of

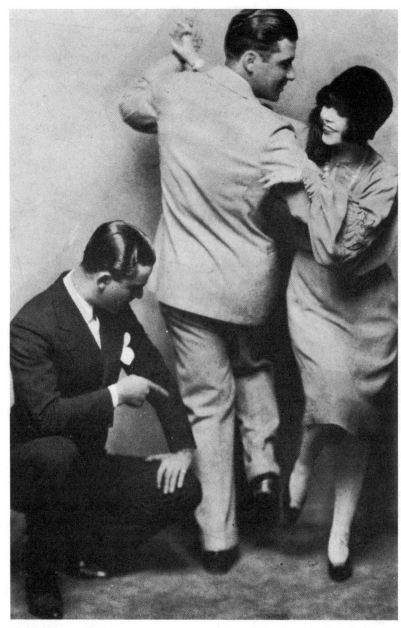

Culver Pictures, Inc.

George White's Scandals (1926).
Producer-director George White teaching the intricacies of "The Black Bottom" to Tom Patricola and Ann Pennington.

Mine" (lyric by Billy Rose and Mort Dixon), "Bye Bye Blackbird" (lyric by Dixon alone), "Five Foot Two, Eyes of Blue" and "I'm Sitting on Top of the World" (the last two with Sam Lewis and Joe Young). The first Henderson melody mated to words by Buddy De-Sylva (in collaboration with Bud Green) was "Alabamy Bound," identified with both Al Jolson and Eddie Cantor. The song was introduced early in 1925, the same year DeSylva, Brown and Henderson were united for their first *George White's Scandals.*

Surprisingly, the special DeSylva-Brown-Henderson chemistry took a little while to become apparent. The maiden effort for the *Scandals* produced nothing memorable at all—not even with the inspiration of Helen Morgan in her Broadway debut. But the trio's second score the following year turned out to be one of the glories of the mid-Twenties revues, contributing much to achieving what Wells Root dubbed in the *World*, "the master *Scandals* of the series."

George White was determined, right from the outset, to make it exactly that. He was so confident that he would have the triumph of his career that he charged $55.00 per ticket for the first nine rows on opening night (thereafter it dropped to the still steep price of $5.50). No one was heard demanding his money back. The show had, for its day, everything. There was Harry Richman, in straw hat and cane, strutting through "Lucky Day" (in which "horseshoe" rhymed with "of course you"), rimmed by lovelies apparelled as a Wishbone, a Horseshoe, a Four-Leaf Clover, a Star, a New Moon, and a Haystack. There were the Howard brothers, Willie and Eugene, cavorting through a wild sketch about a woman barber (Frances Williams), and another one about their dear old days at the Winter Garden. There was the eye-boggling "Triumph of Women" montage, with the likes of Mme. Sans-Gene, Salome, Mme. DuBarry, Lucretia Borgia,

Cleopatra, and Eve serenaded to the tune of "Lady Fair." There were Richman and Miss Williams mutually cooing "The Girl Is You and the Boy Is Me." There was dimple-kneed Ann Pennington, the *Scandals'* celebrated dancing doll. There was the new dance craze (Mr. White had to have one every year), "The Black Bottom," "a slap-foot, drag-foot, oozy sort of dance (to quote John Anderson in the *Post*) from the mud flats of the Suwanee River, moaning a little swampily as it lags through its sinuous gyrations."

And there was, most certainly, "The Birth of the Blues." In the first act finale, a jazz-versus-classics duel, Willie Howard played Beethoven, brother Eugene was Liszt, and Harry Richman was the champion of that native musical form, the blues, assisted by the McCarthy sisters personifying the "St. Louis Blues" and the "Memphis Blues." To prove to the obdurate longhairs that this was indeed music worthy of their admiration, Richman offered in evidence, "The Birth of the Blues," tracing its genesis to the breeze in the trees singing weird melodies, the wail of a downhearted incarcerated frail, and a note from a whippoorwill high on a hill. In addition to these disparate pregenital origins, there was a further evidential piece, Gershwin's "Rhapsody in Blue" (with lyrics!). That did it. The immortals of music grandly let open the heavenly gates, and the curtain fell on a glimpse of Paradise with indigo-spotlighted angels perched on a flight of steps trilling the final notes.

There was no official *George White's Scandals* in 1927. However, to many, the DeSylva-Brown-Henderson almost book-less book show, *Manhattan Mary*, produced by George White, was an acceptable substitute. It had a great clown (Ed Wynn), a new dance step ("The Five Step"), and, as part of its slender story, the heroine (Ona Munson) actually ended up as the queen of the *Scandals*.

All the principal performers of the 1926 *George White's Scandals*—plus the song-writing trio—were reunited for the ninth edition of the revue in 1928. Again in full-throated command of most of the songs was the ebullient Harry Richman, sailing into "Crest of a Wave" ("Do I theem to efferveth!"), and, in "What D'Ya Say?," crooning into Frances Williams' ear, "You're so very cute you're/Bound to have a future." According to Richman's autobiography, *A Hell of a Life*, "It seems hard to realize that song writers could have written material so perfectly styled to an entertainer. It was as though they somehow had got inside my skin and joined forces with my brains and lungs."

Sandwiched in between the last two editions of the *Scandals* that all three writers did together was their first major book musical, *Good News!* The show was unquestionably the quintessence of the DeSylva-Brown-Henderson musical comedy genre, and set the stage for no less than three successes in the general mold—*Hold Everything, Follow Thru* and *Flying High. Good News!* did it simply by taking a lively modern subject—collegiate life—as a peg to hang any

Good News *(1927).*
College roommates Gus Shy and John Price Jones sing the praises of Jones' latest flame. (Costumes by Kiviette; setting by Donald Oenslager.)

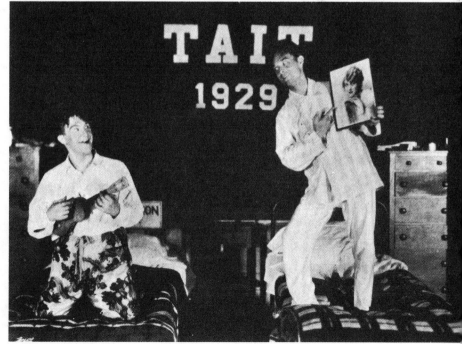

Hold Everything *(1928). Cook Victor Moore, trainer Harry T. Shannon and prize-fighter Bert Lahr have their problems at the training camp. (Setting by Henry Dreyfuss.)*

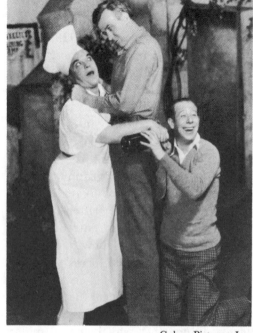

Culver Pictures, Inc.

number of situations and songs that reflected the naively hedonistic attitude of the period. It was all speed and youth and fun, and those concerned made sure the audience got into the proper spirit right from the start: before the show began, George Olsen's band filed down the aisles in college sweaters, and gave out with a rah-rah cheer before settling down to playing the overture. The story line concerned one Tom Marlowe (played by John Price Jones), dear old Tait's football star and ladies' man (he had a song called "He's a Ladies' Man"), his romantic entanglements, scholastic hurdles, and eventual gridiron victory. (Tom was allowed to play in the big game, despite a failing grade in astronomy, simply because the professor liked him.)

The presentation of the show, somewhat akin to a series of highly animated John Held cartoons, was perfectly complemented by the musical episodes. The opening number lost no time, lest there be any lingering doubt, in establishing the prevailing point of view: "Learning to sin—not how to think. How to mix our gin right in the sink." Other pieces were

equally sturdy examples of musical comedy requirements of the period: 1) A number about flaming youth (titled "Flaming Youth"). 2) A new dance routine, the combustible down-on-the-heels-up-on-the-toes "Varsity Drag." 3) A revivalistic chorale, the pie-in-the-sky harbinger, "Good News." 4) A philosophical interlude, "The Best Things in Life Are Free," which they managed to shoehorn into a scene by having the poor heroine (played by Mary Lawlor) admit her lower social station in order that our hero might advise her, in song, that a lot of things make up for a shortage of money. The show received honor grades from the critics, with most of them getting into the proper descriptive spirit. "They sway from the hips," described Burns Mantle in the *News*. "They wear their trousers baggy and their panties short. They sing with raucous abandon and dance like all get out. They rah-rah with gusto. They are very collegiate. Oh, very!" Mantle went on to admire the musical's "flaming, flaring, infectious youth," an alliterative bent that also overtook Walter Winchell who proclaimed the evening "flip, fast, furious, free and flaming festive."

With a good thing going for them, De-Sylva, Brown and Henderson next found inspiration in another youthfully energetic subject, prize fighting. *Hold Everything* (the title makes one wonder if the original idea might not have dealt with wrestling) was held together by the slender thread of a plot involving a handsome boxer (Jack Whiting), whose knockout victory resulted from a mistaken notion that his adversary had insulted his beloved. But the story counted for little. For the show had in its corner the new clown prince of Broadway, Bert Lahr, to gnong-gnong his way through a maze of hilarious boxing routines and one-line gags (when asked in the locker room what book he is reading, Lahr blinked his beady eyes and answered haughtily, "Da Woiks, by William

Shakespeare"). The notices weren't quite as enthusiastic as they had been for *Good News!*, but there was enough journalistic approval to help keep audiences in attendance for over 400 performances. To wit, Percy Hammond in the *Herald Tribune*: "... a likeable jamboree, boisterous, light on its feet, and with a flair for minor melody and romance. Its grim story of the wars in Madison Square Garden is mitigated by pretty girls in leggy maneouvers, nonsense both quiet and loud, and a velvet love affair involving a tony pugilist and a soubrette of the better type."

The songs continued to be lively, contagious variations on themes expressing emotions ranging from the universal to the up-to-the-minute. The reverse title song, "Don't Hold Everything" ("Just let everything go") was a peppy panegyric to unrestricted behavior based, according to the verse, on the teachings of Sigmund Freud. There were love songs, both simpering ("To Know You Is to Love You") and exuberant ("Too Good to Be True"). But nothing quite caught the public fancy as did "You're the Cream in My Coffee," that engaging, pre-Cole Porter compilation in which the individual serenaded is likened to those everyday adjuncts designed to add taste and convenience to the necessities of life.

College football, then boxing, then . . . golf. *Follow Thru* was the name of the new game, billed as "A Musical Slice of Country Club Life," and guaranteed to be a fitting successor to its athletic precursors. The score, apart from the musical banality of "My Lucky Star" and the lyrical banality of "You Wouldn't Fool Me, Would You?," contained such bright new pieces as the latest flapper confession, "I Want to Be Bad" ("What can you do when you're loaded with hell-th and vigor?") and the adoitly worded hymn to postponed romance, "Then I'll Have Time for You." Again it was a novelty love song, "Button Up Your Over-

coat," that became the most reprised number, with audiences responding readily to its healthful prescriptions to eat proper food, be careful crossing streets ("oo-oo"), get to bed by three (!), and keep away from bootleg hootch. Gilbert Gabriel echoed the critical consensus in the *American*: "They seem dedicated to the task of making youth flame and love shout out, with crisp, crazy, lusty, ankle-loosing, hip-seizing songs, and lyrics that give this whole razzing, jazzing society circus its cue to get gay. Wild-faced, free-legged kids shouted catch lines across the footlights that fairly roped and yanked the audience onto the stage."

Flying High, presented in 1930, turned the boys away from the sporting page to an equally topical tale about aviation. Luckily, Bert Lahr was on hand again to play the role of an aviator who sets a world record for time in the air simply because he doesn't know how to get his plane to land. In spite of the generally conventional story, the musical did break with tradition by not having the chorus appear until the third scene. The show opened on the roof of an apartment

Follow Thru (1929).
The antics of Jack Haley attract the attention of Constance Lane, Dorothy Christy and Yvonne Grey. (Costumes by Kiviette; setting by Donald Oenslager.)

Culver Pictures, Inc.

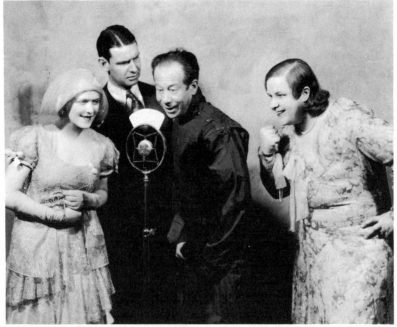

Culver Pictures, Inc.

Flying High *(1930).*
Wrote Gilbert Gabriel in the "American": "By the sweat of his crazily corrugated brows and all the Indian contortions of his comical mug and his grotesquely quaky shoulder blades, Bert Lahr wrung such laughter out of the audience as no clown of this season's lot could." Here is Bert, surrounded by Grace Brinkley, Henry Whittemore and Kate Smith, broadcasting the story of his record-breaking flight. (Costumes by Charles LeMaire.)

house in Manhattan, with wide-eyed Grace Brinkley pining away for an unknown love in the song "I'll Know Him." Then, on cue, there is an explosion above her head, she looks up in fear and amazement, and a handsome pilot (Oscar Shaw) parachutes to her feet.

The song writers contributed a moody, insistently throbbing tune in "Without Love"; a tasteless teasing number in "Good for You—Bad for Me" (containing, as an inside joke, the line, "But some things in life are not free"); a rhythmic ode, "Red Hot Chicago," in which that metropolis is celebrated as the origin of jazz ("If you think I'm wrong then you're a nincompoop! Poop-poop-a-doop!"); and another one of their justly popular roundabout love songs, "Thank Your Father." In this one, the boy's love is conveyed through his gratitude for the girl's conception which, if the lyric is to be taken literally, was apparently illegitimate.

After writing songs for three early "talkies" (Al Jolson's *The Singing Fool* and *Say It with Songs*, and also *Sunny Side Up*), DeSylva, Brown and Henderson decided to make a permanent move to the West Coast in 1930. But within a year irreconcilable differences forced the trio to break up. DeSylva remained in Hollywood (except for a temporary interruption to coproduce *Take a Chance* in New York and to write its lyrics), and rose rapidly in his new career as a film producer. Brown and Henderson, however, stuck together as song writers; their first DeSylva-less assignment brought them back to Broadway for the 1931 *George White's Scandals.* Confounding the Sardi set, they did initially well as a duo, turning out such once popular numbers as "This Is the Missus" for Rudy Vallee, "The Thrill Is Gone" and "That's Why Darkies Were Born," both for Everett Marshall, as well as that stirring antidote to the Depression, "Life Is Just a Bowl of Cherries," trumpeted by Ethel Merman, who had been rushed into the show just before its Broadway

Culver Pictures, Inc.

George White's Scandals (1931).
Rudy Vallee, surrounded by bridesmaids, about to croon "This Is the Missus." Note bridesmaid Alice Faye on the extreme right. (Costumes by Charles LeMaire; setting Joseph Urban.)

première. Other pleasures: Ray Bolger as a fleetfooted Al Smith, Willie and Eugene Howard in their classic "Pay the Two Dollars" sketch, and the musical stage debut of Ethel Barrymore Colt, whose one duet with Vallee, "My Song," turned out to be Merman's song by the time the revue officially opened.

A second Brown-Henderson offering, *Hot-Cha!*, incredibly subtitled "Laid in Mexico," opened the same season as the *Scandals*. With Bert Lahr and Lupe Velez in the cast, and a fast-moving story about bullfighting, the show was an obvious attempt to revive the same sort of book musical that had established the team's reputation during their heyday with DeSylva. But times had changed. In a season that had produced *The Cat and*

the Fiddle, *Of Thee I Sing* and *Face the Music*, the anything-for-a-laugh *Hot-Cha!* was an anachronism.* The following year, Brown and Henderson were back with a revue, *Strike Me Pink*. It had Jimmy Durante, Hope Williams, Lupe Velez, and mobster Waxey Gordon's $150,000, but it didn't last more than three months. The show also marked the termination of the partnership of Lew Brown and Ray Henderson.

In 1934, Henderson joined lyricist Ted Koehler in writing the score for a short-lived Harry Richman opus, *Say When,*

*Brown and Henderson were not particularly happy about the new trend toward politically slanted musicals. In one of their *Hot-Cha!* songs, they derided "Park Avenue librettos by children of the ghettos," an obvious swipe at the creators of *Of Thee I Sing* and *Face the Music*.

Photo by Graphic House, Inc.

Ziegfeld Follies *(1943)*.
Inspired by Carmen Jones,
the first act finale, Carmen in
Zoot, *had Milton Berle as a
peg-trousered Escamillio
(sic)*. *(Costumes by Miles
White)*.

and Brown teamed with composer Harry Akst for a revue, *Calling All Stars*, which turned out to be more of a cry for help than a prideful announcement. That same year, Brown went to Hollywood and, like DeSylva, became a film producer.

After an absence of over four years, George White brought back his *Scandals*—the twelfth in line—in 1935. Rudy Vallee was in it, along with the Howard brothers and Bert Lahr, and the occasion also introduced the new song writing team of Ray Henderson and Jack Yellen. But the revue was dismissed as being too much of an echo of the past and it had a run of only 110 performances. Henderson's whilom partner, Lew Brown, returned to Broadway in 1939. He teamed with co-lyricist Charles Tobias and composer Sam Stept to produce a cornball musical yclept *Yokel Boy*, best recalled for Phil Silvers' musical comedy debut and an insistent song, "Comes Love."

1939, however, was a particularly important year in the career of the Hollywood-based Buddy DeSylva. Brooding over his lack of public acclaim as a film executive, DeSylva was anxious to see his name back in lights on Broadway. His friend, librettist Herbert Fields, outlined a rough story idea, suitable for someone like Mae West, about an up-to-date Mme. DuBarry. At the same time DeSylva was dreaming about a tale of a washroom attendant in a swank night club smitten with the likes of Brenda Frazier. Together the two men pooled and altered their respective outlines; within two weeks they were ready to sign Bert Lahr to play the part of a washroom attendant who dreams about being Louis XV to Ethel Merman's DuBarry. All that was needed was Cole Porter to supply words and music and *voilà*—*DuBarry Was a Lady*. In December, 1939, the name "B. G. DeSylva" was blinking above the marquee at the 46th Street Theatre as both producer and co-librettist of the season's biggest smash.

The biggest smash, that is, until De-Sylva's next musical, *Louisiana Purchase*, came along the following May. For this one he hired the services of librettist Morrie Ryskind (adapting his story from an original DeSylva concept), composer-lyricist Irving Berlin, and performers William Gaxton, Vera Zorina and Victor Moore. Then, in October, 1940, DeSylva made it three hits in a row. Intrigued by the song, "Katie Went to Haiti," in *DuBarry*, Herbert Fields and Buddy DeSylva decided to expand its basic idea into an entire Merman musical. The Haitian locale, however, was switched to Panama, which conveniently lent itself to a ready-made show title, *Panama Hattie*. Again they finished the book within two weeks, and again they had Cole Porter to join them in another DeSylva-Fields-Merman festival. For about a month and a half after the show's opening, DeSylva became the first producer since Ziegfeld to have three musical successes running simultaneously in New York.*

Once satisfied that his personal prestige had been fully restored, DeSylva was content to quit while he was ahead. There also may have been a more practical reason. Within a month after the opening of *Panama Hattie*, he was California-bound to succeed William LeBaron, another ex-lyricist-librettist, as head of Paramount

Studios. DeSylva held the post for about four years, then turned to independent film production, and finally retired because of ill health. On July 11, 1950, at the age of 55, he died of a heart attack in Los Angeles. Lew Brown, whose last Broadway assignment had been as director-writer of a revised 1941 revue, *Crazy with the Heat*, also succumbed to a heart attack. That was on February 5, 1958, when he was 64.

Ray Henderson returned to Broadway in 1943 as composer—with Jack Yellen as lyricist—of one of the last successful large-scale revues, the *Ziegfeld Follies*. Starring the unlikely trio of Milton Berle, Ilona Massey and Arthur Treacher, it turned out to be a particularly gala wartime treat, possibly made all the more so by stirring memories of a bygone era when shows such as this were the rule rather than the exception. It was Henderson's final effort for the theatre. He died of a heart attack on December 31, 1970, at the age of 74.

Although the team of DeSylva, Brown and Henderson flourished for not quite five years, the unique personality of the theatre they represented is still savored today. They personified a form of musical comedy that was bound to disappear in a rapidly changing and brutal world. Only during the Twenties was there time for just fun and games along Broadway. And when it came to fun-and-games musicals, no writers were more adept at calling the tune than DeSylva, Brown and Henderson.

---

*From March 13 through April 7, 1928, Ziegfeld's three concurrently running musicals were *Rio Rita*, *Show Boat* and *The Three Musketeers*.

Cole Porter. Photo by Leo Friedman

CHAPTER TWELVE

COLE PORTER

THE LIVES OF the most prominent theatre composers have been distinguished by extreme dedication to their occupations. Apart from Rodgers, who got his apprenticeship writing amateur shows, the leading figures during the Twenties generally followed a set routine as they went from song plugger (usually for Max Dreyfus), to vaudeville accompanist, to rehearsal pianist. Then, if they were lucky, they would have a song interpolated in a show, or, if they were even luckier, they would be asked to compose an entire score. But no matter what the exact path may have been, all the major talents first decided on their goal when they were in their early or middle teens, and then went after it with diligence and determination.

Cole Porter was the notable exception. He never had to struggle or to perform lowly tasks either in Tin Pan Alley or in Shubert Alley. He never had to bother with amateur shows to attract attention. He never had to make the rounds of producers and publishers. Competition never disturbed him, nor was he particularly concerned about money. He was twenty-three when his first Broadway show, *See America First*, opened in 1916,

but for the next twelve years he spent most of his time living in Europe, traveling around the world, and, in general, making sure that there was not one pleasurable place anywhere that he had not visited. Chronologically, his initial offering places Porter after Romberg, Friml, and Berlin, and before Gershwin, Youmans, and Rodgers, but his theatrical career only began in earnest at the very end of the 1920's. From then on, however, Porter's rise was rapid. He turned out a series of scores—both words and music—for musical comedies celebrated for their glossy opulence, outstanding performances, melodic inventiveness, and sophisticated wit.

During the Thirties, when other composers were writing social satires and experimenting with new and different theatrical forms, Porter was creating songs that did what they could do to perpetuate all that was glamorous in the Twenties. For Porter, that was the decade of luxurious apartments in Paris, special trains to the Lido, ballets staged by Diaghilev for his own private parties, years spent at the Palazzo Rezzonico in Venice (at a rental of $4,000 a month), cruises down the Rhine, and incessant traveling

143

to distant, exotic places. During this period, whenever a friend would suggest that he try Broadway again, Porter's answer was that he much preferred writing his songs for the amusement of his friends. His attitude was summed up once when, to an entreaty that he turn professional song-writer, he answered simply, "Suppose I had to settle down on Broadway for three months just when I was planning to go to the Antibes."

Nonetheless, wherever Porter was, or whatever he was supposed to be doing, he was always busily composing songs. These songs, among them "Two Little Babes in the Wood," "Let's Do It," and "What Is This Thing Called Love?," were certainly not the product of an amateur or a dabbler. In melody and in lyrics, his work at the time showed a professionalism made all the more impressive by his absence from Broadway. For though he was aware of what the Gershwin brothers and Rodgers and Hart were accomplishing, he was not directly under the influence of the rising young generation of songwriters of the Twenties. Completely independently and far from the Broadway scene, Cole Porter was creating his own distinctive style, one that would later characterize all his contributions to the musical theatre.

Cole Albert Porter was born on a 750-acre farm in Peru, Indiana, on June 9, 1891. His parents were Samuel Fenwick and Kate (Cole) Porter. By the time he was ten, young Cole had already composed two songs, a feat that so delighted his proud mother that she had one of them, "The Bobolink Waltz," published in Chicago. This musical interest, however, did not please Porter's wealthy grandfather, J. O. Cole. Cole, who had made a fortune in the lumber business in West Virginia, was anxious to leave his grandson a large inheritance, but only on the condition that the boy become a lawyer.

Porter's grandfather sent him to Worcester Academy in Massachusetts, and to Yale, with the hope that he would become interested in his studies and get his mind off music. Porter still found time to write. When he was nineteen, Remick published an early effort called "Bridget," and within the next two years he created those immortal college tunes, "Bingo Eli Yale" and "Yale Bulldog Song." Although music interested him far more than his regular studies, Porter dutifully entered Harvard Law School. His obvious lack of interest in the law soon became apparent to the dean, who suggested that he might make a more impressive scholastic record at the Harvard School of Music. Once grandfather Cole finally gave his grudging consent, Porter enthusiastically began his study of music.

While still at Harvard, Porter and a fellow student, T. Lawrason Riggs, collaborated on a professional Broadway show, *See America First*. On one of his frequent trips to visit friends in East Hampton, Porter had met Elisabeth Marbury, the socially prominent literary agent who had recently cosponsored the immensely successful *Very Good Eddie*. Hoping to do as much for Porter's career as she had for Kern's, Miss Marbury agreed to produce the show that Porter and Riggs had recently written. *See America First* ("A Patriotic Comic Opera") may have seemed like a clever idea on paper, but when it was performed on the stage it was a complete failure. The story dealt with the efforts of an anti-British U. S. senator to keep his daughter from meeting anyone from across the Atlantic. Of course, inevitably, after being taken out West, the girl does meet a titled though rugged Englishman, they fall in love, and, eventually, the senator loses his prejudices. Apparently, the fact that this was a spoof of the George M. Cohan flag-wavers—particularly *George Washington, Jr.*—was lost on the unnamed critic of the *New York Dramatic Mirror*, who wrote: "The lyrics are studiously copied after the Gilbertian pattern in the long and complicated rhyme effects achieved. The music, however, gives the impression that its composer, after the first hour, gave up the task of recreating a Sullivan atmosphere, preferring to seek his inspiration in our own George M. Cohan."

Following the demise of *See America First**, Porter stayed in New York for a mostly indolent year and a half. In the fall of 1917, boredom—and perhaps conscience—prompted him to sail for war-ravaged France. There he served in a relief mission, two American military advisory units, and, for a brief and undistinguished period, the French Foreign Legion. He always managed, though, to find time to enjoy the social life of Paris, where he entertained friends by performing on a zither-like, custom-made portable piano. After the war, he decided to remain in Paris.

Although he was rather well provided for, Porter felt that he needed a still larger allowance from his grandfather, especially since he wanted to marry the wealthy Linda Lee Thomas. Such an important request required a personal confrontation, and Porter sailed back to the United States in 1919. Also on board ship was Raymond Hitchcock, the popular comedian and producer. After hearing Porter play some of his songs (and possibly not unmindful of the young man's financial status), Hitchcock commissioned the young composer to write the music and lyrics for the third edition of his *Hitchy-Koo* revues. Joe Cook made his New York debut in the show singing "When I Had a Uniform On," but it was the uncharacteristically sentimental "An Old-Fashioned Garden" that gave Cole Porter his first song hit.

Grandfather Cole's refusal to allow him more money was of little concern to Porter now. With his royalty checks from "An Old-Fashioned Garden" giving his bank account a much-needed boost, he

returned to Paris, married Linda Lee, and began his life of party-giver and pleasure-seeker. He did not abandon music, however, devoting much time to the study of harmony and counterpoint under Vincent d'Indy at the Schola Cantorum in Paris. In 1923, Porter's affluence was enhanced even more when J. O. Cole died and left his grandson over $1 million. Then, as Porter once put it, "I could go to Venice."

During the early Twenties, Porter interrupted his life of ease only twice: to write songs for another *Hitchy-Koo* revue that never came to New York, and to contribute the score for John Murray Anderson's *Greenwich Village Follies of 1924*. Of the numbers in the *Follies*, "I'm in Love Again," sung by the Dolly Sisters and danced by future Broadway choreographer Robert Alton, was the only one to win popularity.

Among the many people who never gave up their efforts to induce Porter to return to the Broadway theatre, the only one to succeed was E. Ray Goetz. Goetz, an enterprising producer and occasional song-writer himself, journeyed to the

*Paris (1928).
Irene Bordoni surrounded by Irving Aaronson's Commanders. (Setting by William Castle.)*

**T. Lawrason Riggs gave up thoughts of a theatrical career after *See America First*. He soon entered the priesthood, and later became Roman Catholic chaplain at Yale.*

Lido in the summer of 1928 with the express purpose of talking the reluctant composer into creating another score. Finding Porter sunning himself on the beach, the producer introduced himself and immediately offered what he was sure would be an attractive proposal. The score would be for a musical that was so Parisian it was actually called *Paris*, the star of the show would be Goetz's vivacious wife, Irene Bordoni, and Porter would only have to compose eight songs. Somewhat to his own surprise, Porter found himself agreeing to take the assignment.

Paris, though it was billed, *Time*-fashion, as "A Musicomedy," and though it did well at the box office, was little more than an incidental comedy with incidental music. In fact, of the eight Cole Porter songs, only five were used, with two others supplied by the producer. All the numbers were sung by Miss Bordoni accompanied by Irving Aaronson's Commanders, an eleven-piece orchestra seated on stage in what was supposed to be a hotel suite.

In the song, "Let's Misbehave" (cut from *Paris* before it reached New York), Porter's lyric mentioned briefly the love life of lovebirds, bears, and camels. This interest in the animal kingdom was slight compared to the zoölogical survey in "Let's Do It," the number that replaced "Let's Misbehave." Bluebirds, bluebells, sponges, oysters, clams, jellyfish, electric eels, shad, sole, goldfish, dragonflies, centipedes, mosquitoes, katydids, lady bugs, moths, locusts, bees, fleas, chimpanzees, kangaroos, giraffes, hippopotamuses, sloths, guinea pigs, bears, and Pekinese dogs—in addition to various types of humans—all had their amatory habits covered in a manner that immediately established Cole Porter as one of the most ingenious creators of sly and imaginative lyrics.

The reception to his songs for *Paris* convinced Porter that there were plea-sures to be had in the world of musical comedy as well as in the world of international society. The next year, he and Goetz again worked together on another musical with a Parisian locale, *Fifty Million Frenchmen*. Featuring William Gaxton, Genevieve Tobin, and Helen Broderick, it was the first of seven Cole Porter musicals to have librettos written or co-written by Herbert Fields. It was also the first musical directed by Edgar Montillion "Monty" Woolley, who had been an instructor at Yale while Porter was an undergraduate.

Fifty Million Frenchmen, a bigger box office hit than *Paris*, had a score that abounded in unhackneyed sentiments. "I Worship You" (unaccountably cut) revealed Porter's interest in the mythology of the Greeks, Phoenicians, and Egyptians, while "Find Me a Primitive Man" went back to an earlier age for inspiration. There was even a jaunty, insouciant air about the more traditional love duets, "You Do Something to Me" and "You've Got That Thing." "When it comes to lyrics," wrote George Jean Nathan in *Judge*, "this Cole Porter is so far ahead of the other boys in New York that there just is no race at all."

Just one month after the première of *Fifty Million Frenchmen*, an English show, *Wake Up and Dream!*, opened with Jack Buchanan, Jessie Matthews, and Tilly Losch. Porter did not contribute all the songs to it, but he was responsible for the dark, brooding "What Is This Thing Called Love?," which was based on a native chant he had first heard in Marrakech, Morocco, and the somewhat more emotionally fulfilling "Looking at You." Although the eternal dilemma of the modern maiden called "Which?" had been intended originally for *Paris*, it was first sung on Broadway by Miss Matthews in *Wake Up and Dream!*

The New Yorkers, in 1930, was another Porter musical written by Herbert

Fields for E. Ray Goetz. Monty Woolley again directed. There were some interpolations in it from the repertory of Clayton, Jackson, and Durante, and also that of Fred Waring's Pennsylvanians, but the score was chiefly Porter's. Hope Williams and Charles King sang "Where Have You Been?," a rather heavy ballad, and Kathryn Crawford intoned the dolorous pitch of a street walker in "Love for Sale." The composer also described the rival pleasures of staying at home ("The Great Indoors") and of taking off for a tropical island ("Let's Fly Away").

Porter's skill at combining opposites within a single song was strikingly demonstrated in "Night and Day," which was first sung by Fred Astaire in the 1932 success, *Gay Divorce*. The song, a somewhat extended piece, was another example of a less ethereal, more carnal approach to love, with its verse suggesting a heartbeat and its release a tegumentary revelation of the yearning burning under one's hide. Luella Gear and Eric Blore contributed most of the comedy, with Miss Gear making something both funny and touching of the mad life of the social-climbing "Mister and Missus Fitch."

After the debacle of the Gershwin brothers' *Pardon My English* ended the Alex A. Aarons–Vinton Freedley partnership in 1934, Freedley and his wife took a lengthy ocean voyage to enable him to reflect on the possibility of a career as a solo producer. As Freedley recalls: "The idea came to me when I was fishing peacefully in the Pacific Ocean near the Pearl Islands. While waiting for a bite, I began, with no special purpose, to consider the ideal people for a musical show." William Gaxton and Victor Moore were obvious choices, particularly as a result of their Wintergreen and Throttlebottom characterizations in *Of Thee I Sing* and *Let 'Em Eat Cake*. So was Ethel Merman, whom Freedley had

Culver Pictures, Inc.

Brown Bros.

Fifty Million Frenchmen (1929).
William Gaxton and a bevy of beauties. (Costumes by James Reynolds.)

Gay Divorce *(1932).*
There were many complications in this tale of an unhappy wife who hires a professional corespondent to help her secure a divorce. In this scene, Luella Gear discovers the wife (Claire Luce) with both the presumed corespondent (Fred Astaire) and the real one (Erik Rhodes). (Setting by Jo Mielziner.)

discovered for *Girl Crazy*. George and Ira Gershwin would have been the logical song-writers, but it was apparent from their toiling over *Porgy and Bess* that they would have little interest in doing another musical comedy. The bright and brittle rhythms of Cole Porter suggested themselves immediately; so did the idea of having a book created by the Princess Theatre masters, P. G. Wodehouse and Guy Bolton.

The more he thought of the idea, the more plausible it became. When he arrived back in New York, Freedley immediately signed the stars, the composer, and, finally, the librettists. In those days, as Ethel Merman wrote in her autobiography, *Who Could Ask for Anything More*, "the writers who used to think up the books that were wrapped around Gershwin or Cole Porter scores, started from scratch, with only their bare cupboards and an unmanageable sense of humor to guide them. First a producer signed a cast; then he hired writers to rustle up some material for that cast to use. 'I've got Bert Lahr,' he'd say; 'write me a part for Bert Lahr.' Or 'I've signed Victor Moore. Get goin' buddy. Make with the Moore-type yoks.' "*

The story Wodehouse and Bolton concocted for the new show was based on some general ideas Freedley had given them. The producer wanted it to take place on board a ship, but when the script arrived he found that the authors had written a libretto about a shipwreck. Such a theme would not have been disastrous in itself, but just two months before the scheduled opening of the musical, the *S.S. Morro Castle* went down in flames off Asbury Park, New Jersey, with a loss of 125 lives. With Wodehouse in London and Bolton in Paris, the harried producer had to find someone quickly to rewrite the book. His director, Howard Lindsay, had had some experience as a playwright, but with so little time Lind-

say insisted on having a collaborator. Through a mutual friend he was introduced to Russel Crouse, a Theatre Guild press agent and occasional librettist. The two agreed to be partners. "We went into rehearsal with only two-thirds of a first act and there was no second act at all," Lindsay later admitted. Somehow, everything was miraculously pulled into shape before the opening night; once the curtain went up on November 21, 1934, there was little doubt that *Anything Goes* would become one of the decade's superior achievements in musical comedy.

"A thundering good song-and-dance show," thundered Brooks Atkinson, and so it was. With Moore in the incongruous role of Public Enemy Number 13 (a superstitious man, he was anxious to bump off Number 12 so that he might rise in the hierarchy), with Gaxton bursting with kinetic energy, and with Ethel Merman trumpeting her way through some of Cole Porter's most inspired numbers, *Anything Goes* was the quintessence of the lavish, bawdy, swift-paced, uninhibited Music Comedy of the mid-Thirties. Almost every musical number was a highly polished gem, including "All Through the Night," with its throbbing description of an imaginary nocturnal romance; the propulsive "Blow, Gabriel, Blow"; the blasé, but sincere "I Get a Kick out of You"; and "You're the Top," the classic of catalogued superlatives set to music.

Most of the songs for *Anything Goes* were written while Porter was cruising down the Rhine. For *Jubilee*, the following year, he extended his quest for geographical inspiration by composing the score during a worldwide tour with librettist Moss Hart. Wherever he went, Porter was able to find ideas for his songs. The melody for "Begin the Beguine" came to him as he was listening to native music on the island of Kalabahi, in the Dutch East Indies; the advice-giving "Kling-Kling Bird on the Divi-Divi Tree" was actually seen and heard in

* From *Who Could Ask for Anything More* by Ethel Merman. Garden City, N.Y.: Doubleday & Company.

Aruba, Dutch West Indies; the music for the "Judgment of Paris" ballet emanated from ethnic themes heard on the island of Bali. Among the less exotic rhythms, "A Picture of Me without You" strung out a varied list of improbable separations to affirm love's constancy (Fritzi Kreisler without his fiddle, Philadelphia without a Biddle); "Why Shouldn't I?" expressed the youthful desire for even a temporary romance; and "Just One of Those Things" conveyed a disillusioned, though realistic, acceptance of a passing affair.

Mary Boland and Melville Cooper were the queen and king of an Anglified (though unspecified) country in *Jubilee*. Members of the royal family included Charles Walters, Margaret Adams, and fifteen-year-old Montgomery Clift. Unfortunately, when a film contract forced Miss Boland to return to Hollywood, her replacement proved unsatisfactory, and the musical was closed after only 169 performances.

In 1936, hoping to repeat the success of *Anything Goes*, Vinton Freedley signed Cole Porter, Howard Lindsay, and Russel Crouse to create *Red, Hot and Blue!* It was originally intended as a vehicle for Ethel Merman, Jimmy Durante, and William Gaxton, but, according to Miss Merman, Gaxton refused to appear in it after overhearing Lindsay and Crouse telling her what a big part she would have. To replace Gaxton, Freedley hired Bob Hope, who had previously revealed his comic talent in *Roberta* and the *Ziegfeld Follies of 1936*.

In spite of its authors and performers, *Red, Hot and Blue!* was not a success. The chief fault was the book, a fairly elementary piece concerned with the search for a missing heiress whose identity could only be determined by a waffle-iron mark on her behind. Porter's contributions were more inspired. "Down in the Depths (on the 90th Floor)," sung by Miss Merman in a gold lamé gown illuminated by a single gold spotlight, brilliantly heightened the heroine's loneli-

Photo by Vandamm

Photo by Alfredo Valente

Anything Goes *(1934).*
Ethel Merman sings "Anything Goes" accompanied by Marshall Smith, Ray Johnson, Dwight Snyder, and Del Porter. (Costume by Jenkins.)

Jubilee *(1935).*
The collaborators: Cole Porter (music and lyrics) and Moss Hart (libretto).

Jubilee (1935).
King Melville Cooper is momentarily distracted from his rope trick to glance at a picture of Queen Mary Boland's favorite Hollywood star. (Costumes by Irene Sharaff and Connie De Pinna; setting by Jo Mielziner.)

Red, Hot and Blue! (1936).
Vivian Vance, Jimmy Durante, Ethel Merman, Bob Hope, and Grace Hartman have a large audience for their conversation. (Costumes by Constance Ripley; setting by Donald Oenslager.)

Photo by Vandamm

Photo by Vandamm

ness by contrasting it with her surrounding luxury. The exultant "Ridin' High," however, brought Miss Merman back to her more accustomed sanguine emotions. There was also the cleverly intricate "It's De-Lovely," which told, via a self-kidding verse and four choruses, the blissful saga of a boy and girl from the night they fell in love, through their marriage and wedding trip, and right up to the arrival of their first born.

Apart from its songs, *Red, Hot and Blue!* is remembered today chiefly because of the ridiculous battle of the billing. Both Miss Merman's and Durante's agents wanted their clients to have top billing, i.e., the name on the left-hand side above the title of the show. Although it still seemed to give the preferential billing to Durante, the following compromise was finally worked out:

In the summer of 1937, while Porter was horseback riding on a friend's estate on Long Island, his horse suddenly slipped, threw him, and then fell on top of him. Both of his legs were broken, and extreme damage was done to his nervous system. After submitting to thirty-one operations over a period of about twenty years in order to save his legs, Porter eventually had to have his right leg amputated in 1958.

Shortly after the accident, the Shubert brothers tried to take Porter's mind off his misfortune by commissioning him to supply the score for *You Never Know.* It was not, however, one of his—or their—major efforts. The next year, the composer had far better luck with *Leave It to Me!*, which was also written while he was bed-ridden. Adapted by Sam and Bella Spewack from their play *Clear All Wires*, the musical had a stellar cast including William Gaxton, Victor Moore, Sophie Tucker, and Tamara. While Moore, as usual, was singled out for his hilarious performance as Alonzo P. Goodhue, the American ambassador to the Soviet Union, a twenty-four-year-old singer named Mary Martin made an auspicious Broadway debut as she sang, and coyly stripped to, "My Heart Belongs to Daddy," while waiting at a freezing Siberian railway station. (Some people even noticed a dancer in that scene named Gene Kelly, who was also appearing on the New York stage for the first time.)

Leave It to Me! was a generally funny spoof of communism and American diplomacy, with such irreverences as "The Internationale" performed as the first-act finale and Stalin dancing around in true musical comedy fashion. The sight of the timid Mr. Moore kicking the Nazi ambassador in the stomach was treasured by audiences as both a wish-fulfillment and a reminder of the unique freedom that the Broadway theatre has always enjoyed.

From December, 1939, to January, 1944, Cole Porter created the songs for five box-office smashes in a row—*DuBarry Was a Lady, Panama Hattie, Let's Face It!, Something for the Boys,* and *Mexican Hayride.* Each one of these shows ran over 400 performances, and all were co-authored by Herbert Fields (he wrote the first two with B. G. De-Sylva, the other three with his sister, Dorothy Fields). Although only *Let's Face It!* was produced by Vinton Freedley, all five musicals seemed to capture the bright, star-studded, flavor of the Gershwin shows that Aarons and Freedley had offered in the Twenties. Like Gershwin at that time, Porter was particularly adept at writing for star personalities (Ethel Merman, Bert Lahr, Danny Kaye, Bobby Clark) without too

Leave It to Me! *(1938).* *"A new girl named Mary Martin is gay, fresh, and attractive," wrote Richard Watts, Jr., in the* Herald Tribune. *Here at a freezing Siberian railroad station she sings "My Heart Belongs to Daddy," accompanied by a quintet including (to her immediate right) Gene Kelly. (Costumes by Raoul Pène du Bois; setting by Albert Johnson.)*

Photo by Vandamm

DuBarry Was a Lady *(1939).* *Bert Lahr, as the washroom attendant at the Club Petite, dreams that he is King Louis XV and that Ethel Merman is DuBarry. (Costumes by Raoul Pène du Bois.)*

Photo by Hermann-Pix

DuBarry Was a Lady *(1939).*
Charles Walters and Betty
Grable in a burlesque routine
at the Club Petite. (Costumes
by Raoul Pène du Bois.)

N.Y. Public Library

Photo by Vandamm

Brown Bros.

Panama Hattie *(1940).*
Rags Ragland registers
complete approval of Ethel
Merman's rather garish outfit.
(Costumes and setting by
Raoul Pène du Bois.)

Let's Face It! *(1941).*
Extra marital entanglements
among three discontented
wives and three eager
servicemen. Eve Arden,
Danny Kaye, Edith Meiser,
Benny Baker, Jack Williams,
and Vivian Vance. (Costumes
by John Harkrider; setting by
Harry Horner.)

*Mexican Hayride (1944).
Bobby Clark (alias Joe
Bascom, alias Humphrey
Fish) and June Havoc as the
bullfighter known as
Montana. (Costumes by Mary
Grant.)*

Photo by Bob Golby

much concern for the logic of plot development or the manner in which the songs were suited to the story. But just as the early Gershwin entertainments were attuned to the period in which they were presented, so the five Porter musicals of the early Forties could offer the amusement-seeking audiences of the Second World War a much-needed escape into a spangled, melodic, and glamorous world.

DuBarry Was a Lady was described by John Mason Brown as "a rowdy, boisterous, high-spirited extravaganza which stops at just this side of nothing and makes much of little." Ethel Merman played May Daley, a nightclub singer, and Bert Lahr was the washroom attendant at the Club Petite who dreams that he is Louis XV and Ethel is DuBarry. Among the songs, "Do I Love You?" was another beguine-styled ballad; "Katie Went to Haiti" related the rhythmic saga of a girl who was, according to critic John Anderson, "obviously a business and musical relation of the immortal Eadie"; and "Well, Did You Evah?" was made up of a series of gossipy social

notes, delivered by Betty Grable (in her first stage role) and Charles Walters. Surprisingly, the song with the greatest popular appeal was the mocking hillbilly duet in which Miss Merman and Mr. Lahr vowed their eternal "Friendship."

Ethel Merman received solo star billing for the first time in *Panama Hattie*. Again she played the part of a nightclub singer (this time called Hattie Maloney) whose heart of gold could only be revealed through a voice of brass. In "I've Still Got My Health," she gaily proclaimed that her physical soundness was ample compensation for her lack of social graces, but in "Make It Another Old Fashioned, Please," she sadly concluded that the only thing to do with her sorrow was to drown it. The most fondly remembered sequence in the show involved Miss Merman and eight-year-old Joan Carroll, an occasion so touching that Brooks Atkinson predicted: "Gruff old codgers are going to choke a little this winter when tot and temptress sing 'Let's Be Buddies' and bring down the house."

The performance that Danny Kaye had given in *Lady in the Dark* fully merited the stardom he won in *Let's Face It!* Its tale of three middle-aged married ladies who go on a spree with three young servicemen was found to be, in the words of John Mason Brown, "an exuberant and irresistible show which does not hesitate to call a shovel a spade." In addition to Kaye, the cast was comprised of a superior roster of musical comedy talent, including Mary Jane Walsh, Eve Arden (with Carol Channing as understudy), Edith Meiser, Vivian Vance, Nanette Fabray, and Benny Baker. Among the outstanding Porter songs were "Farming," which ridiculed celebrities who had just discovered the soil; "Ev'rything I Love," a straight love duet for Kaye and Miss Walsh; and "You Irritate Me So," a comic love duet sung by Miss Fabray and Jack Williams.

Cole Porter's two musicals for Michael Todd, *Something for the Boys* and *Mex-*

ican Hayride were successful as money-makers, though neither one represented the composer's best work. Originally known as *Jenny Get Your Gun*, *Something for the Boys* doubtlessly benefited from the presence of Ethel Merman who was cast as a defense worker who could receive wartime radio messages through the fillings in her teeth. The show-stopping routine was one in which Miss Merman and Paula Laurence, decked out as squaws for no apparent reason, romped through a number about their husbands who wait for them "By the Mis-sis-sis-sis-sis-sis-sis-sis-sin-e-wah."

Just as *Something for the Boys* was indebted to Ethel Merman for its success, so *Mexican Hayride* was equally indebted to Bobby Clark. As Joe Bascom (alias Humphrey Fish), Clark was cast as a numbers racketeer who flees to Mexico, assumes various disguises, and becomes involved with a female bullfighter (played by June Havoc). "I Love You," which followed the pattern of "Do I Love You?", has been the most durable song from the score, but two others, "Sing to Me, Guitar" and "Carlotta," were especially successful in capturing

Photo by Eileen Darby—Graphic House

Kiss Me, Kate *(1948)*.
"We open in Venice," sing Patricia Morison, Alfred Drake, Lisa Kirk, and Harold Lang as a group of strolling players about to appear in Shakespeare's The Taming of the Shrew. *(Costumes and setting by Lemuel Ayers.)*

Photo by Eileen Darby—Graphic House

Fred Graham (Alfred Drake) gives vent to his feelings toward his leading lady, Lilli Vanessi (Patricia Morison), by administering a sound spanking during a performance of The Taming of the Shrew. *Lisa Kirk is beneath the balcony at the right.*

the atmosphere of a languid and romantic Mexico.

By the mid-Forties, the belief was that Cole Porter was no longer capable of creating the outstanding scores that had distinguished most of his early musicals. Neither *Something for the Boys* nor *Mexican Hayride* was a major effort, and there was little of merit in Porter's music and lyrics for Billy Rose's revue, *Seven Lively Arts*, or Orson Welles's adaptation of Jules Verne's *Around the World in Eighty Days*. Few, therefore, had high expectations when it was announced in 1948 that librettists Sam and Bella Spewack were collaborating with Porter on *Kiss Me, Kate*, a musical based on Shakespeare's *The Taming of the Shrew*. Nor did the stars indicate success. Since his first important role in *Oklahoma!*, Alfred Drake had appeared in four failures in a row, and Patricia Morison, who was to play opposite him, had not been in a Broadway musical in over ten years. (Her last appearance had been in *The Two Bouquets*, in which Drake also had had a part.)

Like Irving Berlin with regard to *Annie Get Your Gun*, Porter was apprehensive about the new project, which was completely unlike the usual gossamer star vehicles with which he was customarily associated. Moreover, in common with everyone else in the musical theatre, he was well aware of the strides taken since the formation of the Rodgers and Hammerstein partnership. "The librettos are much better," he once told reporter Gilbert Millstein, "and the scores are much closer to the librettos than they used to be. Those two made it much harder for everybody else." Nevertheless, partially spurred on by Berlin's example ("His having so much music in *Annie Get Your Gun* made me feel like trying a similar thing"), Porter created a score for *Kiss Me, Kate* that is universally conceded to be his masterpiece. Although, as was his customary professional habit, he still remained somewhat aloof from the actual production, he was extremely con-

cerned with the way his music and lyrics fit the characters and the situations, and frequently called upon the Spewacks for opinions and suggestions.

Porter's unique accomplishment in *Kiss Me, Kate* lay in his facility for creating melodies and lyrics of uncommonly high standards while, at the same time, successfully bridging the completely different worlds of Broadway and the Bard. From the general area of Times Square, he produced "Another Op'nin', Another Show," a rousing show business anthem to rival Berlin's "There's No Business like Show Business"; the plaintive torch ballad, "Why Can't You Behave?"; "Too Darn Hot," with its galvanic melody in direct contrast to the inaction proposed in the lyric; and the tender confession, "So in Love," another melody in Porter's soft beguine style. "Always True to You in My Fashion" was pure Broadway also, even though its title stemmed from a line in a poem by Ernest Dowson. In its avowel of fidelity to one true love, the song expressed a reverse sentiment to the composer's previous "My Heart Belongs to Daddy," in which fidelity was pledged to the wealthy "daddy."

The Taming of the Shrew itself provided the direct inspiration for four of the songs. "I've Come to Wive It Wealthily in Padua" was based on Petruchio's first revelation of his quest for a rich wife, in which the concluding lines were:

> . . . were she as rough
> As are the swelling Adriatic
> seas:
> I come to wive it wealthily in
> Padua;
> If wealthily then happily in
> Padua.

"Where Is the Life That Late I Led?" was a line in a song actually sung by Shakespeare's hero, while the rather mystical "Were Thine That Special Faee" was prompted by Bianca's admission:

> Believe me, sister, of all the men
> alive,

I never yet beheld that special face
Which I could fancy more than any
other.

For the last number in the show, "I Am
Ashamed That Women Are So Simple,"
Porter set almost all of Shakespeare's
original words to music for the reformed
Kate to explain how women should be-
have toward their husbands.

Such numbers as "Tom, Dick or
Harry," "We Open in Venice," and "I
Hate Men," while they are all com-
pletely Porter, fit perfectly into the story
and spirit of the ancient tale. Indeed,
Brooks Atkinson has termed "I Hate
Men" "the perfect musical sublimation
of Shakespeare's evil-tempered Kate."

"Wunderbar" is, of course, far from
either Shubert Alley or Shakespeare.
Though Porter wrote the melody in strict
three-quarter time, the song is actually a
satire on all the sentimental waltzes ever
performed in a Viennese operetta. This
is immediately revealed in the first line of
the verse, "Gazing down on the
Jungfrau," a rather difficult feat since
the Jungfrau is one of the highest peaks
in the Alps.

Arnold Saint Subber and Lemuel
Ayers, the producers of *Kiss Me, Kate*,
also produced Cole Porter's next musical,
Out of This World. As *Kiss Me, Kate* had
contrasted show business with Shakespeare, so *Out of This World* combined
the Amphitryon legend with the adventures of a modern American couple visit-
ing Greece on their wedding trip. In the
role of Juno, Charlotte Greenwood made
a gangling, triumphal return to the musical stage after an absence of almost
twenty-four years.

The now-standard "From This Moment On" was dropped from the score
before the musical opened in New York,
but there were still many superb songs
among those left—"Where, Oh
Where?," with its sweet, lilting melody
mated to a coldly calculating lyric; the
ever-present beguine, "I Am Loved"
(with a release almost identical to that of

the earlier "I Love You"); the forthright
stand of the contented wife called "No
Lover"; and the paean to the satisfactions
of old age, "I Sleep Easier Now," which
Miss Greenwood sang with particular
relish. There were also some delightful
Cole Porter incongruities: "I Jupiter,
I Rex" ("Breck-eck-o-weck-o-wex!")
brought the spirit of the Yale cheering
section to Mount Olympus, while "Climb
Up the Mountain" turned a quasi-Negro
spiritual into the perfect musical expression for gods and goddesses. Two
bright sagas of itemization were "Cherry
Pies Ought to Be You" (in the "You're
the Top" vein), and the Rabelaisian,
rapid-fire account of Mercury's romantic
conquests, "They Couldn't Compare to
You."

Can-Can (1953) and *Silk Stockings*
(1955) were presented by Cy Feuer and
Ernest Martin, the team that had previously produced *Where's Charley?* and
Guys and Dolls. Both shows were written
and directed by Abe Burrows, although in
the case of *Silk Stockings* he revised a
script already completed by George S.
Kaufman and Leueen McGrath. *Can-
Can* dealt with Parisian life in the days of
Toulouse-Lautrec. Its story may have
been inconsequential, but the dances created by Michael Kidd and the show's
breezy pace helped make it a huge financial success. The songs, if not among Porter's best work, nonetheless enabled him
to recapture the Parisian flavor of some of
his earliest scores with such pieces as "Allez-Vous-En," "I Love Paris" (written,
according to Porter, because Jo Mielziner
had designed such a beautiful scenic sky-
line of the city), "Montmart'," and "C'est
Magnifique." Of the rest, "I Am in Love"
was constructed from the "Do I Love
You?—I Love You—So in Love—I Am
Loved" matrix, and "It's All Right with
Me" was a wry serenade sung by a disillusioned young man whose heart still
longs for another.

Lilo, the French star, was imported especially to play La Mome Pistache,
which she did in a strikingly ebullient

Can-Can *(1953)*.
Gwen Verdon, Hans Conried, and Lilo. (Costumes by Motley.)

Photo by Eileen Darby—Graphic House

Silk Stockings *(1955)*.
Don Ameche as Steve Canfield and Hildegarde Neff as Ninotchka in the musical version of one of Garbo's most popular films. (Costumes by Lucinda Ballard.)

Photo by Eileen Darby—Graphic House

manner. However, a greater success was scored by a twenty-eight-year-old dancer named Gwen Verdon, despite the fact that her part had been cut drastically to please the star. Miss Verdon's two previous Broadway appearances had been as a dancer in *Alive and Kicking*, a revue, and in the Villa-Lobos operetta, *Magdalena*.

Silk Stockings, an adaptation of the movie, *Ninotchka*, was set in modern Paris, with the leading roles played by Hildegarde Neff, Don Ameche, and Gretchen Wyler. Porter's lyrics had fun at the expense of the movies ("Josephine," "Stereophonic Sound") and the Russians ("Too Bad," "Siberia," and the exercise in verbal frugality, "The Red Blues"). Amatory emotions were expressed cartographically in "All of You," selflessly in "Without Love," and dispassionately in "It's a Chemical Reaction."

After almost thirty years of physical suffering, Cole Porter died on October 15, 1964, in Santa Monica, California. He succumbed at the age of 73 following surgery for a kidney stone. Of all the major musical comedy composers and lyricists, Porter possessed a style that was least affected by the passage of time. If we listen to his earliest efforts and compare them with the songs he wrote toward the end of his career, we can find little change in their basic attitudes or musical construction. There was an undeniable aura of the glittering Twenties about almost everything he ever wrote. For in spite of developments within the theatre, in spite of changes in world conditions, Cole Porter's art remained completely personal, completely impervious to outside influence.

In his so very civilized outlook, revealed through his urbane verses and his compelling music, Cole Porter never stopped writing the kind of songs he once did merely to amuse his friends. In fact he never ceased writing to amuse his friends. This did not mean he was a dilettante; on the contrary, he was always a meticulous, painstaking craftsman. Yet his detached manner toward the theatre (which kept him far from the day-to-day problems of actual production) did allow him to take pleasure in his own works in much the same ingenuous manner of George Gershwin. The premières of Cole Porter musicals invariably found the composer, surrounded by the smartest of the smart set, enjoying himself thoroughly from an orchestra seat as if he were listening to his own creations for the very first time. Nor was he above leaning over to one of his guests after a particular number and whispering, with guileless relish, "Good, isn't it?"

As Jule Styne once said, "Cole Porter has a brand of sophistication that is commercial, the type that makes a shopgirl know 21 or El Morocco without ever having been there." This communication was possible because there was nothing ever spurious or derivative about his style. It was simply the genuine expression of what always was, to Cole Porter, the only way of life.

Arthur Schwartz and Howard Dietz.   Photo by Alfredo Valente

CHAPTER THIRTEEN

HOWARD DIETZ
ARTHUR SCHWARTZ
DOROTHY FIELDS

THE OPPORTUNITIES AVAILABLE to aspiring young writers of the musical theatre have always been limited. By the mid-Twenties, they could no longer depend on the heavy European operettas of the kind that had served Jerome Kern so propitiously in the early decades of the century. However, there were still the revues. Whether extravagant or intimate, on-Broadway or off-Broadway, hackneyed or imaginative, these shows were the chief outlets for the budding talents of young composers and lyricists, their first chance to get their work on the professional stage.

The lyricist and composer most closely identified with the revue form of musical theatre were Howard Dietz and Arthur Schwartz. Moreover, from their very first collaboration, *The Little Show*, they were among the leaders in creating a new form of revue. Eschewing the opulence of Ziegfeld or the make-shift modesty of the off-Broadway attractions, the new shows were closer to the spirit of the impeccably produced *Charlot's Revues*, which had introduced Beatrice Lillie, Gertrude Lawrence, and Jack Buchanan to American audiences in the mid-Twenties. Intimate, sophisticated, and callid, these revues were marked by the brilliant performances of their stars, some revolutionary innovations in stagecraft, and a general air of sleek but exuberant professionalism.

In addition to *The Little Show*, Dietz and Schwartz were associated with other memorable revues—*Three's a Crowd*, *The Band Wagon*, *Flying Colors*, *At Home Abroad*, and *Inside U.S.A.* All of these attractions were well suited to the skillful cohesion of words and music created by the team. For both men were of similar background and outlook, and their urbane, literate songs caught perfectly the flavor of the shows for which they were created. Though his music has always shown great variety, Schwartz's most distinguished ballads are frequently marked by a brooding soulfulness that is perhaps matched only by some of Cole Porter's work. Dietz's lyrics are characterized by their brittle wit and subtle poetic imagery; while they may lack a certain warmth, they nevertheless contain a keenness and originality that make them ideally suited to Schwartz's music.

Arthur Schwartz was born in Brooklyn, on November 25, 1900. His father, a lawyer, was so strongly opposed to his son's early interest in music that he punished the youth whenever he found him trying to play the family piano. Secretly encouraged by his mother, young Arthur learned to play well enough to make his professional debut at the age of fourteen when he was hired to furnish musical accompaniment to silent films at the Cortelyou Movie Emporium in Flatbush.

After graduating from New York University, Schwartz continued his studies at Columbia University. Although he briefly considered a writing career, he acceded to his father's wishes and entered Columbia Law School. During his four years there, he helped support himself by teaching English at various high schools in New York. He also began to devote whatever free time he had to composing popular songs. At twenty-three, he wrote his first published song, "Baltimore, Md., You're the Only Doctor for Me." It netted him about eight dollars, but the urge to write melodies continued to be strong. One thing was obvious even from the title: he needed a good lyricist.

At first, Schwartz hoped to form a partnership with Lorenz Hart. The summer after graduating from Columbia Law School, he took a job as a counselor at a summer camp for the sole reason that Hart was also a counselor there. They wrote several songs together for camp shows, plus one, "I Know My Girl by Her Perfume," that was later used in a vaudeville act.

The success Hart achieved with Rodgers when they wrote the scores for *The Garrick Gaieties* ended the possibility of a permanent Schwartz-Hart collaboration. In 1926, Schwartz had some songs in *The Grand Street Follies* and the following year he was one of three composers responsible for another off-Broadway revue, *The New Yorkers* (not to be confused with the Cole Porter musical of three years later). Finding

himself being drawn more to music than to law, Schwartz felt that he had to make a definite choice between the two. Encouraged by Larry Hart, he quit his law practice in 1928 to devote himself exclusively to music and the theatre.

Although some of his earliest assignments—for vaudeville acts and "tab" shows (tabloid versions of Broadway plays that played the vaudeville circuits)—were not profitable, he continued to feel that things would change once he found the right lyricist. The man he eventually decided on was a part-time writer for the theatre and a full-time publicist for M-G-M named Howard Dietz.

Dietz was born in New York City, on September 8, 1896. He attended Columbia University at the same time as Oscar Hammerstein II and Lorenz Hart. While still an undergraduate, he had his first light verse published in Franklin P. Adams' *Conning Tower* and Don Marquis' *Sun Dial* newspaper columns. He also won a $500 prize for submitting the winning advertising copy in a contest sponsored by Fatima cigarettes, which led to his getting a job as copywriter for an advertising agency. One of the agency's accounts was the Goldwyn Pictures Corporation, and one of Dietz's first assignments was to give the new company a trademark (Leo the Lion, inspired by the mascot of Columbia University) and a slogan (*Ars Gratia Artis*). After serving in the Navy during World War I, Dietz did free-lance publicity for various film companies until Samuel Goldwyn appointed him director of advertising and publicity. When, in 1924, the Goldwyn company merged with Metro and Mayer, Dietz continued with the new company in a similar capacity. (Goldwyn, however, sold his interest soon after the merger to continue as an independent producer.) Dietz remained an executive at M-G-M for over thirty years; during that period he also wrote sketches, librettos, and lyrics for twelve

Broadway musicals, plus English versions of *La Bohème* and *Fledermaus* for the Metropolitan Opera.

Dietz first began to write for the theatre in 1923, when he fashioned a lyric to Arthur Samuel's music for the song "Alibi Baby." It was sung by Luella Gear in *Poppy*, one of W. C. Fields's greatest stage successes. (Fame was not Dietz's, however, because Dorothy Donnelly, the librettist-lyricist of the show, would not allow his name on either the program or the sheet music.)

The following year, Jerome Kern agreed to collaborate with the young lyricist on the score for *Dear Sir*. One evening when Dietz reported to the composer at his home in Bronxville, Kern played twelve numbers of the score on the piano, and asked him to get to work and return in a few days. Somewhat overawed by writing his first complete score with such an illustrious composer, Dietz thought he was expected to have all twelve sets of lyrics completed by that time. He then worked for fifty hours straight to finish the assignment, only to discover upon his return to Kerns's home that the composer had expected him to have just one lyric ready.

Dear Sir was a quick failure, but *Merry-Go-Round*, a revue which Dietz wrote with Jay Gorney and Morrie Ryskind in 1927, did have a long enough run to make many people recognize his talent. One of those most impressed was Arthur Schwartz.

Schwartz became convinced that in Dietz he would have a partner equally as inventive and as bright as Larry Hart. So determined was he to form a collaboration that he barraged the lyricist with telegrams and telephone calls. Dietz, however, was not receptive to the entreaties; he felt that since both men were relatively new to the theatre they would benefit more from associating with writers of greater experience.

The matter was allowed to rest until 1929 when Tom Weatherly joined with

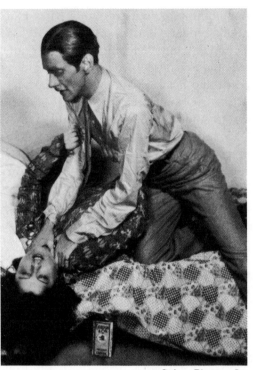

William A. Brady, Jr., and Dwight Deere Wiman to produce a revue called *The Little Show*. This was the outgrowth of a series of Sunday evening *Divertissements* that Weatherly and James Pond had presented at the Selwyn Theatre. "They were really nothing more than high-class vaudeville shows," recalls Weatherly, "but they were far more artistic than the Sunday night variety programs then being offered at the Winter Garden. They became so successful that I was convinced there would be an audience for a really smart and sophisticated revue." Upon reading the first newspaper announcement of the plans for *The Little Show*, Schwartz immediately went to see Weatherly. After some further persuasion on Schwartz's part, Dietz finally yielded and agreed to become associated with the project.

The Little Show, which played at the Music Box, was an elegantly intimate affair featuring Clifton Webb, Libby Holman, and Fred Allen. Most of the songs were composed by Schwartz and Dietz, but, as in most revues, there were many interpolated numbers. In fact, Schwartz

The Little Show (1929). "One of the most striking things in the revue," wrote critic Richard Lockridge, "is a song that is neither amusing nor forgettable. It is 'Moanin' Low,' which Libby Holman sings in that powerfully throbbing voice of hers while Clifton Webb dances with her in mad grotesque." The climax of that dance is shown here. (Costumes by Ruth Brenner.)

had nothing to do with two of Miss Holman's biggest hits, "Can't We Be Friends?" and "Moanin' Low." "Can't We Be Friends?" was written by Kay Swift and her husband, James Warburg, a banker and occasional lyricist who wrote under the name of Paul James; "Moanin' Low" was the work of Howard Dietz and Ralph Rainger, one of the two featured pianists in the pit orchestra. During the out-of-town tryout of the revue, prospects did not seem very promising until Dietz suggested that "Moanin' Low" be given the next-to-closing spot on the program; somehow this strengthened the entire entertainment and helped assure its success. The scene in which Libby Holman expressed this excruciating sentiment was a squalid Harlem tenement flat. After rousing her lover (Clifton Webb) from a drunken stupor, she brings him to his feet and they perform a particularly torrid dance. As a climax to the scene, and to prove the line in the song about being mean as can be, Webb strangles his devoted paramour.

The Dietz-Schwartz creations, however, were not completely overlooked.

Among them was the open-hearted tribute to New York's celebrated nuts-and-bolts emporium, "Hammacher Schlemmer, I Love You," and the debonair admission of the spurned lover, "I Guess I'll Have to Change My Plan."*

With *The Little Show* such an impressive hit, Messrs. Brady, Wiman, and Weatherly soon made plans for a sequel to be produced in the fall of 1930. At first they considered starring Webb, Holman, and Allen again. Then, remembering that even with Lillie, Lawrence, and Buchanan, the second *Charlot's Revue* had run less than half the number of performances of the first, the producers decided upon an entirely new cast for *The Second Little Show*. The show lasted just two months.

Once it became known that Webb, Holman, and Allen would not be in the new production, Max Gordon, a former agent and associate of Sam Harris, promptly signed the three for his own production, *Three's a Crowd*. He also hired Dietz and Schwartz to supply most of the songs, and gave Dietz the additional task of selecting all the material and the other performers to be in the show.

Again, although Dietz and Schwartz wrote most of the songs together, Dietz also collaborated on numbers with Phil Charig, Burton Lane, and Vernon Duke. The piece that made the biggest hit, however, was the only one that Dietz was not associated with—"Body and Soul," by Johnny Green, Robert Sour, and Edward Heyman. As intoned by Libby Holman, this masochistic lament became the "Moanin' Low" of the new revue. The best of the Dietz and Schwartz inspirations was "Something to

Photo by Vandamm

Three's a Crowd *(1930).*
Clifton Webb, Libby Holman, and Fred Allen.

*"I Guess I'll Have to Change My Plan" was based on a melody Schwartz had written the summer he spent at the camp with Lorenz Hart. Hart's original lyric went, in part:

> I love to lie awake in bed.
>   Right after taps
>   I pull the flaps
>   Above my head . . .

The Band Wagon *(1931).* "I Love Louisa," *sung by the cast on a merry-go-round at a Bavarian amusement park, was the first act finale. Adele and Fred Astaire are seated on the tortoise, Frank Morgan wears the lederhosen, and Helen Broderick is on the lamb. (Costumes by Kiviette; setting by Albert Johnson.)*

Photo by Vandamm

Remember You By,"* a ballad of unhappy leave-taking sung by Miss Holman to a sailor who stood with his back to the audience. He was played by Fred MacMurray. Fred Allen achieved new stature as a comedian with his uproarious sketch about Admiral Byrd at the South Pole.

By the time they signed with Max Gordon to supply the songs for *The Band Wagon,* Dietz and Schwartz were the acknowledged masters of the revue form. Dietz again agreed to supervise the production but only on two conditions: George S. Kaufman would have to write most of the sketches, and Fred and Adele Astaire would have to be signed for the leads. "In many ways, it was an experimental production," Dietz has observed, "combining as it did the best features of the so-called intimate type of revue that had come into vogue with *The Garrick Gaieties* and *The Little Show,* with the

*"Something to Remember You By," with a much faster tempo, was called "I Have No Words" when it was first sung in an English musical, *Little Tommy Tucker,* the previous year.

more spectacular backgrounds associated with the productions of Ziegfeld."

One of its most unusual innovations was the use of the revolving stage, which before that had been used mainly to change scenery. Now, as created by Albert Johnson, it was employed to enhance the musical and dramatic effectiveness of a scene. The sketches by Kaufman and Dietz were well above the average in wit and substance, particularly the satire on the Old South called "The Pride of the Claghornes."

Shortly after the June 3, 1931, opening of *The Band Wagon,* Olin Downes, the music critic of the New York *Times,* handed down the following verdict: "Each scene or episode serves to display a new angle of approach and craftsmanship. And—mirabile dictu—we have a composer whose melodic vein is not only graceful but characterized at its best by refinement and artistic quality. . . . He is able in many places to deliver a quality of musical workmanship which would command the respect of the most serious composer, and perhaps also the envy."

The still-enviable score—possibly the finest ever written for a revue—included the gaily optimistic "New Sun in the Sky" for Astaire to sing as he preened before a mirror; the saucy "Hoops" for Fred and Adele as two frolicking Parisian *enfants*; the almost ethereal "High and Low"; and the contagious oom-pah rhythm of "I Love Louisa," which ended the first act on a roistering Bavarian scene with the cast astride a swirling, festively decorated merry-go-round.

During rehearsals one day, it was discovered that there was need for what Schwartz describes as a "dark song, somewhat mystical, yet in slow, even rhythm." The following morning, he awoke with the entire melody so fixed in his mind that he was able to go immediately to the piano and play it through without faltering. The song, "Dancing in the Dark," was sung by John Barker, and danced by Tilly Losch on a slanted, mirrored floor illuminated by continually changing colored lights.

The third and final Max Gordon revue was *Flying Colors*. Judging by its cast (Clifton Webb, Tamara Geva, Patsy Kelly, Charles Butterworth, Larry Adler), it was the equal of *Three's a Crowd* and *The Band Wagon*. Yet, though Dietz (chief sketch writer, director, and lyricist) and Schwartz made notable contributions, there were many who felt that the show was merely repeating some of the proven formulas of their previous offerings. "Meine Kleine Akrobat," for example, sought to recapture the flavor of "I Love Louisa," while the sultry "Alone Together" was performed in a manner so similar to "Dancing in the Dark" that John Mason Brown referred to it as "Dancing in the Schwartz." "A Shine On Your Shoes," a piece of didactic exuberance tapped out by Monette Moore and Vilma and Buddy Ebsen around a shoe-shine stand, and the joyous chorale, "Louisiana Hayride," were also originally heard in this revue.*

The sameness that was creeping into their revues and their natural desire to try something fresh prompted Dietz and Schwartz to write their first book musical, *Revenge with Music*, in 1934. Inspired by a trip to Spain, Dietz adapted his libretto from the same Spanish novel, *El Sombrero de Tres Picos* by Pedro de Alarcón, that had previously served as the basis for Manuel de Falla's ballet of the same name and Hugo Wolf's comic opera, *Der Corregidor*. The story, a fairly elementary tale, concerned the attempt of a governor of a Spanish province to make love to the wife of a poor miller, and the miller's counter (and more successful) attempt to make love to the governor's wife.

Schwartz's score was distinguished by its melodic richness and its faculty for capturing all the fire and romance of Spain. Because Libby Holman, as the miller's wife, was given the fervent "You and the Night and the Music," it was necessary to have an equally strong solo for Georges Metaxa, as her husband. Among the many songs Dietz and Schwartz had written the previous year

Revenge with Music (1934). Libby Holman and Georges Metaxa as the young Spanish couple in a musical based on an old Spanish tale of cuckolds and cuckolders. (Costumes by Constance Ripley.)

Culver Pictures, Inc.

*Agnes de Mille was to have done the choreography—her first for a Broadway musical—for *Flying Colors*, but because of differences with almost everyone but Howard Dietz, she quit during the tryout and was succeeded by Albertina Rasch.

for a radio serial, *The Gibson Family*, was one called "If There Is Someone Lovelier Than You," which they felt would be perfectly suited to the requirements of *Revenge with Music*. Although melodically it may have lacked the proper Spanish coloration, Mr. Metaxa's European accent and the orchestral arrangement combined to give it just the right atmosphere for the locale.

There were two other collaborations by the team in the Thirties. *At Home Abroad* (1935) used one of the oldest frameworks for a revue, the around-the-world tour. Thus, Beatrice Lillie was given the opportunity to extoll the charms of "Paree," become hopelessly confused in London ordering "two dozen double-damask dinner napkins," and, in "Get Yourself a Geisha," slyly reveal some of the quaint customs of Japan, the land where "it's better with your shoes off." Ethel Waters, Eleanor Powell, Herb Williams, and Reginald Gardiner (he mimicked trains and gave an impersonation of wallpaper) were also members of the tour.

Between the Devil (1937), the last Dietz-Schwartz musical for eleven years, was their second book show. Its tale of an English bigamist whose life was complicated by an English wife (Evelyn Laye) and a French wife (Adèle Dixon) was a time-worn farce situation (it turned up again twenty-one years later in *Oh Captain!*), and neither the authors nor the players could extract much life from it. As the bigamist, Jack Buchanan sang the jauntily self-pitying "By Myself" while being pursued by bobbies through London's foggy streets. The show ran three months.

Because of increased pressure on Dietz to concentrate on his salaried chores at M-G-M, Schwartz was compelled to seek other collaborators during the latter part of the Thirties. Shortly before *Between the Devil*, he became associated with an elaborate production called *Virginia* which the Rockefeller family pro-

duced at the Center Theatre in Radio City. As the Rockefellers had already invested a considerable sum toward the restoration of the Colonial village of Williamsburg, Virginia, they thought it would be a fine idea to offer a musical set in that locale during the American Revolution. To write the book they chose Laurence Stallings (later succeeded by Owen Davis), and as Schwartz's partner they assigned Albert Stillman, the Radio City staff lyricist.

The musical, a costly but dull extravaganza, was the next to last stage musical shown at the theatre. After becoming a showplace for Sonja Henie's ice revue and then a television studio, the Center Theatre was gutted in 1954 and converted into office space.

Stars In Your Eyes, in 1939, was Schwartz's first score with Dorothy Fields. Miss Fields, the daughter of producer-comedian Lew Fields and the sister of librettist Herbert and librettist-playwright Joseph, was born on July 15, 1904 in Allenhurst, New Jersey, where her parents had rented a summer home. Determined that none of his children would suffer the inherent agonies of a theatrical career, Papa Fields at first

Herbert and Dorothy Fields.

Photo by G. Maillard Kesslere

Photo by Jerome Robinson

Stars in Your Eyes (1939). Every night, in the midst of the song called "It's All Yours," Ethel Merman and Jimmy Durante would break each other up with supposedly spontaneous wisecracks and stories. (Costumes by John Hambleton.)

vainly tried to steer them into other pursuits. Dorothy attended the Benjamin School for Girls and, following graduation, became the school's drama instructor. Her first literary efforts were light verses she submitted to magazines, and her first lyrics were improvisations she made up to fit the classical piano pieces she was studying. When she was twenty-two, Dorothy met composer Jimmy McHugh, who had already written a number of hits, including "When My Sugar Walks Down the Street" and "I Can't Believe that You're in Love with Me," both for Harlem's famed Cotton Club. Impressed by Dorothy's poems and lyrics, McHugh took her on as a collaborator for the next Cotton Club revue, featuring Duke Ellington and his Orchestra. Their work attracted the attention of producer Lew Leslie who was convinced they would be the perfect combination to write the score for his all-Negro Broadway revue, *Blackbirds of 1928*, starring Adelaide Hall and Bill

Robinson. The show contained a remarkable string of song hits—"I Can't Give You Anything but Love, Baby" (allegedly inspired by a remark made by an indigent swain while peering into Tiffany's window), "Diga Diga Doo," "I Must Have that Man," and "Porgy" (a pre-Gershwin plaint prompted by the Dorothy and DuBose Heyward play).

The great success of *Blackbirds* (among the longest-running Negro shows ever presented on Broadway*) assured the song-writing partners of steady employment in a variety of locales and media. Ziegfeld hired them to write songs for his final *Midnight Frolic* (1928), headlining Eddie Cantor and Helen Morgan. Lew Fields put them to work on *Hello, Daddy*, which he kept pretty much of a family affair by starring in it himself and assigning son Herbert to do the book. Leslie next signed McHugh and Fields for his *International Review*, a Broadway flop despite the stellar presence of Gertrude Lawrence, Harry Richman and Jack Pearl, plus songs such as "Exactly Like You" and "On the Sunny Side of the Street." The team also did the songs for Leslie's Chicago revue, *Clowns in Clover* (including "Don't Blame Me"), for New York's Palais Royale night club floorshow, and for the opening bill at Radio City Music Hall.

During most of the period between 1930 and 1939, Dorothy Fields worked in Hollywood, writing film songs primarily with McHugh ("I'm in the Mood for Love," "Dinner at Eight") and Jerome Kern (scores for *I Dream Too Much* and *Swing Time*). This movie background made her particularly well equipped to collaborate on Arthur Schwartz's new musical comedy project, *Stars in Your Eyes*. For this was to be a movie satire with a particularly novel

*Leslie had first presented a *Blackbirds* revue in London in 1926, with Florence Mills starred. His attempts to mount subsequent *Blackbirds* editions on Broadway in 1930, 1933, and in 1939—even with Lena Horne in the last—were failures. West End audiences, however, continued to prove receptive in 1934 and 1936.

idea. It was Schwartz's notion that a very funny show could be built around the making of a Hollywood musical by leaders of New York's left-wing theatre, with the humor derived from superimposing social significance on a glamorous Hollywood production. After J. P. McEvoy completed the script—then called *Swing to the Left*—Dwight Deere Wiman agreed to produce it with Ethel Merman as a movie queen and Jimmy Durante as a labor-union organizer. Upon reading the book and listening to the songs, however, director Joshua Logan objected to the social commentary. Liberal themes were fine for revues, he told the authors, but why clutter up a gay story with anything so weighty? Eventually, Schwartz, Fields and McEvoy capitulated. The labor leader became a studio idea man, a song about the South's economy was thrown out, and, in general, what might have been a sharp, unconventional spoof of the movies became a standard product by the time *Swing to the Left* was transformed into *Stars in Your Eyes* Nevertheless, with all the concessions to what the public was supposed to want, the show lasted only 127 performances.

Soon after *Stars in Your Eyes* opened, Schwartz accepted an offer to work in Hollywood. He remained there until 1946. Among the films for which he wrote complete scores were *Thank Your Lucky Stars* (lyrics by Frank Loesser) and *The Time, the Place and the Girl* (lyrics by Leo Robin). For Columbia, he produced the Gene Kelly–Rita Hayworth *Cover Girl* (score by Jerome Kern and Ira Gershwin), and for Warners, the romanticized biography of Cole Porter, *Night and Day*.

By the mid-Forties, the Broadway musical theatre had become saturated with serious costume musical plays. As something of an antidote to *Bloomer Girl*, *Song of Norway*, *Up in Central Park*, *Carousel*, and the like, George S. Kaufman and Nunnally Johnson decided to collaborate on a sophisticated modern musical comedy. *Park Avenue*, the show

they wrote, was concerned with nothing more serious than the compulsion of socialites to shed their mates with as much frequency as possible. As the production was also to mark the return to Broadway of both Arthur Schwartz and Ira Gershwin in their first assignment as a team, there was, understandably, great expectation for the enterprise. Unfortunately, although the songs were attractive, the book was too much of a one-joke affair, and the show had a very brief run.

Schwartz's duties both in New York and in Hollywood required that he cross the country many times. Yet it was not until the summer of 1947, when he drove from the East Coast to the West Coast, that he actually saw something of the country and the people. This gave him an idea: a musical revue that, instead of using the format of an around-the-world tour as in *At Home Abroad*, would be restricted to topics and locales indigenous to the United States. John Gunther presented him with a perfect title for it—*Inside U.S.A.*

Inside U.S.A. *(1948).*
The gay opening number of the second act with Beatrice Lillie as the queen of the Mardi Gras. The kneeling swain at the right is Jack Cassidy. (Costumes by Eleanor Goldsmith and Castillo; setting by Lemuel Ayers.)

Photo by Eileen Darby—Graphic House

Inside U.S.A., which co-starred Beatrice Lillie and Jack Haley, was the only musical Schwartz ever produced himself. It also reunited him with Howard Dietz, and their score gave undeniable proof that in the wit and originality of their songs the collaborators had lost none of the skill that had marked their earlier efforts. In "Haunted Heart," they returned to the kind of throbbing torch ballad to which they have always given a certain distinction; in "Rhode Island Is Famous for You," they created a punning inventory of the most famous products of almost every state in the Union; in "Come, O Come to Pittsburgh," they supplied Beatrice Lillie with a mocking madrigal celebrating the industrial wonders of that city. Two particularly original musical notions were "Blue Grass," the lament of a girl who has lost her boy friend to the horses at Churchill Downs, and "My Gal Is Mine Once More," a loping Western number sung by a cowboy celebrating his remarriage to his first wife.

For his next two undertakings, *A Tree Grows in Brooklyn* in 1951, and *By the Beautiful Sea* in 1954, Schwartz again became affiliated with lyricist Dorothy Fields. Both shows starred Shirley Booth (whose previous musical comedy experience had been as Louhedda Hopsons in *Hollywood Pinafore* five years earlier),

both were set in Brooklyn just after the turn of the century, and both lasted exactly 270 performances.

Judged on musical merits, *A Tree Grows in Brooklyn* was the more impressive work. The famous Betty Smith novel provided both Schwartz and Miss Fields with the opportunity to create songs of far greater depth and meaning than they had previously done. In place of sophisticated patter and soulful ballads of the type they had provided for *Stars in Your Eyes*, the writers produced a score overflowing with nostalgia and sentiment, one that caught all the poignance and emotion of the gallant Nolan family. For Schwartz, it was an opportunity to return to the people and the places he had once known during his boyhood in Brooklyn, and he took long walks through the tenement areas of the city in order to steep himself in the proper atmosphere. Miss Fields also strove for authenticity. "The lyrics reflect the simplicity of these people," she once said. "There are no high-flown poetic sentiments." Yet, though there may not be any deliberate attempts at poetry, there is a rich vein of the poetry of everyday speech in the lyrics, just as there is a feeling of genuine eloquence in the music. Indeed, the characters and locale came more vividly to life in the songs than in the somewhat awkward libretto devised by George Abbott and Betty Smith.

Because it had a weaker book and score, *By the Beautiful Sea* was much more dependent on the charm and personality of Shirley Booth. As Lottie Gibson, a vaudeville performer who owned a theatrical boarding house in Coney Island, her performance was so disarming that Brooks Atkinson had to confess, "Everyone has long since lost his heart to Miss Booth."

Dorothy Fields never again collaborated on a Broadway show with Arthur Schwartz. In 1959, she worked with composer Albert Hague on the Gwen

A Tree Grows in Brooklyn (1951).
Aunt Cissy breaks out into a spirited rendition of "Look Who's Dancing." The scene is a furniture store where she and newlyweds Kate and Johnny Nolan have gone to purchase a bed. Shirley Booth, Marcia VanDyke, and Johnny Johnston. (Costumes by Irene Sharaff.)

Photo by Eileen Darby—Graphic House

Verdon vehicle, *Redhead*; seven years later she teamed with Cy Coleman on another Gwen Verdon musical, *Sweet Charity*, and seven years after that, again with Coleman, on a similar work, *Seesaw*. She died in New York on March 28, 1974, of a heart attack.

In 1960, Howard Dietz retired from his duties at Metro-Goldwyn-Mayer to devote himself full time to writing with Arthur Schwartz. The first product of their resumed partnership, *The Gay Life*, adapted from Schnitzler's *Affairs of Anatol*, was a slightly frayed bedroom farce redeemed by a score of unfailing melodic richness and lyrical grace. The Italian comic Walter Chiari was miscast as the roving Anatol, but the lovely Barbara Cook made the most of such musical delights as "Magic Moment" and "Who Can? You Can!" Another Dietz-Schwartz collaboration, *Jennie*, starring Mary Martin as a fictitious Laurette Taylor, suffered through a brief life in 1963.

The striking irony in the career of Arthur Schwartz is that in spite of the high quality of his melodic creations for such book musicals as *Revenge with Music*, *Virginia*, *Between the Devil*, *Stars in Your Eyes*, *Park Avenue*, *The Gay Life*, and especially *A Tree Grows in Brooklyn*, the composer's only commercial successes have been the revues he wrote in partnership with Howard Dietz. The fault has seldom been his or his lyricist's; in almost every case it has been the librettist who has somehow failed to supply a script worthy of its score.

The contributions of Dietz and Schwartz to the revue form are still their most significant collaborative achievement in the development of the musical theatre. Chiefly due to their efforts, the revue reached a peak of perfection that has never been surpassed. Indeed, in the event that this form of entertainment ever does return to its former eminence, it will need the very qualities of smartness, originality, wit and melody that have so distinguished the works of Howard Dietz and Arthur Schwartz.

CHAPTER FOURTEEN

E. Y. HARBURG
VERNON DUKE
HAROLD ARLEN
BURTON LANE

IN ADDITION TO Arthur Schwartz, there were many other composers who first won recognition for their work in the Broadway revues of the late Twenties and early Thirties. Chief among them were Vernon Duke, Harold Arlen, and Burton Lane, though none of these men was as closely identified with this form of entertainment as Schwartz.

In fact, each one of these composers won far more lasting fame with serious musical plays during the Forties—Duke with *Cabin in the Sky*, Arlen with *Bloomer Girl*, and Lane with *Finian's Rainbow*. Apart from the similarity of their progress in the theatre, what is interesting about these men is that they were part of the rising group of writers—which included Schwartz—who were inspired by George Gershwin. Just as Jerome Kern had been the idol of Rodgers, Gershwin, and other composers of the Twenties, so it was now Gershwin himself who was the inspiration for the new generation. The relationship of these men to the Gershwin family has even been professional, as all have collaborated with George's brother, Ira. The lyricist, however, who has been most closely associated with the careers of Duke, Arlen, and Lane—and who has also been a close friend of the Gershwins—is the prodigious E. Y. Harburg.

E. Y. Harburg

E. Y. (Edgar "Yip") Harburg was born on April 8, 1898, in New York City. His parents were poor, and as a boy he sold newspapers, lighted street lamps, and did other odd jobs to help pay for his education. At Townsend Harris High School, he was co-editor with Ira Gershwin of the literary column in the school newspaper. The friendship of the two men continued when they both attended the City College of New York. While at college, Harburg, like Ira Gershwin and Howard Dietz, began to contribute light verse to Franklin P. Adams' *Conning Tower* column. After graduation, he traveled through South America for about three years, spending a year writing for a newspaper in Montevideo, Uruguay.

While in South America, he made up his mind to become a lyricist. On his return to New York in the early Twenties, he was advised by Ira Gershwin that he would do well to find a more remunerative way of earning a living. Harburg then started an electrical appliance business and did well until the 1929 stock market crash wiped him out. "I had my fill of this dreamy abstract thing called business," he once said, "and I decided to face reality by writing lyrics."

Fortunately, at that time, composer Jay Gorney was looking for a lyricist. A few years before, having read some poems in F.P.A.'s column signed "Freckles," Gorney had discovered the man behind the nickname to be Howard Dietz, and an informal partnership had developed. But because Gorney had recently been appointed head of the music department of Paramount Picture's Astoria Studio and Dietz was the chief publicist for M-G-M, the composer had to find another lyricist. Again he scanned F.P.A.'s column, where some verses signed "Yip" attracted his attention. Abetted by a high recommendation from Ira Gershwin, Harburg soon had both a

partner and a contract with a motion picture company. About the same time, five songs by Gorney and Harburg were accepted for *Earl Carroll's Sketchbook*, an extremely successful revue which ran for a year and one-half. So outstanding were Harburg's initial efforts that he was given assignments to contribute the major share of lyrics to *The Garrick Gaieties*, *Earl Carroll Vanities of 1930*, *Shoot the Works*, *Ballyhoo*, and *Americana*. In *Americana*, produced in 1932, Harburg was represented by contributions written with Vernon Duke ("Let Me Match My Private Life with Yours"), Harold Arlen and Johnny Mercer ("Satan's Li'l Lamb"), and Burton Lane ("You're Not Pretty but You're Mine"). The biggest hit of the show was the memorable Depression anthem, "Brother, Can You Spare a Dime?," which Harburg wrote with Jay Gorney. The song was one of the first examples of the kind of socially conscious viewpoint that would mark many of Harburg's later lyrics.

Vernon Duke.

Photo by Atelier Von Behr

Vernon Duke

Along with Kurt Weill, Vernon Duke had the most thorough musical education of any of the leading theatre composers who won recognition during the Thirties. Yet, unlike most well-trained composers, Duke has led a somewhat schizophrenic musical life, writing symphonies, ballets, and concertos in a style completely unlike that employed in his musical comedies and revues. Indeed, for many years, he even used two different names: his real name, Vladimir Dukelsky, for the concert hall, and Vernon Duke, a pseudonym suggested by George Gershwin, for Broadway.

Duke was born in Parafianovo, Russia, on October 10, 1903. His early studies were under Reinhold Glière and Marian Dombrovsky, and at the age of thirteen was admitted to the Kiev Conservatory of Music. After the Russian

Revolution, his family fled the country. For a time, Duke tried to pursue his musical career in the United States, but found few opportunities. He returned to Europe, where he soon became acquainted with Sergei Diaghilev, the director of the Ballet Russe. Diaghilev was so impressed with the twenty-year-old composer that he commissioned him to write the music for the ballet, *Zéphyr et Flore*, which was subsequently performed throughout Europe. In the mid-Twenties, Duke moved to London, where his first assignment for the musical theatre was to supply additional music for *Katja, the Dancer*. The following year he performed a similar task for *Yvonne*, which won immortality when Noël Coward dubbed it "*Yvonne* the Terrible." Duke's first complete score was written in 1928 for *The Yellow Mask*, an English musical with a book by Edgar Wallace.

Soon after settling permanently in the United States in 1929, Duke wrote his first "American" song, "I Am Only Human After All," with a lyric by Ira Gershwin and E. Y. Harburg. Although the song was accepted for Ruth Selwyn's *9:15 Revue*, it was dropped from the score even before rehearsals began. Later, it was introduced in the 1930 edition of *The Garrick Gaieties* and became Duke's first commercial success.

Duke's romantic background as a Russian emigré soon made him a popular figure in the social life of New York. Courtney Burr, a wealthy young man with a great interest in the theatre, was anxious to produce a revue in the sophisticated style inaugurated by *The Little Show*. Burr was impressed by Duke's musical talent and hoped to induce Dorothy Parker to contribute the lyrics. On Duke's insistence, however, the assignment went to Harburg. The revue, *Walk a Little Faster*, opened in December, 1932, with the leading parts played by Beatrice Lillie and Clark and McCullough. The show may have been hindered by its continual striving for

Walk a Little Faster (1932). Bobby Clark, Beatrice Lillie, and Paul McCullough.

Culver Pictures, Inc.

unusual artistic effects, but there was no sign of strain in the smoothly constructed melodies or in their deft lyrics.

"April in Paris," which quickly established the reputation of Duke and Harburg (even though Evelyn Hoey, who introduced it, had laryngitis on opening night), was written one April afternoon while Duke and some friends were reminiscing about Paris in a small restaurant in New York. Suddenly, someone paraphrased Browning by crying out, "Oh, to be in Paris now that April's here." "April in Paris" struck the composer as a perfect title for a song; he dashed over to an upright piano and, within a relatively short time, created the refrain that still remains the most popular melody he ever composed.

In the mid-Thirties, the Shuberts were the successors to Ziegfeld in the creation of elaborate revues. In fact, after Ziegfeld's death in 1932, his former rivals secured the rights to produce the *Ziegfeld Follies*. The first Shubert-sponsored *Follies* was presented in 1934, with Mrs. Billie Burke Ziegfeld as titular producer. Duke and Harburg created most of the score for this revue. Two years later, an equally resplendent edition reunited

Duke with Ira Gershwin. Fanny Brice was the stellar attraction in both productions, though the second served to introduce Broadway audiences to the charms of the St. Louis-born and Paris-acclaimed Josephine Baker. The 1936 *Follies* was also the first Broadway attraction to have choreography by George Balanchine.

On Christmas night, 1936, the Shuberts offered another opulent revue, *The Show Is On*, which was designed and directed by Vincente Minnelli. The bulk of the score was the product of Vernon Duke and Ted Fetter (Cole Porter's cousin). By the time the show reached New York, however, many of their numbers had been cut and replaced by contributions by some of the most illustrious song-writers of the theatre: George and Ira Gershwin, "By Strauss"; Rodgers and Hart, "Rhythm" (for an aggressively rhythmic Beatrice Lillie); Hoagy Carmichael and Stanley Adams, "Little Old Lady"; and Harold Arlen and E. Y. Harburg, "Song of the Woodman" (bellowed out by Bert Lahr). Among the remaining Duke-Fetter songs was one of

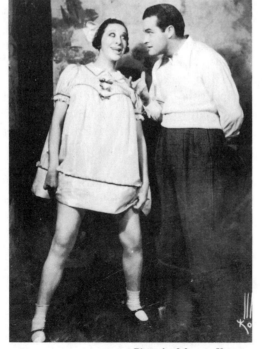

Ziegfeld Follies of 1936. The irrepressible Baby Snooks (Fanny Brice) is beginning to get on the nerves of a Hollywood director (Bob Hope) in one of the sketches from the revue. This was Miss Brice's last appearance on the Broadway stage.

Photo by Murray Korman

their loveliest inspirations, the graceful, economically titled "Now."

Although his previous works would not have indicated his suitability for the task, Vernon Duke became associated in 1940 with a musical fantasy of Negro life called *Cabin in the Sky*. The Lynn Root libretto was initially brought to George Balanchine, who was anxious to do it as his first assignment as director of an entire Broadway production. Balanchine took the script to Duke, who became fascinated by the story. Nevertheless, he hesitated to write the music as he feared that his lack of familiarity with the Negro people would be too much of a handicap. (The word around Broadway at the time was that the wrong Duke had been chosen.)

The more he thought about it, however, the more Duke became intrigued by the challenge. Because both he and Balanchine were Russian and Root was a Hollywood script-writer, the composer wanted a lyricist with some direct contact with Southern Negroes. Duke first thought of Ira Gershwin because of *Porgy and Bess*, but Gershwin was already committed to *Lady in the Dark*. E.Y. Harburg, Duke's second choice, diplomatically told the composer that he thought the story lacked significance, though his true feeling was that the composer was incapable of writing the kind of score the play required. (Later, Harburg readily admitted he was wrong.) Finally, Duke turned to the willing John Treville Latouche, a twenty-three-year-old poet from Richmond, Virginia, whose lyric to *Ballad for Americans* (music by Earl Robinson) had recently won wide acclaim.

When it was finally presented in October, 1940, *Cabin in the Sky* offered audiences an imaginative tale that combined elements of both *The Green Pastures* and *Liliom*. As a parable of the struggle between good and evil, the play may have been, as Richard Watts, Jr.,

Photo by Alfredo Valente

The Show Is On *(1936). Beatrice Lillie invites the audience to "Buy yourself a balloon, fly up to the moon," as she is swung way out over the orchestra. As a climax to the number, Miss Lillie unfastened a garter and flung it to a favored gentleman. (Costume by Vincente Minnelli.)*

wrote, "merely a white man's self-conscious attempt to write a pseudo-folk fable of another race." Yet in its pioneering effort to create something bold and unconventional, it did provide Ethel Waters with her only dramatic role in the musical theatre, while also demonstrating the remarkable versatility of the composer. Despite the fact there were no blues or rhythm songs to convey the authentic emotions of American Negroes, the score was still authentic enough as purely theatre music to delineate characters skillfully and to set the proper mood. Such varied, yet appropriate creations as the deeply felt "Cabin in the Sky," or the slinky "Honey in the Honeycomb" (for temptress Katherine Dunham), or the hedonistic "Do What You Wanna Do," all demonstrated their creators' talents for using music and lyrics to achieve maximum dramatic effectiveness.

Photo by Bob Golby

Cabin in the Sky *(1940). Dooley Wilson listens as Ethel Waters sings "Cabin in the Sky." Without once stepping out of character or assuming the airs of a star performer,"* wrote Brooks Atkinson, "Miss Waters captures all the innocence and humor of a storybook character, investing it also with that rangy warmth of spirit that distinguishes her acting."

Shortly before the New York opening, the authors felt that a comic number was badly needed for Miss Waters to offset some of her more impassioned solos. With the New York première only three days off, Duke came up with a song called "Foolin' Around with Love," which he had once written with Ted Fetter. Latouche retitled it "Taking a Chance on Love" and wrote the reprises. With Miss Waters delivering it through chorus after chorus, it became one of the most memorable show-stoppers in the history of Broadway musicals.

One of the great enigmas of the American musical theatre is that Vernon Duke was never able to follow up his work for *Cabin in the Sky* with anything else that has revealed so much creative talent for the stage. As in the case of Arthur Schwartz, Harold Arlen, and other gifted composers, the fault was not the quality of Duke's contributions but rather in the quality of the productions for which they were written. Just one year after *Cabin in the Sky*, Duke agreed to work on a minor vehicle for Eddie Cantor called *Banjo Eyes*, which was also Cantor's final Broadway appearance. In 1944, great expectations were held for *Sadie Thompson*, a musical version of Somerset Maugham's *Rain* that had a libretto by Howard Dietz (he also did the lyrics) and Rouben Mamoulian (he also directed). However, the production was foredoomed when Ethel Merman, the intended star, refused to appear in it because she objected to Dietz's lyrics. June Havoc was a satisfactory replacement, but the damage had been done: *Sadie Thompson* lasted only two months on Broadway.

In the Fifties, Duke became involved in the ill-advised Bette Davis revue, *Two's Company*, which also included an abbreviated musical treatment of *Rain* as the first-act finale. Two of the composer's most exquisite numbers, "Roundabout" and "Out of the Clear Blue Sky" (both with lyrics by Ogden Nash), were also sung in this revue. On January 16, 1969, in Santa Monica, California, Duke succumbed to lung cancer at the age of 65.

Probably no other composer, with the possible exception of Arthur Schwartz, contributed more quality songs to the revues of the Thirties than Vernon Duke. With *Cabin in the Sky*, however, he showed definite indications of the broadening of his scope as a creator of well-integrated scores for adult, meaningful book musicals. The bad luck that plagued him in the commercial theatre cannot obliterate the sound musicianship and superior quality that distinguished his work for the musical stage. Graceful, elegant, imaginatively constructed, the songs of Vernon Duke have a durability and individuality that have made them part of the permanent literature of American popular music.

Harold Arlen

Harold Arlen became a composer almost by accident. He was born in Buffalo, New York, on February 15, 1905. At seven, he sang in the choir of the synagogue where his father was a cantor. Because his parents wanted him to become a music teacher, they encouraged young Harold's interest in music. In his early teens, Arlen began to play piano at local clubs and on lake steamers. When he was fifteen, he helped organize an instrumental group known as The Snappy Trio. He later joined another group, The Yankee Six, which eventually expanded into a full-sized dance orchestra known as the Buffalodians. While performing as a pianist, vocalist, and arranger for the group during an engagement at a New York nightclub, Arlen attracted the attention of Arnold Johnson, a well-known orchestra leader. Johnson liked Arlen's singing and playing so much that he hired him for his own orchestra, which was then about to appear in *George White's Scandals of 1928*.

Because Arlen's chief ambition at the time was to become a singer, Johnson allowed him to sing one of the songs from the DeSylva-Brown-Henderson score during the intermission. Thus for the six-and-one-half-month run of the *Scandals*, Arlen serenaded nonsmoking spectators with his crooning of Harry Richman's hit song, "On the Crest of a Wave." One of those who were impressed with the twenty-three-year-old between-the-acts entertainer was Vincent Youmans, who was just beginning to organize the cast for his forthcoming production, *Great Day!* Youmans promptly hired Arlen to play the role of Cokey Joe, the piano player, in the musical. Arlen never quite made it on the Broadway stage, however; after the first tryout performance on Long Island, both the character and the song he sang, "Doo-Dah-Dey," were eliminated.

Great Day! may have ended Arlen's career as a performer, but it was responsible for beginning his career as a full-time composer. One day at rehearsal, the regular pianist had become ill. As Arlen recalls: "I was asked to sit at the piano and play ta-tum, ta-tum-tum, TUM—the phrase that's always used to start a dance chorus off at rehearsals. I gave them the standard pick-up the first day, but the next day I played it a little differently. On the third day, I worked it around a bit more, and suddenly the whole company was asking, 'Say, what *is* that you're playing?'"

Urged to turn his variation into a commercial song, the neophyte composer took the piece to his friend, Harry Warren, then on the staff at Remick's. Warren introduced Arlen to Ted Koehler, who gave the melody a lyric and the title, "Get Happy." When they learned of Ruth Selwyn's plans for the *9:15 Revue*, the two men auditioned the song. Unlike the less-fortunate team of Duke, Harburg, and Gershwin, whose "I Am Only Human after All" had not been used, Arlen and Koehler had their new song

accepted and given to Ruth Etting to sing in the first-act finale. George Gershwin, who saw the show during its tryout, was so impressed with "Get Happy" that he told the composer it was the most exciting finale he had ever heard. After receiving such encouragement—especially since the *9:15 Revue* was a dismal failure—Arlen promptly decided to end his career as a singer and pianist to devote all his time to composing.

Though he contributed songs to a few minor Broadway attractions in the early 1930's, Harold Arlen first won fame for the songs he and Koehler wrote for a series of Cotton Club revues. These were probably the only nightclub floor shows ever to produce so many numbers of enduring appeal, among them "Between the Devil and the Deep Blue Sea," "Kickin' the Gong Around," "I Love a Parade," "I've Got the World on a String," "Stormy Weather," and "Ill Wind."

In 1938, "Yip" Harburg had an idea for a musical that was eventually turned

Harold Arlen.

into a successful vehicle for Ed Wynn and called *Hooray for What!* Concerned with the chaotic world situation at that time, the lyricist was anxious to become associated with a musical comedy that would not only be entertaining but would also have something to say about the need for preserving peace and the dangers of the armament race. Unsure of his own ability as a librettist, he took the idea to Howard Lindsay and Russel Crouse, who agreed to write the book. Arlen then joined Harburg to write the score. In spite of its overtones of a message (it even made reference to the atom bomb), *Hooray for What!* was still very much within the framework of conventional musical comedy. Ed Wynn again played his customary zany clown, although this time the character was called upon to save the world from destruction by using laughing gas. In the score were many superior numbers, including "God's Country," a merry flag-waver in which Popeye and Gypsy Rose Lee were extolled as ample compensation for being deprived of Mussolini and Oswald Mosley.*

From the Thirties to the mid-Forties, the uncertain condition of the Broadway theatre forced most of the creative musical talent, including Arlen and Harburg, to accept Hollywood contracts. By the early Forties, however, writers on the West Coast were becoming eager to return to a Broadway that was being transformed as a result of the impact of *Cabin in the Sky, Pal Joey, Lady in the Dark,* and, most significantly, *Oklahoma!* A book show now had to have a really sturdy libretto, with songs and dances an inseparable part of the entire production. During World War II, there was also a greater emphasis on American themes from which audiences might derive some measure of hope for the future.

---

*Hooray for What! was the second musical intended to begin the Broadway career of choreographer Agnes de Mille. As in *Flying Colors,* however, she withdrew prior to the show's New York opening.

While still in California, "Yip" Harburg became intrigued with the idea of doing a musical with a Civil War setting. Lilith and Dan James had written a play about the introduction of bloomers during that period. Harburg liked the story, but he felt the theme needed further development and suggested to writers Sig Herzig and Fred Saidy that they strengthen it by putting greater emphasis on the issues of women's rights and Negro rights. In that way, he felt, audiences of 1944 could accept the theme as pertaining to the struggle for freedom everywhere. To provide the score, Harburg was joined by Arlen, with whom he had last collaborated on the film *The Wizard of Oz.*

Bloomer Girl emerged as a charming and colorful musical play with an almost inescapable kinship to *Oklahoma!* This, however, was due more to its cast and production staff than to its subject matter or music. Both Celeste Holm (in her first starring role) and Joan McCracken had previously been in the Rodgers and Hammerstein musical and both plays shared the same set designer (Lemuel Ayers), costume designer (Miles White), choreographer (Agnes de Mille), and orchestral arranger (Robert Russell Bennett). Miss de Mille's chief contribution, a Civil War ballet, was particularly impressive in its moving depiction of the anguish of women who must wait at home while their men are at war.

The songs by Arlen and Harburg caught the mood and the spirit of the story. "The Eagle and Me" and "I Got a Song" sang eloquently of the Negro's yearning for freedom, while "It Was Good Enough for Grandma" burst out in animated defiance of old-fashioned convention. The eternal subject of love was melodiously treated in "Evelina," with its quasi-folk flavor, and in the more conventional "Right as the Rain." "Sunday in Cicero Falls" was a mocking, stately march that conveyed so perfectly the starched atmosphere of the Sabbath in a small, mid-

Bloomer Girl *(1944).* *Agnes de Mille's eloquent Civil War ballet. Joan McCracken is the girl with her arms upraised, third from the left. (Costumes by Miles White; setting by Lemuel Ayers.)*

Photo by Vandamm

nineteenth-century American town.

After *Bloomer Girl*, Harold Arlen continued to divide his time between film assignments and Broadway. In 1946, he joined Johnny Mercer in creating the songs for *St. Louis Woman** an all-Negro musical in which Pearl Bailey made an auspicious Broadway debut singing "Legalize My Name" and "A Woman's Prerogative." In spite of a superior score, however, the show was not a success. Neither was Arlen's next musical, *House of Flowers*, produced almost nine years later. Truman Capote made the adaptation from his own short story, and collaborated with Arlen on the lyrics. Although the idea was promising, the story of an innocent girl living in a brothel on a Caribbean island proved to be too weak and undramatic to be successful as a musical comedy libretto. This was particularly

*St. Louis Woman was subsequently expanded into a "blues opera," *Free and Easy*, which incorporated some early songs by the composer. After opening in Amsterdam, Holland, in the fall of 1959, it was forced to close soon afterward in Paris.

unfortunate; Arlen's score was one of his most distinguished, the Oliver Messel décor was stunning, and the cast, headed by Pearl Bailey and Diahann Carroll, was widely acclaimed.

When Harburg first approached Arlen to write the music for *Jamaica*, the composer was reluctant. The Caribbean locale of the story was almost identical with that of *House of Flowers*, and, though his music has always shown a certain Negroid influence, he was understandably anxious to try something different. But the prospect of again working with Harburg was hard to resist, and he was intrigued by the simple charm of the story. Originally, Harburg's script was about a poor fisherman on a tropical island (to be played by Harry Belafonte) who was unique among his fellow islanders in that he had no desire to live in the United States. Why, he reasoned, should he trade his values for those of the people on the mainland when tourists obviously liked his way of life so much that they continuously visited his island?

St. Louis Woman *(1946).*
Pearl Bailey made her first
appearance on Broadway in
this musical. Here she is seen
urging Fayard Nicholas to
"Legalize My Name."
(Costumes by Lemuel Ayers.)

Photo by Eileen Darby—Graphic House

Photo by Zinn Arthur

House of Flowers *(1954).*
Ottilie (Diahann Carroll) and
the townspeople of a
Caribbean island give a joyous
welcome to Royal (Rawn
Spearman), who has just
barely escaped being drowned
at sea. (Costumes and setting
by Oliver Messel.)

Because the producer, David Merrick, had different ideas about the show, this theme was completely lost by the time *Jamaica* opened on Broadway in the fall of 1957. The character of the fisherman (now played by Ricardo Montalban) was made subordinate to that of the leading female character (Lena Horne), and the plot was almost nonexistent. Although the show was a financial success because of the lure of Miss Horne in her first starring role, in almost every department it was a curiously heavy-handed production.

Faults of production were also apparent in *Saratoga*, for which Arlen was joined by his *St. Louis Woman* lyricist, Johnny Mercer. In his first attempt as librettist, director Morton Da Costa evolved a rather plodding book out of Edna Ferber's novel, *Saratoga Trunk*, which left Cecil Beaton's almost overpoweringly elegant settings as the chief feature of the attraction.

In Harold Arlen, the musical theatre has, quite possibly, the most distinguished native composer to emerge since the Twenties. George Gershwin called him "the most original of us all." Irving Berlin, with typical succinctness, has said, "Harold's best *is* the best." To E. Y. Harburg, Harold Arlen is a genius. "He writes with his own genes. An Arlen song is completely individual, completely uninfluenced by anyone else. His songs are the kind that last. His contributions are colorfast."

Though he can write in a variety of moods, Arlen is best known for his blues and rhythm songs that have a strong affinity with the emotions of Negroes. Many of his numbers have been written specifically for shows with all-Negro or predominantly Negro casts—the Cotton Club revues, *St. Louis Woman* (and *Free and Easy*), *House of Flowers*, and *Jamaica*. Other musicals, such as *Bloomer Girl* and *Saratoga*, were concerned with Negro themes. Yet Arlen's ability to invest his songs with so much inventiveness and musicianship has kept them from seeming repetitive, and his great theatrical sense has endowed them with an indisputable fitness for the stage.

"Does it work theatrically?" was the question Arlen continually asked himself about his music. "Does it motivate the action? Is the song, in a sense, a part of the dialogue? Does the music capture character without getting out of the framework of the show?" The hard, relentless questioning of the requirements of his music happily resulted in songs that can be appreciated even apart from the circumstances for which they were written. For though he understood fully the theatrical requirements of music, Arlen frequently associated with enterprises that did not always utilize his gifts to their fullest. A dedicated, sensitive artist, he has the stamp of his own creativity far more on the songs he wrote than he did on the productions for which they were created. The obstacles of a weak libretto could not be surmounted even by a composer such as Harold Arlen. That so many of his songs have outlasted their original surroundings is a testament to the inherent quality with which they were endowed.

Photo by Friedman-Abeles

Jamaica *(1957).* *Ricardo Montalban and Lena Horne. Of Miss Horne,* Life Magazine *wrote, "She shines like a tigress in the night, purring and preening and pouncing into the spotlight." (Costumes by Miles White.)*

Saratoga *(1959).* *"Cecil Beaton's sets and costumes depicting New Orleans and the title resort in the lavish glories of the '80s provide a really breathtaking pictorial loveliness," was the opinion of Richard Watts, Jr. The scene shows Howard Keel, Carol Lawrence, Odette Myrtil, Tun Tun, and Carol Brice at the Waterfront Market in New Orleans.*

Courtesy C.B.S.

Burton Lane

Although *Bloomer Girl* was a success, commitments in Hollywood forced Harburg to remain on the West Coast for the next few years. While there, he continued to think of ideas for the stage. He had tentative ideas for two nonmusical plays, but neither one seemed to work out. One was about a bigoted Southern senator who miraculously turns black and thus becomes a victim of his own discriminatory laws. The other was a fantasy about a leprechaun with three wishes. "Then it occured to me," Harburg recalls, "why not combine the two stories by having one of the leprechaun's wishes be to turn the senator black? Then I knew I had something!"

Harburg decided to write the story himself in collaboration with Fred Saidy.

After finishing the libretto, he approached composer Burton Lane to supply the music. "All it needs is something like *Porgy and Bess*," Harburg told him. Lane, a highly regarded song-writer, but one who had never before attempted anything of this scope, at first felt that Harburg had gone to the wrong man. But Harburg was so positive that Lane eventually joined the project that resulted in *Finian's Rainbow*.

Burton Lane was another composer who had begun his career in the early Thirties by having songs interpolated in revues. He was born in New York City, on February 2, 1912, of well-to-do parents. While still in high school, he showed so much musical talent that J. J. Shubert hired him to compose the score for a proposed edition of the *Greenwich Village Follies*. The sixteen-year-old composer had more than twenty songs ready for the show, but when the intended star, James Barton, fell ill, Shubert abruptly cancelled the production. After getting a job as a pianist at Remick's, Lane became acquainted with many rising young songwriters. One of them, Howard Dietz, liked two of his melodies so much that he put words to them and added the songs to *Three's a Crowd*. The composer was still in his teens when "Forget All Your Books" and "Out in the Open Air" were sung in the revue.

Many of the numbers for the 1931 edition of the *Earl Carroll Vanities* were written by Lane in collaboration with lyricist Harold Adamson. Two years later, Lane went to Hollywood. He remained there until 1954, creating many film songs with such lyricists as Adamson, Harburg, Ted Koehler, Frank Loesser, Alan Jay Lerner, and Ira Gershwin.

During the twenty-one years he lived in California, Lane returned to New York for three Broadway assignments. In 1940, he and Harburg wrote a bright score for *Hold On to Your Hats*, a satire on radio Westerns, in which Al Jolson made a highly acclaimed return to the stage after an absence of almost ten years. Jolson scored a personal hit, but the show lasted only about four months because of the star's ill health at the time. It was his last appearance in a musical comedy. Lane returned to Broadway again in 1944 when he contributed both words and music to Olsen and Johnson's madhouse variety show, *Laffing Room Only*. Created from the same mold as the immensely successful *Hellzapoppin* and *Sons o' Fun*, the attraction is probably best remembered for the song "Feudin' and Fightin'," later made famous by Dorothy Shay.

In 1947, *Finian's Rainbow* brought Lane back to New York for the third time. That its intermingling of fantasy and social comment could cohere so smoothly into a unified musical attests to the uncommon skill brought to it by all those responsible for its creation. The feeling of a message may have been apparent throughout, but *Finian's Rainbow* was never allowed to become a sermon. It was light, it was imaginative, and it had its own brand of simple-minded logic. For example, Finian, an Irishman newly arrived in the state of Missitucky, is anxious to bury a crock of

gold at Fort Knox. His reason is that if gold is buried there it will have to grow, for what other purpose would the United States government have to put all of its gold in the ground? Harburg was anxious to make two important points in the story: one was that people would find riches not in burying gold but in trusting one another more, and the other, as exemplified by the situation of the senator, was the inanity of racial intolerance.

The score aided immeasurably in keeping the various elements complementing rather than competing with each other. The Irish motif was found in the wistful "How Are Things in Glocca Morra?" and "Look to the Rainbow," both sung by Ella Logan in her customary Scottish burr. The whimsical spirit of the leprechaun, played by David Wayne, came through in "Something Sort of Grandish" and "When I'm Not Near the Girl I Love." Two rousingly optimistic numbers describing the vision of a bright future were the satirical "When the Idle Poor Become the Idle Rich," and the more impassioned "That Great Come-and-Get-It-Day."

Almost eighteen years elapsed before Burton Lane was once again represented on Broadway. This time it was as collaborator with Alan Jay Lerner on the score

Finian's Rainbow *(1947). Og, a leprechaun (played by David Wayne), sings a reprise of "Something Sort of Grandish" to the children of Rainbow Valley, Missitucky. (Costumes by Eleanor Goldsmith.)*

John Springer Collection

Photo by Bert Andrews

On a Clear Day You Can See Forever *(1965)*.
Dr. Mark Bruckner (John Cullum) trying to cure Daisy Gamble (Barbara Harris) of the smoking habit. Wrote Ted Kalem in Time: *"Barbara Harris can fumble a cigarette between her teeth like a crazed nicotine addict and fire off machine gun bursts of smoke . . . She can chew grammar like bubble gum, or make English ring with the elegance of George III's crystal."*

for Lerner's production of *On a Clear Day You Can See Forever*. Although faults were found in the book, Lane's contributions were among the most noteworthy of the season. According to Howard Taubman's verdict in the *Times*, his tunes have "more melodic grace and inventive distinction than has been heard in some years."

Lane has been active in the musical theatre far less frequently than any other major composer who first won recognition in the Thirties. Nevertheless, his scores for *Finian's Rainbow* and *On a Clear Day* unquestionably place him among the most gifted and original of the post-Twenties composers. It was Yip Harburg who gave him the ultimate accolade. Of all the modern composers, Harburg once said, Burton Lane comes closest to capturing that special effervescence so characteristic in the songs of George Gershwin.

Of the composers discussed in this chapter, Arlen has been the most prolific, though the contributions of Duke and Lane, particularly with respect to their work for *Cabin in the Sky* and *Finian's Rainbow*, have ensured their lasting fame. Yet the inability of these men to continue the pursuit of their careers in the theatre with the constancy of the composers of the first three decades of the century is unfortunate. The drastic reduction in the number of musicals being produced, the length of time that it takes to prepare a musical, and the almost prohibitive cost of such a venture have all been factors resulting in the relative infrequency of their efforts on Broadway.

Another important change has been the growing importance of the librettist. No other writer has appreciated this more than E. Y. Harburg. His entire career has reflected the transformations through which the musical theatre has gone. Starting as a writer of sophisticated lyrics for revues in the early Thirties, he soon moved away from revues to concentrate his attention on book musicals. In the Forties, he originated the plot of *Bloomer Girl* and also directed it. With *Finian's Rainbow*, he became his own librettist, in collaboration with Fred Saidy. The Harburg-Saidy team was also responsible for the books of *Flahooley* (music by Sammy Fain) and *Jamaica* (music by Arlen). In 1961, Harburg supplied both inspiration and outline for *The Happiest Girl in the World*, a short-lived musical satire for which he mated his lyrics to melodies by Jacques Offenbach. Harburg's last work for Broadway, *Darling of the Day* (1968), adapted from Arnold Bennett's *Buried Alive*, was his only collaboration with composer Jule Styne.

Because of his deep concern with every phase of a production, Harburg was able to make his musicals more totally an expression of his own personality and point of view than were the composers with whom he worked. Rather than merely setting words to melodies or blocking out the rudiments of a story to hold the songs together, more often than not he was the motivating force behind each production. Moreover, particularly in the cases of Harold Arlen and Burton Lane, he was able to furnish composers with concepts that helped them turn out their most successful efforts.

Although occasionally accused of injecting too much social consciousness in his plays, "Yip" Harburg is one of the most consistently adventurous men of the musical theatre, both in his lyrics and his librettos. To him, his purpose in writing for the musical stage is neither to provide escapist entertainment nor to depict life realistically. "I don't believe the theatre is a place for photographic reproduction," he says. "That's why I'm attracted to fantasy, to things with a poetic quality. Through fantasy, I feel that a musical can say things with greater effectiveness about life. It's great for pricking balloons, for exploding shibboleths. Of course, I want to send people out of the theatre with the glow of having had a good time, but I also believe the purpose of a musical is to make people think."

Harold Rome.   Photo by Alfredo Valente

CHAPTER FIFTEEN

HAROLD ROME

THE ECONOMIC CLIMATE of the early Thirties inevitably nurtured the socially conscious revues and musical comedies that came along during the second half of the decade. Of course, there had been such pioneering work as *Strike Up the Band*, *Of Thee I Sing*, and *Face the Music*, but these did not hit specific individuals or situations; the country had to wait until after the worst years of the Depression for serious topics to again be treated with a certain amount of detachment and humor.

Parade, in 1935, was intended as the first revue of social significance, though its edge was considerably blunted by its sponsor, the Theatre Guild. The season of 1937–1938 provided theatregoers with four political musicals containing viewpoints ranging from mildly liberal to radical: *I'd Rather Be Right* (President Roosevelt and his administration); Marc Blitzstein's *The Cradle Will Rock* (the evils of capitalism and the virtues of the working class); *Hooray for What!* (the need for international disarmament); and *Pins and Needles*.

Of them all, it was *Pins and Needles* that won the largest following. Produced by the International Ladies Garment Workers Union and with a cast composed entirely of union members, the revue ran for more than three years, went through at least three editions, toured the major cities of the United States, and was responsible for giving composer-lyricist Harold Jacob Rome the most auspicious debut of any song-writer of the decade.

Rome was born in Hartford, Connecticut, on May 27, 1908. He began to play the piano at an early age and, in his teens, joined many local dance bands. At Yale, he was a member of the University Orchestra, with which he made four trips to Europe. After graduation, he spent a year at the Yale Law School. Like Cole Porter, he had little interest in poring over law books, and soon switched to the School of Architecture. In 1934, he became a draftsman with an architectural firm in New York. As the Depression was then at its most severe, he augmented his small salary by playing the piano at social functions.

After quitting his job as a draftsman, Rome joined the entertainment staff at Green Mansions, an adult summer camp in upstate New York. There he wrote many topical songs for camp revues. Encouraged by the reception the guests gave

Pins and Needles (1937).
*Two of the "Four Little Angels
of Peace": Berni Gould as
Hitler and Harry Clark as
Stalin. (Setting by S.
Syrjala.).*

his efforts, he returned to New York determined to succeed as a song-writer. Producers and publishers, however, were almost unanimous in their reactions: Nobody, they chorused, wanted to hear songs about the nation's current problems while the economic situation was still so serious. Though he did manage to get a few numbers published—one was sold to Gypsy Rose Lee—it was not until Louis Schaffer, the head of the I.L.G.W.U. drama activities, heard his songs that Rome at last was given his opportunity.

Schaffer was then preparing a revue to be shown at the Labor Stage (the new name of the Princess Theatre), with the cast recruited entirely from the ranks of the union. After assembling all the sketches and songs necessary for the show, Schaffer discovered that his union actors were against doing anything so frivolous as a musical revue. They wanted a grim drama depicting the hardships of the economically exploited masses. In order to convince them that a song-and-dance show would be even more effective in presenting the union's point of view, Schaffer hired a group of W.P.A. actors to perform the show exclusively for the benefit of the cast. With Harold Rome and Earl Robinson providing two-piano accompaniment, the first showing of *Pins and Needles* took place on June 14, 1936, in a small studio above the regular Labor Stage auditorium.

As soon as they saw the sketches and heard Rome's bright, pungent music and lyrics, those who had objected to the entertainment were won over. For a year and a half, the I.L.G.W.U. Players rehearsed almost every night after they had finished their day's work in New York's garment center. They were eager to learn, but their lack of experience and the brevity of rehearsal periods were responsible for many delays. When the show finally had its première, neither critics nor a large audience turned out to greet it. Within weeks, however, word-of-mouth reports turned *Pins and Needles* into such a popular attraction that the small playhouse soon had a hit equal to those it had once enjoyed during the days of Bolton, Wodehouse, and Kern.

The revue was intelligent and funny, with the enthusiasm of the cast making up for what it may have lacked in professional skill. Perhaps the show's most winning trait was the ability to laugh at the labor movement itself while also, of course, taking jabs at the foibles of those on the other side of the bargaining table. After running about a year and one-half, a somewhat altered version, *Pins and Needles 1939*, was introduced. Later that year, it moved uptown to the larger, on-Broadway Windsor Theatre ($1.65 top) where a third edition, *New Pins and Needles*, was presently displayed. Including all its versions, the show had a run of 1,108 performances, though this impressive record must be "weighted" as the Labor Stage seated only about 300.

"Sing me a song with social significance" demanded the opening chorus in feigned earnestness. Rome obliged with a group of songs that were remarkable in their ability to express a fresh, original viewpoint within a colloquial speech pattern that was completely natural for the untrained performers. "It's Better with a Union Man" was a turn-of-the-century tearjerker given a sly, up-to-date twist; "Nobody Makes a Pass at Me" revealed the plight of the girl whose love life is completely unaided by any of the advertised products she tries; "Sunday in the Park" proclaimed the verdant pleasures of Central Park as a haven for the working man; and "One Big Union for Two" expressed eternal love through the language of collective bargaining.

The sketches and songs tried to keep up with the daily headlines as much as possible. "Four Little Angels of Peace" were Hitler, Mussolini, Eden, and an unnamed Japanese. After Munich, the composer substituted Chamberlain for Eden. With the signing of the Hitler-Stalin nonaggression pact, another angel was added. "Britannia Waives the Rules" had to be cut when World War II started. In "The Red Mikado," Rome and sketch-writer Joseph Schrank had fun at the expense of both communism and the two jazz versions of the same Gilbert and Sullivan operetta, *The Hot Mikado* and *The Swing Mikado*, then running concurrently in New York.

Even before *Pins and Needles* ended its run, *Sing Out the News*, another topical revue with words and music by Harold Rome, was offered on Broadway. This time, although the view was still from the left of the political stage, the show was a completely professional affair produced by Max Gordon in association with George S. Kaufman and Moss Hart. Rome's observations continued to be remarkably trenchant, but the novelty of this kind of revue had apparently already worn off. Although *Sing Out the News* lasted only three months, it did contain one truly electric number—the exultant "F.D.R. Jones," sung by Rex Ingram and chorus at a joyous Harlem christening.

Rome was inducted into the Army in 1943. During most of his time in the service, he wrote and organized soldier shows. While still in uniform, Rome and Arnold Auerbach, a former radio script-writer, began planning a Broadway revue. The show's theme would be soldiers returning to civilian life, with songs and sketches depicting in a generally light-hearted manner various aspects of life in and out of the Army. Only ex-servicemen, ex-WACs, and ex-USO entertainers would be in the cast, which was headed by Betty Garrett. (Her credentials were numerous appearances in the *G.I. Jane* shows that toured Army bases and hospitals.)

Titled *Call Me Mister*, the revue was presented in the spring of 1946 under the

Call Me Mister *(1946).*
Betty Garrett, as a U.S.O.
hostess, expresses her opinion
of Latin American music in
"South America, Take It
Away." The attentive soldiers
are Alan Manson, Chandler
Cowles, George Hall, and
Harry Clark.

Photo by Eileen Darby—Graphic House

Wish You Were Here *(1952).*
Joshua Logan directing.

Photo by Slim Aarons

combined sponsorship of Herman Levin (who was to produce *My Fair Lady* ten years later) and Melvyn Douglas. The mood of the show was almost completely optimistic. Although Rome's songs were less concerned with the class struggle, they were equally as original as those of his previous revues. "The important element of a song is neither the words nor the tune, but the basic idea," Rome explained at the time *Call Me Mister* opened. "Take 'Little Surplus Me.' Once I had the picture of the girl pleading with the President to bring back her uniformed boy friends, the rest was merely a matter of variations on the original thesis. Similarly with 'Military Life.' Having conceived the notion that the soldier who went away a jerk might return still a jerk, all that remained was improvisations on the established theme."

The two serious numbers (both sung by Lawrence Winters) in *Call Me Mister* illustrated the composer's sociopolitical outlook. Contrasted with the jubilation of "F.D.R. Jones" in *Sing Out the News*, was the quietly touching tribute to Roosevelt called "The Face on the Dime." There was also a bitter sequence in which Winters, a Negro, after singing of the wartime exploits of the Transportation Corps in the stirring "Red Ball Express," was the only one of a group of applicants to be refused a job.

Harold Rome was the last of the major revue writers of the Thirties to compose a score for a book musical. In 1950, he and Arthur Kober decided to adapt Kober's play *Having Wonderful Time* into a musical appropriately called *Wish You Were Here*. The story dealt with middle-class New Yorkers on a two-week vacation at a summer camp in the mountains, and it gave Rome the chance to

Wish You Were Here (1952). Happy vacationers at Camp Karefree, a summer camp for adults, "where friendships are formed to last a whole lifetime through." In the center are Jack Cassidy, Patricia Marand, and Sheila Bond. (Costumes by Robert Mackintosh; setting by Jo Mielziner.)

draw from his youthful experiences at Green Mansions. *Wish You Were Here* was also an early example of the importance that directors were to assume in the musical theatre during the Fifties. When Joshua Logan agreed to produce the show, he also became its director, co-librettist, and choreographer. His insistence on putting in a $15,000 swimming pool made it impossible to take the musical on the customary tryout tour. Consequently, without the necessary "break-in" period, the paly was greeted with generally unfavorable reviews following its June 25, 1952, première.

Logan still thought he had a potential hit. With the cooperation of Kober and Rome, he completely rewrote the script, changed many songs, and had the dances restaged by Jerome Robbins. *Wish You*

Were Here became a sell-out within three weeks, and ran for two years. (So many alterations had taken place after its faltering start that Harold Clurman once called it the only experimental theatre left in New York.)

Logan was also associated with Rome in his next musical, *Fanny*. In 1951, Producer David Merrick had bought the property, which was based on Marcel Pagnol's trilogy *Marius, César,* and *Fanny*. The musical took three years of preparation before it reached Broadway, with Ezio Pinza and Walter Slezak in the leads. After working more than a year with other writers and composers, Merrick called in Logan, who promptly became co-producer, co-author (with S.N. Behrman), and director. Because of their association on *Wish You Were Here*, Logan brought in Rome.

The score of *Fanny* presented the composer with a greater challenge than any other work for which he had written. Previously, he had been more celebrated for the ingenuity and wit of his lyrics than for his gifts as a composer. For *Fanny* he was called upon to create an expansive, melodious score, matched by lyrics that expressed deep emotions. As Marseilles was the locale and the people were uneducated waterfront characters, it was necessary to give the music a certain French feeling, while keeping the lyrics both simple and direct. Another major problem, according to Logan, was ". . . how to get jubilation into an essentially tragic story. Here was the tale of two lovers who are so completely separated that it is difficult to dream of them ever getting together. The songs in *Fanny* did not solve the problem completely, but Harold Rome's resourceful score was able to satisfy the audience's need for happy music without sacrificing the integrity of the story."

During the run of *Fanny*, it occurred to David Merrick that there had never been a real western musical comedy in the classic good-guys-versus-bad-guys movie tradition. He immediately decided that

*Fanny (1954).
Ezio Pinza as César and Walter Slezak as Panisse. This was Pinza's last role in the theatre.*

Photo by Zinn Arthur

the time had come to musicalize that durable sagebrush saga, *Destry Rides Again*, and secured both the rights to the story from Universal Pictures and the services of Harold Rome for the score. The musical opened in the spring of 1959 with Andy Griffith as the violence-hating deputy sheriff, and Dolores Gray as the frontier saloon singer. While the show added neither satire nor a new dimension to the familiar tale, it was skillfully staged by Michael Kidd, whose crackling dance routines were among the most exciting of the season. Rome's songs ably captured the spirit of the terrain but, unfortunately, the book offered him little inspiration for a distinguished score.

For *I Can Get It for You Wholesale*, produced by Merrick three years later, Rome returned to the more familiar *Pins and Needles* milieu of New York's garment district. This time, however, he and librettist Jerome Weidman (who had adapted his own novel) were more concerned with skullduggery among employers than with the social slant of the workers. Seldom has a composer been more perfectly in tune with his subject, with both music and lyrics beautifully conveying the pains and pleasures of toiling along Manhattan's Seventh Avenue. But little could be done to atone for the lack of appeal of the central characters. Wrote John Chapman in the *News*: "I couldn't find one to whom I could give either affection or admiration. Well, I guess there was one—but she is just a minor mouse in the story. She is a harried, frantic, put-upon, homely frump of a secretary, and she is hilariously played by a nineteen-year-old newcomer, Barbra Streisand. Her song, 'Miss Marmelstein,' is the happiest number in Rome's copious score."

The revues that Harold Rome was identified with during the Thirties and Forties were reactions to current events. *Pins and Needles* and *Sing Out the News* were outgrowths of the Depression. *Call Me Mister* reflected the spirit of the country immediately after the war.

When timely revues were no longer in style, and Rome at last began to write scores for book shows, he was able to bring to them the same understanding and natural warmth that had shown through in his earlier works. Moreover, to his already well established skill with words, Rome soon added a greater richness of musical style, one that served him with equally winning effect in his scores for *Wish You Were Here*, *Fanny* and *I Can Get It for You Wholesale*. The ability to express in songs the honest emotions of those who are least articulate has been one of his most distinguishing characteristics. For Rome is, essentially, a people's composer and lyricist, one who, without being sentimental or patronizing, provides the common man with uncommon musical expressions.

Destry Rides Again *(1959). Tom Destry (Andy Griffith) causes Frenchie (Dolores Gray) some momentary embarrassment by accidentally tearing off part of her skirt. The villainous Kent (Scott Brady) thinks it's all rather amusing. (Costumes by Alvin Colt.)*

Photo by Friedman-Abeles

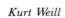

Kurt Weill   Photo by Hoyningen-Huene. Courtesy New York City Opera

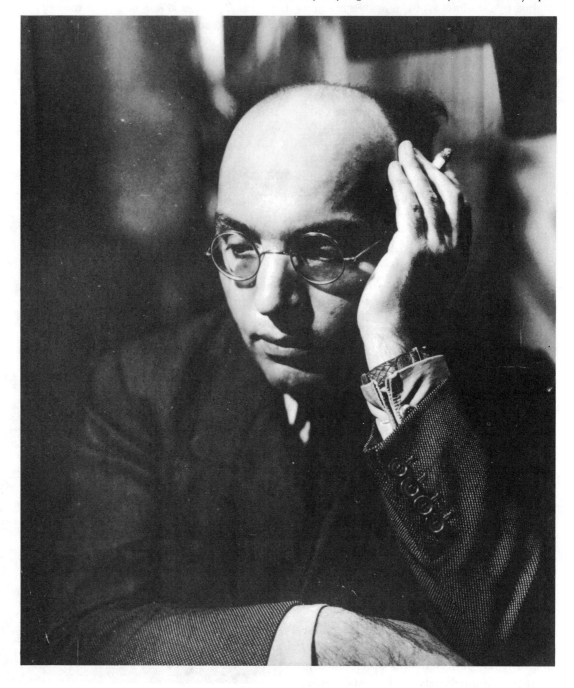

CHAPTER SIXTEEN

KURT WEILL

UNLIKE OTHER EUROPEAN-BORN composers who have settled in the United States, Kurt Weill had achieved a worldwide reputation even before he began to write for the American musical theatre. His *Die Dreigroschenoper* (*The Threepenny Opera*), written in 1928, was performed over 10,000 times throughout Central Europe within a period of five years. It was translated into eighteen languages and, in 1933, even had a brief run on Broadway. The musical was universally accepted as the most revealing depiction of the moral decadence that was then eating away the fabric of society at almost every level all over Europe. Bertolt Brecht's libretto may have been a social preachment but, particularly when combined with Weill's jangly, beer-hall tunes, it emerged as popular entertainment that reflected the cynicism and desperate gaiety of the times.

To the Nazis, however, the work was that of a *Kultur-Bolshevist*, and one of the first things the new regime did when it came to power in Germany in 1933 was to ban the production. Weill and his wife, Lotte Lenya, were soon forced to flee the country. For a time they settled in Paris where the composer quickly learned the techniques of the French theatre. Within two years, he had collaborated with French playwright Jacques Deval on *Marie Galante* and, with fellow-refugee Bertolt Brecht, he composed the ballet *The Seven Deadly Sins*.

Though his career in France seemed assured, Weill was anxious to leave Europe as quickly as possible. He had little confidence that France or England could stand up to Hitler; only in the United States, he felt, was there hope for the future. His opportunity to leave the Continent came in 1935. Max Reinhardt, the Viennese director and producer, was then preparing a Biblical pageant, *The Eternal Road*, for a Broadway production. Knowing of Weill's urgent desire to go to America, he offered the composer the commission of creating the background music.

Almost as soon as he arrived in New York, Weill became so much a part of his adopted country that he made up his mind never to return to Europe. Indeed, it was characteristic of the man, in both his work and in his personal life, that he never looked backward. The challenge of the present was what concerned him,

Photo by Alfredo Valente

Johnny Johnson (1936).
The scene in the French
churchyard in which Johnny
Johnson, an American soldier,
captures a German sniper who
has been hiding behind a
statue of Christ. When Johnny
learns that the German
(whose name is also Johnny)
longs for peace, he releases
him. John Garfield played the
German and Russell Collins
had the title role. (Setting by
Donald Oenslager.)

whether it was a new country or a new musical project. His impatience with self-pity, combined with his complete disinterest in anything that was not of immediate concern, enabled him to adjust to every new situation within the shortest possible time and with the most efficient results.

Kurt Weill was born in Dessau, Germany, on March 2, 1900. Like Irving Berlin and Harold Arlen, he was the son of a cantor. As a youth, he showed such musical aptitude that at sixteen he was sent to Berlin to study under Engelbert Humperdinck. When Humperdinck retired from teaching, Weill accepted the post of director of a small opera company at Ludenscheid. During his one year there, he gained valuable experience in every phase of theatrical production.

Weill returned to Berlin in the early Twenties to continue his studies under Ferruccio Busoni. His first important attempts at composition resulted in many concert pieces greatly influenced by the modern atonal technique. At the time, Weill cared little for audience acclaim. His ideas began to change, however, when he was commissioned to compose a children's ballet, *Die Zaubernacht.* Upon seeing the reactions of the children to the work, Weill, with characteristic decisiveness, made up his mind to devote his career to creating music that would make a direct appeal to the largest number of people. "I am not struggling for new forms or new theories," he said in the mid-Twenties. "I am struggling for a new public."

Three years later, Weill's first opera, *Der Protagonist,* with a libretto by playwright Georg Kaiser, won such favorable notice that he received a commission from the Berlin State Opera. This resulted in *Royal Palace,* in which may be detected some of the earliest influences of jazz in an opera.

With *Die Dreigroschenoper* and the even more sardonic *Aufstieg und Fall der Stadt Mahagonny (Rise and Fall of the*

City of Mahagonny), the composer broke completely with the classical past. Even the opera house had become too confining for these examples of *Zeitoper*, a form of popular opera created to reflect the spirit of the times in which it was written.

After he had come to America in 1935, Weill found that the Broadway theatre offered him a greater latitude than he had ever had before. There was no censorship, no storm troopers, nothing to stand in his way of reaching the wide public he so fervently desired. He reacted to this freedom by shedding some of the astringent pessimism inherent in his German works and by revealing a far greater lyricism than had previously been apparent.

One of the exciting developments of the Broadway theatre during the mid-Thirties was the formation of the Group Theatre, a repertory company dedicated to introducing new works by promising playwrights. Because he admired the aims of the organization, Weill confided in Lee Strasberg, one of the Group's directors, that he would like to work on an original musical play with a dramatist Strasberg would recommend. Strasberg suggested Paul Green. The result of the Weill-Green collaboration was *Johnny Johnson*, a bitter yet funny anti-war "folk legend," with a cast including many who later won fame as both actor and directors: Russell Collins (in the title role), Lee J. Cobb, John (then Jules) Garfield, Robert Lewis, Elia Kazan, Luther Adler, and Morris Carnovsky. The production also marked the first Broadway assignment of musical director Lehman Engel.

Although *Johnny Johnson* was not a commercial success, its daring fusion of music and satiric fantasy won many champions. At the opening-night performance, Lorenz Hart, who was seated behind Weill, tapped the composer on the shoulder and inquired in mock rage: "What are you trying to do, put people

like me out of business?" And Robert Benchley, indignant at the indifference of both critics and the public, particularly in a mediocre theatrical season, exclaimed: "My God, if we don't grab onto something really big when it comes along, even if it does have flaws, the theatre may go right on as it started this year. This is the first anti-war play to use laughing gas in its attack on the stupidity of mankind, and to my mind it is the most effective of all satires in its class."

Knickerbocker Holiday, in 1938, united Kurt Weill with playwright Maxwell Anderson. As both men were deeply concerned with the world situation, they longed to say something pertinent, yet entertaining, about the evils of dictatorship and the value of freedom. To express their convictions they drew modern parallels with the attempts of the tyrannical Pieter Stuyvesant to suppress the liberties of the people of New Amsterdam.

Knickerbocker Holiday (1938).
Led by Councilman Roosevelt (George Watts), the City Council of New Amsterdam turns against Governor Pieter Stuyvesant (Walter Huston) and refuses to pull the rope that would hang the outspoken Brom Broeck (Richard Kollmar). (Costumes by Frank Bevan; setting by Jo Mielziner.)

Photo by Lucas-Pritchard

The theme of the play was posed in the song, "How Can You Tell An American?" To Anderson and Weill, the answer was simple: An American is someone who loves freedom and hates any restrictions on his thoughts or on his actions.

At the suggestion of director Joshua Logan, the role of Stuyvesant was given to the fifty-four-year-old Walter Huston, a former vaudeville song-and-dance man who had never before appeared in a Broadway musical. Because Huston was living in California when he signed the contract, Weill sent him the following telegram: "WHAT IS RANGE OF YOUR VOICE?" The actor's reply came promptly: "I HAVE NO RANGE STOP APPEARING TONIGHT ON BING CROSBY PROGRAM WILL SING SONG FOR YOU." Upon hearing Huston's transcontinental radio audition that night, Weill turned to Anderson and said, "Let's write a sentimental, romantic song for him." Both men went to work at once and within a few hours produced the most enduring number of the show, "September Song."

In spite of its brief run of about four months, *Knickerbocker Holiday* is generally accepted as a significant milestone in the development of the American musical theatre. Apart from its close integration of music and story, it was one of the first musicals to use a historical subject as a means through which pertinent observations could be made about contemporary political problems.

Moss Hart was the one who first thought of the idea of *Lady in the Dark*. Having recently undergone psychoanalysis, he was anxious to write a serious play about the subject and to cast Katharine Cornell in the central role of an emotionally disturbed fashion-magazine editor. As the work progressed, however, he found it taking shape more as a musical. With Miss Cornell eliminated by the play's metamorphosis, the author could think of no other actress for the part than Gertrude Lawrence. Kurt

Weill, who was to have written some incidental music for the original concept, readily agreed to supply the entire score, and Ira Gershwin was signed as lyricist for his first Broadway musical since the death of his brother.

Lady in the Dark was an advanced work in both theme and music. Even allowing for the convenient device of keeping the musical portions within the dream sequences until the final scene, the music and lyrics, as Moss Hart has written, were "part and parcel of the basic structure of the play. One cannot separate the play from the music, and vice versa. More than that, the music and lyrics carry the story forward dramatically and psychologically."

The most memorable scene of *Lady in the Dark* takes place in the Circus Dream during the second act. Here the inability of the magazine editor, Liza Elliott, to make up her mind becomes the motivation for a trial presided over by the Ringmaster (Danny Kaye), with the handsome movie star (Victor Mature) as Liza's lawyer. For no apparent reason (except that tongue-twisting numbers were a Danny Kaye specialty), the Ringmaster rattles off the names of forty-nine Russian composers in thirty-nine seconds in a piece called "Tschaikowsky."* Soon after this feat of vocal dexterity, Liza follows it with her own lubriciously uninhibited "Saga of Jenny," in which she relates all the misfortunes that once befell a lady because she "would make up her mind." Doing "Jenny" so soon after Kaye's ovation-winning rendition was a challenge to Miss Lawrence; she met it by giving an interpretation of such unbounded magnetism that audiences were once again brought to their feet.

* "Tschaikowsky" was based on a humorous poem called "The Music Hour," which Ira Gershwin had written under the pen name of Arthur Francis. It was published in the June 12, 1924, issue of the old *Life* magazine. Before listing the Russian composer's names, Gershwin introduced them with the following couplet:
    I'll mention some composers who are known to us as Russian.
    Please note them down. Tomorrow we shall have them for discussion.

Lady in the Dark *(1941)*.
*Musical director Maurice
Abravanel, composer Kurt
Weill, and lyricist Ira
Gershwin.*

Photo by Eileen Darby—Graphic House

*"As for Gertrude Lawrence,"
wrote Brooks Atkinson in his
review, "she is a goddess,
that's all." Miss Lawrence is
shown here in the Circus
Dream sequence as she related
all the misadventures of the
unfortunate lady known as
Jenny. (Costumes by Irene
Sharaff.)*

Photo by Richard Tucker

Lady in the Dark, which opened January 23, 1941, was the third major musical to move onto Broadway within a period of three months. Following so soon after *Cabin in the Sky* and *Pal Joey*, it inspired Brooks Atkinson to predict: "The American musical stage is a sound basis for a new centrifugal dramatic form, and *Lady in the Dark* takes a long step forward in that direction."

If *One Touch of Venus* was not the daring work usually associated with Kurt Weill, the musical nevertheless provided many unusual touches on the familiar Pygmalion-Galatea theme. The S. J. Perelman libretto may have floundered occasionally between low comedy and highly polished wit, but the songs by Weill and poet-lyricist Ogden Nash maintained a high level of musicianship and verbal ingenuity. Although *One Touch of Venus* was originally written with Marlene Dietrich in mind, the part was eventually given to Mary Martin as her first starring role on Broadway. Apart from the brooding, haunting "Speak Low," the most impressive musical interlude came when Miss Martin, in elegant simplicity, leaned over the back of an ordinary straight chair to describe her ideal man in the tender, amusing (and intentionally ungrammatical) "That's Him."

From the very beginning of his theatrical career, Kurt Weill zealously recruited outstanding writers from other fields to become active in the musical theatre. By the time he began work on the musical version of *Street Scene*, some of his American collaborators had been playwrights Paul Green, Maxwell Anderson, and Edwin Justus Mayer (with whom Weill had adapted the short-lived *Firebrand of Florence* from Mayer's own play, *The Firebrand*), humorist S. J. Perelman, and poet Ogden Nash. For *Street Scene*, produced in 1947, the composer persuaded Elmer Rice to supply the libretto based on his own Pulitzer

Prize-winning play, and secured Langston Hughes to write the lyrics. "Not until *Street Scene*," Weill once wrote, "did I achieve a real blending of drama and music in which the singing continues naturally where the speaking stops, and the spoken word, as well as the dramatic action, is embedded in the over-all musical structure."

Even though it was billed as "A Dramatic Musical," *Street Scene* was very close to genuine opera. Taking a compassionate look at the varied inhabitants of a single New York tenement (much as DuBose Heyward and George and Ira Gershwin had done with the citizens of Catfish Row in *Porgy and Bess*), the authors created a work that was, in the opinion of critic Olin Downes, "the most important step toward significant American opera yet encountered in the musical theatre." Of its arias, "Somehow I Never Could Believe" (sung by Polyna Stoska) was an overpowering exposition of the causes of a woman's bitterness and frustration, and there were deeply affecting passages in Anne Jeffrey's and Brian Sullivan's duets, "Remember That I Care" and "We'll Go Away Together." The musical even had a "pop" hit, "Moon-Faced, Starry-Eyed," energetically danced by Sheila Bond and Danny Daniels over fire hydrants, garbage pails, and a front stoop.

A temporary cessation in the partnership of Alan Jay Lerner and Frederick Loewe enabled Lerner to become associated with Weill for an imaginative musical called *Love Life*. Designated simply as "A Vaudeville," it depicted the disintegration of marriage in the United States—from the colonial era up to that time (1948)—in a series of sketches and vaudeville acts. The couple through whom the story was told never grew any older during the entertainment; they were still the same age in the last scene, when the tensions of modern life had made it increasingly difficult for them to

One Touch of Venus *(1943).*
Mary Martin singing "That's
Him." (Costume by
Mainbocher; setting by
Howard Bay.)

Photo by Vandamm

Street Scene *(1947).*
Norman Cordon, as the
suspicious husband, threatens
his wife, Polyna Stoska, as
Anne Jeffreys, their daughter,
tries to intervene. (Costumes
by Lucinda Ballard; setting by
Jo Mielziner.)

John Springer Collection

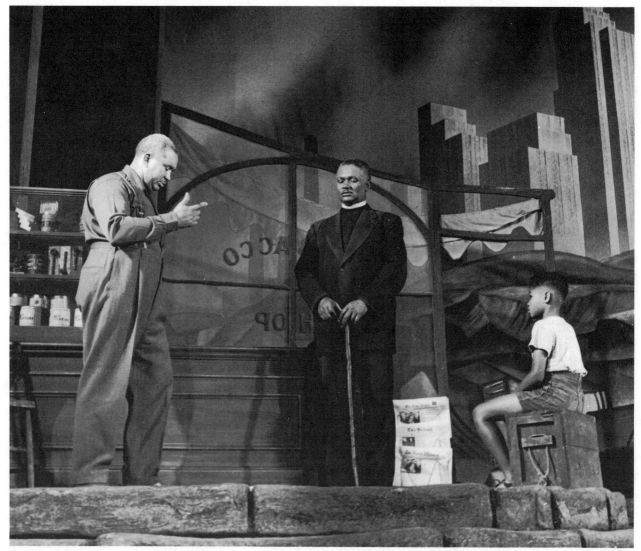

Photo by Karger-Pix

Lost in the Stars *(1949).*
Rev. Stephen Kumalo (Todd
Duncan) visits his brother
(Warren Coleman) in
Shantytown, outside of
Johannesburg, in a vain
attempt to enlist his help in
finding his missing son.
(Setting by George Jenkins.)

remain in the same blissful matrimonial state as they had been at the play's beginning. If its stagecraft technique occasionally seemed like too much of a theatrical device, *Love Life* was nevertheless a welcome departure from conventional musical fare, containing many sharp observations on marital mores in America.

Weill was reunited with Maxwell Anderson for his last work, *Lost in the Stars*, produced in 1949. For years, Weill and Anderson had been looking for the right story on which to base a musical dealing with racial problems. At the recommendation of Mrs. Oscar Hammerstein II, they read Alan Paton's novel, *Cry, the Beloved Country*, and immediately felt that it was the story they needed. Through this drama of Negro-white relations in South Africa, Weill sought to convey a "message of hope that people, through a personal approach, will solve whatever racial problems exist." Avoiding obvious "native" devices in his score, the composer made effective use of music to set the proper emotional atmosphere, though the integration of music as part of the action of the story was never completely realized.

Kurt Weill was only fifty years old when he died of a heart attack on April 3, 1950. During the fifteen years that he devoted himself to the American musical theatre, he brought to it an affection and pride that was, perhaps, partly motivated by the circumstances responsible for his becoming part of it. His undeviating faith in the commerical theatre was effectively summed up when, in an interview, he said, "You hear a lot of talk about the 'American opera' that's going to come along some day. It's my opinion that we can and will develop a musical-dramatic form in this country, but I don't think it will be called 'opera,' or that it will grow out of the opera which has become a thing separate from the commercial theatre. It will develop from, and remain a part of, the American theatre—'Broadway' theatre, if you like. I'm convinced

that many modern composers have a feeling of superiority toward their audiences. But the great 'classic' composers wrote for their contemporary audiences. As for myself, I write for today. I don't give a damn about writing for posterity."

Posterity, however, does give a damn about the writing of Kurt Weill. *Street Scene* and *Lost in the Stars* have become part of the repertory of the New York City Opera Company, and *The Seven Deadly Sins* is one of the most popular attractions of the New York City Ballet Company. *Down in the Valley*, a half-hour opera based on American themes that Weill wrote with Arnold Sundgaard, is continually being performed in schools throughout the country. In 1979, the Metropolitan Opera mounted a new production of the forty-nine-year-old *Rise and Fall of the City of Mahagonny*.

Just four years after the composer's death, Stanley Chase and Carmen Capalbo raised $10,000 to present an off-Broadway production of Marc Blitzstein's English adaptation of *The Threepenny Opera*. With Lotte Lenya appearing in the same role she had created in Berlin in 1928, the show ran for twelve weeks before it was forced to vacate the theatre due to a prior booking of another play. But interest in *The Threepenny Opera* would not die. In response to genuine public demand, it reopened, a year and a half later, on September 20, 1955, and ran a total of 2,611 performances. An even more astringent version was offered by Joseph Papp in 1976, which ran both off and on Broadway.

What is the reason for its continued durability? In the twilight years of the Weimar Republic in Germany, audiences could see in its raffish, sardonic story all the venality and bitterness then so much a part of daily life in Central Europe. An empathy was created between the play and audience that no other work of that period could approach. The social illnesses within the United States many years later may not be so pronounced, but

The Threepenny Opera
(1954).
Lotte Lenya, Kurt Weill's
widow, as Jenny. As Jay
Harrison wrote: "During the
second act, Lotte Lenya
stepped to the front of the
stage to sing her air about
Pirate Jenny. At that moment
the miniature confines of the
theatre stretched and were
replaced by a broad and
sweeping arena of genuine
sentiment. For that's what art
can do, and that's what an
artist does."

they have caused many sociologists to express concern at the decline of moral values within an apparently healthy society. Thus, *The Threepenny Opera* still has something pertinent to say, while, at the same time, delivering its message with broad humor, a certain romantic charm, and an unflagging musical appeal.

Kurt Weill was a complete man of the theatre. The only major composer since Victor Herbert to do his own orchestrations, he was also vitally interested in every phase of theatre production. Moreover, from his very first American score, he was a motivating force in organizing and giving direction to every musical with which he was associated. Never lured to Hollywood for a lengthy stay, this soft-spoken, timid-looking man was able to devote all his considerable energies to the creation of a popular musical theatre that, he felt, had as its essence "a simple, strong story told in musical terms, interweaving the spoken word and the sung word so that the singing takes over naturally whenever the emotion of the spoken word reaches a point where the music can 'speak' with greater effectiveness."

Weill's devotion to the commercial theatre never made him deaf to uncommercial ideas. In fact, the theory of the *Zeitoper* theatre that he had brought to such acceptance in Germany continued to dominate his thinking in his American works. Though he believed in the mass appeal of music, he would never condescend to his audiences. Nothing was too daring for him. He built his musicals around such "unpopular" subjects as war, dictatorship, psychoanalysis, tenement living, race relations, and political and moral decay. That so many of his works are still performed today attests not only to the durability of the popular theatre in which Weill had so much faith, but also to his own indestructible place in it.

Richard Rodgers and Oscar Hammerstein II.

CHAPTER SEVENTEEN

RICHARD RODGERS
and OSCAR HAMMERSTEIN II

AT A FEW SECONDS past eight-thirty on the evening of March 31, 1943, the house lights at the St. James theatre dimmed, the excited chatter of the audience died down, musical director Jacob Schwartzdorf* raised his baton, and the orchestra struck up the overture to the first New York performance of *Oklahoma!*

Everyone connected with the production had reason to feel especially apprehensive at that moment. To Theresa Helburn and Lawrence Langner, the co-directors of the Theatre Guild which produced it, the new work represented their last hope. The once affluent Guild had only $30,000 in the bank when it occurred to Miss Helburn that a twelve-year-old play by Lynn Riggs, *Green Grow the Lilacs*, might make a good musical. A series of theatrical failures had depleted the number of financial backers who would even consider investing in a Guild project; countless time-consuming auditions had to be given before, little by little, the required amount was raised.

To actors Alfred Drake, Joan Roberts, and Celeste Holm, *Oklahoma!* was their

first opportunity to be seen in major roles in a Broadway musical. To director Rouben Mamoulian, it was a challenge to repeat the great success he had achieved with *Porgy and Bess*, his last Broadway assignment more than seven years before. To choreographer Agnes de Mille, it was the first real chance to create something meaningful in the musical theatre.

To composer Richard Rodgers and librettist-lyricist Oscar Hammerstein II, *Oklahoma!* had probably the greatest significance of all. For twenty-five years, Rodgers had never written a note with any lyricist other than Lorenz Hart. They had been an inseparable team that had created some of the greatest musical comedy scores ever heard on Broadway. It was almost impossible to think of one without the other. As for Hammerstein, though he had had many successes in the Twenties, his record since *Music in the Air*, in 1932, had consisted of an almost unbroken chain of failures.

The new partners also knew they were giving the public a work that broke with conventional musical comedy on many levels. While it was no longer an innovation to begin a show without a high-kicking chorus line, it was unusual for the

*During the run of *Oklahoma!*, Mr. Schwartzdorf Anglicized his name to Jay S. Blackton.

Oklahoma! *(1943).*
The Post Cards in Agnes de Mille's dream ballet, "Laurey Makes Up Her Mind": Joan McCracken, Kate Friedlich, Margit DeKova, Bobby Barrentine, and Vivian Smith. (Costumes by Miles White; setting by Lemuel Ayers.)

Photo by Vandamm

curtain to rise on a simple farm scene of a woman sitting alone on the stage churning butter, with the opening song, "Oh, What a Beautiful Mornin'," begun offstage by the leading baritone. About forty minutes later, when the dancing girls finally did arrive, they were all garbed in correct, though less-than-appealing, period costumes. No great conflicts were posed in Act I; the action was concerned primarily with finding out which man, Curly McLain or Jud Fry, would take Laurey Williams to a dance. The second act introduced only three new songs, all the others being reprised from the first.

Many of the facts concerning the production were known to the audience at the first-night performance. Indeed, as the reports from Boston—where the show had opened under the title of *Away We Go!*—were not overwhelmingly enthusiastic, there were empty seats at the première. But almost as soon as they heard the rich, true baritone of Alfred Drake singing "Oh, What a Beautiful Mornin'," the audience succumbed to the

open-air charm of the production. After the intermission, as the people were returning to their seats for the second act, Hammerstein recalls that "the glow was like the light from a thousand lanterns. You could *feel* the glow, it was that bright."

The critical reception the next morning was equally incandescent. "Wonderful," exclaimed Lewis Nichols of the *Times*. "Jubilant and enchanting," cheered Howard Barnes of the *Herald Tribune*. "The most thoroughly and attractive American musical comedy since *Show Boat*," was the verdict of the *News's* Burns Mantle. To Burton Rascoe of the *World-Telegram*, it was "fresh, lively, colorful and enormously pleasing." Wolcott Gibbs of *The New Yorker* happily admitted, "I feel nothing but the greatest affection for everybody in it. To the Theatre Guild my gratitude is practically boundless."

Oklahoma! ran for five years and nine weeks, to achieve a total run of 2,212 performances. Until it was surpassed by *My Fair Lady*, this held the record as the

Photo by Vandamm

Oklahoma! *(1943).*
*The final scene just before
Curly and Laurey (Alfred
Drake and Joan Roberts)
drive off in the surrey with the
fringe on top. Kneeling in
front of the happy couple is
Joseph Buloff as Ali Hakim,
the peddler. Other well-wishers
are Marc Platt (Chalmers),
George Church (Jess),
Katharine Sergava (Ellen),
Lee Dixon (Will Parker),
Celeste Holm (Ado Annie),
Betty Garde (Aunt Eller),
Owen Martin (Cord Elam),
and four of the bridesmaids.
(Costumes by Miles White;
setting by Lemuel Ayers.)*

*The lively "Farmer and the
Cowman" dance at the party
at the Skidmore ranch. Photo
is of the National Company
which toured for ten and a half
years, beginning in New
Haven, October 15, 1943, and
ending in Philadelphia, May
1, 1954. It was seen in 153
cities in the United States and
10 in Canada, with frequent
return performances in most of
the larger cities. In 1951, it
was presented in Berlin,
Germany, as part of the
International Theatre Festival.
The longest run of the
National Company was 60
weeks in Chicago.*

Photo by Vandamm

greatest number of continuous performances ever achieved by a musical on
Broadway.

The first lyric Hammerstein wrote for
Oklahoma! was for "Oh, What a Beautiful Mornin'." "When Oscar handed it to
me," Rodgers recalled, "and I read it for
the first time, I was a little sick with joy
because it was so lovely and so right.

When you're given words like 'the corn
is as high as an elephant's eye,' you've
got something to say musically." In its
happy description of a sun-drenched
morning on a farm in the American
Southwest, the song set the proper mood
for both play and audience.

The mood continued throughout.
Early in the first act there was need for a

love duet between the hero and the heroine. As they had just had a quarrel, however, it was necessary for them to express their emotions in an indirect way. Rodgers and Hammerstein adroitly solved the problem in "People Will Say We're in Love" by having the boy and girl warn each other against appearing too friendly lest they give people the impression that they are really in love. "The Surrey with the Fringe on Top" was a brilliant piece of scene painting in the way it fused music and lyric to convey the simple pleasures of a young couple riding in a horse and buggy. In "Pore Jud," the authors succeeded in creating something both ludicrous and touching in the imagined death of the story's villain. As a finale, they produced a roaring title song that was so charged the audience could almost feel the wind come sweeping down the plain.

Apart from the charm and inventiveness of the individual songs, what was unique about *Oklahoma!* was the synthesis of its component parts into a complete theatrical entity of great beauty and imagination. Everything fit into place. For the first time, not only were songs and story inseparable, but the dances devised by Agnes de Mille heightened the drama by revealing the subconscious fears and desires of the leading characters.

One factor in the success of *Oklahoma!* that cannot be overlooked was the attitude of the American people at the time it was presented. World War II was more than a year old when the musical opened, and those who remained at home were becoming increasingly aware of the heritage they enjoyed as a free people. Seeing the happier, sunnier days that were so much a part of this heritage gave spectators both an escape from daily headlines and a feeling of optimism for the future.

Rodgers was forty years old and Hammerstein was forty-seven when *Oklahoma!* began its historic run on Broadway. Though they had never written together professionally before, they had known each other almost all of their lives. In fact, Rodgers had met Hammerstein about a year before he met Larry Hart. Mortimer Rodgers, Dick's older brother and Oscar's fraternity brother, had taken Dick to see a Columbia Varsity Show in which Hammerstein was appearing. Later, backstage, the awestruck fourteen-year-old Rodgers was introduced to his future partner, then a worldly twenty-one year-old Junior.

Oscar Greeley Clendenning Hammerstein was born July 12, 1895, in New York City. Named for his paternal grandfather, the opera impressario and producer of *Naughty Marietta*, young Oscar soon adopted the "II" in order to rid himself of the cumbersome middle names. His father, William Hammerstein, was the manager of the Victoria Theatre, a vaudeville house owned by Oscar I. It was there that the youth first experienced the fascination of the theatre. But his parents were well aware of the hazards of show business and thought that their son might be happier if he became a lawyer. At Columbia, Oscar's first writing for the stage was an additional scene in the Varsity Show of 1916, *The Peace Pirates*, in which both he and Lorenz Hart appeared.

Even though the theatre was becoming increasingly important to him, Hammerstein acceded to his parents wishes and entered Columbia Law School. After a few months, however, he left to enter the professional theatre. His uncle, producer Arthur Hammerstein, gave him his first jobs as stage manager for three Rudolf Friml musicals—*You're in Love*, *Sometime*, and *Tumble In*.

Hammerstein also continued to be active in Columbia Varsity Shows. He shared credit for writing the book and lyrics of the 1917 edition, *Home, James*, and the following year assumed full responsibility for the book, lyrics, and direction of the "War Show," *Ten for Five*. He was also on the committee that chose

Rodgers and Hart's *Fly with Me* as the Varsity Show of 1920. In addition to having the first complete Rodgers and Hart score, the musical also had the first song by Rodgers and Hammerstein, "There's Always Room for One More," a debonair piece with a touch of John Donne in the lyric:

My heart is an airy castle
   Filled with girls I adore.
My brain is a cloud of memories
   of peaches galore.
There were Jane and Molly,
   And Ruth and Sue;
Camilla, Kit,
   and Patricia, too.
My heart is filled to the brim with you—
But there's always room for one more!

In 1919, Hammerstein created his first professional work for the theatre, a non-musical play called *The Light*. It lasted four performances in New Haven, where it was described by one critic as "*The Light* that failed." The following year, Hammerstein wrote the book and lyrics for his first musical, *Always You*, with music by Herbert Stothart. The show had a very brief Broadway run. Because Hammerstein exhibited far greater talent as a lyricist than as a librettist, Arthur Hammerstein, who had produced both of his nephew's plays, suggested that he collaborate with the more experienced Otto Harbach, who had written both book and lyrics for most of the early Friml operettas. Their maiden effort, *Tickle Me*, had a good run due chiefly to its star, Frank Tinney. Later they worked on four of the leading musicals of the Twenties—*Wildflower, Rose-Marie, Sunny*, and *The Desert Song*. Still later, as the sole author of both libretto and lyrics, Hammerstein joined Jerome Kern in creating *Show Boat, Sweet Adeline, Music in the Air*, and *Very Warm for May*.

When Rodgers first proposed to Hammerstein that they collaborate on the musical version of *Green Grow the Lilacs*, the librettist was immediately enthusias-tic since he had already tried to interest Jerome Kern in the same project. Rodgers believed that their basically similar outlook on the theatre and on life itself would help to make theirs a harmonious partnership. With Larry Hart, it had been a matter of combining warm, tender melodies with frequently biting lyrics. With Hammerstein, it would now be a matter of combining these same musical qualities with lyrics that also possessed great warmth and tenderness. This fact, coupled with Rodgers' sound musicianship, his explorative nature, and his maturity as a composer, indicated how well he would be able to suit his style to that of his new collaborator. To a writer of such innate gifts, turning from the sardonic quality of a *Pal Joey*, or the slickness of a *By Jupiter*, to the rustic pleasures of an *Oklahoma!* was both natural and, perhaps, even inevitable.

The lyrics of Oscar Hammerstein II differ from those of Lorenz Hart in many ways, just as in appearance, working habits, and temperament the men themselves were entirely different. For example, unless it is something like "Thou Swell," it is hard to recall a dialect lyric by Hart. Hammerstein, however, has always made use of dialects and idioms; his rare gift for enchancing the varied, colloquial speech patterns of an Oklahoma cowboy or a Siamese monarch is equally as brilliant as Hart's more facile ability with polysyllabic and internal rhymes. A Hammerstein lyric seldom calls attention to itself; at its best it seems to be the spontaneous and honest expression of the character who sings it. Yet there is always an inherent quality that once prompted Irving Berlin to remark, "The difference between Oscar and the rest of us lyric writers is that he is a poet." Moreover, Hammerstein was able to convey his basic philosophy more directly through his work than Hart. "I believe not that the whole world and all of life is good," he once said, "but I do believe that so much of it is good, and my inclination is to emphasize that side of life. It's a natural inclination, not one that I've developed."

Shortly after *Oklahoma!* opened, the team split up temporarily—Rodgers to produce the new version of *A Connecticut Yankee* and Hammerstein to complete work on *Carmen Jones*, adapted from Georges Bizet's opera *Carmen*. While adhering faithfully to the original tempos (except in the wildly exciting "Beat out Dat Rhythm on a Drum"), Hammerstein updated the story more than one hundred years and changed the characters and locale from Basques in southern Spain to Negroes in the southern United States. What resulted was a vividly idiomatic theatrical piece, beautifully sung and acted, and stunningly produced.

Rodgers and Hammerstein resumed their partnership to create *Carousel*, a musical version of Ferenc Molnar's play, *Liliom*. As in *Oklahoma!*, it was Theresa Helburn of the Theatre Guild who first suggested the idea. Initially, the partners thought it was too tragic for the musical stage, but they finally decided that the story could be made acceptable by adding a strong note of hopefulness at the end. They also felt that the play's locale of Budapest should be changed to somewhere in the United States; Rodgers' suggestion of the New England coast met with a favorable response because they could then have choruses of mill workers, sailors, and fishermen. Another task was in keeping the leading character, a carnival barker, basically sympathetic even though he is shiftless and frequently unattractive. But the authors were able to treat the theme with so much insight and compassion that the work emerged as a remarkably affecting musical drama, one that could be accepted on its individual merits without comparison to the play from which it had been adapted.

The use of music as an integral part of the story was maintained to an even greater degree than in the authors' first collaboration. Early in the play, when two young girls, Julie Jordan and Carrie Pipperidge, are seated on a park bench, their dialogue is first synchronized over the music. As their conversation continues, it develops naturally into song: first the duet, "You're a Queer One, Julie Jordan," and then Carrie's starry-eyed revelation that she is in love with Mr. Snow. Shortly thereafter, Julie meets Billy Bigelow, the barker. Because it is too soon for them to admit their love, Rodgers and Hammerstein created "If I Loved You," a song in which the characters imagined how they would act if they really were in love.

As with "Oh, What a Beautiful Mornin'," "June Is Bustin' Out All Over" was inspired by the effect of weather. However, while the song in *Oklahoma!* was a lazy, arm-stretching ode to the beauties of a farm in summertime, the song in *Carousel* is a sprightly account of the odd effects summer has on the behavior of normally well-adjusted individuals. The final feeling of hope, so essential to the story, is conveyed through the simple, moving hymn, "You'll Never Walk Alone."

The most ambitious musical undertaking of the score was Billy Bigelow's "Soliloquy," which had taken Hammerstein several seeks to write and Rodgers just two hours to compose. The song contains many contrasting melodic and emotional themes as the barker imagines what it would be like to be the father of a boy and what it would be like to be the father of a girl. Expressing the frequently conflicting feelings of the joys and fears of fatherhood, the authors created one of the most probing expositions of a man's inner thoughts ever written for the Broadway stage.

In addition to its Theatre Guild sponsorship, *Carousel* kept intact most of the production staff that had worked on *Oklahoma!* Rouben Mamoulian directed, Agnes de Mille did the choreography, and Miles White designed the costumes.

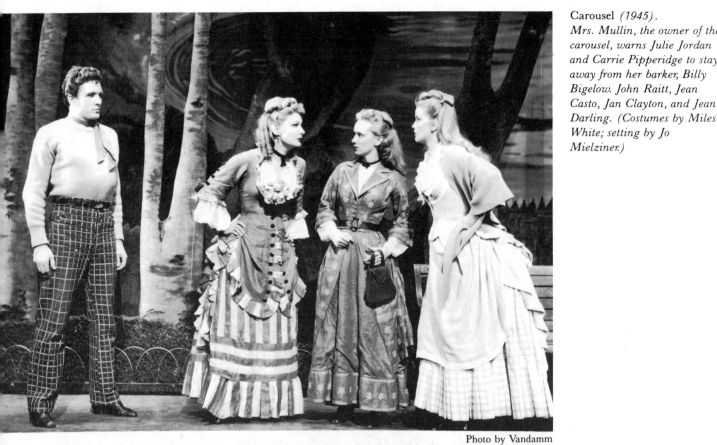

Photo by Vandamm

Carousel *(1945).*
Mrs. Mullin, the owner of the carousel, warns Julie Jordan and Carrie Pipperidge to stay away from her barker, Billy Bigelow. John Raitt, Jean Casto, Jan Clayton, and Jean Darling. (Costumes by Miles White; setting by Jo Mielziner.)

Photo by Vandamm

The final scene of the musical in which the graduating class of a local school sings "You'll Never Walk Alone." Bambi Linn, as Louise, is seated at the far right of the front row. At the far right of the stage are Jan Clayton and John Raitt.

Allegro *(1947)*.
"Yatata, yatata, yatata, yatata" sing the guests at a party at the home of Dr. and Mrs. Joseph Taylor. John Battles and Roberta Jonay, as the host and hostess, are in the center foreground. John Conte, as Joe's best friend, is third from the left holding the brandy snifter. (Costumes by Lucinda Ballard.)

Photo by Vandamm

Again the cast consisted of comparatively unknown performers, among them John Raitt, Jan Clayton, Murvyn Vye, Jean Darling, and, from *Oklahoma!*, Bambi Linn. The new musical opened on April 19, 1945, at the Majestic Theatre, directly across the street from the St. James where *Oklahoma!* was playing. Thus, for about two years, Rodgers and Hammerstein had two musicals facing each other on West 44th Street.

Allegro, produced by the Theatre Guild in 1947, was Rodgers and Hammerstein's first original musical play. Directed entirely by Agnes de Mille, it was a boldly experimental work detailing the life of a young doctor from his birth to his thirty-fifth year. The authors used the story to probe the reasons why dedicated men sometimes begin to lose their integrity after they have won success. "I wanted to write a large, universal story, and I think I overestimated the psychological ability of the audience to identify itself with the leading character," Hammerstein admits.

The story was told with many original theatrical effects, particularly in the elimination of formal sets and in the use of a modern Greek chorus to comment on the happenings in the play. The authors also made a deliberate attempt to make the score serve the function of the plot, although some pieces, "A Fellow Needs a Girl," "So Far" (the only number that was not germane to the story), and "The Gentleman Is a Dope," have won favor as individual popular songs.

Allegro had the critics divided. Brooks Atkinson thought it "just missed the final splendor of a perfect work of art," while Howard Barnes felt it was a "show to be remembered with *Show Boat* and *Oklahoma!*" However, Wolcott Gibbs referred to it as "spectacular banality," and George Jean Nathan called it "as pretentious as artificial jewelry, and just as valuable."

South Pacific, which opened in 1949, is probably the most universally admired achievement of Rodgers and Hammerstein. In a realistic wartime setting, they created a warm, credible romance between a worldly French planter and a naïve Army nurse from Little Rock, while managing to keep this somewhat idyllic relationship in perfect balance with the far-from-idyllic circumstances that brought them together.

The idea of turning James A. Michener's collection of stories, *Tales of the South Pacific*, into a dramatic work first occurred to Kenneth MacKenna, then the head of M-G-M's story department. When the studio decided against filming it, MacKenna suggested to his friend, Joshua Logan, that it would make an excellent property for the stage. Logan read the book and took the idea to producer Leland Hayward; when it seemed to be developing into a musical, they approached Rodgers and Hammerstein. All four men agreed to become associated as co-producers, with Logan also serving as director. Originally, the libretto was to have been written entirely by Hammerstein, but Logan, after making certain contributions to the script, demanded—and received—credit as coauthor. One thing everyone was agreed on from the start: there would be no formal choreography to jar the mood.

Almost four months were devoted to conferences before a word or a note was put on paper. The tale they decided to use for the story was the one called "Fo' Dollah," which related the unhappy love affair between Lieutenant Joe Cable and a Tonganese girl, Liat. The writers soon felt, however, that there was too much *Madama Butterfly* in the romance to make it acceptable as the main plot. Another tale, "Our Heroine," about the planter Emile DeBecque and the nurse Nellie Forbush, seemed to work out better. The story of Cable and Liat was retained as a secondary theme and the two stories were fused by adding the dramatic situation of Cable and DeBecque going off together on a secret mission behind enemy lines.

For the part of DeBecque, Rodgers and Hammerstein needed a mature man with an excellent singing voice. When they heard that Metropolitan Opera basso Ezio Pinza was anxious to appear in a Broadway musical, they promptly signed him to a contract. For Nellie, they chose Mary Martin, who had just finished touring in the National Com-

pany of *Annie Get Your Gun*, another Rodgers and Hammerstein production.

The skill with which the action flowed from the music just as smoothly as the music flowed from the action prompted some music critics to liken Rodgers' technique to that of an operatic composer. Moreover, the authors created each song to fit perfectly with the occasion and the character singing it. Nellie's straightforward, buoyant, warmhearted quality is expressed through "A Cockeyed Optimist," "I'm Gonna Wash That Man Right Outa My Hair," and "I'm in Love with a Wonderful Guy." In fact, this last song had such a contagious effect on audiences that Harold Clurman once wrote: "When Mary Martin tells us, with radiant good nature, 'I'm in love, I'm in love, I'm in love with a wonderful guy,' one doesn't murmur 'Who cares?' but 'Congratulations, congratulations, congratulations to you both!'"

DeBecque's impulsive, romantic emotions come through in his ardent affir-

South Pacific (1949). Mary Martin, Ezio Pinza, and "Some Enchanted Evening."

mation of love at first sight, "Some Enchanted Evening," and in the touching song of a fleeting romance, "This Nearly Was Mine." The raucous, restless Seabees beautifully contrast this idealized attitude with their single-minded desires in the rollicking "There Is Nothin' Like a Dame." The haunting dissonance of "Bali Ha'i" (which the composer wrote in less than ten minutes during lunch one day) captures the flavor of the entire South Pacific, while "Younger Than Springtime" and the plea for understanding, "Carefully Taught," give meaning to the character of the earnest young Joe Cable.

South Pacific had a New York run of 1,925 performances and, until *My Fair Lady*, held the record for the highest gross receipts ($9,000,000) of any Broadway musical. In 1950, it became the second musical ever to win the Pulitzer Prize for drama. As the *Herald Tribune* editorialized, it was one award that "will receive confirming cheers from coast to coast."

After traveling to Oklahoma, New England, the Middle West, and the South Pacific, Rodgers and Hammerstein journeyed to the Far East in 1951 for *The King and I*. The play was adapted from the book, *Anna and the King of Siam* by Margaret Landon, which had been based on the real adventures of a Victorian Englishwoman who went to Siam to become tutor and governess to the royal children. The novel made such an impression on Gertrude Lawrence that she approached Rodgers and Hammerstein about adapting it as a musical for her. Miss Lawrence was persuasive, and the partners were especially intrigued by the prospect of doing a play with an Oriental locale.* Finding an actor to play the part of the king proved to be more difficult. They finally decided on a little-known, bald-headed actor named Yul Brynner who, for his audition, sat cross-legged on the stage, played a guitar, and sang gypsy songs.

The possibility of creating a story around the characters of the straight-laced Anna Leonowens and the semibarbaric monarch fascinated Rodgers and Hammerstein. "The intangibility of their strange union," they once wrote, "was a challenge to us as librettist and composer. In dealing with them musically, we could not write songs which said 'I love you' or even 'I love him' or 'I love her.' We were dealing with two characters who could indulge themselves only in oblique expressions of their feeling for each other, since they themselves do not realize exactly what these feelings mean."

Again Rodgers and Hammerstein created a score to implement the action and to reveal characters and motivations, but at times with even greater effectiveness than in previous works. The king's soliloquy, "A Puzzlement," so different from the emotional outpouring of Billy Bigelow in *Carousel*, illuminates much of the personality of the untutored yet crafty ruler; "My Lord and Master" is a moving expression of pent-up secret defiance; the light, dainty "Getting to Know You" is an affirmative answer to Cable's troubled "Carefully Taught" in

*Gertrude Lawrence died on September 6, 1952, during the run of *The King and I*. She was succeeded by Constance Carpenter.

South Pacific (1949). Myron McCormick leads the Seabees in singing "There Is Nothin' Like a Dame." (Setting by Jo Mielziner.)

Photo by Vandamm

The King And I *(1951)*.
The royal Siamese children bow down as the king enters their classroom. Standing are Gertrude Lawrence, Yul Brynner, and Dorothy Sarnoff. (Costumes by Irene Sharaff; setting by Jo Mielziner.)

The King and I *(1977)*.
With Yul Brynner again playing the Asian monarch, the musical was successfully revived in 1977. To the music of "Shall We Dance?" Constance Towers teaches the king how couples dance in Western countries. (Costumes by Stanley Simmons from originals by Irene Sharaff.)

Photo by Michael Baumann, Fuji

Photo by Eileen Darby—Graphic House

Me And Juliet *(1953).*
A tense moment backstage, as Bob, the electrician (Mark Dawson), warns Larry, the assistant stage manager (Bill Hayes), to keep away from his girl. In the center of the group of onlookers are Joan McCracken and Arthur Maxwell. (Costumes by Irene Sharaff.)

South Pacific; Anna's "Hello, Young Lovers" is a gentle, eloquent song of consolation and encouragement.

No better example of the way Rodgers and Hammerstein use a song to illuminate a dramatic situation can be found than the scene from *The King and I* in which Lady Thiang, the king's number-one wife, pleads with Anna to remain at court after she has decided to leave. Nothing can sway the determined governess. Then, as a final effort, Lady Thiang sings "Something Wonderful." In the song, while admitting all the ruler's faults, she emphasizes his hopes and aspirations and expresses her own belief that with Anna's help he could accomplish "something wonderful." This alone changes Anna's mind, and she agrees to stay in Siam.

The exotic locales of *South Pacific* and *The King and I* made Rodgers and Hammerstein anxious to try something completely different. As both men had been stagestruck from early youth, they decided to express their feelings about the theatre in a modern musical comedy. *Me and Juliet*, produced in 1953, was their valentine to show business. For their cast, they chose such bright young performers as Isabel Bigley, Bill Hayes, and Joan McCracken, and for their director, George Abbott.

Hammerstein's libretto was his first original script since *Allegro*. Unfortunately, it was an occasionally awkward combination of backstage story and onstage story that never quite succeeded in fitting together as a completely realized plot. The real distinction of the production was the spectacular scenic effects devised by Jo Mielziner, which enabled audiences to see both backstage and onstage simultaneously. "No Other Love," originally written as a theme for Rodgers' thirteen-hour television score for *Victory at Sea*, was the song with the greatest popularity.

Pipe Dream, in 1955, had the shortest run of any Rodgers and Hammerstein musical—246 performances. Originally, the rights to do a musical version of John Steinbeck's *Sweet Thursday* were held by producers Cy Feuer and Ernest Martin; when they were unable to secure Frank Loesser to write the score, they suggested to Rodgers and Hammerstein that it might be suitable for them. R & H agreed, but the public did not. A leisurely story with little conflict, *Pipe Dream* took such a warmhearted look at the denizens of a West Coast skid row that there was little opportunity for theatrical excitement or genuine gaiety. In the leading female role of the owner of a brothel, the Metropolitan's Helen Traubel found herself in rather strange surroundings.

In 1957, playwright Joseph Fields read the novel, *The Flower Drum Song*, by Chin Y. Lee, and felt that it was an almost-perfect property for the stage. After securing the rights, he and his friend Oscar Hammerstein discussed the possibility of turning it into a musical. Hammerstein believed that while it did not have a strong plot, it was "strong on character and background, like a Chinese *Life with Father*. I just fell in love with it." With Rodgers in agreement, Hammerstein and Fields then became collaborators on the libretto.

Flower Drum Song opened on December 1, 1958. It told a placid, somewhat predictable tale of the conflicts between Old World and New World Chinese living in San Francisco's Chinatown. Miyoshi Umeki, who was born in Japan, played the part of a tradition-bound Chinese girl, while Pat Suzuki, an American of Japanese descent, played a Chinese-American strip-tease dancer. Of the songs, the masterfully constructed "I Enjoy Being a Girl" has probably become the most popular, but the gliding, pseudo-Oriental "You Are Beautiful" and the searching lament, "Love, Look Away," are equally fine examples of the art of Rodgers and Hammerstein. *Flower Drum Song* was a box-office success in

spite of wide differences among the critics—from Robert Coleman's "everything about it is just right," to Brooks Atkinson's "a pleasant interlude," to Kenneth Tynan's "a world of woozy song."

Even before the opening of *Flower Drum Song*, Rodgers and Hammerstein had become associated with one of those rare productions that seems, from the outset, to be incapable of failure. Theatre director Vincent J. Donehue, after being approached by Paramount Pictures to direct a movie based on a German film, *The Trapp Family Singers*, became convinced that the story should be done only as a Broadway musical. Once the film company allowed its option to lapse, Donehue contacted Mary Martin; as soon as she saw the German film, she too became excited about the project.

Securing the rights, however, turned out to be rather difficult. Miss Martin's husband, Richard Halliday, spent eight fruitless months trying to locate Baroness Von Trapp, who was somewhere in the South Pacific doing missionary work. Eventually, he found her in an Austrian hospital, where she was being treated for malaria. Co-producer Leland Hayward made six trips to Munich before he came

*Pipe Dream (1955).
Helen Traubel leads the group in "The Bums' Opera." Seated at the left are Mike Kellin and George Wallace. (Costumes by Alvin Colt; setting by Jo Mielziner.)*

Photo by Karger—Pix

Flower Drum Song *(1958).*
Oscar Hammerstein II leans
across the footlights to polish a
lyric.

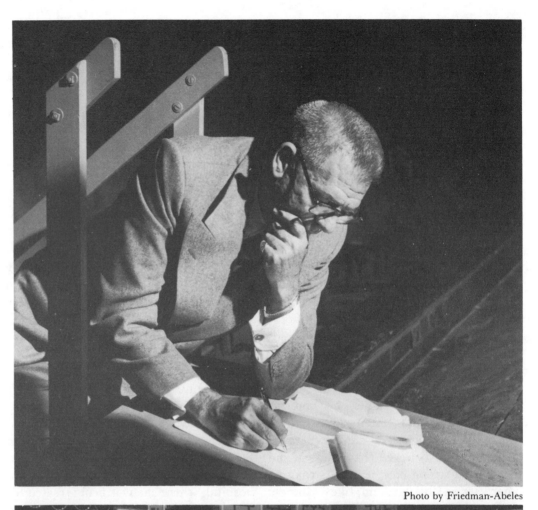

Photo by Friedman-Abeles

Pat Suzuki and the chorus of
the Celestial Bar singing of the
wonders of Grant Avenue, the
main street of San Francisco's
Chinatown. (Costumes by
Irene Sharaff; setting by
Oliver Smith.)

to terms with the German film company that had made the original movie. Then the producer had to search for the widely scattered Trapp children to secure their permission to be portrayed on the stage.

After all of this preliminary work was over, there was still the important task of finding the writers best suited to tell the story of the courageous Trapp family. The first to be signed were librettists Howard Lindsay and Russel Crouse. For the score, the producers wanted to use the authentic folk and religious songs that the family actually sang in its concerts, plus some additional songs. When Hayward suggested to Rodgers and Hammerstein that they supply the new material, the partners were against the idea. If you are going to use authentic Trapp family music, that's fine, Rodgers told the producer; the important thing is that old songs should never be mixed

with new. It did not take Hayward long to come to a decision: if Rodgers and Hammerstein would supply an entirely new score, he would be glad to postpone production until they had completed *Flower Drum Song*.

The effect of the new alliance was not hard to foresee. The combination of Mary Martin and Rodgers and Hammerstein (who also became co-producers) was enough to guarantee an advance ticket sale for *The Sound of Music* of $3,325,000, the highest ever achieved for a Broadway production.

Opening on November 16, 1959, the play that audiences waited for so eagerly was cheerful, wholesome entertainment, possibly more in the style of a Sigmund Romberg operetta than in the integrated style that Rodgers and Hammerstein themselves had done so much to develop. Wisely, the team decided against a for-

The Sound Of Music *(1959). To allay the Von Trapp children's fears during a storm, Maria (Mary Martin) teaches them a song about "The Lonely Goatherd." (Costumes by Lucinda Ballard; setting by Oliver Smith.)*

Photo by Friedman-Abeles

The Sound Of Music *(1959).*
Maria (Mary Martin) and
Capt. Von Trapp (Theodore
Bikel) first begin to realize
that they are in love as they
dance to the "Laendler"
during a party at the captain's
home. (Costumes by Lucinda
Ballard.)

mal overture. Instead, nuns at an abbey sang a moving *a capella* "Preludium," which helped set the tone and spirit of the play. The title song told appealingly of the beauties of music and nature, while a bubbly quartet, "Maria," was described by Walter Kerr as having "the lilt and sprightliness proper to lucky princesses living in an enchanted castle." Of the numbers Miss Martin sang with the seven Trapp children, the most popular has become "Do-Re-Mi," a brisk march that served to teach the children the rudiments of music by having the lyric develop from the notes on the scale. "My Favorite Things," possibly the loveliest song in the play, deftly employed an abruptly contrasting release to emphasize the wistfulness of the chief melodic line. The moving theme of the story, "Climb Ev'ry Mountain," had something of the simple faith expressed in "You'll Never Walk Alone" from *Carousel.*

Again, as in most recent Rodgers and Hammerstein works, the critics were divided. Although he lamented the book, Brooks Atkinson found that "the sound of music is always moving. Occasionally, it is also glorious." Richard Watts, Jr., thought the entire production "wonderfully endearing," and John McClain of the *Journal-American* called it "the most mature product of the Rodgers-Hammerstein team." However, Walter Kerr felt that it "will be most admired by people who have always found Sir James M. Barrie pretty rough stuff," and Henry Hewes of the *Saturday Review* questioned whether everything about the play "was decided by a committee of craftsmen all too willing to please each other and to avoid risk." Nevertheless, audiences were far less divided, and *The Sound of Music* became one of the longest-running musicals in Broadway history.

Oscar Hammerstein's death, as a result of cancer, on August 23, 1960, terminated the most successful partnership in theatre history. From the beginning of their association, Rodgers and Hammerstein made their influence felt both in the audience and behind the footlights. Once, when Cole Porter was asked to name the most profound changes in musical comedy in forty years, he replied simply, "Rodgers and Hammerstein." Chiefly because of them, writers for the musical stage who might have spent the rest of their lives in Hollywood suddenly began to think again of the challenge and the opportunities inherent in the Broadway musical theatre. By their pioneering, Rodgers and Hammerstein conditioned the public to accept the kind of adventurous musicals that have been presented since *Oklahoma!* For in spite of the gradual changes that were taking place before that memorable production, it was *Oklahoma!* that demonstrated to composers, lyricists and librettists the indisputable truth that if they do create a work of merit, no matter how unconventional, there will be a large and responsive audience waiting for it.

As did the team of Rodgers and Hart, the team of Rodgers and Hammerstein always avoided formula musicals. "We believe that writers who repeat themselves will eventually bore themselves," they once wrote. "And this condition is a short and automatic step toward boring the public." In spite of the variety of their plays, however, there was always something of the basic philosophy of the two men present in their works. Ironically, although they helped bring about a more mature musical theatre through their contributions both before and after their partnership, Rodgers and Hammerstein were frequently accused of radiating too much of an unreal aura of sweetness and light. Rodgers was always quick to answer. "What's wrong with sweetness and light? It's been around quite a while. Even a cliché has a right to be true. I'm not interested in cracking out at anything, and I'm certainly not interested in kicking sentiment around. I love satire but I just couldn't write it." For his part, Hammerstein readily ad-

mitted he was a sentimentalist. "There's nothing wrong with sentiment because the things we're sentimental about are the fundamental things in life—the birth of a child, the death of a child, or anybody falling in love. I couldn't be anything but sentimental about these basic things. To be anything else is being a poseur."

Apart from their influence and philosophy, Rodgers and Hammerstein were particularly concerned about creative integrity. Once they decided upon their subject and the manner in which it would be developed, they proceeded in a direction that conformed solely to their own convictions. "I think it is disaster to try to do what the public wants if you don't feel that way yourself," Rodgers once said. "It's only when you and the public have the same mind that you are successful." To which Hammerstein added, "You can't deliberately say, 'I will please the public although I don't like what I'm doing.' There must be a faith behind every work to make it succeed."

Following Hammerstein's death, Rodgers waited over a year before announcing his future plans—a collaboration with Alan Jay Lerner (which never materialized) and an original musical, *No Strings*, which, for the first time, would have lyrics as well as music by Richard Rodgers. *No Strings* proved to be an especially daring undertaking in many ways. Impressed with the talents of singer Diahann Carroll, the composer joined with playwright Samuel Taylor to fashion a vehicle expressly for her. Their conception took the form of an interracial love affair, set amid the elegant world of modern Paris and St. Tropez, but with the racial angle deliberately de-emphasized. Then with relative newcomers Joe Layton as director, Peter Matz as music director, and Ralph Burns as arranger, Rodgers worked out a scheme for taking the orchestra out of the pit, placing it backstage, and utilizing the services of specific instrumental soloists on stage

No Strings *(1962).*
Diahann Carroll and Richard
Kiley strolling down a stylized
Parisian boulevard. (Costumes
by Fred Voelpel and Donald
Brooks; setting by David
Hays.)

both as part of the action and to lend appropriate atmosphere. He further did away with conventional scene changes by having the ladies of the chorus serve as decorative stage hands shifting sets and properties within full view of the audience. Then, as a touch of whimsy, he even had the instrumentation—save for a harp and bass violin—live up to the play's title by consisting of nothing that could be bowed or plucked. But there was more than mere whimsy in the overall concept. "I wanted the orchestra on stage," Rodgers explained, "in order to blend the orchestral sounds with the other elements so completely that they would seem to be an integral part of the proceedings, just as much as the dialogue, the lyrics, or the action. I also wanted to eliminate the chasm between the audience and the stage that has always existed because of the orchestra pit."

There was general rejoicing at the boldness of the presentation, though some critical reservations were expressed regarding the book itself. As for the music, Howard Taubman happily announced in the *Times* that the composer was "still a magician of the musical theatre," who had "written a score full of romance and vivacity" with lyrics that "have a touch of the wholesome ease of Hammerstein and a soupcon of the peppery impertinence of Lorenz Hart." As for Miss Carroll, she was unquestionably the most electric personality appearing on Broadway that season—though, unfortunately, she hasn't been back since.

Somewhat less friendly receptions have greeted Rodgers' more recent efforts, *Do I Hear a Waltz?* (with lyricist Stephen Sondheim), *Two by Two* (in which Danny Kaye played Noah), *Rex* (in partnership with Sheldon Harnick), and *I Remember Mama* (starring Liv Ullmann). Praiseworthy elements in all—with the last most closely capturing the honest warmth and optimism so characteristic of the Rodgers musicals with Hammerstein—yet none viewed as representing the master at his most masterful.

In the history of the American musical theatre, there has simply never been anyone whose level of creativity remained so high for so long as Richard Rodgers, who died in New York on December 30, 1979, at the age of 77. It is, in fact, a bit staggering to realize that if all his Broadway musicals—including their mainstem revivals—could be presented consecutively, they would, so far, have an unbroken run of over 43½ years.

Leonard Bernstein.   Photo By Vandamm. Courtesy N.Y. Philharmonic

CHAPTER EIGHTEEN

LEONARD BERNSTEIN

WITH THE STRONG emphasis on well-constructed book shows, young theatre writers since the Forties have no longer been able to rely on the disappearing revue as a means of getting their first songs on Broadway. Diverse media of entertainment, however, were still able to provide training for many aspiring composers and lyricists. The profusion of movie musicals in the Thirties and Forties gave Jule Styne and Frank Loesser the opportunity to write their first hits. Betty Comden and Adolph Green began their careers performing their own material in night clubs. Radio script-writing was Alan Jay Lerner's first professional job. For many years, Meredith Willson was known coast to coast as a radio conductor and composer. The most ancient training locale of all, Tin Pan Alley, was responsible for the emergence of Richard Adler and Jerry Ross, and Bob Merrill.

Although it is no longer a rarity for the concert hall to produce composers for the musical stage, not since Victor Herbert has there been anyone quite as successful in both areas as Leonard Bernstein. As a conductor, pianist, lecturer, and composer for the concert hall, he is an ac-knowledged leader in the world of classical music; as the composer of *On The Town*, *Wonderful Town*, *Candide*, and *West Side Story*, he is also an ac-knowledged leader in the world of musical comedy.

Born in Lawrence, Massachusetts, on August 25, 1918, Leonard Bernstein first became interested in music at a relatively advanced age. He was ten when an aunt presented his parents with a discarded upright piano; the gift so fascinated the youth that his father eventually yielded to his entreaties and permitted him to take lessons. At Harvard, where he majored in music, Bernstein became acquainted with Dimitri Mitropoulos, who was so impressed by the young man's talents that he urged him to become a conductor. After graduating from Harvard, Bernstein studied under Fritz Reiner at the Curtis Institute of Music in Philadelphia. In the summer of 1940, Serge Koussevitzky hired him as an assistant at the Tanglewood Summer Music Festival. The famed conductor soon developed a fatherly affection for Bernstein, who returned to Tanglewood for the next two summers.

Artur Rodzinski, then the musical director of the New York Philharmonic, thought the twenty-five-year-old conductor showed so much promise that he made him his assistant. One evening in the fall of 1943, Bruno Walter, the scheduled guest conductor of the Philharmonic, was suddenly taken ill. With Rodzinski out of town, and with no time for a rehearsal, Bernstein was suddenly called on to take over as conductor of the concert. His success prompted a front page story in the New York *Times* and an editorial in the *Daily News*. Hailed as a *Wunderkind*, Bernstein quickly found himself sought after for a wide variety of musical commissions.

The first one he accepted was to compose the music for a ballet, *Fancy Free*, choreographed by a young man named Jerome Robbins. The work, which depicted the escapades of three brash sailors on a twenty-four-hour spree in New York, became such a popular attraction of the Ballet Theatre that its creators decided to enlarge it into a Broadway musical. At Bernstein's suggestion, producers Oliver Smith and Paul Feigay signed Betty Comden and Adolph Green to write the libretto and lyrics.

Bernstein and Green had known each other since 1937 when Bernstein had been the music counsellor at a summer camp where Green had been hired to play the pirate king in a production of *The Pirates of Penzance*. Two years later, they shared an apartment in Greenwich Village. At the time, Green wrote for a nightclub act, The Revuers, which consisted of himself, Betty Comden, and Judy Holliday. Bernstein spent almost every evening with the group, which was then performing at the Village Vanguard.

Because of the inexperience of all those connected with *On the Town*, they chose as over-all director one of the most experienced men in the theatre, George Abbott. The show, which opened in December, 1944, was bright, swift-paced, and engagingly youthful. Its skillful blending

of music, lyrics, book, and dances was the result of the unusually close rapport among the creators. The score was not only melodically and rhythmically appealing, but it had a technical mastery and unity of design that was uncommon. For example, the melody of "New York, New York," which opens the show and sets its invigorating pace, was later used by Bernstein in a much slower tempo to establish the proper mood for the contrasting expression, "Lonely Town." Comden and Green also had parts in the show (to bellow out their song of suppressed desires, "I Get Carried Away"), and Nancy Walker, as a female taxi driver, was especially funny as she boasted of her culinary and amatory prowess in "I Can Cook, Too."

Bernstein's major occupation as a conductor (with the short-lived New York City Symphony and, between 1956 and 1966, with the New York Philharmonic) had limited his theatrical output since *On the Town*. His second musical, *Wonderful Town*, was written eight years later and came about when he was called in to replace another composer. Because of differences with Joseph Fields and Jerome Chodorov (who had adapted the story from their play, *My Sister Eileen*), composer Leroy Anderson and lyricist Arnold Horwitt had quit five weeks before rehearsals were to start. This posed a problem; if rehearsals did not begin by December 15, 1953, producer Robert Fryer would lose his star, Rosalind Russell. In desperation, director George Abbott called in Betty Comden and Adolph Green. They agreed to write the lyrics on the condition that Leonard Bernstein would compose the music.

According to Green, neither he nor Miss Comden was optimistic about the show. *My Sister Eileen* had seemed to him "so awfully Thirties-bound, sort of a post-Depression play, full of overexploited plot lines and passé references." Bernstein, however, was bursting with enthusiasm. "The Thirties! My God,

On the Town *(1944).*
The collaborators at work.
Leonard Bernstein
(composer), Jerome Robbins
(choreographer), Betty
Comden, and Adolph Green
(co-librettists and co-lyricists).

Three sailors enjoying the
night life of New York. Adolph
Green, Cris Alexander, and
John Battles are the sailors,
Allyn Ann McLerie, Betty
Comden, and Nancy Walker
are the girls. (Costumes by
Alvin Colt; setting by Oliver
Smith.)

Photo by Vandamm

Wonderful Town *(1953).*
Rosalind Russell, in the arms of a Brazilian naval officer, gives some pointers on the American dance called the conga. Wrote Walter Kerr: "Instead of attacking a song, she inhabits it, moving around in it with such confidence, grace, and honest exuberance as to make it entirely her own."

Photo By Bob Golby

West Side Story *(1957).*
Larry Kert and Carol Lawrence, as the Romeo and Juliet lovers, use a fire escape as a balcony as they sing "Tonight." (Costumes by Irene Sharaff; setting by Oliver Smith.)

Photo By Fred Fehl

those were the years! The excitement that was around! The political awareness! F. D. R.! Fiorello! Real personalities! And the wonderful fashions! Glorious! And the songs! What beat!" The composer's attitude proved so contagious that the trio seldom left his studio during the five weeks it took to finish the score.

All the numbers in *Wonderful Town* caught the pace and spirit of New York of the mid-Thirties, with such tunes as "Swing!" and "Conga!" written in the specific style of the then-current rhythmic phenomena. "Conversation Piece," in which five people at a party make self-conscious, embarrassed attempts at conversation, has always been one of the composer's favorites. "That's the kind of thing I like to do in the theatre. The background is pure theatre music, operating exclusively in theatre terms, not with an eye on Tin Pan Alley, and not to create a memorable tune, but something which is an integral part of the story."

As in *On the Town*, Bernstein used many devices to give the score unity. For example, themes from "What a Waste" were adroitly repeated at the beginning of "Pass that Football" and "A Quiet Girl," while the melody of "A Little Bit in Love" was used in the introductions to "Conversation Piece" and "It's Love."

The most important single element that assured the box-office success of *Wonderful Town* was the performance of Rosalind Russell. After eighteen years in Hollywood, the forty-five-year-old actress romped through her part with such magnetic verve that audiences happily overlooked her limitations as a singer and dancer.

Being a thorough musician, Bernstein has not been limited by either subject matter or locale. For the unsuccessful *Candide* in 1956 he was able to capture the flavor of the Voltaire classic in a score that abounded in melodic grace and satiric invention. Such rhythms as the

tango, mazurka, waltz, gavotte, and schottische were employed with striking effect, as were parodies of the styles of various classical composers. In particular, "Glitter and Be Gay" provided a delightful coloratura aria in which the heroine, now a *demimondaine*, trills gaily of the materialistic compensations of her sad life. In 1974, a greatly revised version directed by Harold Prince at last earned *Candide* recognition as a musical-theatre classic.

For many years, Bernstein and Jerome Robbins had discussed the idea of doing a special kind of musical. Was it possible, they wondered, to tell a tragic story with a theme of some depth in terms of musical comedy without becoming operatic? A specific idea occurred to Robbins early in 1949: an up-to-date version of *Romeo and Juliet*, with the lovers played by a Jewish girl and an Italian Catholic boy living on the lower East Side of Manhattan. Playwright Arthur Laurents, a friend of Robbins, was called in to write the libretto of *East Side Story*, as it was then called, but the project soon had to be abandoned because of conflicting schedules.

About six years later, the writers decided to try again. By this time, it was apparent that the original concept was dated; the clashes between native-born teenagers and newly arrived Puerto Ricans offered them a far more timely and dramatic conflict. Now, in partnership with a young television writer named Stephen Sondheim as lyricist, they moved the play's locale across town and retitled it *West Side Story*. Although the work had to be interrupted because of Bernstein's commitment to compose the score for *Candide*, the four men were reunited early in 1957.

To Bernstein, creating *West Side Story* was like walking on a tightrope. The important thing was to keep it from ever getting too poetic or too realistic. In the "Rumble," for instance, the composer felt that if it "had been too balletic, we

*West Side Story (1957).
The Jets and their girls dance
in the local drugstore just
before their rumble with the
rival gang known as the
Sharks. Larry Kert, seated
alone at a table, is worried
about the outcome. (Costumes
by Irene Sharaff; setting by
Oliver Smith.)*

Photo By Fred Fehl

would have fallen off on one side—all you'd have is just another ballet. And if it had been too realistic, we would have fallen off on the other side—there would have been no poetry to it, no art."

The great triumph of *West Side Story*, which was presented on Broadway in September 1957, was that the subject was treated impressionistically while at the same time giving the illusion of reality. The costumes, the settings, the dialogue, the music, and the dances were all combined with a theatrical expressiveness that transcended mere naturalism to establish a mood of genuine lyricism. Here were young city toughs moving with agility through the dance patterns, spewing out their pent-up frustrations and revealing secret longings through music that could be, by turns, both nervously agitated ("America," "Cool") and almost ethereal ("Maria," "Tonight"). It made few compromises, yet *West Side Story* did enjoy a two-year run on Broadway and returned in 1960 after a successful cross-country tour.

With time for only six Broadway scores in thirty-three years, Bernstein has nevertheless left a strong mark on the theatrical scene, particularly as something of a *minnesinger* of Manhattan. The brash spirit of *On the Town*, the nostalgia of *Wonderful Town*, and the jagged impact of *West Side Story* reveal a city of many faces and a composer of many facets. Perhaps only one not native to the city could capture it so well in music. "This town still gets me," Bernstein exclaims. "No wonder I keep composing about it. It's so dramatic and alive. New York! The amazing, confusing beauty of the place!"

Paradoxically, this concern with one geographical locale has not endowed Bernstein's creations with any discernible personal style. Partly due to his knowledge of, and his involvement in, all kinds of music, Bernstein has shown a certain eclecticism in his work for the theatre that has made it less of an individual expression than highly technical, remarkably effective music with each score sounding almost as if it were the work of a different man.

"Out of our natural musical theatre," the composer once said, "which is wholly an outgrowth of our culture, is emerging our opera, intelligible to all." The firmness of this belief would suggest that Bernstein is the successor to Kurt Weill, and, indeed, *West Side Story* is a direct extension of the *Zeitoper* that Weill had been instrumental in creating in Germany. Unfortunately, Bernstein has been unable to devote all his prodigious energies to the musical theatre. In spite of his multiple activities, however, he has always brought to his work for the Broadway stage the same kind of affection, originality, and painstaking care that has distinguished his career in every one of the numerous musical pursuits to which he is devoted.

Frederick Loewe and Alan Jay Lerner.

Photo by Karsh

CHAPTER NINETEEN

ALAN JAY LERNER
and FREDERICK LOEWE

THE SPECIAL CHEMISTRY that takes place between two individuals to enable them to produce a successful blending of words and music has never been distilled in any laboratory's test tube. Some famous song-writing teams—Rodgers and Hammerstein, for example, or Schwartz and Dietz—have had markedly similar backgrounds and outlooks; others—Rodgers and Hart, the Gershwin brothers—may have had similar, and even identical, backgrounds, but they have been made up of men with almost completely different personalities and tastes.

In background, in personality, and in temperament, Alan Jay Lerner and Frederick Loewe would seem to be two of the most dissimilar men in the theatre. Loewe, Lerner's senior by fourteen years, was born in Berlin, on June 10, 1904. He was the son of Edmund Loewe, a well-known Viennese tenor who sang in the popular operettas of the day. By the time he was seven, young Fritz could pick out tunes on the piano. He studied in Berlin under Ferruccio Busoni (Kurt Weill's teacher), Eugène d'Albert, and Emil Nikolaus von Reznicek. At thirteen, he was the youngest piano soloist ever to appear with the Berlin Symphony. Two years later, he wrote a popular song, "Katrina," which became one of the biggest song hits throughout Europe.

In 1924, Frederick Loewe confidently journeyed to New York to continue his career. His difficulties with the English language and his seeming inability to write in an "American" style made it extremely hard for him to adjust to the new country. Instead of continuing his career as a composer, he was soon forced to take a job as a pianist at a Greenwich Village nightclub, and, for a time, he was even a bus boy in a cafeteria.

With his career in music apparently over, Loewe, a solidly built, athletic man, next became a riding instructor at a New Hampshire resort and, later, a prize fighter at a Brooklyn athletic club. His pugilistic career, however, was painfully terminated when his teeth were knocked out in his ninth bout. After a few years in the West (where he was a cow puncher, gold prospector, and horseback mail deliverer), Loewe took a job as a pianist on board ships transporting thirsty citizens from Miami to Havana during Prohibition. When repeal ended this ferrying service in the early Thirties, he became a pianist at a *Brauhaus* in Yorkville, New York City's German section.

During this period, he again began to compose. As one acquaintance remembers, "Even though Fritz wasn't doing well in those days, I knew he had a tremendous inner fire just burning to create great songs." To help his career, Loewe joined the Lambs, the famous theatrical club. There he became friendly with Dennis King, who was so fond of one of Loewe's songs, "Love Tiptoed Through My Heart," that he sang it in the play *Petticoat Fever*.

The following year, 1935, Loewe formed a partnership with Earle Crooker, a radio and Hollywood script-writer, who had contributed lyrics to *The Little Show*. Their first song, "A Waltz Was Born in Vienna," was danced by Gomez and Winona in the unsuccessful *Illustrators' Show*. It was subsequently added to the score for *Salute to Spring*, an original musical Loewe and Crooker wrote for the St. Louis Opera Association.

Salute to Spring was one of the most popular attractions offered in St. Louis in the summer of 1937. Producer Dwight Deere Wiman was so delighted with their work that he signed Loewe and Crooker to create the songs for *Great Lady*, a costly operetta which he produced on Broadway the following year. Neither music nor lyrics were distinguished, nor was there much merit in the story of how Eliza Bowan, a notorious adventuress of the early nineteenth century, broke into New York society by marrying the wealthy Stephen Jumel. Musical comedy sentimentalists may have been delighted to see Norma Terris, Irene Bordoni, and Helen Ford in the same play, but the future stars of the ballet, opera, and musical theatre were in the singing and dancing groups. The dancers, led by André Eglevsky, included Alicia Alonso, Nora Kaye, Paul Godkin, and Jerome Robbins;

Dorothy Kirsten and Walter Cassel were among the singers.

It had taken Loewe almost fourteen years to get the opportunity to compose his first Broadway score. Unfortunately, *Great Lady* closed after twenty performances, and he was once again forced to return to his job as a piano player in a restaurant. Then, one day in 1942, he introduced himself to a young writer named Alan Jay Lerner.

Unlike Loewe, Lerner had never had to spend years toiling at strange occupations in an alien country. He was born in New York City, on August 31, 1918, the son of the founder of a chain of women's specialty shops, the Lerner Shops. Instead of smothering his ability, the advantages of wealth and education only instilled in him a strong determination to succeed unaided by any parental assistance. Lerner was only eight when he first made up his mind to become a writer for the theatre. His father neither opposed nor encouraged this ambition; his only advice to his son was that he would have to work hard at his profession if he really wanted to succeed. Young Lerner learned to play the piano at an early age, and later took courses at the Juilliard School of Music. At Harvard, he wrote music and lyrics for two Hasty Pudding shows. Two songs were even considered worthy enough to be commercially published: "Chance to Dream" from the 1938 production, *So Proudly We Hail*, and "From Me to You" from the 1939 show, *Fair Enough*. After graduating Lerner became a radio script-writer, turning out about five hundred scripts in two years.

Desperation brought Loewe to Lerner in 1942. Henry Duffy, a producer, wanted to present a series of original musical comedies at a theatre he owned in Detroit. The previous year he had offered a musical adaptation of Barry Conners' play, *The Patsy*, in San Francisco, but he wanted an entirely different treatment of the same story for the Detroit production. Two weeks before rehearsals were to begin, Duffy met with Loewe at the Lambs Club to discuss the possibility of using the bulk of the Loewe-Crooker score for *Salute to Spring*. What Loewe needed to ensure the commission, however, was a librettist who could also update some of the earlier lyrics. Because he admired the sketches and lyrics Lerner had contributed to *The Lambs Gambol*, a revue put on by Lambs Club members, Loewe immediately thought of him for the new project. Seeing Lerner at the club that day playing cards, the composer introduced himself with the businesslike: "You are Alan Jay Lerner? You write good lyrics. I am Frederick Loewe. I have something to say to you."

Two days later, they were on a train bound for Detroit, the show was written within the prescribed two weeks, and in October, 1942, Detroit audiences saw the initial collaboration of Alan Jay Lerner and Frederick Loewe—*Life of the Party*, starring Dorothy Stone and Charles Collins. There was nothing memorable about the musical, but Lerner's work convinced Loewe that they might succeed as a team. For their next musical, *What's Up*—and for every one of their collaborations since then—Alan Jay Lerner wrote the book and lyrics and Frederick Loewe composed the music.

What's Up opened in November, 1943. Even with Jimmy Savo in the cast and George Balanchine as director, it was not an auspicious debut. Their next work, however, *The Day Before Spring*, turned out to be a highly literate and imaginative fantasy which just missed being a hit. Wolcott Gibbs called it "my kind of show," adding that "the songs that go with it are fresh and bright and seem to spring spontaneously from the action rather than from spasmodic impulses on the part of the singers."

The Day Before Spring was more of an artistic than a commercial success.

Photo by Eileen Darby—Graphic House

What's Up *(1943).*
Johnny Morgan as an American sergeant and Jimmy Savo as an East Indian potentate.

Brigadoon was both. Lerner, long fond of the works of Sir James M. Barrie, had been eager to write a musical with a Scottish setting. "One day, while working on *The Day Before Spring*, Fritz mentioned something about faith moving mountains. This started me thinking. For a while, I had a play about faith moving a mountain. From there we went to all sorts of miracles occurring through faith, and, eventually, faith moved a town."

In less skilled hands, the legend of the sleeping Scottish town that awakens once in every one hundred years could easily have been too precious or maudlin, but so ably were the theatrical ingredients blended—story, music, lyrics, dancing, settings, costumes—that the result became what Brooks Atkinson unequivocably labeled a "vibrant work of art." Never before had Agnes de Mille's talents been better realized than in the way she made each dance sequence an integral part of the story, most notably in the Sword Dance, the Chase, and the Funeral Dance. Robert Lewis directed *Brigadoon* with rare sensitivity, and

Photo by Vandamm

Oliver Smith's evocative settings enhanced the total effect.

The score that Frederick Loewe and Alan Jay Lerner created was especially distinguished for its appropriateness to locale, story, and characters. Lerner's lyrics captured much of the highland flavor, and his ability to use simple, genuine imagery was marked in the songs "Brigadoon," "Come to Me, Bend to Me," and "The Heather on the Hill." Loewe's music was equally suffused with the atmosphere of the play, and, when required, attained a certain eloquence. The wisdom of the authors' approach was notably demonstrated in the way the one sophisticated song, "Almost Like Being in Love," was first introduced by the rich American tourist (played by David Brooks) before being reprised by the simple highland maid (Marion Bell).

Soon after writing *Love Life* with Kurt Weill in 1948, Lerner began thinking of an idea for a musical he could write with Loewe. He was determined that it would have a story with a positive point of view, "a musical that would embrace all the robustness and vitality and cockeyed courage that is so much a part of our American heritage." To both Lerner and Loewe, the saga of the California gold rush filled that specification.

Paint Your Wagon opened in New York in November, 1951. With the exception of director Daniel Mann, almost all of the principal members of the production staff had been associated with *Brigadoon*—producer Cheryl Crawford, choreographer Agnes de Mille, designer Oliver Smith, musical director Franz Allers, and musical arranger Ted Royal. James Barton, who had not appeared in a Broadway musical in over twenty years, played the part of a grizzled old prospector, and Olga San Juan appeared as his daughter. Throughout the score, the songs projected a genuine flavor of Americana; many of them, in fact, seemed to be not Broadway show tunes but authentic folk ballads handed down from the miners themselves. The booming theme song, "Wand'rin' Star," sung at the beginning and end of the play, served as an appropriate frame for such numbers as the ardent "I Talk to the Trees"; the rushing legend "They Call the Wind Maria"; the misty-eyed "I Still See Elisa," touchingly sung by Barton; the rousing dances "Whoop-Ti-Ay" and "Hand Me Down That Can o' Beans";

and the almost chilling expression of loneliness, "Another Autumn."

In their research for *Paint Your Wagon*, Lerner and Loewe became so steeped in the subject that they incorporated actual incidents and miners' dialogue as part of the play. Possibly, as Lerner later admitted, they may have done too much research. According to Walter Kerr, "Writing an *integrated* musical comedy— where people are believable and the songs are logically introduced—is no excuse for not being funny from time to time. But the librettist of *Paint Your Wagon* seems to be more interested in the authenticity of his background than in the joy of his audience."

Including *Paint Your Wagon*, Lerner's books for his first five musicals had all been based on original stories. He became convinced that the main reason why some of his musicals were not more successful was that they had faulty librettos. Quite logically, he decided that henceforth he would adapt his stories from plays or novels that had already won favor with both critics and the public. His opportunity came in 1952, when Gabriel Pascal, the celebrated Hun-

garian movie producer, suggested to him that he transform Bernard Shaw's *Pygmalion* into a musical play.

Pascal, the only man ever to win Shaw's permission to film his plays, had made a motion picture of *Pygmalion* in the mid-Thirties. Sometime after that he became interested in producing a musical version of the work. Shaw, who had voiced public indignation over Oscar Straus's *The Chocolate Soldier* (based on his *Arms and the Man*), had always been unalterably opposed to the idea of a musical *Pygmalion*. In 1948, when a friend once interceded in behalf of two other writers, the playwright shot back a typically Shavian response: "I absolutely forbid such outrage. If *Pygmalion* is not good enough for your friends with its own verbal music, their talent must be altogether extraordinary. Let them try Mozart's *Cosi fan tutti*, or at least Offenbach's *Grand Duchess*."

After Shaw's death in 1950, Pascal felt free to proceed with his plan. In rapid succession, he importuned such distinguished writers of the musical stage as Noël Coward, Cole Porter, E. Y. Harburg and Fred Saidy, Schwartz and

Paint Your Wagon (1951). Agnes de Mille's lively dance to "Hand Me Down That Can o' Beans." (Costumes by Motley; setting by Oliver Smith.)

Photo by Karger—Pix

Dietz, and Rodgers and Hammerstein. Each one, however, turned him down.* When Lerner and Loewe finally agreed to undertake the project, the producer did not even have the rights to present the play as a musical. So persuasive were his arguments, however, that the Shaw estate granted him a two-year option.

Lerner and Loewe at first could not agree on the proper approach to the Shaw work. After struggling with it for about three months, they had to admit to Pascal that they saw no way in which the adaption could be accomplished. For the next two years, Lerner and Loewe went their separate ways, each becoming involved in projects that were never realized. Lerner tried to transform *Li'l Abner*† into a musical, first with Arthur Schwartz, and later with Burton Lane. Loewe joined with Joseph Fields, Jerome Chodorov, and Leo Robin in attempting a musical version of Paul Vincent Carroll's *Saints and Sinners*.

While Lerner and Loewe were occupied with other pursuits, Pascal continued his vain hunt for other writers who might be induced to make a musical of *Pygmalion*. It had become such an obsession with him that he obtained a two-year extension after his option had expired. The tenacious producer, however, never lived to see his dream fulfilled. He died in New York in the summer of 1954, soon after beginning another search.

Ironically, it was about the time of Pascal's death that Lerner and Loewe resumed their partnership to make one last attempt at setting *Pygmalion* to music. The problem, according to Lerner, "was how to enlarge it into a big musical without hurting its content. It was a big sur-

prise—we hardly had to enlarge the plot at all. We just added what Shaw had happening offstage." Once they found the way to do it, the authors went ahead with their adaptation, even though they no longer had Pascal or the rights. Herman Levin, who was to have produced *Li'l Abner*, became the new sponsor— but only after clearing a number of legal hurdles involving the Pascal estate.

From the very beginning, Rex Harrison was the choice of Lerner and Loewe to play Professor Higgins. Following Shaw's specifications that Eliza Doolittle should be played by an actress between eighteen and twenty, the authors diligently auditioned every girl in her late teens they could find. While so occupied, they received word that Mary Martin was interested in the part. "Forgetting Shaw's directions," Levin recalls, "we paged Mary. She wasn't twenty, but she was box-office dynamite. Mary quickly dissipated any qualms we may have had about flouting Shaw's blueprint. Lerner and Loewe played five songs for her and she didn't like any of them." They next tested a young English actress, Julie Andrews, then making an impressive Broadway debut in Sandy Wilson's *The Boy Friend*. Although she fitted Shaw's concept perfectly, they still were not completely sure that she was right for the part. After auditioning about fifty English girls in London, however, the producer and the writers returned to New York and signed Miss Andrews to a two-year contract.

In October, 1955, a press release announced the forthcoming adaptation, then known as *My Lady Liza*. Rehearsals began early the following January. Moss Hart was the director, Hanya Holm the choreographer, Oliver Smith the set designer, Cecil Beaton the costume designer, and Franz Allers the musical director. The supporting cast was headed by Stanley Holloway (Alfred P. Doolittle), Cathleen Nesbitt (Professor Higgins' mother), and Robert Coote (Col. Picker-

---

*Harburg refused to do the adaptation because he felt *Pygmalion* was a perfect work of art and should not be touched. Hammerstein's reason was based on Shaw's insistence that it was not a love story, and he did not want to oppose the author's wishes.

†The rights to *Li'l Abner* were presently acquired by Norman Panama, Melvin Frank, and Michael Kidd. With a score by Johnny Mercer and Gene de Paul, the musical opened in New York in the fall of 1956. It had a run of almost 700 performances.

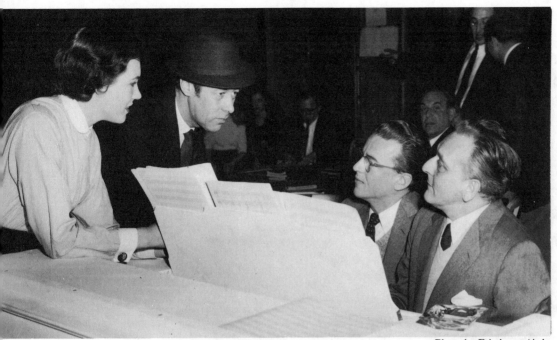

My Fair Lady (1956).
The first day of rehearsals on
the roof of the New
Amsterdam Theatre. Julie
Andrews, Rex Harrison, Alan
Jay Lerner, and Frederick
Loewe. Moss Hart can be seen
just behind Lerner and Loewe.

Photo by Friedman-Abeles

ing). In New Haven, two songs, "Say a Prayer" (later in the film, *Gigi*) and "Come to the Ball," and a ballet, "Decorating Eliza," were cut. The New York première took place March 15, 1956, at the Mark Hellinger Theatre.

"For years, Fritz and I floundered around, trying to find our natural way of writing," Lerner once confessed in an interview in the New York *Times*. "*My Fair Lady* revealed it to us. The property dictates it. The characters in the story. We are the means by which they express themselves, not vice versa. When we felt we really knew them, then we began to work on the score. We try to find some thought of a character that motivates him and, in turn, the story."

This approach is evident throughout. In the songs for Professor Higgins, there is the biting disdain for his inferiors in "Why Can't the English?"; his witty defense of his own way of life in "I'm an Ordinary Man"; his petulant admiration for masculine traits in "A Hymn to Him"; and, in the simply stated "I've Grown Accustomed to Her Face," his admission that he has finally fallen in love with Eliza. Eliza's character is also revealed through song. First, as a poor flower-seller, she dreams only of a life of physical comforts in "Wouldn't It Be Loverly?" Later, after having gone through the rigors of the professor's speech classes, she expresses her secret defiance in "Just You Wait," and her thrill at having succeeded in speaking correctly in "I Could Have Danced All Night." The girl's impatience with all men bursts through in "Show Me," and, at the end, in a bolt of sarcastic fury, she tells Higgins her real opinion of him in "Without You."

The secondary characters are equally well served by the songs. For Alfred Doolittle, Eliza's philosophical, high-spirited father, Lerner and Loewe created two appropriate music-hall turns, "With a Little Bit of Luck" and "Get Me to the Church on Time." For the faithful Freddy Eynsford-Hill (played by Dennis King's son, John Michael King) they wrote the worshipful ballad "On the Street Where You Live."

The most musically and dramatically effective episode comes midway through the first act when Eliza is at last able to say, "The rain in Spain stays mainly in the plain," without a Cockney accent. As Walter Kerr described the scene, "You

Photo by Friedman-Abeles

My Fair Lady *(1956).*
The first scene between Eliza Doolittle (Julie Andrews) and Professor Higgins (Rex Harrison), as they meet outside the Royal Opera House at Covent Garden. (Costumes by Cecil Beaton.)

Stanley Holloway (as Alfred P. Doolittle) explains his philosophy in "With a Little Bit of Luck" to cronies Gordon Dilworth and Rod McLennan.

Eliza (Julie Andrews), Professor Higgins (Rex Harrison), and Col. Pickering (Robert Coote) join in a spontaneous dance to the tune of "The Rain in Spain." This was, in Wolcott Gibbs's opinion, "just about the most brilliantly successful scene I remember seeing in a musical comedy."

Photo by Friedman-Abeles

listen astonished—because you believe in her so completely that you didn't really suppose she could make it. Suddenly, her delight becomes yours. And when Mr. Harrison, together with an equally astonished Robert Coote, bounces irresistibly to the center of the stage and begins to kick out a tango rhythm to the sound she has just made, there is no controlling the joy in the theatre."

The unprecedented success of *My Fair Lady*, which gave Lerner and Loewe a stature almost equal to that of Rodgers and Hammerstein, produced a philosophical attitude in both men. "Neither Fritz nor I believe we're *that* good," said Lerner. "It's just that the time was ripe for something gay and theatrical, something that was not two lonely people finding each other in a dark alley. *My Fair Lady* filled the bill."

How does one follow *My Fair Lady*? If a tale originally inspired by the legendary Pygmalion, King of Cyprus, could succeed so spectacularly, why not a musical based on another legendary king, Arthur of Britain? Lerner's specific source was T. H. White's *The Once and Future King*, though he was indebted to it more for approach and style than for plot. In partnership with director Moss Hart, Lerner and Loewe produced the musical themselves, and gave it the name of Arthur's court and castle, Camelot.

Trouble plagued the enterprise from the start. During the out-of-town tryout Lerner was hospitalized with bleeding ulcers and Hart was felled by a heart attack. Once Lerner was well enough to be discharged, he assumed responsibility for the direction which, among other things, included slicing off more than an hour from the show's original four-hour running time. After two months on the road, the cost of the production had soared to a record $635,000. But these *were* the people who had created *My Fair Lady*, and there *was* Fair Lady Julie Andrews, *plus* Richard Burton. Little wonder that ex-

pectations ran so high that the pre-opening ticket sale was well over $3 million.

A distinct let-down was felt following the December, 1960, première at the Majestic Theatre. The reviews ran the gamut, with the majority praising the richness of the decor but decrying the poverty of the plot. Obviously the play wasn't ready for the opening and obviously something had to be done—fast. Within a month a partially recovered Moss Hart began the major task of overhauling. Lerner wrote and rewrote, shaved another twelve minutes from the script, and, at the suggestion of critic John Chapman, substituted a more upbeat but still consistent ending. The result was that—aided by the huge advance ticket sale—*Camelot* soon found its audience, and ended its Broadway run nearly 900 performances later.

Few of the songs seemed to be fully appreciated when the musical was first unveiled. The stirring saga of "Camelot" and the jaunty "What Do the Simple Folk Do?" caused a slight stir and, thanks to a pop recording, "If Ever I Would Leave You," that throbbing declaration of multi-seasonal devotion managed to catch on. After a while, "How to Handle a Woman," "The Lusty Month of May," "Follow Me," and "I Wonder What the King Is Doing Tonight" became better known and won deserved favor.

Except for the 1973 stage adaptation of their film, *Gigi*, for which Lerner and Loewe contributed four additional songs, *Camelot* remains the team's last stage collaboration. On reviewing their contributions, we find that their musicals were, to a great extent, modern counterparts of the Viennese school of Lehár and Strauss and Herbert. But instead of pasteboard characters, theirs were believable and three-dimensional. Instead of illogical, absurd stories, theirs dealt coherently with a variety of adult themes. Instead of bland, predictable lyrics mated to fre-

My Fair Lady *(1956).*
The scene at the Ascot Races.
Freddy Eynsford-Hill and
Henry Higgins's mother are
amused at Liza's difficulties
with the English language.
John Michael King, Julie
Andrews, and Cathleen
Nesbitt. (Costumes by Cecil
Beaton.)

Photo by Friedman-Abeles

Photo by Friedman-Abeles   Camelot *(1960).*
As the queen, Julie Andrews
listens while King Arthur
(Richard Burton) sings
"What Do the Simple Folk
Do?" (Costumes by Adrian
and Tony Duquette.)

quently unmotivated melodies, their songs were created to serve a dramatic purpose and to spring naturally from the characters who sang them.

Modern though their plays were in approach and execution, the distinguishing trait of Lerner and Loewe was their ability to preserve the traditions and values of a distant past—the innocent faith of a 200-year-old Scottish village that had vanished in the highland mist . . . the foolhardy determination of gold prospectors in mid-nineteenth century California . . . the triumph of will that can break down London's social barriers in the period before World War I . . . the doomed chivalry of King Arthur's round table . . . the changing social structure of a bubbling *fin-de-siècle* Paris. Through these works, bygone places and people come excitingly alive, eternally romantic and appealing.

Apart from sporadic reunions, Lerner and Loewe, chiefly because of temperamental differences, dissolved their partnership in 1962. Loewe has remained relatively inactive, but Lerner is still very much a part of the musical-theatre scene, though with considerably diminished success. He attempted a collaboration with Richard Rodgers that didn't work out, then joined Burton Lane for *On a Clear Day You Can See Forever*. Though the songs were radiantly melodious and Barbara Harris scored a personal success, the show itself was a somewhat uneasy amalgam of *Bridey Murphy* and *Berkeley Square* and barely lasted the 1965/66 season. Four years later, Lerner joined with composer Andre Previn for a suitably stylish musical based on the life of fashion designer Coco Chanel. *Coco*, however, was almost entirely dependent upon its star, Katharine Hepburn, whose magnetic drawing power enabled the show to remain open almost a year. The ambitious *1600 Pennsylvania Avenue*, which teamed Lerner with Leonard Bernstein, was an awkward history lesson dealing with various White House occupants. It tarried a week in 1976. The resolutely old-fashioned *Carmelina* (1979), reuniting Lerner with Burton Lane, was a frothy look at postwar Italy that fared only slightly better.

Despite setbacks and even without Frederick Loewe, it is evident that the past continues to hold an irresistible fascination for one of the most forward looking and painstaking of contemporary theatre craftsmen.

Jule Styne, Betty Comden and
Adolph Green.

CHAPTER TWENTY

JULE STYNE
BETTY COMDEN
and ADOLPH GREEN

THERE ARE MANY REASONS for the reduction in the number of Broadway musicals since the 1920's and the corollary lessening in the output of major theatrical composers. Among the most apparent have been the increasingly longer runs of hit shows, the greater time spent on all the component parts of the production, the competition from other entertainment media, and, possibly the strongest deterrent of all, the mounting production costs.

As a consequence, some striking paradoxes emerge regarding the musical theatre of the Twenties and the Fifties, particularly as reflected in the career of composer Jule Styne. By working on twelve Broadway musicals over a period of about eleven and a half years, Vincent Youmans was the least prolific among the leading composers of his day; by working on eight Broadway musicals over a similar period of time, Styne established himself as the most prolific composer of the post-World War II years. In fact, judging by the popularity of his shows, he is undoubtably one of the most successful musical-comedy composers of all time. The total number of original Broadway performances of Styne's first sixteen musi-cals easily exceeds that of the entire seventeen musicals with complete scores by Irving Berlin, or the twenty-three with scores by George Gershwin, or the twenty-five with scores by Rodgers and Hart.

No yardstick is intended here other than to point out the changing face of Broadway both in the productivity of its writers and the longevity of their creations. Yet it is strange that with a record of accomplishment such as this that the name Jule Styne is still less familiar to the average person than the aforementioned Messrs. Youmans, Berlin, Gershwin or Rodgers. Here, too, the reason is tied in with the theatrical changes that have developed through the years. Today it isn't just enough to create a varied and tuneful collection of songs to keep a show running. The composer and lyricist contribute only one part—an indispensable one to be sure, but still only a part—of the total creation. A musical succeeds because of its overall style and the way all the components have been pulled into shape, not, generally speaking, because of the predominance of any single factor.

Except possibly the star. And that's another reason for Styne's lack of due recognition. Almost every one of his hits has been dominated by the personality of an authentic star—or two authentic stars. *High Button Shoes* had the swaggering clowning of Phil Silvers and the vivacity of Nanette Fabray. *Gentlemen Prefer Blondes* became a vehicle for a saucer-eyed comedienne named Carol Channing. *Two on the Aisle* gave us both Bert Lahr and Dolores Gray. *Peter Pan* relied for much of its appeal on the charms of Mary Martin. *Bells Are Ringing* owed its marathon run primarily to the incandescent Judy Holliday. *Gypsy* offered Ethel Merman at the height of her powers. *Funny Girl* revealed the magnetism of Barbra Streisand. *Fade Out—Fade In* was known as "the Carol Burnett Show." And *Hallelujah, Baby!*, though it aimed at significance, owed its limited success to the sparkling performance of Leslie Uggams.

There is, of course, ample evidence that the stature of Jule Styne is being more and more recognized despite the enumerated roadblocks. Surely his work for *Gypsy* and *Funny Girl* has clearly

High Button Shoes *(1947). Phil Silvers, as Harrison Floy, and Nanette Fabray, as Sara Longstreet. Of Mr. Silvers, Brooks Atkinson wrote: "He is an uproarious comic. He has the speed, the drollery, and the shell-game style of a honky tonk buffoon." (Costumes by Miles White; setting by Oliver Smith.)*

demonstrated that musical scores such as these are equally as important to the artistic merits of their respective productions as the stars. In these two musicals especially, it is evident that in quality as well as in proficiency and popularity, Jule Styne is in the front ranks of composers for the modern musical theatre.

Styne was born Jules Stein in London, England, on December 31, 1905. He had his first taste of the theatre at the age of three when he bounded up on the stage to sing a duet with Sir Harry Lauder, the legendary Scottish entertainer. When he was eight, young Jule and his parents moved to Chicago. There the youth quickly showed such musical talent that within a year he was guest piano soloist with the Chicago and Detroit symphonies. At thirteen, he won a scholarship to the Chicago College of Music where he studied piano, harmony, composition and theory.

In the Twenties, Styne became fascinated by the songs being written by the rising young composers of Tin Pan Alley and Broadway. Responding to this kind of music to a far greater extent than he did to the works of classical composers, he abandoned his concert career to become a pianist in a dance band. In 1931, he organized his own orchestra, for which he served not only as leader but also as arranger and occasional song writer (his first song and his first hit, "Sunday," had been composed in 1926). Writing eventually became more important to Styne than fronting an orchestra; in the mid-Thirties he disbanded his group to sign a contract with Twentieth Century-Fox as both composer and vocal coach.

During the Thirties and Forties, Styne turned out many hits for the movies. With lyricist Frank Loesser, he wrote "I Don't Want To Walk Without You, Baby"; later, with Sammy Cahn, he created a string of Hit Parade leaders including "I've Heard That Song Before," "I'll Walk Alone," "It's Been a Long

Long Time," "Time After Time," and "It's Magic." Living in California was pleasant and profitable, but Styne deeply felt the lack of recognition or of any artistic fulfillment. He had only one ambition: he wanted to write a Broadway score. (As Styne once said, "In Hollywood you're a song writer; in New York you're a composer.") Styne and Cahn received their first opportunity in 1944, when they supplied the songs for the Broadway-bound *Glad to See You*, but the show never made it any closer to New York than Boston.

High Button Shoes, three years later, not only opened on Broadway but remained there for about two and one-half years. With a book by Stephen Longstreet, it was a bright, funny, though formula musical heavy with nostalgic charm. Its main appeal was the brash performance of Phil Silvers as con man Harrison Floy and the hilarious Keystone Kops ballet devised by Jerome Robbins. Of the songs, "Papa, Won't You Dance with Me?" and "I Still Get Jealous," both engagingly performed by Nanette Fabray and Jack McCauley, are still recalled for their infectious period flavor.

Despite the success of *High Button Shoes*, Cahn preferred to return to the sunkissed hills of Hollywood, and Styne formed a winning but brief partnership with lyricist Leo Robin. For *Gentlemen Prefer Blondes*, produced in 1949, they contributed a lively, atmospheric score perfectly suited to Anita Loos's hedonistic tale of the torrid Twenties. Yet it was Carol Channing, as gold-digging Lorelei Lee, who captivated both critics and public, particularly with her renditions of "Diamonds Are a Girl's Best Friend" and "A Little Girl from Little Rock." Miss Channing, whose only previous experience on Broadway had been as Eve Arden's understudy in *Let's Face It!* and in the Charles Gaynor revue, *Lend an Ear*, was elevated to stardom during the run.

Culver Pictures, Inc.

In 1951, Jule Styne began his association with his most frequent collaborators, Betty Comden and Adolph Green. The inseparable lyricists had met thirteen years before while Miss Comden was a drama major at New York University and Green was a self-styled bum. From then on, neither one has ever written a lyric or a libretto or a screenplay without the other, surely the most remarkable example of tenacious teamwork in the annals of the musical stage.

Betty Comden was born in Brooklyn on May 3, 1915; Adolph Green first saw daylight in the Bronx on December 2, 1915. Originally their mutual ambition was to scale the heights of thespian stardom and, to that end, they formed a quintet of acting and singing comedians known as The Revuers. Another member of the troupe, Judy Tuvim, a bright-eyed, baby-voiced blonde, later changed her last name to Holliday. Because they couldn't afford writers, Comden and Green found themselves dreaming up most of the scripts and the lyrics. The act was a hit at the Village Vanguard, flopped at the Rainbow Room, and disbanded after a disastrous fling at the movies.

Gentlemen Prefer Blondes (1949).
Lorelei Lee (Carol Channing) demonstrates her prowess on a diminutive Frenchman (Mort Marshall). Looking on is another Frenchman (Howard Morris). According to John Chapman, Miss Channing "got the most enthusiastic notices of any musicomedienne of this generation." (Costumes by Miles White; setting by Oliver Smith.)

Comden and Green, however, stuck together. It was while appearing at the Blue Angel, a New York supperclub, that they were approached by a young composer named Leonard Bernstein to collaborate on the score for a musical that would become known as *On the Town*. Bernstein, a former roommate of Green's, had been asked to expand his ballet, *Fancy Free*, into a musical comedy, and he was firm in his conviction that none but Comden and Green would do for the story and lyrics. The team promptly gave up their night club performing career in favor of writing—but they also made sure that two fat parts in the show would be played by Betty Comden and Adolph Green.

On the Town was a resounding smash, and Comden and Green were immediately hailed as the freshest, brightest lyric writers of the year. But the cheers quickly died. In December 1945, almost exactly one year after *On the Town*, the team had a less-than-brilliant entry in *Billion Dollar Baby*, a spoof of the Twenties with a score by Morton Gould. Even more disastrous was *Bonanza Bound*, which they wrote two years later with composer (later movie producer) Saul Chaplin. It folded in Philadelphia. Hollywood—finally—beckoned, and for about two years Comden and Green were gainfully employed as scenarists and/or lyricists for such M-G-M musicals as *Good News, On the Town*, and *The Barkleys of Broadway*.

The team returned to New York in 1951. That year saw the first Broadway score with lyrics by Comden and Green, music by Jule Styne. The musical, *Two on the Aisle*, was a revue with a show biz

Bells Are Ringing (1956). Sydney Chaplin and Judy Holliday perform an impromptu entertainment for passersby in New York's Central Park. (Costumes and setting by Raoul Pène du Bois.)

Photo by Friedman-Abeles

slant for which the lyricists also contributed most of the sketches. The entertainment's main attraction was Bert Lahr hilariously ranging from impersonating Queen Victoria to playing a member of New York's Sanitation Department who lives in constant dread of being demoted to the dump. Among the songs blasted out by Dolores Gray was an inspired creation, "If You Hadn't but You Did," a rapid-fire apologia detailing the reasons why a distraught woman has just bumped off her husband.

Styne was both producer and composer of *Hazel Flagg*, a disappointing musical version of the celebrated movie, *Nothing Sacred*. Ben Hecht adapted the story from his own screenplay, and Bob Hilliard supplied the lyrics. The score was not on a level with most of Styne's work, but it did contain an especially affectionate tribute to New York City, "Every Street's a Boulevard in Old New York," sung and soft-shoed by Jack Whiting as a dapper Jimmy Walker-type mayor. Just fourteen days after the opening of *Hazel Flagg*—on February 25, 1953, to be exact—Comden and Green plus Leonard Bernstein had their second smash in a row, *Wonderful Town*.

The following year, when Jerome Robbins decided to stage a new production of Sir James M. Barrie's *Peter Pan* with Mary Martin as Peter and Cyril Ritchard as Captain Hook, he initially planned to use only a few incidental songs by composer Mark ("Moose") Charlap and lyricist Carolyn Leigh. When the production began to evolve into a full-scale musical, he went to Styne, Comden and Green to supply the additional songs. Following its world première in San Francisco, *Peter Pan* opened in New York in October. The reviews were generally favorable and Miss Martin won special acclaim for her ability to sing and fly through the air at the same time. The play's disappointing run (152 performances) was due primarily to the fact that it had opened only about

four and one-half years after the highly successful Jean Arthur-Boris Karloff version. That one had five songs written by Leonard Bernstein. (A 1979 revival of the Styne-Comden-Green-Charlap-Leigh musical, starring Sandy Duncan, became the longest running—or flying— *Peter Pan* ever staged on Broadway.)

Styne, Comden, Green and Robbins were reunited in 1956 for *Bells Are Ringing*. Ever since Betty Comden and Adolph Green first worked with Judy Holliday in their night club act, they had hoped someday to write a musical especially for her. Their inspiration came when they thought of casting Judy as a meddlesome switchboard operator at a telephone answering service. The resultant libretto owed much to the already proven *Wonderful Town* formula of depicting New York as just a gay, warm-hearted small town, where people dance and sing in subways, and where a mousey telephone operator can find both adventure and the man of her dreams.* Miss Holliday, in her first musical, had an irresistible winsomeness that helped audiences overlook many of the sophomoric twists of the plot. Even her untrained singing voice proved remarkably suitable at interpreting the sentiments of such diverse musical contributions as "Is It a Crime?" which satirizes pathetic pleas for happiness, the poignant "The Party's Over," and the rousing "Mammy"-styled "I'm Going Back" ("To The Bonjour Tristesse Brassière Company").

Say, Darling, the fourth Jule Styne-Betty Comden-Adolph Green collaboration, was something of a theatrical oddity. After having co-authored *The Pajama Game*, a musical version of his novel, *7½ Cents*, Richard Bissell wrote another novel based on his adventures in

---

*The leading character in *Bells Are Ringing* was not too dissimilar from the one in *The Five O'Clock Girl*, a Bert Kalmar-Harry Ruby musical comedy hit of 1927. In that show, the heroine worked in a cleaner's shop and carried on a telephone flirtation with an unknown man every day at five.

Photo by Friedman-Abeles

Say, Darling *(1958).*
Director Abe Burrows
explaining a scene to Johnny
Desmond, Vivian Blaine and
David Wayne. (Setting by
Oliver Smith.)

the world of musical comedy. Called *Say, Darling*, it too was converted into a musical, or to be precise, "A Comedy About a Musical." Nine songs were in it, none really distinguished.

Once *Say, Darling* was unveiled on Broadway in the spring of 1958, audiences took special pleasure in trying to identify some of the individuals who had been connected with *The Pajama Game*. David Wayne, as the smalltown author, was obviously Bissell himself. Robert Morse, as a young producer, was doubtlessly Harold Prince, and Jerome Cowan, as an experienced musical comedy director, could be none other than George Abbott. Whether the egotistical song writer (played by Johnny Desmond) was a composite of Richard Adler and Jerry Ross was never made clear, nor was the true identity of the glamorous star of the show (played by Vivian Blaine).

Producer David Merrick first saw the musical possibilities in *Gypsy*, the autobiography of Gypsy Rose Lee, when he read only a chapter from it in *Harper's Magazine*. Without even bothering to read the entire book, he went ahead and secured the theatrical rights. Ethel Merman, who did read the complete biography, was so determined to play the part of Gypsy's ambitious mother that she threatened to shoot anyone else who got the part. She got it without firing a shot. At first *Gypsy* was supposed to have been another Styne, Comden and Green enterprise, but after working on it for some time, all three came to the conclusion that it could not be adapted. Director Jerome Robbins, however, was sure it could—if librettist Arthur Laurents, with whom he had worked on *West Side Story*, were given a crack at it. Then, according to Stephen Sondheim, the eventual lyricist, "they auditioned a number of song writers, including Cy Coleman and Carolyn Leigh, Marshall Barer and Dean Fuller, and myself. I was chosen to do both music and lyrics. That was in April of 1958; Arthur and I began preliminary discussions on the play, awaiting Ethel Merman's approval. She came to New York in August and announced that since she had just been burned by two young writers in *Happy Hunting*, she didn't want to take a chance on an unknown again. Her agent suggested Jule. Arthur and Jerry said they'd accept him if I would. I said no, since I didn't want to be pigeonholed as a lyricist forever. But Oscar Hammerstein, who brought me up, and Arthur, who said that he wouldn't do the show with any other lyricist, persuaded me to stop licking my wounds. And I *did* like the project."

The book of *Gypsy* may have been another variation on the familiar rags-to-riches Cinderella tale, but all those responsible resisted the temptation to make it just another backstage saga about a domineering mother. "This woman is a classic," says Laurents. "What we've got here is a mother who has to learn that if you try to live your children's lives, you'll end up by destroying yourself." Creating music to match the uncompromising libretto was the most severe challenge Styne ever faced as a composer. To achieve the proper musical setting, Styne and Sondheim evolved a superbly congruous score that illuminated all the courage, misplaced ambition, and singleness of purpose of the central character. They achieved this principally through three numbers—"Some People," "Ev'rything's Coming Up Roses," and "Rose's Turn"—each individually compelling, yet each firmly linked to the other, with the haunting "I had a dream" passage effectively used as a leitmotif.

On a lighter though equally meaningful level, the composer and lyricist were able to capture all the tinselled gaudiness of small-time vaudeville and big-time burlesque. One particularly original and striking touch was their variations on a single melody, "May We Entertain You?" (later called "Let Me Entertain You"), which was the "onstage" music for all scenes involving Gypsy Rose Lee and her sister, June Havoc. First, it was sung by two frightened kids as they auditioned for a seedy vaudeville show; later it became a more aggressive invitation as the girls acquired greater experience; finally, it turned into the slinky, blaring accompaniment to Gypsy's first strip tease. Other remarkably effective pieces dealing with varied aspects of show business were "All I Need Is the Girl," the slightly pathetic attempt of a young hoofer to do the suave Fred Astaire bit,

Gypsy (1959).
Rose, the ambitious stage mother, coaches her children, Louise and June, in the first scene of the play. Karen Moore, Ethel Merman, and Jacqueline Mayro. (Costumes by Raoul Pène du Bois.)

Photo by Friedman-Abeles

Gypsy *(1959).*
"Salute to Christmas" à la
Minsky. (Costumes by Raoul
Pène du Bois; setting by Jo
Mielziner.)

and the vulgar, riotous show-stopper, "You Gotta Have a Gimmick," in which three strippers offered highly animated expatiations on their art.

Gypsy did win Jule Styne a measure of long-delayed recognition. It may have had Ethel Merman to attract the customers, but the show could not be called a Merman vehicle. For just as the musical required more of Styne, it also required more of Merman; both met the challenges of the story with gifts never before revealed because they had never before been tested.

For his next two musicals, *Do Re Mi* and *Subways Are for Sleeping*, Styne was rejoined by Comden and Green. Both shows dealt with aspects of modern-day big city life. The former, with a book by Garson Kanin based on his own novel, was a wild satire on the music business with special emphasis on the jukebox industry. The latter, a Comden and Green adaptation of Edmund Love's novel, was a wacky look at the city's disaffected and indigent. Both productions, though cut pretty much to formula, did have rewarding features. *Do Re Mi*, which was reminiscent of *Guys and Dolls* and a few other recent musicals (the solo breast-beating ending was right out of *Gypsy*), gave us two brilliant clowns in Phil Silvers, as Hubie Cram, the pushiest of patsies, and Nancy Walker, as a long-suffering spouse. At a recording session, Phil knowledgeably instructed a group of musicians how and what to play ("You hang around, you learn," was his bland explanation for such expertise), and, at a flashy night club, went into hilariously full details of gangland behavior gleaned from watching old movies on television's Late Late Show. Miss Walker was at her slack-jawed best in the rampageous musical account, "Adventure," in which she contrasted her abandoned middle class security with her frenetic, unpredictable life with Phil. Apart from such specialties, the score contained two standout pieces, the folkish "Cry Like the Wind," sung by Nancy Dussault, and that bit of homey philosophy, "Make Someone Happy," sung by John Reardon.

While *Subways Are for Sleeping* was a far less skillful piece of stagecraft ("woebegone," "painful" and "vapid" were among the critical adjectives used in the press), it did give audiences the opportunity—as did *On the Town, Wonderful Town* and *Bells Are Ringing*—of going along on another of Comden and Green's wide-eyed, affectionate guided tours through the brick and concrete playground called Manhattan. With composer Styne, they revealed the lonely heart of a big-city office worker ("Girls Like Me"), showed how astonishingly agile are the city's George Price-ish street-corner Santas ("Be a Santa"), and, in a truly inspired creation, "Ride Through the Night," cut through the babble of subway riders' voices to reveal the magic carpet wonders of a twisting, turning express ride underground. Two other appealing items, "Taking My Time" and "Comes Once in a Lifetime," prescribed proper attitudes for achieving happiness in the tough but of course basically friendly city.

At various times before its opening, Jule Styne's next musical was called *A Very Special Person, My Man* and *The Luckiest People.* At various times, the leading role was announced—or rumored—for Mary Martin, Anne Bancroft and Carol Burnett. But when *Funny Girl* did, after much pre-Broadway travail, arrive at the Winter Garden late in March, 1964, there was no doubt

Do Re Mi *(1960).*
"Watch Nancy Walker,"
advised critic Walter Kerr, "as
she larrups into a honey of a
lyric called 'Adventure,'
whipping husband Phil
Silvers' wardrobe like a lariat
beneath her feet while she
sends forth the mating call of a
triumphant coyote."
(Costumes by Irene Sharaff;
setting by Boris Aronson.)

Photo by Friedman-Abeles

Funny Girl (1964).
Composer Jule Styne and
lyricist Bob Merrill go over
the score with Sydney Chaplin
and Barbra Streisand.

that the musical and its star, Barbra Streisand, would be as inextricably linked as if the one had been created specifically for the other.

Mounting a dramatic work based on the life of comedienne Fanny Brice had long been the dream of producer Ray Stark, an understandable ambition since he also happens to be the husband of Fanny's daughter, Frances. But since Stark was—and still is—primarily a Hollywood executive, he first visualized it as a screen adaptation. It was only after reading scenarist Isobel Lennart's first draft that he saw it emerging as a musical for the stage. Styne and lyricist Bob Merrill, who heretofore had written music as well as words for the theatre, were then signed to supply the songs. By the time rehearsals began in November, 1963, a year and a half had already been spent in writing. By the time the show opened on Broadway four months later, there had been four changes of directors (Jerome Robbins, Bob Fosse, Garson Kanin, and back to Robbins), innumerable script alterations including forty rewrites of the final scene alone (main problem: should Fanny leave husband Nicky Arnstein after he gets out of prison or should he leave her?), and five postponements of the première. But once the show opened, nothing that had gone on before really mattered. For *Funny Girl*, thanks mainly to its dynamic star and its superior score, was a boxoffice smash that continued to attract customers for almost 1,400 performances.

Most of the attention was focused, quite logically, on the twenty-one-year-old Barbra Streisand, whose only previous theatrical experience had been in a short-lived off-Broadway revue, *Another Evening with Harry Stoones* (whence also came Diana Sands and Dom De-Luise), and in her brief but memorable role in *I Can Get It for You Wholesale*. Melvin Gussow in *Newsweek* commented that the actress was given "plenty of elbow room to prove she's a star—and she seems to have a dozen elbows," and described her movements as "more gnu than gazelle." A similarly physical appraisal of Miss Streisand's performance was voiced by *Time* critic Ted Kalem, who both heralded the actress as "the theatre's new girl for all seasons," and called her "an anthology of the awkward graces, all knees and elbows, or else a boneless wonder, a seal doing an unbalancing act." But it was Walter Kerr of the *Herald Tribune* who outdid everyone by likening the lady to a grasshopper, an oak with the spine of a willow inside, an eel, and a second cousin to an octopus. Oh, yes, he also proclaimed her a star.

Musically and lyrically, Styne and Merrill had to balance their score between personal expressions and songs that were supposedly part of the theatrical productions—just as Styne and Sondheim had done in *Gypsy*. Indeed,

there were a few parallels between the two scores that were perhaps impossible to avoid. In *Gypsy*, the spirit of out-of-my-way determination was revealed early in the show through "Some People"; in *Funny Girl*, "I'm the Greatest Star" carried a similar message as, after a tentative start, it builds to a blaring declaration of self-confidence. Both musicals brought down their first act curtains on their respective stars, all alone at deserted railway terminals, in self-deluding affirmations of their single-minded goals. Just as "I had a dream" became part of "Ev'rything's Coming Up Roses," so an interpolation from "I'm the Greatest Star"—the staccato buildup beginning, somewhat anachronistically, "Who is the pip with piz-azz?"—was added, with a different lyric, to the curtain dropper, "Don't Rain on My Parade." As for the endings of both shows, each contained throat-catching bits in which the star appeared solo on stage to strip herself emotionally bare. Merman in *Gypsy* had the explosive "Rose's Turn"; Streisand in *Funny Girl* the equally affecting, though more conventional, "The Only Music that Makes Me Dance" (also serving as substitute for the real Fanny Brice's tear-stained theme, "My Man"). But the song from *Funny Girl* that became most closely identified with the "new" Fanny was unquestionably "People," a soaring, wide-ranged testament to the brotherhood of man that was that theatrical rarity, a show-stopping ballad.

Just two months after the opening of *Funny Girl*, Jule Styne had another show on the boards, *Fade Out—Fade In*, an original Comden and Green concept spoofing Hollywood in the Thirties. The musical, both tailor-made and jerry-built, spotlighted the gawky gamboling of Carol Burnett, and received a generally favorable press. Though slated for a good run, the show was forced to close after only a few months because of Miss Burnett's back injuries. It faded in again the following February, but faded out

Funny Girl *(1964).*
Barbra Streisand, as Fanny
Brice, is hoisted by her friends
and neighbors following her
rendition of the song of the
happy newlywed, "Sadie,
Sadie." (Costumes by Irene
Sharaff; setting by Robert
Randolph.)

Fade Out—Fade In *(1964).*
Tiger Haynes and Carol
Burnett do the Bill Robinson
and Shirley Temple bit as they
strut through the number, "You
Mustn't Be Discouraged."
(Costumes by Donald
Brooks.)

permanently after two months—this time because of Miss Burnett's pregnancy. The score tried hard for nostalgia and satire, and succeeded most impressively in a starry-eyed clarion, "The Usher from the Mezzanine."

Hallelujah, Baby!, at this writing the most recent Styne-Comden-Green musical, had a bright, imaginative idea behind it—a lighthearted look at the Negro's struggle for equality since the turn of the century, but with none of the characters aging a day.* What looked particularly promising was that the trio was being joined in the venture by *West Side Story* and *Gypsy* librettist, Arthur Laurents. But regrettably the musical turned out to be rather patronizing, with ill-defined characters, a fuzzy point of view, and a story that simply gave up midway in the second act. The show, however, did have one important thing in its favor. Leslie Uggams, in her Broadway debut, was, in the words of Walter Kerr, "One of the most complete personalities to have descended upon us in many a mournful moon, ready-made, able for anything, proud as silk, intimate as velvet, cheery as gingham." Apart from one hand-me-down item ("Witches Brew," with a different lyric, had been "Call Me Savage" in *Fade Out—Fade In*), the song writers matched her personality with such fresh expressions as: "My Own Morning," a suitably lofty air for the show's hope-for-the-future theme; "Being Good Isn't Good Enough," an almost excruciatingly intense personal credo; and the foot-stomping, hand-clapping, tambourine-jangling title song.

In 1970, Comden and Green limited their efforts to supplying only the libretto for *Applause* (Strouse and Adams did the score), and in 1978 they turned out both book and lyrics for *On the Twentieth Century*, with music by Cy Coleman. Both assignments found the team in the

familiar company of volatile show-business types. Styne, however, branched out unexpectedly in 1970 when he joined with his *High Button Shoes* collaborator, Sammy Cahn, to create the songs for *Look to the Lilies*. This gentle tale of the influence of a Catholic order on an itinerant Negro starred Shirley Booth and had an affecting score, but the customers didn't come. Two years later, Styne was in more accustomed territory with *Sugar*, adapted from the film, *Some Like It Hot*. With Bob Merrill as lyricist, he turned out a competent if scarcely compelling score to accompany the farcical tale of two innocents who, having witnessed a gangland slaying in Chicago, don female garb as disguise and pass themselves off as musicians in an all-girl orchestra. The show's five hundred-plus performances were due primarily to the silken direction of Gower Champion and the clowning of Robert Morse and Cyril Ritchard.

"Without the rendition there is no song," maintains Jule Styne emphatically, and his career proves it. With Nanette Fabray, Carol Channing, Dolores Gray, Mary Martin, Judy Holliday, Ethel Merman, Barbra Streisand, Carol Burnett, and Leslie Uggams to sing them, his songs have benefited from some of the most individualistic and compelling renditions ever heard in the theatre. But ovbiously they needed something to render. To compose songs to fit particular talents—especially when they are as outstanding as the ones for whom Styne has written—requires a creativity no less demanding than composing songs ot fit particular characters or situations. When a composer can create a melody that fits all three—the performer, the character and the dramatic situation—he demonstrates the rarest kind of theatrical skill. The measure of Jule Styne's contributions to the world of musical comedy may best be appreciated not alone by what performers have done for his songs, but also by what his songs have meant to the careers of the performers who have sung them.

*A similar technique had been used by Alan Jay Lerner and Kurt Weill in their 1948 collaboration, *Love Life*. In that musical, the principal characters remained the same age from 1791 to the then present.

Frank Loesser.

CHAPTER TWENTY-ONE

FRANK LOESSER
RICHARD ADLER
and JERRY ROSS
MEREDITH WILLSON

DESPITE THE BACK-BITING RIVALRIES for which the theatre has long been celebrated, there are many instances of composers and lyricists showing not only mutual admiration but also assistance. Jerome Kern offered to do what he could to further the career of the fledgling George Gershwin, and Gershwin himself was responsible for getting Vincent Youmans his first Broadway assignment. Otto Harbach was something of a mentor to Oscar Hammerstein; in more recent years, Stephen Sondheim has made much of the debt he owes to Hammerstein's tutelage and guidance. As producers, Rodgers, Hammerstein and Jule Styne were able to be in unique positions to sponsor the works of other writers. In this company, surely none has exerted greater influence than Frank Loesser, whose career was notable not alone for his own creative ability but for his knack of recognizing creative ability in others.

Frank Loesser

The multiple activities of Frank Loesser in the musical theatre—com-poser, lyricist, librettist, producer—gave him a special distinction among his colleagues. Of equal importance to his own accomplishments, however, was his unflagging interest in, and assistance to, new writers for the stage. Loesser was, in fact, able to offer very tangible aid. As president of the Frank Music Company, one of the leading music-publishing companies in the country, he published the works of many promising composers and lyricists—in addition, of course, to his own songs.

It has been a particular mark of his foresight that Frank Loesser was instrumental in furthering the careers of the three most successful songwriters of the theatre to emerge during the Fifties—Richard Adler, Jerry Ross, and Meredith Willson. In 1951, anxious to find the most promising talent among the young writers of Tin Pan Alley, he signed the team of Richard Adler and Jerry Ross to a contract. A few years later, after Loesser was approached to write the score for *The Pajama Game*, he suggested to George Abbott that Adler and Ross would make excellent replacements. In the case of Meredith Willson, it was Loesser who first urged him to turn the story of his Iowa boyhood into a musical. Loesser even introduced Willson to Cy Feuer and Ernest Martin, who were originally to have been the producers of *The Music Man*. Eventually, when it opened in New York in 1957, Frank Productions was the associate producer with Kermit Bloomgarden and Frank Music was the music publisher.

Such a variety of activities was completely natural to the restless, energetic Loesser. A hard-working, hard-driving man, he would get no more than four hours sleep a night and was usually awake by six-thirty in the morning. "I get bored otherwise," he once said. "I like to have a song, a list of figures, and a business problem all around me."

Frank Henry Loesser was born in New York City, on June 29, 1910. His father was a piano teacher whose only interest was in the classics. His older brother, Arthur, has been a concert pianist, critic, and music teacher. In this environment, Loesser became interested in music at an early age. At six, he wrote a song called "The May Party" in celebration of the children's processions he saw in Central Park; a year later, he amused himself by fitting words to the clicking of the elevated railroad as it roared through his neighborhood.

Because his father disapproved of popular music, Loesser had to teach himself how to play the piano when he was in his early teens. After failing in his studies at the City College of New York he took a variety of jobs. One that he particularly liked was as a reporter for a short-lived New Rochelle newspaper. When he was assigned to cover a local dinner of the Lions Club, he obliged one of the officers by supplying rhymed couplets celebrating the exploits of all the members at the dinner. According to his brother Arthur, the local fame he achieved as the author of such lines as "Secretary Albert Vincent, Read these minutes right this instant," gave him his first inspiration to become a lyricist.

Soon Loesser began to write sketches and lyrics for vaudeville acts. During the Depression, he wrote occasional material for radio. In those days, Loesser recalls, "Somehow you had to find a way of getting a job. You had to keep alert all of the time. I suppose that's where this tremendous energy of mine originated."

In 1931, Loesser wrote his first published song, "In Love with a Memory of You." It had a melody by William Schuman, who was to become a celebrated composer of concert music. A few years later, Loesser got a job singing and playing at the Back Drop, a 52nd Street nightclub. Many of the songs he sang were original numbers with music by Irving Actman. Five of these were used in *The Illustrators' Show*, the same revue in which Frederick Loewe's "A Waltz Was Born in Vienna" was first heard.

As a result of their work for *The Illustrators' Show*, Loesser and Actman were signed to a contract by Universal Pictures. Soon afterward, Loesser joined Paramount. His first song hit, "The Moon of Manakoora," was based on Alfred Newman's theme for *The Hurricane* in 1937. Among his most frequent collaborators during his eleven years in Hollywood were Burton Lane, Hoagy Carmichael, Frederick Hollander, Jimmy McHugh, Victor Schertzinger, Jule Styne, and Arthur Schwartz.

Loesser often wrote the words to songs before composers had written the music. Because the very construction of his lyrics almost dictated the melodies that would carry them, many of his collaborators urged him to write music as well as words. The first song with music and lyrics created exclusively by Frank Loesser was "Praise the Lord and Pass the Ammunition," written while he was in the Army during World War II. Its success gave Loesser the confidence to compose all of his own melodies from then on.

After his army stint was over, Loesser returned to Hollywood in 1946. His friends, Cy Feuer, the former head of the music department at Republic Pictures, and Ernest Martin, a former television executive, had formed a partnership to produce musical plays. Through attorney Howard Reinheimer (who was also Rodgers and Hammerstein's lawyer), they had secured the rights to Brandon Thomas' ancient farce, *Charley's Aunt*, as a vehicle for Ray Bolger, and they wanted Loesser to contribute the music and lyrics. In common with many other theatrical beginners, the producers then called upon the experienced George Abbott to serve as director and librettist.

Where's Charley?, as the play was retitled, opened on October 11, 1948, and became an unqualified hit. It was the first of Feuer and Martin's five successful musicals in a row (the other four were *Guys and Dolls*, *The Boy Friend*, *Can-Can*, and *Silk Stockings*), and it also established Loesser as a Broadway composer and lyricist of great promise. His ballads ("My Darling, My Darling" and "Once in Love with Amy") had a simple, direct appeal, though even more impressive musical gifts were revealed in "The Red Rose Cotillion" and "The New Ashmoleon Marching Society and Student Conservatory Band." Moreover, in "Make a Miracle," he created a number in which words and music were brilliantly combined to produce a complete musical vignette as the ardent suitor tries vainly to gain the attention of his daydreaming sweetheart.

For their next musical, Feuer and Martin decided on a more ambitious work. Long fond of Damon Runyon stories and characters, they decided to do a Runyon fable based on a short story, *The Idyll of Miss Sarah Brown*. They also had a good title for it: *Guys and Dolls*. An early choice for librettist was a Hollywood scenarist named Jo Swerling, but the producers were dissatisfied with the result. By the time they approached Abe Burrows, then a radio script-writer, they had already read outlines by eleven dif-

Where's Charley? (1948).
George Abbott directing Ray Bolger.

Photo by Eileen Darby—Graphic House

Photo by Eileen Darby—Graphic House

Guys And Dolls *(1950).*
The oldest established permanent floating crap game in New York takes up temporary residence in a sewer. Throwing the dice is Sky Masterson (Robert Alda), and standing behind him is Big Julie (B. S. Pully). Nicely Nicely Johnson (Stubby Kaye) and Nathan Detroit (Sam Levene) are kneeling on either side of them. (Costumes by Alvin Colt; setting by Jo Mielziner.)

ferent authors. Although the Burrows libretto at last provided the right approach, contractual arrangements compelled them to retain Swerling's name on the program as coauthor.

Feuer and Martin had signed Loesser even before they hired Burrows. Later, they secured George S. Kaufman as director and Michael Kidd to stage the dances. What emerged, when the show opened in 1950, was one of the most tightly coordinated musicals ever created. As Howard Barnes of the *Herald Tribune* wrote: "The work uses music and dancing as embellishments to the libretto, rather than making the latter a loose clothesline for assorted capers and vocal numbers."

In writing the score, Loesser found inspiration in many of the actual guys and dolls he had known when he was a pianist at the Back Drop. It was his ability to capture the racy, hard-shelled, but basically soft-hearted characters of the gamblers and racketeers of the Runyon fable that gave his songs their special distinction. These people speak in awkwardly cultivated tones, their emotions are explosive but unassailably pure, and when Sister Sarah Brown of the Save a Soul Mission comes along to urge them into living more respectable lives, there is never any doubt that she will eventually succeed.

Loesser's score had great variety, yet it also had a singleness of design and purpose that caught the appealing ambivalence of the highminded low-lifes. Dignified and classical forms, such as a Handelian cantata for "The Oldest Established," or the Bachlike fugue for a description of a horse race, were exactly right because, in spite of the incongruity, the characters themselves were essentially dignified and classical. So, too, a grandly operatic duet, "Sue Me," was used with unerring effect as Adelaide, a nightclub singer (played by Vivian Blaine) flails away at Nathan Detroit (Sam Levene), her fiancé of fourteen

years, only to be met by his unnerving acquiescence. Two highlights were the production numbers at the Hot Box nightclub. "A Bushel and a Peck" was a purposely inane down-on-the-farm routine squealed by the chorus "Farmerettes," while "Take Back Your Mink," under the pretext of shocked innocence, offered an ensemble strip tease as the virtuous recipients of various articles of apparel return them rather than submit.

One song, "Adelaide's Lament," was written well before the final libretto was completed. Originally, Adelaide was to have been a stripper who catches cold from overexposure; later, when it was decided that she would be more sympathetic as a singer, Loesser changed the lyric to make her suffer from psychosomatic ailments because her marriage to Nathan has been postponed so often. "Adelaide's Lament," one of the most brilliant of all comic love songs, is a perfect example of Loesser's dictum: "I try to examine characters, not events."

In 1952, a friend suggested to Loesser that he create a musical out of Sidney Howard's *They Knew What They Wanted.* Loesser read it and was immediately intrigued with the idea. "I figured, take out all this political talk, the labor talk, and the religious talk. Get rid of all that stuff and you have a good love story." The tender tale of the elderly Italian winegrower in California who falls in love at first sight with a waitress seemed to Loesser to have an emotional intensity especially well suited to a musical adaptation. "Go spell what you sound like when you're laughing or crying. You have to say it in music."

Writing *The Most Happy Fella*—music, lyrics, libretto—took Loesser more than four years. He felt like giving it up many times, but inevitably a period of depression would be followed by one of extreme enthusiasm, and he would again plod forward. Once the work was finished, there still remained the problem of finding a suitable actor for the leading role of the winegrower. Loesser even made a trip to Italy in a vain search for someone with the right quality of voice and acting ability. Eventually, he engaged Robert Weede, formerly of the Metropolitan Opera, who made his Broadway debut in the musical.

The Most Happy Fella, which opened in New York on May 5, 1956, was one of the most ambitiously operatic works ever written for the Broadway musical theatre. Included among its more than thirty separate musical numbers were recitatives, arias, duets, trios, quartets, and choral passages, yet all of them were created to fit within the framework of the commercial musical theatre. Big, booming arias, such as "Rosabella" and "My Heart Is So Full of You," are interspersed with such traditional Broadway specialty numbers as "Big 'D'" and "Standing on the Corner." Other selections, particularly "Abbondanza" and "Benvenuta," reveal their composer's knack of parodying the effulgences of Neapolitan singers. Perhaps most charming of all are the duet between Weede and Jo Sullivan (as his mail-order bride), "Happy to Make Your Acquaintance," and the evocative quartet, "How Beautiful the Days."

Although in the manner of an opera, the program for *The Most Happy Fella* did not list the individual songs; the work was designated simply as "A Musical." To those who prodded him on the matter, Loesser said, "I may give the impression this show has operatic tendencies. If people feel that way—fine. Actually all it has is a great frequency of songs. It's a musical with music." Or, as arranger Don Walker put it, "This is a musical comedy expanded. Not an opera cut down."

Apparently, once Frank Loesser became identified with a particular type of music or musical, he felt compelled to move on to something more challenging. In his next production, *Greenwillow*, starring Anthony Perkins in his first ap-

The Most Happy Fella *(1956).*
Robert Weede as Tony, the aging winegrower of Napa Valley, California, and Jo Sullivan as Rosabella, his mail-order bride.

Photo by Arthur Cantor

Photo by Friedman-Abeles

The "Big D" number led by Texans Susan Johnson and, at the far right, Shorty Long. (Costumes by Motley.)

pearance in a musical, Loesser abruptly abandoned the colorful big-city world of Damon Runyon and the melodramatic world of Sidney Howard in favor of the pastoral world of novelist B. J. Chute. This time, Loesser (and co-librettist Lesser Samuels) sought to capture the elusive flavor of an imaginary community located somewhere along the banks of the Meander River. With little plot, the musical relied on a certain synthetic

Photo by Fred Fehl

charm derived from imaginary, quaint, rural customs (the baptism of a cow, for example) that were perhaps somewhat difficult to accept on the musical stage. "Folklore," wrote Walter Kerr following its March 8, 1960, première, "may just be one dish that can't be cooked to order."

Loesser's score provided a rich variety of bucolic themes, demonstrating again that the composer was a master at recreating familiar musical styles, while still endowing his songs with his own individual style. Included are wistful old English ballads ("Walking Away Whistling," "Faraway Boy"), a religious hymn (an amusing bit in which two ministers offer contrasting sermons on the same theme), and a Christmas carol ("Greenwillow Christmas"). Loesser also created two moving songs for Mr. Perkins, "Summertime Love," which fairly bursts out its message of love's constancy, and the touching renunciation, "Never Will I Marry." All these numbers have an authenticity and feeling for

mood that somehow escaped the production as a whole.

For his next musical, Loesser had no such problem. *How to Succeed in Business Without Really Trying* offered a perfect theme for his special musical gifts. Certainly the challenge was still great: to write a score that would hew so closely to this satire on big business shenanigans that it would permit no compromise in the form of dragged-in, commercially-motivated songs. Every number was made to fit. Every number was part of the overall design. "The Company Way" was the organization man's ode to the organization. "I Believe in You" was a narcissistic serenade our hero—to the accompanying buzz of an electric razor—sang to himself while shaving. "Grand Old Ivy" turned out to be every old grad's tribute to every Alma Mater. "A Secretary Is Not a Toy" was a perky compendium of office etiquette ("Her pad is to write in/Not spend the night in"), punctuated by the clatter of typewriters.

Loesser's fidelity to form and content was typical of the integrity of the entire show. The work had originated as a comedy without music by Willie Gilbert and Jack Weinstock, adapted from Shepherd Mead's humorous non-fictional guidebook on how to get ahead in business. But producers Cy Feuer and Ernest Martin had other ideas; they saw it as a musical comedy that was perfect for their *Guys and Dolls* cohorts, composer Frank Loesser and librettist Abe Burrows. Long before they had put a word on paper, Loesser and Burrows held endless sessions thrashing out the vital questions posed by the specific nature of the project. How do you sing a show about big business? What kind of songs would business people sing? When and why would they sing them? Bob Fosse, who had been hired to do the musical staging, ventured the idea that a soft-shoe number would have the right sound for a business office. That became "A Secretary Is Not a Toy." Burrows came up with the notion of having the musical's big love song sung by the leading man to himself. That became "I Believe in You." Only after working out about nine or ten musical ideas—not even knowing exactly where they would go—did Loesser and Burrows then sit down to write the songs and the libretto. "We declared," declared Burrows, "that our show would be as impudent as we could make it. We wanted it to be funny and sharp. Our people were going to be interesting and exciting, not just wilted violets drooping away with fraudulent broken hearts and stems. We promised ourselves that every song would make a point and that no one would stop dead, center stage, in order to sing a song that had no purpose in the story."

After a full year of self-imposed discipline, the men eventually came up with a working script. Everything connected with the mores and morals of corporation life—from the mailroom to the board room—became frequently devasted targets, with shots aimed at such institutions and fixtures as the coffee break, the office party (in which all the girls show up in the identical "Paris Original"), the fawning yes men, and even the prestigious confines of the executive washroom.

From the very beginning of the project, there was agreement that the role of the baby-faced, two-timing "hero," J. Pierpont Finch, would go to Robert Morse, who had been in only two previous musicals. Despite a tendency toward mugging, Morse was unquestionably the season's musical comedy find. The part of the stuffy tycoon, J. B. Biggley, president of World Wide Wicket Co., Inc., was played by Rudy Vallee in his first Broadway appearance since the *George White's Scandals of 1936*. The general hat-tossing reception the musical received following its October, 1961, opening, fully justified the determination of the authors to keep their work free from moralizing or sentimentality. Howard

How To Succeed in Business Without Really Trying *(1961).*
Alma Mater "Grand Old Ivy" is ardently sung by old-grad J. B. Biggley (Rudy Vallee) and would-be young-grad J. Pierpont Finch (Robert Morse).

Taubman of the *Times* ranked it among "the blue chips of modern musicals," and Walter Kerr in the *Herald Tribune* found it "crafty, conniving, sneaky, cynical, irreverent, impertinent, sly, malicious, and lovely, just lovely." So did the Pulitzer Committee, which handed the show its prize as the best play of the year—the fourth musical so honored.

Frank Loesser's multiple activities limited him to only six musicals (one, *Pleasures and Palaces* in 1965, didn't make it to New York) since he first began his theatre career in 1948. Yet he was universally acknowledged to be among the most creative practitioners in the field. Moreover, his work was marked by the most steady advance of any composer since George Gershwin. From formula musical comedy (*Where's Charley?*), he plunged right into a modern comic opera (*Guys and Dolls*). Then, in *The Most Happy Fella*, he proceeded to write the first successful Broadway opera since Gershwin's *Porgy and Bess*. *Greenwillow*, despite its faults, was still commendably daring in subject and treatment, and *How to Succeed in Business Without Really Trying* capped Loesser's career to date with a second modern comic opera

even more unconventional than the first. Also noteworthy is that, just as he extended himself in themes, Loesser also expanded his creative activities—from lyricist to composer-lyricist to composer-lyricist-librettist-producer.

Frank Loesser, who died July 28, 1969, at the age of 59, was an original who established his own high standards in the Broadway theatre. Combining the sensitivity of the artist with the acumen of the businessman, he labored to preserve these standards not alone through his own works but through the works of others whom he encouraged and sponsored.

Richard Adler and Jerry Ross

When, in 1951, Frank Loesser asked another music publisher to send him the most promising young song-writers he knew, the publisher immediately thought of Richard Adler and Jerry Ross. Loesser was so impressed with their songs that he promptly signed the two young composers to an exclusive contract with his publishing company. Many things about the versatile team—each man could write both music and lyrics—made Loesser confident that they would eventually fulfill his expectations. Their music showed both originality and a rhythmic accessibility that indicated commercial appeal. Their lyrics were full of the argot of modern, idiomatic speech that Loesser himself has captured so well. Above all, both men, like Loesser, were anxious to break down the walls that had, for so many years, created barriers between Tin Pan Alley and the Broadway theatre.

During their relatively brief partnership, these "two young Loessers," as Leonard Bernstein once called them, showed a special aptitude for communicating with contemporary audiences. "Subconsciously, and from our training, we're writing for the man in the street,"

Richard Adler and Jerry Ross.

Photo by Talbot

Ross once remarked. To which Adler added: "We try to write universal truths in colloquial terms. We're just trying to bring out the expression of the times in which we live in terms of the people with whom we're dealing. We're writing the way our generation demands we write."

Both men were born in New York—Adler on August 23, 1923, and Ross on March 9, 1926. Adler's family life was quite similar to Frank Loesser's, as his father, Clarence Adler, was a concert pianist and music teacher. Classical music, however, never interested the young Adler; in fact, his original ambition was to become a writer. After graduating from the University of North Carolina (where he studied playwrighting under Paul Green), he spent three years in the Navy. Upon his discharge, he got a job writing advertising copy for a large corporation. About this time he began to compose songs; at first, during his spare time and later even during office hours. Inevitably, this resulted in his dismissal, but, as Adler had already decided to become a song-writer, he welcomed the opportunity to devote all of his time to music. He met with little success, however, until he met Jerry Ross in 1950.

Ross was born in the East Bronx of poor parents. At ten, while singing in a synagogue choir, he was approached to join the Bronx Art Theatre, a Yiddish acting company. After acting in one of its productions, he joined other companies then presenting plays on the Jewish stage. Because Ross attended high school in the Bronx and most of these groups were on the lower East Side of Manhattan, he was forced to stay up until all hours commuting. As a result, during this period he developed chronic bronchietasis, which was eventually responsible for his death. Ross was still in his teens when he wrote his first song. He continued composing at New York University, where he took courses in music, and at summer resorts in the Catskills. Like Adler, Ross had little luck as a song-writer until he met his partner.

Adler and Ross's first success for Frank Loesser was "Rags to Riches," which they wrote in 1953. The same year they were signed to write most of the songs for *John Murray Anderson's Almanac*, a revue starring Hermione Gingold, Billy DeWolfe, and Harry Belafonte. Even before this show opened, the team was hired by George Abbott to create the entire score for *The Pajama Game*. Adler and Ross had previously auditioned for Abbott on two occasions; each time, though he was encouraging, the old master told them that they were not yet ready. When Loesser recommended them for *The Pajama Game*, the partners again auditioned. This time, the director was so excited about their work that he rushed over to Frederick Brisson, Robert Griffith, and Harold Prince, the show's producers, and insisted that the team be hired.

The Pajama Game opened in May, 1954. Following the frequent pattern of George Abbott musicals, most of the people responsible for the production were newcomers to the theatre—including the producers (Griffith and Prince had been stage managers for many of Abbott's pro-

The Pajama Game *(1954).*
Eddie Foy, Jr., Janis Paige, and John Raitt.

ductions) and choreographer Bob Fosse. Apart from Abbott, the only other experienced member of the staff was Jerome Robbins, the co-director, though this marked his first assignment directing an entire show. By thus dividing the directing chores, Abbott was given more time to work on the libretto with Richard Bissell, the author of 7½ Cents, the novel from which the book was adapted.*

The Pajama Game was a fast-paced, human story based on the unlikely subject of a threatened strike in a pajama factory. There was, however, nothing socially conscious about it in the manner of *Pins and Needles*; the rights of the workers were not nearly as important as their fun and romantic complications. Although the unmistakable George Abbott touch was evident throughout, the contributions of Adler and Ross were of sufficient merit to establish them as the brightest new song-writing team to emerge during the decade. *The Pajama Game* also provided new opportunities for its stars, John Raitt, Janis Paige, and Eddie Foy, Jr., as well as for Carol Haney, a young dancer making her

*Bissell subsequently based his novel, *Say, Darling*, on his experiences working on *The Pajama Game*. This, in turn, became "A Comedy about a Musical," with songs by Jule Styne, Betty Comden, and Adolph Green.

Broadway debut. (For a few performances soon after the opening, Miss Haney was replaced by her understudy, Shirley MacLaine.)

The flavor—if not the ingredients—of *Damn Yankees*, produced exactly one year later, was similar to *The Pajama Game*. It had the same production staff—producers, choreographer, musical director (Hal Hastings), arranger (Don Walker)—plus director George Abbott and Adler and Ross. Abbott also collaborated on the libretto with Douglass Wallop, whose novel, *The Year the Yankees Lost the Pennant*, furnished the basis for the musical. Again, the swift-moving show had the style and the spirit that has long distinguished its director's work; even the Faustian overtones of the story were treated in a breezy manner, particularly with Ray Walston playing the devil and Gwen Verdon (in her first starring role) as his most efficient temptress. The Adler and Ross contributions, while not as striking as those in their first score, nevertheless provided such commercially successful pieces as "Whatever Lola Wants" and "Heart."

There is little doubt that the firm hand of director and co-librettist George Abbott was chiefly responsible for the lengthy runs of both *The Pajama Game* and *Damn Yankees*. Yet the work of Adler and Ross cannot be overlooked in appraising their success. Just as Frank Loesser had before them, they brought a new commercial flair to the Broadway theatre; with their special ability at combining a wide range of catchy, familiar rhythms—plus original sound effects—within the framework of a single score. Thus, in *The Pajama Game* there was a lively march ("7½ Cents"), a roaring Western ballad ("There Once Was a Man"), a novelty item with a hissing noise as part of its lyric ("Steam Heat"), a lilting waltz ("I'm Not at All in Love"), a solo love song that became a duet when played back over a dictaphone ("Hey, There"), and a spooky tango

Damn Yankees (1955). *Choreographer Bob Fosse rehearsing the chorus.*

Photo by Talbot

("Hernando's Hideaway"). For *Damn Yankees*, the team created a satirical barbershop quartet ("Heart"), a spirited hoedown ("Shoeless Joe from Hannibal, Mo."), a sultry tango ("Whatever Lola Wants"), a soft-shoe vaudeville number ("Those Were the Good Old Days"), and a comic mambo ("Who's Got the Pain?").

The Adler-Ross partnership was tragically ended on November 11, 1955, when Ross died of a lung ailment at the age of 29. Since then, except for the worthy but short-lived *Kwamina* (1961) and *Music Is* (1976), Adler has devoted most of his energies to writing television commercials and, more recently, orchestral works for concerts and ballets. But in the team's two remarkable hits, *The Pajama Game* and *Damn Yankees*, Adler and Ross made a major—if brief—breakthrough. By proving conclusively that good theatre music could also become good commercial music, they succeeded in closing the ever-widening gulf between the world of Broadway and the world of pop.

Meredith Willson

One day in 1949, Meredith Willson was indulging in one of his favorite indoor pastimes: reminiscing to a group of friends about his boyhood in Mason City, Iowa. Among his listeners was Frank Loesser. Suddenly, Loesser jumped to his feet. "What an idea!" he shouted, "Why don't you write a musical about it?" Then he started to pace up and down. "Maybe you can start with the fire chief. Let's make him the leader of the town band. Maybe *you* can play the fire chief. And maybe instead of a pit orchestra, you can have a real brass band in the pit. And you're the leader of the band. You could also be sort of a narrator and talk directly to the people in the audience. That way you could tell every-

Photo by Arthur Cantor

Rini and Meredith Willson.

body about your town. It would be real Americana!"

When *The Music Man* finally opened on Broadway eight years later, it bore little resemblance to Loesser's original concept. But Loesser had planted an idea in Willson's mind about doing a musical with an Iowa background, something that would capture all the nostalgia and warmth inherent in a story of a small Midwestern town in the early days of the century. "Innocent, that was the adjective for Iowa," Willson has said. "I didn't have to make anything up for *The Music Man*. All I had to do was remember."

Meredith Willson was born in Mason City, on May 18, 1902. His mother gave piano lessons, and young Meredith dutifully studied that instrument as well as the piccolo and the flute. In his youth, he played piccolo in the high-school band, enjoyed the county fairs, had a job pumping water for Saturday night baths, and, in general, absorbed everything he could of the folklore of his small Iowa community. After high school, he went to New York to pursue a career in music. There he studied at the Institute of Musical Art (later Juilliard School of Music), and, at the age of nineteen, was hired by John Philip Sousa as first flutist in his band.

The Music Man *(1957).*
In "Seventy Six Trombones,"
Robert Preston, as a bogus
instrument salesman, wins
over the children of River City,
Iowa, with his description of
the most mammoth parade of
all times. "Though he never
danced or sang before on
stage," wrote **Life Magazine,**
"he displays both zing and
polish and follows
triumphantly in the tradition
of George M. Cohan."
(Costumes by Raoul Pène du
Bois.)

Three years later, he joined the New York Philharmonic, where he played under Toscanini. In 1929, Willson became musical director of the Northwest Territory for the American Broadcasting Company; soon afterward, he joined the staff of the National Broadcasting Company.

Willson's first symphony ("San Francisco") was written when he was thirty-three. From 1937 on, with the exception of the years spent in the Army during World War II, he was associated with many radio programs as both conductor and performer. His first song hit, "You and I," was written in 1941; nine years later, he wrote the popular "May the Good Lord Bless and Keep You" as the theme song for Tallulah Bankhead's radio program, *The Big Show*.

Because of his other work, Willson did not begin to write the musical about Iowa until nearly three years after Loesser had first suggested it. After abandoning the idea of the fire chief and also of appearing in the show himself, Willson then thought of telling a story about a kindly music teacher. Later, the main character was changed to a traveling salesman of nonexistent musical instruments. The leading female part, a librarian who also gives piano lessons, was modeled after Willson's mother.

Through Loesser, Willson met producers Cy Feuer and Ernest Martin. They became so enthusiastic about the script that they promised to put it into production immediately after the opening of *Silk Stockings* in February, 1955. They even suggested *The Music Man* as the title. Soon, however, the producers lost interest because of what they felt were basic weaknesses in the story. This was a serious blow to Willson, but he had already put so much effort and time on the musical by then that he was determined to continue to work on it and try to interest other producers. In the summer of 1956, he rewrote much of the libretto with playwright Franklin Lacey.

By the following November, Willson had already gone through thirty-two drafts of *The Music Man* and he was still unable to find a producer. Then, remembering that Kermit Bloomgarden had co-sponsored Frank Loesser's *The Most Happy Fella*, he telephoned the producer from California. When Bloomgarden agreed to let him audition, Willson and his wife, Rini, flew to New York, and played and sang the entire production the following evening. The next morning, Bloomgarden called Willson to his office. "Meredith," he asked, "may I have the privilege of producing your beautiful play?"

Many actors were considered for the leading role of Professor Harold Hill, the persuasive but unscrupulous music man. According to Willson's book, *But He Doesn't Know the Territory*, Danny Kaye was the original choice, but Kaye did not feel he was right for the part. Dan Dailey never kept his appointment to discuss the matter with Willson. Phil Harris did not even return his telephone call. Gene Kelly just was not interested. Finally, at the insistence of director Morton DaCosta and musical director Herbert Greene, Robert Preston, best known for his performances in movie Westerns, was signed for the part.

In his score for *The Music Man*, Willson made great use of the technique of rhythmic, but not rhyming, lyrics. This is apparent in the very first number of the show, "Rock Island," in which the rhythm of a moving train is simulated in dialogue as a group of traveling salesmen discuss the problems of their trade. The same device later occurs in both "Piano Lesson," which uses the musical scale as accompaniment to a conversation between Barbara Cook, as the librarian-music teacher, and Pert Kelton, as her mother, and in "Trouble," a rousing sermon exploded into the midst of the townspeople by the fast-talking Professor Hill. Willson also adds a dramatic touch by employing the same melody for both

Photo by Friedman-Abeles

The Unsinkable Molly Brown
(1960).
*Harve Presnell and Tammy
Grimes cavorting to "I Ain't
Down Yet." (Costumes by
Miles White; setting by Oliver
Smith.)*

Miss Cook's wistful "Goodnight, My Someone" and Preston's spirited "Seventy-Six Trombones," in order, as he has explained, "to suggest that these two people have something more in common than meets the eye."

Despite the fears of those who felt that *The Music Man* would be too old-fashioned for Broadway, it received unanimously favorable reviews following its December 19, 1957, opening. It then settled down for the first marathon run since *My Fair Lady*. What distinguished the show were the qualities of conviction and affection that so obviously went into its creation. Every type of musical expression used—soft-shoe, ragtime, barbershop quartet, march—had a feeling of genuineness that helped to bring alive the flavor of a naïve American town circa 1912. In his capacity as composer, lyricist, and librettist, Willson brought to his work a musical proficiency and a unity of purpose that made *The Music Man* a completely irresistible show.

The play's successful combination of breeziness and sentimentality was reminiscent of the works of another man of the theatre who also wrote books, music and lyrics—George M. Cohan. There was the same fondness for typically American characters and locales, the same electric excitement in the swiftly paced production, the same theatrical contrast between the city slicker and various rural types. *The Music Man* even took place on Cohan's favorite holiday, the Fourth of July. Thus, in spite of the skills of production and the advances in theatrical techniques, the musical theatre could still find welcome room for a production with the same basic appeal of the earliest examples of strictly American musicals based on strictly American themes.

Willson's two subsequent musicals, *The Unsinkable Molly Brown* (book by Richard Morris) and *Here's Love* (book by Willson), were equally representative—though not equally felicitous—examples of the composer's general style and outlook. *Molly Brown*, which provided Tammy Grimes with her most rewarding role to date, retold the saga of a near-legendary figure of the Colorado silver mines, who pulled herself up from poverty by marrying a lucky prospector named Leadville Johnny Brown. Here the situation was something of a reversal of *The Music Man*. Harold Hill had been a big city con man who made a living bilking rubes; Molly Brown was a rustic who triumphed over the big city swells. Also, perhaps coincidentally, Molly's saga took her from the turn of the century to late April, 1912—just two months short of the period in which the story of *The Music Man* was set. Musically, the new work had the by-now familiar Willson trademarks—an optimistically breezy march ("I Ain't Down Yet"), a boisterous male chorale ("Belly Up to the Bar, Boys"), a back country dance number ("Keep a-Hoppin' "), and a revivalistic exhortation ("Are You Sure?") that almost matched the feverous pitch of "Trouble."

In *Here's Love*, which arrived in the fall of 1963, Willson jumped from the rural past to the urban present. Just as he had found inspiration in the Fourth of July celebration in *The Music Man*, he now made full and colorful use of another indigenously American holiday, Thanksgiving. Shunning an overture, the show simply took off by presenting, to the tune of a lighter-than-air march, "The Big Calown Balloons," the Macy's Parade in New York. The festive opening, of course, was almost inevitable since Willson had adapted his story from that happy cinema fantasy, *The Miracle on 34th Street*, which was all about a real Santa Claus who gets a job in a department store. Again the composer had provided parents with a suitable-for-the-kiddies show, possibly less congenial to his muse than his previous works, but still retaining much of the innocent charm and freshness of the original.

All three Meredith Willson musicals revealed his world to be a thoroughly affirmative one, full of simple faith easily reinforced by a miracle or two. Although his roots may be in the rich soil of the heartlands of America, Willson proved that, with conviction and talent, they could be transplanted successfully to the steel and concrete of Broadway.

Bob Merrill.   Photo by Friedman-Abeles

CHAPTER TWENTY-TWO

BOB MERRILL

I T MAY NOT HAVE guaranteed his success, but it surely was no hindrance to his career that in his early years Bob Merrill was able to gain experience in more areas of entertainment than any other leading writer for the Broadway musical stage. He started out as an actor, then became a radio writer and producer, went on to become a film director, and later a television casting director and production consultant. Oh, yes, he was also a Tin Pan Alley songwriter. While that last calling should have logically been the one that led to his career as a stage composer and lyricist, it was in fact the chief reason why Merrill took so long to become established.

For the songs with which he was initially almost exclusively identified were juvenile novelty items of the early Fifties; the greatest stigma they bore was not that they were flops but that they were hits. Following "If I Knew You Were Comin' I'd've Baked a Cake" (written with Al Hoffman and Clem Watts), Merrill—unaided—came up with another gastronomical ditty, "Candy and Cake," and from then on the airwaves were filled with such catchy if transitory pieces as "Sparrow in the Treetop," "My

Truly Truly Fair," "Belle, Belle, My Liberty Belle," "Mambo Italiano," "Honeycomb," and that yelping query, "How Much Is That Doggie in the Window?" Nary a harbinger among them that they had been created by a talent that would later musicalize two plays by Eugene O'Neill or furnish Barbra Streisand with lyrics for the songs that helped launch her career.

Bob Merrill (né Henry Robert Merrill Lavan) was born in Atlantic City, New Jersey, on May 17, 1921. Raised in Philadelphia, he had a brief fling at an acting career before being drafted in the Army in World War II. His experience writing and producing GI radio shows encouraged him to try to find similar work in Hollywood after the war, but the best he could get was a job as porter at CBS. One day, during lunch hour, he put on his only suit and walked boldly into the writers' department at NBC where he passed himself off as a CBS writer anxious to switch to the rival network. Hired on the spot, he took no more than three weeks to become supervisor of the entire department. In the mid-Forties, he became a dialogue director at Columbia Pictures, which allowed him enough free time to pursue his new hobby—song writing. With less training than he had to become an NBC writer, Merrill found that he had a knack of picking out tunes on a toy xylophone, a method of composing he continued to use in later years. He returned to CBS in 1948, spent a year as a television casting director, then became television production consultant to the Liggett and Myers Tobacco Company.

But the urge to write songs made him quit to devote himself to it full time. Publishers, however, told him his stuff was too sophisticated for the commercial market, so Merrill simply changed his style and soon became the nation's top purveyor of novelty tunes. Though the financial rewards were great, he was fired by a new ambition: to write for the musical theatre. Here it turned out his experience was the reverse of what it had been when he first began writing pop songs: as the master of "Doggie in the Window," his work was simply dismissed out of hand.

Undaunted, Merrill tried Hollywood again in 1956. John Green, the head of M-G-M's music department, was so im-

New Girl In Town *(1957).*
Gwen Verdon and companions
Harvey Hohnecker and
Harvey Jung have a high-
kicking time at the Check
Apron Ball. (Costumes by
Rouben TerArutunian.)

pressed with his efforts that he helped him get a contract to write, compose, and produce up to ten musicals over a seven-year period. The first was to have been based on O'Neill's *Anna Christie*, retitled *A Saint She Ain't*, and Merrill had already completed sixteen songs when the company abruptly scrapped the entire project. Maybe it was that title.

Director George Abbott, then filming the screen version of *The Pajama Game*, auditioned the songs and promptly got Broadway producers Robert Griffith and Harold Prince to secure the rights to *Anna Christie* from M-G-M. For various reasons, the only song retained for the stage adaptation, renamed *New Girl in Town*, was "It's Good to Be Alive," and Merrill had to come up with a virtually brand new score.

Transforming the dour saga of the woebegone Anna into a frisky, flavorsome musical presented too many problems to be solved to everyone's complete satisfaction. Following the May 1957 opening, Wolcott Gibbs wrote in *The New Yorker*, "Abbott and Merrill have done their best to say that incest, prostitution, and terrible despair are simultaneously the stuff of high tragedy and also somehow of low comedy, but it is uphill work." Still, the musical did have the stellar presence of Gwen Verdon as Anna and the appealing abrasiveness of Thelma Ritter as Marthy. As for the score, while the romantic expressions never really added very much to the story or to the characters, there were a number of atmospheric pieces that caught the raffish, turn-of-the-century flavor—"Roll Yer Socks Up," "At the Check Apron Ball," and the lachrymose barbershop ballad, "The Sunshine Girl" ("has raindrops in her eyes"). And the production did have one well-remembered directorial touch. The first-act curtain fell as Miss Verdon was leading the dancers in the middle of "There Ain't No Flies on Me"; after the intermission, the second act began with the same dancers continuing the routine from the exact positions at which they had last been seen.

Eugene O'Neill again furnished the basis for Merrill's second musical, *Take Me Along*, which came along in September 1959. Since the original, *Ah, Wilderness!*, was just about the sunniest play the doom-obsessed playwright ever wrote, the work was far more congenial to a musical treatment than was *Anna Christie*. This one, however, suffered from casting problems. Although Eileen Herlie as Aunt Lily and Robert Morse as teenager Richard Miller were ideal for their roles, Jackie Gleason's excessively flamboyant Uncle Sid dominated the proceedings and shifted the focus from the head of the family, Nat Miller (played by Walter Pidgeon), who was almost relegated to a supporting character.

Take Me Along found Bob Merrill at his most skillful. Again he showed his flair for creating a turn-of-the-century mood, particularly in the soft-shoe title song performed so engagingly by Gleason and Pidgeon. The character songs, however, were even more felicitous. Pidgeon's "Staying Young" said almost as much about growing old as did the classic in the field, "September Song." Gleason's "Sid Ol' Kid" and "Little Green Snakes" were splendidly realized comic pieces. Miss Herlie was given two selections, "We're Home" and "Promise Me a Rose," that contained just the right combination of pathos and imagination. Morse had two, "I Would Die" and "Nine O'Clock," that beautifully caught the proper adolescent spirit. All fine, fresh musical ideas without a false note. The musical-dramatic highpoint, however, occurred when Gleason, in a more or less sincere mood, dropped to one knee to propose marriage to the fluttery Miss Herlie. In their duet, "I Get Embarrassed," he delivered a fairly ribald proposal to which the lady responded in hysterical spasms, alternating genuine embarrassment with ill-concealed delight

in anticipating the carnal pleasures of matrimony.

Opening in the spring of 1961, *Carnival* offered the composer a special kind of challenge. Since the work was based on that cinematic lollipop, *Lili*, the problem was in coming up with a theme song reminiscent of—but just different enough from—"Hi Lili, Hi Lo." "Love Makes the World Go Round" (also called "Theme from Carnival") proved a worthy if by no means obliterating substitute. Also for the first time, Merrill was called upon to create songs with a wide range to suit the vocal prowess of the stage Lili, Anna Maria Alberghetti. The results, including "Mira" and "Yes, My Heart," were not only melodically affecting but also particularly fitting for the dramatic requirements of the story of a waif in a circus world.

Carnival was the second musical staged by Gower Champion and written by

Take Me Along *(1959).* *"There are many quite wonderful moments in* Take Me Along," *Richard Watts, Jr., wrote in his review, "but the one I think I treasure most is that in which the Messrs. Gleason and Pidgeon go into a soft-shoe dance to the accompaniment of the title song."*

Carnival *(1961).*
Pierre Olaf in a pensive
moment with Anna Maria
Alberghetti. (Costumes by
Freddy Wittop.)

Michael Stewart, both of whom had begun their Broadway careers with *Bye Bye Birdie* the previous year. The new production firmly established Champion as the stage's most inventive director-choreographer of the Sixties. For openers, he did away with the overture. *Carnival* begins on a bare, predawn stage with the theme music first heard from a wheezing concertina as, one by one, the members of a down-at-the-heels French carnival troupe wearily stagger on to arrange the lighting, hang the bunting, and set up the tents. In a later scene, Champion had the disillusioned, somnolent performers snap wide awake with bright-eyed, high-kicking anticipation as Pierre Olaf describes the fame that will be theirs once they are again hailed as the Grand Imperial Cirque de Paris. By the time they're finished, not a soul in the audience could possibly doubt their eventual triumph. *Carnival*'s 719-performance run was a well-deserved success for a work that, as Howard Taubman wrote in the *Times*, turned "sentiment and show business razzle-dazzle into a flashy, eye-filling and occasionally touching entertainment."

Prior to *Funny Girl*, Bob Merrill's record as a composer-lyricist was solid enough to have easily erased any lingering memories of his "Candy-in-the-Window, Doggie-in-the-Treetop" output. Yet the new project gave him two new firsts: it marked the first time in the theatre that he had set his lyrics to another composer's melodies (in this case Jule Styne's), and it marked the first time—with "People" and "Don't Rain on My Parade"—that he had two juicy show-tune hits.

Since that memorable production, however, Merrill's career has had more disappointments than satisfactions. One score had the distinction of having been written for what was probably the most publicized flop of all times, David Merrick's *Breakfast at Tiffany's*. Amid fanfare comparable to that heralding a success, the show packed up its diamond-surrounded cornflakes without even risking an official Broadway opening. Dazed but unfazed, Merrill next contributed the score for *Henry, Sweet Henry*, which Nunnally Johnson adapted from his own screenplay, *The World of Henry Orient*. The musical opened in the fall of 1967 with Don Ameche as the temperamental, amorous concert pianist, and is perhaps best remembered for Alice Playten's belting "Nobody Steps on Kafritz" (in which "pick a kid" rhymes with "indicative" and "miser'ble" with "visible"), and a manic first-act finale with the whole company disrupting Ameche's rendezvous with Carol Bruce. The rest of Merrill's score was noticeably deficient in its suitability to the modern, youthful spirit of the story. A return to composer Jule Styne five years later for *Sugar* gave the lyricist an unexpected two-year hit.

As of this writing, Bob Merrill has been represented on Broadway by six musicals during a period of over twenty years. At his best, he has shown a laudable dramatic gift for creating the right song for the right person in the right place, with the emotional directness and lyricism of his melodies especially well suited to the simple, uncomplicated drifters and dreamers who inhabit his most appealing works.

Stephen Sondheim.

CHAPTER TWENTY-THREE

STEPHEN SONDHEIM

ONE OF THE MORE obvious commentaries on the current state of the musical theatre is that it has become dominated by directors and choreographers. Possibly the only writer today with a prestige and influence on a par with the best of them is composer-lyricist Stephen Sondheim. People speak of a Sondheim show the way they once referred to a Gershwin show or a Rodgers and Hammerstein show. Sondheim has a style and stamp that have given his musicals—diverse though they may be—a special identity, and his willingness to experiment within the basic form has profoundly affected the works of young writers in the field.

Yet Sondheim too is associated with a director, Harold Prince (who has also been a producer but never a choreographer). To date, there have been five musicals with scores by Sondheim directed by Prince, all of which represent both men at a level of artistic achievement that set the hallmark of musical-theatre creativity during the Seventies.

The form of musical theatre that Sondheim and Prince have been involved in has been dubbed by critics the concept musical: that is, one in which style of pre-

sentation takes precedence over the story itself. But the Sondheim-Prince style is as equally concerned with matter as it is with manner. In show after show, they have sought to illuminate a variety of major themes—the stresses of urban living in *Company*; the conflict between reality and illusion in *Follies*; the ways in which social position and age affect romantic relationships in *A Little Night Music*; America's baleful influence on Oriental culture in *Pacific Overtures*; even the grim view that man has no other choice than to eat or be eaten in *Sweeney Todd*.

There have, of course, been compromises along the way and at times the metaphors have become somewhat blurred. Indeed, more often than not the songs have transcended their librettos to establish their own world of social commentary and character revelation. In so doing, Sondheim utilizes every suitable musical and poetical form, yet he still leaves his own personal imprint of melodic expression, philosophical viewpoint, and verbal agility that has clearly altered the course of our musical stage.

Stephen Joshua Sondheim came to his calling under expert tutelage. Born in New York on March 22, 1930, he attended the George School in Newtown, Pennsylvania, where he became friendly with fellow student James Hammerstein, son of Oscar II. Through his friend, the fifteen-year-old Sondheim first met the elder Hammerstein who promptly took a paternal interest in his work and served for many years as both critic and mentor. At Williams College, where he majored in music, Sondheim first began to write musicals and to think seriously of making the theatre his life's work.

Following graduation, he was awarded the Hutchinson Prize to study composition with Milton Babbitt. During this two-year period, he won his bread by turning out scripts for the *Topper* television series. His first theatrical breakthrough occurred in 1954 when his musical, *Saturday Night* (book by Julius Epstein) was earmarked for production by Lemuel Ayers. Although Ayers died before the work could be mounted, the many backers' auditions gave Sondheim the chance to make his work familiar to people in the theatre. Among the most impressed was playwright Arthur Laurents, at that time working on the script of the musical that would eventually become *West Side Story*. The show's composer, Leonard Bernstein, then desperately looking for a lyricist, heard Sondheim's songs and enthusiastically welcomed the twenty-seven-year-old writer as his collaborator. Sondheim more than held his own—even though he now looks back on his lyrics for the show as too pretentious. When *West Side Story* was followed by *Gypsy* (music by Jule Styne), there was general agreement that a major talent was at work in the Broadway musical theatre.

Sondheim's ambition, however, was still to compose. He got the opportunity in 1961 when writer Burt Shevelove, a close friend, came to him with an idea—turning some of the characters and stories by the Roman playwright Plautus into a farcical musical to be called *A Funny Thing Happened on the Way to the Forum*.

Though the assignment at last gave him the chance to write music as well as lyrics, Sondheim found the task surprisingly difficult. Songs in musicals are usually inserted at moments of extreme emotional pitch, when, in effect, feelings can no longer be contained in prose but must erupt in melody. But *Forum* had no emotional highs; its relentless pace called for songs primarily to provide rest periods between the fast-moving comic episodes. As Sondheim has commented, "The score interrupts the action instead of carrying it on, because there are no songs that develop the characters and the story. They simply pinpoint moments of joy or desire or fear, and they give the performers a chance to perform."

When originally tried out, the show opened with the leading character singing a dainty, bucolic piece, "Love Is in the Air"—and nothing seemed to work after that. Director George Abbott, though a veteran of farces, was completely stumped and a hurry call went out to Jerome Robbins. His solution: begin the show with a number that tells the audience the kind of entertainment it is about to see (which, curiously, was what Abbott himself had done in *The Pajama Game*). Overnight, Sondheim came up with the proper slambang opener, "Comedy Tonight" ("No royal curse, no Trojan Horse,/ And a happy ending, of course!"), and overnight an apparent disaster became a surefire hit.

The mood of lighthearted, satirical fun was maintained throughout the entire score as it gave voice to man's ambivalent desire for freedom ("Free"), offered detailed instructions for two lovers to make their getaway ("Pretty Little Picture"), sang the praises of domestic service ("Everybody Ought to Have a Maid"), and provided a trumpeting command ("Bring Me My Bride") for the impatient war hero, Miles Gloriosus. For the beauteous but dimwitted heroine, there were two particularly fetching sentiments—the ingenuously self-praising "Lovely" and

A Funny Thing Happened on the Way to the Forum (1962). Four gentlemen of ancient Rome—Lycus (John Carradine), Hysterium (Jack Gilford), Senex (David Burns) and Pseudolus (Zero Mostel)—lustily agree "Everybody Ought to Have a Maid." (Costumes and setting by Tony Walton.)

Photo by Van Williams

A riotous complication in the plot finds Jack Gilford mistaken for a honey-haired virgin. Here Miles Gloriosus (Ronald Holgate), Senex (David Burns) and Erronius (Raymond Walburn) attempt to prevent the beauty from fleeing.

Photo by Friedman-Abeles

the love-starved "Love I Hear" ("I pine, I blush, I squeak, I squawk,/Today I woke too weak to walk").

With a cast headed by such seasoned buffoons as Zero Mostel (in a role originally intended for Phil Silvers and then announced for Milton Berle), Jack Gilford and David Burns, the musical madhouse was greeted rapturously upon its opening in May 1962, and ran for over 1,000 performances. Though Plautus was the inspiration, coauthors Shevelove and Larry Gelbart, after researching all twenty-one of his surviving comedies, ended up with an original story that used only a few of the playwright's characters and situations. One concerned a doddering old man who is kept from entering his house because he is tricked into believing that it is haunted. Prophetically, the scene was found in a play titled *Mostellaria*.

"I wouldn't mind putting my name to a flop if it had done something that hadn't been tried before," Sondheim said in an interview in 1961. His chance came three years later, with *Anyone Can Whistle*. The show, with an original, satirical book by Arthur Laurents, was welcomed by an unmerciful clobbering by the reviewers: "Exasperating"—Kerr, *Herald Tribune* . . . "Acute pretentiousness"—Thompson, *Life* . . . "Sick"—Taubman, *Times* . . . "Ponderously heavy-handed"—Watts, *Post* . . . "Boxoffice dodo"—Morrison, *Variety*.

Although some claimed that the show was ahead of its time, a more rational view was that the musical, concerned as it was with the fairly adolescent theme that madness is the only hope for world sanity, had an almost impossible task of winning over an audience. It lasted a week. Sondheim's score, however, was found worthy enough to merit an original-cast album even after the show had closed. His choral numbers were especially effective, and surely two of the songs—the emotionally frustrated title piece and the pathetically defiant "A Parade in Town"—would have added luster to any score.

One distinctive aspect of the Sondheim style was introduced in *Anyone Can Whistle*. While all other characters were given music and lyrics that expressed exactly how they felt, the venal mayoress (Angela Lansbury in her first musical) had songs that revealed her personality not through the words she sang but through their rhythm and musical accompaniment. The lyric of "Me and My Town," for example, may have expressed sincere concern about the ruination of her city, but the music's flip, finger-snapping beat left no doubt that her real concern was only herself. This use of a song to say one thing and mean another would show up in various forms in subsequent Sondheim musicals.

Sondheim wrote only lyrics for *Do I Hear a Waltz?*, his sole collaboration with Richard Rodgers and his fourth association with librettist Arthur Laurents. Though unappreciated, the show was in many ways an adult work of considerable charm and integrity.

Company, the first Sondheim musical directed by Harold Prince, opened in 1970. To probe its theme of urban living, the production invaded the lives of five Manhattan couples held together by their rather excessively protective feelings about a bachelor friend. While their virtually ceaseless attachment to Bobby, Bobby, Bobby put a strain on the show's believability, *Company* did offer a frequently corruscating cross section of marital attachments and detachments among the financially affluent but emotionally deprived high-rise city dwellers. Particularly effective was the use of designer Boris Aronson's skeletal set and projections as an integral part of the concept.

Fortunately, wherever the script was weakest, the songs carried the themes and filled in the plot holes. Since the characters were largely ambivalent in their feelings about what they really wanted for their bachelor friend—as well as in their attitudes toward each other—the words and music mirrored their confused, contradictory emotions in such insightful expressions as "The Little Things You Do Together," "Sorry-Grateful," and "Getting Married Today." And seldom has the desperate, frantic, lonely world of New Yorkers been so effectively limned as in "Another Hundred People" ("And they meet at parties through the friends of friends who they never know./ Will you pick me up or do I meet you there or shall we let it go?").

Though its mood was far different and its theme more complex, *Follies* (1971) was, like *Company*, structurally built on the foundation of a party. In the previous musical it had been a birthday party that brought the characters together in the opening scene; in *Follies* it was a reunion of ladies who had at one time or another appeared in a *Ziegfeld Follies*-type series of revues. The form, however, was excessively cumbersome, with the story dealing not only with the conflict between the reality of life and the unreality of the theatre but also with the somewhat confusing youthful alter egos of the four principals.

Yet for all its busyness, *Follies* had moments of incredible theatricality, offering audiences the kind of emotional lift that can only be experienced in a stage production. "Who's that Woman?" found a half dozen former chorus girls tap dancing with their supposed mirrored reflections as they looked as young girls. In "I'm Still Here," Yvonne DeCarlo belted out her song of indestructibility ("I've been through Herbert and J. Edgar Hoover,/ Gee, that was fun and a half"), and in "Broadway Baby," Ethel Shutta caught the strident urgency of the stagestruck hopeful. All the principals had effective character-revealing pieces, such as John McMartin's self-questioning "The Road You Didn't Take," or Dorothy Collins' self-deceptive "In Buddy's Eyes" (with the true emotion conveyed not through the music but through Jonathan

Photo by Zodiac

Company (1970).
Pamela Myers, Susan Browning and Donna McKechnie harmonize to "You Could Drive a Person Crazy." (Costumes by D. D. Ryan.)

Follies *(1971)*.
*With their youthful selves
mirrored in the background,
Ethel Barrymore Colt, Alexis
Smith, Dorothy Collins, Helon
Blount, and Yvonne DeCarlo
perform their old* Follies
*routine, "Who's that
Woman?" (Costumes by
Florence Klotz.)*

Photo by Martha Swope

Tunick's orchestration) and her torchy, tortured "Losing My Mind" (melodically reminiscent of both Gershwin's "The Man I Love" and André Previn's "You're Gonna Hear from Me"). Possibly the number that cuts deepest is "Could I Leave You?," in which Alexis Smith, her nerve ends exposed, builds to a bitter frenzy as she lays bare the hollowness of her life.

Both *Company* and *Follies*, because of their construction, modern Manhattan settings and emotionally confused characters, were somewhat allied. *A Little Night Music* was a departure for Sondheim and Prince. It was their first work to be based on a previous source, in this case the Ingmar Bergman film, *Smiles of a Summer Night*, and its setting was Sweden at the turn of the century. Though the musical was peopled by rueful, introspective characters, they were a warmer, more attractive group than those in the previous Sondheim-Prince shows, with a healthier view of living and loving. And the score brought out new aspects of Sondheim's restless imagination.

Having established his skill at creating

wry, witty, sardonic songs with an unmistakably modern texture, he now set himself a new goal of creating wry, witty, sardonic songs exclusively in three-quarter time (or multiples thereof). The score for *A Little Night Music*, in fact, was so redolent of the classical past that it prompted theatre critics to reveal their musical erudition. To Clive Barnes in the *Times*, despite the play's Mozart-inspired title, Sondheim was "aiming at the lilt of Mahler." Theodore Kalem in *Time* discovered its "rarified musical sources" to be Ravel, Rachmaninoff, and Brahms. The *News'* Douglas Watt felt that its music had "something of the effect of Ravel's *Valses Nobles et Sentimentales* equipped with superior Broadway rhymes." In the *Sunday Times*, Walter Kerr likened "In Praise of Women" to "something verging on Johann Strauss." Years later, Martin Gottfried wrote in the *Post* of its "music filled with obscure and not so obscure references to Richard Strauss, Franz Liszt, and especially Ravel."

In "Send in the Clowns," Sondheim had the first song hit for which he wrote both words and music. In a scene toward the end of the play, Desirée Armfeldt, a worldly actress (played by Glynis Johns), believing that she will never win back her lover, Fredrik Egerman (Len Cariou), sadly points out to him the incompatibility of their relationship. To a remarkably compelling melodic line, she uses theatrical terms ("making my entrance again," "sure of my lines," "losing my timing") to describe a situation so ludicrous that it can only be saved by letting the clowns take over. Curiously, the song attained its popularity despite a lyric—at least when heard out of context—that seems ambiguous with regard to the identity of the clowns and the meaning of the last line, "Well, maybe next year . . ." (It refers not to the clowns' arrival but to the possibility of a reunion.)

If their first three joint efforts ventured into unaccustomed areas of musical theatre, Sondheim and Prince practically dared the public to follow them down their next two theatrical paths. *Pacific Overtures*, presented in 1976, was nothing less than an attempt to relate the story of the Westernization of Japan from 1856, the year of Commodore Perry's arrival, to the commercialized present. Not only was this a subject for which there certainly could be no sizeable presold audience, the creators—including librettist John Weidman, son of Jerome—elected to present their agitprop musical both from the Japanese point of view and in a Broadway facsimile of the ancient Japanese theatrical form of Kabuki.

Yet those who were put off by its didacticism missed a work of soaring imagination and stunning visual effects (thanks in part to another collaborator, designer Boris Aronson). The work, however, may have been structurally marred by its indecision between being an elaborate historical panorama and a more personal story of the ways two men respond to cultural shock (a tradition-bound samurai becomes westernized and

Photo by Martha Swope

decadent, a westernized fisherman reverts to the traditions of the samurai).

Sondheim again showed his ability to write in an adopted style while still maintaining his own individuality of expression. Though contrary to Japanese custom he did use harmony, his music contained a strong oriental feeling which he achieved after discovering that the Japanese pentatonic scale has a minor modal texture that reminded him of the Spanish composer, Manuel de Falla. "I was able to relate to it," he has said, "because suddenly it had a Western feeling and at the same time an Eastern feeling." As for lyrics, he managed to capture the simple eloquence of Haiku poetry, while at the same time displaying his own ability at narrative description ("Someone in a Tree") and intricate construction ("Chrysanthemum Tea").

Throughout his career there has always been something of a dark side to Stephen Sondheim, though nothing in his past quite prepared audiences for anything like the stygian quality of *Sweeney Todd*. The melodramatic story of the

A Little Night Music (1973). Len Cariou and Glynis Johns in the Harold Prince musical based on the Ingmar Bergman film, Smiles of a Summer Night. *(Costumes by Florence Klotz; setting by Boris Aronson.)*

Pacific Overtures *(1976).*
Isao Sato and Sab Shimono
(in small boat) on their way
to deal with the invading
Americans led by Comm.
Perry . (Costumes by Florence
Klotz; setting by Boris
Aronson.)

Photo by Zoe Dominic

"Demon Barber of Fleet Street" had been around for well over a century. On the stage, it was first shown in London in 1842 as *A String of Pearls, or the Fiend of Fleet Street*, written by one George Dibden Pitt. Under the title *Sweeney Todd* a number of versions followed, the latest being an adaptation by Christopher Bond in 1973. To Bond, Sweeney was more than a crazed, murder-obsessed barber mindlessly slitting the throats of customers whose corpses are then turned into meat pies by the obliging Mrs. Lovett. Bond saw him as a victim of nineteenth century social order, a poor, devoted husband and father who was sent away to prison simply because a rich and powerful judge fancied his wife. Escaping and returning to London, the barber takes indiscriminate revenge until he does away with the man who wronged him. In the end Sweeney kills Mrs. Lovett by throwing her into her oven and is himself done in by a deranged assistant.

Conceivably because of the ambivalence of a leading male character

who is both sympathetic and terrifying and a leading female character who is both comic and terrifying, Sondheim became intrigued by the play's musical possibilities and brought the idea to Harold Prince (though the actual production was handled by others). The show opened in March 1979, and was greeted by generally enthusiastic notices that had high praise for the score, the gripping theatricality of Prince's staging, and the strong performances of Len Cariou as Sweeney and Angela Lansbury as Mrs. Lovett.

Together with librettist Hugh Wheeler, Sondheim and Prince approached the work as something of a Grand Guignol with social conscience, a Brechtian, Dickensian view of class repression and mass revenge. To symbolize the oppressiveness of the Industrial Revolution, a huge, hulking framework of a real iron foundry was installed on the stage to replace the theatre's actual proscenium arch. Prince has been quoted as saying that the musical was really about "the incursion of the industrial age and its influence on souls, poetry and people," though the idea of expressing this theme (which could also apply to *Pacific Overtures*) by means of rampant killings and cannibalism seems an attempt at significance not entirely justified by the material.

In creating the score, Sondheim, aided by arranger Jonathan Tunick, met what was probably his most difficult challenge by contributing a rich, near-operatic flow of melody, with almost continuous underscoring and a constant interweaving of musical themes. One of the most affecting examples of this occurs early in the second act when Sweeney, about to slit the throats of his victims, sings dreamily about his daughter, Johanna, while the girl's lover calls her name as he searches for her through the streets of London. Dramatically, the composer is strikingly effective at the end of the first act when the barber, swearing vengeance upon everybody, lets loose a torrent of pent-up fury ("Epiphany"), then immediately follows it with a gruesomely comic waltzing duet with Mrs. Lovett as they imagine the kinds of pies to be made from men of various professions ("A Little Priest"). Of note too is the subtly chilling effect in "Not While I'm Around," during which the strings are properly lush when a simpleminded cockney lad sings of his devotion to Mrs. Lovett, then go jarringly dissonant when the same piece is sung by the homicidal accomplice herself.

Though Sondheim has been the dominant theatre composer-lyricist of the seventies, his musicals do not always enjoy the kind of commercial success achieved by more conventional enterprises. "There is something about my shows," he said some months before *Sweeney Todd* opened, "that make people a little uncomfortable in the theatre—which is, incidentally, not my intention. But that's the way it comes out, because what's interesting to write is something you haven't done before. I *have* to go for something I haven't done before. The result is people don't know what to expect from show to show."

Photo by Martha Swope

Sweeney Todd *(1979).* Mrs. Lovett (Angela Lansbury) and Sweeney (Len Cariou) vow to wreak vengeance on the world. (Costumes by Franne Lee; setting by Eugene Lee.)

Jerry Bock and Sheldon Harnick.

CHAPTER TWENTY-FOUR

JERRY BOCK and SHELDON HARNICK

CERTAIN COMPOSERS AND LYRICISTS for the musical theatre, no matter how durable their careers may be, seem to be forever identified with specific decades. This has to do not only with their periods of greatest productivity but also with the style and flavor of the theatre in which they worked most compatibly. George Gershwin, Vincent Youmans and DeSylva, Brown and Henderson primarily conjure up the Twenties; Cole Porter, Dietz and Schwartz and Rodgers and Hart recall the Thirties; Rodgers and Hammerstein and Lerner and Loewe the Forties and Fifties. Though they started a few years earlier and ended their collaboration about a year later, composer Jerry Bock and lyricist Sheldon Harnick were unquestionably the dominant team of the Sixties, with all their major works save *The Rothschilds* shown on Broadway during that decade.

The partners were, moreover, the logical successors to the two illustrious teams that had immediately preceded them. Like Rodgers and Hammerstein and Lerner and Loewe, they had the particular affinity for recreating a bygone world made meaningful to modern audiences through evenings brimming with honest sentiment and compelling melodic appeal. To an even greater extent, however, they strove to create musical expressions that were so absolutely right for their periods and locales as to be almost irremovable from the texts for which they had been conceived. As a team, they almost invariably dealt with—and showed their abiding sympathy for—the problems of ordinary people and the way their determination, humanity and humor helped them cope with misfortunes ranging from losing a job to losing a loved one to losing a homeland.

Harnick, the older of the two, was born in Chicago, on April 30, 1924. As a child he showed his musical talent by learning to play the violin and his lyric-writing talent by making up verses honoring family celebrations. After a hitch in the army during World War II, he attended Northwestern University where he contributed songs—both words and music—to the undergraduate Waa-Mu shows. After college, Harnick became a professional violinist in dance orchestras in the Chicago area; he abruptly abandoned this calling, however, when he was fired by Xavier Cugat after working for the band leader only one night.

By this time he had a new ambition—he wanted to write songs for the theatre. He came to New York in 1950, getting most of his theatrical experience initially at Green Mansions, the same summer resort where Harold Rome had first tried out *his* earliest efforts. The reception accorded "The Boston Beguine," sung by Alice Ghostley in *New Faces of 1952*, led to opportunities to contribute to other revues. Most notably: "The Merry Minuet" ("They're rioting in Africa . . ."), which Orson Bean introduced in *John Murray Anderson's Almanac*.

Harnick was building a reputation if not a bank account. It was "Yip" Harburg who convinced him that while his lyrics were good, he'd better start looking around for a composer to work with. Harnick found him at a bar the night of June 13, 1956. The lyricist had gone there following the opening of *Shangri-La*, a short-lived musical for which he had made some last-minute, uncredited interpolations. Also at that particular bar was Jack Cassidy, a member of the cast, who introduced Harnick to his future partner, Jerry Bock.

Bock was born in New Haven, on November 23, 1928. His father, a machine salesman, moved the family to Flushing, New York, when Jerry was a tot. He studied piano with local teachers, and soon discovered that he could play songs by ear—even venturing variations on their themes. At high school, he won limited fame by writing the words and music for a war bond show, *My Dream*. At the University of Wisconsin, Bock wrote another original musical, *Big as Life*, which toured the surrounding cities. Following graduation, he returned to New York where he got a job writing for Max Liebman's television revues starring Sid Caesar and Imogene Coca. Summers were spent mastering his craft at Tamiment, an adult summer camp in the Pennsylvania Poconos. There he turned out ten revue scores each season for three years.

Bock's first lyric-writing collaborator was Larry Holofcener, with whom he contributed three songs to the Broadway revue, *Catch a Star*. The team of Bock and Holofcener—augmented by George Weiss—did well enough with their first book musical, *Mr. Wonderful*, a Sammy Davis vehicle co-produced by Jule Styne. The show even spawned two durable hits—the title song and "Too Close for Comfort." *Mr. Wonderful* opened just three months before Bock and Harnick met for the first time.

Tommy Valando, who published the *Mr. Wonderful* score, sent the newly allied team to Richard Kollmar, then preparing a musical about prize fighters called *The Body Beautiful*. Bock and Harnick were hired but their partnership debut was less than auspicious. The show was panned and so were the songs, though at least two, "Summer Is" and "All of These and More," became part of the audition repertory of aspiring young singers.

One of the few who was impressed with the songs for *The Body Beautiful* was George Abbott, then about to go into production on a musical based on the life of New York's peppery Mayor, Fiorello H. LaGuardia. Producers Robert Griffith and Harold Prince had secured the rights to a musical dramatization of LaGuardia's life, and Griffith had persuaded his Connecticut neighbor, novelist Jerome Weidman, to write the adaptation with Abbott. But no one was signed for the songs. What Abbott wanted was a new team who could write with a satirical slant but who could also give the score the period flavor it required. As an audition Bock and Harnick wrote a nostalgic waltz suggestive of the World War I period of LaGuardia's younger days. Abbott hired them on the basis of that number, "Till Tomorrow," one of the memorable moments in the score.

Casting an actor who could sing and dance and look and act like New York's "Little Flower" was an even bigger problem. About two hundred—ranging

Photo by Friedman-Abeles

Mr. Wonderful *(1956).*
In a nightclub scene from
Jerry Bock's first book
musical, Sammy Davis Jr., his
father and uncle, Will Mastin,
perform "Jacque d' Iraq."
(Costumes by Robert
Mackintosh.)

Courtesy Capital Records

Fiorello! (1959).
A young New York lawyer named Fiorello LaGuardia shows picketing workers how to put some spirit in what they are doing. In the opinion of critic Henry Hewes, "Actor Tom Bosley, as a fine artist should, captures more of LaGuardia's essence than the man did himself when he was alive." (Costumes by William and Jean Eckart.)

from Mickey Rooney to Eli Wallach—were tested before the producers settled on 32-year-old Tom Bosley who had never appeared in a Broadway play before. In voice, stance and general magnetism he caught the spirit of LaGuardia to an uncanny degree, and scored a resounding success. As for Bock and Harnick, there was no question that they too had arrived. Apart from the romantic contributions, their score admirably captured all the ward-heeling double-dealing of New York politics, particularly with "Politics and Poker," a waltzing tribute to the interrelationship of the two games, and "Little Tin Box" (written two weeks before the Broadway opening). In the latter, various politicos, found with their hands in the till, explain their wealth in shocked innocence by detailing how they saved their pennies by giving up smoking, returning empty bottles to the grocer, and going without lunches for a week. There was also wonderful contrast in the campaign songs—a thumpingly idealistic march, "The Name's LaGuardia" for the pugnacious

reformer and a razzmatazz Charleston, "Gentleman Jimmy" to describe the incumbent mayor, Jimmy Walker.

The press greeted *Fiorello!* with all the affection the New York electorate had once bestowed on its subject, with the *Herald Tribune's* Walter Kerr calling it "a song-and-dance jamboree with a curious streak of honest journalism, and a strong strain of rugged sobriety about it." It not only won the votes of the New York Drama Critics Circle as the year's best musical, it also was elected the year's best drama by the Pulitzer Prize committee.

Everyone connected with the creation of *Fiorello!*—Griffith, Prince, Abbott, Weidman, Bock and Harnick—got along so well that they decided to stick together for their next musical, *Tenderloin*. The show, which gave Maurice Evans his first singing role since *Ball at the Savoy* in London, 1933, again dealt with a stubbornly crusading white knight battling corruption in a bygone, wicked New York. But Dr. Parkhurst's fight against the red light section known as the Tenderloin suffered from a stuffy leading character and a wavering point of view—and from the inevitable comparison with *Fiorello!* The Bock-Harnick contributions, however, were delectable recreations of a bawdy and sentimental era, particularly in the tear-stained "Artificial Flowers," the jolly tale of the virtues of vice known as "The Picture of Happiness," and the innocent compilation of childhood games, "Good Clean Fun."

On April 23, 1963, producer Harold Prince became producer-director Harold Prince with the opening of *She Loves Me.** It also reunited him with Jerry Bock and Sheldon Harnick. Initially, however, the producers were to have been Lawrence Kasha and Philip McKenna who had wanted to put on a musical version of Ernst Lubitsch's film, *The Shop Around the Corner*, ever since

* Prince's first Broadway directorial assignment had been *A Family Affair*, presented by Andrew Siff early in 1962.

Photo by Graphic House, Inc.

Tenderloin *(1960).*
Maurice Evans, as a crusading
minister, puts on a disguise to
learn from first hand
experience all about New
York's most sinful section, the
Tenderloin. (Costumes and
setting by Cecil Beaton.)

they had seen a revival of it. The musical version of the film (which in turn had been based on a play called *Parfumerie* by Miklos Laszlo) deserved a far better fate than its relatively meager three hundred or so performances. Perhaps in the waning theatrical season the play was just too gentle, too intimate, and too free from Broadway razzle-dazzle to attract the customers. Critics could find no adjectives more helpful to the show's press agents than "charming," "delightful," "enjoyable," and "darling." And surely the lone nay-sayer, Walter Kerr, in the *Herald Tribune,* didn't help with his crack, "things seem a little shopworn around the corner."

But for eyes that could see and ears that could hear, *She Loves Me* will stand as a model in its use of songs as an indispensable adjunct to the plot. It was, in fact, a musical told *through* music and

lyrics, with no less than twenty-three set musical pieces. This in no way diminishes the worthy contribution of librettist Joe Masteroff, in his first assignment in the musical theatre. It was agreed from the start that he would write a complete play—not a libretto—in order that Bock and Harnick could best find areas in which to substitute songs for dialogue, as well as utilizing the dialogue itself as a springboard for the musical expressions. In keeping with the proper spirit, most of the songs were done as solos and duets, only occasionally by the rather limited chorus. Everything jelled, nothing stood out in applause-milking desperation. Little wonder that Jerry Bock could later recall, "It was a show that we dearly loved doing. There was a feeling of give and take throughout. There was a feeling of inspiration throughout. A feeling of group chemistry."

She Loves Me (1963). *After much misunderstanding, boy (Daniel Massey) finally gets girl (Barbara Cook) on Christmas day in front of Maraczek's Parfumerie.*

Photo by Graphic House, Inc.

Even before starting work on *She Loves Me*, Bock and Harnick had begun laying the groundwork for the musical that was to become *Fiddler on the Roof*. They had read a novel by Sholom-Aleichem, thought it had theatrical possibilities, and had turned it over to librettist Joseph Stein, with whom they had worked on *The Body Beautiful*. Though Stein did not think that this particular story could be converted into a musical, Bock and Harnick had become completely hooked on doing something by Sholom Aleichem. At a friend's suggestion, they read another one of his books, *Tevye's Daughters*. There was no question about it. This was it. For the first time in their careers, both composer and lyricist had the satisfaction of initiating a project rather than having a producer call them in to work on an already-scheduled show.

Fiddler on the Roof became the fourth Bock and Harnick musical to be produced by Harold Prince. In many ways it was a far from commercial undertaking. Recalling the famous telegram that Mike Todd sent after seeing *Oklahoma!* during its tryout ("NO GAGS NO GALS NO CHANCE"), here was a musical that had no pretty scenery, no pretty costumes, no pretty girls, and no pretty story. Its plot dealt with a people vainly trying to keep alive traditions in an alien, hostile world, and of their hopeless attempts to establish roots in a place where they had none and from which they are eventually forced to flee. But though the libretto was concerned specifically with impoverished Jews in Czarist Russia, its theme is so universal that audiences of all backgrounds have responded to it. Notwithstanding its special ethnic quality, *Fiddler on the Roof* has managed to create an empathetic bond with everyone who has ever had to deal with mindless cruelty, or has ever been compelled to leave a home or a family.

The guiding hand of director Jerome Robbins was in evidence throughout in soaking the production in authentic atmosphere—despite an occasional intrusion of a line or piece of business that seemed like unnecessary concessions to musical comedy taste. In the central role of Tevya, the dairyman, Zero Mostel scored the unquestioned theatrical triumph of the year, with many critics, incorrectly as it turned out, crediting him for the production's success. Bock and Harnick, who initially conceived of Tevya as a thin, wasted little man, not only had to rethink the role along physical lines but also were inspired to create songs with Mostel specifically in mind. Of one of them, "If I Were a Rich Man," and the way it was performed, the *Herald Tribune's* Walter Kerr wrote, "Mr. Mostel dreams his dreams in vocalized snuggles, not in words. For every other line of the lyric he simply substitutes gratifying gargles and cascading coos un-

*Fiddler on the Roof (1964).
Zero Mostel leads his fellow
villagers in the joyful toast,
"To life, to life, l'chaim."*

Photo by Friedman-Abeles

*The men of Anatevka do a
traditional bottle dance at the
wedding of Tevya's daughter ,
Tzeitel. (Costumes by Patricia
Zipprodt.)*

Photo by Eileen Darby-Graphic House

til he has arrived, mystically, at a kind of cabalistic coloratura. The effect is what we all had in mind when we last thought of satisfaction in depth." There is much color and emotion too in the foot-stomping opening number, "Tradition," in the wistful "Matchmaker, Matchmaker," in the robust "To Life" ("L'Chaim"), and, in the excruciatingly poignant, "Sunrise, Sunset," the gentlest of all commentaries on the unbelievability of passing years.

The fiddler remained perched on the roof of Tevye's house until July 2, 1972, for a record-breaking total of 3,242 performances. Mostel played the role of Tevye a little under a year, was followed by Luther Adler for three months, by Herschel Bernardi for two years, by Harry Goz for almost two years, and also by Jerry Jarrett, Paul Lipson and Jan Peerce. Lipson, who originated the part of the Bookseller, played Tevye

The Apple Tree *(1966).*
In The Lady or the Tiger, *the second of three one-act musicals offered on the same program, Larry Blyden played the Balladeer, Alan Alda Captain Sanjar, and Barbara Harris the seductive Princess Barbára. (Costumes by Tony Walton.)*

more performances—both on the road and in New York—than any other actor.

In mid-1965, Bock and Harnick ventured on a musical path that was not only daring but previously untrodden: a show that would contain three separate one-act stories connected by a unifying thread which, originally, was to have been man, woman, and the devil. After trying out stories by de Maupassant, Bernard Malamud, and Marcel Aymé, they settled on Bruce Jay Friedman's *Show Biz Connections* (illustrating modern-day permissiveness), Nathaniel Hawthorne's *Young Goodman Brown* (early American Puritanism), and Mark Twain's *Diary of Adam and Eve* (dawn of humanity and innocence). The original title was *Come Back! Go Away! I Love You!*, the original director was Jerome Robbins, and the original librettist was Jerome Coopersmith. But things didn't work out as planned. Robbins was replaced by Mike Nichols (his first Broadway musical), who drastically altered both concept and contents. Frank Stockton's *The Lady or the Tiger* was substituted for the Hawthorne, Jules Feiffer's *Passionella* for the Friedman, the order of the stories was reversed, and Coopersmith's work was taken over by Bock and Harnick themselves. Under the new title of *The Apple Tree*, the finished product, when it was premiered in the autumn of 1966, turned out to be three musical vignettes with hardly a discernable link. Sharp ears, though, could spot certain interrelating musical themes—the melody of the lullaby, "Go to Sleep Whatever You Are," in *Adam and Eve*, showed up as the final song in *Passionella*, and the music for the snake's "Forbidden Fruit," was likewise repeated for the Balladeer's song in *The Lady or the Tiger*. There was also whimsical reference to the color brown that cropped up in all three stories.

Just as *Tenderloin* was the successor to *Fiorello!*, so *The Rothschilds*, which opened in 1970, was the successor to *Fid-*

dler on the Roof. In this adaptation of Frederic Morton's best-selling saga of the rise of the European banking dynasty, we were again treated to an affectionate look at a large Jewish family—Mayer Rothschild (played by Hal Linden) had five sons to Tevye's five daughters—and its struggle against religious persecution. But unlike the impoverished, powerless Jews of *Fiddler,* the family Rothschild was able to triumph over its oppressors through the weapon of money.

Bock and Harnick were first approached by producer Hillard Elkins to write the score in 1963. At the time they were occupied with *Fiddler,* though purely on speculation, but they decided to stick with that musical chiefly because of their dissatisfaction with the original treatment of the Rothschild story. Five years and six librettists later, they were finally won over by the adaptation submitted by Sherman Yellen. Another factor in their decision was that the texture of the score would be more akin to eighteenth and nineteenth Century European music than it would be to the traditional Hebraic and Russian themes of *Fiddler.* Still, *The Rothschilds* could not help but be perceived as Tevye's wealthy relatives, and though the musical had a respectable run of over 500 performances, it was—ironically—unable to earn a profit.

One of the play's memorable scenes concerned an anti-Semitic rampage in the Rothschild home. Before the attack, Mayer's young boys are herded into the cellar and the looting and wrecking occur in the dark. Once the attack is over and the lights go on, the boys emerge from the cellar—only now they are all young men. Thus through director Michael Kidd's ingenious method of telescoping the passage of time, we became vividly aware that the attacks never ceased during the years that the boys were growing up.

Whatever their reasons (which have never been revealed to the public), Bock and Harnick terminated their partner-

ship after *The Rothschilds.* Bock then concentrated on writing lyrics as well as music but his efforts, so far, have gone unproduced. Harnick has been occupied with fashioning lyrics for operas (including Jack Beeson's *Captain Jinks of the Horse Marines*), an operetta (a new version of Lehar's *The Merry Widow*), a Broadway musical (the short-lived *Rex,* with music by Richard Rodgers), and a limited-run off-Broadway musical (the stage adaptation of the Michel Legrand-Jacques Demy cinema soufflé, *The Umbrellas of Cherbourg*).

The Rothschilds *(1970).* Hal Linden as Mayer Rothschild. *(Costume by John Bury.)*

Charles Strouse and Lee Adams.

Courtesy ASCAP

CHAPTER TWENTY-FIVE

CHARLES STROUSE
LEE ADAMS
MARTIN CHARNIN

"I LOVE MUSICALS like *A Little Night Music* or *My Fair Lady*," says Charles Strouse, "but, on the other hand, they're not the kind of things I'd be interested in doing myself. All of my musicals, starting with *Bye Bye Birdie*, take place in America and are about Americans."

Though no one would ever accuse Strouse of the kind of flag-waving chauvinism that was once so much a part of the theatre of George M. Cohan, it is equally true that no other composer for the Broadway stage since the fabled George M. has ever shown such single-minded concern for the American experience.* In *Bye Bye Birdie*, the setting is Sweet Apple, Ohio, and the story deals with the effect of an Elvis Presley-type idol on swooning adolescents. In *All American* (nothing left to chance with *that* title), the theme is the Americanization of a Hungarian professor at a southern football college. In *Golden Boy*, a Harlem youth battles to win recognition in the fight ring. In *It's a Bird It's a Plane It's Superman*, superhuman hero-

ics triumph in the campy, comic strip world of Metropolis, U.S.A. In *Applause*, the backstage world of the Broadway theatre becomes the battleground for an ingenue-vs-star encounter. In *Annie*, another comic strip musical, youthful innocence conquers adversity in New York.

It will certainly not escape notice that Strouse's Broadway musicals to date—all scores written with lyricist Lee Adams except for *Annie*, which he wrote with Martin Charnin—not only have dealt with American subjects but have been characterized largely by contemporary themes concerning the youth of our land. Since our musical stage contains so many of the attributes most often associated with young people—optimism, romantic excess, energetic movement, colorful attire—it is little wonder that their crushes, crises, and cartoons should provide highly appropriate inspiration. And surely through the talents of Strouse, Adams, and Charnin those whose years are still tender have been supplied with especially winning and perceptive musical expressions.

Charles Strouse, who was born in New York, June 7, 1928, began his composing career at the age of twelve. Music

* This, it should be quickly noted, applies exclusively to Strouse's work so far in New York. In London in 1972, he joined with lyricist Lee Adams to create the score for *I and Albert*, which was all about the royal romance between Queen Victoria and her consort.

Bye Bye Birdie *(1960).*
His teenage fans swoon
whenever they hear rock and
roll idol, Conrad Birdie (Dick
Gautier), sing "Honestly
Sincere." Michael J. Pollard
and Susan Watson are at the
left. (Costumes by Miles
White).

Golden Boy *(1964).*
"Into the ring," wrote Walter
Kerr in the Herald Tribune,
"choreographer Donald
McKayle throws Sammy Davis
and dancer Jaime Rogers with
nothing but drums to guide
them. There are instant
haymakers but on metronome
beat . . . The view from the
ringside is breath-taking as
Mr. Rogers spins his last spin
and drops; it is as though
rhythm had died while you
were looking."

was his life from then on, though initially his goal was in the area of the concert hall. He attended the Eastman School of Music at Rochester, received a scholarship to study with Aaron Copland at Tanglewood, and later studied in Paris with Nadia Boulanger. Once his student days were over, however, Strouse discovered, without too much surprise, that popular music offered more gainful employment, both as performer and as composer. At first he played piano in dance bands; soon he gravitated toward the theatre—in the Jerome Kern-George Gershwin tradition—via the rehearsal pianist route.

Lee Adams, a native of Mansfield, Ohio, was born on August 14, 1924. At Ohio State University, where he was a journalism major, he wrote occasional lyrics for the varsity shows though with nary a thought about song writing as anything else but a hobby. Upon graduation, Adams came to New York where he did graduate work at Columbia University's Pulitzer School of Journalism. For almost four years he served on the staff of *Pageant* magazine, which he left to become articles editor of *This Week.*

Strouse and Adams met through a mutual friend in 1949. Their first collaborative efforts for the theatre were heard at the Green Mansions summer resort, where they followed the customary training route of preparing a new revue score every week for ten weeks. In all, they wrote songs for some ten revues both off-Broadway and in London, including three for Ben Bagley—*Shoestring Revue* in 1955 (for which Strouse doubled as music director), *The Littlest Revue,* and *Shoestring '57.*

It was Edward Padula who ended Strouse's career as a rehearsal pianist and Adams' career as a magazine editor. He wanted the team to collaborate on the songs for *Bye Bye Birdie,* his first venture as a Broadway producer. Padula's aim was to do an original story about modern teenagers, but one that would show their healthier, sunnier, far from the *West Side Story* side. And he wanted the songwriting team to come up with a fresh, youthful score to match the fresh, youthful script being devised by Michael Stewart, another Green Mansions alumnus. In all, over two and a half years were devoted to creating some fifty-five songs for three separate versions of the story—as well as holding over eighty-five backers' auditions. "Our problem," Strouse has said, "was to satirize a kind of music—rock-and-roll—that was so new it was hard to maintain a perspective about it as we could, say, the Charleston or swing. And not only did we have to satirize it, we also had to use the form for real musical value. In 'The Telephone Hour,' we did a kind of fugal development, with real rock-and-roll harmonies and rhythm. In 'One Last Kiss,' we satirized it by going overboard, the way we imagined our singing idol, Conrad Birdie, would do it." Other songs also captured the spirit of a restless but not alienated youth. In "One Boy" ("One boy to laugh with, to joke with, have Coke with"), an adolescent girl dreams of the pleasures of going steady. The rhythmic "A Lot of Livin' To Do" was a beltable ode to a future life of uninhibited pleasure. And "Kids" gave the adult point of view as the elders bewailed, "Why can't they be like we were, perfect in every way?"

What added greatly to the show's style were the contributions of director Gower Champion. For "The Telephone Hour," for example, he had his teenagers wriggling and writhing through telephone conversations staged in a huge honeycomb set representing their rooms. Memorable too was the madcap disruption of a Shriners' convention in which Chita Rivera enticed all of the befezzed celebrants under the table. "Everything about the musical," gushed Kenneth Tynan in *The New Yorker*, "was filled with a kind of affectionate freshness that we have seldom encountered since Mr.

Rodgers collaborated with Mr. Hart on *Babes in Arms*." (Mr. Tynan, bless his faultless memory, was all of eleven at the time and living in England.)

The high school kids of *Bye Bye Birdie* gave way to the college kids of *All American*, which came along two years later. Ray Bolger, absent from Broadway musicals since *Where's Charley?*, made a none too auspicious return in the role of an immigrant engineering professor who comes to this country to teach at Southern Baptist Institute of Technology and ends up as the football coach. Many opportunities for spoofing American education and huckstering were somehow lost in the Mel Brooks libretto, which simply deteriorated into an old-fashioned star vehicle. The score, surprisingly, was strongest in the sentimental pieces—including "Once Upon a Time" sung by Bolger and Eileen Herlie as the dean of women.

The inspiration for transforming Clifford Odets' drama, *Golden Boy*, into a musical drama originated with Hillard Elkins, a personal manager, who was anxious to break into the ranks of producers. It occurred to him that switching the central part of an Italian-American boxer named Joe Bonaparte into a Negro American boxer named Joe Wellington would give the story the same significance for modern audiences as had the earlier concept for the audiences of the Thirties. Once Sammy Davis had become enthusiastic about doing the part, Elkins signed Strouse and Adams (two of his former clients) for the songs, and then managed to talk a slightly startled Clifford Odets into writing the adaptation.

The work did not proceed smoothly or quickly. Then, with the second revision almost completed, Odets died of cancer in August, 1963. At first Adams, who had worked closely with the playwright, tried taking over the book-writing assignment, but in August, 1964, with only two months to go before the Broadway opening, playwright William Gibson, a close friend of Odets, was persuaded to do a complete rewrite. Disagreements forced the replacement of director Peter Coe by Arthur Penn, and there were some major cast changes. Nerves were frayed and no one seemed to have a clear idea of exactly what was going on from one day to the next. But the miracle happened; the show opened on schedule, got respectable notices, and, thanks largely to the appeal of Sammy Davis, had a run of over 500 performances.

There was no question that the production suffered from its too numerous changes, and that the seams showed quite obviously. Yet the show captured its audience through the dynamic performance of its star and its inherent theatricality (highlighted by a musicalized gym workout as an opener, and a stunner of a choreographed fight sequence). The Strouse-Adams score caught just the right qualities of pathos and impending doom in the love songs, particularly in "I Want to Be with You" and "Lorna's Here." But larger issues were not overlooked. In "Night Song," the writers gave musical dimension to the feelings of frustration and tension of Negro youth; in "127th Street," they turned out a lively, nose-thumbing salute to Harlem, made all the more telling through its parodying of sentimental home-and-hearth ballads.

In *It's a Bird It's a Plane It's Superman*, produced and directed by Harold Prince in 1966, Strouse and Adams ventured into the camp camp via a takeoff on the well-known comic strip. Everyone connected with the show—including librettists Robert Benton and David Newman—was scrupulous in avoiding the above-it-all, exaggerated approach; everything was done to make the ridiculous appear natural and matter-of-fact. The musical contributions worked well within the show's framework, allowing for some wonderfully foursquare statements for the hero ("Every man has a job to do, and my job is doing good") that beautifully contrasted with the generally breezy pieces Strouse and Adams gave to almost everyone else.

With *Applause* (1970), Strouse and Adams became involved in the back-scratching, back-stabbing world of the New York theatre. In adapting the film, *All About Eve*, co-librettists Betty Comden and Adolph Green (for the first time responsible for the libretto but not the lyrics) managed to convey an aura of show-business authenticity as they chronicled the manner in which mousy but sharp-clawed Eve Harrington is befriended by doyenne Margo Channing, and, through equal measures of guile and talent, displaces her at the theatrical top. Despite some glaringly illogical plot devices (critics would hardly have covered an understudy's single appearance nor is it likely that an ambitious actress would spurn a producer in favor of a married playwright, to name two), the authors did take the unexpected step of making their leading characters dramatic rather than musical-comedy actresses, thereby avoiding the obvious of inserting the song numbers into the productions being performed. Instead, apart from those pieces directly related to the plot, specialty numbers were brought in through scenes in a Greenwich Village gay bar (for the propulsively affirmative "But Alive") and in Joe Allen's restaurant, a "gypsy"—or chorus dancer—hangout (for two rousing odes to the world of greasepaint—"Applause" and "She's No Longer a Gypsy").

What was perhaps the most important element in the success of the musical was the sizzling performance of Lauren Bacall, making her musical-stage debut as Margo. Neither a trained singer nor dancer, she projected so much sheer magnetism that it required more than the normal amount of willing disbelief suspension to accept the premise that she could be overshadowed by anyone else within stalking distance of Shubert Alley. She was, in the view of *The New Yorker*'s Brendan Gill, "the be-all and end-all. Tall, tigerishly restless, blazing with energy and humor, she gathers the show up in her arms and from time to time, gives it a good, hard, motherly shake. She is in charge, and it is plain that she enjoys her responsibilities."

Charles Strouse took seven years after *Applause* to return to Broadway. It was worth the wait.

Shortly before Christmas 1971, Martin Charnin, a lyricist and director, bought a bound collection of *Little Orphan Annie* comic strips—and immediately began visualizing the waif's saga taking shape as a musical comedy. Charnin, a native New Yorker who was born on November 24, 1934, had made his Broadway debut as an actor (in the role of Big Deal) in *West Side Story*, and also appeared in the revue, *The Boys Against the Girls*. As lyricist, he contributed songs to off-Broadway revues, then collaborated with Mary Rodgers (daughter of Richard) on *Hot Spot*, starring Judy Holliday, and with Richard Rodgers himself on *Two by Two*, starring Danny Kaye. At the time he became hooked on *Little Orphan Annie*, Charnin was primarily involved in television.

For his librettist and composer, the writer turned to two friends, Thomas Meehan, a *New Yorker* contributor who had adapted his piece, "Yma, Ava; Yma, Aga; Yma, Uta; Yma, Ida," for a Charnin-produced television special featuring Anne Bancroft, and Charles Strouse, whom he had known ever since Strouse contributed vocal arrangements for *The Boys Against the Girls*.

Though neither Meehan nor Strouse was initially enthusiastic about the project (their identical first reaction was "Ughhh"), Charnin won them over by explaining that he didn't plan to use anything specific from the strip but rather to fit the three major characters—Annie, Daddy Warbucks, and Annie's dog, Sandy—into an original story. Meehan decided to set his tale late in 1933, with the plot centering around Annie's search for her missing parents and her eventual adoption by millionaire Warbucks. This

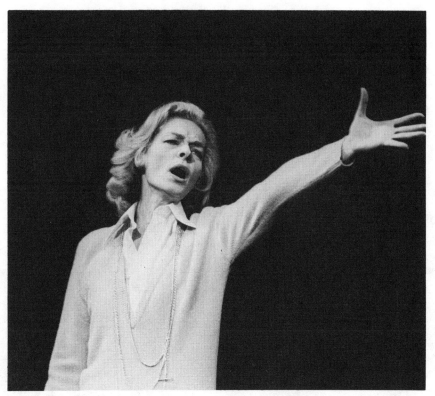

Applause (1970).
"Welcome to the theatre,"
sings Lauren Bacall as
Broadway star Margo
Channing.

approach, he felt, would keep the fable within the quaint, even Dickensian quality of the Harold Gray cartoon (others would later note more than a twist of *Oliver!* in his characters and plot). As the writing progressed, Meehan began thinking of Annie as "a metaphorical figure standing for innate decency, courage and optimism in the face of hard times, pessimism and despair"—in short, an antidote to the prevailing mood of the Vietnam-Nixon-Watergate years during which the script was written. For his part, Charles Strouse found a great deal of affinity in composing music for this kind of story. "A comic strip is an ideal basis for a musical comedy," he has said, "because they are similar forms of popular American culture, both dealing in broad strokes, telling simple stories in as few words as possible."

The writing of *Annie* took fourteen months, but it took another four and a half years for it to arrive on Broadway. The reason was fundamental: no producer thought it stood a chance. Finally, in the summer of 1976, Michael P. Price of the

Photo by Martha Swope

Annie (Andrea McArdle) gets a paddling from Miss Hannigan (Dorothy Loudon) for trying to run away from the orphanage.

*Annie (1977).
The men responsible: composer Charles Strouse, lyricist-director Martin Charnin, and librettist Thomas Meehan.*

The birth of the New Deal— or the day Little Orphan Annie sang "Tomorrow" to President Roosevelt. Charmed by Andrea McCardle are, left to right, Laurie Beechman, Reid Shelton (Daddy Warbucks), Richard Ennslen, Donald Craig, James Hosbein, Raymond Thorne (F.D.R.), and Bob Freschi. (Costumes by Theoni V. Aldredge; setting by David Mitchell.)

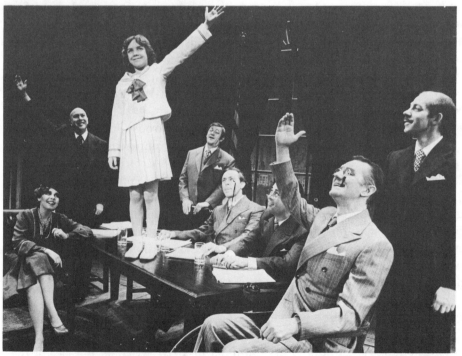

Photo by Martha Swope

Goodspeed Opera House in East Haddam, Connecticut, gave it a showing at his theatre, where the results were encouraging even though the show needed more work in the areas of tightening the plot and giving it a more consistent viewpoint. The road to Broadway was considerably smoothed when Mike Nichols joined the venture as producer and uncredited guiding hand. By the time *Annie*· played Washington before its New York opening at the Alvin Theatre (April 21, 1977), the show had become such a predestined hit that it was virtually critic-proof.

Aware of this, most of the critics seemed to be as concerned with analyzing *Annie*'s appeal as they were to offering their own views. To Martin Gottfried in the *Post*, it was simply because "the damn thing works"—despite its "greasepaint sentimentality," "mawkishness," "cheap nostalgia," and "unabashed corniness." The *News*' Douglas Watt felt that it was being accepted by audiences as "a kiddie show for adults," even if he couldn't recommend it to anyone over eleven. *New York* magazine's Alan Rich didn't see how it could miss with "six preteen foundlings as chorus line, a mongrel dog, a love song to New York City, and a Christmas tree"—though he considered the show "pretty much of a grab bag overall." According to Theodore Kalem in *Time*, the musical was "wholesome family fare," notwithstanding its "aridity of mood." And in *Cue*, Marilyn Stasio credited its success to "an uncanny insight into what people need right now—strong new parent figures who are gonna make their boo-boos all better." As for herself, she found it "a pedestrian show of minor theatrical merit."

It is also true that any serious appraisal of *Annie* cannot help but detect that the story is virtually without conflict, since it takes no time at all for our heroine to melt the tycoon heart of Daddy Warbucks, and that the chief villain (originally Dorothy Loudon) is played more for laughs than for menace. Also, the sight of an ineffectual President Roosevelt being roused into creating the New Deal after hearing Annie sing "Tomorrow" unfortunately belittles the man and distorts history.

Perhaps, after all, the appeal of *Annie* is simply that it makes audiences believe the unbelievable, that faith and hope will be rewarded not by mere charity but by riches, security, and love. That the show's heroine has already become something of a theatrical legend there can be no doubt. As a direct descendent of Dorothy of *The Wizard of Oz* (and *The Wiz*), *Sally*'s Sally, *Carnival*'s Lili—not to mention *Oliver!*'s Oliver—she has unquestionably taken her place as Broadway's most beloved waif of all times.

Verve, vitality, honest emotion, and, above all, a thorough understanding of the function of songs in the modern musical theatre have marked the output of the three writers discussed in this chapter. In addition, they are all deeply committed to the song as an entity, as an inextricable union of music and lyrics. "What we are aiming for," Strouse once said of his work with Adams, "is to make the lyric almost indistinguishable from the music. Not merely a wedding of words and music, but the words and music as a total concept, a complete and inevitable part of the character's expression at the moment. As we see it, neither the melody nor the lyric should be able to exist without the other."

Cy Coleman.

CHAPTER TWENTY-SIX

CY COLEMAN
CAROLYN LEIGH
MICHAEL STEWART

To MANY COMPOSERS and lyricists in the musical theatre, it is reward enough to hear their songs performed and appreciated in the context for which they were created. To others, however, true personal satisfaction comes only through personal identification—through singing, playing, or conducting their own works before paying customers in theatres, concert halls and cabarets. This tradition goes back to the earliest days of our Broadway theatre. George M. Cohan starred in his own productions, and both Victor Herbert and Sigmund Romberg loved to conduct. Since then, through Gershwin, Bernstein, Comden and Green, and on up to the more recent writers such as Bacharach, Hamlisch, Gretchen Cryer, and Elizabeth Swados, the creator-interpreter has been very much a part of the theatre scene.

In this dual capacity, none has carved so firm a niche in our contemporary theatre as Cy Coleman, who, since 1969, has been an active and innovative composer, but who also, since many years before that, has been a sought-after supperclub and concert-hall soloist. Performing, in fact, is the area that Coleman professes to enjoy most. "When you sit down and write," he once observed, "it's in a lonely room and you spend a great deal of time just staring at your collaborator. That's why it's so great to get out and perform in clubs. Your social life is taken care of and, best of all, you're able to get instant reaction to what you're doing."

Though his musical direction would later take a far different course, Cy Coleman started out—and at a remarkably tender age—to become a concert pianist. Born in the Bronx, New York, on June 14, 1929, he began playing when he was four, picking out tunes he heard on the radio. This feat so impressed his family that they arranged to get him a piano scholarship. By the time he was six, he had already given recitals at both Steinway Hall and Town Hall. He continued his piano studies under Rudolph Gruen, attending the New York College of Music at the same time he was going to classes at the High School of Music and Art. In his mid-teens, Coleman played in servicemen's canteens where he found himself becoming increasingly involved in jazz. After graduating from high school, he

Carolyn Leigh.

Photo by Friedman-Abeles

served as the first act finale of *John Murray Anderson's Almanac.*

About four years later, Coleman accidentally met lyricist Carolyn Leigh on the street. They had known each other slightly before and, partly to make conversation, Cy asked Carolyn if she'd like to write a song with him sometime. "How about right now?" she suggested, and off they went. "A Moment of Madness," the tune that resulted, was written in two days, was published almost immediately, and was quickly recorded by Sammy Davis, Jr. Convinced that they had a good thing going, Coleman and Leigh soon began turning out songs on a regular basis. Among their pre-Broadway hits: "Witchcraft," "Firefly" (written as a Twenties-type production number for *Gypsy,* for which they auditioned but lost out to Styne and Sondheim), "I Walk a Little Faster," "You Fascinate Me So" (sung in the Julius Monk supper club revue, *Demi-Dozen*), "The Best Is Yet to Come," and "It Amazes Me."

Carolyn Leigh's debut as a writer for the theatre occurred some six years before her first score with Coleman. Born on August 21, 1926, also in the Bronx, she started writing poems and doggerel when she was nine. After attending Queens College and New York University, she entered the literary world by writing continuity for WQXR and serving as chief—because she was the only—copywriter at an advertising agency. In 1951, a music publisher, impressed with some verse she had written, offered her a year's contract to write song lyrics. Her first big success, "Young at Heart" (music by Johnny Richards), came along two years later.

While driving home one night following a theatre performance, Mary Martin heard the song on her automobile radio. Struck with the quality of the words, she felt that the person who had written them would be ideal to write the lyrics for her next musical, *Peter Pan.* The following day, Miss Martin's husband, producer

formed a trio and promptly got a booking at the Little Club. The success of this engagement insured steady work and made his name well known even before his composing skills were recognized.

Cy Coleman's first lyric writing partner was Joe McCarthy (his father, also named Joe McCarthy, had been the lyricist of *Irene, Kid Boots* and *Rio Rita*). Their biggest hits were "I'm Gonna Laugh You Right Out of My Life" and "Why Try to Change Me Now?" In 1953, the Coleman-McCarthy song, "Tin Pan Alley" ("Just think of a catchy tune/ Come up with a rhyme for June")

Richard Halliday, telephoned Miss Leigh and simply asked her if she'd be interested in the assignment. With a new partner, composer Mark ("Moose") Charlap, she wrote about ten pieces for what was then a "play with music." When, however, during the production's West Coast break-in, director Jerome Robbins decided to increase the musical content, he turned to the more seasoned team of Jule Styne, Betty Comden and Adolph Green for the additional songs. Still, the best-remembered songs from *Peter Pan*, "I've Gotta Crow" and "I'm Flying," were the work of Leigh and Charlap.

Despite her skill with words dealing with the emotions of the young, Carolyn Leigh, once she had begun writing with Cy Coleman, showed she could match the rhythmically sophisticated music of her partner with suitably adult, worldly lyrics. Their Broadway debut as a team was prompted by a long distance telephone call from director Michael Kidd. Kidd, then in Hollywood, was about to

co-produce a musical in partnership with librettist N. Richard Nash, that would star the reigning queen of video, Lucille Ball. Coleman and Leigh eagerly snapped at the chance. Unfortunately, *Wildcat*, when it was unveiled on Broadway in December, 1960, was met by a generally lukewarm press. Due to the boxoffice appeal of the star, however, the show did well enough financially, but then had to shut down in June because of Miss Ball's illness.

The Coleman-Leigh score had several attractive pieces and one smash hit—"Hey, Look Me Over." This was the first song in the show sung by Lucille Ball, and the writing of it posed many serious problems. Originally, the team was thinking of something very sophisticated, very Broadway, but whatever they tried always came out sounding like an Ethel Merman opener. Finally, after two weeks, Carolyn said, "Cy, if you didn't care at all, if it wasn't the opening number and it wasn't for Lucille Ball making

Wildcat *(1960).*
Flanked by Swen Swenson and Al Lanti, Lucille Ball does her own version of the Mexican Hat Dance in "El Sombrero." (Costumes by Alvin Colt.)

Photo by Friedman-Abeles

her stage debut, and it was just a simple number for the scene and the character, what would you write?" And Cy replied, "If this number weren't so important, I'd just write something as corny and as simple as this . . ." And he played the opening measures of "Hey, Look Me Over." They laughed and quickly vetoed the idea, but Carolyn couldn't get the melody out of her head. Two days later, she called her partner, "Remember that tune you played for Lucy's opening number? As long as we're making jokes, how's this for a lyric, 'Hey, look me over, lend me an ear/ Fresh out of clover, mortgaged up to here . . .' Isn't that funny, Cy?"

There were fewer uncertainties about the next Coleman-Leigh venture, *Little Me*, which opened two years later. The hilarious saga of the rise of Belle Poitrine, née Schlumpfert, had been a successful novel by Patrick Dennis, the libretto was the work of Neil Simon, and the star was Sid Caesar playing no less than seven roles. The reviews ranged from mild to wild approval, but somehow the customers didn't come in the expected drove-like packs. The musical contributions were certainly superior to the work Coleman and Leigh had done for *Wildcat*. The ethereal "Real Live Girl," a striking contrast to the generally brash, spoofing nature of the rest of the score, provided a memorable ballet for soldiers in a World War I dugout. "The Other Side of the Tracks" emerged from a sentimental daydream into a clarion battle cry. The slinky "I've Got Your Number" was a show-stopping, tantalizing mating call for the gracefully agile Swen Swenson. Mr. Caesar had five comic turns, most notably "I Love You," in which a snobbish young man ardently professes his love for the heroine, "Considering you're riffraff and I am well-to-do."

Two Broadway scores and over twenty published songs—and the team of Cy Coleman and Carolyn Leigh decided to call it quits. Of the two, the composer has fared considerably better on Broadway since the breakup. (Miss Leigh's only post-Coleman effort to date, the 1967 *How Now, Dow Jones*, written with Hollywood's Elmer Bernstein, received a more bearish than bullish reception.) Coleman began the second phase of his writing career in much the same way that he had begun the first: one day he simply called veteran lyricist Dorothy Fields and asked her if she'd like to write a song with him. Miss Fields was willing, and before long they were hard at work creating the score for *Sweet Charity*, starring Gwen Verdon.

Coleman was working on two film scores at the time he agreed to supply the music for the new musical, and, in setting about the new task, he injected some of the techniques he had picked up in Hollywood. In true cinematic fashion, he deliberately composed a perky, chipper instrumental piece as an identifying

Little Me *(1962).*
Sid Caesar as Mr. Pinchley, the richest man in the world, takes a shine to our little Belle (Virginia Martin.)

Photo by Friedman-Abeles

*Sweet Charity (1966).
Composer Cy Coleman and
lyricist Dorothy Fields talk
over a problem backstage with
director-choreographer Bob
Fosse.*

*Gwen Verdon, Helen
Gallagher and Thelma Oliver
belting out "There's Gotta Be
Something Better than This."
(Costumes by Irene Sharaff.)*

theme everytime Miss Verdon, as Charity, appeared on the stage. He also made great use of underscoring to heighten the dramatic situations of the story. As for the set pieces, Coleman and Fields constructed a musically unified score that dramatically exposed the heroine's variety of moods and emotions—"Where Am I Going" to point up her frustration, "There's Gotta Be Something Better than This" her determination to seek a better life, "If My Friends Could See Me Now" her amazement at fleeting good fortune. In one memorably atmospheric number, "Big Spender," the dance hall hostesses at the Fan-Dango Ballroom draped themselves around a railing in awkwardly seductive poses to coax the audience, as lethargically as possible, to "spend a little time with me."

The origin of the musical had been Federico Fellini's *Nights of Cabiria*, but on Broadway in the newly refurbished Palace Theatre the prostitute of the film had become a presumably more sympathetic dime-a-dance girl. Initially conceived to be presented with another one-act musical written by Elaine May, *Sweet Charity* was subsequently fleshed out to two acts by Neil Simon when the other concept was abandoned. The padding, however, was all too apparent, with many scenes extended beyond their proper lengths and with seemingly endless, though excitingly staged, dance routines by Bob Fosse.

It took seven years before Coleman and Fields were back again on Broadway. The extended absence may possibly have helped audiences overlook the fact that their next project, *Seesaw* (adapted from the William Gibson play, *Two for the Seesaw*), was almost a continuation of the romantic adventures of their previous heroine. Again we had a kookie, trusting, tarnished innocent in New York (played by Michele Lee) who smiles bravely through a brief romantic affair with a squarish lover (Ken Howard). Again the tale gave them the chance to meet various oddball characters in different parts of Manhattan. Even one of the songs, "Poor Everybody Else," had been intended for the Gwen Verdon musical, and the librettist, who replaced Michael Stewart on the road, turned out to be Neil Simon (though he refused program credit). Despite director Michael Bennett's salvaging efforts (the original director, Edwin Sherin, was another road casualty), the blending of the intimate scenes with the rather garish exteriors and ensembles never quite meshed. A well-publicized onstage appearance of Mayor John Lindsay (who bore a slight resemblance to the play's hero) did, however, help keep the show running for almost three hundred performances.

Coleman and Fields caught the many faces of modern New York in their score. Two of the heroine's numbers stood out: "Nobody Does It Like Me," a confession of chronic ineptitude in affairs of the heart, and "Welcome to Holiday Inn" (melodically recalling "Walking My Baby Back Home") in which all sorts of special amenities are proffered to the lady's overnight guest. There was also a colorful cakewalk, "It's Not Where You Start (It's Where You Finish)," a choreographer's dream that ends with the stage knee-deep in balloons as the director (Tommy Tune) high-kicks up a flight of hastily supplied stairs.

A year or so after the death of Dorothy Fields in 1974, Coleman became involved with Michael Stewart on the project that would eventually be known as *I Love My Wife*. Stewart, though initially a lyricist, had made his name as librettist for such notable attractions as *Bye Bye Birdie*, *Carnival* and *Hello, Dolly!* His chance to combine both talents came when he saw a French farce with music, *Viens, Chez Moi, J'Habite Chez une Copine (Come to My Place, I'm Living with a Girlfriend)*. What especially appealed to the writer was the direct, artless way the songs were introduced: when one was needed, an actor simply stopped the show, took a microphone off a hook at the side of the stage, lip-synched the song, and then hung up the mike and resumed the story.

In creating the score for their American adaptation, Coleman and Stewart followed the concept of purposely avoiding any attempt at integrating songs within the story line. Instead, the four characters in the plot—plus four highly visible singing and dancing musicians in a variety of costumes—sang the numbers as a series of pointed commentaries on the theme. And what was this brave new theme that inspired this brave new concept? Mate-swapping in Trenton, New Jersey.

The great challenge for the writers, of course, was to try to rid the story of its inherent tastelessness and to offer it as a basically innocent romp involving two normal married couples who decide to catch up on the sexual revolution by enjoying a *menage à quatre*. Under the guidance of director Gene Saks it succeeded better than might have been expected. Critics used such adjectives as "bright, inventive, amusing and breezy"

I Love My Wife *(1977).
The opening number, "We're
Still Friends," sung by the
company. On the floor are
Kenny Baker, Ilene Graff,
Joanna Gleason, and James
Naughton; behind them the
onstage instrumentalists are
Ken Bichel, Michael Mark,
Joseph Saulter, and John
Miller. (Costumes by Ron
Talsky.)*

(Barnes, *Times*), and "healthy, well-adjusted, sentimental, and cheerful" (Gottfried, *Post*), though there was a minority that found the goings-on and takings-off far less appealing. Brendan Gill, in *The New Yorker*, termed the book "a monotonous and mildly unsavory series of variations on a single witless joke," while Marilyn Stasio, in *Cue*, held the entertainment "hopelessly dated in subject and shockingly skimpy in execution."

The score, however, won nothing but praise. Coleman's music offered a variety of pieces that, despite their eclecticism, had a commendable unity of mood and purpose—from the country-ballad type "Someone Wonderful I Missed" to the happy jazz beat of "Hey There, Good Times"; from the Jacques Brel-type declaration, "Sexually Free," to the vaudeville turn, "Everybody Today Is Turning On"; and from the sophisticated cabaret revue-type "Lovers on Christmas Eve" to the romantic, waltzing avowal, "I Love My Wife" (despite the crudity of the lines, "If I should shake, break out in spots,/ Don't fret, my dear, it's not swine fever/ You're swine has got the hots").

Coleman's problems in writing the score for *On the Twentieth Century* (which, though it opened almost a year later, had been in the works before *I Love My Wife*) were of a far different nature. "What I decided to do," the composer once said, "was to take my model from the characters—flamboyant, larger-than-life, outrageous people. I decided to go to the comic-opera form because those were the days, in the early Thirties, when people flung out their arms and bared their chests and acted in that style. It accented the glamour, and it also influenced our casting the show with real singers as well as actors."

The most outrageously flamboyant people of the story were producer-director Oscar Jaffee (John Cullum) and actress Lily Garland (first Madeline

On the Twentieth
Century *(1978).*
Movie idol Kevin Kline
threatens producer John
Cullum over glamorous star
Judy Kaye. (Costumes by
Florence Klotz; setting by
Robin Wagner.)

Photo by Martha Swope

Michael Stewart

Kahn, later replaced by Judy Kaye) whose frenzied antagonisms aboard the speeding Chicago-to-New York deluxe train provided both the humor and the conflict of the story. Though the work was based on the durable farce, *Twentieth Century*, theatre buffs could also detect in the leading characters something of the relationship between Fred Graham and Lili Vanessi in *Kiss Me, Kate*, and Mack Sennett and Mabel Normand in *Mack and Mabel*.

On the Twentieth Century teamed Coleman for the first time with the libretto-and-lyrics writing team of Betty Comden and Adolph Green. In adapting the text, the writers eliminated two Oberammergau actors, built up the character of a religious nut and changed him into a woman (so the part could be played by elfin Imogene Coca in her first Broadway musical role in thirty-eight years), and, as an excuse to leave the train periodically, added a flashback audition sequence and an episode in which a new play is performed.

With Harold Prince directing, the musical arrived at the St. James Theatre in February 1978. Audiences were treated to a dazzlingly pell-mell production featuring, as much as any of the actors, designer Robin Wagner's gleaming art deco reproduction of the Twentieth Century Limited, which was able to do just about everything short of singing and dancing. As in the case of Stephen Sondheim's music for *A Little Night Music*, Coleman's comic-opera score again gave critics the chance to display their musical knowledge. "There are grandiloquent and amusing suggestions of everything from Tchaikowsky through Puccini and Friml and on up through Kurt Weill," itemized the *Times'* Richard Eder. "It runs a gorgeous gamut from Jacques Brel to Menotti," traced the *Post's* Clive Barnes. It was "a sometimes effective pastiche, with deft echoes of everything from Offenbach to Jerome Kern to

Gilbert and Sullivan," reported *Newsweek's* Jack Kroll. And Douglas Watt, in the *News*, could detect styles a century apart as he found the music "alternating much of the time between early nineteenth-century comic-opera mannerisms and early twentieth century operetta."

For *Barnum*, which opened at the St. James Theatre a little over two years later, Coleman returned to Broadway with the saga of another flashy impresario, the legendary sponsor of such attractions as George Washington's alleged 160-year-old nurse, the midget Tom Thumb, the elephant Jumbo, the diva Jennie Lind, and, finally, the three-ring circus. Reunited with lyricist Michael Stewart, the composer came up with a prancing parading score, abetted by Stewart's diamond-sharp, tongue-twisting words. Though it tried to jam too much into its 45-year time span, the entertainment provided full scope for he dynamic, multi-talented Jim Dale (his Barnum could sing and walk a tightrope at the same time), while also allowing director Joe Layton to create a total circus concept, with the entire cast continually in motion juggling, tumbling, clowning, twirling, marching, strutting, and flying through the air.

Coleman's work to date has clearly established him as one of the theatre's preeminent of the current scene. Once distinguished for his brisk, jazz influenced, sophisticated rhythms, he has shown a wider range and greater dramatic gifts in his most recent works, a sure sign that the Cy Coleman of the future will reveal untapped facets of both his skills as a craftsman and his dedication as a theatre composer. "My feeling about musicals is that very often the score is the sub-text of the entire piece," he has said. "It is the characters, the texture of the skin, the color of the eyes. You have to have a book that will work, of course, but it's the score that gives it the overall flavor and emotional quality."

Jerry Herman.   Photo by Friedman-Abeles

CHAPTER TWENTY-SEVEN

JERRY HERMAN

WHILE OTHERS CELEBRAT-
ED in this book may have found inspiration in swashbuckling romance, or in
the joys of nature, or in youthful Americana, or in the seamier side of life, Jerry
Herman—so far—has been most closely
identified with musicals dealing with optimistic characters well into their middle
years, with the emphasis on larger-than-
life, independent-minded women. In five
of his seven book shows to date, he has
involved audiences in two mature romances in *Milk and Honey*, the machinations of an aging fraud in *Madame
Aphrodite*, the madcap careers of those
antic postdebs, Dolly Gallagher Levi and
Mame Dennis Burnside, and the sane in-
sanity of an ancient French *grande dame*
in *Dear World*.

Perhaps his preoccupation with subjects dealing with characters of advanced
age may be partly explained by the Herman style. Though very much of a writer
for today's audience, he is neither an innovator in form nor is he influenced by
so-called modern sounds. He is our theatre's leading traditionalist in that he still
believes music should have melody and
memorability, and that lyrics should be
concerned with basic, uncomplicated

emotions. In an age when many writers
purposely submerge their musical personality in favor of the book or "concept," Herman's output has an identifiable exuberance and directness. As he
himself once expressed in song, he revels
in the show tune in two-four. When
questioned about this, he readily admits,
"I really don't understand the current
sound as well as I understand the sound
of the Thirties and Forties. I know my
limitations, and I don't want to get into
areas that other people do better."

Jerry, né Gerald, Herman was born in
New York on July 10, 1932, but moved
with his family to Jersey City, New
Jersey, at an early age. Though Herman's mother was a piano and voice
teacher, she never forced him to take lessons; he picked up his musical knowledge
by playing piano by ear and never did
have a formal musical education (a condition he shares with, among other composers, Irving Berlin, Frank Loesser,
Richard Adler, Bob Merrill, and Harvey
Schmidt). At Miami University, which
he attended primarily because of its experimental drama department, Herman
was active as a composer, lyricist, author,
director and designer.

Milk and Honey *(1961).*
The principals: Mimi Benzell,
Robert Weede, and Molly
Picon. (Costumes by Miles
White.)

mance run spurred producer Lawrence Kasha to commission Herman to whip up another off-Broadway revue, *Parade,* though its success was only moderate.

That was early in 1960. Herman, with three revues—plus assorted television and nightclub assignments—now felt himself ready for Broadway. His agent introduced him to another client, playwright Don Appell, and the two began tossing ideas around. Suddenly, Appell blurted out, "How about a musical set in Israel?" With no idea of what they would put into a musical set in Israel, the two men agreed to collaborate. Aided by a financial assist from realtor-turned-producer Gerard Oestreicher, they took off for Israel where they spent five weeks soaking up atmosphere and dreaming up a story and the songs to go with it. Because Herman didn't want to confine himself to writing an entire score in a minor key, the writers decided to make their principal characters Americans rather than Israelis, with appropriately indigenous music added for local color.

When it opened in October, 1961, *Milk and Honey* won respectable notices, with generous praise for the performances of Robert Weede, Mimi Benzell and Molly Picon, and the bright, travel poster way the Israeli spirit was captured. As for Jerry Herman, Howard Taubman wrote in the *Times,* "He has provided songs that range from functional to exultant. His hora has the necessary rhythmic fervor; his 'Shalom' and 'Milk and Honey' pay genial respects to Israel, and in 'That Was Yesterday' and 'I Will Follow You,' he conveys the conviction of personal emotion."

Notwithstanding the gay, satirical pieces Jerry Herman had written for revues, he now found, as a result of *Milk and Honey,* that his creative image had become so altered that he was besieged with scripts dealing with somber romances between men and women of the post-forties generation. What he needed

One of Jerry Herman's college revues was called *I Feel Wonderful.* Apparently, it gave enough patrons a similarly affirmative attitude; in 1954, after Herman had graduated from Miami, the show was bankrolled by local enthusiasts and presented at an off-Broadway theatre. Not too many customers came, but the reviews were favorable ("Fresh and entertaining without a tedious number in it," opined Louis Kronenberger). *Nightcap,* a night club revue, was offered at the Showplace, where Herman was earning steady money as a pianist. Its 400-perfor-

was a quick change of pace. Hearing that David Merrick was about to produce a musical version of Thornton Wilder's slam-bang farce, *The Matchmaker*, Herman went about getting the song writing assignment in the most direct manner possible. He simply auditioned. After listening to four songs, Merrick, in fabled Hollywood style, turned to Herman and said, "Kid, the show is yours."

Because he had also sponsored *The Matchmaker*, Merrick had an especially proprietary attitude about the musical adaptation, and he was determined to do everything he could to insure that it would be the biggest success of his career. For librettist, he hired Michael Stewart, and for director, Gower Champion, both of whom had worked on two previous winners, *Bye Bye Birdie* and *Carnival*. His star was the superpowered, larger-than-life Carol Channing. Couldn't miss? Well, it almost did. The prospects looked so bleak, in fact, during the Detroit tryout that Merrick almost shut down the production.

But major alterations were quickly and skillfully made. Three songs were dropped, three were added (including the Act I finale). Possibly the most significant change was in holding up Miss Channing's second act entrance until the second—or "Hello, Dolly!"—scene. Following the January 16, 1964, New York première at the St. James Theatre, *Hello, Dolly!* was joyously welcomed by hat-tossing but not completely uncritical critics. While proclaiming it "a musical shot through with enchantment," Howard Taubman in the *Times* nevertheless objected to its "unnecessarily vulgar and frenzied touches." The *Post*'s Richard Watts, Jr., although hailing it as "big, bouncing, handsome, rapid-paced and filled with the shrewdest ingredients of successful showmanship," still lamented the lack of "whimsically playful humor and charm it had originally." Theodore Kalem of *Time*, however, disagreed. He

found "it has eye appeal, ear appeal, love appeal, and laugh appeal, but its most insinuating charm is its nostalgic appeal." As for Henry Hewes, the *Saturday Review* reviewer called it "a triumph of staging over a book, lyrics, and music that are not in themselves extraordinary."

Among other touches that helped him score his triumph, director Champion made use of a circular runway around the rim of the orchestra pit which was particularly effective in the show's biggest applause-catcher, the "Hello, Dolly" number. It is useless to cavil, of course, that the scene advances the story not a whit, or that Dolly Levi's return to a once-favored haunt is hardly a significant enough event to warrant such riotous celebrating. What counts, obviously, is the exciting theatricality of the number—the waiters strutting and racing through a split-second whirlwind gallop, manipulating trays, food and shish-kebab skewers ... the descent down the center staircase of the scarlet-gowned, plume-topped mistress of the revels ... the opening up of the scene practically in the audience's lap as Dolly

Hello, Dolly! (1964). Carol Channing and her welcoming committee at the Harmonia Gardens. (Costumes by Freddy Wittop; setting by Oliver Smith.)

Hello, Dolly! *(1964).*
Horace Vandergelder (David Burns) is rather distracted by the ability of Dolly Levi (Carol Channing) to consume endless quantities of dumplings.

leads her fleet-footed admirers across the runway. It was an electric occasion, one that Walter Kerr summed up as "the best single piece of sheer musical comedy staging I have ever seen since I went to my first minstrel show."

After Miss Channing had relinquished her role on Broadway to tour in the musical for over a year, the part was taken over by a succession of ex-movie queens—Ginger Rogers (year and a half), Martha Raye (four months), Betty Grable (five months), and, in a touring edition, Dorothy Lamour. In October 1967, Pearl Bailey and Cab Calloway headed a spirited all-black company that played on Broadway for twenty-six months. When that company went on the road, the last two Dolly's of the original run were Phyllis Diller (three months) and Ethel Merman (nine). Two subsequent revivals were mounted in New York: Pearl Bailey and Billy Daniels led a company in 1975, Carol Channing and Eddie Bracken headed one in 1978.

Following the success of *Hello, Dolly!*, Jerry Herman had no further image problem. Obviously no longer in need of proving his versatility, he next became involved with the saga of another zany, flamboyant female, Auntie Mame. Jerome Lawrence and Robert E. Lee had already turned Patrick Dennis' novel into a play that had somehow given the impression of being a musical comedy without music; now Lawrence and Lee were taking the inevitable step of converting it into a musical comedy *with* music. After flirting with the title *My Best Girl*, they eventually settled for the simplest appellation possible, *Mame*.

Herman worked closely with the librettists at all times, almost as a third book collaborator. What the authors were determined to do was to try to forget everything that they had done in fashioning *Auntie Mame* as a play. They wanted *Mame* to have a life of her own, not merely be a blaring, overblown cartoon of the previous incarnation. With Angela Lansbury as the redoubtable

Mame (after almost forty ladies of the theatre had been considered or tested), they achieved a laudable blending of music, lyrics, and story that, if anything, made the leading character and her escapades more human and fully developed than they had been before.

Mame offered Jerry Herman an inescapable challenge—to write another high-stepping title song. For the new number—slotted as the first-act finale—he came up with a prancing, cake-walking, dear-old-Southland tribute to the heroine, with such lines as, "You make our black-eyed peas and our grits, Mame,/Seem like the bill of fare at the Ritz, Mame." But the composer's own favorite, and understandably so, was Mame's tender "If He Walked into My Life," in which the hedonistic heroine muses about the things she may have done wrong in bringing up young Patrick Dennis. "It's Today," reworked from

Herman's earlier "No Tune Like a Show Tune" in *Parade*, was an effulgent credo to life, while "Open a New Window" sounded a challenge to risk the unknown.

None of Herman's subsequent musicals enjoyed anything like the success of *Hello, Dolly!* and *Mame*, yet none was without musical merit or audience appeal. *Dear World*, which opened in 1969, reunited the composer with three of his *Mame* associates, librettists Jerome Lawrence and Robert E. Lee and star Angela Lansbury. Their story, adapted from Jean Giradeux's *The Madwoman of Chaillot*, offered the opportunity for social commentary as it pitted dreamers, idealists, and assorted eccentrics against the forces of cold materialism. The work failed, according to Herman, because of its somewhat dichotomous combination of a small-scaled, poetic fantasy and a large-scale, flashy Broadway production. This was also noticeable in the score. For

Mame (1966).
"It's Today!," sings Angela Lansbury, and all the invited guests at her party are in exuberant agreement. (Costumes by Robert Mackintosh; settings by William and Jean Eckart.)

Photo by Roger Greenwalt

The Grand Tour *(1979).
Much to the discomfort of a
Polish aristocrat (Ronald
Holgate) and the amusement
of his orderly (Stephen
Vinovich), they are joined by
S. K. Jacobowski (Joel Grey)
as they flee the Nazis.
(Costumes by Theoni V.
Aldredge; setting by Ming
Cho Lee.)*

the tender, touching waltz, "I Don't Want to Know," or the three-part, contrapuntal "Tea Party," there was a genuine Parisian delicacy, while the high-spirited, high-kicking title song gave us another variation on the by-now familiar Herman trademark (though this one was addressed to a sick world rather than an idolized woman).

The romance between movie pioneer Mack Sennett and leading lady Mabel Normand might have been expected to provide a framework for a fondly nostalgic look at the early days of movie-making, enlivened by Keystone Kops, custard pies, and mincing bathing beauties. But *Mack and Mabel* (1974), starring Robert Preston and Bernadette Peters, had a libretto by Michael Stewart that was so downbeat it worked at cross-purpose with the highjinks of the two-reelers being produced. Herman's score, though, caught the right flavor, with such standout pieces as Mabel's torchy "Time Heals Everything," with its emotion building in intensity through the enumeration of days, months and seasons; Mack's anti-romantic yet poignant "I Won't Send Roses"; and the parody cure-for-the-blues number, "Tap Your Troubles Away," both a distillation and a commentary on early talkie routines. Yes,

there was also a signature tune, "When Mabel Comes in the Room," performed at a joyous welcome-home party on a movie set and ending with our heroine flying high in the air while seated on a camera crane.

The Grand Tour, in 1979, the third Herman-Stewart collaboration, was adapted from Franz Werfel's *Jacobowsky and the Colonel*. It offered Joel Grey as a spunky Jewish refugee whose fortune it is to team up with a fleeing Polish aristocrat during World War II. Despite its appealing theme and reliably hummable Herman songs (i.e. "I'll Be Here Tomorrow," "Marianne," "I Belong Here"), the largely negative critical reception helped cancel the *Tour* after only two months.

"Aside from being a songwriter," Jerry Herman once said, "I'm a composer-lyricist for the musical theatre. That's not being redundant. There's an enormous difference. For me the greatest satisfaction comes from taking over from the playwright and heightening an emotion that might not be reached by the spoken word alone. It is this rollercoaster between dialogue and song, this homogenization of the spoken and the sung word, that makes a career in the American musical theatre so fascinating."

John Kander and Fred Ebb.   Courtesy BMI Archives

CHAPTER TWENTY-EIGHT

JOHN KANDER and FRED EBB

Because of the impor-
tance of the script—or at least the
"concept"—in determining the sound of
today's musical theatre, composers and
lyricists must often submerge their own
personal, identifiable styles in the interest
of the productions as a whole. In this regard, no collaborators on the current
scene have more successfully adjusted
their creative signatures to conform to
the dictates of their musicals than have
composer John Kander and lyricist Fred
Ebb. They have, in fact, managed to
adapt their songs to the required period
or ethnic flavor with such self-effacing
skill that their contributions often go un-
noticed while attention is focused on the
pantheon directors—George Abbott,
Harold Prince, Gower Champion, Bob
Fosse—with whom they have been associated. Kander and Ebb, it seems, show
the kind of dedication that makes them
more concerned with distinction in their
musicals than distinctiveness in their music and lyrics.

They also have a distinction of another
kind: no other composer and lyricist in
the theatre today enjoy a closer partnership. John Kander, born in Kansas City,
Missouri, on March 18, 1927, studied

music at both Oberlin College and Columbia University. He received his master's degree in 1953. During the next
nine years his theatrical training included
conducting at summer theatres, serving as
rehearsal pianist and, eventually, creating the dance arrangements for *Gypsy*
and *Irma la Douce*. In 1962, Kander
joined with James and William Goldman
to fashion songs and story for *A Family
Affair*, Harold Prince's first directorial
assignment. Though the presentation was
short-lived, Kander's score won the
"sleeper of the year" prize from fellow
composer Vernon Duke, who wrote in his
book, *Listen Here!*: "The music bristles
with delightful surprises, new departures
in song construction, and a sort of unre-
strained lust for tonal adventure exceed-
ingly rare to come by these days."

The same year, Kander was introduced
to Ebb by their mutual publisher, Tommy
Valando, and their first song, "My Coloring Book," went on to long-playing popularity via a recording by Sandy Stewart.
The second Kander-Ebb song, "I Don't
Care Much," became a Barbra Streisand
specialty. It also helped put the partnership on a permanent basis.

A native New Yorker, Fred Ebb was

born on April 8, 1932, and attended both New York University and Columbia. With his first collaborator, Paul Klein, he turned out some strikingly fresh nightclub pieces, among them "The Insecure Tango" (a girl's confession that she's not even sure she's insecure) and a hilarious look at communal psychiatry called "Group Therapy." In 1960, in partnership with both Klein and Norman Martin, Ebb contributed material to the revue, *From A to Z*, starring Hermione Gingold.

The first musical-comedy score written by Kander and Ebb was for *Flora, the Red Menace*, a nostalgic look at the Depression years, which gave Liza Minnelli her first leading role on Broadway. Under the sponsorship of Harold Prince and the direction of George Abbott, the show had a brief stay in 1965. Despite the musical's limited run, Prince signed Kander

and Ebb to write the songs for *Cabaret*, which he produced and directed, and which opened late in 1966. It turned out to be a daringly innovative venture on a number of levels.

As the audience enters the theatre the curtain is already up so that the theatregoers can see themselves reflected in a huge, slanted, distorted mirror, the only prop on the darkened stage. To the left of the proscenium arch is a spiral staircase. Dimly seen receding street lamps are on both sides. Suddenly, an illuminated sign blinks on, letter by letter—C A B A R E T. As it is hoisted away, there is a low, ominous roll on the drums, the cymbals clash, and the Master of Ceremonies enters. His patent leather hair is parted in the middle, his face is clown white, his cheeks rouged, his lips scarlet, his eyes mascaraed, his smile leering. To an oompah, beerhall

Cabaret (1966).
The Master of Ceremonies (Joel Grey) bidding one and all "Willkommen, bienvenue, welcome." (Costumes by Patricia Zipprodt; setting by Boris Aronson.)

Photo By Friedman-Abeles

beat, he bids us in a steely German-accented voice, "Willkommen, bienvenue, welcome im Cabaret, au Cabaret, to Cabaret!" Here in the Kit Kat Klub, he tells us, "life is beautiful . . . even the orchestra is beautiful!"—and a platform containing a quartet of musical harpies, pounding and blasting away at their instruments, is rolled onstage. With another effusive introduction ("each and every one a virgin"), the bra-less, bare-thighed, black-stockinged, frozen-faced doxies of the chorus appear to join in the song of welcome, as the slanted mirror tilts upward now reflecting the performers. Then, to the wail of tenor saxes, the tables—complete with telephones—roll onstage, as does the bar, and out come the waiters, busboys, bartenders, entertainers, customers. Willkommen, bienvenue, welcome, they all sing, high-kicking their way down to the footlights—and we are right there in the frenzied midst of a garish Berlin night club of the late Twenties.

Thus *Cabaret* begins, making it perfectly clear that, despite the desperate gaiety of the opening number, there will be nothing truly gay or escapist about the musical. From then on, it proceeds to an ending of complete despair as our cabaret master of ceremonies, his enthusiasm drained, his voice husky and his face now a death mask, welcomes us for the last time. Hitler has now come to power, the dancers goosestep wearing swastika armbands, and the music is nightmarish and discordant. At the end of *Man of La Mancha*, Don Quixote may still dream his impossible dream. At the end of *Fiddler on the Roof*, Tevya may still have his faith. But when the curtain falls on *Cabaret*, no one is left with anything. Hero has left heroine to her doomed life and the world is about to plunge into its most devastating war. The fact that *Cabaret* has succeeded so well on a commercial level indicates that audiences accept it as reflecting more than a decadent period of the past. Despotism and discord will not

disappear, it seems to say, if we close our eyes and heed only the beckoning call to come to the cabaret old chum, come to the cabaret . . .

The musical was adapted by Joe Masteroff from both the play, *I Am a Camera* by John van Druten, and the play's source, Christopher Isherwood's *Berlin Stories*. Masteroff and producer-director Harold Prince began working on a treatment even before they approached composer John Kander and lyricist Fred Ebb to write the score. As the musical began to take shape, little of *I Am a Camera*,

Cabaret (1966).
Overcome by the gift of a pineapple, Lotte Lenya conveys her thanks to Jack Gilford in "It Couldn't Please Me More."

except for the character of Sally Bowles, was retained; increasingly, the collaborators found themselves going back to the flavor and situations of the Isherwood stories. But the form of the musical began to jell only when they hit upon the idea of the Master of Ceremonies, an entirely original character, who provided the thematic thread woven through a series of vulgar night club specialties.

Cabaret won praise for the jangling, sardonic, Kurt Weill-influenced score, as well as the George Grosz atmosphere of the decor and some memorable performances by Joel Grey (as the epicene Master of Ceremonies), Lotte Lenya (as a pragmatic landlady), and Jack Gilford (as a mushy Jewish fruit dealer). Tying the elements together into a unified concept was the accomplishment of director Harold Prince as he recreated so chillingly the atmosphere of a world in decay.

Walter Kerr, writing in the N.Y. *Times*, found something even more noteworthy in the production—a breakthrough in musical theatre form. Here, he held, was a rarity, a musical that did not really concern itself with the integration of song into the story; the musical numbers for the most part were done within the framework of set pieces in the night club—which itself provided the framework for the entire production. "Instead of putting the narrative first," wrote Kerr, "and the singers and dancers wherever a small corner can be found for them, it pops the painted clown and gartered girls directly into our faces, making them, in effect, a brightly glazed window—with a musical staff scrawled all over it—*through* which we can perceive the people and the emotional pattern of the plot."

What Kerr described, without giving it a name, was an early example of what has come to be known as the concept musical, a stylized approach with which Kander and Ebb would become increasingly associated. Though their next musical, *The Happy Time* (early 1968),

was more conventional, director Gower Champion did make imaginative use of photographic enlargements to set the mood for this sentimental view of a small French Canadian town, and the folkish, gentle charms of the songs helped greatly to sustain it.

Zorbá (late 1968) reunited Kander and Ebb with their *Cabaret* producer-director, Harold Prince. The musicalization of Nikos Kazantzakis' novel, however, seemed more akin to *Fiddler on the Roof* with its larger-than-life hero and its stageful of earthy, ethnic types. In fact, it was put together by virtually the same staff: producer Prince (here also directing), librettist Joseph Stein, set designer Boris Aronson, and costume designer Patricia Zipprodt, and it co-starred the third Tevye (Herschel Bernardi) with the first Golde (Maria Karnilova). But the Greek peasants were a colder, more menacing lot than *Fiddler*'s open-hearted villagers, and the work was too spare and gloomy to win more than a season's run. Kander and Ebb moved with apparent ease to their Cretan surroundings, bringing to it fire, strength, humor ("No Boom-Boom"), and tenderness ("Happy Birthday" was both a childhood recollection and a threnody), colored by instrumentation that made the score sound as true to bouzouki as it did to Broadway. In his conceptual approach, Prince unfolded his story as a tale told by a group of café entertainers and used its Leader and singers to interrupt the play's action with dramatically effective musical commentary. (Variations on this would show up in a number of subsequent Prince-directed musicals.)

Seventy Girls Seventy in 1971 may have been structurally confusing but it did allow Kander and Ebb to deal with a relatively light subject for one of the few times in their career. The authors have always felt affection for this tale of a group of aging but spry New Yorkers who embark on a life of crime, and feel that it might have had a longer run had it

Courtesy Capitol Records

Zorbá (1968).
*Gathered round composer
Kander and lyricist Ebb are
librettist Joseph Stein,
choreographer Ronald Field,
co-stars Maria Karnilova and
Herschel Bernardi, and
producer-director Harold
Prince.*

Photo by Friedman-Abeles

*The "Y'assou" number danced
by Maria Karnilova and
Herschel Bernardi. (Costumes
by Patricia Zipprodt.)*

Chicago *(1975).*
The musical closes with Chita
Rivera and Gwen Verdon, as
two acquitted murderesses,
acknowledging the applause
after their vaudeville act.
(Costumes by Patricia
Zipprodt.)

The Act *(1977).*
Liza Minnelli and dancers
performing "City Lights."
(Costumes by Halston.)

been mounted on the intimate scale that they had first envisaged.

Over four years later, the team was on Broadway again with *Chicago*, their second most successful endeavor next to *Cabaret*. *Chicago* had a lengthy gestation. In 1956, Bob Fosse first tried to get the rights to the Twenties play but it was not until thirteen years later that the way was cleared to begin turning it into a musical for Gwen Verdon, who was then his wife. The tale of murderess Roxie Hart and the way she managed not only to avoid prison but also to become a vaudeville headliner was adapted into a bitterly sardonic commentary on all the huckstering, immorality, and decadence of the period. Fosse's concept converted the story into a gaudy vaudeville show, a valid enough approach since the musical's aim was to reveal how various aspects of American life reflect show business at its tawdriest.

Many, however, felt that the play's relentless cynicism amounted to dramatic overkill and that its place and period had more of the depraved atmosphere of a Brechtian Berlin than a Caponean Chicago. Indeed, the show had an inescapable aura of Kander and Ebb's own *Cabaret*, with an occasional suggestion of Fosse's own *Pippin*. In the score, the mood-setting "All That Jazz" conjured up *Pippin*'s prancing Ben Vereen, Mary McCarty's "When You're Good to Mama" recalled Kurt Weill, and "Mr. Cellophane" found Barney Martin, as Roxie's cuckold, decked out like Emil Jannings in *The Blue Angel* while singing the self-mocking Bert Williams-type number. More authentic parodies of the era were Miss Verdon's "Funny Honey," in the "Man I Love" tradition; the pseudo-sentimental "All I Care About Is Love," in which Jerry Orbach, as a shady lawyer, made like Harry Rich-

man; and Orbach's soft-shoed, finger-snapping "Razzle-Dazzle," his credo on how to deceive the public. Though *Chicago* conveyed the general feeling that it was indicting the audience for the moral decay of the world, that didn't stop Broadway theatregoers from willingly accepting their lumps for over two years.

If the concept of *Chicago* dictated a certain stylistic dislocation in the score, there was no question of the locale that inspired the songs for *The Act* (1977). Surely one of the most vehicularly shaped of modern musicals, this one was little more than a series of flashy Las Vegas production numbers created by Kander and Ebb to show off the blazing talents of Liza Minnelli. Faced with a multitude of problems during the pre-Broadway tryout (for one thing, director Martin Scorsese was replaced by Gower Champion), the show was somehow pulled together in time to win Miss Minnelli a unanimously enthusiastic reception. Though *The Act* ran through the season, the production is perhaps best recalled as the first musical with a twenty-five-dollar top ticket price, and also the first to permit its star to prerecord some of the numbers.

"We're strictly theatre guys, writing the moment as it happens in the play," Ebb has said, by way of explaining why the team has written so few hit songs. Theirs have seldom been structured songs in the commercial sense, but they have been eminently dramatic, conveying whatever the desired mood and flavor is called for. If, like their creators, the songs have escaped individual acclaim, they have nevertheless performed the demanding function of heightening the emotion and strengthening the texture of the varied dramatic works for which they were created.

Harvey Schmidt and Tom Jones.

CHAPTER TWENTY-NINE

TOM JONES and
HARVEY SCHMIDT
MITCH LEIGH and JOE DARION
GALT MacDERMOT
BURT BACHARACH and
HAL DAVID

THIS CHAPTER AND THE TWO following are devoted to those composers and lyricists who, though their output has been relatively limited, have created at least one notable work or sizable hit since 1960. Each writer is taken up in more or less chronological order, without regard to his or her relationship to the other writers discussed within the same chapter. Chapter 29 covers the contributions of those whose theatre scores first attracted notice during the period 1960 through 1968; Chapter 30 those from 1969 through 1971; chapter 31 those from 1972 through 1978.

Tom Jones and Harvey Schmidt

As the first two sons of Texas to achieve renown in the musical theatre, lyricist Tom Jones and composer Harvey Schmidt might well have been expected to reflect something of the tone of excess and elaboration for which the Lone Star State has long been celebrated. Yet Jones (born in Littlefield on February 17, 1928) and Schmidt (born in Dallas on September 12, 1929) have made it big by doing things small. The theatre in which they have been most active and to which they have been artistically dedicated has been the theatre of the intimate and the compressed, whether it be in playing area, in casting, or in time span.

To date, Jones and Schmidt have written the scores for five commercial book musicals, four of them with Jones also supplying librettos. Their first, *The Fantasticks*, still playing at the 149-seat Sullivan Street Playhouse, has a cast of eight (shaved down from the original nine). Their second, *110 in the Shade*, more conventional in size and their first on Broadway, kept the action within the span of one day. Their third, *I Do! I Do!*, became the first Broadway musical to have a cast consisting of only two actors. Their fourth, *Celebration*, took place entirely during New Year's Eve and had four principals. Their fifth, *Philemon*, was presented at Jones and Schmidt's tiny Portfolio Studio with a cast of seven.

This preoccupation with stylistic frugality is, of course, very much a part of the team's philosophy. "I'm convinced," Jones has said, "that the simpler you do a thing the better it's going to be. All too often in the musical theatre a great deal of effort is expended on things that have only a momentary effect without producing a genuine emotional response. The proper words and music can evoke a spectacle in the mind that's so much more satisfying than anything the most skillful scenic designer could possibly devise."

Tom Jones and Harvey Schmidt met when they were both students at the University of Texas. Tom, who was studying to be a stage director, was anxious to become part of the world of music; Harvey, an art major, was able to play piano by ear and was anxious to become part of the world of the theatre. They were brought together by their activities in a campus theatrical group, the Curtain Club, and their first show was something called *Hippsy-Boo*. Harvey wrote the title song and Tom the sketches. A second collegiate effort, *Time Staggers On* (an inherited title) was their maiden attempt at writing words and music together.

Following graduation, both men served time in the army—at different camps—and continued to collaborate via mail. Jones reached New York first. He began his professional career writing and directing a night club act featuring Tom Posten and Gerry Matthews. The act was booked into the Reuben Bleu, a since deceased bistro, whose revelries were presided over by Julius Monk. By the time Schmidt had arrived to join his partner, Monk had moved to the Upstairs at the Downstairs, where he offered his series of numerically progressive revues (*Four Below, Demi-Dozen, Pieces of Eight*, etc.). These were frequently studded with the efforts of Jones and Schmidt. (At the time, Schmidt, who had become a much sought-after commercial artist, also co-authored, with Robert

Benton, the bible of the trivia set known as *The In and Out Book*.)

Early in June, 1959, Word Baker, a fellow Texas U. graduate, telephoned Tom and Harvey. He knew that they had been struggling for years over a musical adaptation of Edmond Rostand's first play, *Les Romanesques*, and he was wondering if they could possibly whip it into shape in about two months. He thought it might do nicely at a summer theatre then being run at Barnard College. But Baker, who was to direct the show, insisted that the play be cut down to a one-act musical. This presented a real problem. Originally, true to their Lone Star heritage, Jones and Schmidt had conceived of the work as an elaborate spectacle called *Joy Comes to Dead Horse*. They had reset the story in the American southwest, and had concerned it with the rivalry between a Mexican family and an Anglo family living on adjoining ranches. The Mexican girl was named Maria, and there was even a song about her with that title. What they had, of course, was a Texas version of *West Side Story*—only theirs had come first.

It wasn't until Jones and Schmidt got together with Baker in New York that the musical finally crystallized. It was all too easy. They just decided to do an uncluttered version of the Rostand play, without elaborate staging or nationalistic overtones. The rewriting took three weeks, and, as a one-act musical, *The Fantasticks* (the title of an earlier translation of the play) had a week-long run at Barnard. Among the most enthusiastic members of the first night audience was a young producer, Lorenzo "Lore" Noto, who offered the boys a proposition: expand the show into a full evening entertainment and he'd produce it off Broadway. They did and he did nine months later.

The Fantasticks takes up the whimsical notion that a girl and boy can fall in love only if their feelings are expressly forbidden by their parents. To aid romance, two neighboring and friendly fathers not only appear to be enemies (arch enemies?) but even hire an itinerant bandit named El Gallo (who also doubles as Narrator) to stage a pretend rape in the moonlight so that the boy can be a hero. When the sun comes up, however, humdrum reality intrudes, the lovers quarrel and the boy runs away. Guided by El Gallo, he comes up against the cruelty of the world, an experience that sends him back gratefully to his beloved. To librettist Jones, the play's underlying theme is that of vegetation, of seasonal rebirth, which is expressed so poetically in the Narrator's delicate, mood-setting ballad, "Try to Remember."

The musical cost a mere $16,500 to open. After steadily declining business during the first nine weeks, the producer was ready to post the closing notice. But word-of-mouth comments helped, and within eight months the show had repaid its entire investment. One year later it had turned a 100% profit. At the present writing, with the run now over twenty years, *The Fantasticks* has shown a net profit of over $1,900,000, or more than 5,600% on the original capitalization.

Those who look to critics as omnipotent arbiters would do well to reread the opening-night reviews of *The Fantasticks*. Brooks Atkinson in *The Times* found it "the sort of thing that loses magic the longer it endures." Walter Kerr summed up his feelings in the *Herald Tribune* with: "It attracts you, settles back a bit limply, wakes you up again and averages out a little less than satisfactory." The *Post*'s Richard Watts Jr. held that "So much that is pleasant goes on in *The Fantasticks* that I feel almost ungrateful for adding my quibbles about its lack of consistent effectiveness." The *News*, however, gave it a brief but glowing notice, and Henry Hewes, in *Saturday Review*, went all out: "Jones and Schmidt have worked with a professional expertness equalling the best Broadway has to offer

and with a degree of artistic taste that Broadway seldom attains anymore."

Broadway, in the person of David Merrick, apparently thought it could use a little of that artistic taste itself. Merrick signed the team for a musical version of N. Richard Nash's play, *The Rainmaker*, first renamed *Rainbow*, then finally *110 in the Shade*. The theme of an unattractive girl whose brief fling with a fast-talking rainmaker helps rid her of her insecurity was, in fact, even more congenial to the song writers than to Nash, who fashioned the libretto out of his own play. The private longings of the touching ballad, "Love Don't Turn Away," and the controlled exultation of "Is It Really Me?" reached the height of

Photo by Friedman-Abeles

The Fantasticks *(1960).*
Jerry Orbach, as El Gallo,
crosses swords with hero
Kenneth Nelson, as heroine
Rita Gardner watches with
apprehension.

American art songs. So too the vivid contrast of the rainmaker's fantastic saga of "Melisande" and the girl's explanation of her desire for "Simple Little Things" were almost spine-tinglingly effective. As the awkward Lizzie, Inga Swenson gave a shiningly memorable performance, though Robert Horton's rainmaker failed to make the character thoroughly convincing.

I Do! I Do!, also produced by Mr. Merrick, came along in December, 1966. At first the prospect of turning Jan de Hartog's two-character play, *The Fourposter*, into a two-character musical did

I Do! I Do! *(1966).*
Mary Martin and Robert Preston doing their shoeless old soft shoe to the tune of "I Love My Wife."

not light any sparks. But director Gower Champion was persistent, and soon Jones and Schmidt began seeing the possibilities in the concept. Mary Martin had agreed to play the role of Agnes almost from the very start; in June, 1966, Robert Preston agreed to play Michael. Thus the musical took shape with the most important advantage a two-character musical could possibly have—two authentic superstars.

Keeping things hopping for a meandering, crisis-free saga of a half century of wedded bliss was a severe test for Jones, Schmidt and Champion. They dreamed up a soft shoe routine without shoes. They devised a top hat and cane strutaway for Preston, and an uninhibited whatever-it-was in a big hat for Miss Martin. They created a lark happy duet for both of them called "When the Kids Get Married," and topped it off with Preston playing a saxophone and Miss Martin doing her stuff on a violin. To show the aging of the two stars, Champion simply had them come down to the footlights and apply wrinkle lines and grey wigs out of their makeup kits. *I Do! I Do!*, despite its theatrical ingenuity, received a mixed press; critics, for the most part, appreciated the high points but questioned the play's basic sentimentality.

With *Celebration* (1969), Jones and Schmidt returned to the theme of seasonal rebirth that had proved so successful in *The Fantasticks*. The setting and title were fortuitously provided by a *New York Times* editorial about the Winter Solstice. Intrigued with the idea that the first day of Winter heralds both the coldest months and also the period when the Earth moves closest to the sun, Jones and Schmidt decided to focus on their theme of youth and age through that most hopeful of occasions, a New Year's Eve celebration ("Beneath the snow/ There's a tiny seed/ And it's gonna grow!"). The critical verdict ranged from "welcome, merry, tuneful, and imaginative" (Brendan Gill, *The New Yorker*), to "helpless, hapless, hopeless" (John Chapman, *News*), and the celebrants departed after three months.

Shortly before the opening of *Celebration*, the partners rented a brownstone on West 47th Street, dubbed it the Portfolio Studio, and set about creating experimental musicals that would conform to their artistic canon of maximum imagination and minimum size. During the 1974/75 season, which turned out to be the studio's last, they unveiled a program of four works, of which *Philemon* was the best received and the only one given an extended though brief commercial run.

Mitch Leigh and Joe Darion

It is symptomatic of the times that, in addition to the popular music field, summer resorts, off-Broadway, night clubs, films, and the concert hall, there has emerged a new training ground for musical theatre composers—radio and television commercials. To date, Mitch Leigh, the composer of the score for *Man of La Mancha*, is the most celebrated practitioner but many others have been following. "Writing a jingle or a pop song or a symphony or a Broadway score," he insists, "involves a profound training in the craft and that's exactly what Madison Avenue gives a writer."

Leigh, however, has not been artistically limited to Madison Avenue. Born in Brooklyn, New York, on January 31, 1928, he studied music at Yale University under Paul Hindemith and earned his master's degree. In 1954, in collaboration with another writer, he sold his first television commercial to Revlon. After completing their assignment, the two men asked the advertising agency how much they could expect for their labors. When they were told "seven-fifty," Leigh was shocked. He had figured at least ten dollars, with five apiece. How could they split $7.50? When it was explained that the fee would be seven hundred and fifty,

Leigh was no longer concerned about simple division. Three years later, he founded Music Makers, Inc., which became the largest company in the country specializing in television and radio musical commercials.

Leigh first ventured into the theatre in 1963 when he composed the background music for an all-star cast revival of Bernard Shaw's *Too True to Be Good*. Albert Marre was the director. In August of the same year, *The New York Times* announced that Music Makers was about to enter the Broadway production ranks by sponsoring a musical treatment of Dale Wasserman's television play, *I, Don Quixote*, to be called *Man of La Mancha*. Albert Marre would do the staging, and the score would be written by Mitch

Mitch Leigh.

Joe Darion.

Growing Up Tree" (music by George Kleinsinger) for the Camp Fire Girls, plus assorted pop hits. He has written words to song cycles and cantatas, and his oratorio, *Galileo*, with music by Ezra Laderman, was commissioned by CBS-TV. For the theatre, he was praised for the lyrics—to George Kleinsinger's music—of *Shinbone Alley*, a musical version of Don Marquis' *archie and mehitabel*, which was seen briefly in 1957. Darion was also the lyricist of the 1967 musical, *Illya Darling*, starring the explosive Melina Mercouri. Manos Hadjidakis, who had created the background score for the film *Never on Sunday*, the basis of the musical, was the composer.

Playwright Wasserman first thought of writing a play about Cervantes' *Don Quixote* when, in Madrid, he read a totally erroneous newspaper account that that was his purpose for being in Spain. This spurred him to read the book, which convinced him to attempt, not a dramatization, but a play that would be "a tribute to the spirit of Don Quixote's creator. The motif of the attempt I found in a quotation by another brilliant writer, Miguel Unamuno, who said: 'Only he who attempts the ridiculous may achieve the impossible.' In that quixotic spirit the play was written, a deliberate denial of the prevailing spirit of our time which finds its theatrical mood in black comedy and the deification of despair."

Once his television play had been presented, Wasserman rewrote it as a play for Broadway. But director Albert Marre, to whom he showed it, persuaded him to rewrite it again as a musical. This opened up many new problems in construction, staging and style. For composer Leigh and lyricist Darion, the challenge was primarily to write songs that *sounded* authentic, without necessarily being authentic in music or lyrics. Leigh spent hours researching the music of the early seventeenth century, the period of

Leigh and, as co-lyricists, W. H. Auden and Chester Kallman. Michael Redgrave was then the likeliest prospect for the title role. By the time the production was unveiled two years later, the production had been turned over to Albert W. Selden and Hal James, Richard Kiley was the Don, and the lyrics had become the work of Joe Darion.

Like Mitch Leigh, Joe Darion has felt at home in all areas of writing. A native New Yorker, born January 30, 1917, he attended the City College of Journalism, and has written for radio, television, films, and the concert hall. He is responsible for "The Ho-Ho Song" (music by Jack Wolf) for Red Buttons, and "The

the story, but found it totally uninteresting. Then he turned to Flamenco, which, though only about one hundred and fifty years old, seemed to have the proper period flavor and theatrical effectiveness. "It became evident," the composer has explained, "that a single continuing sound was required, on which variations would have to be 'leaned.' The humorous songs and the wilder numbers could not stray too far from the emotional content of the piece."

Apart from these considerations, the music and lyrics had a rightness about them in content as well as in form. Don Quixote's innocent faith was never permitted to become farcical, whether in his declaration of his mission ("I am I, Don Quixote, the Lord of La Mancha/My destiny calls and I go"), or in extolling the whore Aldonza as his spotless Dulcinea, or in dreaming his impossible dream. Aldonza actually did come to believe herself to be Dulcinea, a transformation calling for musical emotions ranging from bitter resignation in "It's All the Same" to her final, anguished plea, as the knight lay dying, to "bring me back the bright and shining glory of Dulcinea."

Man of La Mancha was tried out at the Goodspeed Opera House, in East Haddam, Connecticut, in the summer of 1965. After much alteration, it opened five months later far from the theatre district at the ANTA Washington Square Theatre, on East 4th Street. In March, 1968, it transferred to the Martin Beck Theatre, where it remained until the end of June, 1971. Its total New York run was 2,328 performances.

Surely, few musicals have ever matched *Man of La Mancha* for the sheer theatricality of its physical production—at least in its original home. The suspended stage platform, jutting out into 'the banked, semi-circular auditorium, was tilted toward the audience. Behind it towered a huge staircase sus-

pended whenever necessary to provide a link between the outer world and the dungeon into which Cervantes and his servant have been thrown. The orchestra was split in two and placed on both sides of the arena stage. The transformation of Cervantes into Don Quixote and his servant into Sancho Panza was done simply with makeup kits in full view of the audience, and their subsequent horseback ride was accomplished on two wooden frames attached to two dancers wearing horse head masks.

Photo by Arthur Cantor.

Man of La Mancha (1965).
"I am I, Don Quixote," booms
the Don (Richard Kiley), as
he and his servant, Sancho
Panza (Irving Jacobson), set
off on their adventure astride
two remarkable steeds.
(Costumes by Howard Bay
and Patton Campbell.)

Despite the geographical inconvenience of the theatre's location and the physical inconvenience to theatregoers of running without an intermission, the play soon found its audience. This is, perhaps, even more surprising when we reread some of the reviews that greeted it. Though Richard Watts and John Chapman were unstinting in their praise, Howard Taubman of the *Times* and Walter Kerr of the *Herald Tribune* took strong exception to what both called its vulgarities. However, former *Times* appraiser Brooks Atkinson came out of retirement to dub it "one of the most imaginative theatre events of the decade." Others were quick to fault the production for distorting Cervantes; instead of making the work a satire on the foolishness of the dying age of knight errantry, it now became a pathetic tale of

the need for vision and faith in a world of cynicism, cruelty, and greed. The universal success of *Man of La Mancha* is evidence that this theme strikes a chord in audiences everywhere who wishfully empathize with a dreamer who dares see people as better than they are.

Leigh and Darion never collaborated again—nor did either win popular successes with anyone else. The Darion-Manos Hadjidakis musical, *Illya Darling*, ran nine months mainly on the strength of Melina Mercouri's name, and none of Leigh's last three musicals did that well. Yet one of these, *Cry for Us All* (1970), with lyrics by William Alfred and Phyllis Robinson, had a particularly rich, robust, and atmospheric score that easily transcended the musty melodrama for which it was created.

Galt MacDermot

The American musical theatre received something of a jolt the night of October 29, 1967, when a new production cryptically titled *Hair* became the first attraction at Joseph Papp's New York Shakespeare Festival Public Theatre. For a ticket price of $2.50, theatregoers were rattled, roused, shocked, and cajoled by a scruffy, energetic group of social misfits who reveled in their disdain for the establishment, hatred of war, and love of pot. Both onstage and in the aisles, they unremittingly proclaimed their determination to live their own life and do their own thing—never mind about the brain-damaging effect of drugs, the irresponsibility of promiscuous sex, or the inherent selfishness of copping out. Still, there was something appealingly unorthodox about this ebullient evening with a tribe of ingenuous, irrepressible hippies, an undeniable breakthrough in form, spirit, social attitude, and musical expression.

The composer of this so-called "American Tribal Love-Rock Musical" was

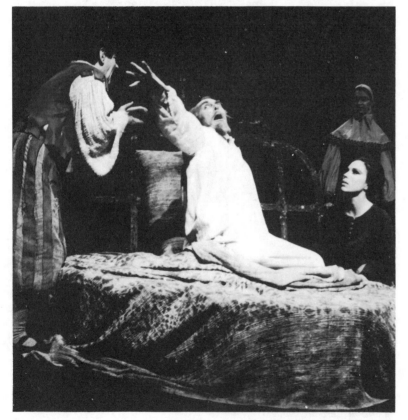

Man of La Mancha (1965). The deathbed scene—Sancho (Irving Jacobson), the Don (Richard Kiley), and Aldonza (Joan Diener).

Canadian-born Galt MacDermot. Unlike co-librettists and co-lyricists Gerome Ragni and James Rado, whose very appearance proclaimed their kinship with the flower-power world, MacDermot turned out to be a soft-spoken, business-suited, relatively short-haired, classically trained musician. And it was not from an East Village pad but from Staten Island suburbia that the propulsively rhythmic yet hauntingly melodic sound of America's counter culture first made its way successfully to the musical stage.

MacDermot was born in Montreal on December 18, 1928, the son of a member of Canada's diplomatic corps. At an early age he studied violin and piano, but what really interested him was the sound of jazz and boogie-woogie. During his father's assignment in South Africa, young Galt attended the Capetown College of Music, where he wrote a rhythm opera based on Joyce Carey's *Mister Johnson*, and from which came MacDermot's first song hit (at least in England), "African Waltz." After returning to Montreal, MacDermot spent seven years as the organist at a Baptist church and contributed songs to a touring collegiate musical, *My Fur Lady* (which had absolutely nothing to do with the Lerner and Loewe heroine). He lived in London for a while, then settled in Staten Island where he wrote songs by day and played piano in local bars by night.

Early in 1967, MacDermot met Ragni and Rado through music publisher Nat Shapiro. The librettists had already written the script of *Hair* and had offered it to Joseph Papp, who promised to present it if they could provide someone to supply the music. MacDermot found the concept challenging and promptly went to work. "I wrote fast enough," he once said, "so that in two weeks or so we had enough to take to Papp and play for him. He liked it and said, 'Go ahead.'"

Under Papp's guidance, *Hair* was offered for a limited run at the Public Theatre. Gerald Freedman was the director

Galt MacDermot

and the cast included Walker Daniels as an unwilling draftee, Jill O'Hara as the girl whose favors he seeks, and co-librettist Ragni as the leader of the tribe. For the music, MacDermot went back to the sounds he'd heard while living in Capetown. "*Hair* is very African," he claims. "Particularly in the rhythms. Really, rock and roll is sort of African, although the beat is basically a cha-cha—the accents and the way you feel make the difference." Little time was lost before the songs began winning popularity, and such pieces as the willowy, lyrical "Good Morning, Starshine," "Let the Sunshine in" and "Aquarius" not only became hits but also showed how a contemporary sound could also be affectingly melodic and adapt itself to the requirements of the theatre.

Though young people were attracted by the musical, others were put off by the obscenity of the language, the moral attitudes expressed, and the squalor of the locale. Papp, however, felt there was an audience for the show and, after the brief run at the Public, reopened it at Cheetah, a huge Broadway discotheque. It floundered there and might have died without a trace had it not been for Michael Butler, a wealthy Chicagoan who opened the show for the third time on April 29, 1968, at the Biltmore Theatre.

But not before it was rewritten so that there was even less of a coherent story line than before, and redirected—by Tom O'Horgan—so that it became even more uninhibited in style and more outspoken in dialogue. It was also redesigned, recostumed, and largely recast, with Daniels succeeded by coauthor James Rado, Jonelle Allen by Melba Moore, and Jill O'Hara by Lynn Kellogg (later by Diane Keaton). The result was that on Broadway, *Hair* was wilder, bolder, and more perverse (the middle-class woman of the original production, for example, was now being played by a man in drag). Added to this was the well-publicized act-one finale featuring Broadway's first, though hardly visible, frontal male and female nudity.

Whatever the reason, *Hair* quickly became a legendary musical, running over four years on Broadway and spawning numerous touring and foreign-language companies. When it was first unveiled in 1967, Edith Oliver observed in *The New Yorker*: "*Hair* simply could not have existed ten years ago, and it is conceivable that it could mystify audiences ten years from now." Well, it *was* revived on Broadway ten years later, but audiences found it not so much mystifying as dated and it folded after less than two months.

MacDermot retained his association with Joseph Papp, composing background music for two of the producer's free Shakespeare presentations in Central Park. For a third, *Two Gentlemen of Verona*, he was initially to write only a new musical setting for "Who Is Silvia?," but when Papp replaced the original director, his successor, Mel Shapiro, felt that since the play was also to be shown on the streets of poor neighborhoods, their audiences would find little relevance in a tale of romantic rivalry set in renaissance Italy. With playwright John Guare called in to revise the Shakespearean text with modern colloquialisms, the play was reconstructed as an exuberantly colorful, racially mixed musical in which Milan and Verona became the equivalent of San Juan and New York. Three months after the show's tour, in December 1971, Papp opened *Two Gentlemen* on Broadway where it settled down to a run of over 600 performances. MacDermot, with Guare as lyricist, contributed a richly varied, distinctive score of over thirty pieces that again revealed the composer's ability to fuse a contemporary beat within the framework of a dramatic story.

Since *Two Gentlemen of Verona*, MacDermot has been represented by two ambitious failures, *Dude* and *Via Galectica*, which both appeared briefly in the fall of 1972.* The following spring he indited a sparkling collection of pieces for Rochelle Owens' *Karl Marx Play*. More recently, he collaborated with playwright Derek Walcott on three musicals that have been presented in Trinidad by Walcott's own company.

*MacDermot has the distinction of being the only composer to have written the scores for two musicals that were the inaugural attractions at two theatres: *Hair* at the Public in 1967 and *Via Galectica* at the Uris in 1972.

James Rado and Gerome Ragni, authors of and actors in Hair.

Hair *(1968).*
Emmaretta Marks, Melba
Moore and Lorri Davis
(above) sing the praises of
"White Boys," while
Suzannah Norstrand, Diane
Keaton and Natalie Mosco
(below) show equal
enthusiasm for "Black Boys."
(Costumes by Nancy Potts;
setting by Robin Wagner.)

Photo by Friedman-Abeles

Two Gentlemen of Verona
(1971).
The "Night Letter" number
with Jonelle Allen and Clifton
Davis. (Costumes by Theoni
Aldredge; setting by Ming
Cho Lee.)

Burt Bacharach and Hal David

Toward the end of the 1960s, two composers were universally credited with bringing a new sound to the Broadway musical. One was Galt MacDermot, the other Burt Bacharach. MacDermot was virtually unknown before *Hair* propelled his special brand of pop-rock into worldwide acclaim. Bacharach, however, was widely celebrated as the country's premier contemporary pop song writer well before he and lyricist Hal David invaded Broadway with *Promises, Promises*. In fact, composer and lyricist had won notice as early as 1957 with their first hit, "Magic Moments." After that the team turned out a high percentage of successes—usually recorded by Dionne Warwick—bearing such titles as "Don't Make Me Over," "Wives and Lovers," "Walk on By," "What the World Needs Now," "What's New Pussycat?" (from Bacharach's first film score), and the title song from *Alfie*.

What gives Bacharach's music its individuality is the composer's ability to combine the popular sounds he absorbed as a youth with the rock beat that had taken over in the Fifties. His formula was to add such ingredients as Latin flavoring (with emphasis on the bossa nova, the bolero, and calypso), distinctively original and unpredictable time changes, and a certain inner tension that gives his work dramatic impact. Bacharach's tunes have a modern kind of sophistication, both propulsive and provocative, but always adhering to the advice he once received from Darius Milhaud: "Never be afraid to write a tuneful melody." Somewhat overshadowed by Bacharach's innovative music have been the equally innovative lyrics of Hal David, whose sensitive, adaptable style is notable for its originality, literacy, and poetic imagination.

Burt Bacharach (his father was the syndicated columnist) was born in Kansas City, Missouri, on May 12, 1928. When Burt was young, the family moved

Burt Bacharach and Hal David.

Courtesy ASCAP

to Forest Hills, New York, where the lad went to school and where he first learned to play the piano. He continued his musical studies at McGill University, spent a summer at Tanglewood, and also studied under Henry Cowell and Bohislav Martinu. Following a stint in the army, Bacharach chose to pursue a career in pop rather than classical music partly, he has admitted, because of the financial rewards. His song writing began in earnest during a period as accompanist to such singers as Vic Damone, the Ames Brothers, and Polly Bergen. Between 1958 and 1963 he served as Marlene Dietrich's pianist, conductor and arranger—and occasional writer—during her international tours.

Bacharach met Hal David in the late Fifties. David, a brother of lyricist Mack David ("Moon Love," "Falling Leaves"), was born in Brooklyn on May 25, 1921. Educated at New York University, he originally planned a career in journalism, but switched to lyric writing while serving in an Army entertainment unit during World War II. Following his discharge, David had early successes with

"The Four Winds and the Seven Seas" (music by Don Rodney), "My Heart Is an Open Book" (with Lee Pockriss), and "Broken-Hearted Melody" (with Sherman Edwards, who would later create the score for *1776*). But these were only prelude to the string of winners he had with Bacharach, both in the pop field and in films. The next logical step was Broadway.

In 1966, while in London scoring the film *Casino Royale*, Bacharach met producer David Merrick at a party. Merrick who had recently acquired the stage rights to the film *The Apartment*, offered the composer the opportunity of writing the score. Almost immediately, Bacharach and David began working on the musical that would eventually become *Promises, Promises*.

The team's Broadway debut took place December 1968, with high critical praise for their contributions to what was generally hailed as an adult and witty musical. Jack Kroll in *Newsweek* wrote, "Bacharach has that unmistakable mark of the musical-comedy master; his tunes seem to speak, sing and dance at the

Photo by Friedman-Abeles

Promises, Promises (1968). To help buck up the spirits of Jill O'Hara, who has just tried to commit suicide, A. Larry Haines and Jerry Orbach clown through "A Young Pretty Girl Like You." (Setting by Robin Wagner.)

same time." And from Douglas Watt in *The New Yorker*: "(David is) a lyricist of unusual sensibility ... The score expands the familiar materials of the Broadway musical in several directions and in such a manner that the genre appears to have been reborn overnight."

The *Promises, Promises* score delivered one undeniable hit, "I'll Never Fall in Love Again," a plaintive ballad of disillusionment that Bacharach and David wrote during the Boston tryout. Even more intriguing, both musically and lyrically, was "Whoever You Are," in which a lovesick girl reveals—to an impassioned, compelling melody—that her beloved's physical appearance changes according to the way he treats her. But perhaps the most daring piece of music was the title song, whose nervous, driving quality was accentuated by no less than sixteen changes in time signals.

Neil Simon's cynical yet touching book was concerned with one path up the corporate success road that had not been traveled in *How to Succeed in Business Without Really Trying*. Prompted by the promises, promises of advancement at Consolidated Life, Chuck Baxter (Jerry Orbach), a faceless drone, makes his apartment available to assorted executives for their extramarital dalliances. Two of the dalliers are Fran Kubelik (Jill O'Hara), whom Chuck loves, and J. D. Sheldrake (Edward Winters). After being spurned by Sheldrake, the girl is saved from her suicide attempt by Chuck, which goes a long way toward making her return his affection.

Following the show's opening, Bacharach admitted that it had been such an emotional drain that he never wanted to work on another Broadway score. So far he has kept his word. David, who became president of ASCAP in 1980, still plans to come back. At this writing, however, both men remain members of that select but frustrating group of creative people whose record on the Broadway scoreboard tallies one show and one hit.

Courtesy ASCAP

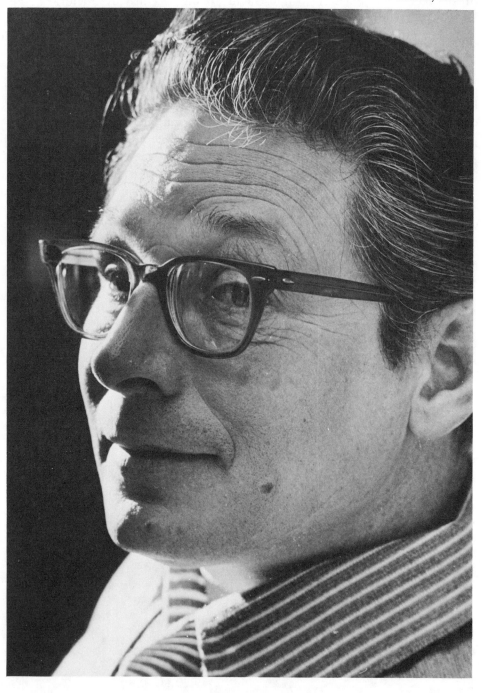

CHAPTER THIRTY

SHERMAN EDWARDS
GRETCHEN CRYER and
NANCY FORD
GARY GELD and PETER UDELL
STEPHEN SCHWARTZ

THERE HAVE BEEN any number of Broadway musicals that utilized historical events as part of their stories, but no musical before or since *1776* was ever created with the sole purpose of depicting, with as much fidelity as dramatically possible, the actual event itself. The event here, of course, was the signing of the Declaration of Independence, with the cast of characters made up almost entirely of delegates to the second Continental Congress, and the libretto concerned with the debates and compromises that occurred during three stifling, momentous summer months in Philadelphia. Leaders of the drive for independence, such as John Adams (played by William Daniels), Benjamin Franklin (Howard DaSilva) and Thomas Jefferson (Ken Howard), and their opponents, including John Dickinson (Paul Hecht) and Edward Rutledge (Clifford David), were not only brought to theatrical life but made to sing and dance without lessening their stature or the seriousness of their undertaking.

Sherman Edwards

Perhaps a subject so unlikely could only have been undertaken successfully by a writer inexperienced in the musical theatre. In July 1966, *The New York Times* broke the news that a pop song composer named Sherman Edwards, whose previous Broadway association had been as an actor in Harold Rome's labor revue, *Pins and Needles*, had created book, music, and lyrics based on the activities leading up to the adoption of the Declaration of Independence. What's more, it was actually scheduled for Broadway production.

Academically, at least, Edwards did have solid credentials. Born in New York on April 4, 1919, he grew up in Newark, N.J., majored in history at New York University and did graduate work in the field at Cornell. For a while he taught American history in high school, but he gave up teaching to play piano in the bands of Benny Goodman, Louis Armstrong, and Tommy Dorsey. Along the way he also became a songwriter, credited with such temporal hits as "Wonderful! Wonderful!" (lyric by Ben Raleigh), "See You in September" (with Sid Wayne), "Broken-Hearted Melody" (with Hal David, who would later be the lyricist of *Promises, Promises*), and "Johnny Get Angry" (with Earl Shuman). While thus gainfully occupied, Edwards began spending his spare time

Photo by Martha Swope

*1776 (1969).
Thomas Jefferson (Ken Howard), Benjamin Franklin (Howard Da Silva) and John Adams (William Daniels) are waiting for the "Chirp! Chirp! Chirp! Of an eaglet being born. . . ." (Costumes by Patricia Zipprodt.)*

at the Morristown, New Jersey, Public Library near his home, where he pored over whatever material he could find relating to the American Revolution. Soon he became so obsessed with the idea of writing a musical about the signing of the Declaration of Independence that he quit all other endeavors to devote himself exclusively to the project.

Though the *Times* announcement of the *1776* production indicated a Broadway opening late in 1966, Edwards's libretto was soon found to be unworkable and Peter Stone, librettist of *Kean* and *Skyscraper*, was brought in to rewrite the book. Delays forced the New York premiere to take place in March 1969. It was generally hailed by the press, became the unexpected hit of the season, and went on to achieve a total run of 1,217 performances.

1776 may have been based firmly on historical fact, but the authors found that a certain amount of dramatic license was necessary. One major alteration was having the debate on the wording of the Declaration take place before, not after, the vote for independence. Another was to have the play end with the thrilling sight of each delegate, as his name is called and as the Liberty Bell tolls away, rise and affix his signature to the document on the Fourth of July. Actually, the

Declaration was signed over a period of months with most of the signing taking place August second. Perhaps the most criticized historical tampering was having Martha Jefferson, Thomas' young bride, brought to Philadelphia at the instigation of John Adams so that lovesick Tom might be romantically inspired to write the Declaration. Jefferson apparently did go to Virginia to be with his wife during this period, but the authors felt that having Martha make the journey worked better dramatically.

Without deliberately recreating an eighteenth century sound, the score (apparently Edwards' hail and farewell to the theatre) sounded right for the period, while the lyrics evolved naturally from the situations and the dialogue. This is indicated by such titles as "Sit Down, John," "Fiddle, Twiddle and Resolve," and "But, Mr. Adams-" (even if the last did go in for such modern rhyming as "etiquette," "predicate" and "Connecticut"), and by the dramatic exhortation, "Molasses to Rum," in which South Carolina's Rutledge flays his Northern adversaries for their hypocrisy on the issue of slavery. John Adams' summation of his dream of independence, "Is Anybody There?" (a quote from one of General Washington's messages), was based directly on a letter that the real Adams had written to his wife, Abigail. One of its original lines—"Through all the gloom, I can see the rays of ravishing light and glory"—was even repeated unchanged in the lyric. Also in the letter, Adams exultantly expressed his views on the ways Independence Day should be celebrated in the future: "It should be solemnized with pomp and parade, with shows, games, sports, guns, balls, bonfires, and illumination." Building on those words, Sherman Edwards rephrased Adams' prophesy in the stirring lines:

I see fireworks!
I see the pageant and pomp and parade!
I hear the bells ringing out!
I hear the cannons roar!

Gretchen Cryer and Nancy Ford

The personal stamp that has marked the contributions of Gretchen Cryer and Nancy Ford has increasingly distinguished them as the foremost exponents of the woman's experience in the musical theatre today. While this may have something to do with the fact that they are the only female lyricist-composer team that has ever, to anyone's knowledge, written for the Broadway stage, it is also a very natural development of two writers who have always brought an intensely individual voice to all of their works. They have never been, nor are they ever likely to be, creators who can adapt themselves to concepts other than their own; their songs and librettos have all shown marked originality in both subject matter and viewpoint, as they have consistently reflected the collaborators' mutual attitudes and deep concerns.

Lyricist-librettist Gretchen Cryer (born Gretchen Kiger in Dunreith, Indiana, on October 17, 1935) and composer Nancy Ford (born in Kalamazoo, Michigan, on October 1, 1935) first met when they were attending DePauw University. At college, they collaborated on two musical productions, married classmates and, after graduation, accompanied their husbands to New Haven where the men briefly studied at the Yale Divinity School. Nancy and her husband were soon divorced; Gretchen's husband, David Cryer, pursued a career as actor, singer, and producer. In New York, Gretchen appeared in the choruses of *Little Me* and *110 in the Shade*, and Nancy became the pianist of the long-running *Fantasticks* (where she met her second husband, Keith Charles, then playing El Gallo).

During this period, the women began writing together again and their efforts resulted in their first professional musical, *Now Is the Time for All Good Men*. The motivation for this 1967 off Broad-

Nancy Ford and Gretchen Cryer.

way effort was the experience of Gretchen's brother who had served two years in prison as a conscientious objector during the Vietnam War. In the musical, a pacifist English instructor (played by David Cryer, who was also coproducer) gets into trouble in a small Indiana town by teaching Thoreau's concept of civil disobedience. When he is revealed as an army deserter who has served a prison term, he loses his job, his girl (Gretchen Cryer under the name of Sally Niven) and his life (though soon after the opening his melodramatic murder was changed so that he is merely run out of town). While the plot was preachy and the score conventional, the work won applause for daring to grapple with a serious contemporary issue and it had a moderately successful run.

A more lighthearted, though equally contemporary musical was *The Last Sweet Days of Isaac*, which opened off Broadway early in 1970. Actually, the work combined two one-act musicals to illuminate the overall theme that excessive documentation of life gets in the way of living. In the stories, the hero is so busy tape recording and photographing himself into a permanent record that he is incapable of personal contact. The musical was both appealingly ridiculous and insightful, while the softly rocking score gave the show a buoyant and lyrical tone that helped it achieve a run of over 500 performances. The Cryer-Ford *Shelter*, the team's first Broadway offering three years later, was something of an extension of the *Isaac* theme as it told the story of a young man's relationship with three women while enduring a synthesized existence living in a television studio with a talking computer. Too fantastic and slight for Broadway was the general verdict.

I'm Getting My Act Together and Taking It on the Road (1978) was, by far, the most personal expression of the team. As if to make the identification unmistakable, Gretchen Cryer herself originated the central role, that of a divorced thirty-nine-year-old pop singer defiantly attempting a comeback. (The Cryers had been divorced some years before.) Through the new songs that she tries out on her skeptical manager, she becomes the embodiment of the outspoken, liberated woman, absolutely honest in emotion, attitude, and unglamorized appearance. The manager reacts with increasing irritation to what he calls her "angry, confused and offensive" songs; as the show ends she is on her own, gallantly celebrating her birthday through the belated discovery of her true self.

While most of the critics were only moderately sympathetic, the show's treatment of the modern woman's dilemma has won enthusiastic female support; at this writing, over two years after the opening, it is still playing at an off Broadway house. Its success is testament that the catharsis Gretchen Cryer and Nancy Ford have experienced through their songs can also be felt by a wide spectrum of women today, no matter their divergence in backgrounds or interests.

I'm Getting My Act Together and Taking It on the Road *(1978)*.
Gretchen Cryer auditioning her new act with Lee Grayson and Dean Swenson.
(Costumes by Pearl Somner.)

Gary Geld and Peter Udell

Although the musical theatre has long been used to trodding many an off-the-beaten path, there is something notably singleminded about the careers of composer Gary Geld and lyricist-librettist Peter Udell. In their three Broadway musicals to date, these two Northern writers of urban backgrounds have specialized in musicals that dealt with themes of substance that were all set in a bygone, rural Southland: black and white relations in the backwoods of Georgia (in the long-running *Purlie*); the devastating effects of war on a pacifist farmer in Virginia (in the longer-running *Shenandoah*); and the conflict between youth and age in a small town in South Carolina (in the nonrunning *Angel*). Throughout they have managed to treat complex, emotional subjects in broad, dramatic strokes that have helped shed light on issues that are still very much with us today.

Gary Geld was born in Paterson, New Jersey, on October 18, 1935, and received his education at New York University and at Juilliard. Peter Udell was born in Brooklyn, on May 24, 1934, and studied—at least for a while—at the University of Chicago. Both men were stage-struck at early ages. They met in 1960 and decided on a ten-year plan that they felt would equip them to realize their theatrical goals. Surprisingly this involved writing not show scores but pop tunes, a field that found them winning fleeting successes with such items as "Tear of the Year," "He Says the Same Things to Me," "Getting Married Has Made Us Strangers," and "Sealed with a Kiss." In their range of styles, Geld and Udell demonstrated their knack of writing not only in the pop idiom of the day but also in such specialized areas as rhythm and blues and country and western.

This experience served them particularly well in *Purlie*, their first theatrical assignment, since the story called for music and lyrics that stemmed from these

Gary Geld and Peter Udell.

three areas. Based on Ossie Davis's folkish play, *Purlie Victorious*, the musical was the idea of Philip Rose, who took on the dual capacity of producer and director (as he also would for the next two Geld-Udell collaborations). The tale of how the good but simple southern Negroes turn the tables on the nasty but simpler southern Whites arrived with little fanfare in March 1970, and quickly became the sleeper of the year. Spurred by favorable reviews by the *Times*' Clive Barnes ("*Purlie* is victorious") and the *News*' John Chapman ("*Purlie* is victorious"), the show had no trouble finding its audience, despite the reactions of those who felt its story both dated and partronizing. Cleavon Little cut an exuberant figure as the "new-fangled preacher-man," while the rousing, revivalistic opening chorale, "Walk Him Up the Stairs," and Melba Moore's singing of "I Got Love" became the nightly show-stoppers. *Purlie* chalked up an impressive run of almost 700 performances.

Shenandoah, which the partners began writing soon after finishing *Purlie*, was tried out at the Goodspeed Opera House in East Haddam, Connecticut (whence

Shenandoah *(1975)*.
"This farm don't belong to Virginia; my sons bleed but not for the South," sings John Cullum in his impassioned "Meditation." (Costume by Pearl Somner.)

Photo by Friedman-Abeles

also came *Man of La Mancha* and *Annie*). Closely following the scenario of a film that had starred James Stewart as a war-resisting farmer during the Civil War, the musical opened early in 1975. It was greeted by a mixed critical reception ranging from the *News'* Douglas Watt ("dull . . . gloomy . . . insipid songs") to Clive Barnes ("lusty . . . lovely ballads . . . very likeable") and from *The New Yorker's* Brendan Gill ("conventional claptrap . . . the songs don't invite repeating") to the *Times'* Walter Kerr ("singularly beautiful . . . I wound up in tears"). With John Cullum giving a touching, robust performance and with a homespun texture and moral tone recalling Rodgers and Hammerstein, *Shenandoah* managed to affect audiences deeply. Surely its run of over 1,000 performances was ample confirmation of the credo which both Gary Geld and Peter Udell believe in so strongly: "Simple is good— also very difficult."

Stephen Schwartz

Rodgers and Hammerstein spent almost forty years in the theatre before achieving their so-far unmatched record of four musicals (*Oklahoma!*, *South Pacific*, *The King and I*, *The Sound of Music*) that ran over 1,000 performances. To date, the only other writer to come close is composer-lyricist Stephen Schwartz, whose three musicals to run more than 1,000—*Godspell*, *Pippin* and *The Magic Show*—also happen to be the first three he ever wrote. And all were produced before his twenty-seventh birthday.

It may, of course, be argued that *Godspell* achieved 2,124 performances at small, off-Broadway houses, that *Pippin* owed its longevity to the inventive skills of director-choreographer Bob Fosse, and that *The Magic Show* would have quickly disappeared without a trace had it not been for the legerdemain of illusionist Doug Henning. But though the achievement can be explained it cannot be denied—nor can Schwartz's talent. What the composer has brought to the theatre is a modern, youthful, crisp sound, primarily influenced by rock but also endowed with sensitivity and melodic grace. As he has put it, "Generally, I write in what I prefer to call contemporary style. That's how I hear music. I don't understand why some people feel that that sort of style cannot be applied to the theatre, that it cannot tell a story, or communicate an emotion, or further an event. Why should music in a 1940s style be intrinsically more capable of performing a dramatic function than rock music?"

Stephen Schwartz was born in New York on March 6, 1948. He grew up in Roslyn Heights, Long Island, where he began taking piano lessons at six. During his high school years he wrote and directed plays, and also found time to study composition at Juilliard. Schwartz attended Carnegie Tech's drama school; as a Sophomore he collaborated on a musical called *Pippin Pippin*, based on the exploits of Charlemagne's son. After graduation he tried unsuccessfully to get the show presented off Broadway, then spent two years as a record producer at RCA. In 1969, his title song for the play, *Butterflies Are Free*, became his first piece heard on Broadway.

Schwartz became associated with *Godspell* when he saw John-Michael Tebelak's nonmusical play (written as a master's thesis) at Ellen Stewart's experimental Café LaMama theatre. Producers Edgar Lansbury and Joseph Beruh thought that the childlike, contemporary resetting of Saint Matthews' Passion might work as an off Broadway musical; with Schwartz supplying the score, they got it on the boards some five months before *Jesus Christ Superstar*, the flashier Broadway variation of the same Biblical source.

Godspell began its run at the Cherry Lane Theatre in May 1971. While Clive Barnes's review in the *Times* was grudgingly unfavorable ("There may well be those who will find freshness and originality here where I could discover only a naive but fey frivolity"), other notices were more helpful, and patrons kept coming. Within three months it had transferred to the Promenade Theatre where it remained for over five years. It also had a healthy Broadway run at the Broadhurst beginning in June 1976.

Though the show depicted Jesus as an innocent clown with a Superman "S" on his shirt and his disciples as a troupe of nine ragamuffins, there were few complaints of sacrilege. There were, however, complaints of the cutes, though most audiences readily responded to the show's frolicsome appeal and general air of amiable piety. Throughout the evening, the cast enacted the parables in antic, colloquial style, with the songs conveying the spirit of the entertainment, perhaps most effectively in the contrapuntal, vaudeville turn, "All for the Best." The only piece to emerge with a life of its own was the rather lugubrious "Day by Day," based on an ancient Episcopal hymn.

Stephen Schwartz.

Godspell proved a godsend for Schwartz. Leonard Bernstein enlisted his aid as collaborator on the English text of his *Mass*. And suddenly producers began showing an interest in his college musical, *Pippin Pippin*. The one presenting it on Broadway was Stuart Ostrow who signed playwright Roger O. Hirson as librettist and Bob Fosse as director-choreographer. One of their first acts was to throw away half the title.

By gaining Fosse, the show also gained a concept, that of a magic show, in which a variety of theatrical forms would be used to emphasize the razzle-dazzle nature of the entertainment. In addition, Fosse conceived the idea of offering the story within the framework of a Commedia dell'Arte performance. For the remarkable opening, "Join Us," a group of players led by Ben Vereen first showed only their illuminated hands weaving patterns through the enveloping smoke that covered the entire stage area. Also fitting into the Fosse scheme were Irene Ryan's "No Time at All," done as a vaudeville sing-along complete with bouncing ball (in place of Schwartz's

Godspell *(1971).*
David Haskell as Judas and
Stephen Nathan as Jesus with
the members of the company.
(Costumes by Susan Tzu.)

Photo by Metropolitan Photo

Pippin *(1972).*
Pippin (John Rubinstein)
decides it's time to start living
and stop worrying. (Costumes
by Patricia Zipprodt.)

original rock version) and "War Is a Science" as a minstrel show (instead of the original Gilbert-and-Sullivan takeoff). In depicting the saga of Pippin's Candide-like search for glory through a number of experiences dealing with war, sex, politics, and family, the story was still basically Schwartz's tale of a boy who tries for greatness but must eventually find fulfillment in compromise. The composer, however, felt the stunning theatrical effects obfuscated his theme and his relationship with Fosse was stormy. The New York reception, at least, justified the director's approach and, aided by a skillful television advertising campaign, *Pippin* remained on Broadway over four and a half years.

Pippin was a magic show in concept and execution; *The Magic Show* was a sleight-of-hand act awkwardly combined with a light-in-the-head story set in a seedy Passaic, N.J., nightclub. Packaging the remarkable illusionist, Doug Henning, within the framework of a musical-comedy libretto may have seemed totally wrong-headed—except for the fact that the show did become an extremely popular family entertainment. Even though the star was succeeded by Joe Adalbo for about half the run, it wound up with an astonishing 1,920 performances.

Success with his first three shows has given Stephen Schwartz the independence to devote himself only to subjects that he feels strongly about. (Such as the worthy but uncommercial *Working*, which he adapted from Studs Terkel's book and also directed.) In the composer's words, "I can't understand people who say, 'Gee, let's do this show because I think it'll be a hit.' It takes two years out of your life, at the least, to do a show. It should be something meaningful to you. I write about what interests me, what concerns me. All of my shows are about compromise, which is very much part of my life. Usually, whenever I have a serious problem I just write a show about it."

Jim Jacobs and Warren Casey.

CHAPTER THIRTY-ONE

JIM JACOBS and WARREN CASEY
CHARLIE SMALLS
MARVIN HAMLISCH
EDWARD KLEBAN
CAROLE BAYER SAGER
ELIZABETH SWADOS
CAROL HALL

IT BEGAN AS a five-hour-long amateur show presented in a Chicago trolley barn in the summer of 1971. Two young New York producers saw it, made the authors cut the show down to normal length, and opened it at the Eden Theatre on Second Avenue on February 14, 1972. It won general approval from an indulgent press, moved uptown to the Broadhurst in June and to the Royale in November. And it remained there for almost seven-and-a-half years.

Jim Jacobs and Warren Casey

The musical, of course, is *Grease* and the question, of course, is "Why?" In this recreation of the mores, morals, and music of 1950s adolescents, the characters are unappealing, foulmouthed, self-indulgent and self-pitying, with nary a thought in their oleaginous heads to anything other than hanging out and making out. Individuality is mocked, conformity is the only conduct tolerated, illegitimacy is philosophically defended, and every pubescent trauma is explored through such lachrymose sentiments as "Alone at a Drive-In Movie," "It's Raining on Prom Night" and "Beauty School Dropout."

But obviously the musical hit a nerve. Though the air was primarily one of parody, *Grease* let us see with unerring authenticity and a total lack of sentimentality the way kids actually looked and acted and felt during those witch-hunting, Korean War days that we look back on as somehow being both placid and plastic. The songs caught the beat and pathos of their inane but catchy originals, the dialogue and situations got laughs, Patricia Birch's choreography had style, and the cast (originally led by Barry Bostwick and Carole Demas) was infused with a spirit that audiences found contagious. For anyone who grew up in the Sandra Dee-James Dean decade, there was total identification with the Palace Burger Boys and Pink Ladies of Rydell High and their pajama parties, proms, garishly decorated hot rods, angora sweaters, and ducktail hair styles. For kids in their teens—who made up

Grease *(1972).*
The Pink Ladies and the
Burger Palace Boys singing
the first-act finale, "We Go
Together" ("Like rama-lama-
lama, ka-dinga da ding-
dong"). (Costumes by Carrie
Robbins; setting by Douglas
Schmidt.)

most of *Grease*'s audience and who frequently paid return visits—it spoke and sang a language they related to despite a time gap of some twenty years.

Grease was the creation of Jim Jacobs and Warren Casey (they both worked on the book, music, and lyrics) who wrote it for a Chicago community theatre called the Kingston Mines. Jacobs, who was born in Chicago on October 7, 1942, was a self-admitted greaser at Taft High School and a guitarist with several rock and roll groups. Casey was born in Yonkers, on April 2, 1935, and became an art major at Syracuse University. After teaching in upstate New York, he moved to Chicago, where he held a variety of jobs but soon gravitated toward acting and writing songs. Though the team first met in 1963, they followed other paths, including an appearance by Jacobs in the Broadway play, *No Place to Be Somebody*. One day in the early seventies, they got together again and soon began tossing ideas around about doing a modest, inexpensive show that would take an affectionate but honest look at the world of their youth. . . .

Charlie Smalls

The annals of the American musical theatre are crammed with case histories of productions that appeared to have only the slimmest chance for survival before opening on Broadway, but somehow managed to be pulled, tugged, and molded into such healthy condition that they went on to achieve lengthy runs, earn pots of money, and win eternal glory. Among those near-hopeless cases that come readily to mind: *No, No, Nanette* (both the 1925 and 1971 versions), *The New Moon, Funny Face, Anything Goes, Camelot, Hello, Dolly!,* and *Funny Girl.* In 1975, that illustrious company was joined by *The Wiz.*

Consider. It had to compete for affection with *The Wizard of Oz*, the legendary, beloved film version of the same Frank Baum children's story on which it was based. Neither the composer nor the librettist had ever before had his name on a Broadway book musical, nor had the producer ever produced before. It had an all-black cast of such anonymity that its best-known member was Butterfly McQueen—and her part was cut on the road. Before the first tryout performance, in Baltimore, the technical rehearsal was so disastrous that the producer was advised by his stage manager to close the show. In Detroit, the musical was in such desperate need of pruning and polishing that the director was replaced by the costume designer. During the Broadway previews, the show turned no profit, attracted neither advance ticket sale nor theatre-party booking, and had no money in reserve. The closing notice was posted backstage on opening night (January 5, 1975), and the reviews the next day, while mostly favorable, were still not exactly the kind to make anyone unduly optimistic.

And then what happened? And then what happened was that the show ran for four solid years on Broadway, spawned touring companies that traveled for over three years, won any number of ego-gratifying prizes, and was brought to the screen at a record cost of almost $35 million.

The genesis of *The Wiz* began in 1970

when Ken Harper, a young radio executive, chucked his job to pursue his dream of turning the turn-of-the-century fairy tale into an up-to-date all-black rock musical. Among those enlisted early in the preparation was Charlie Smalls, a songwriter-musician Harper had first met at a recording session, who was signed for both music and lyrics.

Born in Long Island City on October 25, 1943, Charlie Smalls was a child prodigy who gave concerts at five, won a scholarship to Juilliard at eleven, and went on to master the drums, bass, guitar, organ, and harpsichord at the High School of Performing Arts. After a stint with a U.S. Air Force band, he became music director at various New York night spots and a featured singer and pianist on records. He has also scored and appeared in films, including John Cassavetes' *Faces*.

In the summer of 1973, Harper approached Geoffrey Holder to play the part of the Wiz. Holder, a man of many theatrical parts, became so intrigued by the project that he also offered himself as costume designer, and submitted sketches that were both imaginative and functional, showing how each of the major characters would move and walk. The Lion, for example, would be a dude in his new fur coat, while the Tinman would become the spirit of Harlem with a garbage-can torso. Since the costumes determined the style of the show, the producer handed Holder the additional responsibilities of directing and choreographing. Now with sketches, libretto (the work of William F. Brown, a white television writer) and music and lyrics, Harper was able to win the financial backing of Twentieth Century-Fox ("I knew we had 'em," said Smalls, "when nine grown men cried when I sang 'Home' "), but the executives balked at entrusting so much authority to Holder. While remaining as costume designer, he was replaced as director and choreographer by Gilbert Moses and George Faison, and as The Wiz by André DeShields.

Charlie Smalls.

Under Moses, the creative staff embellished the ancient fable with a number of inventive touches. Faison conceived the idea of the Tornado Ballet, which inspired Holder to create a dazzling costume with one hundred yards of black silk streaming from a dancer's head. Set designer Tom H. John suggested having four dancers personify the Yellow Brick Road, for which Holder supplied the design of the frizzy-haired clowns in their yellow tailcoats. During tryouts, serious problems developed that forced Harper to dismiss his director (who thus became the second Moses to be kept from leading his people to the Promised Land) and replace him with . . . Geoffrey Holder. Holder pulled the show together and gave it focus, but since many of his more flamboyant concepts were dropped before Broadway, the show New Yorkers saw was basically the same one that had been laid out by Moses and Faison.

The wizardry that turned *The Wiz* into a boxoffice hit relied at first on distributing free tickets in exchange for air plugs and newspaper stories, plus contacting church and civic groups in black communities. Once word of mouth and cut-rate tickets had helped boost attendance, Twentieth Century-Fox agreed to pump additional funds into a television and radio saturation advertising campaign that proved incredibly effective. One week after the initial airing, *The Wiz* took in $100,000. Two weeks after that—and for two years after *that*—the show that almost died before it was born never played to an empty seat.

The Wiz *(1975).*
The Wiz *(André DeShields) bids farewell to his fellow Ozians ("Y'All Got It") before sailing off in a balloon. (Costumes by Geoffrey Holder; setting by Tom H. John.)*

Marvin Hamlisch, Edward Kleban, Carole Bayer Sager

It was unprecedented. Even before its official opening on May 21, 1975, even before the critics had given their seal of approval or any kind of drum-beating had been heard, *A Chorus Line* was being hailed as the most exciting new musical New York had seen in years. Ever since mid-April, when previews had begun at Joseph Papp's Public Theatre near Astor Place, cheering, overflowing audiences had been sending the word uptown about a new kind of musical that dared to be concerned with nothing more world-shaking than the everyday lives of chorus dancers. The unanimously enthusiastic critical response simply confirmed the public's verdict; within two months the production was moved uptown to the Shubert Theatre where it remains, at this writing, one of Broadway's most admired and honored attractions.

The credit for conceiving the show and leading it to triumph goes to one man, director-choreographer Michael Bennett. Bennett, a former chorus "gypsy" himself, had long wanted to do a musical celebrating the contributions of those faceless toilers in this unappreciated area of the performing arts. Though still undecided about the form it would take, he rented a dance studio in January 1974, where he brought together twenty-four other dancers to spend the night talking about themselves into a tape recorder. After a second session had produced a total of some thirty hours of taped autobiographies, it began to dawn on Bennett that "what these kids had been doing was auditioning their lives for me," and that the only possible dramatic form for the musical would be an audition. That summer he and Nicholas Dante, one of the dancers at the sessions, began editing the tapes and organizing their contents. What they did so impressed producer Papp that he offered to sponsor the project as a workshop production of his New York Shakespeare Festival. It was at this stage that Bennett acquired a composer and lyricist. For the score, he secured Marvin Hamlisch, whose talents he had admired ever since they had worked together on the 1967 musical, *Henry, Sweet Henry*, for which Bennett served as choreographer and Hamlisch was the dance-music arranger. For the lyrics it was Edward Kleban, a virtually unknown writer who won the assignment after, appropriately, an audition.

Hamlisch, a native New Yorker born on June 2, 1944, was blessed with such prodigious musical gifts that he won a Juilliard scholarship at the age of seven. He wrote his first song hit at seventeen ("Sunshine, Lollipops and Rainbows," with lyricist Howard Liebling), and the following year had his initial Broadway assignment, as assistant vocal arranger for *Funny Girl*. After majoring in music at Queens College, Hamlisch met film producer Sam Spiegel who was so impressed with his work that he hired the composer to create the background score for *The Swimmer*, starring Burt Lancaster.

The score won sufficient notice to open doors to other Hollywood commissions such as *Take the Money and Run*, *Bananas*, and *Save the Tiger*, as well as the chance to compose Las Vegas numbers for the likes of Liza Minnelli, Ann-Margret, and Joel Grey. At the time Bennett contacted him, Hamlisch was enjoying his first taste of popular acclaim, having recently won the Academy Awards' first Triple Crown—as arranger of Scott Joplin's music for *The Sting*, and as composer of the background music and title song for *The Way We Were* (lyric by Alan and Marilyn Bergman). Since accepting Bennett's proposal meant turning down lucrative offers, it took some soul-searching before the composer agreed—largely, as he has said, because "it offered me the challenge to write classical, ballet, rock, jazz, and Broadway music all in one show."

There was no such soul-searching on the part of Kleban, whose career at that

Marvin Hamlisch.

Edward Kleban.

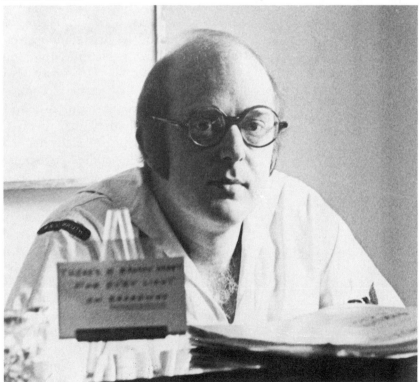

Courtesy Chappell Music

Courtesy BMI Archives

A Chorus Line *(1975).*
Performing the number called
"One"—Sammy Williams,
Pamela Blair, Michel Stuart,
Nancy Lane, Cameron
Mason, Renee Baughman,
Ron Kuhlman, Patricia
Garland, Thomas J. Walsh,
Carole (later Kelly) Bishop,
Don Percassi. (Costumes by
Theoni V. Aldredge.)

time was showing hardly any signs of progress. A composer as well as lyricist, Kleban, who was born on April 30, 1939, grew up in The Bronx and was educated at the High School of Music and Art and at Columbia University. Not long out of college he became a producer at Columbia Records, a position he quit in 1968 to devote himself exclusively to song writing. During a relatively lean seven-year period, he studied at Lehman Engel's BMI Theatre Workshop, contributed songs to experimental theatre groups and television, and was "emergency" lyricist for the 1973 revivals of *Irene* and *The Desert Song.* One of the unusual aspects of the Hamlisch-Kleban collaboration on *A Chorus Line* was that, because of the very nature of the musical, many of the songs were worked out right in the theatre as the show was being put together.

The rehearsals were temporarily halted at the end of September, then re-sumed in December after playwright James Kirkwood had been brought in to work with Dante. (Another playwright to help out along the way was Neil Simon.) By the time the musical opened, it had cost Papp $300,000—or about a quarter of what it would have cost on Broadway. (That is, if Broadway could have found anyone to finance so questionable a venture.)

In the story of *A Chorus Line,* twenty-seven dancers (thirty-one by the time the show moved uptown) vie with each other to be chosen for a chorus line requiring four girls and four boys. The applicants are quickly winnowed down to eighteen, who are then obliged by the largely unseen and somewhat sadistic director to reveal truths about themselves to help him make the final selection. At least three members of the original cast—Donna McKechnie, Priscilla Lopez, and Kelly (then Carole) Bishop—had been in the rap sessions and related experiences similar to their own; one cast member, Sammy Williams, told the humiliating real-life story of co-librettist Dante's experience as a drag queen. Though the show must end with the acceptance of eight dancers and the heartbreaking rejection of ten, it then turns into a wish-fulfillment for the audience as the entire step-kicking company—with a background mirror doubling the number—comes out in salmon-colored satin costumes and top hats for a rousingly up-beat finale.

The great appeal of *A Chorus Line* unquestionably lies in the empathetical bond that it achieves right from the start. No matter what our field may be, we have all had to undergo the dreaded experience of being forced to stand in a real or symbolic line as a stranger passes judgment on our qualifications. Although the musical has a show-business setting, it is, as Bennett has said, "a metaphor for life."

A Chorus Line was conceived as an "opera-ballet," which the director has defined as a work in which the music stops whenever talk is really necessary, rather than something in which talk is stopped for the singing and dancing. Actually, the show contains an almost continuous flow of music which comes to a complete halt only three times during the evening. As Martin Gottfried pointed out in the *Post*, "Hamlisch's music is that rare animal, a theatre *score*. It isn't just a series of songs but an evening's worth of music designed to function as part of a stage work. It captures the very spirit and essence of rehearsal music."

Notwithstanding such praise or the fact that Hamlisch, on his first try, had written the score for a Pulitzer Prize-winner, he felt that his contributions to the production were generally overlooked. "The problem was to write theme songs for eighteen people so you'd know the lives of every chorus gypsy in thirty-two bars. If I had written hit songs, the audience would root only for the people with the hit songs and it

Courtesy Chappell Music

Carole Bayer Sager.

would throw the show off balance. I sacrificed like hell for the sake of the show."

No such sacrifice was needed for Hamlisch's second Broadway endeavor, *They're Playing Our Song*, which arrived four years later. For just as his first musical had been based on real-life show and tell, so the second was based on real-life kiss and tell—but in this case the inspiration was the composer's own romance with his frequent lyric-writing partner, Carole Bayer Sager. And since the show was about a song-writing duo, their songs and the way they write them and feel about them became a vital part of the relationship between the two characters in the story. (Like *I Do! I Do!*, there were only two, but each had three singing alter egos.)

Although in 1970 she had provided lyrics to George Fischoff's music for the short-lived musical, *Georgy*, Carole Bayer Sager is far more a part of the current pop scene than she is of the Broadway musical scene. Born in New York on March 8, 1944, she began writing songs at fifteen while still a student at the High School of Performing Arts. Her first hit, in 1966, was "A Groovy Kind of Love," written with Toni Wine, and she has since contributed material for such major performers as Frank Sinatra, Liza Minnelli, Carly Simon ("Nobody Does It Better," taken from the main theme of Hamlisch's score for the film, *The Spy who Loved Me*), and Melissa Manchester (with whom she has also written songs). In addition to writing, Miss Sager (though divorced, she still keeps her married name) has been a featured singer on a number of albums.

The idea for *They're Playing Our Song* began around the time Hamlisch and playwright Neil Simon were attempting to make a musical out of Simon's play, *The Gingerbread Lady*. During this period, the composer's running account of

his occasionally tempestuous relationship with his lyricist-in-residence so intrigued the playwright that *Lady* was abandoned and *Song* was born.

In the musical, Lucie Arnaz (daughter of Lucy and Desi, making her Broadway debut) played an aspiring, wise-cracking, neurotic lyricist named Sonia Walsk who has a penchant for wearing salvaged costumes from old stage productions, and Robert Klein (son of Frieda and Ben, in his first major stage role) played a successful, wise-cracking, neurotic composer named Vernon Gersch (for Duke and Gershwin?) who has a penchant for telling his troubles into a tape recorder. The main device for causing their romantic crises is the persistent telephoning of Sonia's former lover for whom she still feels deep concern.

The Hamlisch-Sager score that punctuates the Hamlisch-Gersch and Sager-Walsk story is less tightly functional than that for *A Chorus Line* since it is a parade of highly polished pop songs created as much for chart-busting as for character exposition and plot development. In its use of novelty effects within the basically pop structure, the score occasionally sounds like updated Frank Loesser. This is apparent in "They're Playing My Song" in which first Vernon and then Sonia explode in dithyrambic self-esteem upon hearing their songs being played in a night club. Or "Fill in the Words," which finds the play's composer, accompanied by his alter egos, writing a new song at a toy piano but leaving some lines unsung because of his inability to find the right expression. And despite a lyric that rhymes "another" with "cover" and "clever" with "together," the propulsive "Working It Out" manages to deal ingeniously with the dual problems of working out a new song and working out the emotional strains of ending a love affair. Whatever other virtues the score possesses, Marvin Hamlisch has made sure that it cannot be overlooked—or leave any doubt about whose song is being played.

They're Playing Our Song (1979).
Lucie Arnaz and Robert Klein in the final clinch. (Costumes by Ann Roth.)

Photo by Jay Thompson

Elizabeth Swados

Although she has yet to create a box office-jamming smash, Elizabeth Swados has established herself within a relatively brief time as a major innovative force in the contemporary musical theatre. Not only is she both composer and lyricist with a highly eclectic style ranging from ragas to rock and from country to bird calls, but she has also conceived and directed all of her musicals to date (at least those that fall within the scope of this survey), and has performed in two of them. Moreover, since all three Swados offerings have shunned single narrative stories in favor of collages of songs, choral pieces, and monologues, she has been credited by Clive Barnes for having given the musical theatre a new direction—"she has invented the Broadway cantata"—and she has done it with themes deliberately far from the convenient and the conventional. "It's so difficult," the composer has said, "to get people to believe in what can be done in the musical theatre. I'm scared by the lack of risk in theatre."

Taking risks has always been part of the Swados approach. Born in Buffalo, New York, on February 5, 1951, she was able to play piano and compose music at five and to give folk-song recitals by the time she was eleven. After studying composition with Henry Brant at Bennington—and then dropping out of college—she sang in coffee houses in New York City and created songs for experimental works at Ellen Stewart's Café LaMama. There she met director Andrei Serban with whom, in 1971, she collaborated on a highly original music-drama concept of Euripides' *Medea*. Following a tour with the production in Europe, Miss Swados joined Peter Brook's International Theatre Group as composer and music director during its African tour. Upon her return to the United States, she resumed her association with Serban, first on two more Greek tragedies, Sopho-

Photo by Martha Swope

Elizabeth Swados.

cles' *Electra* and Euripides' *Trojan Women*, then on a new version of Brecht's *Good Woman of Setzuan*. In 1977, she again teamed with Serban, this time at Joseph Papp's New York Shakespeare Festival at Lincoln Center, where they worked on new interpretations of Chekhov's *Cherry Orchard* and Aeschylus's *Agamemnon*.

Before undertaking the last two projects, Miss Swados found time to create, assemble, and stage the first of her own musicals, *Nightclub Cantata*. The work, which was favorably received by the press, was a diverse collection of musical pieces, poems, and pantomimes, including such highlights as the choked-up, staccato reading of Sylvia Plath's "The Applicant," the improvised comic takeoff

Runaways *(1978).*
With Bruce Hlibok and Karen
Evans accompanying her in
sign language, Trini Alvarado
sings "Lullaby from Baby to
Baby." (Costumes by Hilary
Rosenfeld.)

on the acrobatically inept Pastrami Brothers and "Dibarti," a husband-wife clash in the form of a Hebrew chant.

Nightclub Cantata inaugurated the genre that Elizabeth Swados then used in a more thematically concentrated form in *Runaways.* Here the concept was a musical production that would deal with various aspects of runaway adolescents and the way they cope with living in the streets. It would also be concerned with the more universal situation that, as the composer puts it, "everyone runs away from certain things in life, if only symbolically. Sometimes it takes guts, sometimes it's cowardly." (Swados herself had run away from home a number of times and her mother ran away by committing suicide.)

In May 1977, the composer took her idea to Joseph Papp, who agreed to sponsor its development as a workshop production. She spent the next four months interviewing children at schools and community centers; from the thousands she saw, she recruited her multi-

racial cast of twenty-one consisting mostly of those with some acting experience, including a deaf mute and a skateboard champion (an actual runaway), plus three professional actors. Improvisational sessions and rehearsals consumed another five months before the show was ready to open at the Public Theatre. In the manner of its evolution under Papp's aegis and in its use of songs and narratives to relate experiences based on real situations, *Runaways* was viewed as following in the creative and confessional tradition of *A Chorus Line,* with other antecedents being *Hair* and *The Me Nobody Knows* (a 1970 musical based on poems by ghetto children). In its music, the rhythms showed strong influences of salsa, samba, blues, country, calypso, and punk rock, all accompanying themes dealing with loneliness, child prostitution, hero-worship, comradeship, street-smart ingenuity, the joys of being a kid, and the need for greater understanding on the part of both parents and children. The newspaper verdicts proved so encouraging that Papp transferred *Runaways* to a Broadway house where it remained almost eight months.

With *Dispatches* (which Miss Swados worked on after her musical treatment of *Alice in Wonderland* had to be shelved), the focus was once more on a single basic topic, in this case nothing less than the effects of the Vietnam War on American combat troops. With the words extracted from only one source, Michael Herr's graphic and sensitive book, it covered to a predominantly rock beat all the contrasting emotions of desperation, pride, fear, grief, and exhilaration that are felt by men at war.

Daring and uncompromising, Elizabeth Swados is a creative writer of such intense imagination that she is able to discover lyricism and beauty in areas where others find only depressingly prosaic squalor. "Some people," she says, "don't want intensity, they want entertainment. That's not what I'm about."

Carol Hall

Beginning in the late sixties, one of the most noteworthy developments in the theatre has been the number of Broadway successes that were first tried out—in one form or another—in playhouses and workshops located off Broadway and beyond. Joseph Papp's Public Theatre developed *Hair, A Chorus Line,*and *Runaways*; Ellen Stewart's Café LaMama begat *Godspell*; Chicago's Kingston Mines sent us *Grease*; the Manhattan Theatre Club originated *Ain't Misbehavin'*. And from Lee Strasberg's Actor's Studio came *The Best Little Whorehouse in Texas*.

The genesis of the musical had started some years before in a magazine article by Larry L. King about a crusading, oilier-than-thou Houston television commentator and the way he caused the demise of a legendary brothel known as the Chicken Ranch (so-called because cashless patrons were allowed to pay with poultry). Turning the account into a stage musical was the idea of Peter Masterson, a Texas-born actor and director, after fellow-Texan Carol Hall had expressed interest in writing a show about their native state that would be "funny and nostalgic and tender." They got in touch with King (another Texan), who told them he hated musicals—and then promptly began the first draft ("But ah don' want no tippy-toed tap dancers stompin' on mah dialogue!"). With Masterson to help structure the material and Miss Hall to create both words and music, the show was put together, the composer recalls, "like a patchwork quilt because the things that turned each of us on were the things we did. Larry wrote what he wanted to, Pete edited, and, on my own, I came up with the songs I felt would be right."

Carol Hall's involvement with all forms of music began at an early age. She was born in Abilene on April 3, 1936, where her mother, a piano and violin

Carol Hall.

teacher, made sure that she had a thorough training in the classics. After graduating from Sarah Lawrence in 1960, she turned to pop song writing—first (unsuccessfully) in the adult field, then (successfully) with her children songs for television's *Free to Be You and Me* and *Sesame Street*. Her theatrical experience began about a year before *Whorehouse* when her musical, *Wonderful Beast*, was tried out at Café LaMama.

The first performance of *The Best Little Whorehouse in Texas* was a reading, under Masterson's direction, at the Actor's Studio. Carlin Glynn (Mrs. Masterson) played Miss Mona (don't call her madam!) and Henderson Forsythe was blunt-talking Sheriff Ed Earl Dodd. After a more complete version had been

Photo by Ilene Jones

The Best Little Whorehouse
in Texas *(1978)*.
*A confrontation between
crusading television
commentator Clint Allmon
and brothel owner Carlin
Glynn and her ally, Sheriff
Henderson Forsythe.
(Costumes by Ann Roth.)*

staged at the studio, Universal Pictures took over the production, thus becoming the first film company to be an official sponsor of a theatrical work. The show opened off Broadway early in 1978 at the Entermedia Theatre (previously known as the Phoenix and the Eden); two months later Broadway had a *Whorehouse* on it.

The Best Little Whorehouse in Texas has won deserved praise for its authentic atmosphere, unblushing country humor, basic innocence, high-spirited choreography (by Texas' own Tommy Tune), and immensely appealing score. Among Tune's inspirations: a comic number in which six blank-faced, blond football cheerleaders prance about with each girl holding a pair of bouncing, life-sized dummy replicas of herself. The songs, with their twangy, rustic instrumentation, cover a variety of styles and themes, ranging from gospel ("Twenty-Four Hours of Lovin'"), to square dancing ("Texas Has a Whorehouse in It"), to narrative ballad ("Bus from Amarillo"), and on to the wistful chorale, in which the girls, with the ranch shut down, ponder their future while preparing for a "Hard Candy Christmas." "Let's just say," says Carol Hall in summing up her musical influences, "that the music was written by someone with a classical background who absorbed the Nashville sound and who always wanted a career on Broadway."

MUSICAL PRODUCTIONS & DISCOGRAPHY

The following lists include opening dates, theatres, number of performances, collaborators, producers, directors, choreographers, leading cast members, and principal songs of every Broadway (and off-Broadway) musical with scores written by the composers and lyricists discussed in this book. Director-choreographers are credited only as directors. In addition to productions with complete scores by these writers, others with four or more interpolated songs have been included.

All original cast (O.C.), film version cast (F.V.), television cast (TV), and studio cast (S.C.) 12-inch long playing records are noted and discussed briefly. Only the most recently assigned catalogue numbers of authorized American albums are included. All Reader's Digest versions—each one digested to one side of a record—are part of a ten-record package, *Treasury of Great Operettas*.

The exact number of performances is often difficult to determine. In general, references have been *The Best Plays* series, *The Billboard*, *Variety*, and *Theater World* series. Wherever a noticeable discrepancy exists in these sources, the number has been used that most closely corresponds to the total months a show has played on Broadway.

Names of cast members have been listed according to the spelling found in programs of each musical. In cases where actors or writers have since changed their names so that they are no longer identifiable by this listing, the more familiar names appear in parentheses.

Chapter Two
VICTOR HERBERT
Composer

PRINCE ANANIAS
Opened: Nov. 20, 1894, Broadway Th.
(No record of performances)
Book & lyrics by Francis Neilson.
Produced by The Bostonians.
Cast included: Mena Cleary, W. H.
MacDonald, Eugene Cowles, Henry Clay
Barnabee, George Frothingham, Jessie
Bartlett Davis, Josephine Bartlett.
Principal songs: Ah! Cupid, Meddlesome
Boy!; Ah! List to Me; It Needs No Poet; I Am
No Queen; Amaryllis.

THE WIZARD OF THE NILE
Opened: Nov. 4, 1895, Casino Th.
105 *performances.*
Book & lyrics by Harry B. Smith.
Produced by Kirke LaShelle & Arthur F.
Clark; directed by Napier Lothian, Jr.
Cast included: Frank Daniels, Walter Allen,
Edwin Isham, Dorothy Morton, Helen
Redmond.
Principal songs: Pure and White Is the Lotus;
Star Light, Star Bright; My Angeline;
Stonecutters' Song.

THE GOLD BUG
Opened: Sept. 21, 1896, Casino Th.
1 *week.*
Book & lyrics by Glen MacDonough.
Produced by Thomas Canary & George W.
Lederer; directed by Max Freeman.
Cast included: Marie Cahill, Max Figman,
Molly Fuller, Bert Williams & George
Walker.
Principal songs: One for Another; The Owl
and the Thrush; Gold Bug March.

THE SERENADE
Opened: Mar. 16, 1897, Knickerbocker Th.
79 *performances.*
Books & lyrics by Harry B. Smith.
Produced by The Bostonians; directed by W.
H. Fitzgerald.
Cast included: Alice Nielsen, Eugene Cowles,
Henry Clay Barnabee, Josephine Bartlett, W.
H. MacDonald, George Frothingham, Jessie
Bartlett Davis.
Principal songs: With Cracking of Whip and
Rattle of Spur; I Love Thee, I Adore Thee;
The Monk and the Maid; Cupid and I.

THE IDOL'S EYE
Opened: Oct. 25, 1897, Broadway Th.
7 *weeks.*
Book & lyrics by Harry B. Smith.
Produced by Frank Daniels; directed by
Julian Mitchell.
Cast included: Frank Daniels, Helen
Redmond, Maurice Darcy, Alf. C. Whelan,
Will Danforth.
Principal songs: I'm Captain Cholly Chumley

of the Guards; The Lady and the Kick; Song
of the Priestess; Cuban Song.

THE FORTUNE TELLER
Opened: Sept. 26, 1898, Wallack's Th.
40 *performances.*
Book & lyrics by Harry B. Smith.
Produced by Frank L. Perley; directed by
Julian Mitchell.
Cast included: Alice Nielsen, Eugene Cowles,
Joseph Herbert, Joseph Cawthorn, Frank
Rushworth, May Boley.
Principal songs: Always Do as People Say
You Should; Romany Life; Gypsy Love Song;
Czardas.

CYRANO DE BERGERAC
Opened: Sept. 18, 1899, Knickerbocker Th.
28 *performances.*
Book by Stuart Reed; lyrics by Harry B.
Smith.
Produced by Francis Wilson; directed by A.
M. Holbrook.
Cast included: Francis Wilson, Lulu Glaser,
Josephine Intropidi, Charles H. Bowers.
Principal songs: Since I Am Not For Thee;
Cadets of Gascony; I Wonder; Let the Sun of
My Eyes.

THE SINGING GIRL
Opened: Oct. 23, 1899, Casino Th.
80 *performances.*
Book by Stanislaus Stange; lyrics by Harry B.
Smith.
Produced by Fred J. Perley; directed by Julian
Mitchell.
Cast included: Alice Nielsen, Eugene Cowles,
Joseph Herbert, Joseph Cawthorn, Richie
Ling.
Principal songs: If Only You Were Mine;
Love Is Tyrant; Well Beloved; The Song of the
Danube.

THE AMEER
Opened: Dec. 4, 1899, Wallack's Th.
51 *performances.*
Book & Lyrics by Frederic Ranken & Kirke
La Shelle.
Produced by Frank Daniels; directed by John
Stapleton.
Cast included: Frank Daniels, Helen
Redmond, George Devoll, Will Danforth,
Josephine Bartlett.
Principal songs: Sweet Clarissa; Fond Love,
True Love.

THE VICEROY
Opened: Apr. 9, 1900, Knickerbocker Th.
28 *performances.*
Book & Lyrics by Harry B. Smith.
Produced by The Bostonians; directed by
William H. Fitzgerald.
Cast included: Henry Clay Barnabee, Helen
Bertram, Grace Cameron, William H.
MacDonald, Frank Rushworth, George B.
Frothingham, William H. Fitzgerald.
Principal Songs: The Robin and the Rose; Tell

Me; 'Neath The Blue Neapolitan Skies; Just for Today.

BABES IN TOYLAND
Opened: Oct. 13, 1903, Majestic Th.
192 performances.
Book & Lyrics by Glen MacDonough.
Produced by Fred R. Hamlin & Julian Mitchell; directed by Mitchell.
Cast included: George W. Denham, Mabel Barrison, William Norris, Bessie Wynn, Amy Ricard, Nella Webb.
Principal songs: Never Mind, Bo Peep; I Can't Do the Sum; Go to Sleep, Slumber Deep; March of the Toys; Toyland; Barney O'Flynn.
Recorded Versions
Decca DL 8458 (S.C.).
Reader's Digest S 40 (S.C.).
Buena Vista S 4022 (F.V.) (1962).
   The same 6 pieces from the charming score sung on the Decca (Kenny Baker, Karen Kemple) are also on the RD (Peter Palmer, Mary Ellen Pracht), plus "Barney O'Flynn." The soundtrack, with Tommy Sands, Annette, Ray Bolger & Ed Wynn, is pretty bowdlerized.

BABETTE
Opened: Nov. 16, 1903, Broadway Th.
59 perfomances.
Book & lyrics by Harry B. Smith.
Produced by Charles Dillingham; directed by Fred G. Latham & A. M. Holbrook.
Cast included: Fritzi Scheff, Eugene Cowles, Richie Ling, Louis Harrison, Erroll Dunbar, Josephine Bartlett.
Principal songs: Letters I Write All the Day; I'll Bribe the Stars; There Once Was an Owl.

IT HAPPENED IN NORDLAND
Opened: Dec. 5, 1904, Lew Fields Th.
154 performances.
Book & lyrics by Glen MacDonough.
Produced by Fred R. Hamlin, Julian Mitchell, Lew Fields; directed by Mitchell.
Cast included: Marie Cahill, Lew Fields, Joseph Herbert, Harry Davenport, May Robson, Bessie Clayton, Pauline Frederick.
Principal songs: Absinthe Frappé; Commanderess-in-Chief; Al Fresco; The Knot of Blue; Bandanna Land.

MISS DOLLY DOLLARS
Opened: Sept. 4, 1905, Knickerbocker Th.
56 performances.
Book & lyrics by Harry B. Smith.
Produced by Charles Dillingham; directed by A. M. Holbrook.
Cast included: Lulu Glaser, Melville Stewart, Carter DeHaven, Elsie Ferguson, Ralph Herz.
Principal songs: A Woman Is Only a Woman but a Good Cigar Is a Smoke; An American Heiress; Ollendorff Duet.

WONDERLAND
Opened: Oct. 24, 1905, Majestic Th.
73 performances.
Book & lyrics by Glen MacDonough.
Produced & directed by Julian Mitchell.
Cast included: Sam Chip, Lotta Faust, Eva Davenport, Bessie Wynn.
Principal songs: The Nature Class; Love's Golden Day; The Only One.

MLLE. MODISTE
Opened: Dec. 25, 1905, Knickerbocker Th.
202 performances.
Book & lyrics by Henry Blossom.
Princpal Songs: Kiss Me Again; The Time, the Place and the Girl; When the Cat's Away; I Want What I Want when I Want It; The Mascot of the Troop; The Nightingale and the Star; Love Me, Love My Dog.
Cast included: Fritzi Scheff, William Pruette, Walter Percival, Claude Gillingwater, Josephine Bartlett, Leo Mars, Howard Chambers, Bertha Holly, George Schaeder, Edna Fassett, Blanche Morrison.
Recorded Version
Reader's Digest S 40 (S.C.).
   Eight selections from Herbert's romantic score sung by a cast headed by Jeanette Scovotti & Arthur Rubin.

THE RED MILL
Opened: Sept. 24, 1906, Knickerbocker Th.
274 performances.
Book & lyrics by Henry Blossom.
Produced by Charles Dillingham; directed by Fred G. Latham.
Cast included: Fred Stone, David Montgomery, Augusta Greenleaf, Joseph Ratliff, Allene Crater.
Principal songs: The Isle of Our Dreams; When You're Pretty and the World Is Fair; Everyday Is Ladies' Day With Me; The Streets of New York; Because You're You; Moonbeams; If You Love but Me.
Recorded Versions
Capitol T 551 (S.C.).
Decca DL 8458 (S.C.).
Reader's Digest S 40 (S.C.).
   The Capitol (Gordon MacRae, Lucille Norman) manages to get almost twice as many songs on one side as either the Decca (Eileen Farrell, Wilbur Evans) or the RD (Mary Ellen Pracht, Richard Fredricks).

DREAM CITY AND THE MAGIC KNIGHT
Opened: Dec. 25, 1906, Weber's Th.
102 performances.
Book & lyrics by Edgar Smith.
Produced by Joe Weber; directed by Al. Holbrook.
Cast included: Joe Weber, Otis Harlan, Cecilia Loftus, Maurice Farkoa, Lillian Blauvelt.
Principal songs: I Don't Believe I'll Ever Be a Lady; In Vaudeville; Nancy, I Fancy You.

THE TATTOOED MAN
Opened: Feb. 18, 1907, Criterion Th.
59 *performances.*
Book by Harry B. Smith & A. N. C. Fowler;
lyrics by Smith.
Produced by Charles Dillingham; directed by
Julian Mitchell.
Cast included: Frank Daniels, Sallie Fisher,
Herbert Waterous, Harry Clark, May Vokes.
Principal songs: Boys Will Be Boys and Girls
Will Be Girls; The Land of Dreams; Nobody
Loves Me.

ALGERIA
Opened: Aug. 31, 1908, Broadway Th.
48 *performances.*
Book & lyrics by Glen MacDonough.
Produced by Frank McKee; directed by
George Marion.
Cast included: Ida Brooks Hunt, William
Pruette, George Marion, George Leon Moore,
Harriet Burt.
Principal songs: Rose of the World; Twilight
in Barakeesh; Love Is Like a Cigarette; Ask
Her While the Band Is Playing.

LITTLE NEMO
Opened: Oct. 20, 1908, New Amsterdam Th.
111 *performances.*
Book & lyrics by Harry B. Smith.
Produced by Klaw & Erlanger; directed by
Herbert Gresham.
Cast included: Joseph Cawthorn, Billy B. Van,
Harry Kelly, Master Gabriel, Florence
Tempest, Sunshine Ijames (Marion Sunshine),
Rose Beaumont.
Principal songs: Won't You Be My
Valentine?; The Happy Land of Once-Upon-
a-Time; In Happy Slumberland.

THE PRIMA DONNA
Opened: Nov. 30, 1908, Knickerbocker Th.
72 *performances.*
Book & lyrics by Henry Blossom.
Produced by Charles Dillingham; directed by
Fred G. Latham.
Cast included: Fritzi Scheff, William
Raymond, William K. Harcourt, St. Clair
Bayfield, Josephine Bartlett.
Principal songs: I'll Be Married to the Music
of a Military Band; A Soldier's Love;
Espagnola; If You Were I and I Were You.

THE ROSE OF ALGERIA
(revised version of *Algeria*)
Opened: Sept. 20, 1909, Herald Square Th.
40 *performances.*
Book & lyrics by Glen MacDonough.
Produced by Lew Fields; directed by Ned
Wayburn.
Cast included: Lillian Herlein, Eugene
Cowles, Anna Wheaton, Frank Pollock.
Principal songs: Same as *Algeria.*

OLD DUTCH
Opened: Nov. 22, 1909, Herald Square Th.
88 *performances.*
Book by Edgar Smith; lyrics by George V.
Hobart.
Produced by Messrs. Shubert & Lew Fields;
directed by Ned Wayburn.
Cast included: Lew Fields, Alice Dovey, Ada
Lewis, Charles Judels, John Bunny, Eva
Davenport, Vernon Castle, John E. Henshaw,
William Raymond, Helen Hayes.
Principal songs: I Want a Man to Love Me;
Climb, Climb; U, Dearie.

NAUGHTY MARIETTA
Opened: Nov. 7, 1910, New York Th.
136 *performances.*
Book & lyrics by Rida Johnson Young.
Produced by Oscar Hammerstein; directed by
Jacques Coini.
Cast included: Emma Trentini, Orville
Harrold, Edward Martindel, Marie Duchene,
Peggy Wood.
Principal songs: Tramp! Tramp! Tramp!;
Naughty Marietta; 'Neath the Southern
Moon; Italian Street Song; I'm Falling in Love
with Someone; Ah! Sweet Mystery of Life; It
Never Never Can Be Love.
Recorded Versions
Capitol T 551 (S.C.).
Reader's Digest S 40 (S.C.).
Columbia P 13707 (S.C.).
    A bit more of the enduring score may be
heard on the Capitol with Marguerite Piazza
& Gordon MacRae than on the RD with
Anna Moffo & William Lewis. Nelson Eddy
& Nadine Connor sing on the Columbia.

WHEN SWEET SIXTEEN
Opened: Sept. 14, 1911, Daly's Th.
12 *performances.*
Book & lyrics by George V. Hobart.
Produced by Harry J. Everall & Samuel A.
Wallach; directed by R. H. Burnside &
Hobart.
Cast included: Harriet Standon, Josie
Intropidi, Roy Purviance, Frank Belcher,
William Morris.
Principal songs: The Wild Rose; In the
Golden Long Ago; Laughs.

THE DUCHESS
Opened: Oct. 16, 1911, Lyric Th.
24 *performances.*
Book by Joseph Herbert; lyrics by Joseph
Herbert & Harry B. Smith.
Produced by Messrs. Shubert; directed by J.
C. Huffman.
Cast included: Fritzi Scheff, George Anderson,
John E. Hazzard, May Boley.
Principal songs: Cupid, Tell Me Why; The
Land of Sultans' Dreams; It's the Bump.

THE ENCHANTRESS
Opened: Oct. 19, 1911, New York Th.
72 *performances.*
Book by Fred DeGresac; lyrics by Harry B.
Smith.
Produced by Joseph M. Gaites; directed by
Fred G. Latham.

Cast included: Kitty Gordon, Harold (Hal) Forde, Ralph Riggs, Hattie Arnold.
Principal songs: To the Land of My Own Romance; Rose, Lucky Rose; All Your Own Am I; They All Look Good when They're Far Away.

THE LADY OF THE SLIPPER
Opened: Oct. 28, 1912, Globe Th.
232 *performances.*
Book by Anne Caldwell & Lawrence McCarty; lyrics by James O'Dea.
Produced by Charles Dillingham; directed by R. H. Burnside.
Cast included: Fred Stone, David Montgomery, Elsie Janis, Vernon Castle, Queenie Vassar, Peggy Wood, Allene Crater, Douglas Stevenson, Vivian Rushmore, Lydia Lopokova.
Principal songs: Bagdad; Meow! Meow! Meow!; Punch Bowl Glide; Drums of All Nations.

SWEETHEARTS
Opened: Sept. 8, 1913, New Amsterdam Th.
136 *performances.*
Book by Harry B. Smith & Fred DeGresac; lyrics by Robert B. Smith.
Produced by Werba & Luescher; directed by Fred G. Latham; dances by Charles S. Morgan, Jr.
Cast included: Christie MacDonald, Thomas Conkey, Tom McNaughton, Edwin Wilson.
Principal songs: Sweethearts; Angelus; Every Lover Must Meet His Fate; Jeannette and Her Little Wooden Shoes; Pretty as a Picture; The Cricket on the Hearth.
Recorded Version
RCA Camden CAL 369 (S.C.).
   With Al Goodman conducting, soloists sing 6 numbers from the operetta, plus "To the Land of My Own Romance" & "I Might Be Your Once-in-a-While."

THE MADCAP DUCHESS
Opened: Nov. 11, 1913, Globe Th.
71 *performances.*
Book & lyrics by David Stevens & Justin Huntly McCarthy.
Produced by H. H. Frazee; directed by Fred G. Latham.
Cast included: Ann Swinburne, Glenn Hall, Josephine Whittell, Peggy Wood, Harry Macdonough.
Principal songs: Aurora Blushing Rosily; Love and I Are Playing; The Deuce, Young Man; Goddess of Mine.

THE ONLY GIRL
Opened: Nov. 2, 1914, 39th St. Th.
240 *performances.*
Book & lyrics by Henry Blossom.
Produced by Joe Weber; directed by Fred G. Latham.
Cast included: Thurston Hall, Wilda Bennett, Jed Prouty, Ernest Torrence, Adele Rowland, Josephine Whittell, Richard Bartlett.
Principal songs: When You're Away; Tell It All Over Again; You're the Only Girl for Me; Personality; When You're Wearing the Ball and Chain.

THE DÉBUTANTE
Opened: Dec. 7, 1914, Knickerbocker Th.
48 *performances.*
Book by Harry B. Smith; lyrics by Robert B. Smith.
Produced by John C. Fisher; directed by George Marion; dances by Allan K. Foster.
Cast included: Hazel Dawn, Wilmuth Merkyl, Zoe Barnett, Robert G. Pitkin, William Danforth.
Principal songs: All for the Sake of a Girl; The Golden Age; The Love of the Lorelei; The Springtime of Life.

THE PRINCESS PAT
Opened: Sept. 29, 1915, Cort Th.
158 *performances.*
Book & lyrics by Henry Blossom.
Produced by John Cort; directed by Fred G. Latham.
Cast included: Eleanor Painter, Joseph R. Lertora, Al Shean, Eva Fallon, Robert Ober, Doris Kenyon, Ralph Riggs.
Principal songs: Love Is the Best of All; Neapolitan Love Song; All for You; Two Laughing Irish Eyes.

THE CENTURY GIRL
Opened: Nov. 6, 1916, Century Th.
200 *performances.*
Sketches uncredited; Herbert lyrics by Henry Blossom; music & lyrics also by Irving Berlin.
Produced by Charles Dillingham & Florenz Ziegfeld, Jr.; directed by Fred G. Latham, Leon Errol, Edward Royce, Ned Wayburn.
Cast included: Hazel Dawn, Sam Bernard, Marie Dressler, Leon Errol, Elsie Janis, Harry Kelly, Gus Van & Joe Schenck, Frank Tinney, John Slavin, Lillian Tashman, Irving Fisher, James Doyle & Harland Dixon, Maurice & Florence Walton.
Principal Herbert-Blossom songs: The Century Girl; When Uncle Sam Is Ruler of the Sea; You Belong to Me (lyric by Harry B.Smith).

EILEEN
Opened: Mar. 19, 1917, Shubert Th.
64 *performances.*
Book & lyrics by Henry Blossom.
Produced by Joe Weber; directed by Fred G. Latham.
Cast included: Walter Scanlan, Greek Evans, Edward Martindel, Olga Roller, Grace Breen.
Principal songs: Free Trade and a Misty Moon; When Shall I Again See Ireland?; When Love Awakes; Thine Alone; The Irish Have a Great Day Tonight; Eileen Alanna Asthore.
Recorded Version
RCA Camden CAL 210 (S.C.).
   Six pieces from Herbert's own favorite score are heard on one side of the LP.

MISS 1917
Opened: Nov. 5, 1917, Century Th.
48 *performances.*
Sketches by Guy Bolton & P. G. Wodehouse; lyrics by Wodehouse; music also by Jerome Kern.
Produced by Charles Dillingham & Florenz Ziegfeld, Jr.; directed by Ned Wayburn.
Cast included: Lew Fields, Cecil Lean, Cleo Mayfield, Vivienne Segal, Andrew Tombes, Harry Kelly, Elizabeth Brice, Marion Davies, Charles King, Peggy Hopkins, Bessie McCoy Davis, Gus Van & Joe Schenck, Irene Castle, Lilyan Tashman, George White, Ann Pennington, Bert Savoy & Joe Brennan, Emma Haig, Herbert Fields.
Principal Herbert songs: The Society Farmerettes; The Singing Blacksmith of Curriclough (based on songs by Samuel Lover).

HER REGIMENT
Opened: Nov. 12, 1917, Broadhurst Th.
40 *performances.*
Book & lyrics by William Le Baron.
Produced by Joe Weber; directed by Fred G. Latham.
Cast included: Donald Brian, Audrey Maple, Hugh Chilvers, Frank Moulan, Josie Intropidi.
Principal songs: Soldier Men; 'Twixt Love and Duty; Art Song.

THE VELVET LADY
Opened: Feb. 3, 1919, New Amsterdam Th.
136 *performances.*
Book & lyrics by Henry Blossom.
Produced by Klaw & Erlanger; directed by Edgar MacGregor & Julian Mitchell.
Cast included: Fay Marbe, Alfred Gerrard, Ray Redmond, Ernest Torrence, Georgia O'Ramey, Jed Prouty, Eddie Dowling, Minerva Coverdale, Marie Flynn.
Principal songs: Life and Love; Fair Honeymoon; Spooky Ookum.

ANGEL FACE
Opened: Dec. 29, 1919, Knickerbocker Th.
57 *performances.*
Book by Harry B. Smith; lyrics by Robert B. Smith.
Produced & directed by George W. Lederer; dances by Julian Alfred.
Cast included: Marguerite Zender, John E. Young, Tyler Brooks, Emilie Lea, George Schiller, Jack Donahue, Mary Milburn.
Principal songs: I Might Be Your Once-in-a-While; Someone Like You; Angel Face.

MY GOLDEN GIRL
Opened: Feb. 2, 1920, Nora Bayes Th.
105 *performances.*
Book & lyrics by Frederic Arnold Kummer.
Produced by Harry Wardell; directed by J. Clifford Brooke.
Cast included: Victor Morley, Marie Carroll, Helen Bolton, George Trabert, Ned A. Sparks, Edna May Oliver.

Principal songs: Darby and Joan; I Want You; A Song Without (Many) Words; Ragtime Terpsichore.

THE GIRL IN THE SPOTLIGHT
Opened: July 12, 1920, Knickerbocker Th.
56 *performances.*
Book & lyrics by Richard Bruce (Robert B. Smith).
Produced & directed by George W. Lederer; dances by Julian Alfred.
Cast included: Mary Milburn, Ben Forbes (Bechtel Alcock), Johnny Dooley, Hal Skelly, John Reinhard.
Principal songs: I Cannot Sleep Without Dreaming of You; I Love the Ground You Walk On; Catch 'Em Young, Treat 'Em Rough, Tell 'Em Nothing.

ZIEGFELD FOLLIES
(15th Edition)
Opened: June 21, 1921, Globe Th.
119 *performances.*
Sketches by Willard Mack, Raymond Hitchcock, James Reynolds; Herbert lyrics by Gene Buck; music & lyrics also by Henry Creamer & Turner Layton, James Hanley & Grant Clarke, David Stamper, Rudolf Friml & B. G. DeSylva, Maurice Yvain & Channing Pollock, Harry Carroll & Ballard Macdonald.
Produced by Florenz Ziegfeld, Jr.; directed by Edward Royce & George Marion.
Cast included: Gus Van & Joe Schenck, Fannie Brice, Raymond Hitchcock, Mary Milburn, W. C. Fields, Mary Eaton, Vera Michelena, Ray Dooley, Florence O'Denishawn, Channing Pollock, Consuelo Flowerton.
Principal Herbert-Buck songs: Princess of My Dreams; The Legend of the Golden Tree.

ORANGE BLOSSOMS
Opened: Sept. 19, 1922, Fulton Th.
95 *performances.*
Book by Fred DeGresac; lyrics by B. G. DeSylva.
Produced & directed by Edward Royce.
Cast included: Edith Day, Queenie Smith, Hal Skelly, Robert Michaelis, Pat Somerset, Jack Whiting, Robert Fischer.
Principal songs: A Kiss in the Dark; This Time It's Love; The Lonely Nest; A Dream of Orange Blossoms.

ZIEGFELD FOLLIES
(18th Edition)
Opened: Oct. 20, 1923, New Amsterdam Th.
233 *performances.*
Sketches by Eddie Cantor & Gene Buck; Herbert lyrics by Buck; music & lyrics also by David Stamper, Harry Tierney & Joe McCarthy, Rudolf Friml, Bert Kalmar & Harry Ruby, Leo Edwards & Blanche Merrill.
Produced by Florenz Ziegfeld; directed by Ned Wayburn.
Cast included: Bert & Betty Wheeler, Fannie

Brice, Brooke Johns, Harland Dixon, Lew Hearn, Olga Steck, Edna Leedom, David Stamper, Roy Cropper, Robert Quinault, Paul Whiteman Orchestra.
Principal Herbert-Buck songs: That Old-Fashioned Garden of Mine; I'd Love to Waltz Through Life with You; Legend of the Drums.

THE DREAM GIRL
Opened: Aug. 20, 1924, Ambassador Th.
117 *performances.*
Book by Rida Johnson Young & Harold Atteridge; lyrics by Mrs. Young.
Produced by Messrs. Shubert; directed by J. C. Huffman; dances by David Bennett.
Cast included: Fay Bainter, Walter Woolf, George Lemaire, Billy B. Van, Maude Odell, William O'Neal, John Clarke.
Principal songs: My Dream Girl; If Somebody Only Would Find Me; Bubble Song.

Chapter Three
GEORGE M. COHAN
Composer-lyricist

All books, music & lyrics by Mr. Cohan unless otherwise noted.

THE GOVERNOR'S SON
Opened: Feb. 25, 1901, Savoy Th.
32 *performances.*
Produced by L. C. Behman & Cohan; directed by R. A. Roberts.
Cast included: The Four Cohans, Ethel Levey, Will Sloan, Josephine Kirkwood.
Principal songs: Too Many Miles from Broadway; The Story of the Wedding March; A Regular William Gillette.

RUNNING FOR OFFICE
Opened: Apr. 27, 1903, 14th St. Th.
48 *performances.*
Produced by Fred Niblo; directed by C. W. Valentine.
Cast included: The Four Cohans, Ethel Levey.
Principal songs: If I Were Only Mr. Morgan; I Want to Go to Paree, Papa; I'll Be There in the Public Square.

LITTLE JOHNNY JONES
Opened: Nov. 7, 1904, Liberty Th.
52 *performances.*
Produced by Sam H. Harris; directed by Cohan.
Cast included: George M. Cohan, Jerry Cohan, Helen Cohan, Ethel Levey, Donald Brian, Tom Lewis, Truly Shattuck, Sam J. Ryan.
Principal songs: The Yankee Doodle Boy; Good-Bye Flo; Give My Regards to Broadway; Life's a Funny Proposition After All; If Mr. Boston Lawson Had His Way; I'm Mighty Glad I'm Living and That's All.

FORTY-FIVE MINUTES FROM BROADWAY
Opened: Jan. 1, 1906, New Amsterdam Th.
90 *performances.*
Produced by Klaw & Erlanger; directed by Cohan.
Cast included: Fay Templeton, Victor Moore, Donald Brian, Julia Ralph, Lois Ewell, Marion Singer.
Principal songs: I Want to Be a Popular Millionaire; Mary's a Grand Old Name; So Long, Mary; Forty-Five Minutes from Broadway; Stand Up and Fight Like H---.

GEORGE WASHINGTON, JR.
Opened: Feb. 12, 1906, Herald Square Th.
81 *performances.*
Produced by Sam H. Harris; directed by Cohan.
Cast included: George M. Cohan, Jerry Cohan, Helen Cohan, Ethel Levey, Truly Shattuck, Eugene O'Rourke, Willis Sweatman.
Principal songs: You're a Grand Old Flag; I Was Born in Virginia; All Aboard for Broadway; If Washington Should Come to Life; Washington, He Was a Wonderful Man.

THE HONEYMOONERS
(revised version of *Running for Office*)
Opened: June 3, 1907, Aerial Gardens.
167 *performances.*
Produced by Sam H. Harris; directed by Cohan.
Cast included: George M. Cohan, Jerry Cohan, Helen Cohan, Gertrude Hoffman.
Principal songs: I'm a Popular Man; If I'm Going to Die I'm Going to Have Some Fun; I'll Be There in the Public Square.

THE TALK OF NEW YORK
Opened: Dec. 3, 1907, Knickerbocker Th.
157 *performances.*
Produced by Cohan & Harris; directed by Cohan.
Cast included: Victor Moore, Emma Littlefield, Gertrude Vanderbilt, Jack Gardner, Rosie Green, Stanley Forde.
Principal songs: When We Are M-A- Double R-I-E-D; When a Fellow's on the Level with a Girl that's on the Square; I Want the World to Know I Love You; Under Any Old Flag at All.

FIFTY MILES FROM BOSTON
Opened: Feb. 3, 1908, Garrick Th.
32 *performances.*
Produced by Cohan & Harris; directed by Cohan.
Cast included: Edna Wallace Hopper; Lawrence Wheat, Emma Janvier, George Parsons, James C. Marlowe.
Principal songs: Harrigan; A Small Town Girl; Ain't It Awful.

THE YANKEE PRINCE
Opened: Apr. 20, 1908, Knickerbocker Th.

128 *performances.*
Produced by Cohan & Harris; directed by
Cohan.
Cast included: The Four Cohans, Tom Lewis,
Stella Hammerstein, Jack Gardner, Donald
Crisp.
Principal songs: Come On Down Town; I'm
Awfully Strong for You; I'm to Marry a
Nobleman; The ABC's of the U.S.A.; Cohan's
Rag Babe.

THE AMERICAN IDEA
Opened: Oct. 5, 1908, New York Th.
64 *performances.*
Produced by Cohan & Harris; directed by
Cohan.
Cast included: George Beban, Gertrude
Vanderbilt, Stella Hammerstein, Trixie
Friganza, Rosie Green, Robert Daly.
Principal songs: Too Long from Longacre
Square; That's Some Love; F-A-M-E;
Cohan's Pet Names.

THE MAN WHO OWNS BROADWAY
Opened: Oct. 11, 1909, New York Th.
128 *performances.*
Produced by Cohan & Harris; directed by
Cohan.
Cast included: Raymond Hitchcock, Flora
Zabelle, Stanley Forde.
Principal songs: There's Something About a
Uniform; The Man who Owns Broadway;
I've Always Been a Good Old Sport.

THE LITTLE MILLIONAIRE
Opened: Sept. 25, 1911, George M. Cohan Th.
192 *performances.*
Produced by Cohan & Harris; directed by
Cohan.
Cast included: George M. Cohan, Jerry
Cohan, Helen Cohan, Tom Lewis, George
Parsons, Donald Crisp.
Principal songs: Barnum Had the Right Idea;
Any Place the Old Flag Flies; Oh, You
Wonderful Girl.

HELLO, BROADWAY!
Opened: Dec. 25, 1914, Astor Th.
123 *performances.*
Produced by Cohan & Harris; directed by
Cohan; dances by Ned Wayburn & James
Gorman.
Cast included: George M. Cohan, William
Collier, Louise Dresser, Peggy Wood,
Lawrence Wheat, Rozsika Dolly, Florence
Moore, Tom Dingle.
Principal songs: Hello, Broadway; My Flag;
Pygmalion Rose.

THE COHAN REVUE 1916
Opened: Feb. 9, 1916, Astor Th.
165 *performances.*
Produced by Cohan & Harris; directed by
Cohan; dances by James Gorman.
Cast included: Elizabeth Murray, Fred
Santley, Charles Winninger, Valli Valli,

Richard Carle, Harry Bulger, Harry Delf,
Miss Juliet.
Principal songs: It's a Long Way from
Broadway to Edinboro Town; You Can Tell
that I'm Irish; Julia, Donald and Joe; Won't
You Let Me Be Your Little Edna May?

THE COHAN REVUE 1918
Opened: Dec. 31, 1917, New Amsterdam Th.
96 *performances.*
Music and lyrics also by Irving Berlin.
Produced by Cohan & Harris; directed by
Cohan; dances also by Jack Mason & James
Gorman.
Cast included: Nora Bayes, Charles
Winninger, Irving Fisher, Fred Santley,
Sydney Jarvis.
Principal Cohan songs: The Eyes of Youth
See the Truth; Their Hearts Are Over Here;
Our Acrobatic Melodramatic Home.

THE VOICE OF McCONNELL
Opened: Dec. 25, 1918, Manhattan Opera
House.
30 *performances.*
Produced by Cohan & Harris; directed by
Cohan & Sam Forrest.
Cast included: Chauncey Olcott, Arthur
Shields, Roy Cochrane.
Principal songs: Ireland, the Land of My
Dreams; You Can't Deny You're Irish; When
I Look in Your Eyes, Mavourneen.

THE ROYAL VAGABOND
Opened: Feb. 17, 1919, Cohan & Harris Th.
208 *performances.*
Book by Stephen Ivor Szinnyey; music &
lyrics also by Anselm Goetzl & William Cary
Duncan.
Produced by Cohan & Harris; directed by
Cohan, Julian Mitchell & Sam Forrest.
Cast included: Tessa Kosta, Fred Santley,
Mary Eaton, Dorothy Dickson, Carl Hyson.
Principal Cohan songs: Opera, Comic Opera;
In a Kingdom of Our Own; Goodbye,
Bargravia.

LITTLE NELLIE KELLY
Opened: Nov. 13, 1922, Liberty Th.
276 *performances.*
Produced & directed by Cohan; dances by
Julian Mitchell.
Cast included: Elizabeth Hines, Robert Pitkin,
Georgia Caine, Charles King, Arthur Deagon,
Frank Parker, Barrett Greenwood, Jack
Oakie.
Principal songs: You Remind Me of My
Mother; Till Good Luck Comes Rolling
Along; Nellie Kelly, I Love You; The Voice in
My Heart.

THE RISE OF ROSIE O'REILLY
Opened: Dec. 25, 1923, Liberty Th.
87 *performances.*
Produced by Cohan; directed by Cohan &
John Meehan; dances by Julian Mitchell.
Cast included: Virginia O'Brien, Jack

McGowan, George Bancroft, Mary Lawlor, Emma Haig, Georgie Hale, Margaret Dumont, Bobby Watson, Ruby Keeler.
Principal songs: Born and Bred in Brooklyn; When June Comes Along with a Song; Let's You and I Say Goodbye; Ring to the Name of Rose.

THE MERRY MALONES
Opened: Sept. 26, 1927, Erlanger's Th.
208 *performances.*
Produced by Cohan; directed by Edward Royce & Sam Forrest; dances by Jack Mason.
Cast included: George M. Cohan, Polly Walker, Alan Edwards, Robinson Newbold.
Principal songs: Molly Malone; God's Good to the Irish; Like a Wandering Minstrel; Like a Little Ladylike Lady Like You; The Bronx Express.

BILLIE
Opened: Oct. 1, 1928, Erlanger's Th.
112 *performances.*
Produced by Cohan, directed by Edward Royce & Sam Forrest.
Cast included: Polly Walker, Robinson Newbold, Joseph Wagstaff, June O'Dea, Charles Sabin, Al Stanton, Ernie Stanton, Chantall Sisters (duo-pianists).
Principal songs: Every Boy in Town's My Sweetheart; Where Were You, Where Was I?; Billie; Go Home Ev'ry Once in a While.

GEORGE M!
Opened: Apr. 10, 1968, Palace Th.
427 *performances.*
Book by Michael Stewart, John & Fran Pascal.
Produced by David Black, Konrad Matthaei, Lorin E. Price; directed by Joe Layton.
Cast included: Joel Grey, Betty Ann Grove, Jerry Dodge, Jill O'Hara, Bernadette Peters, Jamie Donnelly, Jacqueline Alloway, Danny Carroll.
Principal songs: Ring to the Name of Rose; Give My Regards to Broadway; Forty-Five Minutes from Broadway; So Long, Mary; Mary's a Grand Old Name; Yankee Doodle Dandy; Over There; You're a Grand Old Flag.
Recorded Version
Columbia KOS 3200 (O.C.).
    Almost all the Cohan favorites are given the proper razzle-dazzle treatment.

Chapter Four
RUDOLF FRIML
Composer

THE FIREFLY
Opened: Dec. 2, 1912, Lyric Th.
120 *performances.*
Book & lyrics by Otto Hauerbach.
Produced by Arthur Hammerstein; directed by Fred G. Latham.
Cast included: Emma Trentini, Roy Atwell,

Melville Stewart, Sammy Lee, Audrey Maple, Craig Campbell.
Principal songs: Giannina Mia; When a Maid Comes Knocking at Your Heart; Love Is Like a Firefly; Sympathy.

HIGH JINKS
Opened: Dec. 10, 1913, Lyric Th.
213 *performances.*
Book & lyrics by Otto Hauerbach.
Produced by Arthur Hammerstein; directed by Frank Smithson.
Cast included: Elaine Hammerstein, Robert Pitkin, Mana Zucca, Tom Lewis, Elizabeth Murray, Gladys Feldman, Ignacio Martinetti.
Principal songs: Love's Own Kiss; Not Now but Later; The Bubble; Something Seems Tingle-ingleing.

THE PEASANT GIRL
Opened: March 2, 1915, 44th St. Th.
111 *performances.*
Book by Edgar Smith; lyrics by Herbert Reynolds (M. E. Rourke) & Harold Atteridge; music also by Oskar Nedbal.
Produced by Messrs. Shubert; directed by J. H. Benrimo; dances by Jack Mason.
Cast included: Emma Trentini, Clifton Crawford, Ernest Hare, John Charles Thomas.
Principal Friml songs: Listen, Dear (Reynolds); Love Is Like a Butterfly (Reynolds); The Flame of Love (Atteridge); And the Dream Came True (Atteridge).

KATINKA
Opened: Dec. 23, 1915, 44th St. Th.
220 *performances.*
Book & lyrics by Otto Hauerbach.
Produced by Arthur Hammerstein; directed by Frank Smithson.
Cast included: Adele Rowland, Franklyn Ardell, May Naudain, Samuel Ash, A. Robbins, Count Lorrie Grimaldi.
Principal songs: 'Tis the End So Farewell; Allah's Holiday; Rackety Coo; My Paradise.

YOU'RE IN LOVE
Opened: Feb. 6, 1917, Casino Th.
167 *performances.*
Book & lyrics by Otto Hauerbach & Edward Clark.
Produced by Arthur Hammerstein; directed by Clark.
Cast included: Lawrence Wheat, Clarence Nordstom, May Thompson, Harry Clarke.
Principal songs: I'm Only Dreaming; You're in Love; That's the Only Place Where Our Flag Shall Fly.

KITTY DARLIN'
Opened: Nov. 7, 1917, Casino Th.
14 *performances.*
Book by Otto Hauerbach; lyrics by Hauerbach & P. G. Wodehouse.
Produced by William Elliott, F. Ray Comstock, Morris Gest; directed by Edward Royce.

Cast included: Alice Nielsen, Glen Hall, Jackson Hines, Edwin Stevens, Frank Westerton.
Principal songs: When She Gives Him a Shamrock Bloom (Hauerbach); The Land Where Dreams Come True (Wodehouse); Dear Old Dublin (Wodehouse); Kitty Darlin' (Hauerbach).

SOMETIME
Opened: Oct. 4, 1918, Shubert Th.
283 *performances.*
Book & lyrics by Rida Johnson Young.
Produced by Arthur Hammerstein; directed by Oscar Eagle; dances by Allan K. Foster.
Cast included: Ed Wynn, Mae West, Francine Larrimore, Beatrice Summers, Betty Stivers.
Principal songs: Sometime; Spanish Maid; The Tune You Can't Forget; Keep on Smiling.

GLORIANNA
Opened: Oct. 26, 1918, Liberty Th.
96 *performances.*
Book & lyrics by Catherine Chisholm Cushing.
Produced by John Cort; directed by Clifford Brooke.
Cast included: Eleanor Painter, Alexander Clark, Ralph Whitehead, Dorothy South.
Principal songs: When a Girl; Toodle-oo; My Climbing Rose.

TUMBLE IN
Opened: Mar. 24, 1919, Selwyn Th.
128 *performances.*
Book & lyrics by Otto Hauerbach.
Produced by Arthur Hammerstein; directed by Bertram Harrison; dances by Bert French.
Cast included: Peggy O'Neil, Charles Ruggles, Zelda Sears, Edna Hibbard, Johnny Ford.
Principal songs: The Thoughts I Wrote on the Leaves of My Heart; I've Told My Love; Snuggle and Dream.

THE LITTLE WHOPPER
Opened: Oct. 13, 1919, Casino Th.
224 *performances.*
Book by Otto Harbach; lyrics by Bide Dudley & Harbach.
Produced by Abraham Levy; directed by Oscar Eagle; dances by Bert French.
Cast included: Vivienne Segal, David Torrence, Harry C. Browne, Sydney Grant, Rose & May Wilton, Inez Courtney.
Principal songs: You'll Dream and I'll Dream; 'Round the Corner; Oh! What a Little Whopper.

JUNE LOVE
Opened: Apr. 25, 1921, Knickerbocker Th.
50 *performances.*
Book by Otto Harbach & W. H. Post; lyrics by Brian Hooker.
Produced by Sherman Brown; directed by George Vivian.
Cast included: Else Alder, Clarence Nordstrom, Johnny Dooley, W. B. Davidson.
Principal songs: Dear Love, My Love; June Love; The Flapper and the Vamp; Don't Keep Calling Me Dearie.

ZIEGFELD FOLLIES
(15th Edition)
Opened: June 21, 1921, Globe Th.
119 *performances.*
Sketches by Willard Mack, Raymond Hitchcock, James Reynolds; Friml lyrics by Gene Buck, Brian Hooker, B. G. DeSylva; music & lyrics also by Henry Creamer & Turner Layton, James Hanley & Grant Clarke, David Stamper, Victor Herbert, Maurice Yvain & Channing Pollock, Harry Carroll & Ballard Macdonald.
Produced by Florenz Ziegfeld, Jr.; directed by Edward Royce & George Marion.
Cast included: Gus Van & Joe Schenck, Fannie Brice, Raymond Hitchcock, Mary Milburn, W. C. Fields, Mary Eaton, Vera Michelena, Ray Dooley, Florence O'Denishawn, Channing Pollock, Consuelo Flowerton.
Principal Friml songs: Bring Back My Blushing Rose (Buck-Hooker); Four Little Girls with a Future and Four Little Girls with a Past (DeSylva).

THE BLUE KITTEN
Opened: Jan. 13, 1922, Selwyn Th.
140 *performances.*
Book & lyrics by Otto Harbach & William Cary Duncan.
Produced by Arthur Hammerstein; directed by Edgar Selwyn, Leon Errol, Julian Mitchell.
Cast included: Joseph Cawthorn, Lillian Lorraine, Lorraine Manville, Victor Morley, Robert Woolsey, Marion Sunshine, Douglas Stevenson, Frances Grant & Ted Wing, Dallas Welford.
Principal songs: Cutie; I Found a Bud Among the Roses; Blue Kitten Blues; When I Waltz with You.

CINDERS
Opened: Apr. 3, 1923, Dresden Th.
31 *performances.*
Book & lyrics by Edward Clark.
Produced & directed by Edward Royce.
Cast included: Queenie Smith, Nancy Welford, Jack Whiting, Douglas Stevenson, George Bancroft, Margaret Dale, Roberta Beatty, Kitty Kelly, Ralph Riggs.
Principal songs: Cinders; One Good Time; I'm Simply Mad About the Boys; Belles of the Bronx.

ROSE-MARIE
Opened: Sept. 2, 1924, Imperial Th.
557 *performances.*
Book & lyrics by Otto Harbach & Oscar Hammerstein II; music also by Herbert Stothart.
Produced by Arthur Hammerstein; directed by Paul Dickey; dances by David Bennett.
Cast included: Mary Ellis, Dennis King, William Kent, Edward Ciannelli, Dorothy Mackaye, Pearl Regay, Arthur Deagon.

Principal Friml songs: Rose-Marie; The Mounties (with Stothart); Indian Love Call; Totem Tom-Tom (with Stothart); The Door of My Dreams; Pretty Things.
Recorded Versions
RCA LSO 1001 (S.C.).
Reader's Digest S 40 (S.C.).
MGM 2 SES 41 (F.V.) (1954).
Columbia P 13878 (S.C.).

The RCA release, starring Julie Andrews & Giorgio Tozzi, remains the only complete version of this robust score. RD (Anna Moffo, Richard Fredricks) offers 7 numbers, & MGM (Howard Keel, Ann Blyth) retains 3 & adds 4 new ones by Friml & Paul Francis Webster. Nelson Eddy & Dorothy Kirsten are the Columbia singers.

THE VAGABOND KING
Opened: Sept. 21, 1925, Casino Th.
511 *performances.*
Book by Brian Hooker, W. H. Post, Russell Janney; lyrics by Hooker.
Produced by Janney; directed by Max Figman; dances by Julian Alfred.
Cast included: Dennis King, Carolyn Thomson, Max Figman, Herbert Corthell, Herbert Delmore, Jane Carroll.
Principal songs: Song of the Vagabonds; Some Day; Only a Rose; Huguette Waltz; Love Me Tonight; Nocturne; Love for Sale; Tomorrow.
Recorded Versions
RCA LSC 2509 (S.C.).
Reader's Digest S 40 (S.C.).
Capitol T 219 (S.C.).
Decca DL 8362 (S.C.).
RCA LSC 2004 (F.V.) (1956).

The Mario Lanza-Judith Raskin version on the first RCA is the most nearly complete. Other choices: the RD with Sara Endich & William Lewis, the Capitol with Gordon MacRae & Lucille Norman & the Decca with Alfred Drake & Mimi Benzell. Oreste & Jean Fenn (not in film) are on the 2nd RCA.

NO FOOLIN'
(Title changed during run to *Ziegfeld's American Revue of 1926).*
Opened: June 24, 1926, Globe Th.
108 *performances.*
Sketches by J. P. McEnvoy & James Barton; lyrics by Gene Buck & Irving Caesar; music also by James Hanley.
Produced by Florenz Ziegfeld; directed by John Boyle & Walter Wilson.
Cast included: James Barton, Charles King, Andrew Tombes, Ray Dooley, Irving Fisher, Arthur "Bugs" Baer, Moran & Mack, Barbara Newberry, Louise Brown, Edna Leedom, Polly Walker, Peggy Fears, Claire Luce, Paulette Goddard.
Principal Friml songs: Florida, the Moon and You (Buck); Wasn't It Nice? (Caesar); Gentlemen Prefer Blondes (Caesar).

THE WILD ROSE
Opened: Oct. 20, 1926, Martin Beck Th.
61 *performances.*
Book & lyrics by Otto Harbach & Oscar Hammerstein II.
Produced by Arthur Hammerstein; directed by William J. Wilson; dances by Busby Berkeley.
Cast included: William Collier, Desirée Ellinger, Joseph Santley, Joseph Macaulay, Gus Shy, Inez Courtney, Nana Bryant, Fuller Mellish.
Principal songs: Brown Eyes; Wild Rose; One Golden Hour; We'll Have a Kingdom.

THE WHITE EAGLE
Opened: Dec. 26, 1927, Casino Th.
48 *performances.*
Book & lyrics by Brian Hooker & W. H. Post.
Produced by Russell Janney; directed by Richard Boleslavsky; dances by Busby Berkeley.
Cast included: Allan Prior, Marion Keeler, Jay Fassett, Blanche Fleming.
Principal songs: Give Me One Hour; Gather the Rose; Regimental Song; Silver Wing.

THE THREE MUSKETEERS
Opened: Mar. 13, 1928, Lyric Th.
319 *performances.*
Book by William Anthony McGuire; lyrics by Clifford Grey.
Produced by Florenz Ziegfeld; directed by McGuire & Richard Boleslavsky; dances by Albertina Rasch.
Cast included: Dennis King, Vivienne Segal, Lester Allen, Yvonne D'Arle, Douglass Dumbrille, Detmar Poppen, Louis Hector, Reginald Owen, Clarence Derwent, Harriet Hoctor.
Principal songs: March of the Musketeers (lyric with P. G. Wodehouse); Ma Belle; Your Eyes (lyric by Wodehouse); My Sword and I; Queen of My Heart; Gascony; One Kiss.
Recorded Version
M-E 7050 (London O.C.) (1930).

Repeating his original role, Dennis King leads the Londoners in 8 swashbuckling selections.

LUANA
Opened: Sept. 17, 1930, Hammerstein Th.
21 *performances.*
Book by Howard Emmett Rogers; lyrics by J. Keirn Brennan.
Produced by Arthur Hammerstein; directed by Hammerstein & Rogers; dances by Earl Lindsey.
Cast included: Ruth Altman, Joseph Macaulay, Donald Novis, Lillian Bond, Marguerita Silva, Robert Chisholm, Doris Carson, Sally Rand.
Principal songs: Luana; My Bird of Paradise; Son of the Sun; Aloha.

MUSIC HATH CHARMS
Opened: Dec. 29, 1934, Majestic Th.

29 *performances.*
Book by Rowland Leigh & George Rosener;
lyrics by Leigh & John Shubert.
Produced by Messrs. Shubert; directed by
Rosener; dances by Alex Yakovleff.
Cast included: Natalie Hall, Robert Halliday,
Andrew Tombes, Paul Haakon, Constance
Carpenter, William Kent.
Principal songs: My Palace of Dreams; My
Heart Is Yours; It's You I Want to Love
Tonight; Sweet Fool.

OTTO HARBACH

Lyricist
*All books & lyrics by Mr. Harbach unless
otherwise noted.*

THREE TWINS
Opened: June 15, 1908, Herald Square Th.
288 *performances.*
Book by Charles Dickson; music by Karl
Hoschna.
Produced by Joseph M. Gaites; directed by
Gus Sohlke.
Cast included: Bessie McCoy, Clifton
Crawford, Joseph Allen, Stella Tracy, Joseph
Kaufman.
Principal songs: Cuddle Up a Little Closer,
Lovey Mine; Hypnotic Kiss; Boo-Hoo, Tee-
Hee; Little Miss Up-to-Date; The Yama-
Yama Man (lyric by Collin Davis).

BRIGHT EYES
Opened: Feb. 28, 1910, New York Th.
40 *performances.*
Book by Charles Dickson; music by Karl
Hoschna.
Produced by Joseph M. Gaites; directed by
Frederick A. Bishop.
Cast included: Florence Holbrook, Cecil Lean,
Adelaide Sharp, Arthur Conrad.
Principal songs: Good Old Days of Yore; For
You Bright Eyes; Cheer Up My Honey.

MADAME SHERRY
Opened: Aug. 30, 1910, New Amsterdam Th.
231 *performances.*
Music by Karl Hoschna.
Produced by A. H. Woods, H. H. Frazee &
George Lederer; directed by Lederer.
Cast included: Lina Abarbanell, Ralph Herz,
Elizabeth Murray, Frances Demarest, Ignacio
Martinetti, Dorothy Jardon, Jack Gardner.
Principal songs: Every Little Movement; The
Smile She Means for Me; The Birth of
Passion; We Are Only Poor Weak Mortals.

DR. DELUXE
Opened: Apr. 17, 1911, Knickerbocker Th.
32 *performances.*
Music by Karl Hoschna.
Produced by Joseph M. Gaites; directed by
Frank Smithson.
Cast included: Ernest Truex, Ralph Herz,
William Pruette, Lillian Berry.
Principal songs: The Accent Makes No

Difference in the Language of Love; War Is
Hell, but Oh You Jealousy; For Every Boy
that's Lonely There's a Girl that's Lonely
Too.

THE GIRL OF MY DREAMS
Opened: Aug. 7, 1911, Criterion Th.
40 *performances.*
Book with Wilbur Nesbit; music by Karl
Hoschna.
Produced by Joseph M. Gaites; directed by
Frank Smithson.
Cast included: Leila McIntyre, John Hyams,
Harry Humphreys, Harry Clark, Ethel
Marston.
Principal songs: The Girl who Wouldn't
Spoon; Girl of My Dreams; Every Girlie
Loves Me but the Girlie I Love.

THE FASCINATING WIDOW
Opened: Sept. 11, 1911, Liberty Th.
56 *performances.*
Music by Karl Hoschna.
Produced by A. H. Woods; directed by George
Marion.
Cast included: Julian Eltinge, June Mathis,
Winona Winter, Ed Garvie.
Principal songs: Don't Take Your Beau to the
Seashore; You Built a Fire Down in My
Heart; The Ragtime College Girl.

THE FIREFLY
(*See* Rudolf Friml).

HIGH JINKS
(*See* Rudolf Friml).

THE CRINOLINE GIRL
Opened: Mar. 16, 1914, Knickerbocker Th.
88 *performances.*
Lyrics by Julian Eltinge; music by Percy
Wenrich.
Produced by A. H. Woods; directed by John
Emerson.
Cast included: Julian Eltinge, Maidel Turner,
Herbert McKenzie.

SUZI
Opened: Nov. 3, 1914, Casino Th.
55 *performances.*
Music by Aladar Renyi.
Produced by Lew Fields; directed by George
Marion.
Cast included: Jose Collins, Melville Stewart,
Lew Hearn, Tom MacNaughton.
Principal songs: I'll Not Let Love Disparage
Marriage; Life Is a Garden.

KATINKA
(*See* Rudolf Friml).

YOU'RE IN LOVE
(*See* Rudolf Friml).

KITTY DARLIN'
(*See* Rudolf Friml).

GOING UP
Opened: Dec. 25, 1917, Liberty Th.

351 *performances.*
Music by Louis A. Hirsch.
Produced by George M. Cohan & Sam H.
Harris; directed by Edward Royce & James
Montgomery.
Cast included: Edith Day, Frank Craven,
Ruth Donnelly, Donald Meek, Marion
Sunshine.
Principal songs: The Tickle Toe; Kiss Me;
Going Up; If You Look in Her Eyes.

TUMBLE IN
(*See* Rudolf Friml).

THE LITTLE WHOPPER
(*See* Rudolf Friml).

TICKLE ME
(*See* Oscar Hammerstein II).

MARY
Opened: Oct. 18, 1920, Knickerbocker Th.
219 *performances.*
Book with Frank Mandel; music by Louis A.
Hirsch.
Produced by George M. Cohan; directed by
Cohan, Julian Mitchell & Sam Forrest.
Cast included: Jack McGowan, Janet Velie,
Charles Judels, Georgia Caine.
Principal songs: The Love Nest; Mary;
Anything You Want to Do, Dear; That Might
Have Satisfied Grandma.

JIMMIE
(*See* Oscar Hammerstein II).

JUNE LOVE
(*See* Rudolf Friml).

THE O'BRIEN GIRL
Opened: Oct. 3, 1921, Liberty Th.
164 *performances.*
Book with Frank Mandel; music by Louis A.
Hirsch.
Produced by George M. Cohan; directed by
Julian Mitchell.
Cast included: Elizabeth Hines, Robinson
Newbold, Edwin Forsberg, Georgia Caine,
Ada Mae Weeks, Andrew Tombes, Carl
Hemmer.
Principal songs: I Wonder How I Ever Passed
You By; The Conversation Step; That
O'Brien Girl.

THE BLUE KITTEN
(*See* Rudolf Friml).

MOLLY DARLING
Opened: Sept. 1, 1922, Liberty Th.
99 *performances.*
Book with William Cary Duncan; lyrics by
Phil Cook; music by Tom Johnstone.
Produced by Moore & Mesley; directed by
Julian Mitchell & Walter Wilson.
Cast included: Mary Milburn, Jack Donahue,
Clarence Nordstrom, Hal Forde, Albert
Roccardi.

WILDFLOWER
(*See* Vincent Youmans).

JACK AND JILL
Opened: Mar. 22, 1923, Globe Th.
92 *performances.*
Book with Frederic Isham; lyrics also by John
Murray Anderson, Augustus Barratt, Robert
A. Simon, Irving Caesar; music by Alfred
Newman, William Daly, Muriel Pollock,
Augustus Barratt.
Produced by Chelsea Productions; directed by
John Murray Anderson; dances by Larry
Ceballos & Leon Barté.
Cast included: Ann Pennington, Clifton Webb,
Brooke Johns, Georgia O'Ramey, Lennox
Pawle, Roger Imhof, Leon Barté.
Principal Harbach songs: Voodoo Man
(Newman); I Want a Pretty Girl (Daly).

KID BOOTS
Opened: Dec. 31. 1923, Earl Carroll Th.
479 *performances.*
Book with William Anthony McGuire; lyrics
by Joseph McCarthy; music by Harry
Tierney.
Produced by Florenz Ziegfeld; directed by
Edward Royce.
Cast included: Eddie Cantor, Mary Eaton,
Jobyna Howland, Robert Barrat, Paul
Everton, Harry Fender, Ethelind Terry,
Harland Dixon, George Olsen Orch.

ROSE-MARIE
(*See* Rudolf Friml).

BETTY LEE
Opened: Dec. 25, 1924, 44th St. Th.
111 *performances.*
Lyrics also by Irving Caesar; music by Louis
A. Hirsch, Con Conrad.
Produced by Rufus LeMaire; directed by
Bertram Harrison; dances by David Bennett.
Cast included: Joe E. Brown, Hal Skelly,
Gloria Foy, Jack Kearns.
Principal Harbach songs: Arabian Dreams
(Caesar-Hirsch); Betty Lee (Caesar-Conrad);
Let's Kiss Goodbye (Caesar-Hirsch-Conrad).

NO, NO, NANETTE
(*See* Vincent Youmans).

SUNNY
(*See* Jerome Kern).

SONG OF THE FLAME
(*See* George Gershwin).

KITTY'S KISSES
Opened: May 6, 1926, Playhouse Th.
170 *performances.*
Book with Philip Bartholomae; lyrics by Gus
Kahn; music by Con Conrad.
Produced by William A. Brady; directed by
John Cromwell; dances by Bobby Connolly.
Cast included: John Boles, Dorothy Dilley,
Nick Long, Jr., William Wayne.

CROSS-CROSS
(*See* Jerome Kern).

THE WILD ROSE
(*See* Rudolf Friml).

THE DESERT SONG
(*See* Sigmund Romberg).

OH, PLEASE!
(*See* Vincent Youmans).

LUCKY
Opened: Mar. 22, 1927, New Amsterdam Th.
71 *performances.*
Book with Bert Kalmar & Harry Ruby;
Kalmar & Harbach music by Ruby; Kalmar
& Ruby music by Jerome Kern.
Produced by Charles Dillingham; directed by
Hassard Short; dances by David Bennett &
Albertina Rasch.
Cast included: Mary Eaton, Richard "Skeet"
Gallagher, Walter Catlett, Ruby Keeler, Ivy
Sawyer, Joseph Santley, Paul Everton, Paul
Whiteman Orchestra (incl. Bing Crosby).
Principal Harbach-Kalmar-Ruby songs:
Cingalese Girls; Dancing the Devil Away;
The Same Old Moon.

GOLDEN DAWN
(*See* Oscar Hammerstein II).

GOOD BOY
(*See* Oscar Hammerstein II).

NINA ROSA
(*See* Sigmund Romberg).

THE CAT AND THE FIDDLE
(*See* Jerome Kern).

ROBERTA
(*See* Jerome Kern).

FORBIDDEN MELODY
(*See* Sigmund Romberg).

Chapter Five
SIGMUND ROMBERG
Composer

THE WHIRL OF THE WORLD
Opened: Jan. 10, 1914, Winter Garden
161 *performances.*
Sketches & lyrics by Harold Atteridge.
Produced by Messrs. Shubert; directed by
William J. Wilson; dances by Jack Mason.
Cast included: Lillian Lorraine, Bernard
Granville, Ralph Herz, Eugene & Willie
Howard, Walter C. Kelly, Rozsika Dolly,
May Boley.
Principal songs: Ragtime Arabian Nights; My
Cleopatra Girl; Life Is Just a Dress Parade.

THE PASSING SHOW OF 1914
Opened: June 10, 1914, Winter Garden
133 *performances.*
Sketches & lyrics by Harold Atteridge; music
also by Harry Carroll.
Produced by Messrs. Shubert; directed by J.
C. Huffman; dances by Jack Mason.
Cast included: Bernard Granville, Jose
Collins, Marilynn Miller, Bessie Crawford,
Robert Emmett Keane, Lew Brice, Frances

Demarest, T. Roy Barnes.
Principal Romberg songs: Omar Khayyam (no
lyric); Dreams of the Past; Bohemian Rag;
California.

DANCING AROUND
Opened: Oct. 10, 1914, Winter Garden
145 *performances.*
Sketches & lyrics by Harold Atteridge; music
also by Harry Carroll.
Produced by Messrs. Shubert; directed by J.
C. Huffman; dances by Jack Mason.
Cast included: Bernard Granville, James
Doyle & Harland Dixon, Al Jolson, Clifton
Webb, Cecil Cunningham, Melville Ellis.
Principal Romberg songs: My Lady of the
Telephone; He Is Sweet, He Is Good; My
Rainbow Beau.

MAID IN AMERICA
Opened: Feb. 18, 1915, Winter Garden
108 *performances.*
Sketches & lyrics by Harold Atteridge; music
also by Harry Carroll.
Produced by Messrs. Shubert; directed by
J. C. Huffman; dances by Jack Mason.
Cast included: Mlle. Dazie, Blossom Seeley,
Harry Carroll, Harry Fox, Hal Forde, Lew
Brice, Nora Bayes, Joe Jackson, Yansci Dolly,
Yvette.
Principal Romberg songs: Sister Susie Started
Syncopation; Only for You; Oh, Those Days;
The Girlie of the Cabaret.

HANDS UP
Opened: July 22, 1915, 44th St. Th.
52 *performances.*
Book by Edgar Smith; lyrics by E. Ray Goetz.
Produced by Messrs. Shubert; directed by
J. H. Benrimo; dances by Jack Mason.
Cast included: George Hassell, Alice Dovey,
Irene Franklin, Ralph Herz, Will Rogers, A.
Robbins, Maurice & Florence Walton.
Principal songs: Orange Blossom Time in San
José; The Levee Along Broadway; Sing Sing
Tango Tea (lyric by Harold Atteridge).

THE BLUE PARADISE
Opened: Aug. 5, 1915, Casino Th.
356 *performances.*
Book by Edgar Smith; lyrics by Herbert
Reynolds (M. E. Rourke); music also by
Edmund Eysler.
Produced by Messrs. Shubert; directed by
J. H. Benrimo; dances by Ed Hutchinson.
Cast included: Cecil Lean, Cleo Mayfield,
Vivienne Segal, Robert Pitkin, Ted Lorraine,
Frances Demarest.
Principal Romberg songs: Auf Wiedersehn;
One Step into Love; My Model Girl (lyric by
Harold Atteridge); A Toast to a Woman's
Eyes.

A WORLD OF PLEASURE
Opened: Oct. 14, 1915, Winter Garden
116 *performances.*
Sketches & lyrics by Harold Atteridge.
Produced by Messrs. Shubert; directed by

J. C. Huffman; dances by Jack Mason.
Cast included: Kitty Gordon, Stella Mayhew,
Clifton Crawford, Lew Holtz, Dan Healy,
Sydney Greenstreet, Venita Fitzhugh, Sahari
Djeli.
Principal songs: I Could Go Home to a Girlie
Like You; The Ragtime Pipe of Pan;
Fascination; Girlies Are Out of My Life.

ROBINSON CRUSOE, JR.
Opened: Feb. 17, 1916, Winter Garden
130 *performances.*
Book & lyrics by Harold Atteridge; music also
by James Hanley.
Produced by Messrs. Shubert; directed by
J. C. Huffman; dances by Allan K. Foster.
Cast included: Al Jolson, Barry Lupino, Kitty
Doner, Lawrence D'Orsay, Claude Flemming.
Principal Romberg songs: When You're
Starring in the Movies; Minstrel Days;
Happy Hottentot; My Pirate Lady.

THE PASSING SHOW OF 1916
Opened: June 22, 1916, Winter Garden
140 *performances.*
Sketches & lyrics by Harold Atteridge; music
also by Otto Motzan.
Produced by Messrs. Shubert; directed by
J. C. Huffman; dances by Allan K. Foster.
Cast included: Ed Wynn, Herman Timberg,
James Hussey, Frances Demarest, Florence
Moore, Fred Walton, Stella Hoban.
Principal Romberg songs: Ragging the
Apache; Sweet and Pretty; Ragtime
Calisthenics.

THE GIRL FROM BRAZIL
Opened: Aug. 30, 1916, 44th St. Th.
61 *performances.*
Book by Edgar Smith; lyrics by Matthew
Woodward; music also by Robert Winterberg.
Produced by Messrs. Shubert; directed by
J. H. Benrimo; dances by Allan K. Foster.
Cast included: Maude Odell, George Hassell,
Hal Forde, Frances Demarest, Anita Baldwin.
Principal Romberg songs: Stolen Kisses; Come
Back Sweet Dream; My Senorita.

THE SHOW OF WONDERS
Opened: Oct. 26, 1916, Winter Garden
209 *performances.*
Sketches & lyrics by Harold Atteridge; music
also by Otto Motzan & Herman Timberg.
Produced by Messrs. Shubert; directed by
J. C. Huffman; dances by Allan K. Foster.
Cast included: Willie & Eugene Howard,
Ernest Hare, Marilynn Miller, McIntyre &
Heath, Lew Clayton, Walter C. Kelly, Sam
White, John T. Murray, Tom Lewis.
Principal Romberg songs: When Pavlova
Starts Buck and Winging; Bring Your Kisses
to Me; Love Is Like a Bubble.

FOLLOW ME
Opened: Nov. 29, 1916, Casino Th.
78 *performances.*
Book uncredited; lyrics by Robert B. Smith.
Produced by Messrs. Shubert; directed by

J. H. Benrimo; dances by Jack Mason &
Allan K. Foster.
Cast included: Anna Held, Edith Day, Paul
Porcasi, Harry Tighe, Wilmer Bentley.
Principal songs: Follow Me; I Am True to
Them All; I Want to Be Good but My Eyes
Won't Let Me; A Tete-à-Tete with You.

HER SOLDIER BOY
Opened: Dec. 6, 1916, Astor Th.
198 *performances.*
Book & lyrics by Rida Johnson Young; music
also by Emmerich Kalman.
Produced by Messrs. Shubert; directed by
J. J. Shubert; dances by Jack Mason.
Cast included: Clifton Crawford, John
Charles Thomas, Adele Rowland, Ralph J.
Herbert.
Principal Romberg songs: Mother; All Alone
in a City Full of Girls; Kiss Waltz; I'd Be
Happy Anywhere with You; A Married Man
Makes the Best Soldier.

THE PASSING SHOW OF 1917
Opened: Apr. 26, 1917, Winter Garden
196 *performances.*
Sketches & lyrics by Harold Atteridge; music
also by Otto Motzan.
Produced by Messrs. Shubert; directed by
J. C. Huffman; dances by Allan K. Foster.
Cast included: DeWolf Hopper, Jefferson De
Angelis, Irene Franklin, Zeke Colvan, Yvette
Rugel, Johnny Dooley, Tom Lewis.
Principal Romberg songs: Won't You Send a
Letter to Me?; The Willow Tree; My Bedouin
Girl.

MY LADY'S GLOVE
Opened: June 18, 1917, Lyric Th.
16 *performances.*
Book by Edgar Smith; lyrics by Edward A.
Paulton; music also by Oscar Straus.
Produced by Messrs. Shubert; directed by
J. C. Huffman; dances by Allan K. Foster.
Cast included: Charles Purcell, Vivienne
Segal, Charles Judels, Maude Odell, Horace
Sinclair, Arthur Geary, Charles McNaughton,
Frances Demarest, Ned Monroe.
Principal Romberg songs: Foolish Little
Maiden, I; No More Girls for Me; Do Buy
Some Candy, Sir.

MAYTIME
Opened: Aug. 16, 1917, Shubert Th.
492 *performances.*
Book & lyrics by Rida Johnson Young.
Produced by Messrs. Shubert; directed by
Edward Temple; dances by Allan K. Foster.
Cast included: Peggy Wood, Charles Purcell,
Ralph J. Herbert, William Norris, Richard
Morgan, Laura Arnold.
Principal songs: The Road to Paradise; Jump
Jim Crow; Will You Remember?; In Our
Little Home Sweet Home.

DOING OUR BIT
Opened: Oct. 18, 1917, Winter Garden
130 *performances.*

Sketches & lyrics by Harold Atteridge; music also by Herman Timberg.
Produced by Messrs. Shubert; directed by J. C. Huffman; dances by Allan K. Foster.
Cast included: Ed Wynn, Frank Tinney, Duncan Sisters, James J. Corbett, Charles Judels, Ada Lewis, Herman Timberg, Sam Ash.
Principal Romberg songs: Doing My Bit; Hello, Miss Tango; For the Sake of Humanity.

OVER THE TOP
Opened: Nov. 28, 1917, 44th St. Th.
78 *performances.*
Book by Philip Bartholomae & Harold Atteridge; lyrics by Charles Manning & Matthew Woodward; music also by Herman Timberg.
Produced by Messrs. Shubert; directed by Joseph Herbert; dances by Allan K. Foster.
Cast included: Justine Johnstone, Mary Eaton, Ted Lorraine, Fred & Adele Astaire, Joe Laurie, T. Roy Barnes, Craig Campbell, Oakland Sisters.
Principal Romberg songs: The Justine Johnstone Rag (music with Frank Carter, lyric by Manning); Oh, Galatea (lyric by Bartholomae); Golden Pheasant (lyric by Woodward).

SINBAD
Opened: Feb. 14, 1918, Winter Garden
164 *performances.*
Book & Romberg lyrics by Harold Atteridge; music & lyrics also by B. G. DeSylva, George Gershwin & Irving Caesar, Jean Schwartz, Joe Young & Sam Lewis.
Produced by Messrs. Shubert; directed by J. C. Huffman; dances by Jack Mason & Alexis Kosloff.
Cast included: Al Jolson, Kitty Doner, Forrest Huff, Mabel Withee, Hazell Cox, Grace Washburn, Edgar Atchinson-Ely.
Principal Romberg-Atteridge songs: A Thousand and One Arabian Nights; The Rag Lad of Bagdad; Beauty and Beast; I Hail from Cairo.

THE PASSING SHOW OF 1918
Opened: July 25, 1918, Winter Garden
124 *performances.*
Sketches & lyrics by Harold Atteridge; music also by Jean Schwartz.
Produced by Messrs. Shubert; directed by J. C. Huffman; dances by Jack Mason.
Cast included: Willie & Eugene Howard, George Hassell, Fred & Adele Astaire, Charles Ruggles, Frank Fay, Lou Clayton, Sam White, Nita Naldi, Dave Dreyer.
Principal Romberg songs: My Baby-Talk Lady; Galli-Curci Rag; The Duchess of Devonshire; My Vampire Girl; I Can't Make My Feet Behave.

THE MELTING OF MOLLY
Opened: Dec. 30, 1918, Broadhurst Th.

88 *performances.*
Book by Maria Thompson Davies & Edgar Smith; lyrics by Cyrus Wood.
Produced by Messrs. Shubert; directed by Oscar Eagle; dances by Allan K. Foster.
Cast included: Charles Purcell, Gladys Walton, Ted Lorraine, Isabelle Lowe, Gloria Goodwin.
Principal songs: Jazz All Your Troubles Away (lyric by Augustus Barratt); Floating Down a Moonlight Stream; You Remember Me.

MONTE CRISTO, JR.
Opened: Feb. 12, 1919, Winter Garden
254 *performances.*
Book & lyrics by Harold Atteridge; music also by Jean Schwartz.
Produced by Messrs. Shubert; directed by J. C. Huffman.
Cast included: Charles Purcell, Ralph Herz, Chic Sale, Sam Ash, Rose Rolando, Clem Bevins, Tom Lewis, William & Gordon Dooley.
Principal songs: Are You Stepping Out Tonight?; Broadway Butterfly; Jazzamarimba; There's a World of Beauty in You.

THE PASSING SHOW OF 1919
Opened: Oct. 23, 1919, Winter Garden
144 *performances.*
Sketches & lyrics by Harold Atteridge; music also by Jean Schwartz.
Produced by Messrs. Shubert; directed by J. C. Huffman; dances by Allan K. Foster.
Cast included: James Barton, Charles Winninger, Blanche Ring, Reginald Denny, Avon Comedy 4, Walter Woolf, George & Dick Rath, Harry Turpin, Ralph Riggs, Hazel Cox, Olga Cook, Haley Sisters.
Principal songs: So Long, Sing Song; Dreamy Florence; The Kiss Burglar.

THE MAGIC MELODY
Opened: Nov. 11, 1919, Shubert Th.
143 *performances.*
Book & lyrics by Frederic Arnold Kummer.
Produced by Max R. Wilner & Romberg; directed by J. C. Huffman; dances by Allan K. Foster.
Cast included: Charles Purcell, Fay Marbe, Julia Deane, Carmel Myers, Flavia Arcaro, Tom McNaughton.
Principal songs: The Little Church 'Round the Corner (lyric by Alex Gerber); Down by the Nile; Once Upon a Time; Dream Girl, Give Back My Dreams.

POOR LITTLE RITZ GIRL
Opened: July 28, 1920, Central Th.
119 *performances.*
Book by George Campbell & Lew Fields; Romberg lyrics by Alex Gerber; music & lyrics also by Richard Rodgers & Lorenz Hart.
Produced by Lew Fields; directed by Ned Wayburn.
Cast included: Charles Purcell, Eleanor

Griffith, Lulu McConnell, Andrew Tombes, Aileen Poe, Grant Simpson.
Principal Romberg-Gerber songs: I Love to Say Hello to the Girls; When I Found You; In the Land of Yesterday.

LOVE BIRDS
Opened: Mar. 15, 1921, Apollo Th.
105 *performances.*
Book by Edgar Allan Woolf; lyrics by Ballard Macdonald. Produced by Max R. Wilner & Romberg; directed by Edgar MacGregor; dances by Julian Alfred.
Cast included: Pat Rooney, Marion Bent, Elizabeth Hines, Elizabeth Murray, Vincent Lopez.
Principal songs: I Love to Go Swimmin' with Wimmen; Is It Hard to Guess?; Trousseau Incomplete; Two Little Love Birds.

BLOSSOM TIME
Opened: Sept. 29, 1921, Ambassador Th.
516 *performances.*
Book & lyrics by Dorothy Donnelly; music based on Franz Schubert themes.
Produced by Messrs. Shubert; directed by J. C. Huffman.
Cast included: Bertram Peacock, Olga Cook, Howard Marsh, William Danforth, Roy Cropper.
Principal songs: Song of Love; Tell Me Daisy; Only One Love Ever Fills the Heart; My Springtime Thou Art; Three Little Maids.

BOMBO
Opened: Oct. 6, 1921, Al Jolson Th.
219 *performances.*
Book & Romberg lyrics by Harold Atteridge; music & lyrics also by B. G. DeSylva, Con Conrad, Cliff Friend, Walter Donaldson, Sam Lewis & Joe Young.
Produced by Messrs. Shubert; directed by J. C. Huffman; dances by Allan K. Foster.
Cast included: Al Jolson, Janet Adair, Forrest Huff, Vivian Oakland, Russell Mack, Portland Hoffa.
Principal Romberg-Atteridge songs: Oh, Oh, Columbus; In Old Granada; Jazza-Da-Dadoo; The Very Next Girl I See.

THE BLUSHING BRIDE
Opened: Feb. 6, 1922, Astor Th.
144 *performances.*
Book & lyrics by Cyrus Wood.
Produced by Messrs. Shubert; directed by Frank Smithson.
Cast included: Cecil Lean, Cleo Mayfield, Tom Lewis, Clarence Nordstrom, Edythe Baker, Robert O'Connor, William Holbrook.
Principal songs: Mister and Missus; Rosy Posy; I'll Bet on Anything but Girls.

THE ROSE OF STAMBOUL
Opened: Mar. 7, 1922, Century Th.
111 *performances.*
Book & lyrics by Harold Atteridge; music also by Leo Fall.

Produced by Messrs. Shubert; directed by J. C. Huffman.
Cast included: Tessa Kosta, Marion Green, James Barton, Felicia Sorel.
Principal Romberg songs: My Heart Is Calling; Lovey Dove; Mazuma.

SPRINGTIME OF YOUTH
Opened: Oct. 26, 1922, Broadhurst Th.
68 *performances.*
Book uncredited; lyrics by Cyrus Wood.
Produced by Messrs. Shubert; directed by John Harwood; dances by Allan K. Foster.
Cast included: Olga Steck, J. Harold Murray, Harry K. Morton, George MacFarlane, Eleanor Griffith, Harry Kelly.
Principal songs: Starlight of Hope; Just Like a Doll; Pretty Polly.

THE DANCING GIRL
Opened: Jan. 24, 1923, Winter Garden
126 *performances.*
Book & lyrics by Harold Atteridge; music also by Alfred Goodman.
Produced by Messrs. Shubert; directed by J. C. Huffman.
Cast included: Trini, Marie Dressler, Jack Pearl, Arthur Margetson, Edythe Baker, Lou Holtz, Ted & Kitty Doner, Benny Leonard, Nat Nazzaro, Jr.
Principal Romberg songs: Cuddle Me as We Dance; That Romance of Mine; Why Am I Sad?

THE PASSING SHOW OF 1923
Opened: June 14, 1923, Winter Garden
118 *performances.*
Sketches & lyrics by Harold Atteridge; music also by Jean Schwartz.
Produced by Messrs. Shubert; directed by J. C. Huffman; dances by Allan K. Foster.
Cast included: George Hassell, Walter Woolf, George Jessel, Barnett Parker, Helen Shipman, Alex Morrison, Nancy Carroll, Jack Oakie.
Principal Romberg songs: Lotus Flower (lyric by Cyrus Wood); Lovelit Eyes; The Ball Begins.

INNOCENT EYES
Opened: May 20, 1924, Winter Garden
126 *performances.*
Book by Harold Atteridge; lyrics by Atteridge & Tot Seymour; music also by Jean Schwartz.
Produced by Messrs. Shubert; directed by Frank Smithson; dances by Jack Mason & Seymour Felix.
Cast included: Mistinguett, Cecil Lean, Cleo Mayfield, Frances Williams, Lew Hearn, Edythe Baker, Ted Doner, Vera Lavrova (Baroness Michael Royce Garrett), Vanessi, Jack Oakie, Lucille Le Sueur (Joan Crawford).
Principal Romberg songs: Love Is Like a Pinwheel; Day Dreams.

THE PASSING SHOW OF 1924
Opened: Sept. 3, 1924, Winter Garden

106 *performances.*
Sketches by Harold Atteridge; lyrics by
Atteridge & Alex Gerber; music also by Jean
Schwartz.
Produced by Messrs. Shubert; directed by
J. C. Huffman; dances by Max Scheck &
Seymour Felix.
Cast included: James Barton, George Hassell,
Allan Prior, Lulu McConnell, Olga Cook,
Harry McNaughton, Lucille Le Sueur (Joan
Crawford).
Principal songs: When Knighthood Was in
Flower (Atteridge); Dublinola (Atteridge);
Mooching Along (Gerber).

ARTISTS AND MODELS OF 1924
Opened: Oct. 15, 1924, Astor Th.
261 *performances.*
Sketches mostly by Harry Wagstaff Gribble;
lyrics by Sam Coslow & Clifford Grey; music
also by J. Fred Coots.
Produced by Messrs. Shubert; directed by
J. J. Shubert; dances by Seymour Felix.
Cast included: Trini, Frank Gaby, Barnett
Parker, Mable Withee.
Principal songs: Tomorrow's Another Day;
Take Me Back to Samoa Some More.

ANNIE DEAR
Opened: Nov. 4, 1924, Times Square Th.
103 *performances.*
Book by Clare Kummer; lyrics by Clifford
Grey; music & lyrics also by Mrs. Kummer.
Produced by Florenz Ziegfeld; directed by
Edward Royce.
Cast included: Billie Burke, Ernest Truex,
Jack Whiting, Alexander Gray, Marion
Green, Spencer Charters, Bobby Watson, May
Vokes, Gavin Gordon, Catherine Littlefield.
Principal Romberg-Grey songs: Whisper to
Me; One Man Is Like Another; Bertie.

THE STUDENT PRINCE IN
HEIDELBERG
Opened: Dec. 2, 1924, Al Jolson Th.
608 *performances.*
Book & lyrics by Dorothy Donnelly.
Produced by Messrs. Shubert; directed by
J. C. Huffman; dances by Max Scheck.
Cast included: Howard Marsh, Ilse
Marvenga, Greek Evans, George Hassell,
Fuller Mellish, Violet Carlson, Roberta
Beatty.
Principal songs: Golden Days; To the Inn
We're Marching; Drinking Song; Deep in My
Heart, Dear; Serenade; Just We Two; Come
Boys, Let's All Be Gay, Boys.
Recorded Versions
Columbia OS 2380 (S.C.).
Columbia CL 826 (S.C.).
Columbia ML 4060 (S.C.).
Angel S 37318 (S.C.).
Decca DL 8362 (S.C.).
Reader's Digest S 40 (S.C.).
M-E 7054 (London O.C.) (1926).
RCA LSC 2339 (F.V.) (1954).

Romberg's nostalgic score is given its best
aural production on the first Columbia with
Jan Peerce, Roberta Peters & Giorgio Tozzi.
The earlier Columbias offer Robert
Rounseville & Dorothy Kirsten on the first,
Nelson Eddy & Risë Stevens on the second.
Other studio casts: Gordon MacRae & Miss
Kirsten on Angel; Lauritz Melchior & Jane
Wilson on Decca; William Lewis & Jeanette
Scovotti on RD. Monmouth-Evergreen
features the London cast with mostly
Americans, while the soundtrack has Mario
Lanza.

LOUIE THE 14TH
Opened: Mar. 3, 1925, Cosmopolitan Th.
319 *performances.*
Book & lyrics by Arthur Wimperis.
Produced by Florenz Ziegfeld; directed by
Edward Royce.
Cast included: Leon Errol, Doris Patston,
Ethel Shutta, Catherine Calhoun Doucet,
Harry Fender, Evelyn Law, Catherine
Littlefield, Lucy Monroe, Peggy Fears, Louise
Brooks.
Principal songs: Little Peach; Homeland;
Edelweiss (lyric by Clifford Grey).

PRINCESS FLAVIA
Opened: Nov. 2, 1925, Century Th.
152 *performances.*
Book & lyrics by Harry B. Smith.
Produced by Messrs. Shubert; directed by
J. C. Huffman; dances by Max Scheck.
Cast included: Harry Welchman, Evelyn
Herbert, John Clarke, Joseph C. Spurin
(Joseph Calleia), William Danforth, Alois
Havrilla, Douglass Dumbrille, Margaret
Breen, Maude Odell.
Principal songs: What Do I Care?; Only One;
I Dare Not Love You; Twilight Voices.

THE DESERT SONG
Opened: Nov. 30, 1926, Casino Th.
465 *performances.*
Book by Otto Harbach, Oscar Hammerstein
II, Frank Mandel; lyrics by Harbach &
Hammerstein.
Produced by Laurence Schwab & Mandel;
directed by Arthur Hurley; dances by Bobby
Connolly.
Cast included: Robert Halliday, Vivienne
Segal, Eddie Buzzell, William O'Neal, Pearl
Regay, Nellie Breen, Margaret Irving, Glen
Dale.
Principal songs: The Riff Song; Margot;
French Military Marching Song; Romance;
Then You Will Know; It; The Desert Song;
Let Love Go; One Flower Grows Alone in
Your Garden; One Alone; I Want a Kiss; The
Sabre Song.
Recorded Versions
Angel S 35905 (S.C.).
Columbia ACL 831 (S.C.).
RCA LSO 1000 (S.C.).
RCA LSC 2440 (S.C.).

Angel S 37319 (S.C.).
Reader's Digest S 40 (S.C.).
M-E 7054 (London O.C.) (1927).

The first Angel release of Romberg's smoldering score, with Edmund Hockridge & June Bronhill, is preferred. Also worthy: Nelson Eddy-Doretta Morrow on Columbia & Mario Lanza-Judith Raskin on the 2nd RCA. The first RCA female lead is vocally weak. Other singing teams include Gordon MacRae & Dorothy Kirsten (2nd Angel), Anna Moffo & William Fredricks (RD), & London leads Edith Day & Harry Welchman (Monmouth-Evergreen).

CHERRY BLOSSOMS
Opened: Mar. 28, 1927, 44th St. Th.
56 *performances.*
Book & lyrics by Harry B. Smith.
Produced by Messrs. Shubert; directed by Lew Morton; dances by Ralph Reader & Michio Ito.
Cast included: Desiree Ellinger, Howard Marsh, Bernard Gorcey, Gladys Baxter.
Principal songs: 'Neath the Cherry Blossom Moon; Tell Me Cigarette; Wait and See.

MY MARYLAND
Opened: Sept. 12, 1927, Al Jolson Th.
312 *performances.*
Book & lyrics by Dorothy Donnelly.
Produced by Messrs. Shubert; directed by J. C. Huffman; dances by Jack Mason.
Cast included: Evelyn Herbert, George Rosener, Nathaniel Wagner, Fuller Mellish, Warren Hull.
Principal songs: Boys in Gray; Won't You Marry Me?; Silver Moon; Mother; Your Land and My Land.

MY PRINCESS
Opened: Oct. 6, 1927, Shubert Th.
20 *performances.*
Book & lyrics by Dorothy Donnelly.
Produced by Alfred E. Aarons; directed by Sam Forrest; dances by David Bennett.
Cast included: Hope Hampton, Leonard Ceeley, Donald Meek, Robert Woolsey, Luis Alberni, Granville Bates.
Principal songs: I Wonder Why; My Mimosa; Follow the Sun to the South.

THE LOVE CALL
Opened: Oct. 24, 1927, Majestic Th.
88 *performances.*
Book by Harry B. Smith & Edward Locke; lyrics by Smith.
Produced by Messrs. Shubert & L. Lawrence Weber; directed by J. C. Huffman & Lew Morton; dances by Earl Lindsay.
Cast included: Berna Dean, John Barker, W. L. Thorne, Barry Lupino, Joseph Macaulay, Veloz & Yolanda.
Principal songs: Eyes that Love; The Ranger's Song; 'Tis Love; I Live, I Die for You.

ROSALIE
Opened: Jan. 10, 1928, New Amsterdam Th.

327 *performances.*
Book by William Anthony McGuire & Guy Bolton; Romberg lyrics by P. G. Wodehouse; music & lyrics also by George & Ira Gershwin.
Produced by Florenz Ziegfeld; directed by McGuire; dances by Seymour Felix.
Cast included: Marilyn Miller, Jack Donahue, Frank Morgan, Bobbe Arnst, Margaret Dale, Oliver McLennan, Clay Clement, Gladys Glad, Hazel Forbes.
Principal Romberg-Wodehouse songs: West Point March; Kingdom of Dreams; The King Can Do No Wrong; Why Must We Always Be Dreaming?

THE NEW MOON
Opened: Sept. 19, 1928, Imperial Th.
518 *performances.*
Book by Oscar Hammerstein II, Frank Mandel, Laurence Schwab; lyrics by Hammerstein.
Produced by Schwab & Mandel; director uncredited; dances by Bobby Connolly.
Cast included: Robert Halliday, Evelyn Herbert, Gus Shy, William O'Neal, Max Figman, Esther Howard, Olga Albani.
Principal songs: Marianne; Softly, as in a Morning Sunrise; Stouthearted Men; One Kiss; Wanting You; Lover, Come Back to Me; Try Her Out at Dances; The Girl on the Prow.
Recorded Versions
Angel S 37320 (S.C.).
Capitol T 219 (S.C.).
Reader's Digest S 40 (S.C.).
Columbia P 13878 (S.C.).
M-E 7051 (London O.C.) (1929).

Angel offers Gordon MacRae & Dorothy Kirsten on 9 selections, Capitol gives us MacRae & Lucille Norman doing 6, Jeanette Scovotti & Peter Palmer head the RD cast, & Nelson Eddy & Dorothy Kirsten are heard on Columbia. The M-E set revives 10 numbers from the Drury Lane production starring Evelyn Laye.

NINA ROSA
Opened: Sept. 20, 1930, Majestic Th.
137 *performances.*
Book by Otto Harbach; lyrics by Irving Caesar.
Produced by Messrs. Shubert; directed by J. C. Huffman; dances by Busby Berkeley (uncredited).
Cast included: Ethelind Terry, Guy Robertson, Leonard Ceeley, Clay Clement, Armida, Cortez & Peggy.
Principal songs: My First Love, My Last Love (lyric with Harbach); Nina Rosa; Serenade of Love; Your Smiles, Your Tears.

EAST WIND
Opened: Oct. 27, 1931, Manhattan Th.
23 *performances.*
Book by Oscar Hammerstein II & Frank Mandel; lyrics by Hammerstein.

Produced by Lawrence Schwab & Mandel; directed by Hammerstein; dances by Bobby Connolly.

Cast included: Charlotte Lansing, J. Harold Murray, Joe Penner, William Williams, Greek Evans, Dennie Moore, Vera Marsh.

Principal songs: Are You Love; East Wind; I'd Be a Fool; You Are My Woman.

MELODY
Opened: Feb. 14, 1933, Casino Th.
79 *performances.*
Book by Edward Childs Carpenter; lyrics by Irving Caesar.
Produced & directed by George White; dances by Bobby Connolly.

Cast included: Evelyn Herbert, Walter Woolf, Everett Marshall, George Houston, Hal Skelly, Victor Morley, Jeanne Aubert, Mildred Parisette, Ina Ray (Hutton), Vivian Fay, Louise Kirtland, Milton Douglas, Rose Louise (Gypsy Rose Lee), Consuelo Flowerton, Barry Hyams.

Principal songs: Give Me a Roll on the Drum; I'd Write a Song; You Are the Song; Tonight May Never Come Again; Melody.

MAY WINE
Opened: Dec. 5, 1935, St. James Th.
213 *performances.*
Book by Frank Mandel; lyrics by Oscar Hammerstein II.
Produced by Laurence Schwab; directed by José Ruben.

Cast included: Walter Slezak, Nancy McCord, Walter Woolf King, Leo G. Carroll, Robert Fischer, Jack Cole, Alice Dudley, Vera Van, Earle MacVeigh.

Principal songs: I Built a Dream; Somebody Ought to Be Told; Something New Is in My Heart; Dance, My Darlings; Just Once Around the Clock.

FORBIDDEN MELODY
Opened: Nov. 2, 1936, New Amsterdam Th.
32 *performances.*
Book & lyrics by Otto Harbach.
Produced by Jack Kirkland & Sam H. Grisman; directed by Macklin Megley & José Ruben.

Cast included: Carl Brisson, Ruby Mercer, Jack Sheehan, Leo Chalzel, June Havoc, Ruth Weston, Joseph Greenwald.

Principal songs: Lady in the Window; You Are All I've Wanted; No Use Pretending; Moonlight and Violins.

SUNNY RIVER
Opened: Dec. 4, 1941, St. James Th.
36 *performances.*
Book & lyrics by Oscar Hammerstein II.
Produced by Max Gordon; directed by John Murray Anderson & Hammerstein; dances by Carl Randall.

Cast included: Muriel Angelus, Bob Lawrence, Helen Claire, Ethel Levey, Tom Ewell, Ivy Scott, Vicki Charles (Vicki Cummings), Richard Huey, Oscar Polk, Dudley Clements, Joan Roberts, William O'Neal, Howard Freeman, Gordon Dilworth.

Principal songs: My Girl and I; Call It a Dream; Along the Winding Road; Let Me Live Today; Sunny River.

UP IN CENTRAL PARK
Opened: Jan. 27, 1945, Century Th.
504 *performances.*
Book by Herbert & Dorothy Fields; lyrics by Miss Fields.
Produced by Michael Todd; directed by John Kennedy; dances by Helen Tamiris.

Cast included: Wilbur Evans, Maureen Cannon, Noah Beery, Betty Bruce, Daniel Nagrin, Robert Field (Robert Rounseville).

Principal songs: The Big Back Yard; When You Walk in the Room; April Snow; Close as Pages in a Book; It Doesn't Cost You Anything to Dream; The Fireman's Bride.

Recorded Version
Decca DL 8016 (S.C.).

Seven songs from the score are well sung by Wilbur Evans, Celeste Holm & Eileen Farrell. Excerpts from Herbert's *The Red Mill* are on reverse.

MY ROMANCE
Opened: Oct. 19, 1948, Shubert Th.
95 *performances.*
Book & lyrics by Rowland Leigh.
Produced by Messrs. Shubert; directed by Leigh; dances by Fred Kelly.

Cast included: Anne Jeffreys, Lawrence Brooks, Luella Gear, Rex Evans, Melville Ruick, Hazel Dawn, Jr., Doris Patston, Hildegarde Halliday, Melton Moore.

Principal songs: From Now Onward; If Only; Desire; In Love with Romance.

THE GIRL IN PINK TIGHTS
Opened: Mar. 5, 1954, Mark Hellinger Th.
115 *performances.*
Book by Jerome Chodorov & Joseph Fields; lyrics by Leo Robin.
Produced by Shepard Traube & Anthony Brady Farrell; directed by Traube; dances by Agnes de Mille.

Cast included: Jeanmaire, Charles Goldner, Brenda Lewis, David Atkinson, Alexander Kalioujny, Joshua Shelley, Dania Krupska, Marni Nixon, Herbert Banke.

Principal songs: Lost in Loveliness; Up in the Elevated Railway; In Paris and in Love; My Heart Won't Say Goodbye; Free to Love.

Recorded Version
Columbia OL 4890 (O.C.).

The only original cast recording of a complete Romberg score, this has some attractive pieces & the dynamic Jeanmaire.

Chapter Six
JEROME KERN
Composer

MR. WIX OF WICKHAM

Opened: Sept. 19, 1904, Bijou Th.
41 *performances.*
Book & lyrics by John Wagner; music also by
Herbert Darnley & George Everard.
Produced & directed by Edward E. Rice.
Cast included: Julian Dalton Eltinge, David
Lythgow, Harry C. Clarke, Frank Lalor,
Thelma Fair.
Principal Kern songs: From Saturday til
Monday; Waiting for You; Angling by the
Babbling Brook.

FASCINATING FLORA

Opened: May 20, 1907, Casino Th.
113 *performances.*
Book by R. H. Burnside & Joseph Herbert;
Kern lyrics by Paul West, James O'Dea,
M. E. Rourke; music & lyrics mostly by
Gustave Kerker & Burnside.
Produced by Burnside & F. Ray Comstock;
directed by Burnside; dances by Jack Mason.
Cast included: Adele Ritchie, Ada Lewis,
Louis Harrison, Fred Bond.
Principal Kern songs: Ballooning (West); The
Subway Express (O'Dea); Little Church
Around the Corner (Rourke).

THE DAIRYMAIDS

Opened: Aug. 26, 1907, Criterion Th.
86 *performances.*
Book by A. M. Thompson & Robert
Courtneidge; Kern lyrics by M. E. Rourke;
music & lyrics mostly by Paul A Rubens,
Frank A. Tours & Arthur Wimperis.
Produced by Charles Frohman; directed by
A. E. Dodson; dances by Ad. Newberger.
Cast included: Julia Sanderson, George
Gregory, Donald Hall, Eugene O'Rourke,
Arthur Conrad, Stella Thomas.
Principal Kern-Rourke songs: The Hay Ride;
I've a Million Reasons Why I Love You; I'd
Like to Meet Your Father.

FLUFFY RUFFLES

Opened: Sept. 7, 1908, Criterion Th.
48 *performances.*
Book by John J. McNally; Kern lyrics by
C. H. Bovill; music & lyrics mostly by
William T. Francis & Wallace Irwin.
Produced by Charles Frohman; directed by
Ben Teal.
Cast included: Hattie Williams, Violet
Heming, John Bunny, Adele Rowland, Jack
Gardner, George Grossmith, Jr.
Principal Kern-Bovill songs: Meet Her with a
Taximeter; Won't You Let Me Carry Your
Parcel?; There's Something Rather Odd About
Augustus.

THE KING OF CADONIA

Opened: Jan. 10, 1910, Daly's Th.
16 *performances.*
Book by Frederick Lonsdale; Kern lyrics
mostly by M. E. Rourke; music & lyrics also
by Sidney Jones & Adrian Ross.
Produced by Messrs. Shubert; directed by

Joseph Herbert.
Cast included: Marguerite Clark, William
Norris, Melville Stewart, William Danforth,
Robert Dempster, Clara Palmer.
Principal Kern-Rourke songs: Come Along,
Pretty Girl; Coo-oo Coo-oo; Catamarang
(lyric by Percival Knight).

LA BELLE PAREE

Opened: Mar. 20, 1911, Winter Garden
104 *performances.*
Sketches by Edgar Smith; lyrics by Edward
Madden; music also by Frank Tours.
Produced by Messrs. Shubert; directed by
J. C. Huffman; dances by William J. Wilson.
Cast included: Mitzi Hajos, Mlle. Dazie,
Kitty Gordon, Stella Mayhew, Al Jolson,
Barney Bernard, Dorothy Jardon, Cliff
Gordon, Edgar Atchison-Ely, Tempest &
Sunshine, Harry Fisher.
Principal Kern-Madden songs: I'm the
Human Brush; Look Me Over, Dearie; Sing
Trovatore.

THE KISS WALTZ

Opened: Sept. 18, 1911, Casino Th.
88 *performances.*
Book by Edgar Smith; lyrics by Matthew
Woodward; music mostly by Carl M. Ziehrer.
Produced by Messrs. Shubert; directed by
J. C. Huffman; dances by Gus Sohlke.
Cast included: Adele Rowland, William
Pruette, Eva Davenport, Charles Bigelow.
Principal Kern songs: Fan Me with a
Movement Slow; Love Is Like a Little Rubber
Band; Ta Ta, Little Girl.

THE GIRL FROM MONTMARTRE

Opened: Aug. 5, 1912, Criterion Th.
64 *performances.*
Book & most lyrics by Harry B. Smith &
Robert B. Smith; music also by Henri Bereny.
Produced by Charles Frohman; directed by
Thomas J. Reynolds.
Cast included: Hattie Williams, Richard
Carle, William Danforth, Lennox Pawle.
Principal Kern songs: Don't Turn My Picture
to the Wall (R. B. Smith); Bohemia (H. B.
Smith); Ooo, Ooo, Lena! (lyric by John
Golden); Hoop-La-La Papa (lyric by M. E.
Rourke).

THE RED PETTICOAT

Opened: Nov. 13, 1912, Daly's Th.
61 *performances.*
Book by Rida Johnson Young; lyrics by Paul
West.
Produced by Messrs. Shubert; directed by
Joseph Herbert.
Cast included: Helen Lowell, William Pruette,
Louise Mink, Frances Kennedy, Allen Kearns.
Principal songs: Little Golden Maid; Since the
Days of Grandmama; The Ragtime
Restaurant.

THE DOLL GIRL

Opened: Aug. 25, 1913, Globe Th.
88 *performances.*

Book & lyrics by Harry B. Smith; music mostly by Leo Fall.
Produced by Charles Frohman; directed by Thomas J. Reynolds; dances by Edward Royce.
Cast included: Hattie Williams, Richard Carle, Charles McNaughton.
Principal Kern songs: If We Were on Our Honeymoon; A Little Thing Like a Kiss; Will It All End in Smoke?

OH, I SAY!
Opened: Oct. 30, 1913, Casino Th.
68 *performances.*
Book by Sydney Blow & Douglas Hoare; lyrics by Harry B. Smith.
Produced by Messrs. Shubert; directed by J. C. Huffman; dances by Julian Alfred.
Cast included: Joseph Herbert, Cecil Cunningham, Nellie King, Walter Jones, Wellington Cross, Clara Palmer, Alice Yorke.
Principal songs: Each Pearl a Thought; Alone at Last; I Can't Forget Your Eyes; Katy-Did.

THE LAUGHING HUSBAND
Opened: Feb. 2, 1914, Knickerbocker Th.
48 *performances.*
Book by Arthur Wimperis; Kern lyrics by Harry B. Smith; music & lyrics mostly by Edmund Eysler & Wimperis.
Produced by Charles Frohman; directed by Edward Royce.
Cast included: Fred Walton, William Norris, Roy Atwell, Josie Intropidi, Venita Fitzhugh, Frances Demarest.
Principal Kern-Smith songs: Take a Step with Me; You're Here and I'm Here; Love Is Like a Violin.

THE GIRL FROM UTAH
Opened: Aug. 24, 1914, Knickerbocker Th.
120 *performances.*
Book by James Tanner; Kern lyrics by Harry B. Smith; music & lyrics also by Paul Rubens, Sidney Jones, Adrian Ross & Percy Greenbank.
Produced by Charles Frohman; directed by J. A. E. Malone.
Cast included: Julia Sanderson, Donald Brian, Joseph Cawthorn, Queenie Vassar, Venita Fitzhugh, George Bishop.
Principal Kern-Smith songs: Same Sort of Girl; Why Don't They Dance the Polka Anymore?; They Didn't Believe Me (lyric by Herbert Reynolds [M. E. Rourke]).

90 IN THE SHADE
Opened: Jan. 25, 1915, Knickerbocker Th.
40 *performances.*
Book by Guy Bolton; lyrics by Harry B. Smith (uncredited).
Produced by Daniel V. Arthur; directed by Robert Milton; dances by Julian Alfred.
Cast included: Richard Carle, Marie Cahill, Edward Martindel, Victor Morley, Otis Harlan, Pedro de Cordoba.
Principal songs: Where's the Girl for Me?; A

Package of Seeds; My Mindanao Chocolate Soldier.

NOBODY HOME
Opened: Apr. 20, 1915, Princess Th.
135 *performances.*
Book by Guy Bolton; lyrics by Schuyler Greene.
Produced by Elisabeth Marbury & F. Ray Comstock; directed by J. H. Benrimo; dances by David Bennett.
Cast included: Adele Rowland, Lawrence Grossmith, Alice Dovey, Charles Judels, Maude Odell, Helen Clarke, George Lydecker, George Anderson.
Principal songs: Any Old Night (music with Otto Motzan, lyric by Greene & Harry B. Smith); In Arcady (lyric by Herbert Reynolds [M. E. Rourke]); The Magic Melody; You Know and I Know; The Chaplin Walk.

MISS INFORMATION
Opened: Oct. 5, 1915, George M. Cohan Th.
47 *performances.*
Book by Paul Dickey & Charles Goddard; lyrics by Elsie Janis.
Produced by Charles Dillingham; directed by Robert Milton.
Cast included: Elsie Janis, Irene Bordoni, Melville Ellis, Maurice Farkoa.
Principal songs: Some Sort of Somebody; A Little Love; Banks of the Wye.

VERY GOOD EDDIE
Opened: Dec. 23, 1915, Princess Th.
341 *performances.*
Book by Philip Bartholomae & Guy Bolton; lyrics by Schuyler Greene.
Produced by Elisabeth Marbury & F. Ray Comstock; directed by Frank McCormack; dances by David Bennett.
Cast included: Alice Dovey, John E. Hazzard, Oscar Shaw, Ernest Truex, Ada Lewis, Helen Raymond.
Principal songs: Babes in the Wood; Some Sort of Somebody (lyric by Elsie Janis); On the Shore at Le Lei Wi (music with Henry Kailimai, lyric by Herbert Reynolds [M. E. Rourke]); Thirteen Collar; Nodding Roses (lyric by Greene & Reynolds); Isn't It Great to Be Married?
Recorded Version
DRG 6100 (O.C.) (1975).
    Kern's earliest recorded score—though with interpolations from other Kern shows—is spiritedly performed by the Goodspeed Opera company.

ZIEGFELD FOLLIES
(10th Edition)
Opened: June 12, 1916, New Amsterdam Th.
112 *performances.*
Sketches by George V. Hobart & Gene Buck; Kern lyrics by Buck; music & lyrics also by Dave Stamper, Louis Hirsch.
Produced by Florenz Ziegfeld, Jr.; directed by Ned Wayburn.

Cast included: Frances White, Sam Hardy, Ina Claire, Carl Randall, Bernard Granville, Fanny Brice, W. C. Fields, Emma Haig, Bert Williams, Ann Pennington, Marion Davies, Lillian Tashman, Justine Johnstone.
Principal Kern-Buck songs: Have a Heart; Ain't It Funny What a Difference Just a Few Drinks Make?; My Lady of the Nile.

HAVE A HEART
Opened: Jan. 11, 1917, Liberty Th.
76 performances.
Book by Guy Bolton & P. G. Wodehouse; lyrics by Wodehouse.
Produced by Henry W. Savage; directed by Edward Royce & George Marion.
Cast included: Louise Dresser, Margaret Romaine, Thurston Hall, Billy B. Van, Flavia Arcaro.
Principal songs: Honeymoon Inn; And I Am All Alone; The Road that Lies Before; You Said Something.

LOVE O' MIKE
Opened: Jan. 15, 1917, Shubert Th.
192 performances.
Book by Thomas Sydney; lyrics by Harry B. Smith.
Produced by Elisabeth Marbury & Lee Shubert; directed by J. H. Benrimo.
Cast included: Peggy Wood, Clifton Webb, Luella Gear, Alan Edwards, George Hassell, Lawrence Grossmith, Helen Clarke.
Principal songs: Drift with Me; Don't Tempt Me; Baby Vampire; Simple Little Tune; It Wasn't My Fault (lyric by Herbert Reynolds [M. E. Rourke]).

OH, BOY!
Opened: Feb. 20, 1917, Princess Th.
463 performances.
Book by Guy Bolton & P. G. Wodehouse; lyrics by Wodehouse.
Produced by William Elliott & F. Ray Comstock; directed by Edward Royce & Robert Milton.
Cast included: Hal Forde, Marie Carroll, Tom Powers, Anna Wheaton, Edna May Oliver, Marion Davies, Justine Johnstone, Dorothy Dickson, Carl Hyson.
Principal songs: Till the Clouds Roll By; An Old-Fashioned Wife; You Never Knew About Me; Nesting Time in Flatbush; A Pal Like You.

LEAVE IT TO JANE
Opened: Aug. 28, 1917, Longacre Th.
167 performances.
Book by Guy Bolton & P. G. Wodehouse; lyrics by Wodehouse.
Produced by William Elliott, F. Ray Comstock & Morris Gest; directed by Edward Royce.
Cast included: Edith Hallor, Robert Pitkin, Oscar Shaw, Georgia O'Ramey, Olin Howland, Ann Orr.
Principal songs: Just You Watch My Step;

Leave It to Jane; The Siren's Song; Cleopatterer; The Crickets Are Calling; The Sun Shines Brighter; Sir Galahad; Wait Till Tomorrow.
Recorded Version
Stet DS 15002 (O.C.) (1959).
 Members of the off-Broadway revival in a scintillating performance.

MISS 1917
Opened: Nov. 5, 1917, Century Th.
48 performances.
Sketches by Guy Bolton & P. G. Wodehouse; lyrics by Wodehouse; music also by Victor Herbert.
Produced by Charles Dillingham & Florenz Ziegfeld, Jr.; directed by Ned Wayburn.
Cast included: Lew Fields, Cecil Lean, Cleo Mayfield, Vivienne Segal, Andrew Tombes, Harry Kelly, Elizabeth Brice, Marion Davies, Charles King, Peggy Hopkins, Bessie McCoy Davis, Gus Van & Joe Schenck, Irene Castle, Lilyan Tashman, George White, Ann Pennington, Bert Savoy & Joe Brennan, Emma Haig.
Principal Kern songs: Go Little Boat; The Land Where the Good Songs Go; Tell Me All Your Troubles, Cutie.

OH, LADY! LADY!!
Opened: Feb. 1, 1918, Princess Th.
219 performances.
Book by Guy Bolton & P. G. Wodehouse; lyrics by Wodehouse.
Produced by F. Ray Comstock & William Elliott; directed by Edward Royce & Robert Milton.
Cast included: Vivienne Segal, Carl Randall, Margaret Dale, Harry C. Browne, Carroll McComas, Janet Velie, Constance Binney.
Principal songs: Before I Met You; Not Yet; When the Ships Come Home; Greenwich Village; You Found Me and I Found You.

TOOT-TOOT!
Opened: Mar. 11, 1918, George M. Cohan Th.
40 performances.
Book by Edgar Allan Woolf; lyrics by Berton Braley.
Produced by Henry W. Savage; directed by Woolf & Edward Rose; dances by Robert Marks.
Cast included: William Kent, Flora Zabelle, Louise Groody, Greek Evans, Alonzo Price.
Principal songs: If You Only Care Enough; Honeymoon Land; When You Wake Up Dancing; Every Girl in All America.

ROCK-A-BYE BABY
Opened: May 22, 1918, Astor Th.
85 performances.
Book by Edgar Allan Woolf & Margaret Mayo; lyrics by Herbert Reynolds (M. E. Rourke).
Produced by Selwyn & Co.; directed by Edward Royce.

Cast included: Louise Dresser, Frank Morgan, Carl Hyson, Dorothy Dickson, Alan Hale, Edna Hibbard, Florence Eldridge.
Principal songs: Little Tune Go Away; No Better Use for Time than Kissing; The Kettle Song.

HEAD OVER HEELS
Opened: Sept. 29, 1918, George M. Cohan Th. 10 *performances.*
Book & lyrics by Edgar Allan Woolf.
Produced by Henry W. Savage; directed by George Marion.
Cast included: Mitzi, Charles Judels, Dorothy Mackaye, Joe Keno, Robert Emmett Keane, Boyd Marshall.
Principal songs: The Big Show; Head Over Heels; Let's Build a Little Nest; Funny Little Something.

SHE'S A GOOD FELLOW
Opened: May 5, 1919, Globe Th. 120 *performances.*
Book & lyrics by Anne Caldwell.
Produced by Charles Dillingham; directed by Fred G. Latham & Edward Royce.
Cast included: Ivy Sawyer, Joseph Santley, Olin Howland, Rosetta & Vivian Duncan, James C. Marlowe, Ann Orr.
Principal songs: First Rose of Summer; I've Been Waiting for You All the Time; The Bullfrog Patrol; Teacher, Teacher.

THE NIGHT BOAT
Opened: Feb. 2, 1920, Liberty Th. 313 *performances.*
Book & lyrics by Anne Caldwell.
Produced by Charles Dillingham; directed by Fred G. Latham; dances by Ned Wayburn.
Cast included: Louise Groody, John E. Hazzard, Hal Skelly, Ernest Torrence, Wellington Cross, Ada Lewis, Lillian Kemble Cooper, Jeanette MacDonald.
Principal songs: Left All Alone Again Blues; Whose Baby Are You?; I Love the Lassies; A Heart for Sale.

HITCHY-KOO 1920
Opened: Oct. 19, 1920, New Amsterdam Th. 71 *performances.*
Sketches by Glen MacDonough; lyrics by Anne Caldwell.
Produced by Raymond Hitchcock; directed by Ned Wayburn.
Cast included: Raymond Hitchcock, Julia Sanderson, Grace Moore, G. P. Huntley, Charles Withers, Florence O'Denishawn, Bobby Connolly, Billy Holbrook.
Principal songs: Buggy Riding; Ding-Dong, It's Kissing Time; Moon of Love.

SALLY
Opened: Dec. 21, 1920, New Amsterdam Th. 570 *performances.*
Book by Guy Bolton; lyrics mostly by Clifford Grey.

Produced by Florenz Ziegfeld, Jr.; directed by Edward Royce.
Cast included: Marilynn Miller, Leon Errol, Walter Catlett, Irving Fisher, Mary Hay, Stanley Ridges, Dolores, Barbara Dean, Catherine Littlefield.
Principal songs: Wild Rose; Sally; The Church 'Round the Corner (lyric by Grey & P. G. Wodehouse); Look for the Silver Lining (lyric by B. G. DeSylva); Whip-Poor-Will (DeSylva); The Lorelei (lyric by Anne Caldwell); The Schnitza Kommiska.
Recorded Version
M-E 7053 (London O.C.) (1921).
   Dorothy Dickson, George Grossmith & Leslie Henson sing 8 numbers from Kern's first major London success.

GOOD MORNING DEARIE
Opened: Nov. 1, 1921, Globe Th. 347 *performances.*
Book & lyrics by Anne Caldwell.
Produced by Charles Dillingham; directed by Edward Royce.
Cast included: Louise Groody, Oscar Shaw, John Price Jones, Ada Lewis, William Kent, Marie Callahan, Harland Dixon, Mary Read, Consuelo Flowerton, Leo Reisman Quartet.
Principal songs: Ka-lu-a; Blue Danube Blues; Easy Pickin's; Rose-Marie; Good Morning Dearie.

THE BUNCH AND JUDY
Opened: Nov. 28, 1922, Globe Th. 63 *performances.*
Book by Anne Caldwell & Hugh Ford; lyrics by Miss Caldwell.
Produced by Charles Dillingham; directed by Fred G. Latham.
Cast included: Fred & Adele Astaire, Ray Dooley, Johnny Dooley, Grace Hayes, Philip Tonge, Six Brown Brothers, Roberta Beatty.
Principal songs: Pale Venetian Moon; Every Day in Every Way; Morning Glory; How Do You Do, Katinka.

STEPPING STONES
Opened: Nov. 6, 1923, Globe Th. 241 *performances.*
Book by R. H. Burnside & Anne Caldwell; lyrics by Miss Caldwell.
Produced by Charles Dillingham; directed by Burnside; dances by Mary Read & John Tiller.
Cast included: Fred Stone, Dorothy Stone, Allene Stone, Jack Whiting, Evelyn Herbert, Oscar Ragland, Roy Hoyer.
Principal songs: In Love with Love; Once in a Blue Moon; Raggedy Ann; Everybody Calls Me Little Red Riding Hood.

SITTING PRETTY
Opened: Apr. 8, 1924, Fulton Th. 95 *performances.*
Book by Guy Bolton & P. G. Wodehouse; lyrics by Wodehouse.

Produced by F. Ray Comstock & Morris Gest; directed by Fred G. Latham; dances by Julian Alfred.
Cast included: Queenie Smith, Frank McIntyre, Dwight Frye, Gertrude Bryan, Rudolph Cameron.
Principal songs: The Enchanted Train; A Year from Today; On a Desert Island with You.

DEAR SIR

Opened: Sept. 23, 1924, Times Square Th.
15 *performances.*
Book by Edgar Selwyn; lyrics by Howard Dietz.
Produced by Philip Goodman; directed by David Burton; dances by David Bennett.
Cast included: Genevieve Tobin, Oscar Shaw, Walter Catlett, Claire Luce, George Sweet.
Principal songs: All Lanes Must Reach a Turning; If You Think It's Love You're Right; A Mormon Life.

SUNNY

Opened: Sept. 22, 1925, New Amsterdam Th.
517 *performances.*
Book & lyrics by Otto Harbach & Oscar Hammerstein II.
Produced by Charles Dillingham; directed by Hassard Short; dances by Julian Mitchell, David Bennett, Alexis Kosloff, John Tiller, Fred Astaire.
Cast included: Marilyn Miller, Jack Donahue, Clifton Webb, Mary Hay, Joseph Cawthorn, Paul Frawley, Cliff Edwards, Esther Howard, Pert Kelton, Marjorie Moss & Georges Fontana, George Olsen Orchestra.
Principal songs: Sunny; Who?; D'Ye Love Me?; Two Little Bluebirds; When We Get Our Divorce; Let's Say Goodnight Till It's Morning.
Recorded Version
Stanyan 10035 (London O.C.) (1926).
Binnie Hale, Jack Buchanan & company go through the numbers (in alphabetical order!) of this lighthearted score.

THE CITY CHAP

Opened: Oct. 26, 1925, Liberty Th.
72 *performances.*
Book by James Montgomery; lyrics by Anne Caldwell.
Produced by Charles Dillingham; directed by R. H. Burnside; dances by David Bennett.
Cast included: Richard "Skeet" Gallagher, Betty Compton, Irene Dunne, George Raft, Frank Doane, Phyllis Cleveland, George Olsen Orchestra.
Principal songs: Sympathetic Someone; Walking Home with Josie; Journey's End (lyric by P. G. Wodehouse).

CRISS-CROSS

Opened: Oct. 12, 1926, Globe Th.
206 *performances.*
Book & lyrics by Anne Caldwell & Otto Harbach.
Produced by Charles Dillingham; directed by

R. H. Burnside; dances by David Bennett & Mary Read.
Cast included: Fred Stone, Dorothy Stone, Oscar Ragland, Roy Hoyer, Dorothy Francis, Lucy Monroe.
Princial songs: You Will, Won't You?; Cinderella Girl; In Araby With You (lyric by Otto Harbach & Oscar Hammerstein II).

LUCKY

Opened: Mar. 22, 1927, New Amsterdam Th.
71 *performances.*
Book by Otto Harbach, Bert Kalmar & Harry Ruby; Kern lyrics by Kalmar & Ruby; lyrics & music mostly by Harbach, Kalmar & Ruby.
Produced by Charles Dillingham; directed by Hassard Short; dances by David Bennett & Albertina Rasch.
Cast included: Mary Eaton, Richard "Skeet" Gallagher, Walter Catlett, Ruby Keeler, Ivy Sawyer, Joseph Santley, Paul Everton, Paul Whiteman Orchestra (incl. Bing Crosby).
Principal Kern - Kalmar - Ruby songs: When the Bo-Tree Blossoms Again; That Little Something; Lucky.

SHOW BOAT

Opened: Dec. 27, 1927, Ziegfeld Th.
575 *performances.*
Book & lyrics by Oscar Hammerstein II.
Produced by Florenz Ziegfeld; directed by Hammerstein (uncredited) & Zeke Colvan; dances by Sammy Lee.
Cast included: Charles Winninger, Norma Terris, Howard Marsh, Helen Morgan, Edna May Oliver, Jules Bledsoe, Eva Puck, Sammy White, Aunt Jemima (Tess Gardella), Charles Ellis.
Principal songs: Make Believe; Ol' Man River; Can't Help Lovin' dat Man; Till Good Luck Comes My Way; I Might Fall Back on You; Life Upon the Wicked Stage; You Are Love; Why Do I Love You?; Bill (lyric with P. G. Wodehouse); After the Ball (by Charles K. Harris).
Recorded Versions
Columbia AC 55 (O.C.) (1932).
Columbia OL 4058 (O.C.) (1946).
RCA LSO 1126 (O.C.) (1966).
Stanyan 10048 (London O.C.) (1971).
RCA LM 2008 (S.C.).
RCA LSO 1505 (S.C.).
Columbia OS 2220 (S.C.).
Stanyan 10036 (S.C.).
Reader's Digest S 40 (S.C.).
MGM 2 SES 44 (F.V.) (1951).
RCA AVM1 1741 (O.C., S.C.).
Columbia's 1932 album of this masterful score features Helen Morgan & Paul Robeson, & its 1946 set stars Jan Clayton, Charles Fredericks & Carol Bruce. RCA's 1966 collection has the Lincoln Center cast (Barbara Cook, Constance Towers, William Warfield). Stanyan's 2-record set of the 1971 London hit offers Cleo Laine as Julie. As for studio casts, the first RCA (Patrice Munsel,

Robert Merrill, Risë Stevens) uses a concert approach; the 2nd RCA (Anne Jeffreys, Howard Keel, Gogi Grant) features stereo placement; the Columbia (Barbara Cook, John Raitt, William Warfield) offers a solid theatrical recreation; the 2nd Stanyan stars Shirley Bassey; the RD spotlights Anna Moffo, Rosalind Elias & Val Pringle. On the soundtrack are Kathryn Grayson, Howard Keel & Ava Gardner (who didn't sing in the film). The last RCA combines previous releases.

SWEET ADELINE
Opened: Sept. 3, 1929, Hammerstein Th.
234 *performances.*
Book & lyrics by Oscar Hammerstein II.
Produced by Arthur Hammerstein; directed by Reginald Hammerstein; dances by Danny Dare.
Cast included: Helen Morgan, Charles Butterworth, Robert Fischer, Irene Franklin, Robert Emmett Keane, Robert Chisholm, John D. Seymour, Violet Carson, Max Hoffman, Jr.
Principal songs: Here Am I; 'Twas Not So Long Ago; Molly O'Donahue; Why Was I Born?; Don't Ever Leave Me; The Sun About to Rise.

THE CAT AND THE FIDDLE
Opened: Oct. 15, 1931, Globe Th.
395 *performances.*
Book & lyrics by Otto Harbach.
Produced by Max Gordon; directed by José Ruben; dances by Albertina Rasch.
Cast included: Bettina Hall, Georges Metaxa, George Meader, Odette Myrtil, Eddie Foy, Jr., José Ruben, Doris Carson, Flora LeBreton, Lawrence Grossmith.
Principal songs: The Night Was Made for Love; She Didn't Say "Yes"; One Moment Alone; Poor Pierrot; Try to Forget; A New Love Is Old; I Watch the Love Parade.
Recorded Version
Epic LN 3569 (S.C.).
    Six selections, all well sung by Doreen Hume & Denis Quilley.

MUSIC IN THE AIR
Opened: Nov. 8, 1932, Alvin Th.
342 *performances.*
Book & lyrics by Oscar Hammerstein II.
Produced by Peggy Fears & A. C. Blumenthal (uncredited), directed by Kern & Hammerstein.
Cast included: Walter Slezak, Natalie Hall, Al Shean, Katherine Carrington, Reinald Werrenrath, Nicholas Joy, Tullio Carminati Ivy Scott, Marjorie Main, Vivian Vance.
Principal songs: There's a Hill Beyond a Hill; I've Told Ev'ry Little Star; And Love Was Born; One More Dance; In Egern on the Tegern See; I'm Alone; The Song Is You; We Belong Together.
Recorded Version
RCA Victor LK 1025.

This was to have been the original cast recording of the 1951 revival. However, because the production was not successful, RCA signed only Jane Pickens to record the songs.

ROBERTA
Opened: Nov. 18, 1933, New Amsterdam Th.
295 *performances.*
Book & lyrics by Otto Harbach.
Produced by Max Gordon; directed by Hassard Short (uncredited); dances by José Limon & John Lonergan (uncredited).
Cast included: Lyda Roberti, Bob Hope, Fay Templeton, Tamara, George Murphy, Sydney Greenstreet, Raymond Middleton, Helen Gray, William Hain, Roberta Beatty, California Collegians (incl. Fred MacMurray).
Principal songs: You're Devastating; Yesterdays; The Touch of Your Hand; Smoke Gets in Your Eyes; Let's Begin; I'll Be Hard to Handle (lyric by Bernard Dougall).
Recorded Versions
Columbia COS 2530 (S.C.).
Decca DL 8007 (S.C.).
Capitol T 384 (S.C.).
Reader's Digest S 40 (S.C.).
MGM 2 SES 50 (F.V.) (1952).
    The preferred version is the Columbia with Jack Cassidy, Joan Roberts & Kaye Ballard. The Decca, with Alfred Drake & Kitty Carlisle, is a bit stiff, the Capitol, with Gordon MacRae & Lucille Norman, is acceptable, & the RD, with Anna Moffo & Stanley Grover, covers only 6 numbers. The soundtrack—called *Lovely to Look At*—offers Howard Keel, Kathryn Grayson & Red Skelton doing pieces from both stage & 1935 film versions.

VERY WARM FOR MAY
Opened: Nov. 17, 1939, Alvin Th.
59 *performances.*
Book & lyrics by Oscar Hammerstein II.
Produced by Max Gordon; directed by Vincente Minnelli & Hammerstein; dances by Albertina Rasch & Harry Losee.
Cast included: Jack Whiting, Eve Arden, Hiram Sherman, Grace McDonald, Frances Mercer, Donald Brian, Richard Quine, Don Loper & Maxine Barrat, Hollace Shaw, Ray Mayer, Robert Shackleton, Evelyn Thawl, Avon Long, Max Showalter, Helena Bliss, June Allyson, Billie Worth, André Charise, Webb Tilton, Vera Ellen, Matty Malneck Orchestra (incl. Milton DeLugg).
Principal songs: In Other Words, Seventeen; All The Things You Are; Heaven in My Arms; That Lucky Fellow; In the Heart of the Dark; All in Fun.

Chapter Seven
IRVING BERLIN
Composer-lyricist

ZIEGFELD FOLLIES
(5th Edition)
Opened: June 26, 1911, Jardin de Paris.
80 *performances.*
Sketches by George V. Hobart; music & lyric also by Maurice Levi, Raymond Hubbell & Hobart, Jerome Kern & Bessie McCoy.
Produced by Florenz Ziegfeld, Jr.; directed by Julian Mitchell; dances by Gus Sohlke & Jack Mason.
Cast included: Leon Errol, Walter Percival, Fanny Brice, Bessie McCoy, Dolly Sisters, Bert Williams, Lillian Lorraine, George White, Harry Watson, Jr., Vera Maxwell, Clara Palmer.
Principal Berlin songs: Ephraham Played Upon the Piano (with Vincent Bryan); Woodman, Woodman, Spare that Tree (with Bryan); Doggone that Chilly Man; You've Built a Fire Down in My Heart.

WATCH YOUR STEP
Opened: Dec. 8, 1914, New Amsterdam Th.
175 *performances.*
Book by Harry B. Smith.
Produced by Charles Dillingham; directed by R. H. Burnside.
Cast included: Vernon & Irene Castle, Frank Tinney, Harry Kelly, Justine Johnstone, Charles King, Elizabeth Brice, Sallie Fisher, Elizabeth Murray.
Principal songs: Play a Simple Melody; Settle Down in a One Horse Town; The Syncopated Walk; When I Discovered You; They Always Follow Me Around; Lock Me in Your Harem and Throw Away the Key.
Recorded Version
Stet DS15029 (London O.C.) (1915).
Ethel Levey & Joseph Coyne are in the oldest cast album represented.

STOP! LOOK! LISTEN!
Opened: Dec. 25, 1915, Globe Th.
105 *performances.*
Sketches by Harry B. Smith.
Produced by Charles Dillingham; directed by R. H. Burnside.
Cast included: Gaby Deslys, Justine Johnstone, Harry Fox, Florence Tempest & Marion Sunshine, Joseph Santley, Frank Lalor, Marion Davies, Marion Harris, Tot Qualters, James Doyle & Harland Dixon, Harry Pilcer, Maurice & Florence Walton.
Principal songs: The Girl on the Magazine Cover; I Love a Piano; When I Get Back to the U.S.A.

THE CENTURY GIRL
Opened: Nov. 6, 1916, Century Th.
200 *performances.*
Sketches uncredited; music & lyrics also by Victor Herbert & Henry Blossom.
Produced by Charles Dillingham & Florenz Ziegfeld, Jr.; directed by Fred G. Latham, Leon Errol, Edward Royce, Ned Wayburn.
Cast included: Hazel Dawn, Sam Bernard, Marie Dressler, Leon Errol, Elsie Janis,

Harry Kelly, Gus Van & Joe Schenck, Frank Tinney, John Slavin, Lillian Tashman, Irving Fisher, James Doyle & Harland Dixon, Maurice & Florence Walton.
Principal Berlin songs: The Chicken Walk; Alice in Wonderland; It Takes an Irishman to Make Love.

THE COHAN REVUE 1918
Opened: Dec. 31, 1917, New Amsterdam Th.
96 *performances.*
Sketches by George M. Cohan; music & lyrics also by Cohan.
Produced by Cohan & Harris; directed by Cohan; dances also by Jack Mason & James Gorman.
Cast included: Nora Bayes, Charles Winninger, Irving Fisher, Fred Santley, Sydney Jarvis.
Principal Berlin songs: Down Where the Jack O'Lanterns Grow; King of Broadway; Polly, Pretty Polly.

YIP, YIP, YAPHANK
Opened: Sept. 2, 1918, Century Th.
32 *performances.*
Sketches by the Boys of Camp Upton.
Produced by Uncle Sam; directed by William Smith.
Cast included: Danny Healy, Harry Green, Bob Higgins, Sammy Lee, Benny Leonard, Irving Berlin.
Principal songs: Bevo; What a Difference a Uniform Will Make; Kitchen Police; Mandy; Oh, How I Hate to Get Up in the Morning; I Can Always Find a Little Sunshine in the Y.M.C.A.

THE CANARY
Opened: Nov. 4, 1918, Globe Th.
152 *performances.*
Book uncredited; music & lyrics also by Ivan Caryll, Anne Caldwell & P. G. Wodehouse.
Produced by Charles Dillingham; directed by Fred G. Latham & Edward Royce.
Cast included: Julia Sanderson, Joseph Cawthorn, Sam Hardy, James Doyle & Harland Dixon, Maude Eburne, Edna Bates, Wilmer Bentley, Marie Callahan.
Principal Berlin songs: You're So Beautiful; Julia and Her Johnnies; I Wouldn't Give That for the Man who Couldn't Dance.

ZIEGFELD FOLLIES
(13th Edition)
Opened: June 16, 1919, New Amsterdam Th.
171 *performances.*
Sketches by Rennold Wolf, George Lemaire, Eddie Cantor, Gene Buck & David Stamper; music & lyrics also by Stamper & Buck, Harry Tierney & Joe McCarthy, Victor Herbert, Albert Von Tilzer, Lew Brown & Eddie Buzzell, Robert Hood Bowers & Francis DeWitt.
Produced by Florenz Ziegfeld, Jr.; directed by Ned Wayburn.
Cast included: Eddie Dowling, Mary Hay, Ray Dooley, Johnny Dooley, Fairbanks

Twins, Delyle Alda, Marilynn Miller, Bert Williams, Gus Van & Joe Schenck, Eddie Cantor, John Steel, George Lemaire, Hazel Washburn, Billie Dove.

Principal Berlin songs: Mandy; A Pretty Girl Is Like a Melody; You Cannot Make Your Shimmy Shake on Tea (lyric with Rennold Wolf); I'm the Guy who Guards the Harem; You'd Be Surprised.

Recorded Version

Smithsonian R 009 (O.C.).

The earliest American "original-cast" album brings together Eddie Cantor, Bert Williams, John Steel, & Van & Schenck.

ZIEGFELD FOLLIES
(14th Edition)

Opened: June 22, 1920, New Amsterdam Th.
123 *performances.*

Sketches by W. C. Fields, George V. Hobart, James Montgomery; music & lyrics also by Victor Herbert, Harry Tierney & Joe McCarthy, David Stamper & Gene Buck, Abner Silver & Alex Gerber, George Fairman & Sidney Mitchell, Harry Carroll & Ballard Macdonald.

Produced by Florenz Ziegfeld, Jr.; directed by Edward Royce.

Cast included: Charles Winninger, Fannie Brice, W. C. Fields, Moran & Mack, Delyle Alda, Ray Dooley, Carl Randall, Bernard Granville, Gus Van & Joe Schenck, Mary Eaton, Jack Donahue, John Steel, Art Hickman Orchestra.

Principal Berlin songs: Bells; The Girls of My Dreams; Tell Me, Little Gypsy; The Syncopated Vamp.

MUSIC BOX REVUE

Opened: Sept. 22, 1921, Music Box Th.
440 *performances.*

Sketches by Frances Nordstrom, William Collier, Thomas Gray, George V. Hobart.

Produced by Sam H. Harris; directed by Hassard Short & William Collier; dances by Bert French.

Cast included: William Collier, Wilda Bennett, Paul Frawley, Sam Bernard, Ivy Sawyer, Joseph Santley, Rose Rolando, Emma Haig, Florence Moore, Brox Sisters, Margaret Irving, Chester Hale, Hugh Cameron, Ethelind Terry, Miriam Hopkins, Irving Berlin.

Principal songs: Everybody Step; Say It With Music; They Call It Dancing; The Legend of the Pearls.

MUSIC BOX REVUE

Opened: Oct. 23, 1922, Music Box Th.
330 *performances.*

Sketches by Frances Nordstrom, George V. Hobart, Walter Catlett, Paul Gerard Smith.

Produced by Sam H. Harris; directed by Hassard Short & Sam Forrest; dances by William Seabury & Stowitts.

Cast included: Charlotte Greenwood, Grace LaRue, William Gaxton, Margaret &

Dorothy McCarthy, Fairbanks Twins, John Steel, Bobby Clark & Paul McCullough, Margaret Irving, Robinson Newbold, Hal Sherman, Ruth Page, Stowitts, Olivette, William Seabury.

Principal songs: Crinoline Days; Pack Up Your Sins and Go to the Devil; Lady of the Evening; Will She Come from the East?; I'm Looking for a Daddy Long Legs.

MUSIC BOX REVUE

Opened: Sept. 22, 1923, Music Box Th.
273 *performances.*

Sketches by Edwin Burke, Stanley Rauh, Irving Strouse, George S. Kaufman, Bertram Block, Robert Benchley.

Produced by Sam H. Harris; directed by Hassard Short & Sam Forrest; dances by Sammy Lee & Alex Oumansky.

Cast included: Frank Tinney, Joseph Santley, Ivy Sawyer, John Steel, Robert Benchley, Phil Baker, Columbus & Snow, Grace Moore, Florence O'Denishawn, Brox Sisters, Florence Moore, Solly Ward, Mme. Dora Stroeva, Hugh Cameron, Dorothy Dilley.

Principal songs: Learn to Do the Strut; An Orange Grove in California; Tell Me a Bedtime Story; The Waltz of Long Ago; Little Butterfly.

MUSIC BOX REVUE

Opened: Dec. 1, 1924, Music Box Th.
184 *performances.*

Sketches by Bert Kalmar & Harry Ruby, Bobby Clark & Paul McCullough, Ralph Bunker, Ned Joyce Heaney, Gilbert Clark.

Produced by Sam H. Harris; directed by John Murray Anderson & Harris; dances by Carl Randall & Mme. Serova.

Cast included: Fannie Brice, Bobby Clark & Paul McCullough, Oscar Shaw, Grace Moore, Carl Randall, Ula Sharon, Brox Sisters, Hal Sherman, Claire Luce, Joseph Macaulay.

Principal songs: Don't Send Me Back to Petrograd; Tell Her in the Springtime; Unlucky in Love; Listening; Rock-a-bye Baby.

THE COCOANUTS

Opened: Dec. 8, 1925, Lyric Th.
276 *performances.*

Book by George S. Kaufman.

Produced by Sam H. Harris; directed by Oscar Eagle; dances by Sammy Lee.

Cast included: The Marx Brothers, Janet Velie, Georgie Hale, Margaret Dumont, Mabel Withee, Basil Ruysdael, Frances Williams, Brox Sisters.

Principal songs: Florida by the Sea; A Little Bungalow; Lucky Boy; Monkey Doodle-Doo.

ZIEGFELD FOLLIES
(21st Edition)

Opened: Aug. 16, 1927, New Amsterdam Th.
167 *performances.*

Sketches by Harold Atteridge & Eddie Cantor.

Produced by A. L. Erlanger & Florenz

Ziegfeld; directed by Zeke Colvan; dances by Sammy Lee & Albertina Rasch.
Cast included: Eddie Cantor, Ruth Etting, Andrew Tombes, Harry McNaughton, Dan Healy, Franklyn Baur, Claire Luce, Irene Delroy, Cliff Edwards, Brox Sisters, Paulette Goddard, Edgar Fairchild & Ralph Rainger (duo-pianists).
Principal songs: It All Belongs to Me; It's Up to the Band; Ooh, Maybe It's You; Shaking the Blues Away; Rainbow of Girls.

FACE THE MUSIC
Opened: Feb. 17, 1932, New Amsterdam Th. 165 *performances.*
Book by Moss Hart.
Produced by Sam H. Harris; directed by Hassard Short & George S. Kaufman; dances by Albertina Rasch.
Cast included: Mary Boland, Hugh O'Connell, J. Harold Murray, Katherine Carrington, Andrew Tombes, Edward Gargan, David Burns, Jack Good.
Principal songs: I Say It's Spinach; Let's Have Another Cup o' Coffee; On a Roof in Manhattan; Soft Lights and Sweet Music.

AS THOUSANDS CHEER
Opened: Sept. 30, 1933, Music Box Th. 400 *performances.*
Sketches by Moss Hart.
Produced by Sam H. Harris; directed by Hassard Short; dances by Charles Weidman.
Cast included: Marilyn Miller, Clifton Webb, Helen Broderick, Ethel Waters, Leslie Adams, Jerome Cowan, Hal Forde, Harry Stockwell, José Limon, Letitia Ide, Hamtree Harrington, Katherine Litz.
Principal songs: Harlem on My Mind; Easter Parade; How's Chances?; Heat Wave; Not for All the Rice in China; Supper Time; Lonely Heart.

LOUISIANA PURCHASE
Opened: May 28, 1940, Imperial Th. 444 *performances.*
Book by Morrie Ryskind.
Produced by B. G. DeSylva; directed by Edgar MacGregor; dances by George Balanchine & Carl Randall.
Cast included: William Gaxton, Vera Zorina, Victor Moore, Irene Bordoni, Carol Bruce, Nick Long, Jr., April Ames, Robert Pitkin, Ralph Riggs, Edward H. Robins, Ray Mayer, Hugh Martin, Ralph Blane, Georgia Carroll.
Principal songs: Fools Fall in Love; It's a Lovely Day Tomorrow; Latins Know How; Louisiana Purchase; You Can't Brush Me Off; You're Lonely and I'm Lonely; The Lord Done Fixed Up My Soul; What Chance Have I?

THIS IS THE ARMY
Opened: July 4, 1942, Broadway Th. 113 *performances.*
Produced by Uncle Sam; directed by Ezra Stone, Joshua Logan; dances by Robert Sidney & Nelson Barclift.
Cast included: Ezra Stone, Fred Kelly, Gary Merrill, Burl Ives, Philip Truex, Julie Oshins, Anthony Ross, Earl Oxford, James MacColl, Robert Sidney, Ross Elliot, Hank Henry, Nelson Barclift, Stuart Churchill, Robert Shanley, Alan Manson, Irving Berlin.
Principal songs: This Is the Army, Mr. Jones; I Left My Heart at the Stage Door Canteen; I'm Getting Tired So I Can Sleep; Mandy; American Eagles; With My Head in the Clouds; The Army's Made a Man out of Me; Oh, How I Hate to Get Up in the Morning.
Recorded Version
Columbia X 14877 (O.C.).
Nine selections from the buoyant flagwaver, including "Oh, How I Hate to Get Up in the Morning" sung by Berlin himself.

ANNIE GET YOUR GUN
Opened: May 16, 1946, Imperial Th. 1,147 *performances.*
Book by Herbert & Dorothy Fields.
Produced by Rodgers & Hammerstein; directed by Joshua Logan; dances by Helen Tamiris.
Cast included: Ethel Merman, Ray Middleton, Marty May, Kenny Bowers, Betty Anne Nyman, William O'Neal, Lea Penman, Ellen Hanley, George Lipton, Milton Watson, Warren Berlinger, Daniel Nagrin, Lubov Roudenko, Harry Bellaver, Christina Lind, Leon Bibb, Franca Baldwin.
Principal songs: Doin' What Comes Natur'lly; The Girl that I Marry; You Can't Get a Man With a Gun; There's No Business Like Show Business; They Say It's Wonderful; My Defenses Are Down; I'm an Indian, Too; I Got Lost in His Arms; I Got the Sun in the Morning; Anything You Can Do; Moonshine Lullaby.
Recorded Versions
MCA 2031 (O.C.).
RCA LSO 1124 (O.C.) (1966).
London XPS 095 (O.C.).
Stanyan 10069 (London O.C.) (1947).
Capitol W 913 (TV) (1958).
MGM 2 SES 42 (F.V.) (1950).
Columbia CS 2360 (S.C.).
The first 3 albums offer the great Merman renditions over a period of 25 years. Stanyan features West End leads Dolores Gray & Bill Johnson; Capitol spotlights TV's twosome Mary Martin & John Raitt; MGM preserves Betty Hutton's ebullience: the Columbia is for Doris Day & Robert Goulet fans.

MISS LIBERTY
Opened: July 15, 1949, Imperial Th. 308 *performances*
Book by Robert E. Sherwood.
Produced by Berlin, Sherwood & Hart; directed by Moss Hart; dances by Jerome Robbins.
Cast included: Eddie Albert, Allyn McLerie, Mary McCarty, Charles Dingle, Philip Bourneuf, Ethel Griffies, Herbert Berghof, Tommy Rall, Dolores (Dody) Goodman,

Janice Rule, Maria Karnilova, Eddie Phillips, Erik Kristen.
Principal songs: A Little Fish in a Big Pond; Let's Take an Old-Fashioned Walk; Homework; Paris Wakes Up and Smiles; Only for Americans; Just One Way to Say I Love You; Give Me Your Tired, Your Poor (poem by Emma Lazarus); You Can Have Him.
Recorded Version
Columbia AOL 4220 (O.C.).
Many attractive pieces in this rather unappreciated score.

CALL ME MADAM
Opened: Oct. 12, 1950, Imperial Th.
644 *performances.*
Book by Howard Lindsay & Russel Crouse.
Produced by Leland Hayward; directed by George Abbott; dances by Jerome Robbins.
Cast included: Ethel Merman, Paul Lukas, Russell Nype, Pat Harrington, Alan Hewitt, Henry Lascoe, Galina Talva, Muriel Bentley, Geoffrey Lumb, Jay Velie, E. A. Krumschmidt, Tommy Rall, Nathaniel Frey.
Principal songs: The Hostess with the Mostes' on the Ball; Marrying for Love; It's a Lovely Day Today; Something to Dance About; They Like Ike; You're Just in Love; The Best Thing for You; Can You Use Any Money Today?
Recorded Versions
RCA CBM1 2032 (O.C.).
MCA 2055 (O.C.).
M-E 7073 (London O.C.) (1952).
Merman's Decca contract kept her from doing the original-cast album for RCA, & she was replaced by Dinah Shore. On the Decca LP (now MCA) she is supported by Dick Haymes. The Monmouth-Evergreen offers 8 numbers sung by the London cast headed by Billie Worth & Anton Walbrook.

MR. PRESIDENT
Opened: Oct. 20, 1962, St. James Th.
265 *performances.*
Book by Howard Lindsay & Russel Crouse.
Produced by Leland Hayward; directed by Joshua Logan; dances by Peter Gennaro.
Cast included: Robert Ryan, Nanette Fabray, Anita Gillette, Jack Haskell, Jack Washburn, Stanley Grover, Jerry Strickler, David Brooks, Charlotte Fairchild, Wisa D'Orso, John Cecil Holm.
Principal songs: Let's Go Back to the Waltz; Meat and Potatoes; Is He the Only Man in the World?; They Love Me; Pigtails and Freckles; Don't Be Afraid of Romance; Empty Pockets Filled With Love; This Is a Great Country.
Recorded Version
Columbia KOS 2270 (O.C.).
Not exactly a landslide, but there are still plenty of winners here.

Chapter Eight
GEORGE GERSHWIN
Composer

IRA GERSHWIN
Lyricist
All music by George Gershwin & lyrics by Ira Gershwin unless otherwise noted.

LA LA LUCILLE
Opened: May 26, 1919, Henry Miller Th.
104 *performances.*
Book by Fred Jackson; lyrics by Arthur Jackson & B. G. DeSylva.
Produced by Alfred E. Aarons; directed by Herbert Gresham; dances by Julian Alfred.
Cast included: Janet Velie, John E. Hazzard, Helen Clark, Eleanor Daniels, Marjorie Bentley, J. Clarence Harvey.
Principal songs: Tee-Oodle-Um-Bum-Bo; There's More to the Kiss than the Sound; Nobody but You.

GEORGE WHITE'S SCANDALS
(2nd Edition)
Opened: June 7, 1920, Globe Th.
134 *performances.*
Sketches by Andy Rice & George White; lyrics by Arthur Jackson.
Produced by White; directed by White & William Collier.
Cast included: Ann Pennington, Lou Holtz, La Sylphe, Lester Allen, George "Doc" Rockwell, Ethel Delmar, George Bickel, George White.
Principal songs: On My Mind the Whole Night Long; Scandal Walk; Idle Dreams; Tum on and Tiss Me.

TWO LITTLE GIRLS IN BLUE
(*See* Vincent Youmans).

GEORGE WHITE'S SCANDALS
(3rd Edition)
Opened: July 11, 1921, Liberty Th.
97 *performances.*
Sketches by Bugs Baer & George White; Lyrics by Arthur Jackson.
Produced by White; directed by White & John Meehan.
Cast included: Ann Pennington, George White, Aunt Jemima (Tess Gardella), George LeMaire, Olive Vaughn, Lou Holtz, Victoria Herbert, Lester Allen, Gene Ford, Charles King, George Bickel, Bert Gordon.
Principal songs: South Sea Isles; Drifting Along with the Tide; She's Just a Baby.

GEORGE WHITE'S SCANDALS
(4th Edition)
Opened: Aug. 28, 1922, Globe Th.
88 *performances.*
Sketches by W. C. Fields, Andy Rice & George White; lyrics by B. G. DeSylva.
Produced & directed by White.
Cast included: Jack McGowan, Winnie Lightner, George White, W. C. Fields, Lester Allen, Pearl Regay, Franklyn Ardell, Olive Vaughn, Dolores Costello, Paul Whiteman Orchestra, Edgar Fairchild, Coletta Ryan, Richard Bold, Charles Wilkens.
Principal songs: Cinderelatives; Where Is the Man of My Dreams? (lyric with E. Ray Goetz); I Found a Four-Leaf Clover; I'll Build

a Stairway to Paradise (lyric with Arthur
Francis [Ira Gershwin]); Argentina; Blue
Monday.
Recorded Version
Turnabout S 34638 (S.C.).

The Gregg Smith Singers devote one side to
Blue Monday, Gershwin's earliest attempt at
opera.

OUR NELL
Opened: Dec. 4, 1922, Nora Bayes Th.
40 *performances.*
Book by A. E. Thomas & Brian Hooker;
lyrics by Hooker; music also by William Daly.
Produced by Hayseed Productions (Ed.
Davidow & Rufus LeMaire); directed by W.
H. Gilmore & Edgar MacGregor; dances by
Julian Mitchell.
Cast included: Mr. & Mrs. Jimmie Barry,
Emma Haig, Olin Howland, John Merkyl,
Thomas Conkey.
Principal songs: Innocent Ingenue Baby;
Walking Home With Angeline; By and By.

GEORGE WHITE'S SCANDALS
(5th Edition)
Opened: June 18, 1923, Globe Th.
168 *performances.*
Sketches by George White & William K.
Wells; lyrics by B. G. DeSylva, E. Ray Goetz,
Ballard Macdonald.
Cast included: Johnny Dooley, Winnie
Lightner, Margaret Breen, Lester Allen, Tom
Patricola, Delyle Alda, Helen Hudson, George
White, Charles Dornberger Orchestra.
Principal songs: The Life of a Rose
(DeSylva); Let's Be Lonesome Together
(DeSylva-Goetz); There Is Nothing Too Good
for You (DeSylva-Goetz); You and I
(DeSylva-Goetz-Macdonald).

SWEET LITTLE DEVIL
Opened: Jan. 21, 1924, Astor Th.
120 *performances.*
Book by Frank Mandel & Laurence Schwab;
lyrics by B. G. DeSylva.
Produced by Schwab; directed by Edgar
MacGregor; dances by Sammy Lee & Michel
Fokine.
Cast included: Constance Binney, Irving
Beebe, Marjorie, Gateson, Franklyn Ardell,
William Holbrook.
Principal songs: Virginia; Someone Believes in
You; The Jijibo; Under a One-Man Top;
Mah-Jongg.

GEORGE WHITE'S SCANDALS
(6th Edition)
Opened: June 30, 1924, Apollo Th.
192 *performances.*
Sketches by William K. Wells & George
White; lyrics by B. G. DeSylva.
Produced & directed by White.
Cast included: Will Mahoney, Winnie
Lightner, Lester Allen, Tom Patricola, Helen
Hudson, Elm City 4, The DeMarcos, Olive
Vaughn, Dolores & Helene Costello, George
White, Louise Brooks.
Principal songs: Somebody Loves Me (lyric by
DeSylva & Ballard Macdonald); Night Time
in Araby; Tune in to Station J.O.Y.; Rose of
Madrid.

BE YOURSELF!
Opened: Sept. 3, 1924, Sam H. Harris Th.
93 *performances.*
Book by George S. Kaufman & Marc
Connelly; lyrics with Kaufman & Connelly;
music by Lewis Gensler & Milton
Schwarzwald.
Produced by Wilmer & Vincent; directed by
William Collier; dances by Vaughn Godfrey &
Jack Mason.
Cast included: Queenie Smith, Jack Donahue,
G. P. Huntley, Georgia Caine, Dorothy
Whitmore, Barrett Greenwood.
Principal songs: I Came Here (Gensler); Uh-
Uh! (Schwarzwald); The Wrong Thing at the
Right Time (Schwarzwald).

LADY, BE GOOD!
Opened: Dec. 1, 1924, Liberty Th.
330 *performances.*
Book by Guy Bolton & Fred Thompson.
Produced by Alex A. Aarons & Vinton
Freedley; directed by Felix Edwardes; dances
by Sammy Lee.
Cast included: Fred & Adele Astaire, Walter
Catlett, Cliff Edwards, Alan Edwards, Gerald
Oliver Smith, Phil Ohman & Vic Arden (duo-
pianists).
Principal songs: Hang on to Me; So Am I;
Fascinating Rhythm; Oh, Lady Be Good!;
"The Half of It, Dearie" Blues; Little Jazz
Bird; Swiss Miss.
Recorded Versions
M-E 7036 (O.C.).
Smithsonian R 008 (O.C.).

Both releases feature Fred & Adele with the
London company. Monmouth-Evergreen fits 7
numbers on one side, with varied Astaire
selections on the other. Smithsonian covers 2
sides with the same pieces (plus "The Man I
Love") by adding performances by Gershwin,
Cliff Edwards & Ohman & Arden.

TELL ME MORE!
Opened: Apr. 13, 1925, Gaiety Th.
100 *performances.*
Book by Fred Thompson & William K. Wells,
lyrics with B. G. DeSylva.
Produced by Alex A. Aarons; directed by John
Harwood; dances by Sammy Lee.
Cast included: Alexander Gray, Phyllis
Cleveland, Andrew Tombes, Lou Holtz,
Emma Haig, Portland Hoffa.
Principal songs: Tell Me More!; Three Times
a Day; Kickin' the Clouds Away; My Fair
Lady; Why Do I Love You?

TIP-TOES
Opened: Dec. 28, 1925, Liberty Th.
194 *performances.*
Book by Guy Bolton & Fred Thompson.

Produced by Alex A. Aarons & Vinton
Freedley; directed by John Harwood; dances
by Sammy Lee.
Cast included: Queenie Smith, Jeanette
MacDonald, Robert Halliday, Allen Kearns,
Andrew Tombes, Harry Watson, Jr., Amy
Revere, Phil Ohman & Vic Arden (duo-
pianists).
Principal songs: Looking for a Boy; When Do
We Dance?; These Charming People; That
Certain Feeling; Sweet and Low-Down;
Nightie-Night; Nice Baby!
Recorded Version
M-E 7052 (London O.C.) (1926).

   These charming people—Dorothy Dickson,
Allen Kearns & Laddie Cliff—sing 8 numbers
from the buoyant score.

SONG OF THE FLAME
Opened: Dec. 30, 1925, 44th St. Th.
219 *performances.*
Book & lyrics by Otto Harbach & Oscar
Hammerstein II; music also by Herbert
Stothart.
Produced by Arthur Hammerstein; directed by
Frank Reicher; dances by Jack Haskell.
Cast included: Tessa Kosta, Guy Robertson,
Greek Evans, Dorothy Mackaye, Hugh
Cameron, Bernard Gorcey, Ula Sharon,
Russian Art Choir.
Principal songs: Cossack Love Song; Song of
the Flame; Midnight Bells (music by
Gershwin alone).

OH, KAY!
Opened: Nov. 8, 1926, Imperial Th.
256 *performances.*
Book by Guy Bolton & P. G. Wodehouse.
Produced by Alex A. Aarons & Vinton
Freedley; directed by John Harwood; dances
by Sammy Lee.
Cast included: Gertrude Lawrence, Oscar
Shaw, Victor Moore, Betty Compton, Gerald
Oliver Smith, Fairbanks Twins, Constance
Carpenter, Harland Dixon, Phil Ohman &
Vic Arden (duo-pianists).
Principal songs: Dear Little Girl; Maybe;
Clap Yo' Hands; Do Do Do; Someone to
Watch Over Me; Fidgety Feet; Heaven on
Earth (lyric with Howard Dietz).
Recorded Versions
Smithsonian R 011 (O.C.).
Columbia ACL 1050 (S.C.).
Stet DS 15017 (O.C.) (1960).

   Smithsonian has brought together Gertrude
Lawrence, George Gershwin, & members of
the London cast. Columbia offers more of the
score sung by Jack Cassidy & Barbara Ruick.
Stet preserves the revised version with David
Daniels, Marti Stevens & company.

FUNNY FACE
Opened: Nov. 22, 1927, Alvin Th.
250 *performances.*
Book by Fred Thompson & Paul Gerard
Smith.
Produced by Alex A. Aarons & Vinton

Freedley; directed by Edgar MacGregor;
dances by Bobby Connolly.
Cast included: Fred & Adele Astaire, Victor
Moore, William Kent, Allen Kearns, Betty
Compton, Phil Ohman & Vic Arden (duo-
pianists).
Principal songs: 'S Wonderful; Funny Face;
High Hat; Let's Kiss and Make Up; He
Loves and She Loves; Tell the Doc; My One
and Only; The Babbitt and the Bromide.
Recorded Versions
M-E 7037 (O.C.).
Smithsonian R 019 (O.C.).
Stet DS 15001 (F.V.) (1957).

   Fred & Adele, plus London cast &
Gershwin, are on both Monmouth-Evergreen
& Smithsonian (latter also has Ohman &
Arden). The soundtrack, with Fred & Audrey
Hepburn, keeps 4 songs, adds 2 from other
Gershwin shows & 2 new ones by Edens &
Gershe.

ROSALIE
Opened: Jan. 10, 1928, New Amsterdam Th.
327 *performances.*
Book by William Anthony McGuire & Guy
Bolton; music & lyrics also by Sigmund
Romberg & P. G. Wodehouse.
Produced by Florenz Ziegfeld; directed by
McGuire; dances by Seymour Felix.
Cast included: Marilyn Miller, Jack
Donahue, Frank Morgan, Bobbe Arnst,
Margaret Dale, Oliver McLennan, Clay
Clement, Gladys Glad, Hazel Forbes.
Principal Gershwin-Gershwin songs: How
Long Has This Been Going On?; Say So!
(lyric with Wodehouse); Oh, Gee! Oh, Joy!
(lyric with Wodehouse).

TREASURE GIRL
Opened: Nov. 8, 1928, Alvin Th.
68 *performances.*
Book by Fred Thompson & Vincent
Lawrence.
Produced by Alex A. Aarons & Vinton
Freedley; directed by Bertram Harrison;
dances by Bobby Connolly.
Cast included: Gertrude Lawrence, Clifton
Webb, Walter Catlett, Mary Hay, Paul
Frawley, Constance Cummings, Peggy
Conklin, Phil Ohman & Vic Arden (duo-
pianists).
Principal songs: I've Got a Crush on You; Oh,
So Nice; I Don't Think I'll Fall in Love
Today; Feeling I'm Falling; Got a Rainbow;
Where's the Boy? Here's the Girl!; K-ra-zy
for You.

SHOW GIRL
Opened: July 2, 1929, Ziegfeld Th.
111 *performances.*
Book by William Anthony McGuire & J. P.
McEvoy; lyrics with Gus Kahn.
Produced by Florenz Ziegfeld; directed by
McGuire; dances by Bobby Connolly &
Albertina Rasch.
Cast included: Ruby Keeler Jolson, Lew

Clayton, Eddie Jackson, Jimmie Durante, Eddie Foy, Jr., Barbara Newberry, Harriet Hoctor, Frank McHugh, Doris Carson, Joseph Macaulay, Nick Lucas, Duke Ellington Orchestra.
Principal songs: Do What You Do!; So Are You!; Liza; An American in Paris (ballet).

STRIKE UP THE BAND
Opened: Jan. 14, 1930, Times Square Th.
191 *performances.*
Book by Morrie Ryskind, based on book by George S. Kaufman.
Produced by Edgar Selwyn; directed by Alexander Leftwich; dances by George Hale.
Cast included: Bobby Clark & Paul McCullough, Blanche Ring, Jerry Goff, Doris Carson, Dudley Clements, Gordon Smith, Margaret Schilling, Red Nichols Orchestra (incl. Benny Goodman, Gene Krupa, Glenn Miller, Jimmy Dorsey, Jack Teagarden).
Principal songs: I Mean to Say; A Typical Self-Made American; Soon; Hangin' Around With You; Strike Up the Band!; Mademoiselle in New Rochelle; I've Got a Crush on You.

GIRL CRAZY
Opened: Oct. 14, 1930, Alvin Th.
272 *performances.*
Book by Guy Bolton & John McGowan.
Produced by Alex A. Aarons & Vinton Freedley; directed by Alexander Leftwich; dances by George Hale.
Cast included: Ginger Rogers, Willie Howard, Ethel Merman, Allen Kearns, Eunice Healey, William Kent, Antonio & Renée DeMarco, Lew Parker, Roger Edens (pianist), Red Nichols Orchestra (incl. Benny Goodman, Gene Krupa, Glenn Miller, Jimmy Dorsey, Jack Teagarden).
Principal songs: Bidin' My Time; Could You Use Me?; Sam and Delilah; Embraceable You; I Got Rhythm; But Not for Me; Treat Me Rough; Boy! What Love Has Done to Me!
Recorded Versions
Columbia COS 2560 (S.C.).
DRG SL 5185 (F.V.) (1943).
The full hit-studded score is sung by Mary Martin & company on Columbia; the 6 numbers retained for the film (Judy Garland & Mickey Rooney) are on DRG.

OF THEE I SING
Opened: Dec. 26, 1931, Music Box Th.
441 *performances.*
Book by George S. Kaufman & Morrie Ryskind.
Produced by Sam Harris; directed by Kaufman; dances by George Hale.
Cast included: William Gaxton, Victor Moore, Lois Moran, George Murphy, Dudley Clements, Edward H. Robins, Ralph Riggs, Florenz Ames, Grace Brinkley, June O'Dea.
Principal songs: Wintergreen for President; Love Is Sweeping the Country; Of Thee I

Sing (Baby); Who Cares?; Hello, Good Morning; The Illegitimate Daughter; Because, Because.
Recorded Versions
Capitol T 11651 (O.C.) (1952).
Columbia S 31763 (TV) (1972).
This tasty political roast is better served by the first revival cast (Jack Carson, Paul Hartman) than by the second (Carroll O'Connor, Cloris Leachman, Jack Gilford).

PARDON MY ENGLISH
Opened: Jan. 20, 1933, Majestic Th.
46 *performances.*
Book by Herbert Fields.
Produced by Alex A. Aarons & Vinton Freedley; directed by John McGowan; dances by George Hale.
Cast included: Jack Pearl, George Givot, Lyda Roberti, Carl Randall, Barbara Newberry, Harry T. Shannon, Gerald Oliver Smith, Cliff Hall, Josephine Huston.
Principal songs: Lorelei; Isn't It a Pity?; My Cousin in Milwaukee.

LET 'EM EAT CAKE
Opened: Oct. 21, 1933, Imperial Th.
90 *performances.*
Book by George S. Kaufman & Morrie Ryskind.
Produced by Sam H. Harris; directed by Kaufman; dances by Ned McGurn & Eugene Van Grona.
Cast included: William Gaxton, Victor Moore, Lois Moran, Dudley Clements, Edward H. Robins, Philip Loeb, Ralph Riggs, Florenz Ames, Consuelo Flowerton.
Principal songs: Tweedledee for President; Mine; Down With Ev'rything that's Up; Let 'Em Eat Cake; On and On and On; Blue, Blue, Blue.

LIFE BEGINS AT 8:40
(*See* Harold Arlen).

PORGY AND BESS
Opened: Oct. 10, 1935, Alvin Th.
124 *performances.*
Book by DuBose Heyward; lyrics also by Heyward.
Produced by The Theatre Guild; directed by Rouben Mamoulian.
Cast included: Todd Duncan, Anne Wiggins Brown, John W. Bubbles, Georgette Harvey, Edward Matthews, Helen Dowdy, Ruby Elzy, Warren Coleman, Ford L. Buck, J. Rosamond Johnson, Eva Jessye Choir.
Principal songs: Summertime (Heyward); A Woman Is a Sometime Thing (Heyward); Gone, Gone, Gone (Heyward); My Man's Gone Now (Heyward); It Takes a Long Pull to Get There (Heyward); I Got Plenty o' Nothin' (lyric with Heyward); What You Want wid Bess? (Heyward); Bess, You Is My Woman Now; Oh, I Can't Sit Down; It Ain't Necessarily So; I Loves You Porgy; A Red Headed Woman; There's a Boat dat's Leavin'

Soon for New York; Bess, Oh Where's My Bess?; I'm on My Way (lyric with Heyward).
Recorded Versions
RCA AR3 2109 (O.C.) (1976).
London OSA 13116 (S.C.).
Odyssey 32360018 (S.C.).
Bethlehem EXPL 1 (S.C.).
Mark56 667 (O.C.).
RCA Camden CAL 500 (S.C.).
MCA 2035 (O.C.) (1942).
RCA LSC 2679 (O.C.) (1952).
Columbia OS 2016 (F.V.) (1959).
Reader's Digest S 40 (S.C.).
   The first 4 are 3-record sets. RCA's with Clamma Dale & Donnie Ray Albert is as definitive as we're likely to get; it's a shade preferable to the concert-type London version conducted by Lorin Maazel. Sonically, they both replace the lowpriced Odyssey with Camilla Williams & Lawrence Winters. Bethlehem's misguided effort offers Frances Faye & Mel Tormé. On the singles, Gershwin is heard conducting a rehearsal on Mark56 with Anne Brown & Todd Duncan (they're also on MCA); Helen Jepsen & Lawrence Tibbett, who made the first commercial set, are on Camden; Leontyne Price & William Warfield are starred on RCA; the soundtrack's dubbers, Robert McFerrin & Adele Addison, are on Columbia; Anna Moffo & Val Pringle give us highlights on RD.

ZIEGFELD FOLLIES OF 1936
(*See* Vernon Duke).

LADY IN THE DARK
(*See* Kurt Weill).

THE FIREBRAND OF FLORENCE
(*See* Kurt Weill).

PARK AVENUE
(*See* Arthur Schwartz).

Chapter Nine
VINCENT YOUMANS
Composer

TWO LITTLE GIRLS IN BLUE
Opened: May 3, 1921, George M. Cohan Th.
135 *performances*.
Book by Fred Jackson; lyrics by Arthur Francis (Ira Gershwin); music also by Paul Lannin.
Produced by A. L. Erlanger; directed by Ned Wayburn.
Cast included: Madeline & Marion Fairbanks, Oscar Shaw, Fred Santley, Olin Howland, Evelyn Law, Julia Kelety, Emma Janvier.
Principal Youmans songs: Oh Me! Oh My!; Dolly (lyric with Schuyler Greene); Who's Who with You?

WILDFLOWER
Opened: Feb. 7, 1923, Casino Th.
477 *performances*.
Book & lyrics by Otto Harbach & Oscar Hammerstein II; music also by Herbert Stothart.
Produced by Arthur Hammerstein; directed by Oscar Eagle; dances by David Bennett.
Cast included: Edith Day, Guy Robertson, Olin Howland, Esther Howard, Charles Judels, James Doyle, Evelyn Cavanaugh.
Principal songs: Wild-Flower; Bambalina; April Blossoms; I Love You, I Love You, I Love You.
Recorded Version
M-E 7052 (London O.C.) (1926).
   Kitty Reidy & Howett Worster head the cast.

MARY JANE McKANE
Opened: Dec. 25, 1923, Imperial Th.
151 *performances*.
Book & lyrics by William Cary Duncan & Oscar Hammerstein II; music also by Herbert Stothart.
Produced by Arthur Hammerstein; directed by Alonzo Price; dances by Sammy Lee.
Cast included: Mary Hay, Hal Skelly, Stanley Ridges, Kitty Kelly, Margaret & Elizabeth Keene, Dallas Welford.
Principal Youmans songs: My Boy and I; Toodle-oo; Flannel Petticoat Gal.

LOLLIPOP
Opened: Jan. 21, 1924, Knickerbocker Th.
152 *performances*.
Book & lyrics by Zelda Sears; additional lyrics by Walter DeLeon.
Produced by H. W. Savage; directed by Ira Hards; dances by Bert French, John Tiller & Mary Read.
Cast included: Ada May, Zelda Sears, Irene Dunne, Leonard Ceeley, Nick Long, Jr., Gus Shy, Harry Puck.
Principal songs: Tie a String Around Your Finger; Take a Little One-Step; Going Rowing; Deep in My Heart.

NO, NO, NANETTE
Opened: Sept. 16, 1925, Globe Th.
321 *performances*.
Book by Otto Harbach & Frank Mandel; lyrics by Irving Caesar.
Produced & directed by H. H. Frazee; dances by Sammy Lee.
Cast included: Louise Groody, Charles Winninger, Georgia O'Ramey, Wellington Cross, Josephine Whittell, Mary Lawlor, Jack (John) Barker, Frank Parker.
Principal songs: No, No, Nanette (lyric by Harbach); Too Many Rings Around Rosie; I Want to Be Happy; Tea for Two; You Can Dance with Any Girl at All; Where Has My Hubby Gone Blues; The Call of the Sea; I've Confessed to the Breeze (Harbach) (revival only).
Recorded Versions
Stanyan 10035 (London O.C.) (1925).

Columbia S 30563 (O.C.) (1971).
Reader's Digest S 40 (S.C.).

This quintessentially 20s score is heard on one side of the Stanyan (with songs in alphabetical order!), sung by Binnie Hale, George Grossmith & company. Columbia offers Ruby Keeler, Patsy Kelly, Bobby Van, Jack Gilford, Helen Gallagher, & Susan Watson in a bubbly aural recreation. The RD company is headed by Jeanette Scovotti & John Vauxhall.

OH, PLEASE!
Opened: Dec. 17, 1926, Fulton Th.
75 performances.
Book by Otto Harbach & Anne Caldwell; lyrics by Caldwell.
Produced by Charles Dillingham; directed by Hassard Short; dances by David Bennett.
Cast included: Beatrice Lillie, Charles Winninger, Charles Purcell, Helen Broderick, Kitty Kelly, Charles Columbus, Nick Long, Jr.
Principal songs: Nicodemus; I Know that You Know; Like He Loves Me; I'm Waiting for a Wonderful Girl.

HIT THE DECK
Opened: Apr. 25, 1927, Belasco Th.
352 performances.
Book by Herbert Fields; lyrics by Clifford Grey & Leo Robin.
Produced by Lew Fields & Youmans; directed by Alexander Leftwich; dances by Seymour Felix.
Cast included: Louise Groody, Charles King, Stella Mayhew, Madeline Cameron, Bobbie Perkins, Brian Donlevy.
Principal songs: Join the Navy; Harbor of My Heart; Why, Oh Why; Sometimes I'm Happy (lyric by Irving Caesar); Hallelujah; Loo-Loo.
Recorded Versions
MGM 2 SES 43 (F.V.) (1955).
Epic LN 3569 (S.C.).

Seven of the 12 songs on the sound-track (Tony Martin, Jane Powell, Debbie Reynolds) were in the original score, & one, "Keeping Myself for You," was from the first film version. Doreen Hume & Denis Quilley sing excerpts on Epic.

RAINBOW
Opened: Nov. 21, 1928, Gallo Th.
29 performances.
Book by Laurence Stallings & Oscar Hammerstein II; lyrics by Hammerstein.
Produced by Philip Goodman; directed by Hammerstein; dances by Busby Berkeley.
Cast included: Allan Prior, Louise Brown, Libby Holman, Charles Ruggles, Brian Donlevy, May Barnes, Harland Dixon, Helen Lynd, Ned McGurn.
Principal songs: I Want a Man; The One Girl; I Like You as You Are; Hay, Straw; The Bride Was Dressed in White.

GREAT DAY!
Opened: Oct. 17, 1929, Cosmopolitan Th.

36 performances.
Book by William Cary Duncan & John Wells; lyrics by William (Billy) Rose & Edward Eliscu.
Produced by Youmans; directed by R. H. Burnside & Frank M. Gillespie; dances by LeRoy Prinz.
Cast included: Mayo Methot, John Haynes, Allan Prior, Walter C. Kelly, Miller & Lyles, Maude Eburne, Ethel Norris, Lois Deppe, Vanessi.
Principal songs: Happy Because I'm in Love; Great Day; More than You Know; Without a Song.

SMILES
Opened: Nov. 18, 1930, Ziegfeld Th.
63 performances.
Book by William Anthony McGuire; lyrics by Harold Adamson, Clifford Grey, Ring Lardner.
Produced by Florenz Ziegfeld; directed by McGuire; dances by Ned Wayburn.
Cast included: Marilyn Miller, Fred & Adele Astaire, Tom Howard, Paul Gregory, Eddie Foy, Jr., Larry Adler, Clare Dodd, Georgia Caine, Bob Hope, Virginia Bruce.
Principal songs: Time on My Hands (lyric by Adamson & Mack Gordon); Carry on, Keep Smiling (Adamson); I'm Glad I Waited (Adamson-Grey); If I Were You, Love (Lardner).

THROUGH THE YEARS
Opened: Jan. 28, 1932, Manhattan Th.
20 performances.
Book by Brian Hooker; lyrics by Edward Heyman.
Produced by Youmans; directed by Edgar MacGregor; dances by Jack Haskell & Max Scheck.
Cast included: Natalie Hall, Michael Bartlett, Charles Winninger, Reginald Owen, Nick Long, Jr.
Principal songs: Kinda Like You; Through the Years; You're Everywhere; Drums in My Heart; Kathleen Mine.

TAKE A CHANCE
Opened: Nov. 26, 1932, Apollo Th.
243 performances.
Book by B. G. DeSylva & Laurence Schwab with Sid Silvers; lyrics by DeSylva; music also by Richard A. Whiting & Herb Brown Nacio (Nacio Herb Brown).
Produced by Schwab & DeSylva; directed by Edgar MacGregor; dances by Bobby Connolly.
Cast included: Jack Haley, Ethel Merman, Jack Whiting, June Knight, Sid Silvers, Robert Gleckler, Mitzi Mayfair, Oscar Ragland.
Principal Youmans songs: Should I Be Sweet?; Rise 'n' Shine; Oh, How I Long to Belong to You.

Chapter Ten
RICHARD RODGERS
Composer
LORENZ HART
Lyricist

POOR LITTLE RITZ GIRL
Opened: July 28, 1920, Central Th.
119 *performances.*
Book by George Campbell & Lew Fields; music & lyrics also by Sigmund Romberg & Alex Gerber.
Produced by Lew Fields: directed by Ned Wayburn.
Cast included: Charles Purcell, Eleanor Griffith, Lulu McConnell, Andrew Tombes, Aileen Poe, Grant Simpson.
Principal Rodgers-Hart songs: You Can't Fool Your Dreams; What Happened Nobody Knows; Mary, Queen of Scots (lyric by Herbert Fields).

THE GARRICK GAIETIES
Opened: May 17, 1925, Garrick Th.
211 *performances.*
Sketches by Benjamin M. Kaye, Edith Meiser, Arthur Sullivan & Morrie Ryskind, Howard Green.
Produced by The Theatre Guild; directed by Philip Loeb; dances by Herbert Fields.
Cast included: Sterling Holloway, Romney Brent, James Norris, June Cochrane, Betty Starbuck, Edith Meiser, Philip Loeb, House Jamieson, Hildegarde Halliday, Lee Strasberg, Rose Rolando, Alvah Bessie, Elizabeth (Libby) Holman, Sanford Meisner, Eleanor Shaler.
Principal songs: Manhattan; April Fool; Sentimental Me; On with the Dance; An Old-Fashioned Girl (lyric by Edith Meiser).

DEAREST ENEMY
Opened: Sept. 18, 1925, Knickerbocker Th.
286 *performances.*
Book by Herbert Fields.
Produced by George Ford; directed by John Murray Anderson; dances by Carl Hemmer.
Cast included: Helen Ford, Charles Purcell, Flavia Arcaro, Harold Crane, Detmar Poppen, Helen Spring.
Principal songs: War Is War; Cheerio; I Beg Your Pardon; Here in My Arms; Where the Hudson River Flows; Bye and Bye; Old Enough to Love; Sweet Peter; Here's a Kiss.

THE GIRL FRIEND
Opened: Mar. 17, 1926, Vanderbilt Th.
301 *performances.*
Book by Herbert Fields.
Produced by Lew Fields; directed by John Harwood; dances by Jack Haskell.
Cast included: Sam White, Eva Puck, June Cochrane, Frank Doane, John Hundley, Evelyn Cavanaugh, Francis X. Donegan.
Principal songs: The Girl Friend; The Blue Room; Why Do I?; Good Fellow Mine.

THE GARRICK GAIETIES
Opened: May 10, 1926, Garrick Th.
174 *performances.*
Sketches by Benjamin M. Kaye, Newman Levy, Marion Page Johnson, Chester Heywood, Edward Hope.
Produced by The Theatre Guild; directed by Philip Loeb; dances by Herbert Fields.
Cast included: Sterling Holloway, Romney Brent, Betty Starbuck, Edith Meiser, Philip Loeb, Bobbie Perkins, Hildegarde Halliday, Eleanor Shaler.
Principal songs: Keys to Heaven; Mountain Greenery; What's the Use of Talking?; Sleepyhead.

PEGGY-ANN
Opened: Dec. 27, 1926, Vanderbilt Th.
333 *performances.*
Book by Herbert Fields.
Produced by Lew Fields & Lyle D. Andrews; directed by Robert Milton; dances by Seymour Felix.
Cast included: Helen Ford, Lulu McConnell, Betty Starbuck, Lester Cole, Edith Meiser, Jack Thompson, Margaret Breen, Grant Simpson, Fuller Mellish, Jr.
Principal songs: A Tree in the Park; A Little Birdie Told Me So; Where's That Rainbow?; Maybe It's Me.

BETSY
Opened: Dec. 28, 1926, New Amsterdam Th.
39 *performances.*
Book by Irving Caesar & David Freedman, revised by William Anthony McGuire.
Produced by Florenz Ziegfeld; directed by McGuire; dances by Sammy Lee.
Cast included: Belle Baker, Al Shean, Jimmy Hussey, Bobbie Perkins, Dan Healy, Allen Kearns, Madeleine Cameron, Barbara Newberry, Evelyn Law, Borrah Minevitch Harmonica Orchestra.
Principal songs: In Our Parlor on the Third Floor Back; If I Were You; This Funny World; Sing; Come and Tell Me; Blue Skies (music & lyrics by Irving Berlin).

A CONNECTICUT YANKEE
Opened: Nov. 3, 1927, Vanderbilt Th.
418 *performances.*
Book by Herbert Fields.
Produced by Lew Fields & Lyle D. Andrews; directed by Alexander Leftwich; dances by Busby Berkeley.
Cast included: William Gaxton, Constance Carpenter, William Norris, June Cochrane, Jack Thompson, Nana Bryant, Paul Everton.
Principal songs: My Heart Stood Still; Thou Swell; On a Desert Island With Thee; I Feel at Home With You.

SHE'S MY BABY
Opened: Jan. 3, 1928, Globe Th.
71 *performances.*
Book by Guy Bolton, Bert Kalmar, Harry Ruby.
Produced by Charles Dillingham; directed by Edward Royce; dances by Mary Read.
Cast included: Beatrice Lillie, Clifton Webb, Jack Whiting, Irene Dunne, Nick Long, Jr., William Frawley, Ula Sharon, Frank Doane.
Principal songs: You're What I Need; A Little House in Soho; A Baby's Best Friend; Try Again Tomorrow.

PRESENT ARMS
Opened: Apr. 26, 1928, Mansfield Th.
155 *performances.*
Book by Herbert Fields.
Produced by Lew Fields; directed by Alexander Leftwich; dances by Busby Berkeley.
Cast included: Charles King, Flora LeBreton, Busby Berkeley, Joyce Barbour, Franker Woods, Fuller Mellish, Jr., Gaile Beverley.
Principal songs: You Took Advantage of Me; Do I Hear You Saying "I Love You"?; A Kiss for Cinderella; Blue Ocean Blues.

CHEE-CHEE
Opened: Sept. 25, 1928, Mansfield Th.
31 *performances.*
Book by Herbert Fields.
Produced by Lew Fields; directed by Alexander Leftwich; dances by Jack Haskell.
Cast included: Helen Ford, William Williams, Betty Starbuck, George Hassell, Philip Loeb, George Houston, Stark Patterson.
Principal songs: I Must Love You; Moon of My Delight; Dear, Oh Dear; Singing a Love Song.

SPRING IS HERE
Opened: Mar. 11, 1929, Alvin Th.
104 *performances.*
Book by Owen Davis.
Produced by Alex A. Aarons & Vinton Freedley; directed by Alexander Leftwich; dances by Bobby Connolly.
Cast included: Glenn Hunter, Lillian Taiz, John Hundley, Charles Ruggles, Inez Courtney, Joyce Barbour, Dick Keene, Lew Parker, Phil Ohman & Vic Arden (duo-pianists).
Principal songs: Yours Sincerely; With a Song in My Heart; Baby's Awake Now; Red Hot Trumpet; Why Can't I?

HEADS UP!
Opened: Nov. 11, 1929, Alvin Th.
144 *performances.*
Book by John McGowan & Paul Gerard Smith.
Produced by Alex A. Aarons & Vinton Freedley; director uncredited; dances by George Hale.
Cast included: Barbara Newberry, Jack

Whiting, Victor Moore, Betty Starbuck, John Hundley, Ray Bolger, Janet Velie, Robert Gleckler, Lew Parker, Atlas & LaMarr, Phil Ohman (pianist).
Principal songs: Why Do You Suppose?; It Must Be Heaven; My Man Is on the Make; A Ship Without a Sail.

SIMPLE SIMON
Opened: Feb. 18, 1930, Ziegfeld Th.
135 *performances.*
Book by Ed Wynn & Guy Bolton.
Produced by Florenz Ziegfeld; directed by Zeke Colvan; dances by Seymour Felix.
Cast includes: Ed Wynn, Ruth Etting, Bobbe Arnst, Will Ahearn, Alan Edwards, Harriet Hoctor, Lennox Pawle, Hazel Forbes.
Principal songs: Send for Me; I Can Do Wonders with You; Ten Cents a Dance; I Still Believe in You; Don't Tell Your Folks.

AMERICA'S SWEETHEART
Opened: Feb. 10, 1931, Broadhurst Th.
135 *performances.*
Book by Herbert Fields.
Produced by Laurence Schwab & Frank Mandel; directed by Monty Woolley; dances by Bobby Connolly.
Cast included: Harriette Lake (Ann Sothern), Jack Whiting, Gus Shy, John Sheehan, Inez Courtney, Jeanne Aubert, Dorothy Dare, Virginia Bruce, Jack Donohue.
Principal songs: I've Got Five Dollars; There's So Much More; We'll Be the Same; How About It?; Sweet Geraldine; Innocent Chorus Girls of Yesterday; A Lady Must Live.

JUMBO
Opened: Nov. 16, 1935, Hippodrome.
233 *performances.*
Book by Ben Hecht & Charles MacArthur.
Produced by Billy Rose; directed by John Murray Anderson & George Abbott; dances by Allan K. Foster.
Cast included: Jimmy Durante, Gloria Grafton, Donald Novis, Poodles Hanneford, Bob Lawrence, Arthur Sinclair, Lipman Duckat (Larry Douglas), Paul Whiteman Orchestra.
Principal songs: Over and Over Again; The Circus Is on Parade; The Most Beautiful Girl in the World; My Romance; Little Girl Blue.
Recorded Version
Columbia AOS 2260 (F.V.) (1962).
    The M-G-M soundtrack (Doris Day, Martha Raye, Jimmy Durante) contains the above 5 songs plus "Why Can't I?" & "This Can't Be Love."

ON YOUR TOES
Opened: Apr. 11, 1936, Imperial Th.
315 *performances.*
Book by Rodgers & Hart & George Abbott.
Produced by Dwight Deere Wiman; directed by Worthington Miner, George Abbott (uncredited); dances by George Balanchine.

Cast included: Ray Bolger, Tamara Geva, Monty Woolley, Doris Carson, David Morris, Luella Gear, Robert Sidney, Demetrios Vilan, George Church, Edgar Fairchild & Adam Carroll (duo-pianists).
Principal songs: It's Got to Be Love; Too Good for the Average Man; There's a Small Hotel; The Heart Is Quicker than the Eye; Quiet Night; Glad to Be Unhappy; On Your Toes; Slaughter on Tenth Avenue (ballet).
Recorded Versions
Stet DS 15024 (O.C.) (1954).
Columbia COS 2590 (S.C.).
   Columbia's LP, with Portia Nelson & Jack Cassidy, was issued before the 1954 revival. The recording of that production (Bobby Van, Elaine Stritch) includes the interpolated "You Took Advantage of Me."

BABES IN ARMS
Opened: Apr. 14, 1937, Shubert Th.
289 *performances.*
Book by Rodgers & Hart.
Produced by Dwight Deere Wiman ; directed by Robert Sinclair; dances by George Balanchine.
Cast included: Mitzi Green, Wynn Murray, Ray Heatherton, Duke McHale, Alfred Drake, Ray McDonald, Grace McDonald, Harold & Fayard Nicholas, Robert Rounseville, Rolly Pickert, Aileen Poe, Dan Dailey, Edgar Fairchild & Adam Carroll (duo-pianists).
Principal songs: Where or When; Babes in Arms; I Wish I Were in Love Again; Way Out West; My Funny Valentine; Johnny One Note; All at Once; The Lady Is a Tramp; Imagine.
Recorded Version
Columbia AOS 2570 (S.C.).
   Probably more hits in this score than in any other by Rodgers & Hart. Mary Martin stars on the record.

I'D RATHER BE RIGHT
Opened: Nov. 2, 1937, Alvin Th.
290 *performances.*
Book by George S Kaufman & Moss Hart.
Produced by Sam H. Harris; directed by Kaufman; dances by Charles Weidman & Ned McGurn.
Cast included: George M. Cohan, Joy Hodges, Austin Marshall, Taylor Holmes, Marion Green, Florenz Ames, Joseph Macaulay, Georgie Tapps, Mary Jane Walsh, Marie Nash, Paul Parks.
Principal songs: Have You Met Miss Jones?; A Little Bit of Constitutional Fun; Sweet Sixty-Five; I'd Rather Be Right; Off the Record.

I MARRIED AN ANGEL
Opened: May 11, 1938, Shubert Th.
338 *performances.*
Book by Rodgers & Hart.
Produced by Dwight Deere Wiman; directed by Joshua Logan; dances by George Balanchine.
Cast included: Dennis King, Vera Zorina, Vivienne Segal, Walter Slezak, Charles Walters, Audrey Christie, Charles Laskey, Morton L. Stevens, Casper Reardon (harpist).
Principal songs: Did You Ever Get Stung?; I Married an Angel; I'll Tell the Man in the Street; How to Win Friends and Influence People; Spring Is Here; A Twinkle in Your Eye; At the Roxy Music Hall.

THE BOYS FROM SYRACUSE
Opened: Nov. 23, 1938, Alvin Th.
235 *performances.*
Book by George Abbott.
Produced & directed by Abbott; dances by George Balanchine.
Cast included: Jimmy Savo, Teddy Hart, Eddie Albert, Ronald Graham, Wynn Murray, Muriel Angelus, Marcy Westcott, Bob Lawrence, Robert Sidney, Burl Ives, George Church, Betty Bruce.
Principal songs: What Can You Do With a Man?; Falling in Love with Love; The Shortest Day of the Year; This Can't Be Love; He and She; You Have Cast Your Shadow on the Sea; Sing for Your Supper; Oh, Diogenes.
Recorded Versions
Columbia COS 2580 (S.C.).
Capitol S TAO 1933 (O.C.) (1963).
Stet DS 15016 (London O.C.) (1963).
   Jack Cassidy, Portia Nelson & Bibi Osterwald are heard in a spirited rendering of the score on Columbia. The successful off-Broadway revival, on Capitol, features Ellen Hanley, Stuart Damon, Julienne Marie & Karen Morrow; the London cast is headed by Bob Monkhouse & Ronnie Corbett.

TOO MANY GIRLS
Opened: Oct. 18, 1939, Imperial Th.
249 *performances.*
Book by George Marion, Jr.
Produced & directed by George Abbott; dances by Robert Alton.
Cast included: Richard Kollmar, Eddie Bracken, Marcy Westcott, Desi Arnaz, Hal LeRoy, Mary Jane Walsh, Leila Ernst, Ivy Scott, Diosa Costello, Van Johnson, James MacColl.
Principal songs: Love Never Went to College; Spic and Spanish; I Like to Recognize the Tune; I Didn't Know What Time It Was; Give It Back to the Indians; She Could Shake the Maracas; Tempt Me Not.
Recorded Version
Painted Smiles 1368 (S.C.).
   Nancy Andrews, Johnny Desmond, Estelle Parsons & Anthony Perkins give their all for dear old Pottawatomie.

HIGHER AND HIGHER
Opened: Apr. 4, 1940, Shubert Th.
104 *performances.*

Book by Gladys Hurlbut & Joshua Logan. Produced by Dwight Deere Wiman; directed by Logan; dances by Robert Alton.
Cast included: Jack Haley, Marta Eggert, Shirley Ross, Leif Erickson, Lee Dixon, Robert Chisholm, Billie Worth, Hollace Shaw, Robert Rounseville, Janet Fox, Jane Ball, Marie Nash, June Allyson, Vera Ellen.
Principal songs: From Another World; Nothing but You; Disgustingly Rich; Ev'ry Sunday Afternoon; It Never Entered My Mind; Mornings at Seven; How's Your Health?

PAL JOEY
Opened: Dec. 25, 1940, Ethel Barrymore Th. 374 *performances.*
Book by John O'Hara.
Produced & directed by George Abbott; dances by Robert Alton.
Cast included: Vivienne Segal, Gene Kelly, June Havoc, Jack Durant, Leila Ernst, Stanley Donen, Jean Casto, Van Johnson, Jerome Whyte.
Principal songs: You Mustn't Kick It Around; I Could Write a Book; That Terrific Rainbow; Happy Hunting Horn; Bewitched, Bothered and Bewildered; The Flower Garden of My Heart; Zip; Den of Iniquity; Take Him.
Recorded Versions
Columbia COL 4364 (S.C.).
Capitol S 310 (O.C.) (1952).
Capitol DW 912 (F.V.) (1957).
　　The Columbia LP helped spark the 1952 revival, with the album's stars, Vivienne Segal & Harold Lang, going into the new production. The first Capitol has the rest of the cast plus Jane Froman & Dick Beavers. The soundtrack features Frank Sinatra & added R&H songs.

BY JUPITER
Opened: June 2, 1942, Shubert Th. 427 *performances.*
Book by Rodgers & Hart.
Produced by Dwight Deere Wiman & Rodgers; directed by Joshua Logan; dances by Robert Alton.
Cast included: Ray Bolger, Constance Moore, Benay Venuta, Ronald Graham, Bertha Belmore, Margaret Bannerman, Mark Dawson, Ralph Dumke, Berni Gould, Vera Ellen.
Principal songs: Jupiter Forbid; Life with Father; Nobody's Heart; Ev'rything I've Got; Careless Rhapsody; Wait till You See Her; Here's a Hand.
Recorded Version
RCA LSO 1137 (O.C.) (1967).
　　The off Broadway cast, headed by Bob Dishy, does exceptionally well by this *Boys from Syracuse*-inspired score.

A CONNECTICUT YANKEE
(revised version)
Opened: Nov. 17, 1943, Martin Beck Th. 135 *performances.*

Book by Herbert Fields.
Produced by Rodgers; directed by John C. Wilson; dances by William Holbrook & Al White, Jr.
Cast included: Dick Foran, Vivienne Segal, Julie Warren, Chester Stratton, Jere McMahon, Robert Chisholm, Vera Ellen.
Principal songs: My Heart Stood Still; Thou Swell; On a Desert Island with Thee; To Keep My Love Alive; Can't You Do a Friend a Favor?; I Feel at Home with You; You Always Love the Same Girl.

Chapter Eleven
B. G. DESYLVA
Lyricist

LEW BROWN
Lyricist

RAY HENDERSON
Composer

This list contains all musicals by Messrs. DeSylva, Brown & Henderson including those written as a team & also those written with other collaborators. For other musicals with books co-authored by Mr. DeSylva, See DuBarry Was a Lady & Panama Hattie *under Cole Porter.*

SINBAD
Opened: Feb. 14, 1918, Winter Garden 164 *performances.*
Book & most lyrics by Harold Atteridge; music mostly by Sigmund Romberg; music & lyrics also by DeSylva, George Gershwin & Irving Caesar, Jean Schwartz, Joe Young & Sam Lewis.
Produced by Messrs. Shubert; directed by J. C. Huffman; dances by Jack Mason & Alexis Kosloff.
Cast included: Al Jolson, Kitty Doner, Forrest Huff, Mabel Withee, Hazell Cox, Grace Washburn, Edgar Atchison-Ely.
Principal DeSylva songs: 'N Everything; I'll Say She Does; I Gave Her That; Chloe.

LA LA LUCILLE (DeSylva)
(*See* George Gershwin).

BOMBO
Opened: Oct. 6, 1921, Al Jolson Th. 219 *performances.*
Book & most lyrics by Harold Atteridge; music mostly by Sigmund Romberg; music & lyrics also by DeSylva, Con Conrad, Cliff Friend, Walter Donaldson, Sam Lewis & Joe Young.
Produced by Messrs. Shubert; directed by J. C. Huffman; dances by Allan K. Foster.
Cast included: Al Jolson, Janet Adair, Forrest Huff, Vivien Oakland, Russell Mack, Portland Hoffa.
Principal DeSylva songs: Avalon (music by

Vincent Rose); April Showers (music by Louis Silvers); Arcady (music by Conrad); Yoo-Hoo.

GEORGE WHITE'S SCANDALS (DeSylva)
(4th Edition)
(*See* George Gershwin).

ORANGE BLOSSOMS (DeSylva)
(*See* Victor Herbert).

THE YANKEE PRINCESS
Opened: Oct. 2, 1922, Knickerbocker Th.
80 *performances.*
Book by William LeBaron; lyrics by DeSylva; music by Emmerich Kalman.
Produced by A. L. Erlanger; directed by Julian Mitchell & Fred G. Latham.
Cast included: Vivienne Segal, John T. Murray, Frank Doane, Colin Campbell, Thorpe Bates, Vivien Oakland.
Principal songs: Roses, Lovely Roses; In the Starlight; I Still Can Dream.

GEORGE WHITE'S SCANDALS (DeSylva)
(5th Edition)
(*See* George Gershwin).

SWEET LITTLE DEVIL (DeSylva)
(*See* George Gershwin).

GEORGE WHITE'S SCANDALS (DeSylva)
(6th Edition)
(*See* George Gershwin).

BIG BOY
Opened: Jan. 7, 1925, Winter Garden
176 *performances.*
Book by Harold Atteridge; lyrics by DeSylva; music mostly by Joseph Meyer & James Hanley.
Produced by Messrs. Shubert; directed by J. C. Huffman & Alexander Leftwich; dances by Seymour Felix & Larry Ceballos.
Cast included: Al Jolson, Edythe Baker, Colin Campbell, Flo Lewis, Ralph Whitehead, Nancy Carroll.
Principal DeSylva songs: It All Depends on You (Brown-Henderson); Hello, 'Tucky (Meyer-Hanley); As Long as I've Got My Mammy (Meyer-Hanley); If You Knew Susie (Meyer); Keep Smiling at Trouble (Jolson-Lewis Gensler).

TELL ME MORE! (DeSylva)
(*See* George Gershwin).

GEORGE WHITE'S SCANDALS
(7th Edition)
Opened: June 22, 1925, Apollo Th.
171 *performances.*
Sketches by William K. Wells & George White; lyrics by DeSylva & Brown; music by Henderson.
Produced & directed by White; dances by Albertina Rasch.
Cast included: Harry Fox, Tom Patricola, Helen Morgan, McCarthy Sisters, Gordon Dooley, Miller & Lyles, Arthur Ball, Helen Hudson, Martha Morton, Elm City 4.

Principal songs: Fly Butterfly; Give Us the Charleston; I Want a Lovable Baby; The Whosis-Whatsis; What a World This Would Be.

CAPTAIN JINKS
Opened: Sept. 8, 1925, Music Box Th.
167 *performances.*
Book by Frank Mandel & Laurence Schwab; lyrics by DeSylva; music by Lewis Gensler.
Produced by Schwab & Mandel; directed by Edgar MacGregor; dances by Sammy Lee.
Cast included: Joe E. Brown, Louise Brown, J. Harold Murray, Max Hoffman, Jr., Marion Sunshine, Nina Olivette.
Principal songs: Sea Legs; Fond of You; I Do; Kiki.

GEORGE WHITE'S SCANDALS
(8th Edition)
Opened: June 14, 1926, Apollo Th.
424 *performances.*
Sketches by George White & William K. Wells; lyrics by DeSylva & Brown; music by Henderson.
Produced & directed by White.
Cast included: Ann Pennington, Willie & Eugene Howard, Tom Patricola, Harry Richman, Buster West, Frances Williams, McCarthy Sisters, Rose Perfect, John Wells, Fairbanks Twins, Portland Hoffa.
Principal songs: Lucky Day; The Birth of the Blues; Black Bottom; The Girl Is You and the Boy Is Me; Rhapsody in Blue (music by George Gershwin).

QUEEN HIGH
Opened: Sept. 8, 1926, Ambassador Th.
378 *performances.*
Book by Laurence Schwab & DeSylva; lyrics by DeSylva; music by Lewis Gensler.
Produced by Schwab; directed by Edgar MacGregor; dances by Sammy Lee.
Cast included: Mary Lawlor, Charles Ruggles, Frank McIntyre, Clarence Nordstrom, Luella Gear, June O'Dea, Gaile Beverly, Edgar Fairchild & Ralph Rainger (duo-pianists).
Principal songs: Cross Your Heart; Gentlemen Prefer Blondes; You'll Never Know; Everything Will Happen for the Best.

PIGGY
(Title changed during run to *I Told You So*)
Opened: Jan. 11, 1927, Royale Th.
83 *performances.*
Book by Daniel Kussell & Alfred Jackson; lyrics by Brown; music by Cliff Friend.
Produced & directed by William B. Friedlander; dances by John Boyle.
Cast included: Sam Bernard, Harry McNaughton, Brooke Johns, Paul Frawley, Wanda Lyons.
Principal songs: Ding Dong Dell; I Need a Little Bit; Let's Stroll Along and Sing a Song of Love; Oh, Baby!

GOOD NEWS!

Opened: Sept. 6, 1927, 46th St. Th.
557 *performances.*
Book by Laurence Schwab & DeSylva; lyrics by DeSylva & Brown; music by Henderson.
Produced by Schwab & Frank Mandel; directed by Edgar MacGregor; dances by Bobby Connolly.
Cast included: Mary Lawlor, John Price Jones, Gus Shy, Inez Courtney, Shirley Vernon, Zelma O'Neal, George Olsen Orchestra.
Principal songs: The Best Things in Life Are Free; Good News; The Varsity Drag; Just Imagine; Lucky in Love; He's a Ladies' Man.
Recorded Version
MGM 2 SES 49 (F.V.) (1947).
  Six songs were retained, two others added (by Roger Edens, Comden & Green) for the film version featuring June Allyson, Peter Lawford, & Joan McCracken.

MANHATTAN MARY

Opened: Sept. 26, 1927, Apollo Th.
264 *performances.*
Book by George White & Billy K. Wells; lyrics by DeSylva & Brown; music by Henderson.
Produced & directed by White.
Cast included: Ed Wynn, George White, Ona Munson, Lou Holtz, Harland Dixon, McCarthy Sisters, Paul Frawley, Paul Stanton, Dorothy Walters, Susan Fleming, Mae Clarke.
Principal songs: Manhattan Mary; The Five-Step; It Won't Be Long Now.

GEORGE WHITE'S SCANDALS
(9th Edition)

Opened: July 2, 1928, Apollo Th.
240 *performances.*
Sketches by William K. Wells & George White; lyrics by DeSylva & Brown; music by Henderson.
Produced & directed by White; dances also by Russell Markert.
Cast included: Ann Pennington, Willie & Eugene Howard, Frances Williams, Harry Richman, Tom Patricola, Rose Perfect, Elm City 4, Arnold Johnson Orchestra (incl. Harold Arlen).
Principal songs: Pickin' Cotton; What D'Ya Say?; I'm on the Crest of a Wave; A Real American Tune.

HOLD EVERYTHING!

Opened: Oct. 10, 1928, Broadhurst Th.
413 *performances.*
Book by DeSylva & John McGowan; lyrics by DeSylva & Brown; music by Henderson.
Produced by Alex A. Aarons & Vinton Freedley; director uncredited; dances by Sam Rose & Jack Haskell.
Cast included: Jack Whiting, Ona Munson, Bert Lahr, Betty Compton, Victor Moore, Nina Olivette, Gus Schilling.

Principal songs: Don't Hold Everything; You're the Cream in My Coffee; To Know You Is to Love You; Too Good to Be True.

THREE CHEERS

Opened: Oct. 15, 1928, Globe Th.
210 *performances.*
Book by Anne Caldwell & R. H. Burnside; lyrics mostly by Caldwell; music mostly by Raymond Hubbell; additional lyrics by DeSylva & Brown; additional music by Henderson.
Produced by Charles Dillingham; directed by Burnside; dances by David Bennett & Mary Read.
Cast included: Will Rogers, Dorothy Stone, Alan Edwards, Oscar Ragland, Patsy Kelly, Janet Velie, Maude Eburne, Andrew Tombes, Edward Allan.
Principal DeSylva-Brown-Henderson songs: Because You're Beautiful; Maybe This Is Love; Pompanola.

FOLLOW THRU

Opened: Jan. 9, 1929, 46th St. Th.
403 *performances.*
Book by Laurence Schwab & DeSylva; lyrics by DeSylva & Brown; music by Henderson.
Produced by Schwab & Frank Mandel; directed by Edgar MacGregor; dances by Bobby Connolly.
Cast included: Irene Delroy, John Barker, Zelma O'Neal, Jack Haley, John Sheehan, Madeline Cameron, Eleanor Powell.
Principal songs: Button Up Your Overcoat; I Want to Be Bad; You Wouldn't Fool Me, Would You?; My Lucky Star.

FLYING HIGH

Opened: Mar. 3, 1930, Apollo Th.
357 *performances.*
Book by Jack McGowan, DeSylva & Brown; lyrics by DeSylva & Brown; music by Henderson.
Produced by George White; directed by Edward Clark Lilley; dances by Bobby Connolly.
Cast included: Bert Lahr, Oscar Shaw, Grace Brinkley, Russ Brown, Kate Smith, Pearl Osgood, Dorothy Hall, Gale Quadruplets, Gus Schilling.
Principal songs: Thank Your Father; Good for You, Bad for Me; Red Hot Chicago; Without Love; Wasn't It Beautiful?

GEORGE WHITE'S SCANDALS
(11th Edition)

Opened: Sept. 14, 1931, Apollo Th.
202 *performances.*
Sketches by George White, Irving Caesar, Harry Conn & Brown; lyrics by Brown; music by Henderson.
Produced & directed by White.
Cast included: Rudy Vallee, Ethel Merman, Willie & Eugene Howard, Everett Marshall, Ray Bolger, Gale Quadruplets, Ethel

Barrymore Colt, Loomis Sisters, Barbara Blair, Alice Faye.
Principal songs: Life Is Just a Bowl of Cherries; This Is the Missus; The Thrill Is Gone; That's Why Darkies Were Born; My Song; Ladies and Gentlemen, That's Love.

HOT-CHA!
Opened: Mar. 8, 1932, Ziegfeld Th.
119 *performances.*
Book by Brown & Henderson, Mark Hellinger, Hy Kraft; lyrics by Brown; music by Henderson.
Produced by Florenz Ziegfeld; directed by Edgar MacGregor & Edward Clark Lilley; dances by Bobby Connolly.
Cast included: Bert Lahr, Lupe Velez, Buddy Rogers, Marjorie White, Lynne Overman, June Knight, June MacCloy, Velez & Yolanda, Antonio & Renée DeMarco, Revva Reyes, Tito Coral, Robert Gleckler, Eleanor Powell, Miriam Battista, Iris Adrian, Rose Louise (Gypsy Rose Lee).
Principal songs: You Can Make My Life a Bed of Roses; Conchita; There I Go Dreaming Again; It's Great to Be Alive.

TAKE A CHANCE
Opened: Nov. 26, 1932, Apollo Th.
243 *performances.*
Book by DeSylva & Laurence Schwab with Sid Silvers; lyrics by DeSylva; music by Richard A. Whiting & Herb Brown Nacio (Nacio Herb Brown), Vincent Youmans.
Produced by Schwab & DeSylva; directed by Edgar MacGregor; dances by Bobby Connolly.
Cast included: Jack Haley, Ethel Merman, Jack Whiting, June Knight, Sid Silvers, Robert Gleckler, Mitzi Mayfair, Oscar Ragland.
Principal songs: Should I Be Sweet? (Youmans); Turn Out the Light (Whiting-Nacio); Oh, How I Long to Belong to You (Youmans); Rise 'n Shine (Youmans); You're an Old Smoothie (Whiting-Nacio); Eadie Was a Lady (Whiting).

STRIKE ME PINK
Opened: Mar. 4, 1933, Majestic Th.
105 *performances.*
Sketches by Brown & Henderson, Jack McGowan, Mack Gordon; lyrics by Brown; music by Henderson.
Produced by Brown & Henderson & Waxey Gordon (uncredited); directed by Brown, Henderson & McGowan; dances by Seymour Felix.
Cast included: Lupe Velez, Jimmy Durante, Hope Williams, Hal LeRoy, Roy Atwell, Eddie Garr, George Dewey Washington, Ruth Harrison & Alex Fisher, Johnny Downs, Gracie Barrie, Milton Watson, Dorothy Dare, Carolyn Nolte.
Principal songs: Strike Me Pink; It's Great to Be Alive; Love and Rhythm; Let's Call It a Day; Home to Harlem.

SAY WHEN
Opened: Nov. 8, 1934, Imperial Th.
76 *performances.*
Book by Jack MacGowan; lyrics by Ted Koehler; music by Henderson.
Produced by Henderson & McGowan; directed by Bertram Harrison; dances by Russell Markert.
Cast included: Harry Richman, Bob Hope, Linda Watkins, Taylor Holmes, Cora Witherspoon, Dennie Moore, Nick Long, Jr., Charles Collins, Michael Romanoff.
Principal songs: When Love Comes Swinging Along; Say When; It Must Have Been the Night; Let's Take Advantage of Now; Isn't It June?

CALLING ALL STARS
Opened: Dec. 13, 1934, Hollywood Th.
36 *performances.*
Sketches by Brown, A. Dorian Otvos, Alan Baxter; lyrics by Brown; music by Harry Akst.
Produced by Brown; directed by Brown & Thomas Mitchell; dances by Sara Mildred Strauss.
Cast included: Lou Holtz, Phil Baker, Everett Marshall, Jack Whiting, Gertrude Niesen, Patricia Bowman, Harry ("Bottle") McNaughton, Al Bernie, Mitzi Mayfair, Judy Canova, Martha Raye, Ella Logan.
Principal songs: If It's Love; Stepping Out of the Picture; Straw Hat in the Rain.

GEORGE WHITE'S SCANDALS
Opened: Dec. 25, 1935, New Amsterdam Th.
110 *performances.*
Sketches by George White, Billy K. Wells, Howard Shiebler, A. Dorian Otvos; lyrics by Jack Yellen; music by Henderson.
Produced & directed by White; dances by Russell Markert.
Cast included: Rudy Vallee, Bert Lahr, Willie & Eugene Howard, Gracie Barrie, Cliff Edwards, Jane Cooper, Hal Forde, Sam, Ted & Ray.
Principal songs: Cigarette; I've Got to Get Hot; I'm the Fellow who Loves You; Life Begins at Sweet Sixteen.

YOKEL BOY
Opened: July 6, 1939, Majestic Th.
208 *performances.*
Book by Brown; lyrics by Brown & Charles Tobias; music by Sam Stept.
Produced & directed by Brown; dances by Gene Snyder.
Cast included: Phil Silvers, Judy Canova, Buddy Ebsen, Dixie Dunbar, Ralph Riggs, Mark Plant, Lew Hearn, Lois January.
Principal songs: Comes Love; A Boy Named Lem; I Can't Afford to Dream.

ZIEGFELD FOLLIES
Opened: Apr. 14, 1943, Winter Garden
553 *performances.*
Sketches by Bud Pearson & Les White,

Charles Sherman & Harry Young, Lester Lawrence, Joseph Erens; lyrics by Jack Yellen; music by Henderson.
Produced by Messrs. Shubert, Alfred Blomingdale & Lou Walters; directed by John Murray Anderson, Arthur Pierson & Fred De Cordova; dances by Robert Alton.
Cast included: Milton Berle, Ilona Massey, Arthur Treacher, Jack Cole, Sue Ryan, Nadine Gae, Tommy Wonder, Dean Murphy, Christine Ayres, The Rhythmaires, Jack McCauley, Imogen Carpenter, Jay Martin, Katherine Meskill, Bill & Cora Baird, Arthur Maxwell, Ben Yost's Vi-Kings, Penny Edwards.
Principal songs: Love Songs Are Made in the Night; Come Up and Have a Cup of Coffee; Hold that Smile.

Chapter Twelve
COLE PORTER
Composer-lyricist

SEE AMERICA FIRST
Opened: Mar. 28, 1916, Maxine Elliott Th.
15 *performances.*
Book by T. Lawrason Riggs; lyrics also by Riggs.
Produced by Elisabeth Marbury; directed by J. H. Benrimo; dances by Ed Hutchinson.
Cast included: Clifton Webb, Clara Palmer, Felix Adler, Jeanne Cartier, Red Eagle.
Principal songs: I've a Shooting Box in Scotland; Buy Her a Box at the Opera; Ever and Ever Yours; See America First.

HITCHY-KOO 1919
Opened: Oct. 6, 1919, Liberty Th.
56 *performances.*
Sketches by George V. Hobart.
Produced by Raymond Hitchcock; directed by Julian Alfred.
Cast included: Raymond Hitchcock, Florence O'Denishawn, Joe Cook, Lillian Kemble Cooper, Billy Holbrook.
Principal songs: When I Had a Uniform on; My Cozy Little Corner in the Ritz; Old-Fashioned Garden; I Introduced; Another Sentimental Song.

GREENWICH VILLAGE FOLLIES
(6th Edition)
Opened: Sept. 16, 1924, Shubert Th.
127 *performances.*
Sketches by John Murray Anderson.
Produced by The Bohemians, Inc.; directed by Anderson & Lew Fields; dances by Larry Ceballos.
Cast included: Dolly Sisters, Moran & Mack, Bobbe Arnst, George Rasely, Georgie Hale, Robert Alton, Don Barclay, Vincent Lopez Orchestra.
Principal songs: I'm in Love Again; Two Little Babes in the Wood; Brittany; Make Every Day a Holiday.

PARIS
Opened: Oct. 8, 1928, Music Box Th.
195 *performances.*
Book by Martin Brown; music & lyrics also by Walter Kollo & E. Ray Goetz.
Produced by Gilbert Miller with Goetz; directed by W. H. Gilmore.
Cast included: Irene Bordoni, Arthur Margetson, Louise Closser Hale, Erik Kalkhurst, Irving Aaronson's Commanders.
Principal Porter songs: Let's Do It; Two Little Babes in the Wood; Don't Look at Me that Way.

FIFTY MILLION FRENCHMEN
Opened: Nov. 27, 1929, Lyric Th.
254 *performances.*
Book by Herbert Fields.
Produced by E. Ray Goetz; directed by Monty Woolley; dances by Larry Ceballos.
Cast included: William Gaxton, Genevieve Tobin, Helen Broderick, Jack Thompson, Betty Compton, Thurston Hall, Evelyn Hoey, Marie Valli (June Knight), Ignacio Martinetti.
Principal songs: You Do Something to Me; You've Got that Thing; Find Me a Primitive Man; You Don't Know Paree; The Tale of an Oyster; Paree, What Did You Do to Me?

WAKE UP AND DREAM!
Opened: Dec. 30, 1929, Selwyn Th.
136 *performances.*
Sketches by John Hastings Turner, Ronald Jeans, Douglas Furber; music & lyrics also by Ivor Novello & Desmond Carter, Arthur Schwartz, Donovan Parsons & Furber, Phil Charig & Joseph Meyer.
Produced by Arch Selwyn with C. B. Cochran; directed by Frank Collins; dances by Tilly Losch, Jack Buchanan, Max Rivers.
Cast included: Jack Buchanan, Jessie Matthews, Tilly Losch, Dave Fitzgibbon, Frances Shelley, William Stephens, Toni Birkmayer, Lance Lister, Marjorie Robertson (Anna Neagle).
Principal songs: I Loved Him but He Didn't Love Me; What Is This Thing Called Love?; Which?; I'm a Gigolo; Looking at You.

THE NEW YORKERS
Opened: Dec. 8, 1930, Broadway Th.
168 *performances.*
Book by Herbert Fields.
Produced by E. Ray Goetz; directed by Monty Woolley; dances by George Hale.
Cast included: Hope Williams, Jimmy Durante, Lew Clayton, Eddie Jackson, Ann Pennington, Frances Williams, Charles King, Richard Carle, Marie Cahill, Oscar Ragland, Kathryn Crawford, Paul Huber, Tammany Young, Fred Waring Pennsylvanians.
Principal songs: Where Have You Been?; I'm Getting Myself Ready for You; Love for Sale; The Great Indoors; Let's Fly Away; Take Me Back to Manhattan; I Happen to Like New York.

GAY DIVORCE

Opened: Nov. 29, 1932, Ethel Barrymore Th.
248 *performances.*
Book by Dwight Taylor with Kenneth Webb
& Samuel Hoffenstein.
Produced by Dwight Deere Wiman & Tom
Weatherly; directed by Howard Lindsay;
dances by Carl Randall & Barbara Newberry.
Cast included: Fred Astaire, Claire Luce,
Luella Gear, Eric Blore, Erik Rhodes, Roland
Bottomley, G. P. Huntley, Jr., Betty Starbuck.
Principal songs: After You; Night and Day;
How's Your Romance?; I've Got You on My
Mind; Mister and Missus Fitch.

ANYTHING GOES

Opened: Nov. 21, 1934, Alvin Th.
420 *performances.*
Book by Guy Bolton & P. G. Wodehouse,
revised by Howard Lindsay & Russel Crouse.
Produced by Vinton Freedley; directed by
Lindsay; dances by Robert Alton.
Cast included: William Gaxton, Ethel
Merman, Victor Moore, Bettina Hall, Vivian
Vance, Helen Raymond, Paul Everton, Leslie
Barrie.
Principal songs: All Through the Night; I Get
a Kick Out of You; You're the Top; Anything
Goes; Blow, Gabriel, Blow; Be Like the
Bluebird; The Gypsy in Me; There'll Always
Be a Lady Fair.
Recorded Versions
Smithsonian R 007 (O.C.).
Epic FLS 15100 (O.C.) (1962).
Columbia AML 4751 (S.C.).
Decca DL 8318 (F.V.) (1955).

Eight songs from the imperishable score are
performed on the Smithsonian by Ethel
Merman, Cole Porter, plus members of the
London company. Eileen Rodgers & Hal
Linden head the spirited revival cast on Epic
(including 6 Porter songs from other shows).
On Columbia, Mary Martin glides through 6
of the original numbers, & on Decca, Bing
Crosby, Mitzi Gaynor & Donald O'Connor
do 5 plus "It's De-Lovely" & 3 by Cahn &
Van Heusen.

JUBILEE

Opened: Oct. 12, 1935, Imperial Th.
169 *performances.*
Book by Moss Hart.
Produced by Sam H. Harris & Max Gordon;
directed by Hassard Short & Monty Woolley;
dances by Albertina Rasch.
Cast included: Mary Boland, June Knight,
Melville Cooper, Derek Williams, May Boley,
Charles Walters, Margaret Adams, Mark
Plant, Richie Ling, Dorothy Fox, Olive
Reeves-Smith, Jackie Kelk, Montgomery Clift,
Leo Chalzell, Ted Fetter, Wyn Cahoon, Adele
Jergens.
Principal songs: Why Shouldn't I?; The
Kling-Kling Bird on the Divi-Divi Tree;
When Love Comes Your Way; Me and
Marie; Just One of Those Things; A Picture

of Me Without You; Begin the Beguine.
Recorded Version
Columbia KS 31456.

On the album called *Cole*, the composer is
heard singing 9 of his most elegant songs.

RED, HOT AND BLUE!

Opened: Oct. 29, 1936, Alvin Th.
183 *performances.*
Book by Howard Lindsay & Russel Crouse.
Produced by Vinton Freedley; directed by
Howard Lindsay; dances by George Hale.
Cast included: Jimmy Durante, Ethel
Merman, Bob Hope, Polly Walters, Paul &
Grace Hartman, Forrest Orr, Dorothy Vernon,
Thurston Crane, Vivian Vance, Lew Parker.
Principal songs: Ours; Down in the Depths;
You've Got Something; It's De-Lovely; Ridin'
High; The Ozarks Are Calling Me Home;
Red, Hot and Blue; You're a Bad Influence on
Me; A Little Skipper from Heaven Above.

YOU NEVER KNOW

Opened: Sept. 21, 1938, Winter Garden
78 *performances.*
Book by Rowland Leigh; music & lyrics also
by Dana Suesse, Robert Katscher & Leigh,
Alex Fogarty & Edwin Gilbert. Produced by
Messrs. Shubert with John Shubert; directed
by Leigh & George Abbott (uncredited);
dances by Robert Alton.
Cast included: Clifton Webb, Lupe Velez,
Libby Holman, Paul & Grace Hartman, Toby
Wing, Rex O'Malley, June Preisser, Roger
Stearns, Charles Kemper, Truman Gaige.
Principal songs: You Never Know; At Long
Last Love; For No Rhyme or Reason; From
Alpha to Omega; What Shall I Do? (lyric by
Leigh).

LEAVE IT TO ME!

Opened: Nov. 9, 1938, Imperial Th.
291 *performances.*
Book by Bella & Samuel Spewack.
Produced by Vinton Freedley; directed by Mr.
Spewack; dances by Robert Alton.
Cast included: William Gaxton, Victor Moore,
Sophie Tucker, Tamara, Mary Martin,
Edward H. Robins, George Tobias, Gene
Kelly, Adele Jergens.
Principal songs: Get Out of Town; Most
Gentlemen Don't Like Love; From Now On;
My Heart Belongs to Daddy; Tomorrow.

DUBARRY WAS A LADY

Opened: Dec. 6, 1939, 46th St. Th.
408 *performances.*
Book by Herbert Fields & B. G. DeSylva.
Produced by DeSylva; directed by Edgar
MacGregor; dances by Robert Alton.
Cast included: Bert Lahr, Ethel Merman,
Betty Grable, Charles Walters, Benny Baker,
Ronald Graham, Janis Carter, Adele Jergens.
Principal songs: When Love Beckoned in
Fifty-Second Street; Do I Love You?; But in
the Morning, No!; Give Him the Oo-La-La;
Katie Went to Haiti; Well, Did You Evah!; It

Was Written in the Stars; Friendship.

PANAMA HATTIE
Opened: Oct. 30, 1940, 46th St. Th.
501 *performances.*
Book by Herbert Fields & B. G. DeSylva.
Produced by DeSylva; directed by Edgar
MacGregor; dances by Robert Alton.
Cast included: Ethel Merman, Arthur
Treacher, James Dunn, Rags Ragland, Pat
Harrington, Frank Hyers, Phyllis Brooks,
Betty Hutton, Joan Carroll, Nadine Gae,
Lipman Duckat (Larry Douglas), Janis
Carter, June Allyson, Jane Ball, Betsy Blair,
Lucille Bremer, Vera Ellen, Doris Dowling.
Principal songs: My Mother Would Love
You; I've Still Got My Health; Fresh as a
Daisy; Let's Be Buddies; Make It Another
Old-Fashioned, Please; Visit Panama; All I've
Got to Get Now Is My Man; I'm Throwing a
Ball Tonight.

LET'S FACE IT!
Opened: Oct. 29, 1941, Imperial Th.
547 *performances.*
Book by Herbert & Dorothy Fields.
Produced by Vinton Freedley; directed by
Edgar MacGregor; dances by Charles Walters.
Cast included: Danny Kaye, Eve Arden,
Benny Baker, Mary Jane Walsh, Edith
Meiser, Vivian Vance, Mary Parker & Billy
Daniel, Sunnie O'Dea, Jack Williams,
Nanette Fabray, Joseph Macaulay, Jane Ball,
Helene Bliss, Garry Davis.
Principal songs: Let's Face It; Farming;
Ev'rything I Love; Ace in the Hole; You
Irritate Me So; A Little Rumba Numba; I
Hate You, Darling; Let's Not Talk About
Love.
Recorded Version
Smithsonian R 016 (O.C.).
    Seven buoyant Porter numbers performed
by Kaye & Walsh, plus Kaye's specialty,
"Melody in 4F."

SOMETHING FOR THE BOYS
Opened: Jan. 7, 1943, Alvin Th.
422 *performances.*
Book by Herbert & Dorothy Fields.
Produced by Michael Todd; directed by
Hassard Short & Herbert Fields; dances by
Jack Cole.
Cast included: Ethel Merman, Bill Johnson,
Betty Garrett, Paula Laurence, Allen Jenkins,
Betty Bruce, Anita Alvarez, Jed Prouty,
William Lynn, Frances Mercer, Bill Callahan,
Murvyn Vye, Dolores (Dody) Goodman,
Herbert Ross.
Principal songs: Something for the Boys; Hey,
Good Lookin'; He's a Right Guy; Could It Be
You; I'm in Love with a Soldier Boy; By the
Mississinewah; The Leader of a Big Time
Band.

MEXICAN HAYRIDE
Opened: Jan. 28, 1944, Winter Garden
481 *performances.*
Book by Herbert & Dorothy Fields.
Produced by Michael Todd; directed by
Hassard Short & John Kennedy; dances by
Paul Haakon.
Cast included: Bobby Clark, June Havoc,
George Givot, Wilbur Evans, Luba Malina,
Corinna Mura, Paul Haakon, Edith Meiser,
Bill Callahan, Candy Jones.
Principal songs: Sing to Me, Guitar; I Love
You; There Must Be Someone for Me;
Abracadabra; Girls; Carlotta; Count Your
Blessings.
Recorded Version
Columbia X 14878 (O.C.).
    Havoc, Evans & Mura—but no Bobby
Clark!—are heard in 8 pieces from this Latin-
flavored Porter score.

SEVEN LIVELY ARTS
Opened: Dec. 7, 1944, Ziegfeld Th.
183 *performances.*
Sketches by Moss Hart, George S. Kaufman,
Robert Pirosh, Joseph Schrank, Charles
Sherman, Ben Hecht; music also by Igor
Stravinsky.
Produced by Billy Rose; directed by Hassard
Short & Philip Loeb; dances by Jack
Donohue & Anton Dolin.
Cast included: Beatrice Lillie, Bert Lahr,
Benny Goodman, Alicia Markova, Anton
Dolin, Doc Rockwell, Dolores Gray, Nan
Wynn, Mary Roche, Albert Carroll, Dennie
Moore, Jere McMahon, Paula Bane, Bill
Tabbert, Billie Worth, Red Norvo, Teddy
Wilson, Helen Gallagher, Temple Texas.
Principal songs: Ev'rytime We Say Goodbye;
Only Another Boy and Girl; When I Was a
Little Cuckoo; Hence, It Don't Make Sense.

AROUND THE WORLD
IN EIGHTY DAYS
Opened: May 31, 1946, Adelphi Th.
75 *performances.*
Book by Orson Welles.
Produced by Mercury Productions; directed by
Welles; dances by Nelson Barclift.
Cast included: Orson Welles, Arthur
Margetson, Mary Healy, Julie Warren, Larry
Laurence (Enzo Stuarti) Victoria Cordova,
Stefan Schnabel, Guy Spaull, Jack Cassidy.
Principal songs: Look What I Found; There
He Goes, Mr. Phileas Fogg; Should I Tell
You I Love You?; Pipe Dreaming; If You
Smile at Me; Wherever They Fly the Flag of
Old England.

KISS ME, KATE
Opened: Dec. 30, 1948, New Century Th.
1,077 *performances.*
Book by Samuel & Bella Spewack.
Produced by Saint Subber & Lemuel Ayers;
directed by John C. Wilson; dances by Hanya
Holm.
Cast included: Alfred Drake, Patricia
Morison, Harold Lang, Lisa Kirk, Harry
Clark, Jack Diamond, Denis Green,

Annabelle Hill, Lorenzo Fuller, Marc Breaux, Rudy Tone.
Principal songs: Another Op'nin', Another Show; Why Can't You Behave?; Wunderbar; So in Love; We Open in Venice; Tom, Dick or Harry; I've Come to Wive It Wealthily in Padua; I Hate Men; Were Thine that Special Face; Too Darn Hot; Where Is the Life that Late I Led?; Always True to You in My Fashion; Bianca; Brush Up Your Shakespeare.
Recorded Versions
Columbia OS 2300 (O.C.).
Capitol STAO 1267 (O.C.).
MGM 2 SES 44 (F.V.) (1953).
RCA LSP 1984 (S.C.).
Columbia CSS 645 (TV) (1968).
Porter's masterpiece is still best served by the original cast on Columbia; Capitol's with the show's leads is almost too aggressively stereophonic. The film soundtrack features Howard Keel, Kathryn Grayson & laundered lyrics. Keel is also on the imaginatively staged RCA release with Anne Jeffreys & Gogi Grant. The second Columbia was a special recording made of the Robert Goulet-Carol Lawrence TV production.

OUT OF THIS WORLD
Opened: Dec. 21, 1950, New Century Th.
157 *performances.*
Book by Dwight Taylor & Reginald Lawrence.
Produced by Saint Subber & Lemuel Ayers; directed by Agnes de Mille; dances by Hanya Holm.
Cast included: Charlotte Greenwood, William Eythe, David Burns, Priscilla Gillette, William Redfield, Barbara Ashley, Janet Collins, George Jongeyans (George Gaynes), Maria Karnilova, Erik Kristen.
Principal songs: Use Your Imagination; Where, Oh Where?; I Am Loved; Climb Up the Mountain; No Lover; Cherry Pies Ought to Be You; Nobody's Chasing Me; They Couldn't Compare to You; I Sleep Easier Now.
Recorded Version
Columbia CML 4390 (O.C.).
This is a sadly unappreciated score with a rich variety of rhymes & rhythms.

CAN-CAN
Opened: May 7, 1953, Shubert Th.
892 *performances.*
Book by Abe Burrows.
Produced by Cy Feuer & Ernest H. Martin; directed by Burrows; dances by Michael Kidd.
Cast included: Lilo, Peter Cookson, Hans Conried, Gwen Verdon, Erik Rhodes, Dania Krupska, Richard Purdy, Phil Leeds, Eddie Phillips, Ralph Beaumont, DeeDee Wood.
Principal songs: Never Give Anything Away; C'est Magnifique; I Am in Love; Allez-vous-en; It's All Right with Me; I Love Paris; Can-Can.
Recorded Versions

Capitol W 452 (O.C.).
M-E 7073 (London O.C.) (1954).
Capitol SW 1301 (F.V.) (1960).
Some attractive performances enliven the original-cast disc. Irene Hilda & Edmund Hockridge are heard on the Monmouth-Evergreen, while the soundtrack, which used only 6 of the songs, (plus 3 others by Porter), features Frank Sinatra, Shirley MacLaine & Maurice Chevalier.

SILK STOCKINGS
Opened: Feb. 24, 1955, Imperial Th.
478 *performances.*
Book by George S. Kaufman, Leueen McGrath & Abe Burrows.
Produced by Cy Feuer & Ernest H. Martin; directed by Kaufman & Feuer (uncredited); dances by Eugene Loring.
Cast included: Hildegarde Neff, Don Ameche, Gretchen Wyler, George Tobias, Leon Belasco, Henry Lascoe, David Opatoshu, Philip Sterling, Julie Newmar, Onna White, Patricia McBride.
Principal songs: Paris Loves Lovers; It's a Chemical Reaction, That's All; All of You; Siberia; Without Love; Satin and Silk; Stereophonic Sound.
Recorded Versions
RCA CBM1 2208 (O.C.).
MGM E 3542 (F.V.) (1957).
Two songs were added to the film & one was cut. Otherwise the choice rests with your preference for the stage leads or the film leads (Fred Astaire & Cyd Charisse's "voice," Carole Richards).

Chapter Thirteen
HOWARD DIETZ
Lyricist

ARTHUR SCHWARTZ
Composer

All lyrics by Mr. Dietz and music by Mr. Schwartz unless otherwise noted.

DEAR SIR
(*See* Jerome Kern).

THE GRAND STREET FOLLIES
(4th Edition)
Opened: June 15, 1926, Neighborhood Playhouse.
55 *performances.*
Sketches & lyrics by Agnes Morgan; music also by Randall Thompson, Lily Hyland, Walter Haenschen.
Produced by the Neighborhood Playhouse; directed by Miss Morgan.
Cast included: Albert Carroll, Agnes Morgan, Dorothy Sands, Paula Trueman, Vera Allen, Jessica Dragonette, Blanche Talmud.
Principal Schwartz songs: Little Igloo for Two; Polar Bear Strut (lyric by Theodore Goodwin).

THE NEW YORKERS

Opened: Mar. 10, 1927, Edyth Totten Th. *52 performances.*

Sketches by Jo Swerling; lyrics by Henry Myers; music also by Edgar Fairchild, Charles Schwab.

Produced by Milton Bender & Myers; directed by Bender.

Cast included: Chester Clute, Tamara Drasin (later known as Tamara), Mona Sorel, Reina Swan.

Principal Schwartz songs: A Song About Love; Floating Thru the Air.

MERRY-GO-ROUND

Opened: May 31, 1927, Klaw Th. *136 performances.*

Sketches & lyrics also by Morrie Ryskind; music by Henry Souvaine & Jay Gorney.

Produced by Richard Herndon; directed by Alan Dinehart; dances by Raymond Midgley.

Cast included: William Collier, Philip Loeb, Marie Cahill, Libby Holman, Leonard Sillman, Etienne Girardot, Frances Gershwin.

Principal songs: Gabriel; Hogan's Alley; New York Town; I've Got a Yes Girl.

THE LITTLE SHOW

Opened: Apr. 30, 1929, Music Box Th. *321 performances.*

Sketches by Dietz, Fred Allen, Newman Levy, Marya Mannes, George S. Kaufman; music & lyrics also by Henry Myers, Morris Hamilton & Grace Henry, Kay Swift & Paul James (James P. Warburg), Herman Hupfeld, Charlotte Kent, Ralph Rainger, Henry Sullivan.

Produced by William A. Brady, Jr., Dwight Deere Wiman & Tom Weatherly; directed by Wiman & Alexander Leftwich; dances by Danny Dare.

Cast included: Clifton Webb, Libby Holman, Fred Allen, Romney Brent, Bettina Hall, Helen Lynd, Portland Hoffa, John (Jack) McCauley, Peggy Conklin, Constance Cummings, Adam Carroll & Ralph Rainger (duo-pianists).

Principal Dietz songs: I Guess I'll Have to Change My Plan (Schwartz); I've Made a Habit of You (Schwartz); Hammacher-Schlemmer, I Love You (Schwartz); Moanin' Low (Rainger); Caught in the Rain (Sullivan).

THE GRAND STREET FOLLIES

(7th Edition)

Opened: May 1, 1929, Booth Th. *93 performances.*

Sketches & most lyrics by Agnes Morgan; music & lyrics also by Max Ewing, Max & Nathaniel Lief.

Produced by Actor-Managers, Inc. & Paul Moss; directed by Miss Morgan; dances by Dave Gould.

Cast included: Albert Carroll, Paula Trueman, Dorothy Sands, James Cagney, Otto Hulett.

Principal Schwartz songs: I Need You So (Dietz); I Love You and I Like You (M. & N. Lief); What Did Della Wear? (Morgan).

THE SECOND LITTLE SHOW

Opened: Sept. 2, 1930, Royale Th. *63 performances.*

Sketches by Norman Clark, Bert Hanlon, Marc Connelly, William B. Miles, Donald Blackwell, James J. Coghlan; music & lyrics also by Del Cleveland & Ted Fetter, Herman Hupfeld.

Produced by William A. Brady, Jr., Dwight Deere Wiman & Tom Weatherly; directed by Wiman & Monty Woolley; dances by Dave Gould.

Cast included: J. C. Flippen, Al Trahan, Gloria Grafton, Ruth Tester, Tashamira, Joey Ray, Arline Judge.

Principal Dietz-Schwartz songs: Lucky Seven; What a Case I've Got on You; I Like Your Face; You're the Sunrise.

PRINCESS CHARMING

Opened: Oct. 13, 1930, Imperial Th. *56 performances.*

Book by Jack Donahue; lyrics by Arthur Swanstrom; music also by Albert Sirmay.

Produced by Bobby Connolly & Swanstrom; directed by Connolly & Edward Clark Lilley; dances by Albertina Rasch.

Cast included: Evelyn Herbert, Robert Halliday, George Grossmith, Victor Moore, Jeanne Aubert, Douglass Dumbrille, Howard St. John, Duke McHale, Paul Huber.

Principal songs: You; I'll Never Leave You; Trailing a Shooting Star.

THREE'S A CROWD

Opened: Oct. 15, 1930, Selwyn Th. *271 performances.*

Sketches by Dietz, Groucho Marx, Laurence Schwab, Corey Ford, William B. Miles & Donald Blackwell, Fred Allen, Arthur Sheekman & Hazel Flynn; music & lyrics also by Alec Wilder & Edward Brandt, Johnny Green & Edward Heyman, Burton Lane, Phil Charig, Charles Schwab & Richard Myers.

Produced by Max Gordon; directed by Hassard Short; dances by Albertina Rasch.

Cast included: Clifton Webb, Libby Holman, Fred Allen, Tamara Geva, Earl Oxford, Portland Hoffa, Margaret Lee, California Collegians (incl. Fred MacMurray).

Principal Dietz songs: The Moment I Saw You (Schwartz); Right at the Start of It (Schwartz); Something to Remember You By (Schwartz); All the King's Horses (Brandt-Wilder); Forget All Your Books (Lane); Practising Up on You (Charig).

THE BAND WAGON

Opened: June 3, 1931, New Amsterdam Th. *260 performances.*

Sketches by George S. Kaufman & Dietz.

Produced by Max Gordon; directed by Hassard Short; dances by Albertina Rasch.

Cast included: Fred & Adele Astaire, Frank Morgan, Helen Broderick, Tilly Losch, Philip Loeb, John Barker.
Principal songs: Dancing in the Dark; New Sun in the Sky; Hoops; I Love Louisa; High and Low; Miserable with You; Where Can He Be?; White Heat; The Beggar Waltz; Confession; Sweet Music.
Recorded Versions
Smithsonian R 021 (O.C.).
MGM 2 SES 44 (F.V.) (1953).
Columbia AML 4751 (S.C.).
    The Smithsonian release, with the Astaires, includes a repressing of the first LP ever made with original Broadway stars. Only 3 of the songs are on the recorded soundtrack, with 7 other Dietz-Schwartz pieces added. Fred Astaire, Jack Buchanan & Nanette Fabray shine. On Columbia, Mary Martin & chorus do 8 numbers.

FLYING COLORS
Opened: Sept. 15, 1932, Imperial Th.
188 *performances.*
Sketches by Dietz.
Produced by Max Gordon; directed by Dietz; dances by Albertina Rasch.
Cast included: Clifton Webb, Tamara Geva, Charles Butterworth, Buddy & Vilma Ebsen, Patsy Kelly, Larry Adler, Philip Loeb, Imogene Coca.
Principal songs: Two-Faced Woman; A Rainy Day; Mother Told Me So; A Shine on Your Shoes; Alone Together; Louisiana Hayride; Fatal Fascination; Smokin' Reefers.

REVENGE WITH MUSIC
Opened: Nov. 28, 1934, New Amsterdam Th.
158 *performances.*
Book by Dietz.
Produced by Arch Selwyn & Harold Franklin; directed by (Theodore) Komisarjevsky, Dietz (uncredited), Worthington Miner (uncredited), Marc Connelly (uncredited); dances by Michael Mordkin.
Cast included: Libby Holman, Charles Winninger, Georges Metaxa, Ilka Chase, Ivy Scott, Rex O'Malley, Joseph Macaulay.
Principal songs: You and the Night and the Music; If There Is Someone Lovelier than You; That Fellow Manuelo; When You Love Only One; Maria; Wand'ring Heart.

AT HOME ABROAD
Opened: Sept. 19, 1935, Winter Garden
198 *performances.*
Sketches by Dietz, Dion Titheridge, Raymond Knight, Marc Connelly.
Produced by Messrs. Shubert; directed by Vincente Minnelli & Thomas Mitchell; dances by Gene Snyder & Harry Losee.
Cast included: Beatrice Lillie, Ethel Waters, Herb Williams, Eleanor Powell, Reginald Gardiner, Eddie Foy, Jr., Paul Haakon, James MacColl, Vera Allen, André Charise, Nina Whitney, John Payne.

Principal songs: That's Not Cricket; Hottentot Potentate; Paree; Farewell, My Lovely; Thief in the Night; Love Is a Dancing Thing; What a Wonderful World; Loadin' Time; Get Yourself a Geisha; Got a Bran' New Suit.
Recorded Version
Smithsonian R 024 (O.C.).
    Recreated musical cruise with Lillie, Waters, Powell, Gardiner, & the composer.

VIRGINIA
Opened: Sept. 2, 1937, Center Th.
60 *performances.*
Book by Laurence Stallings & Owen Davis; lyrics by Albert Stillman.
Produced by the Center Th.; directed by Leon Leonidoff & Edward Clark Lilley; dances by Florence Rogge.
Cast included: Gene Lockhart, Ronald Graham, Anne Booth, Mona Barrie, Ford Buck & John Bubbles, Dennis Hoey, Avis Andrews, Nigel Bruce, Patricia Bowman, Nora Kaye, Bertha Belmore, Lansing Hatfield.
Principal songs: Goodbye, Jonah; If You Were Someone Else; An Old Flame Never Dies (Stillman-Stallings); You and I Know (Stillman-Stallings); My Heart Is Dancing.

BETWEEN THE DEVIL
Opened: Dec. 22, 1937, Imperial Th.
93 *performances.*
Book by Dietz.
Produced by Messrs. Shubert; directed by Hassard Short & John Hayden; dances by Robert Alton.
Cast included: Jack Buchanan, Evelyn Laye, Adele Dixon, Vilma Ebsen, Charles Walters, Eric Brotherson, Tune Twisters.
Principal songs: I See Your Face Before Me; Triplets; By Myself; I'm Against Rhythm; You Have Everything.

STARS IN YOUR EYES
Opened: Feb. 9, 1939, Majestic Th.
127 *performances.*
Book by J. P. McEvoy; lyrics by Dorothy Fields.
Produced by Dwight Deere Wiman; directed by Joshua Logan; dances by Carl Randall.
Cast included: Ethel Merman, Jimmy Durante, Tamara Toumanova, Richard Carlson, Mildred Natwick, Dan Dailey, Jr., Robert Shanley, Roger Stearns, Nancy Wiman, Clinton Sundberg, Mary Wickes, Walter Cassel, Nora Kaye, Alicia Alonso, Jerome Robbins, Maria Karnilova.
Principal songs: This Is It; A Lady Needs a Change; Terribly Attractive; Just a Little Bit More; I'll Pay the Check; It's All Yours.

JACKPOT
(*See* Vernon Duke).

SADIE THOMPSON
(*See* Vernon Duke).

PARK AVENUE
Opened: Nov. 4, 1946, Shubert Th.
72 performances.
Book by Nunnally Johnson & George S. Kaufman; lyrics by Ira Gershwin.
Produced by Max Gordon; directed by Kaufman; dances by Helen Tamiris.
Cast included: Leonora Corbett, Arthur Margetson, Ray McDonald, Martha Stewart, Robert Chisholm, Marthe Errolle, Charles Purcell, Ruth Matteson, Raymond Walburn, Mary Wickes, David Wayne, Kyle McDonnell.
Principal songs: Don't Be a Woman If You Can; Land of Opportunitee; Sweet Nevada; For the Life of Me; There's No Holding Me; Goodbye to All That.

INSIDE U.S.A.
Opened: Apr. 30, 1948, New Century Th.
399 performances.
Sketches by Arnold Auerbach, Moss Hart, Arnold Horwitt.
Produced by Schwartz; directed by Robert H. Gordon; dances by Helen Tamiris.
Cast included: Beatrice Lillie, Jack Haley, John Tyers, Herb Shriner, Valerie Bettis, Eric Victor, Lewis Nye, Carl Reiner, Thelma Carpenter, Estelle Loring, Beverly Bozeman, J. C. McCord, Rod Alexander, Boris Runanin, Jack Cassidy, Tally Beatty.
Principal songs: Inside U.S.A.; Blue Grass; Rhode Island Is Famous for You; Haunted Heart; My Gal Is Mine Once More; At the Mardi Gras; First Prize at the Fair.

A TREE GROWS IN BROOKLYN
Opened: Apr. 19, 1951, Alvin Th.
270 performances.
Book by Betty Smith & George Abbott; lyrics by Dorothy Fields.
Produced by Abbott & Robert Fryer; directed by Abbott; dances by Herbert Ross.
Cast included: Shirley Booth, Johnny Johnston, Marcia Van Dyke, Nomi Mitty, Lou Wills, Jr., Nathaniel Frey, Harland Dixon, Jordan Bentley, James McCracken, Donn Driver.
Principal songs: Mine Till Monday; Make the Man Love Me; I'm Like a New Broom; Look Who's Dancing; Love Is the Reason; If You Haven't Got a Sweetheart; I'll Buy You a Star; Growing Pains; He Had Refinement.
Recorded Version
Columbia AML 4405 (O.C.).
     An inspired collection of songs.

BY THE BEAUTIFUL SEA
Opened: Apr. 8, 1954, Majestic Th.
270 performances.
Book by Herbert & Dorothy Fields; lyrics by Miss Fields.
Produced by Robert Fryer & Lawrence Carr; directed by Marshall Jamison; dances by Helen Tamiris.
Cast included: Shirley Booth, Wilbur Evans, Mae Barnes, Cameron Prud'homme, Richard France, Warde Donovan, Lola Fisher, Cathryn Damon, Libi Staiger, Larry Laurence, Reid Shelton.
Principal songs: Alone Too Long; Happy Habit; I'd Rather Wake Up by Myself; Hooray for George the Third; Hang Up!; More Love than Your Love; The Sea Song; Coney Island Boat.
Recorded Version
Capitol T 11652 (O.C.).
     Another period piece for Shirley Booth.

THE GAY LIFE
Opened: Nov. 18, 1961, Shubert Th.
114 performances.
Book by Fay & Michael Kanin.
Produced by Kermit Bloomgarden; directed by Gerald Freedman; dances by Herbert Ross.
Cast included: Walter Chiari, Barbara Cook, Jules Munshin, Loring Smith, Elizabeth Allen, Jeanne Bal, Yvonne Constant, Leonard Elliott, Lu Leonard.
Principal songs: Why Go Anywhere at All?; Magic Moment; Who Can? You Can!; Oh, Mein Liebchen; Something You Never Had Before; Come A-Wandering With Me; You're Not the Type.
Recorded Version
Capitol S WAO 1560 (O.C.).
     A gay, lilting score that deserves to be better known.

JENNIE
Opened: Oct. 17, 1963, Majestic Th.
82 performances.
Book by Arnold Schulman.
Produced by Cheryl Crawford & Richard Halliday; directed by Vincent J. Donehue; dances by Carol Haney & Matt Mattox.
Cast included: Mary Martin, George Wallace, Robin Bailey, Ethel Shutta, Jack DeLon, Imelda DeMartin.
Principal songs: Waitin' for the Evening Train; When You're Far Away from New York Town; I Still Look at You that Way; Before I Kiss the World Goodbye; Where You Are.
Recorded Version
RCA LSO 1083 (O.C.).
     Not off the top shelf.

DOROTHY FIELDS
Lyricist

For other musicals with books co-authored by Miss Fields, see Let's Face It!, Something for the Boys, Mexican Hayride *under Cole Porter;* Annie Get Your Gun *under Irving Berlin.*

BLACKBIRDS OF 1928
Opened: May 9, 1928, Liberty Th.
518 performances.
Sketches uncredited; music by Jimmy McHugh.
Produced & directed by Lew Leslie.
Cast included: Adelaide Hall, Bill Robinson,

Aida Ward, Tim Moore, Elisabeth Welch, Mantan Moreland, Lois Deppe, Cecil Mack Choir.
Principal songs: Diga Diga Doo; Doin' the New Low-Down; I Can't Give You Anything but Love; I Must Have that Man; Porgy.
Recorded Version
Columbia OL 6770 (O.C.).
  Original cast stars Bill Robinson & Adelaide Hall are joined by Ethel Waters, the Mills Brothers, & the orchestras of Duke Ellington, Cab Calloway & Don Redman. An indispensable reissue.

HELLO, DADDY
Opened: Dec. 26, 1928, Manfield Th.
198 *performances.*
Book by Herbert Fields; music by Jimmy McHugh.
Produced by Lew Fields; directed by John Murray Anderson & Alexander Leftwich; dances by Busby Berkeley & Buddy Bradley.
Cast included: Lew Fields, Betty Starbuck, Allen Kearns, Mary Lawlor, George Hassell, Wilfred Clark.
Principal songs: As Long as We're in Love; Futuristic Rhythm; Let's Sit and Talk About You.

INTERNATIONAL REVUE
Opened: Feb. 25, 1930, Majestic Th.
95 *performances.*
Sketches by Nat Dorfman, Lew Leslie; music by Jimmy McHugh.
Produced by Leslie; directed by Leslie & Edward Clark Lilley; dances by Busby Berkeley & Harry Crosley.
Cast included: Gertrude Lawrence, Harry Richman, Jack Pearl, Argentinita, Anton Dolin, Moss & Fontana, Florence Moore.
Principal songs: Exactly Like You; On The Sunny Side of the Street; Cinderella Brown.

THE VANDERBILT REVUE
Opened: Nov. 5, 1930, Vanderbilt Th.
13 *performances.*
Sketches by Kenyon Nicholson, Ellis Jones, Sig Herzig, Edwin Gilbert & Arthur Burns, James Coghlan; Fields music by Jimmy McHugh; music & lyrics also by Jacques Fray & Edward Eliscu, Mario Braggiotti & E. Y. Harburg, Cole Porter, Ned Washington, Michael Cleary & Herb Magidson.
Produced by Lew Fields & Lyle D. Andrews; directed by Fields & Theodore Hammerstein; dances by John Lonergan & Jack Haskell.
Cast included: Lulu McConnell, Joe Penner, Evelyn Hoey, Richard Lane, Jacques Fray & Mario Braggiotti, Franker Woods, Francesca Braggiotti, Gus Schilling, Olga Markoff, Dorothy Dixon, Teddy Walters.
Principal Fields-McHugh songs: Blue Again; Button Up Your Heart.

STARS IN YOUR EYES
(*See* Arthur Schwartz)

UP IN CENTRAL PARK
(*See* Sigmund Romberg)

ARMS AND THE GIRL
Opened: Feb. 2, 1950, 46th St. Th.
134 *performances.*
Book with Herbert Fields & Rouben Mamoulian; music by Morton Gould.
Produced by The Theatre Guild & Anthony Brady Farrell; directed by Rouben Mamoulian; dances by Michael Kidd.
Cast included: Nanette Fabray, Georges Guetary, Pearl Bailey, John Conte, Florenz Ames, Seth Arnold, Onna White, Peter Gennaro.
Principal songs: That's What I Told Him Last Night; I Like It Here; That's My Fella; A Cow and a Plough and a Frau; Nothin' for Nothin'; You Kissed Me; There Must Be Somethin' Better than Love.
Recorded Version
Columbia X 14879 (O.C.).
  A tale set during the American Revolution inspired some charming music & deft lyrics.

A TREE GROWS IN BROOKLYN
(*See* Arthur Schwartz).

BY THE BEAUTIFUL SEA
(*See* Arthur Schwartz).

REDHEAD
Opened: Feb. 5, 1959, 46th St. Th.
452 *performances.*
Book with Herbert Fields, Sidney Sheldon, David Shaw; music by Albert Hague.
Produced by Robert Fryer & Lawrence Carr; directed by Bob Fosse.
Cast included: Gwen Verdon, Richard Kiley, Leonard Stone, Doris Rich, Cynthia Latham, William LeMassena, Buzz Miller.
Principal songs: Just for Once; Merely Marvelous; The Uncle Sam Rag; 'Erbie Fitch's Twitch; My Girl Is Just Enough Woman for Me; Look Who's in Love; The Right Finger of My Left Hand.
Recorded Version
RCA LSO 1104 (O.C.).
  A worthy addition to anyone's original-cast LP library.

SWEET CHARITY
(*See* Cy Coleman).

SEESAW
(*See* Cy Coleman).

Chapter Fourteen
VERNON DUKE
Composer

THE GARRICK GAIETIES
Opened: June 4, 1930, Guild Th.
170 *performances* (*for 2 editions*).
Sketches by Carroll Carroll, Sally Humason, Benjamin M. Kaye, Newman Levy, Gretchen Damrosch Finletter, Leo Poldine, Landon Herrick, Louis M. Simon & Sterling Holloway; Duke lyrics by E. Y. Harburg, Ira

Gershwin, Newman Levy; music & lyrics also by Richard Myers & Edward Eliscu, Charles M. Schwab & Henry Myers, Ned Lehak & Allen Boretz; Willard Robison, Thomas McKnight, Kay Swift & Paul James (James P. Warburg), Marc Blitzstein, Everett Miller & John Mercer, Peter Nolan & Josiah Titzell, Harold Goldman.
Produced by The Theatre Guild; directed by Philip Loeb; dances by Olin Howard.
Cast included: Albert Carroll, Edith Meiser, Philip Loeb, Sterling Holloway, Nan Blackstone, Ruth Chorpenning, Hildegarde Halliday, William Tannen, Roger Stearns, James Norris, Imogene Coca, Ray Heatherton, Ted Fetter, Otto Hulet. (For 2nd edition, which opened Oct. 16, 1930, following added: Rosalind Russell, Katherine Carrington, Donald Burr, Edgar Stehli.)
Principal Duke-Harburg songs: I Am Only Human After All (lyric with Ira Gershwin); Too Too Divine.

WALK A LITTLE FASTER
Opened: Dec. 7, 1932, St. James Th.
119 *performances.*
Sketches by S. J. Perelman, Robert MacGunigle; lyrics by E. Y. Harburg.
Produced by Courtney Burr; directed by Monty Woolley; dances by Albertina Rasch.
Cast included: Beatrice Lillie, Bobby Clark & Paul McCullough, Dave & Dorothy Fitzgibbon, Evelyn Hoey, Donald Burr, Dorothy McNulty (Penny Singleton), John Hundley, Edgar Fairchild & Ralph Rainger (duo-pianists).
Principal songs: That's Life; April in Paris; So Nonchalant; Speaking of Love; Where Have We Met Before?; A Penny for Your Thoughts.

ZIEGFELD FOLLIES
Opened: Jan. 4, 1934, Winter Garden
182 *performances.*
Sketches by H. I. Phillips, David Freedman, David Turgend, Fred Allen; Duke lyrics by E. Y. Harburg; music & lyrics also by Peter DeRose & Billy Hill, Joe Meyer, Billy Rose & Ballard Macdonald, Dana Suesse, Richard Myers, Sam Pokrass.
Produced by Mrs. Florenz Ziegfeld (Billie Burke) & Messrs. Shubert (uncredited); directed by Bobby Connolly & Edward Clark Lilley; dances by Robert Alton.
Cast included: Fannie Brice, Willie & Eugene Howard, Jane Froman, Everett Marshall, Vilma & Buddy Ebsen, Eve Arden, Cherry & June Preisser, Patricia Bowman, Victor Morley, Vivian Janis, Don Ross, Oliver Wakefield.
Principal Duke-Harburg songs: Water Under the Bridge; I Like the Likes of You; Suddenly; What Is There to Say?

ZIEGFELD FOLLIES
Opened: Jan. 30, 1936, Winter Garden
115 *performances.*
Reopened: Sept. 14, 1936, Winter Garden.

112 *performances.*
Sketches by David Freedman; lyrics by Ira Gershwin.
Produced by Lee Shubert; directed by John Murray Anderson & Edward Clark Lilley; dances by Robert Alton & George Balanchine.
Cast included: Fannie Brice, Josephine Baker, Bob Hope, Gertrude Niesen, Hugh O'Connell, Harriet Hoctor, Eve Arden, Judy Canova, Cherry & June Preisser, John Hoysradt (John Hoyt), Nicholas Brothers, Duke McHale, Stan Kavanaugh, Ben Yost Varsity 8.
Reopened cast included: Fannie Brice, Bobby Clark, Jane Pickens, Ruth Harrison & Alex Fisher, Cherry & June Preisser, Stan Kavanaugh, Gypsy Rose Lee, Cass Daley, Hugh Cameron, Ben Yost Varsity 8.
Principal songs: Island in the West Indies; Words Without Music; That Moment of Moments; I Can't Get Started.

THE SHOW IS ON
Opened: Dec. 25, 1936, Winter Garden
237 *performances.*
Sketches by David Freedman, Moss Hart; Duke lyrics by Ted Fetter; music & lyrics also by Hoagy Carmichael & Stanley Adams, Arthur Schwartz & Howard Dietz, George & Ira Gershwin, Harold Arlen & E. Y. Harburg, Herman Hupfeld, Will Irwin & Norman Zeno, Richard Rodgers & Lorenz Hart.
Produced by Messrs. Shubert; directed by Vincente Minnelli & Edward Clark Lilley; dances by Robert Alton.
Cast included: Beatrice Lillie, Bert Lahr, Reginald Gardiner, Mitzi Mayfair, Paul Haakon, Gracie Barrie, Charles Walters, Vera Allen, Robert Shafer, Jack McCauley, Evelyn Thawl, Ralph Riggs.
Principal Duke-Fetter songs: Now; Casanova.

CABIN IN THE SKY
Opened: Oct. 25, 1940, Martin Beck Th.
156 *performances.*
Book by Lynn Root; lyrics by John Latouche.
Produced by Albert Lewis & Vinton Freedley; directed by George Balanchine & Lewis.
Cast included: Ethel Waters, Todd Duncan, Dooley Wilson, Rex Ingram, Katherine Dunham, J. Rosamond Johnson, Helen Dowdy, Talley Beatty.
Principal songs: Taking a Chance on Love (lyric with Ted Fetter); Cabin in the Sky; Do What You Wanna Do; In My Old Virginia Home (on the River Nile); Love Turned the Light Out; Honey in the Honeycomb.
Recorded Version
Capitol SW 2073 (O.C.) (1964).
 Four new songs were added for the 1964 off-Broadway revival. Rosetta LeNoire and Ketty Lester headed the cast.

BANJO EYES
Opened: Dec. 25, 1941, Hollywood Th.
126 *performances.*

Book by Joe Quillan & Izzy Elinson; lyrics by John Latouche, additional lyrics by Harold Adamson.
Produced by Albert Lewis; directed by Hassard Short & Lewis; dances by Charles Walters.
Cast included: Eddie Cantor, Tony & Sally DeMarco, Lionel Stander, Audrey Christie, June Clyde, Ray Mayer, Morton & Virginia Mayo, Bill Johnson, Richard Rober, Jacqueline Susann, Adele Jergens, Shirl Thomas (Shirl Conway), Doris Dowling, Tommy Wonder.
Principal songs: A Nickel to My Name; Not a Care in the World; I'll Take the City; We're Having a Baby (Adamson).

THE LADY COMES ACROSS
Opened: Jan. 9, 1942, 44th St. Th.
3 performances.
Book by Fred Thompson & Dawn Powell; lyrics by John Latouche.
Produced by George Hale; directed by Romney Brent; dances by George Balanchine.
Cast included: Evelyn Wyckoff, Joe E. Lewis, Ronald Graham, Stiano Braggiotti, Gower Champion & Jeanne Tyler, Mischa Auer, Ruth Weston, Wynn Murray, Marc Platt, Morton L. Stevens, Hugh Martin, Ralph Blane, Lubov Rostova.
Principal songs: Summer Is A-Comin' In; You Took Me by Surprise; This Is Where I Came In.

JACKPOT
Opened: Jan. 13, 1944, Alvin Th.
69 performances.
Book by Guy Bolton, Sidney Sheldon, Ben Roberts; lyrics by Howard Dietz.
Produced by Vinton Freedley; directed by Roy Hargrave; dances by Lauretta Jefferson & Charles Weidman.
Cast included: Nanette Fabray, Allan Jones, Betty Garrett, Jerry Lester, Benny Baker, Mary Wickes, Wendell Corey, Billie Worth, Morton L. Stevens, Jacqueline Susann.
Principal songs: What Happened?; Sugarfoot; I've Got a One-Track Mind; There Are Yanks (from the Banks of the Wabash).

SADIE THOMPSON
Opened: Nov. 16, 1944, Alvin Th.
60 performances.
Book by Howard Dietz & Rouben Mamoulian; lyrics by Dietz.
Produced by A. P. Waxman; directed by Mamoulian; dances by Edward Caton.
Cast included: June Havoc, Lansing Hatfield, Ralph Dumke, Beatrice Kraft, Doris Patston, Milada Mladova.
Principal songs: The Love I Long For; Poor as a Church Mouse; When You Live on an Island.

TWO'S COMPANY
Opened: Dec. 15, 1952, Alvin Th.
90 performances.
Sketches mostly by Charles Sherman & Peter DeVries; lyrics by Ogden Nash, additional lyrics by Sammy Cahn.
Produced by James Russo & Michael Ellis; directed by John Murray Anderson & Jules Dassin; dances by Jerome Robbins.
Cast included: Bette Davis, Hiram Sherman, David Burns, Nora Kaye, Ellen Hanley, Oliver Wakefield, Bill Callahan, Stanley Prager, George S. Irving, Maria Karnilova, Buzz Miller, Peter Kelley, Tina Louise, Ralph Linn.
Principal songs: It Just Occurred to Me (Cahn); Roundabout; Out of the Clear Blue Sky; Haunted Hot Spot; Just Like a Man.
Recorded Version
RCA CBMI 2757 (O.C.).
    Bette Davis' foghorn tends to obscure the attractiveness of the words & music.

THE LITTLEST REVUE
Opened: May 22, 1956, Phoenix Th.
32 performances.
Sketches by Nat Hiken & Billy Friedberg, Mike Stewart, Bud McCreery, George Baxt, Allan Manings & Bob Van Scoyk, Eudora Welty; Duke lyrics by Ogden Nash; music & lyrics also by John Strauss, John Latouche & Kenward Elmslie, Sheldon Harnick, Charles Strouse & Lee Adams, Sol Berkowitz, Michael Brown.
Produced by T. Edward Hambleton & Norris Houghton with Ben Bagley; directed by Paul Lammers; dances by Charles Weidman.
Cast included: Joel Grey, Tammy Grimes, Charlotte Rae, Larry Storch, Beverly Bozeman, Dorothy Jarnac.
Principal Duke-Nash songs: Madly in Love; I Want to Fly Now and Pay Later; You're Far from Wonderful; Love Is Still in Town; Good Little Girls (lyric by Sammy Cahn); Summer Is A-Comin' In (lyric by Latouche).
Recorded Version
Painted Smiles 1361 (O.C.).
    An especially bright, inventive revue score.

HAROLD ARLEN
Composer
EARL CARROLL VANITIES
(8th Edition)
Opened: July 1, 1930, New Amsterdam Th.
215 performances.
Sketches by Eddie Welch & Eugene Conrad; Arlen lyrics by Ted Koehler; music & lyrics also by Jay Gorney & E. Y. Harburg.
Produced by Carroll; directed by Carroll & Priestley Morrison; dances by LeRoy Prinz.
Cast included: Jimmy Savo, Jack Benny, Herb Williams, Harry Stockwell, Patsy Kelly, John Hale, Thelma White, Colette Sisters, Faith Bacon.
Principal Arlen-Koehler songs: Out of a Clear Blue Sky; Hittin' the Bottle; The March of Time.

YOU SAID IT
Opened: Jan. 19, 1931, 46th St. Th.
192 performances.

Book by Jack Yellen & Sid Silvers; lyrics by Yellen.
Produced by Yellen & Lou Holtz; directed by John Harwood; dances by Danny Dare.
Cast included: Lou Holtz, Mary Lawlor, Stanley Smith, Lyda Roberti, Benny Baker.
Principal songs: Sweet and Hot; You Said It; Learn to Croon; If He Really Loves Me; While You Are Young; It's Different With Me.

LIFE BEGINS AT 8:40
Opened: Aug. 27, 1934, Winter Garden
237 *performances.*
Sketches by David Freedman, H. I. Phillips, Alan Baxter, Henry Clapp Smith, Ira Gershwin & E. Y. Harburg, Frank Gabrielson; lyrics by Gershwin & Harburg.
Produced by Messrs. Shubert; directed by John Murray Anderson & Philip Loeb; dances by Robert Alton & Charles Weidman.
Cast included: Bert Lahr, Ray Bolger, Luella Gear, Frances Williams, Dixie Dunbar, Earl Oxford, Brian Donlevy, Robert Wildhack, Josephine Huston, James MacColl.
Principal songs: Shoein' the Mare; You're a Builder-Upper; Things; Fun to Be Fooled; What Can You Say in a Love Song?; Let's Take a Walk Around the Block; I Couldn't Hold My Man.

HOORAY FOR WHAT!
Opened: Dec. 1, 1937, Winter Garden
200 *performances.*
Book by Howard Lindsay & Russel Crouse; lyrics by E. Y. Harburg.
Produced by Messrs. Shubert; directed by Vincente Minnelli & Lindsay; dances by Robert Alton & Agnes de Mille.
Cast included: Ed Wynn, Jack Whiting, June Clyde, Vivian Vance, Paul Haakon, Leo Chalzel, Ruthanna Boris, Meg Mundy.
Principal songs: I've Gone Romantic on You; God's Country; Moanin' in the Mornin'; Down with Love; In the Shade of the New Apple Tree.

BLOOMER GIRL
Opened: Oct. 5, 1944, Shubert Th.
654 *performances.*
Book by Sig Herzig & Fred Saidy; lyrics by E. Y. Harburg.
Produced by John C. Wilson with Nat Goldstone; directed by E. Y. Harburg & William Schorr; dances by Agnes de Mille.
Cast included: Celeste Holm, David Brooks, Dooley Wilson, Joan McCracken, Mabel Taliaferro, Richard Huey, Toni Hart, Matt Briggs, Joe E. Marks, Margaret Douglass, Herbert Ross.
Principal songs: When the Boys Come Home; The Eagle and Me; Right as the Rain; Sunday in Cicero Falls; Evelina; It Was Good Enough for Grandma; The Rakish Young Man with the Whiskers; I Got a Song; T'morra, T'morra.
Recorded Version

MCA 2072 (O.C.).
The Civil War, slavery and women's rights are all dealt with in this attractive period score.

ST. LOUIS WOMAN
Opened: Mar. 30, 1946, Martin Beck Th.
113 *performances.*
Book by Arna Bontemps & Countee Cullen; lyrics by Johnny Mercer.
Produced by Edward Gross; directed by Rouben Mamoulian; dances by Charles Walters.
Cast included: Harold & Fayard Nicholas, Pearl Bailey, Rex Ingram, Ruby Hill, June Hawkins, Juanita Hall, Lorenzo Fuller, Herbert Coleman.
Principal songs: Come Rain or Come Shine; Legalize My Name; Any Place I Hang My Hat Is Home; Cakewalk Your Lady; Sleep Peaceful, Mr. Used-to-Be; Leavin' Time; A Woman's Prerogative; I Had Myself a True Love; Ridin' on the Moon.
Recorded Version
Capitol DW 2742 (O.C.).
A recognized classic in the field.

HOUSE OF FLOWERS
Opened: Dec. 30, 1954, Alvin Th.
165 *performances.*
Book by Truman Capote; lyrics by Capote & Arlen.
Produced by Saint Subber; directed by Peter Brook; dances by Herbert Ross.
Cast included: Pearl Bailey, Diahann Carroll, Juanita Hall, Ray Walston, Dino DiLuca, Rawn Spearman, Geoffrey Holder, Ada Moore, Enid Mosier, Dolores Harper, Frederick O'Neal, Don Redman, Carmen DeLavallade, Alvin Ailey, Arthur Mitchell.
Principal songs: A Sleepin' Bee; Bamboo Cage; Two Ladies in de Shade of de Banana Tree; I'm Gonna Leave Off Wearin' My Shoes; Has I Let You Down?; I Never Has Seen Snow; House of Flowers.
Recorded Versions
Columbia COS 2320 (O.C.).
United Artists 5180 (O.C.) (1968).
Possibly Arlen's supreme achievement for the theatre. The U.A. album is worth getting to hear Josephine Premice sing "Somethin' Cold to Drink."

JAMAICA
Opened: Oct. 31, 1957, Imperial Th.
558 *performances.*
Book by E. Y. Harburg & Fred Saidy; lyrics by Harburg.
Produced by David Merrick; directed by Robert Lewis; dances by Jack Cole.
Cast included: Lena Horne, Ricardo Montalban, Josephine Premice, Adelaide Hall, Joe Adams, Ossie Davis, Erik Rhodes, Augustine Rios, Ethel Ayler, Hugh Bryant.
Principal songs: Savannah; Pretty to Walk With; Push de Button; Cocoanut Sweet; Pity the Sunset; Take It Slow, Joe; Ain't It de

Truth?; Leave the Atom Alone; Napoleon; I Don't Think I'll End It All Today; Little Biscuit.
Recorded Version
RCA LSO 1103 (O.C.).
 Arlen's melodic & rhythmic gifts are amply displayed here.

SARATOGA
Opened: Dec. 7, 1959, Winter Garden
80 *performances.*
Book by Morton DaCosta; lyrics by Johnny Mercer.
Produced by Robert Fryer; directed by DaCosta; dances by Ralph Beaumont.
Cast included: Howard Keel, Carol Lawrence, Odette Myrtil, Edith King, Warde Donovan, Carol Brice, Tun Tun, Truman Gaige, Augie Rios, Virginia Capers.
Principal songs: Petticoat High; A Game of Poker; Love Held Lightly; You or No One; The Man in My Life; Saratoga; Why Fight This? (music & lyric by Mercer).
Recorded Version
RCA LSO 1051 (O.C.).
 The score ably captures the florid atmosphere of the story.

BURTON LANE
Composer

EARL CARROLL VANITIES
(9th Edition)
Opened: Aug. 27, 1931, Earl Carroll Th.
278 *performances.*
Sketches by Ralph Spence & Eddie Welch; Lane lyrics by Harold Adamson; music & lyrics also by Cliff Friend, Ray Klages, Jack Meskill & Vincent Rose, Charlotte Kent, Max & Nathaniel Lief & Michael Cleary.
Produced by Earl Carroll; directed by Edgar MacGregor; dances by George Hale & Gluck Sandor.
Cast included: Will Mahoney, Lillian Roth, Mitchell & Durant, William Demarest, Milton Watson, Helen Lynd, Lucille Page, Slate Brothers.
Principal Lane-Adamson songs: Have a Heart; Heigh-Ho, the Gang's All Here.

HOLD ON TO YOUR HATS
Opened: Sept. 11, 1940, Shubert Th.
158 *performances.*
Book by Guy Bolton, Matt Brooks, Eddie Davis; lyrics by E. Y. Harburg.
Produced by Al Jolson & George Hale; directed by Edgar MacGregor; dances by Catherine Littlefield.
Cast included: Al Jolson, Martha Raye, Jack Whiting, Bert Gordon, Arnold Moss, Gil Lamb, Joseph Vitale, Russ Brown, Jinx Falkenburg, Eunice Healey, Margaret Irving, Joanne Marshall (Joanne Dru), Constance Dowling, Joyce Matthews.
Principal songs: The World Is in My Arms; Would You Be So Kindly?; Don't Let It Get

You Down; There's a Great Day Coming Mañana.
Recorded Version
Painted Smiles 1372 (S.C.)
 Helen Gallagher, Carleton Carpenter, & Arthur Siegel head a cast that captures the score's breezy charm.

LAFFING ROOM ONLY
Opened: Dec. 23, 1944, Winter Garden
233 *performances.*
Sketches by Ole Olsen & Chic Johnson, Eugene Conrad; lyrics by Lane.
Produced by Messrs. Shubert & Olsen & Johnson; directed by John Murray Anderson & Edward Cline; dances by Robert Alton.
Cast included: Olsen & Johnson, Betty Garrett, Frank Libuse, Mata & Hari, J. C. McCord, Lou Wills, Jr., William Archibald, Willie West & McGinty; Fred Waring Glee Club, Kathryn Lee.
Principal songs: Feudin' and Fightin' (lyric with Al Dubin); This Is as Far as I Go.

FINIAN'S RAINBOW
Opened: Jan. 10, 1947, 46th St. Th.
725 *performances.*
Book by E. Y. Harburg & Fred Saidy; lyrics by Harburg.
Produced by Lee Sabinson & William R. Katzell; directed by Bretaigne Windust; dances by Michael Kidd.
Cast included: Ella Logan, Albert Sharpe, Donald Richards, David Wayne, Anita Alvarez, Robert Pitkin, Lorenzo Fuller, J. C. McCord, Lyn Murray Singers.
Principal songs: This Time of the Year; How Are Things in Glocca Morra?; If This Isn't Love; Look to the Rainbow; Old Devil Moon; Something Sort of Grandish; Necessity; When the Idle Poor Become the Idle Rich; When I'm Not Near the Girl I Love; That Great Come-and-Get-It Day; The Begat.
Recorded Versions
Columbia CS 2080 (O.C.).
RCA LSO 1057 (O.C.) (1960).
Warner 2550 (F.V.) (1968).
 Though Columbia's original cast is still something sort of grandish, there are winning performances on RCA by Jeannie Carson & Howard Morris, & on Warner by Fred Astaire & Petulia Clark.

ON A CLEAR DAY YOU CAN SEE FOREVER
Opened: Oct. 17, 1965, Mark Hellinger Th.
280 *performances.*
Book & lyrics by Alan Jay Lerner.
Produced by Lerner; directed by Robert Lewis; dances by Herbert Ross.
Cast included: Barbara Harris, John Cullum, Titos Vandis, William Daniels, Clifford David, Rae Allen, Michael Lewis, Gerry Matthews, Byron Webster.
Principal songs: On a Clear Day (You Can See Forever); On the S. S. Bernard Cohn; She Wasn't You; Melinda; What Did I Have that I Don't Have; Come Back to Me; Wait Till We're Sixty-Five.

Recorded Versions
RCA LSOD 2006 (O.C.).
Columbia AS 30086 (F.V.) (1970).
    A superior score better served by the original cast than by the illmatched Streisand-Montand combination.

CARMELINA
Opened: April 8, 1979, St. James Th.
17 performances.
Book by Alan Jay Lerner & Joseph Stein; lyrics by Lerner.
Produced by Roger L. Stevens, J. W. Fisher, Joan Cullman; directed by José Ferrer; dances by Peter Gennaro.
Cast included: Georgia Brown, Cesare Siepi, Gordon Ramsey, Howard Ross, John Michael King, Virginia Martin, Jossie DeGuzman, Marc Jordan, David Thomas.
Principal songs: It's Time for a Love Song; Someone in April; Yankee Doodles Are Coming to Town; One More Walk Around the Garden; Carmelina; The Image of Me; I'm a Woman.
Recorded Version
Original Cast 7921 (O.C.).
    In a traditional but still appealing vein.

E. Y. HARBURG
Lyricist

EARL CARROLL SKETCHBOOK
Opened: July 1, 1929, Earl Carroll Th.
400 performances.
Sketches by Earl Carroll, Eddie Cantor, Sidney Skolsky, Eddie Welch; Harburg music by Jay Gorney; music & lyrics also by Vincent Rose, Charles & Harry Tobias, Ted Snyder & Benny Davis, Arnold Johnson & Irving Kahal, Abner Silver.
Produced by Carroll; directed by Carroll & Edgar MacGregor; dances by LeRoy Prinz.
Cast included: Will Mahoney, William Demarest, The Three Sailors, Patsy Kelly, George Givot, Dorothy Britton, Don Howard, Faith Bacon.
Principal Harburg-Gorney songs: Kinda Cute; Like Me Less, Love Me More; Crashing the Golden Gate.

THE GARRICK GAIETIES
(*See* Vernon Duke)

EARL CARROLL VANITIES
(8th Edition)
Opened: July 1, 1930, New Amsterdam Th.
215 performances.
Sketches by Eddie Welch & Eugene Conrad; Harburg music by Jay Gorney; music & lyrics also by Harold Arlen & Ted Koehler.
Produced by Carroll; directed by Carroll & Priestley Morrison; dances by LeRoy Prinz.
Cast included: Jimmy Savo, Jack Benny, Herb Williams, Harry Stockwell, Patsy Kelly, John Hale, Thelma White, Colette Sisters, Faith Bacon.

Principal Harburg-Gorney songs: I Came to Life; Ring Out the Blues.

BALLYHOO OF 1932
Opened: Sept. 6, 1932, 44th St. Th.
95 performances.
Sketches by Norman Anthony; music by Lewis Gensler.
Produced by Anthony, Gensler, Bobby Connolly, Russell Patterson; directed by Anthony & Gensler; dances by Connolly.
Cast included: Willie & Eugene Howard, Jeanne Aubert, Lulu McConnell, Bob Hope, Paul Hartman, Donald Stewart, Vera Marche.
Principal songs: Riddle Me This; Falling Off the Wagon; How Do You Do It?; Thrill Me.

AMERICANA
Opened: Oct. 5, 1932, Shubert Th.
77 performances.
Sketches by J. P. McEvoy; Harburg music by Jay Gorney, Richard Myers, Harold Arlen, Burton Lane, Vernon Duke; music & lyrics also by Henry Souvaine & Johnny Mercer.
Produced by Lee Shubert; directed by Harold Johnsrud; dances by John Boyle & Charles Weidman.
Cast included: George Givot, Albert Carroll, Lloyd Nolan, Georgie Tapps, Charles Weidman Dancers (incl. José Limon, Letitia Ide), Doris Humphrey Group, Rex Weber, Francetta Malloy, Peggy Cartwright.
Principal Harburg songs: Brother, Can You Spare a Dime? (Gorney); Let Me Match My Private Life with Yours (Duke); Whistling for a Kiss (Mercer-Myers); You're Not Pretty but You're Mine (Lane); Satan's Li'l Lamb (Mercer-Arlen).

WALK A LITTLE FASTER
(*See* Vernon Duke).

ZIEGFELD FOLLIES (1934)
(*See* Vernon Duke).

LIFE BEGINS AT 8:40
(*See* Harold Arlen).

HOORAY FOR WHAT!
(*See* Harold Arlen).

HOLD ON TO YOUR HATS
(*See* Burton Lane).

BLOOMER GIRL
(*See* Harold Arlen).

FINIAN'S RAINBOW
(*See* Burton Lane).

FLAHOOLEY
Opened: May 14, 1951, Broadhurst Th.
40 performances.
Book by Harburg & Fred Saidy; music by Sammy Fain.
Produced by Cheryl Crawford, Harburg & Saidy; directed by Harburg & Saidy; dances by Helen Tamiris.
Cast included: Yma Sumac, Ernest Truex, Irwin Corey, Jerome Courtland, Edith

Atwater, Barbara Cook, Bil & Cora Baird, Lulu Bates, Fay DeWitt, Marilyn Ross, Louis Nye, Nehemiah Persoff, Laurel Shelby.
Principal songs: You Too Can Be a Puppet; Here's to Your Illusions; Who Says There Ain't No Santa Claus?; The World Is Your Balloon; He's Only Wonderful; Jump, Li'l Chillun; The Springtime Cometh.
Recorded Version
Capitol T 11649 (O.C.).
    An unappreciated score of great charm.

JAMAICA
(*See* Harold Arlen).

THE HAPPIEST GIRL IN THE WORLD
Opened: Apr. 3, 1961, Martin Beck Th.
96 *performances.*
Book by Fred Saidy & Henry Myers; music by Jacques Offenbach.
Produced by Lee Guber; directed by Cyril Ritchard; dances by Dania Krupska.
Cast included: Cyril Ritchard, Janice Rule, Dran Seitz, Bruce Yarnell, Ted Thurston, Michael Kermoyan, Lu Leonard, Lainie Kazan, Maura K. Wedge.
Principal songs: The Happiest Girl in the World; Shall We Say Farewell?; Vive la Virtue; Adrift on a Star; Five Minutes of Spring.
Recorded Version
Columbia KOS 2050 (O.C.).
    The familiar Offenbach melodies seem out of place in this musical approach to the Lysistrata legend.

DARLING OF THE DAY
(*See* Jule Styne).

Chapter Fifteen
HAROLD ROME

Composer-lyricist

PINS AND NEEDLES
Opened: Nov. 27, 1937, Labor Stage.
1,108 *performances.*
Sketches by Charles Friedman, Arthur Arent, Marc Blitzstein, Emanuel Eisenberg, David Gregory.
Produced by the I.L.G.W.U.; directed by Friedman; dances by Gluck Sandor.
Cast included: Members of the I.L.G.W.U.
Principal songs: Sing Me a Song with Social Significance; Sunday in the Park; One Big Union for Two; Chain Store Daisy; Nobody Makes a Pass at Me; It's Better with a Union Man; Doin' the Reactionary.
Recorded Version
Columbia AOS 2210 (S.C.).
    The best-remembered songs from all editions have been preserved by Barbra Streisand, Rose Marie Jun, Jack Carroll & Mr. Rome himself.

SING OUT THE NEWS
Opened: Sept. 24, 1938, Music Box Th.

105 *performances.*
Sketches by George S. Kaufman & Moss Hart (uncredited).
Produced by Max Gordon, Kaufman & Hart; directed by Charles Friedman; dances by Ned McGurn, Dave Gould, Charles Walters.
Cast included: Philip Loeb, Hiram Sherman, Mary Jane Walsh, Will Geer, Dorothy Fox, Michael Loring, Joey Faye, Hazel Scott, Richard Huey, Rex Ingram, June Allyson.
Principal songs: F.D.R. Jones; My Heart Is Unemployed; How Long Can Love Keep Laughing?; Yip-Ahoy; Plaza 6-9423.

LET FREEDOM SING
Opened: Oct. 5, 1942, Longacre Th.
8 *performances.*
Sketches by Sam Locke; lyrics & music also by Marc Blitzstein, Henry Myers, Edward Eliscu & Jay Gorney, Hy Zarat & Walter Kent, Roslyn Harvey & Lou Cooper, Lewis Allan & Earl Robinson.
Produced by Youth Theatre; directed by Joseph Pevney & Robert H. Gordon; dances by Dan Eckley.
Cast included: Mitzi Green, Berni Gould, Lee Sullivan, Betty Garrett, Mordecai Bauman, Phil Leeds.
Principal Rome songs: It's Fun to Be Free; Little Miss Victory Jones.

CALL ME MISTER
Opened: Apr. 18, 1946, National Th.
734 *performances.*
Sketches by Arnold Auerbach, Arnold Horwitt.
Produced by Melvyn Douglas & Herman Levin; directed by Robert H. Gordon; dances by John Wray.
Cast included: Betty Garrett, Jules Munshin, Bill Callahan, Lawrence Winters, George Hall, Harry Clark, Paula Bane, Maria Karnilova, Alan Manson, Danny Scholl, Betty Lou Holland, Chandler Cowles, George S. Irving.
Principal songs: Goin' Home Train; Little Surplus Me; The Red Ball Express; Military Life; The Face on the Dime; Yuletide Park Avenue; South America, Take It Away; Along with Me; When We Meet Again; Call Me Mister.
Recorded Version
Columbia X 14877 (O.C.).
    Rome's satirical yet goodnatured score remains a delight.

ALIVE AND KICKING
Opened: Jan. 17, 1950, Winter Garden
46 *performances.*
Sketches by Ray Golden, Henry Morgan, Jerome Chodorov, Joseph Stein & Will Glickman, Mort Stuart, I.A.L. Diamond; lyrics & music also by Paul Francis Webster, Ray Golden, Hoagy Carmichael, Sonny Burke, Sammy Fain, Irma Jurist & Leonard Gershe.
Produced by William R. Katzell & Ray

Golden; directed by Robert H. Gordon; dances by Jack Cole.
Cast included: David Burns, Lenore Lonergan, Jack Gilford, Carl Reiner, Bobby Van, Jack Cole, Gwen Verdon, Fay DeWitt, Jack Cassidy, Jean Bal, Laurel Shelby.
Principal Rome songs: Love, It Hurts So Good; Cry Baby Cry; French with Tears.

MICHAEL TODD'S PEEP SHOW
Opened: June 28, 1950, Winter Garden
278 *performances.*
Sketches by Bobby Clark, H. I. Phillips, William Roos, Billy K. Wells; lyrics & music also by Chakraband & Bhumibol, Herb Magidson & Sammy Fain, Raymond Scott, Dan Shapiro & Sammy Stept, Bob Hilliard & Jule Styne.
Produced by Michael Todd; directed by Hassard Short & Bobby Clark; dances by James Starbuck.
Cast included: Lina Romay, Lilly Christine, Clifford Guest, "Bozo" Snyder, "Hi Wilberforce" Conley, Peiro Brothers, Corrine & Tito Valdez, "Red" Marshall, "Peanuts" Mann, Art Carroll.
Principal Rome songs: Gimme the Shimmy; Pocketful of Dreams; I Hate a Parade.

BLESS YOU ALL
Opened: Dec. 14, 1950, Mark Hellinger Th.
84 *performances.*
Sketches by Arnold Auerbach.
Produced by Herman Levin & Oliver Smith; directed by John C. Wilson; dances by Helen Tamiris.
Cast included: Mary McCarty, Jules Munshin, Pearl Bailey, Valerie Bettis, Donald Saddler, Robert Chisholm, Byron Palmer, Jane Harvey, Donald McKayle, Swen Swenson, Gene Barry, Garry Davis.
Principal songs: I Can Hear It Now; Little Things Mean So Much to Me; A Rose Is a Rose; Summer Dresses; You Never Know What Hit You.

WISH YOU WERE HERE
Opened: June 25, 1952, Imperial Th.
598 *performances.*
Book by Arthur Kober & Joshua Logan.
Produced by Leland Hayward & Logan; directed by Logan.
Cast included: Sheila Bond, Jack Cassidy, Patricia Marand, Sidney Armus, Paul Valentine, Harry Clark, Richard France, Florence Henderson, Tom Tryon, Larry Blyden, Frank Aletter, Mardi Bayne, Phyllis Newman, Stanley Grover, Reid Shelton, John Perkins, Sammy Smith.
Principal songs: Wish You Were Here; Shopping Around; Could Be; Summer Afternoon; Where Did the Night Go?; Don José of Far Rockaway; Goodbye Love.
Recorded Versions
RCA LSO 1108 (O.C.).
Stet DS 15015 (London O.C.) (1953).

This light, lyrical score may be enjoyed on both the Broadway & West End cast albums (latter with Shani Wallis, Elizabeth Larner & Bruce Trent).

FANNY
Opened: Nov. 4, 1954, Majestic Th.
888 *performances.*
Book by S. N. Behrman & Joshua Logan.
Produced by David Merrick & Logan; directed by Logan; dances by Helen Tamiris.
Cast included: Ezio Pinza, Walter Slezak, Florence Henderson, William Tabbert, Gerald Price, Nejla Ates, Alan Carney, Tani & Dran Seitz, Herbert Banke, Mohammed el Bakkar.
Principal songs: Never Too Late for Love; Octopus Song; Restless Heart; Why Be Afraid to Dance?; Welcome Home; I Have to Tell You; Fanny; To My Wife; Love Is a Very Light Thing; I Like You; Be Kind to Your Parents.
Recorded Version
RCA LSO 1015 (O.C.).
An ambitious, often moving work.

DESTRY RIDES AGAIN
Opened: Apr. 23, 1959, Imperial Th.
473 *performances.*
Book by Leonard Gershe.
Produced by David Merrick; directed by Michael Kidd.
Cast included: Andy Griffith, Dolores Gray, Scott Brady, Jack Prince, Libi Staiger, Swen Swenson, Marc Breaux, Don Crabtree, Rosetta LeNoire.
Principal songs: Hoop-de-Dingle; Ballad of the Gun; I Know Your Kind; Anyone Would Love You; Are You Ready, Gyp Watson?; That Ring on the Finger; Once Knew a Fella.
Recorded Version
Decca DL 79075 (O.C.).
Rome on the range.

I CAN GET IT FOR YOU WHOLESALE
Opened: Mar. 22, 1962, Shubert Th.
300 *performances.*
Book By Jerome Weidman.
Produced by David Merrick; directed by Arthur Laurents; dances by Herbert Ross.
Cast included: Lillian Roth, Elliott Gould, Sheree North, Harold Lang, Jack Kruschen, Ken LeRoy, Marilyn Cooper, Barbra Streisand, Bambi Linn, Luba Lisa.
Principal songs: When Gemini Meets Capricorn; The Sound of Money; Too Soon; Who Knows?; Have I Told You Lately?; Miss Marmelstein; A Funny Thing Happened.
Recorded Version
Columbia AKOS 2180 (O.C.).
The alternately tough and tender songs ably evoke the flavor of New York's Garment District in the 1930s.

THE ZULU AND THE ZAYDA
Opened: Nov. 10, 1965, Cort Th.
179 *performances.*
Play by Howard DaSilva & Felix Leon.

Produced by Theodore Mann & Dore Schary; directed by Schary.
Cast included: Menasha Skulnik, Ossie Davis, Louis Gossett, Joe Silver, Sarah Cunningham.
Principal songs: It's Good to Be Alive; Rivers of Tears; Zulu Love Song; Oisgetzaichnet.
Recorded Version
Columbia KOS 2880 (O.C.).
This "Play with Music" contains a dozen fine Harold Rome songs indigenous to both Zulu and Zayda.

Chapter Sixteen
KURT WEILL
Composer

THE THREEPENNY OPERA
Opened: Apr. 13, 1933, Empire Th.
12 *performances.*
Book & lyrics by Gifford Cochran & Jerrold Krimsky, adapted from the original by Bertolt Brecht.
Produced by John Krimsky & Cochran; directed by Francesco Von Mendelssohn.
Cast included: Steffi Duna, Robert Chisholm, Rex Weber, Rex Evans, Herbert Rudley, Burgess Meredith, George Heller, Harry Bellaver, Josephine Huston.
Principal songs: Legend of Mackie Messer; Wedding Song; Pirate Jenny; Soldier Song; Love Duet; Ballad of the Easy Life; Jealousy Duet; Song of the Aimlessness of Life.

JOHNNY JOHNSON
Opened: Nov. 19, 1936, 44th St. Th.
68 *performances.*
Play and lyrics by Paul Green.
Produced by the Group Theatre; directed by Lee Strasburg.
Cast included: Russell Collins, Roman Bohnen, Phoebe Brand, Sanford Meisner, Robert Lewis, Lee J. Cobb, Art Smith, Albert Van Dekker, Elia Kazan, Luther Adler, Jules (John) Garfield, Morris Carnovsky, Joseph Pevney, Will Lee.
Principal songs: Johnny's Song; O Heart of Love; Song of the Goddess; Oh the Rio Grande; Song of the Guns; Mon Ami, My Friend; Psychiatry Song.
Recorded Version
Heliodor (S) 25024 (S.C.).
Headed by Burgess Meredith, Lotte Lenya, Hiram Sherman & Evelyn Lear, a fine group of singers ably preserves the power of Weill's first American score.

KNICKERBOCKER HOLIDAY
Opened: Oct. 19, 1938, Ethel Barrymore Th.
168 *performances.*
Book & lyrics by Maxwell Anderson.
Produced by The Playwrights' Co.; directed by Joshua Logan; dances by Carl Randall & Edwin Denby.
Cast included: Walter Huston, Jeanne Madden, Ray Middleton, Richard Kollmar,
Mark Smith, Clarence Nordstrom, Howard Freeman, Robert Rounseville.
Principal songs: There's Nowhere to Go but Up; How Can You Tell an American?; September Song; It Never Was You; The Scars.

LADY IN THE DARK
Opened: Jan. 23, 1941, Alvin Th.
467 *performances.*
Book by Moss Hart; lyrics by Ira Gershwin.
Produced by Sam H. Harris; directed by Hassard Short & Hart; dances by Albertina Rasch.
Cast included: Gertrude Lawrence, Victor Mature, Macdonald Carey, Danny Kaye, Bert Lytell, Evelyn Wyckoff, Donald Randolph, Margaret Dale, Natalie Schafer, Virginia Peine, Nelson Barclift, Manfred Hecht.
Principal songs: Oh, Fabulous One; One Life to Live; Girl of the Moment; This Is New; The Princess of Pure Delight; My Ship; The Saga of Jenny; Tschaikowsky.
Recorded Versions
RCA LPV 503 (O.C.).
RCA LM 1882 (TV) (1954).
Columbia COS 2390 (S.C.).
The inimitable Miss Lawrence is heard on one side of the first album. The television adaptation features Ann Sothern & Carleton Carpenter; the Columbia studio version—the most complete—is headed by Risë Stevens, Adolph Green & John Reardon.

ONE TOUCH OF VENUS
Opened: Oct. 7, 1943, Imperial Th.
567 *performances.*
Book by S. J. Perelman & Ogden Nash; lyrics by Nash.
Produced by Cheryl Crawford & John Wildberg; directed by Elia Kazan; dances by Agnes de Mille.
Cast included: Mary Martin, Kenny Baker, John Boles, Paula Laurence, Teddy Hart, Sono Osato, Harry Clark, Lou Wills, Jr., Helen Raymond, Allyn Ann McLerie, Pearl Lang, Nelle Fisher, Jeff Warren.
Principal songs: One Touch of Venus; How Much I Love You; I'm a Stranger Here Myself; Speak Low; West Wind; Foolish Heart; The Trouble with Women; That's Him; Wooden Wedding.
Recorded Version
Decca DL 7 9122 (O.C.).
Bright, breezy, and well worth having.

THE FIREBRAND OF FLORENCE
Opened: Mar. 22, 1945, Alvin Th.
43 *performances.*
Book by Edwin Justus Mayer; lyrics by Ira Gershwin.
Produced by Max Gordon; directed by John Murray Anderson & John Haggott; dances by Catherine Littlefield.
Cast included: Earl Wrightson, Lotte Lenya, Melville Cooper, Marion Green, Bert Freed, Beverly Tyler, John (Jack) Cassidy, Ferdi

Hoffman, Billy (Dee) Williams.
Principal songs: Sing Me Not a Ballad; A Rhyme for Angela; The Cozy Nook Trio; You're Far Too Near Me; There'll Be Life, Love and Laughter.
Recorded Version
Mark56 721.

Ten pieces are performed by Gershwin & Weill in *I Love to Rhyme,* an album devoted to Ira's work.

STREET SCENE
Opened: Jan. 9, 1947, Adelphi Th.
148 *performances.*
Book by Elmer Rice; lyrics by Langston Hughes.
Produced by Dwight Deere Wiman & The Playwrights' Co.; directed by Charles Friedman; dances by Anna Sokolow.
Cast included: Norman Cordon, Anne Jeffreys, Polyna Stoska, Brian Sullivan, Hope Emerson, Irving Kaufman, Don Saxon, Sheila Bond, Danny Daniels, Juanita Hall.
Principal songs: I Got a Marble and a Star; Somehow I Never Could Believe; Ice Cream; Wrapped in a Ribbon and Tied in a Bow; Lonely House; Wouldn't You Like to Be on Broadway?; What Good Would the Moon Be?; Moon-Faced, Starry-Eyed; Remember that I Care; A Boy Like You; We'll Go Away Together.
Recorded Version
Columbia COL 4139 (O.C.).

Weill's most operatic American score is a notable & moving achievement.

LOVE LIFE
Opened: Oct. 7, 1948, 46th St. Th.
252 *performances.*
Book & lyrics by Alan Jay Lerner.
Produced by Cheryl Crawford; directed by Elia Kazan; dances by Michael Kidd.
Cast included: Nanette Fabray, Ray Middleton, Johnny Stewart, Jay Marshall, Lyle Bettger, Cheryl Archer.
Principal songs: Here I'll Stay; Progress; Green-Up Time; Economics; Susan's Dream; Mr. Right.

LOST IN THE STARS
Opened: Oct. 30, 1949, Music Box Th.
273 *performances.*
Book & lyrics by Maxwell Anderson.
Produced by The Playwrights' Co.; directed by Rouben Mamoulian.
Cast included: Todd Duncan, Leslie Banks, Inez Matthews, Warren Coleman, Sheila Guyse, Frank Roane, Herbert Coleman, Georgette Harvey, Robert McFerrin, Guy Spaull, William C. Smith.
Principal songs: The Hills of Ixipo; Thousands of Miles; Train to Johannesburg; The Little Grey House; Trouble Man; Lost in the Stars; Stay Well; Cry, the Beloved Country; Big Mole; A Bird of Paradise.
Recorded Version
MCA 2071 (O.C.).

A frequently impressive work, with dialogue included on the record to bridge the musical selections.

THE THREEPENNY OPERA
Opened: Mar. 10, 1954, Theatre de Lys.
95 *performances.*
Reopened: Sept. 20, 1955, Theatre de Lys.
2,611 *performances.*
Book & lyrics by Marc Blitzstein, adapted from the original by Bertolt Brecht.
Produced by Carmen Capalbo & Stanley Chase; directed by Capalbo.
Cast included: Lotte Lenya, Scott Merrill, Leon Lishner, Jo Sullivan, Charlotte Rae, Gerald Price, Beatrice Arthur.
Principal songs: The Ballad of Mack the Knife; Wedding Song; Pirate Jenny; Army Song; Love Song; Ballad of the Easy Life; Barbara Song; Jealousy Duet; Useless Song; Solomon Song.
Recorded Versions
MGM S 3121 (O.C.).
RCA LSO 1086 (F.V.) (1964).

In addition to the striking MGM release and the less than striking RCA soundtrack with Sammy Davis Jr., there are also recordings with the original German text by Bertolt Brecht: the 1928 Berlin cast (Telefunken 97012) & a complete 2-record version (Odyssey Y2 32977), both with Lotte Lenya, plus the original soundtrack of the above-listed film (London M 76004). In 1976 an even more acerbic translation by Ralph Manheim & John Willett featured Raul Julia & Ellen Greene (Columbia PS 34326).

Chapter Seventeen
RICHARD RODGERS
Composer

OSCAR HAMMERSTEIN II
Lyricist

All lyrics & books by Mr. Hammerstein unless otherwise noted. See separate section for all musicals by Mr. Hammerstein prior to his association with Mr. Rodgers.

OKLAHOMA!
Opened: Mar. 31, 1943, St. James Th.
2,212 *performances.*
Produced by The Theatre Guild; directed by Rouben Mamoulian; dances by Agnes de Mille.
Cast included: Betty Garde, Alfred Drake, Joan Roberts, Howard da Silva, Joseph Buloff, Celeste Holm, Lee Dixon, Katherine Sergava, Joan McCracken, Bambi Linn, George Church, Marc Platt, Ralph Riggs, Diana Adams, George S. Irving, Hayes Gordon.
Principal songs: Oh, What a Beautiful Mornin'; The Surrey with the Fringe on Top; Kansas City; I Cain't Say No; Many a New Day; People Will Say We're in Love; Pore

Jud; Out of My Dreams; All er Nothin'; The Farmer and the Cowman; Oklahoma.
Recorded Versions
MCA 2030 (O.C.).
Capitol SWAO 595 (F.V.) (1955).
Columbia OS 2610 (S.C.).
Harmony 11164 (S.C.).
Stanyan 10069 (London O.C.) (1947).
RCA CBL 1 3572 (O.C.) (1979).

The MCA album (originally on Decca 78s) started the original-cast album vogue in the U.S. Still irreplaceable, though the Capitol soundtrack (Gordon MacRae, Shirley Jones) & the Columbia (John Raitt, Florence Henderson) are better recorded. The low-priced Harmony, with Nelson Eddy & Kaye Ballard, is a good buy. Highlights sung by West End leads Howard Keel & Betty Jane Watson are on Stanyan. The RCA recording of the 1979 revival is the most complete.

CAROUSEL
Opened: Apr. 19, 1945, Majestic Th.
890 *performances.*
Produced by The Theatre Guild; directed by Rouben Mamoulian; dances by Agnes de Mille.
Cast included: John Raitt, Jan Clayton, Jean Darling, Christine Johnson, Jean Casto, Murvyn Vye, Eric Mattson, Bambi Linn, Peter Birch, Pearl Lang, Russell Collins, Robert Pagent, Iva Withers, Jay Velie.
Principal songs: Carousel Waltz; You're a Queer One, Julie Jordan; Mr. Snow; If I Loved You; June Is Bustin' Out All Over; Blow High Blow Low; When the Children Are Asleep; Soliloquy; A Real Nice Clambake; What's the Use of Wond'rin'; You'll Never Walk Alone.
Recorded Versions
MCA 2033 (O.C.).
Capitol SW 694 (F.V.) (1956).
RCA LSO 1114 (O.C.) (1965).
Columbia CSM 479 (TV) (1967).
RCA LPM 1048 (S.C.).
Command RS 843 (S.C.)
Possibly the greatest of all R&H scores. The MCA original cast version has been sonically superceded by the others, which are also more complete. Gordon MacRae & Shirley Jones are on the Capitol soundtrack, John Raitt & Eileen Christy on the RCA Lincoln Center revival, & Robert Goulet & Mary Grover on Columbia's specially-made set of the Armstrong TV production. Both the second RCA (Robert Merrill, Patrice Munsel) & the Command (Alfred Drake, Roberta Peters) studio versions are particularly well sung.

ALLEGRO
Opened: Oct. 10, 1947, Majestic Th.
315 *performances.*
Produced by The Theatre Guild; directed by Agnes de Mille.
Cast included: John Battles, Annamary Dickey, William Ching, John Conte, Muriel

O'Malley, Roberta Jonay, Lisa Kirk, Kathryn Lee, Harrison Muller, Edward Platt, Gloria Wills.
Principal songs: I Know It Can Happen Again; One Foot, Other Foot; A Fellow Needs a Girl; You Are Never Away; So Far; Money Isn't Everything; The Gentleman Is a Dope; Allegro.
Recorded Version
RCA CBM1 2758 (O.C.).
One of the team's least appreciated efforts, the score is still a must for show music buffs.

SOUTH PACIFIC
Opened: Apr. 7, 1949, Majestic Th.
1,925 *performances.*
Book with Joshua Logan.
Produced by Rodgers & Hammerstein, Leland Hayward & Logan; directed by Logan.
Cast included: Ezio Pinza, Mary Martin, Myron McCormick, William Tabbert, Juanita Hall, Betta St. John, Martin Wolfson, Harvey Stephens, Dickinson (Richard) Eastham, Biff McGuire, Sandra Deel, Mardi Bayne, Alex Nicol.
Principal songs: Dites-moi; A Cockeyed Optimist; Some Enchanted Evening; Bloody Mary; There Is Nothin' Like a Dame; Bali Ha'i; I'm Gonna Wash that Man Right Outa My Hair; A Wonderful Guy; Younger than Springtime; Happy Talk; Honey Bun; You've Got to Be Carefully Taught; This Nearly Was Mine.
Recorded Versions
Columbia S 32604 (O.C.).
RCA LSO 1032 (F.V.) (1958).
Columbia OS 3100 (O.C.) (1967).
Rodgers & Hammerstein's ever popular work is still heard at its best on the original cast recording. Columbia's 1967 edition (Florence Henderson, Giorgio Tozzi) is a closer competitor than the RCA soundtrack (Mitzi Gaynor, Giorgio Tozzi).

THE KING AND I
Opened: Mar. 29, 1951, St. James Th.
1,246 *performances.*
Produced by Rodgers & Hammerstein; directed by John van Druten; dances by Jerome Robbins.
Cast included: Gertrude Lawrence, Yul Brynner, Dorothy Sarnoff, Doretta Morrow, Larry Douglas, Johnny Stewart, John Juliano, Gemze de Lappe, Michiko, Yuriko, Gloria Marlowe, Leonard Graves, Stephanie Augustine.
Principal songs: I Whistle a Happy Tune; My Lord and Master; Hello, Young Lovers; March of the Siamese Children; A Puzzlement; Getting to Know You; We Kiss in a Shadow; Something Wonderful; I Have Dreamed; Shall We Dance?
Recorded Versions
MCA 2028 (O.C.).
Stet DS 15014 (London O.C.) (1953).
Capitol SW 740 (F.V.) (1957).
RCA LSO 1092 (O.C.) (1964).

RCA ABL1 2610 (O.C.) (1977).
Columbia OS 2640 (S.C.).

Yul Brynner is on MCA (with Gertrude
Lawrence), Capitol (Marni Nixon), & the
2nd RCA (Constance Towers). This last is the
most complete, though it lacks "The Small
House of Uncle Thomas" ballet, heard on
Columbia (Barbara Cook, Theodore Bikel).
The London cast (led by Valerie Hobson &
Herbert Lom) performs valiantly; the 1964
leads on RCA (Risë Stevens, Darren
McGavin) are vocally unsteady.

ME AND JULIET
Opened: May 28, 1953, Majestic Th.
358 *performances.*
Produced by Rodgers & Hammerstein;
directed by George Abbott; dances by Robert
Alton.
Cast included: Isabel Bigley, Bill Hayes, Joan
McCracken, Ray Walston, Mark Dawson,
Jackie Kelk, Arthur Maxwell, George S.
Irving, Helena Scott, Bob Fortier, Shirley
MacLaine, Michael King, Barbara Carroll
(pianist), Buzz Miller.
Principal songs: That's the Way It Happens;
Marriage Type Love; Keep It Gay; The Big
Black Giant; No Other Love; It's Me; We
Deserve Each Other; I'm Your Girl.
Recorded Version
RCA LSO 1098 (O.C.).
A light, attractive collection of songs.

PIPE DREAM
Opened: Nov. 30, 1955, Shubert Th.
246 *performances.*
Produced by Rodgers & Hammerstein;
directed by Harold Clurman; dances by Boris
Runanin.
Cast included: Helen Traubel, William
Johnson, Judy Tyler, G. D. (George)
Wallace, Mike Kellin, Ruby Braff
(trumpeter), Patricia Wilson, Steve Roland,
Temple Texas, Mildred Slavin, Louise Troy,
Ruth Kobart.
Principal songs: All Kinds of People;
Ev'rybody's Got a Home but Me; A Lopsided
Bus; Sweet Thursday; Suzy is a Good Thing;
All at Once You Love Her; Will You Marry
Me?; The Next Time It Happens.
Recorded Version
RCA LSO 1097 (O.C.).
The cast performs well, but this is one of
the least impressive of the masters'
achievements.

FLOWER DRUM SONG
Opened: Dec. 1, 1958, St. James Th.
601 *performances.*
Book with Joseph Fields.
Produced by Rodgers, Hammerstein & Fields;
directed by Gene Kelly; dances by Carol
Haney.
Cast included: Miyoshi Umeki, Pat Suzuki,
Larry Blyden, Juanita Hall, Ed Kenney, Keye
Luke, Arabella Hong, Jack Soo, Anita Ellis.

Principal songs: You Are Beautiful; A
Hundred Million Miracles; I Enjoy Being a
Girl; Like a God; Chop Suey; Don't Marry
Me; Grant Avenue; Love, Look Away;
Sunday; I Am Going to Like It Here.
Recorded Versions.
Columbia OS 2009 (O.C.).
Angel S 35886 (London O.C.) (1960).
MCA 2069 (F.V.) (1961).
Some charming music, well sung &
orchestrated. The English cast, headed by Yau
Shan Tung & Yama Saki, & the film cast,
headed by Miyoshi Umeki & Nancy Kwan,
have much to recommend.

THE SOUND OF MUSIC
Opened: Nov. 16, 1959, Lunt-Fontanne Th.
1,443 *performances.*
Book by Howard Lindsay & Russel Crouse.
Produced by Leland Hayward, Richard
Halliday, Rodgers & Hammerstein; directed
by Vincent J. Donehue; dances by Joe
Layton.
Cast included: Mary Martin, Theodore Bikel,
Patricia Neway, Kurt Kasznar, Marion
Marlowe, Lauri Peters, Muriel O'Malley,
Karen Shepard, Brian Davies, Joey
Heatherton.
Principal songs: The Sound of Music; Maria;
My Favorite Things; Do-Re-Mi; Sixteen
Going on Seventeen; The Lonely Goatherd; So
Long, Farewell; How Can Love Survive?;
Climb Ev'ry Mountain; Edelweiss.
Recorded Versions
Columbia S 32601 (O.C.).
RCA LSOD 2005 (F.V.) (1965).
Warner Bros. S 1377.
The sugary score is well treated by both the
original cast & film version, with the latter
dropping 3 songs & adding 2 new ones by
Rodgers alone. Warner offers the splendid-
sounding Trapp family.

NO STRINGS
Opened: Mar. 15, 1962, 54th St. Th.
580 *performances.*
Book By Samuel Taylor; lyrics by Rodgers.
Produced by Rodgers; directed by Joe Layton.
Cast included: Richard Kiley, Diahann
Carroll, Noelle Adam, Bernice Massi, Don
Chastain, Alvin Epstein, Mitchell Gregg,
Polly Rowles.
Principal songs: The Sweetest Sounds; Loads
of Love; La, La, La; You Don't Tell Me; Love
Makes the World Go; Nobody Told Me; Look
No Further; Maine; No Strings.
Recorded Versions
Capitol SWAO 1695 (O.C.).
Stet DS 15013 (London O.C.) (1963).
A glossy collection of songs enhanced by
Miss Carroll's vocal sheen. The West End
cast, led by Beverly Todd & Art Lund, is a
worthy alternative.

DO I HEAR A WALTZ?
Opened: Mar. 18, 1965, 46th St. Th.

220 *performances.*
Book by Arthur Laurents; lyrics by Stephen
Sondheim.
Produced by Rodgers; directed by John
Dexter; dances by Herbert Ross.
Cast included: Elizabeth Allen, Sergio
Franchi, Carol Bruce, Madeleine Sherwood,
Julienne Marie, Stuart Damon, Fleury
D'Antonakis, Jack Manning.
Principal songs: Someone Woke Up; This
Week Americans; What Do We Do? We Fly!;
Someone Like You; Here We Are Again; Take
the Moment; Moon in My Window; Do I
Hear a Waltz?; We're Gonna Be All Right.
Recorded Version
Columbia AKOS 2770 (O.C.).
    The short-lived team of Rodgers &
Sondheim turned out a rueful, deftly crafted
score.

TWO BY TWO
Opened: Nov. 10, 1970, Imperial Th.
352 *performances.*
Book by Peter Stone; lyrics by Martin
Charnin.
Produced by Rodgers; directed by Joe Layton.
Cast included: Danny Kaye, Harry Goz, Joan
Copeland, Madeline Kahn, Michael Karm,
Walter Willison, Tricia O'Neil, Marilyn
Cooper.
Principal songs: Put Him Away; Something,
Somewhere; Something Doesn't Happen; Two
by Two; I Do Not Know a Day I Did Not
Love You; When It Dries.
Recorded Version
Columbia S 30338 (O.C.).
    Kaye's Noah & Rodgers' music help make
this a vividly theatrical album.

REX
Opened: April 25, 1976, Lunt-Fontanne Th.
49 *performances.*
Book by Sherman Yellen; lyrics by Sheldon
Harnick.
Produced by Richard Adler; directed by
Edwin Sherin; dances by Dania Krupska.
Cast included: Nicol Williamson, Penny
Fuller, April Shawhan, Ed Evanko, Tom
Aldredge, Barbara Andres.
Principal songs: No Song More Pleasing; The
Chase; Away from You; As Once I Loved
You; Elizabeth; Christmas at Hampton Court;
In Time.
Recorded Version
RCA ABL1 1683 (O.C.).
    The saga of King Henry VIII gave King
Richard one of his shortest reigns on
Broadway.

I REMEMBER MAMA
Opened: May 31, 1979, Majestic Th.
108 *performances.*
Book by Thomas Meehan; lyrics by Martin
Charnin; added lyrics by Raymond Jessel.
Produced by Alexander H. Cohen & Hildy
Parks; directed by Charnin (uncredited), Cy

Feuer; dances by Graciela Daniele, Danny
Daniels.
Cast included: Liv Ullmann, George S. Irving,
George Hearn, Elizabeth Hubbard, Dolores
Wilson, Betty Ann Grove, Maureen Silliman,
Tara Kennedy.
Principal songs: I Remember Mama; A Little
Bit More (Jessel); Ev'ry Day (Comes
Something Beautiful); You Could Not Please
Me More; Easy Come, Easy Go (Jessel); It Is
Not the End of the World; Time.

OSCAR HAMMERSTEIN II
Lyricist

*Musicals by Mr. Hammerstein not written in
collaboration with Richard Rodgers. All books
& lyrics are by Mr. Hammerstein unless
otherwise noted.*

ALWAYS YOU
Opened: Jan. 5, 1920, Central Th.
66 *performances.*
Music by Herbert Stothart.
Produced & directed by Arthur Hammerstein;
dances by Robert Marks.
Cast included: Helen Ford, Walter Scanlan,
Ralph Herz, Edouardo Ciannelli, Julia
Kelety, Bernard Gorcey, Anna Seymour,
Cortez & Peggy, Russell Mack.
Principal songs: Always You; Syncopated
Heart; My Pousse-Café; The Tired Business
Man.

TICKLE ME
Opened: Aug. 17, 1920, Selwyn Th.
207 *performances.*
Book with Otto Harbach & Frank Mandel;
lyrics with Harbach; music by Herbert
Stothart.
Produced by Arthur Hammerstein; directed by
William Collier; dances by Bert French.
Cast included: Frank Tinney, Vic Casmore,
Allen Kearns, Marguerite Zender, Louise
Allen, Frances Grant & Ted Wing.
Principal songs: Until You Say Goodbye;
Tickle Me; If a Wish Could Make It So;
Broadway Swell and Bowery Bum.

JIMMIE
Opened: Nov. 17, 1920, Apollo Th.
71 *performances.*
Book with Otto Harbach & Frank Mandel;
lyrics with Harbach; music by Herbert
Stothart.
Produced by Arthur Hammerstein; directed by
Oscar Eagle; dances by Bert French.
Cast included: Frances White, Ben Welch,
Paul Porcasi, Harry Delf, Hattie Burks, Don
Burroughs.
Principal songs: Cute Little Two by Four;
Baby Dreams; Jimmie; Rickety Crickety.

DAFFY DILL
Opened: Aug. 22, 1922, Apollo Th.
71 *performances.*
Book with Guy Bolton; music by Herbert
Stothart.

Produced by Arthur Hammerstein; directed by Julian Mitchell.
Cast included: Frank Tinney, Guy Robertson, Marion Sunshine, Georgia O'Ramey, Irene Olsen, Frances Grant & Ted Wing, Margaret & Elizabeth Keene.
Principal songs: I'll Build a Bungalow; Two Little Ruby Rings; A Coachman's Heart.

QUEEN O' HEARTS
Opened: Oct. 10, 1922, George M. Cohan Th. *39 performances.*
Book with Frank Mandel; music by Lewis Gensler & Dudley Wilkinson; additional lyrics by Sidney Mitchell.
Produced by Max Spiegel; directed by Ira Hards; dances by David Bennett.
Cast included: Nora Bayes, Harry Richman, Norma Terris, Max Hoffman, Jr., Arthur Uttry, Franker Woods, Georgia Brown, Edna Hibbard, Dudley Wilkinson, Consuelo Flowerton.
Principal Hammerstein songs: Dreaming Alone (Wilkinson); You Need Someone (Gensler); Tom-Tom (Gensler).

WILDFLOWER
(*See* Vincent Youmans).

MARY JANE McKANE
(*See* Vincent Youmans).

ROSE-MARIE
(*See* Rudolf Friml).

SUNNY
(*See* Jerome Kern).

SONG OF THE FLAME
(*See* George Gershwin).

THE WILD ROSE
(*See* Rudolf Friml).

THE DESERT SONG
(*See* Sigmund Romberg).

GOLDEN DAWN
Opened: Nov. 30, 1927, Hammerstein Th. *184 performances.*
Book & lyrics with Otto Harbach; music by Emmerich Kalman & Herbert Stothart.
Produced by Arthur Hammerstein; directed by Reginald Hammerstein; dances by David Bennett.
Cast included: Louise Hunter, Paul Gregory, Marguerita Sylva, Robert Chisholm, Olin Howland, Barbara Newberry, Gil Squires, Hazel Drury, Archie Leach (Cary Grant), Russian Art Choir.
Principal songs: When I Crack My Whip; We Two; Dawn (music by Robert Stolz & Stothart).

SHOW BOAT
(*See* Jerome Kern).

GOOD BOY
Opened: Sept. 25, 1928, Hammerstein Th. *253 performances.*

Book with Otto Harbach & Henry Myers; lyrics by Bert Kalmar; music by Harry Ruby & Herbert Stothart.
Produced by Arthur Hammerstein; directed by Reginald Hammerstein; dances by Busby Berkeley.
Cast included: Eddie Buzzell, Helen Kane, Barbara Newberry, Charles Butterworth, Sam Hearn, Effie Shannon, Dan Healy, Borrah Minevitch, Evelyn Bennett.

THE NEW MOON
(*See* Sigmund Romberg).

RAINBOW
(*See* Vincent Youmans).

SWEET ADELINE
(*See* Jerome Kern).

THE GANG'S ALL HERE
Opened: Feb. 18, 1931, Imperial Th. *23 performances.*
Book with Russel Crouse & Morrie Ryskind; music by Lewis E. Gensler; lyrics by Owen Murphy & Robert A. Simon.
Produced by Morris Green & Gensler; directed by Hammerstein (uncredited) & Frank McCoy; dances by Dave Gould, Tilly Losch.
Cast included: Ted Healy, Tom Howard, Gina Malo, Zelma O'Neal, Shaw & Lee, Ruth Tester, Hal LeRoy, Gomez & Winona, Jack McCauley, Jack Barker.

FREE FOR ALL
Opened: Sept. 8, 1931, Manhattan Th. *15 performances.*
Book with Laurence Schwab; music by Richard A. Whiting.
Produced by Schwab & Frank Mandel; directed by Hammerstein; dances by Bobby Connolly.
Cast included: Jack Haley, Tamara, Lillian Bond, Vera Marsh, Peter Higgins, David Hutcheson, Philip Lord, Seth Arnold, Benny Goodman Orchestra.
Principal songs: I Love Him, the Rat; The Girl Next Door; Not that I Care; When Your Boy Becomes a Man.

EAST WIND
(*See* Sigmund Romberg).

MUSIC IN THE AIR
(*See* Jerome Kern).

MAY WINE
(*See* Sigmund Romberg).

VERY WARM FOR MAY
(*See* Jerome Kern).

SUNNY RIVER
(*See* Sigmund Romberg).

CARMEN JONES
Opened: Dec. 2, 1943, Broadway Th. *502 performances.*
Music by Georges Bizet.
Produced by Billy Rose; directed by Hassard

Short & Charles Friedman; dances by Eugene Loring.

Cast included: Muriel Smith (alternating with Muriel Rahn), Luther Saxon (with Napoleon Reed), Carlotta Franzell (with Elton J. Warren), June Hawkins, Cozy Cole, Glenn Bryant, Inez Matthews.

Principal songs: Dat's Love; Dere's a Café on de Corner; Beat Out dat Rhythm on a Drum; Stan' Up an' Fight; Dis Flower; My Joe; You Talk Just Like My Maw; Whizzin' Away Along de Track.

Recorded Versions
MCA 2054 (O.C.).
RCA LM 1881 (F.V.) (1954).
Heliodor S 25046 (S.C.).

There's much excitement in Hammerstein's resetting of Bizet's *Carmen*. The soundtrack voices on RCA are Marilyn Horne, LeVern Hutcherson, Olga James, Pearl Bailey & Diahann Carroll. The imported Heliodor features Grace Bumbry.

Chapter Eighteen
LEONARD BERNSTEIN
Composer

ON THE TOWN
Opened: Dec. 28, 1944, Adelphi Th.
463 *performances*.
Book & lyrics by Betty Comden & Adolph Green.
Produced by Oliver Smith & Paul Feigay; directed by George Abbott; dances by Jerome Robbins.
Cast included: Nancy Walker, Sono Osato, John Battles, Betty Comden, Adolph Green, Cris Alexander, Alice Pearce, Robert Chisholm, Herbert Greene, Allyn Ann McLerie, Ben Piazza, Nelle Fisher.
Principal songs: New York, New York; I Can Cook, Too; Some Other Time; I Get Carried Away; Lonely Town; Ya Got Me; Lucky to Be Me.
Recorded Versions
Columbia AS 31005 (O.C.).
Decca DL 8030 (O.C.).

With Bernstein conducting, Nancy Walker, Betty Comden & Adolph Green head the cast on Columbia's nearly complete album. Walker, Comden & Green—plus Mary Martin—do 7 numbers on one side of the Decca.

PETER PAN
Opened: April 24, 1950, Imperial Th.
321 *performances*.
Play by James M. Barrie; lyrics by Bernstein.
Produced by Peter Lawrence & Roger L. Stevens; directed by John Burrell; dances by Wendy Toye.
Cast included: Jean Arthur, Boris Karloff, Marcia Henderson, Nehemiah Persoff, Norman Shelly, Peg Hillias, Joe E. Marks.

Songs: Who Am I?; My House; Peter Pan; The Pirate Song; Never Land; The Plank.
Recorded Version
Columbia AOL 4312 (O.C.).

More play with songs than musical play, this is a charmingly abridged view of eternal juvenilia.

WONDERFUL TOWN
Opened: Feb. 25, 1953, Winter Garden
559 *performances*.
Book by Joseph Fields & Jerome Chodorov; lyrics by Betty Comden & Adolph Green.
Produced by Robert Fryer; directed by George Abbott, Jerome Robbins (uncredited); dances by Donald Saddler.
Cast included: Rosalind Russell, George Gaynes, Edith Adams, Henry Lascoe, Dort Clark, Jordan Bentley, Cris Alexander, Ted Beniades, Nathaniel Frey, Dody Goodman, Warren Galjour, Libi Staiger, Joe Layton.
Principal songs: Christopher Street; Ohio; What a Waste; A Quiet Girl; A Little Bit in Love; Conversation Piece; Conga!; My Darlin' Eileen; Swing!; It's Love; Wrong Note Rag; One Hundred Easy Ways.
Recorded Versions
MCA 2050 (O.C.).
Columbia OS 2008 (TV) (1958).

Miss Russell is on both versions, but the cast is better on MCA.

CANDIDE
Opened: Dec. 1, 1956, Martin Beck Th.
73 *performances*.
Book by Lillian Hellman; lyrics by Richard Wilbur.
Produced by Ethel Linder Reiner with Lester Osterman, Jr.; directed by Tyrone Guthrie.
Cast included: Max Adrian, Robert Rounseville, Barbara Cook, Irra Petina, William Olvis, Boris Aplon, William Chapman, Louis Edmonds, Joseph Bernard, Margot Moser, Conrad Bain, Stanley Grover, Jack DeLon.
Principal songs: The Best of All Possible Worlds; Oh, Happy We; It Must Be So; Glitter and Be Gay; You Were Dead, You Know (lyric with John Latouche); I Am Easily Assimilated (lyric by Bernstein); Eldorado (lyric by Miss Hellman); What's the Use?; Gavotte (lyric by Dorothy Parker); Make Our Garden Grow.
Recorded Versions
Columbia OS 2350 (O.C.).
Columbia S2X 32923 (O.C.) (1973).

Though the original production was a boxoffice failure, the first Columbia album kept the superb score alive. The second, on 2 records, contains dialogue plus added pieces with Stephen Sondheim lyrics.

WEST SIDE STORY
Opened: Sept. 26, 1957, Winter Garden
734 *performances*.
Book by Arthur Laurents; lyrics by Stephen Sondheim.

Produced by Robert E. Griffith & Harold S. Prince; directed by Jerome Robbins.
Cast included: Carol Lawrence, Larry Kert, Chita Rivera, Art Smith, Mickey Calin, Ken LeRoy, Lee Becker (Theodore), David Winters, Grover Dale, Martin Charnin, Marilyn Cooper, Reri Grist.
Principal songs: Jet Song; Something's Coming; Maria; Tonight; America; Cool; I Feel Pretty; Somewhere; Gee, Officer Krupke!
Recorded Versions
Columbia S 32603 (O.C.).
Columbia OS 2070 (F.V.) (1961).

There's better placement of songs on the film soundtrack, & the lyric to "America" has been sharpened. The movie voices (Marni Nixon, Jim Bryant, Betty Wand) are at least equal to those in the original cast. Bernstein conducts the ballet music on one side of Columbia MS 6251.

1600 PENNSYLVANIA AVENUE
Opened: May 4, 1976, Mark Hellinger Th.
7 *performances*.
Book & lyrics by Alan Jay Lerner.
Produced by Roger L. Stevens & Robert Whitehead; directed by Gilbert Moses; dances by George Faison.
Cast included: Ken Howard, Patricia Routledge, Gilbert Price, Emily Yancy, Reid Shelton, Edwin Steffe, J. T. Cromwell.
Principal songs: Take Care of This House; President Jefferson Sunday Luncheon Party March; I Love My Wife; Forty Acres and a Mule; Bright and Black; The Red White and Blues.

Chapter Nineteen
ALAN JAY LERNER
Lyricist

FREDERICK LOEWE
Composer

All music by Mr. Loewe & books & lyrics by Mr. Lerner unless otherwise noted.

GREAT LADY
Opened: Dec. 1, 1938, Majestic Th.
20 *performances*.
Book by Earle Crooker & Lowell Brentano; lyrics by Crooker.
Produced by Dwight Deere Wiman & J. H. DelBondio; directed by Bretaigne Windust; dances by William Dollar.
Cast included: Norma Terris, Tullio Carminati, Irene Bordoni, Helen Ford, Joseph Macaulay, Shepperd Strudwick, Annabelle Lyon, Leda Anchutina, André Eglevsky, Robert Shanley, Christine Johnson, Walter Cassel, Dorothy Kirsten, Alicia Alonzo, Nora Kaye, Jerome Robbins, Paul Godkin.
Principal songs: I Have Room in My Heart; There Had to Be the Waltz; May I Suggest Romance?

WHAT'S UP
Opened: Nov. 11, 1943, National Th.
63 *performances*.
Book by Lerner & Arthur Pierson.
Produced by Mark Warnow; directed by George Balanchine & Robert H. Gordon.
Cast included: Jimmy Savo, Gloria Warren, Johnny Morgan, Sondra Barrett, Pat Marshall, Phyllis Hill, William Tabbert, Larry Douglas.
Principal songs: Joshua; You've Got a Hold on Me; You Wash and I'll Dry; My Last Love.

THE DAY BEFORE SPRING
Opened: Nov. 22, 1945, National Th.
165 *performances*.
Produced by John C. Wilson; directed by Wilson & Edward Padula; dances by Antony Tudor.
Cast included: Bill Johnson, Irene Manning, John Archer, Tom Helmore, Pat Marshall, Estelle Loring, Hugh Laing, Mary Ellen Moylan, Bert Freed.
Principal songs: A Jug of Wine; My Love Is a Married Man; I Love You This Morning; The Day Before Spring; You Haven't Changed at All; God's Green World.

BRIGADOON
Opened: Mar. 13, 1947, Ziegfeld Th.
581 *performances*.
Produced by Cheryl Crawford; directed by Robert Lewis; dances by Agnes de Mille.
Cast included: David Brooks, Marion Bell, Pamela Britton, Lee Sullivan, George Keane, William Hansen, James Mitchell, Elliott Sullivan, Hayes Gordon, Helen Gallagher.
Principal songs: Brigadoon; Waitin' for My Dearie; I'll Go Home with Bonnie Jean; The Heather on the Hill; Come to Me, Bend to Me; Almost Like Being in Love; There but for You Go I; My Mother's Wedding Day; From This Day On.
Recorded Versions
RCA LSO 1001 (O.C.).
MGM 2 SES 50 (F.V.) (1954).
Columbia CSM 385 (TV) (1966).
Columbia COS 2540 (S.C.).
RCA LSP 2275 (S.C.).

The most complete, best sung & best recorded version is the Columbia studio cast LP headed by Shirley Jones & Jack Cassidy. Gene Kelly does most of the singing on the soundtrack, while the TV production—available only from Armstrong dealers—spotlights Robert Goulet & Sally Ann Howes. The unlike trio of Jane Powell, Robert Merrill, & Jan Peerce are on the second RCA recording.

LOVE LIFE
(*See* Kurt Weill)

PAINT YOUR WAGON
Opened: Nov. 12, 1951, Shubert Th.
289 *performances*.
Produced by Cheryl Crawford; directed by

Daniel Mann; dances by Agnes de Mille.
Cast included: James Barton, Olga San Juan,
Tony Bavaar, Gemze de Lappe, James
Mitchell, Kay Medford, Marijane Maricle.
Principal songs: I'm on My Way; I Talk to the
Trees; They Call the Wind Maria; I Still See
Elisa; In Between; Carino Mio; There's a
Coach Comin' In; Hand Me Down that Can
o' Beans; Another Autumn; Wand'rin' Star.
Recorded Versions
RCA LSO 1006 (O.C.).
RCA LSP 2274 (S.C.).
Paramount PMS 100 (F.V.) (1969).
    The lusty, flavorsome score is far better
served by the original cast than by the Jane
Powell-Robert Merrill-Jan Peerce combination
on the second RCA. Seven songs were kept for
the film version which also had 5 new ones by
Lerner & André Previn. Cast included Lee
Marvin, Clint Eastwood, Jean Seberg (with
Anita Gordon's voice).

MY FAIR LADY
Opened: Mar. 15, 1956, Mark Hellinger Th.
2,717 *performances*.
Produced by Herman Levin; directed by Moss
Hart; dances by Hanya Holm.
Cast included: Rex Harrison, Julie Andrews,
Stanley Holloway, Cathleen Nesbitt, Robert
Coote, John Michael King, Viola Roache,
Olive Reeves Smith, Christopher Hewett, Lola
Fisher, Margot Moser, Reid Shelton.
Principal songs: Why Can't the English?;
Wouldn't It Be Loverly?; With a Little Bit of
Luck; I'm an Ordinary Man; Just You Wait;
The Rain in Spain; I Could Have Danced All
Night; On the Street Where You Live; Show
Me; Get Me to the Church on Time; A
Hymn to Him; Without You; I've Grown
Accustomed to Her Face.
Recorded Versions
Columbia AOL 5090 (O.C.).
Columbia PS 2015 (London O.C.) (1958).
Columbia 91A 02052 (Mexican O.C.) (1959).
Columbia OS 2660 (Italian O.C.) (1963).
Columbia OL 8050 (Israeli O.C.) (1964).
Columbia PS 2600 (F.V.) (1964).
Columbia PS 34197 (O.C.) (1976).
RCA LSP 2274 (S.C.).
    Columbia's classic original-cast LP is
surrounded by a choice array of satellites,
including foreign language & soundtrack
(Harrison & Marni Nixon). The London set,
with the NY principals, is the first stereo
recording of the score. The loverly 1976
revival starred Ian Richardson, Christine
Andreas, & George Rose. The RCA (Jane
Powell, Robert Merrill, Phil Harris) is
superfluous.

CAMELOT
Opened: Dec. 3, 1960, Majestic Th.
873 *performances*.
Produced by Lerner, Loewe & Moss Hart;
directed by Hart; dances by Hanya Holm.
Cast included: Richard Burton, Julie
Andrews, Robert Goulet, Roddy McDowall,
Robert Coote, M'el Dowd, Bruce Yarnell,
John Cullum, David Hurst, Marjorie Smith,
Michael Kermoyan.
Principal songs: Camelot; C'est Moi; The
Lusty Month of May; If Ever I Would Leave
You; What Do the Simple Folk Do?; I Loved
You Once in Silence; Guenevere; Follow Me;
How to Handle a Woman.
Recorded Versions
Columbia S 32602 (O.C.).
Warner Bros. K 3102 (F.V.) (1967).
Stet DS 15022 (London O.C.) (1964).
    The acceptable soundtrack of this richly
melodic score does not indicate who does the
singing. Laurence Harvey & Elizabeth Larner
had the leads in London.

ON A CLEAR DAY YOU CAN SEE FOREVER
(*See* Burton Lane).

COCO
Opened: Dec. 18, 1969, Hellinger Th.
332 *performances*.
Music by André Previn.
Produced by Frederick Brisson; directed by
Michael Benthall; dances by Michael Bennett.
Cast included: Katharine Hepburn, George
Rose, Gale Dixon, David Holliday, René
Auberjonois, Jeanne Arnold, Jon Cypher, Will
B. Able, Jack Dabdoub, Ann Reinking.
Principal songs: Let's Go Home; On the
Corner of the Rue Cambon; Orbach's,
Bloomingdale's, Best and Saks; Always
Mademoiselle; Gabrielle; When Your Lover
Says Goodbye; Coco.
Recorded Version
Paramount 1002 (O.C.).
    Technically, this is an inferior recording but
the songs do have style.

GIGI
Opened: Nov. 13, 1973, Uris Th.
103 *performances*.
Produced by Saint-Subber; directed by Joseph
Hardy; dances by Onna White.
Cast included: Alfred Drake, Maria
Karnilova, Daniel Massey, Agnes Moorehead,
Karin Wolfe, George Gaynes.
Principal songs: Thank Heaven for Little
Girls; It's a Bore; Paris Is Paris Again; She Is
Not Thinking of Me; The Night They
Invented Champagne; I Remember It Well;
Gigi; I'm Glad I'm Not Young Anymore.
Recorded Version
RCA ABL1 0404 (O.C.).
    The effervescent 1958 film score (MGM SE
3741) was adapted to the stage with 7 of its
original 9 songs plus 4 new ones.

1600 PENNSYLVANIA AVENUE
(*See* Leonard Bernstein).

CARMELINA
(*See* Burton Lane).

Chapter Twenty
JULE STYNE
Composer

BETTY COMDEN
ADOLPH GREEN

Co-lyricists

*All music by Mr. Styne & books or sketches &
lyrics by Miss Comden & Mr. Green unless
otherwise noted. For libretto only by Comden
& Green, see* Applause *under Charles Strouse
& Lee Adams.*

ON THE TOWN
(*See* Leonard Bernstein).

BILLION DOLLAR BABY
Opened: Dec. 21, 1945, Alvin Th.
219 *performances.*
Music by Morton Gould.
Produced by Paul Feigay & Oliver Smith;
directed by George Abbott; dances by Jerome
Robbins.
Cast included: Mitzi Green, Joan McCracken,
William Tabbert, Harold Gary, Robert
Chisholm, Danny Daniels, James Mitchell,
Helen Gallagher.
Principal songs: Broadway Blossom; Bad
Timing; I Got a One Track Mind; I'm Sure of
Your Love.

HIGH BUTTON SHOES
Opened: Oct. 9, 1947, New Century Th.
727 *performances.*
Book by Stephen Longstreet; lyrics by Sammy
Cahn.
Produced by Monte Proser & Joseph Kipness;
directed by George Abbott; dances by Jerome
Robbins.
Cast included: Phil Silvers, Nanette Fabray,
Jack McCauley, Sondra Lee, Joey Faye,
Johnny Stewart, Helen Gallagher, Paul
Godkin, Mark Dawson, Lois Lee, Clay
Clement, Nathaniel Frey.
Principal songs: Can't You Just See
Yourself?; There's Nothing Like a Model
"T"; You're My Girl; Papa, Won't You
Dance with Me?; On a Sunday by the Sea; I
Still Get Jealous.
Recorded Version
RCA LSO 1107 (O.C.).
    Appealing Styne songs.

GENTLEMEN PREFER BLONDES
Opened: Dec. 8, 1949, Ziegfeld Th.
740 *performances.*
Book by Joseph Fields & Anita Loos; lyrics by
Leo Robin.
Produced by Herman Levin & Oliver Smith;
directed by John C. Wilson; dances by Agnes
de Mille.
Cast included: Carol Channing, Yvonne Adair,
Jack McCauley, Eric Brotherson, Alice
Pearce, Rex Evans, Anita Alvarez, George S.
Irving, Reta Shaw, Howard Morris, Mort
Marshall, Peter Birch, Helen Wood.
Principal songs: It's High Time; Bye Bye
Baby; A Little Girl from Little Rock; I Love
What I'm Doing; Just a Kiss Apart; You Say

You Care; Diamonds Are a Girl's Best Friend;
I'm a'Tingle, I'm a'Glow; Sunshine;
Homesick Blues.
Recorded Versions
Columbia AOS 2310 (O.C.).
Stet DS 15005 (F.V.) (1953).
MGM M3G 55 (O.C.) (1973).
MGM MV 5097 (O.C.) (1974).
    The Columbia is the preferred version of
this lively score. The soundtrack keeps 3
numbers & adds 2 by Carmichael &
Adamson, all purred by Marilyn Monroe &
Jane Russell. The 2 MGM sets are both of
Lorelei, the slightly revised remake, starring
Carol Channing. The first album, made at the
start of the year-long tryout, retains 10 songs,
adds 4 with lyrics by Comden & Green; the
second, released after the N.Y. opening, drops
4, adds 2 & a new overture.

TWO ON THE AISLE
Opened: July 19, 1951, Mark Hellinger Th.
281 *performances.*
Produced by Arthur Lesser; directed by Abe
Burrows; dances by Ted Cappy.
Cast included: Bert Lahr, Dolores Gray,
Colette Marchand, Elliott Reid, Stanley
Prager, J. C. McCord, Larry Laurence.
Principal songs: Hold Me, Hold Me, Hold
Me; There Never Was a Baby Like My Baby;
Catch Our Act at the Met; If You Hadn't but
You Did; How Will He Know?
Recorded Version
Decca DL 8040 (O.C.).
    One of the few revue scores recorded & the
only Broadway original cast L.P. featuring the
great Bert Lahr.

HAZEL FLAGG
Opened: Feb. 11, 1953, Mark Hellinger Th.
190 *performances.*
Book by Ben Hecht; lyrics by Bob Hilliard.
Produced by Styne & Anthony Brady Farrell;
directed by David Alexander; dances by
Robert Alton.
Cast included: Helen Gallagher, Thomas
Mitchell, Benay Venuta, John Howard, Jack
Whiting, Sheree North, Jonathan Harris,
John Brascia, Hugh Lambert.
Principal songs: I'm Glad I'm Leaving; Every
Street's a Boulevard in Old New York; How
Do You Speak to an Angel; Everybody Loves
to Take a Bow; I Feel Like I'm Gonna Live
Forever.
Recorded Version
RCA CBMI 2207 (O.C.).
    Apart from "Every Street's a Boulevard,"
there's little to recommend here.

WONDERFUL TOWN
(*See* Leonard Bernstein).

PETER PAN
Opened: Oct. 20, 1954, Winter Garden
152 *performances.*
Play by James M. Barrie; music & lyrics also

by Mark Charlap & Carolyn Leigh.
Produced by Richard Halliday; directed by Jerome Robbins.
Cast included: Mary Martin, Cyril Ritchard, Margalo Gilmore, Kathy Nolan, Heller Halliday, Sondra Lee, Norman Shelly, Joe E. Marks, Joan Tewkesbury.
Principal Styne-Comden-Green songs: Never Never Land; Wendy; Distant Melody; Captain Hook's Waltz.
Recorded Version
RCA LSO 1019 (O.C.).
   The songs for this charming album were divided about evenly between the two teams.

BELLS ARE RINGING
Opened: Nov. 29, 1956, Shubert Th.
924 *performances.*
Produced by The Theatre Guild; directed by Jerome Robbins; dances by Robbins & Bob Fosse.
Cast included: Judy Holliday, Sydney Chaplin, Eddie Lawrence, Jean Stapleton, George S. Irving, Peter Gennaro, Bernie West, Frank Aletter, Steve Roland, Donna Sanders, Billy Wilson.
Principal songs: It's a Perfect Relationship; On My Own; It's a Simple Little System; Is It a Crime?; Just in Time; Long Before I Knew You; The Party's Over; I'm Going Back.
Recorded Versions
Columbia AOS 2006 (O.C.).
Stet DS 15011 (F.V.) (1960).
   A spirited, melodious collection of songs. Miss Holliday & Dean Martin are on the soundtrack.

SAY, DARLING
Opened: Apr. 3, 1958, Anta Th.
332 *performances.*
Play by Richard Bissell, Abe Burrows, Marian Bissell.
Produced by Styne & Lester Osterman; directed by Burrows; dances by Matt Mattox.
Cast included: David Wayne, Vivian Blaine, Johnny Desmond, Jerome Cowan, Constance Ford, Horace McMahon, Robert Morse, Matt Mattox, Mitchell Gregg, Colin Romoff, Elliott Gould, Virginia Martin, Steve Condos, Richard Tone, Robert Downing.
Principal songs: It's the Second Time You Meet that Matters; Say, Darling; Dance Only with Me; Something's Always Happening on the River.
Recorded Version
RCA LSO 1045 (O.C.).
   Hardly memorable.

GYPSY
Opened: May 21, 1959, Broadway Th.
702 *performances.*
Book by Arthur Laurents; lyrics by Stephen Sondheim.
Produced by David Merrick & Leland Hayward; directed by Jerome Robbins.
Cast included: Ethel Merman, Jack Klugman,

Sandra Church, Maria Karnilova, Paul Wallace, Lane Bradbury, Faith Dane, Chotzi Foley, Mort Marshall, Jacqueline Mayro, Joe Silver, Michael Parks; Loney Lewis, Peg Murray.
Principal songs: Let Me Entertain You; Some People; Small World; Little Lamb; You'll Never Get Away from Me; All I Need Is the Girl; Everything's Coming Up Roses; Together; You Gotta Have a Gimmick; Rose's Turn.
Recorded Versions
Columbia S 32607 (O.C.).
Warner Bros. 1480 (F.V.) (1962).
RCA LBL1 5004 (London O.C.) (1973).
   Columbia's is one of the greatest show albums ever made. The soundtrack version stars Rosalind Russell's "voice," the RCA cast is headed by the remarkable Angela Lansbury. But the part is still Ethel's.

DO RE MI
Opened: Dec. 26, 1960, St. James Th.
400 *performances.*
Book by Garson Kanin.
Produced by David Merrick; directed by Kanin; dances by Marc Breaux & Deedee Wood.
Cast included: Phil Silvers, Nancy Walker, John Reardon, David Burns, George Mathews, George Givot, Nancy Dussault, Dawn Nickerson, Steve Roland, Donna Sanders.
Principal songs: I Know About Love; Cry Like the Wind; What's New at the Zoo?; Adventure; Make Someone Happy.
Recorded Version
RCA LSO 1105 (O.C.).
   An average score that is worth the price just to hear Miss Walker describe her life of "Adventure."

SUBWAYS ARE FOR SLEEPING
Opened: Dec. 27, 1961, St. James Th.
205 *performances.*
Produced by David Merrick; directed by Michael Kidd.
Cast included: Sydney Chaplin, Carol Lawrence, Orson Bean, Phyllis Newman, Cy Young, Gordon Connell, Michael Bennett, Valerie Harper.
Principal songs: Girls Like Me; I'm Just Taking My Time; Ride Through the Night; Be a Santa; Comes Once in a Lifetime.
Recorded Version
Columbia AOS 2130 (O.C.).
   An attractive collection of songs, somewhat marred by Mr. Chaplin's vocal inadequacies.

FUNNY GIRL
Opened: Mar. 26, 1964, Winter Garden
1,348 *performances.*
Book by Isobel Lennart; lyrics by Bob Merrill.
Produced by Ray Stark; directed by Garson Kanin & Jerome Robbins; dances by Carol Haney.

Cast included: Barbra Streisand, Sydney Chaplin, Danny Meehan, Kay Medford, Jean Stapleton, Roger DeKoven, Joseph Macaulay, Buzz Miller, Lainie Kazan.
Principal songs: I'm the Greatest Star; Cornet Man; People; You Are Woman; Don't Rain on My Parade; Sadie, Sadie; Who Are You Now?; The Music that Makes Me Dance.
Recorded Versions
Capitol STAO 2059 (O.C.).
Columbia BOS 3220 (F.V.) (1968).
 Styne & Merrill have given Miss Streisand a remarkably rich and varied musical assortment which she interprets superbly. Some musical changes on the soundtrack, including addition of "My Man."

FADE OUT—FADE IN
Opened: May 26, 1964, Mark Hellinger Th.
271 *performances.*
Produced by Lester Osterman & Styne; directed by George Abbott; dances by Ernest Flatt.
Cast included: Carol Burnett, Jack Cassidy, Lou Jacobi, Tina Louise, Dick Patterson, Mitchell Jason, Reuben Singer, Virginia Payne, Tiger Haynes, Aileen Poe, Trish Dwelley.
Principal songs: Call Me Savage; The Usher from the Mezzanine; You Mustn't Be Discouraged; Fade Out—Fade In; Close Harmony.
Recorded Version
ABC Paramount S OC 3 (O.C.).
 Not consistently inspired but entertaining enough.

HALLELUJAH, BABY!
Opened: Apr. 26, 1967, Martin Beck Th.
293 *performances.*
Book by Arthur Laurents.
Produced by Albert W. Selden & Hal James, Jane Nusbaum & Harry Rigby; directed by Burt Shevelove; dances by Kevin Carlisle.
Cast included: Leslie Uggams, Robert Hooks, Allen Case, Lillian Hayman, Barbara Sharma.
Principal songs: My Own Morning; Not Mine; Being Good Isn't Good Enough; Talking to Yourself; I Don't Know Where She Got It; Hallelujah, Baby!
Recorded Version
Columbia KOS 3090 (O.C.).
 Hallelujah, Leslie Uggams.

DARLING OF THE DAY
Opened: Jan. 27, 1968, George Abbott Th.
32 *performances.*
Book uncredited; lyrics by E. Y. Harburg.
Produced by The Theatre Guild & Joel Schenker; directed by Noel Willman; dances by Lee Theodore.
Cast included: Vincent Price, Patricia Routledge, Brenda Forbes, Peter Woodthorpe, Teddy Green.

Principal songs: To Get Out of This World Alive; It's Enough to Make a Lady Fall in Love; Let's See What Happens; That Something Extra Special; Not on Your Nellie.
Recorded Version
RCA LSO 1149 (O.C.).
 The musical deserved a better fate, but we can still enjoy the singing of Miss Routledge and the delights of the score.

LOOK TO THE LILIES
Opened: March 29, 1970, Lunt-Fontanne Th.
25 *performances.*
Book by Leonard Spigelgass; lyrics by Sammy Cahn.
Produced by Edgar Lansbury, Max J. Brown, Richard Levine, Ralph Nelson; directed by Joshua Logan.
Cast included: Shirley Booth, Al Freeman, Jr., Titos Vandis, Taina Elg, Patti Carr, Carmen Alvarez, Maggie Worth.
Principal songs: Follow the Lamb; One Little Brick at a Time; Look to the Lilies; I, Yes, Me, That's Who.

SUGAR
Opened: April 9, 1972, Majestic Th.
505 *performances.*
Book by Peter Stone; lyrics by Bob Merrill.
Produced by David Merrick; directed by Gower Champion.
Cast included: Robert Morse, Tony Roberts, Cyril Ritchard, Elaine Joyce, Sheila Smith, Steve Condos, Igors Gavon.
Principal songs: Beautiful Through and Through; Sun on My Face; November Song; Sugar; Hey, Why Not?; What Do You Give to a Man Who Has Everything?; When You Meet a Man in Chicago.
Recorded Version
United Artists 9905 (O.C.).
 Pretty much in the familiar Broadway mold.

ON THE TWENTIETH CENTURY
(*See* Cy Coleman).

Chapter Twenty-One
FRANK LOESSER
Composer-lyricist

 All music & lyrics by Mr. Loesser unless otherwise noted.

THE ILLUSTRATORS' SHOW
Opened: Jan. 22, 1936, 48th St. Th.
5 *performances.*
Sketches by Max Liebman, Hi Alexander, Kenneth Webb, Otto Soglow, Donald Blackwell, Harry Evans, Frank Gabrielson; Loesser music by Irving Actman; music & lyrics also by others.
Produced by Soc. of Illustrators & Tom Weatherly; directed by Weatherly & Allen Delano; dances by Carl Randall.

Cast included: Helen Lynde, Earl Oxford, Niela Goodelle, Otto Soglow, O. Z. Whitehead, Gomez & Winona.
Principal Loesser-Actman songs: Bang—the Bell Rang!; If You Didn't Love Me.

WHERE'S CHARLEY?
Opened: Oct. 11, 1948, St. James Th.
792 *performances.*
Book by George Abbott.
Produced by Cy Feuer & Ernest Martin with Gwen Rickard; directed by George Abbott; dances by George Balanchine.
Cast included: Ray Bolger, Allyn McLerie, Byron Palmer, Doretta Morrow, Horace Cooper, Jane Lawrence, Paul England, Cornell MacNeil.
Principal songs: The New Ashmoleon Marching Society and Student Conservatory Band; My Darling, My Darling; Make a Miracle; Lovelier than Ever; Pernambuco; Once in Love with Amy; At the Red Rose Cotillion.
Recorded Version
M-E 7029 (London O.C.) (1958).
    The only complete recording of the fondly-remembered score is that of the English company headed by Norman Wisdom.

GUYS AND DOLLS
Opened: Nov. 24, 1950, 46th St. Th.
1,200 *performances.*
Book by Abe Burrows & Jo Swerling.
Produced by Cy Feuer & Ernest Martin; directed by George S. Kaufman; dances by Michael Kidd.
Cast included: Robert Alda, Vivian Blaine, Sam Levene, Isabel Bigley, Pat Rooney, B. S. Pully, Stubby Kaye, Tom Pedi, Johnny Silver, Peter Gennaro, Scott Merrill, Onna White, Eddie Phillips.
Principal songs: Fugue for Tinhorns; The Oldest Established; I'll Know; A Bushel and a Peck; Adelaide's Lament; Guys and Dolls; If I Were a Bell; My Time of Day; I've Never Been in Love Before; Take Back Your Mink; More I Cannot Wish You; Luck Be a Lady; Sue Me; Sit Down, You're Rockin' the Boat; Marry the Man Today.
Recorded Versions
MCA 2034 (O.C.).
Motown 6 876 (O.C.) (1976).
    Though the all-black cast on Motown tries valiantly, the classic score is still served best in the cheesecake & strudel atmosphere of the original original cast.

THE MOST HAPPY FELLA
Opened: May 3, 1956, Imperial Th.
676 *performances.*
Book by Loesser.
Produced by Kermit Bloomgarden & Lynn Loesser; directed by Joseph Anthony; dances by Dania Krupska.
Cast included: Robert Weede, Jo Sullivan, Art Lund, Susan Johnson, Shorty Long, Mona

Paulee, Lee Cass, Zina Bethune.
Principal songs: Somebody Somewhere; The Most Happy Fella; Standing on the Corner; Joey, Joey, Joey; Rosabella; Abbondanza; Sposalizio; Happy to Make Your Acquaintance; Big "D"; Warm All Over; My Heart Is So Full of You; How Beautiful the Days.
Recorded Versions
Columbia CO3L 240 (O.C.).
Angel 35887 (London O.C.) (1960).
    The 3-record set of the entire score reveals many facets of a distinguished musical talent. Highlights are on the single record, Columbia OS 2330. Some fine performances are also turned in by the London company, headed by Inia Wiata, Helena Scott & Art Lund.

GREENWILLOW
Opened: Mar. 8, 1960, Alvin Th.
95 *performances.*
Book by Loesser & Lesser Samuels.
Produced by Robert A. Willey with Frank Productions; directed by George Roy Hill; dances by Joe Layton.
Cast included: Anthony Perkins, Cecil Kellaway, Pert Kelton, Ellen McCown, William Chapman, Lee Cass, Grover Dale, Marion Mercer, Margery Gray.
Principal songs: The Music of Home; Gideon Briggs, I Love You; Summertime Love; Walking Away Whistling; Never Will I Marry; Faraway Boy; Clang Dang the Bell.
Recorded Version
Columbia P 13974 (O.C.).
    Loesser in a bucolic, lyrical, frequently whimsical mood.

HOW TO SUCCEED IN BUSINESS WITHOUT REALLY TRYING
Opened: Oct. 14, 1961, 46th St. Th.
1,417 *performances.*
Book by Abe Burrows, Jack Weinstock, Willie Gilbert.
Produced by Cy Feuer & Ernest Martin with Frank Productions; directed by Burrows & Bob Fosse; dances by Hugh Lambert.
Cast included: Robert Morse, Rudy Vallee, Bonnie Scott, Virginia Martin, Charles Nelson Reilly, Claudette Sutherland, Ruth Kobart, Sammy Smith, Donna McKechnie.
Principal songs: The Company Way; A Secretary Is Not a Toy; Grand Old Ivy; Been a Long Day; Paris Original; Rosemary; I Believe in You; Brotherhood of Man.
Recorded Versions
RCA LSO 1066 (O.C.).
United Artists 5151 (F.V.) (1967).
    With Michele Lee added to original stars Morse & Vallee, the soundtrack LP is a faithful, though decimated version of the long-on-comedy score.

RICHARD ADLER
Composer-lyricist

JERRY ROSS

Composer-lyricist

All music & lyrics by Messrs. Adler & Ross unless otherwise noted.

JOHN MURRAY ANDERSON'S ALMANAC
Opened: Dec. 10, 1953, Imperial Th.
229 *performances.*
Sketches by Jean Kerr, Sumner Locke-Elliott, Arthur Macrae, Billy K. Wells, Herbert Farjeon, Lauri Wylie; music & lyrics also by Cy Coleman & Joseph McCarthy, Sheldon Harnick, Henry Sullivan & John Murray Anderson, Charles Zwar, Michael Grace & Sammy Gallop, John Rox, Harry Belafonte.
Produced by Grace, Stanley Gilkey & Harry Rigby; directed by Anderson & Cyril Ritchard; dances by Donald Saddler.
Cast included: Hermione Gingold, Billy DeWolfe, Harry Belafonte, Orson Bean, Polly Bergen, Nanci Crompton, Carleton Carpenter, Alice Pearce, Elaine Dunn, Celia Lipton, Kay Medford, Monique Van Vooren, Lee Becker (Theodore), Tina Louise, Larry Kert.
Principal Adler-Ross songs: You're So Much a Part of Me; When Am I Going to Meet Your Mother?; Acorn in the Meadow; Fini.

THE PAJAMA GAME
Opened: May 13, 1954, St. James Th.
1,063 *performances.*
Book by George Abbott & Richard Bissell.
Produced by Frederick Brisson, Robert E. Griffith & Harold Prince; directed by Abbott & Jerome Robbins; dances by Bob Fosse.
Cast included: John Raitt, Janis Paige, Eddie Foy, Jr., Carol Haney, Reta Shaw, Stanley Prager, Thelma Pelish, Jack Waldron, Peter Gennaro, Rae Allen, Shirley MacLaine, Buzz Miller, Carmen Alvarez, Virginia Martin.
Principal songs: I'm Not at All in Love; I'll Never Be Jealous Again; Hey, There; Her Is; Once a Year Day; Small Talk; There Once Was a Man; Steam Heat; Hernando's Hideaway; 7½ Cents.
Recorded Versions
Columbia S 32606 (O.C.).
Columbia AOL 5210 (F.V.) (1957).
   Both releases have the same material and almost the same cast. The major change is Doris Day for Janis Paige on the soundtrack.

DAMN YANKEES
Opened: May 5, 1955, 46th St. Th.
1,019 *performances.*
Book by George Abbott & Douglass Wallop.
Produced by Frederick Brisson, Robert E. Griffith & Harold Prince; directed by Abbott; dances by Bob Fosse.
Cast included: Gwen Verdon, Stephen Douglass, Ray Walston, Russ Brown, Shannon Bolin, Jimmy Komack, Robert Shafer, Jean Stapleton, Nathaniel Frey, Eddie Phillips, Rae Allen.
Principal songs: Goodbye, Old Girl; Heart; A Little Brains, a Little Talent; A Man Doesn't Know; Whatever Lola Wants; Who's Got the Pain?; Near to You; Two Lost Souls.
Recorded Versions
RCA LSO 1021 (O.C.).
RCA LSO 1047 (F.V.) (1958).
   There are a few minor changes in the song lineup on the soundtrack, plus the substitution of Tab Hunter for Stephen Douglass.

KWAMINA
Opened: Oct. 23, 1961, 54th St. Th.
32 *performances.*
Book by Robert Alan Aurthur; music & lyrics by Adler.
Produced by Alfred de Liagre; directed by Robert Lewis; dances by Agnes de Mille.
Cast included: Sally Ann Howes, Terry Carter, Brock Peters, Robert Guillaume, Ethel Ayler, Joseph Attles, Norman Barrs, Rex Ingram, Rawn Spearman.
Principal songs: Cocoa Bean Song; Welcome Home; Nothing More to Look Forward To; Ordinary People; What's Wrong with Me?; What Happened to Me Tonight?; Another Time, Another Place.
Recorded Version
Capitol S W 1645 (O.C.).
   A richly colorful score that makes excellent use of native rhythms.

MUSIC IS
Opened: Dec. 20, 1976, St. James Th.
8 *performances.*
Book by George Abbott; lyrics by Will Holt; music by Adler.
Produced by Adler, Roger Berlind & Edward R. Downe, Jr.; directed by Abbott; dances by Patricia Birch.
Cast included: Christopher Hewett, Daniel Ben-Zali, Catherine Cox, Joel Higgins, David Holliday, Marc Jordan, Sherry Mathis, William McClary, Joe Ponazecki, David Sabin.
Principal songs: When First I Saw My Lady's Face; Should I Speak of Loving You?; Sudden Lilac; Sing Hi; No Matter Where.

MEREDITH WILLSON

Composer-lyricist

All books by Mr. Willson unless otherwise noted.

THE MUSIC MAN
Opened: Dec. 19, 1957, Majestic Th.
1,375 *performances.*
Produced by Kermit Bloomgarden with Herbert Greene & Frank Productions; directed by Morton DaCosta; dances by Onna White.
Cast included: Robert Preston, Barbara Cook, David Burns, Pert Kelton, The Buffalo Bills, Iggie Wolfington, Helen Raymond, Paul Reed, Eddie Hodges, Danny Carroll.
Principal songs: Rock Island; Trouble; Piano Lesson; Goodnight, My Someone; Seventy-Six

Trombones; The Sadder-but-Wiser Girl; Marian the Librarian; My White Knight; Wells Fargo Wagon; Shi-poopi; Lida Rose; Will I Ever Tell You?; Gary, Indiana; Till There Was You.

Recorded Versions
Capitol SW 990 (O.C.).
Stanyan 10039 (London O.C.) (1961).
Warner Bros. 1459 (F.V.) (1962).
Capitol ST 1320.

Willson's skillful blend of corn & cacophony gets a thumpingly good production on the original-cast recording. Preston repeats on the soundtrack & Van Johnson is heard in the London replica. On the 2nd Capitol set, the composer & his late wife, Rini, perform the numbers with comments.

THE UNSINKABLE MOLLY BROWN

Opened: Nov. 3, 1960, Winter Garden
532 *performances.*
Book by Richard Morris.
Produced by The Theatre Guild & Dore Schary; directed by Schary; dances by Peter Gennaro.
Cast included: Tammy Grimes, Harve Presnell, Cameron Prud'homme, Mony Dalmes, Edith Meiser, Mitchell Gregg, Christopher Hewett.
Principal songs: I Ain't Down Yet; Belly Up to the Bar, Boys; If I Knew; My Own Brass Bed; Dolce Far Niente; I'll Never Say No.
Recorded Versions
Capitol S W 2152 (O.C.).
MGM S 4232 ST (F.V.) (1964).

A routine score, badly truncated on the Debbie Reynolds-Harve Presnell soundtrack.

HERE'S LOVE

Opened: Oct. 3, 1963, Shubert Th.
334 *performances.*
Produced & directed by Stuart Ostrow; dances by Michael Kidd.
Cast included: Janis Paige, Craig Stevens, Laurence Naismith, Fred Gwynne, Paul Reed, Cliff Hall, David Doyle, Larry Douglas, Valerie Lee, Michael Bennett.
Principal songs: The Big Clown Balloons; Arm in Arm; You Don't Know; Here's Love; Pine Cones and Holly Berries; That Man Over There.
Recorded Version
Columbia KOS 2400 (O.C.).

Some lively moments, though much of the score—and most of the voices—are undistinguished.

Chapter Twenty-Two
BOB MERRILL

Composer-lyricist

All music by Mr. Merrill unless otherwise noted.

NEW GIRL IN TOWN

Opened: May 14, 1957, 46th St. Th.
431 *performances.*
Book by George Abbott.
Produced by Frederick Brisson, Robert E. Griffith & Harold S. Prince; directed by Abbott; dances by Bob Fosse.
Cast included: Gwen Verdon, Thelma Ritter, George Wallace, Cameron Prud'homme, Mark Dawson, Lulu Bates, Eddie Phillips.
Principal songs: Anna Lilla; Sunshine Girl; Flings; It's Good to Be Alive; Look at 'Er; Did You Close Your Eyes?; At the Check Apron Ball.
Recorded Version
RCA LSO 1106 (O.C.).

The atmospheric numbers capture the spirit of the tale better than the romantic pieces.

TAKE ME ALONG

Opened: Oct. 22, 1959, Shubert Th.
448 *performances.*
Book by Joseph Stein & Robert Russell.
Produced by David Merrick; directed by Peter Glenville; dances by Onna White.
Cast included: Jackie Gleason, Walter Pidgeon, Eileen Herlie, Robert Morse, Una Merkel, Susan Luckey, Peter Conlow, Valerie Harper.
Principal songs: I Would Die; Sid Ol' Kid; Staying Young; I Get Embarrassed; We're Home; Take Me Along; Promise Me a Rose; Nine O'Clock; But Yours.
Recorded Version
RCA LSO 1050 (O.C.).

There is great period charm and dramatic appeal in this somewhat neglected score.

CARNIVAL

Opened: Apr. 13, 1961, Imperial Th.
719 *performances.*
Book by Michael Stewart.
Produced by David Merrick; directed by Gower Champion.
Cast included: Anna Maria Alberghetti, James Mitchell, Kaye Ballard, Pierre Olaf, Jerry Orbach, Henry Lascoe, Anita Gillette, Luba Lisa, Will Lee, George Marcy, Paul Sydell, Igors Gavon.
Principal songs: Direct from Vienna; Yes, My Heart; Love Makes the World Go Round; Mira; Beautiful Candy; Always Always You; The Grand Imperial Cirque de Paris.
Recorded Version
MGM SE 3946 (O.C.).

A tender, evocative score.

FUNNY GIRL

(*See* Jule Styne).

HENRY, SWEET HENRY

Opened: Oct. 23, 1967, Palace Th.
80 *performances.*
Book by Nunnally Johnson.
Produced by Edward Spector & Norman Twain; directed by George Roy Hill; dances by Michael Bennett.
Cast included: Don Ameche, Carol Bruce,

Robin Wilson, Neva Small, Louise Lasser, Alice Playten, Milo Boulton, K. C. Townsend.
Principal songs: In Some Little World; Here I Am; I Wonder How It Is; Nobody Steps on Kafritz; Henry, Sweet Henry; Do You Ever Go to Boston?
Recorded Version
ABC SOC 4 (O.C.).
    Little to recommend.

SUGAR
(*See* Jule Styne).

Chapter Twenty-Three
STEPHEN SONDHEIM
Composer-lyricist

All music by Mr. Sondheim unless otherwise noted.

WEST SIDE STORY
(*See* Leonard Bernstein).

GYPSY
(*See* Jule Styne).

A FUNNY THING HAPPENED ON THE WAY TO THE FORUM
Opened: May 8, 1962, Alvin Th.
967 *performances.*
Book by Burt Shevelove & Larry Gelbart.
Produced by Harold Prince; directed by George Abbott & Jerome Robbins (uncredited); dances by Jack Cole.
Cast included: Zero Mostel, Jack Gilford, David Burns, Raymond Walburn, John Carradine, Ruth Kobart, Brian Davies, Preshy Marker, Ronald Holgate, Eddie Phillips.
Principal songs: Comedy Tonight; Love, I Hear; Free; Lovely; Everybody Ought to Have a Maid; Pretty Little Picture.
Recorded Versions
Capitol S W 1717 (O.C.).
United Artists 5144 (F.V.) (1966).
Stet DS 15025 (London O.C.) (1963)
    This delectable score is all but smothered on the soundtrack release. The London cast offers an entertaining substitute.

ANYONE CAN WHISTLE
Opened: Apr. 4, 1964, Majestic Th.
9 *performances.*
Book by Arthur Laurents.
Produced by Kermit Bloomgarden & Diana Krasny; directed by Laurents; dances by Herbert Ross.
Cast included: Lee Remick, Angela Lansbury, Harry Guardino, Gabriel Dell, Arnold Soboloff, James Frawley, Peg Murray.
Principal songs: Me and My Town; Anyone Can Whistle; A Parade in Town; Everybody Says Don't; See What It Gets You; With So Little to be Sure of.
Recorded Version
Columbia AS 32608 (O.C.).
    A "cult" musical that was recorded after the show had closed.

DO I HEAR A WALTZ?
(*See* Richard Rodgers).

COMPANY
Opened: April 26, 1970, Alvin Th.
706 *performances.*
Book by George Furth.
Produced & directed by Harold Prince; dances by Michael Bennett.
Cast included: Dean Jones, Elaine Stritch, Barbara Barrie, George Coe, John Cunningham, Teri Ralston, Donna McKechnie, Charles Braswell, Susan Browning, Steve Elmore, Beth Howland, Pamela Myers.
Principal songs: Company; The Little Things You Do Together; Sorry-Grateful; You Could Drive a Person Crazy; Someone Is Waiting; Another Hundred People; Getting Married Today; Side by Side by Side; What Would We Do Without You?; Barcelona; The Ladies who Lunch; Being Alive.
Recorded Version
Columbia OS 3550 (O.C.).
    Stunning views of urban morals & mores.

FOLLIES
Opened: April 4, 1971, Winter Garden.
522 *performances.*
Book by James Goldman.
Produced by Harold Prince; directed by Prince & Michael Bennett.
Cast included: Alexis Smith, Dorothy Collins, Gene Nelson, John McMartin, Yvonne DeCarlo, Mary McCarthy, Fifi D'Orsay, Ethel Barrymore Colt, Sheila Smith, Michael Bartlett, Ethel Shutta, Arnold Moss, Victoria Mallory, Kurt Peterson, Virginia Sandifur, Harvey Evans, Justine Johnston, Fred Kelly.
Principal songs: Don't Look at Me; Waiting for the Girls Upstairs; Broadway Baby; The Road You Didn't Take; In Buddy's Eyes; Who's That Woman?; I'm Still Here; Too Many Mornings; The Right Girl; One More Kiss; Could I Leave You?; Losing My Mind; The Story of Lucy and Jessie.
Recorded Version
Capitol SO 761 (O.C.).
    Four pieces from this masterful score had to be cut to fit the songs on a single record.

A LITTLE NIGHT MUSIC
Opened: Feb. 25, 1973, Shubert Th.
601 *performances.*
Book by Hugh Wheeler.
Produced & directed by Harold Prince; dances by Patricia Birch.
Cast included: Glynis Johns. Len Cariou, Hermione Gingold, Victoria Mallory, Laurence Guittard, Patricia Elliott, Mark Lambert, D. Jamin-Bartlett, George Lee Andrews, Teri Ralston.
Principal songs: Night Waltz; Now; Later; Soon; The Glamorous Life; Remember?; You Must Meet My Wife; Liaisons; Every Day a Little Death; A Weekend in the Country; It

Would Have Been Wonderful; Send in the
Clowns; The Miller's Son.
Recorded Versions
Columbia KS 32265 (O.C.).
RCA LRL 5090 (London O.C.) (1975).
Columbia JS 35333 (F.V.) (1978).
   Miss Johns' successors—Jean Simmons in
London, Elizabeth Taylor on screen—still
leave her Queen of the "Clowns" in this wry,
witty, waltzing operetta.

PACIFIC OVERTURES
Opened: Jan. 11, 1976, Winter Garden.
193 *performances.*
Book by John Weidman, Hugh Wheeler.
Produced & directed by Harold Prince; dances
by Patricia Birch.
Cast included: Mako, Soon-Teck Oh, Yuki
Shimoda, Sab Shimono, Isao Sato, Alvin Ing.
Principal songs: The Advantages of Floating
in the Middle of the Sea; There Is No Other
Way; Four Black Dragons; Chrysanthemum
Tea; Poems; Welcome to Kanagawa; Someone
In a Tree; Please Hello; A Bowler Hat; Pretty
Lady.
Recorded Version
RCA ARL1 1367 (O.C.).
   The evocative, provocative world of
Sondheim-san.

SWEENEY TODD
Opened: March 1, 1979, Uris Th.
558 *performances.*
Book by Hugh Wheeler.
Produced by Richard Barr, Charles
Woodward, Robert Fryer, Mary Lea Johnson,
Martin Richards; directed by Harold Prince;
dances by Larry Fuller.
Cast included: Angela Lansbury, Len Cariou,
Victor Garber, Ken Jennings, Merle Louise,
Edmund Lyndeck, Sarah Rice.
Principal songs: The Ballad of Sweeney Todd;
The Barber and His Wife; The Worst Pies in
London; Green Finch and Linnet Bird; Ah,
Miss; Johanna; Kiss Me; Pretty Women;
Epiphany; A Little Priest; By the Sea; Not
While I'm Around.
Recorded Version
RCA CBL2 3379 (O.C.).
   A savory Shepard's pie lovingly served on
two platters.

Chapter Twenty-Four
JERRY BOCK
Composer

SHELDON HARNICK
Lyricist

*All music by Mr. Bock & lyrics by Mr.
Harnick unless otherwise noted.*

MR. WONDERFUL
Opened: Mar. 22, 1956, Broadway Th.
383 *performances.*
Book by Joseph Stein & Will Glickman; lyrics

by Larry Holofcener & George Weiss.
Produced by Jule Styne & George Gilbert
with Lester Osterman; directed by Jack
Donohue.
Cast included: Sammy Davis, Jr., Jack Carter,
Pat Marshall, Olga James, Chita Rivera, Hal
Loman, Will Mastin, Sammy Davis, Sr.,
Karen Shepard.
Principal songs: Without You I'm Nothing;
Mr. Wonderful; Ethel Baby; Too Close for
Comfort.
Recorded Version
Decca DL 9032 (O.C.).
   Davis belts out the breezy score with an
exuberance not always warranted by the
material

THE BODY BEAUTIFUL
Opened: Jan. 23, 1958, Broadway Th.
60 *performances.*
Book by Joseph Stein & Will Glickman.
Produced by Richard Kollmar & Albert W.
Selden; directed by George Schaefer; dances by
Herbert Ross.
Cast included: Mindy Carson, Steve Forrest,
Jack Warden, Lonnie Sattin, Barbara
McNair, Brock Peters, William Hickey, Jack
DeLon.
Principal songs: Leave Well Enough Alone;
Uh-Huh, Oh Yeah!; All of These and More;
Summer Is; Just My Luck; A Relatively
Simple Affair.

FIORELLO!
Opened: Nov. 23, 1959, Broadhurst Th.
795 *performances.*
Book by Jerome Weidman & George Abbott.
Produced by Robert Griffith & Harold Prince;
directed by Abbott; dances by Peter Gennaro.
Cast included: Tom Bosley, Patricia Wilson,
Ellen Hanley, Howard DaSilva, Mark
Dawson, Nathaniel Frey, Pat Stanley, Eileen
Rodgers, Bob Holiday, Ron Husmann,
Patricia Harty.
Principal songs: On the Side of the Angels;
Politics and Poker; The Name's LaGuardia; I
Love a Cop; 'Til Tomorrow; When Did I Fall
in Love?; Gentleman Jimmy; Little Tin Box;
The Very Next Man.
Recorded Version
Capitol S WAO 1321 (O.C.).
   New York's beloved Little Flower gets an
affectionate, witty tribute.

TENDERLOIN
Opened: Oct. 17, 1960, 46th St. Th.
216 *performances.*
Book by George Abbott & Jerome Weidman.
Produced by Robert Griffith & Harold Prince;
directed by Abbott; dances by Joe Layton.
Cast included: Maurice Evans, Ron Husmann,
Wynne Miller, Eileen Rodgers, Ralph Dunn,
Irene Kane, Lee Becker (Theodore), Rex
Everhart, Eddie Phillips, Margery Gray.
Principal songs: Little Old New York;
Artificial Flowers; The Picture of Happiness;

Tommy, Tommy; How the Money Changes Hands; Good Clean Fun; My Miss Mary; My Gentle Young Johnny.
Recorded Version
Capitol S. WAO 1492 (O.C.).

Ron Husmann wins vocal honors in this delightfully flavorsome collection.

SMILING THE BOY FELL DEAD
Opened: Apr. 19, 1961, Cherry Lane Th.
22 performances.
Book by Ira Wallach; music by David Baker.
Produced by Theodore Mann & George Kôgel; directed by Word Baker (uncredited) & Mann.
Cast included: Danny Meehan, Phil Leeds, Joseph Macaulay, Claiborne Cary, Louise Larrabee.
Principal songs: Wonderful Future; World to Win; Wonderful Machine; Dear Old Dad.

SHE LOVES ME
Opened: Apr. 23, 1963, Eugene O'Neill Th.
301 performances.
Book by Joe Masteroff.
Produced by Harold Prince with Lawrence J. Kasha & Philip C. McKenna; directed by Prince; dances by Carol Haney.
Cast included: Barbara Cook, Daniel Massey, Barbara Baxley, Jack Cassidy, Ludwig Donath, Nathaniel Frey, Ralph Williams, Jo Wilder, Wood Romoff, Gino Conforti, Peg Murray.
Principal songs: Days Gone By; Tonight at Eight; Will He Like Me?; Ilona; A Romantic Atmosphere; Dear Friend; Ice Cream; She Loves Me; Grand Knowing You; Twelve Days to Christmas.
Recorded Version
Stet DS2 15008 (O.C.).

This remarkably tasty musical confection has been granted the deserved luxury of a 2-record set.

FIDDLER ON THE ROOF
Opened: Sept. 22, 1964, Imperial Th.
3,242 performances.
Book by Joseph Stein.
Produced by Harold Prince; directed by Jerome Robbins.
Cast included: Zero Mostel, Maria Karnilova, Beatrice Arthur, Joanna Merlin, Austin Pendleton, Bert Convy, Julia Migenes, Tanya Everett, Gino Conforti.
Principal songs: Tradition; Matchmaker, Matchmaker; If I Were a Rich Man; To Life; Sunrise, Sunset; Do You Love Me?; Miracle of Miracles; Anatevka.
Recorded Versions
RCA LSO 1093 (O.C.).
Columbia OL 6490 (Hebrew O.C.) (1965).
Columbia OS 3050 (Yiddish O.C.) (1966).
Columbia SX 30742 (London O.C.) (1967).
London SW 99470 (German O.C.) (1968).
United Artists 10900 (F.V.) (1971).
Columbia OS 3010.
London 44121 (S.C.).

In addition to 4 languages, the eloquent score may be savored on a 2-record soundtrack (Isaac Stern is the fiddler), starring Topol. The 4th Columbia features Herschel Bernardi, Mostel's successor; the 2nd London offers Robert Merrill & Molly Picon.

THE APPLE TREE
Opened: Oct. 18, 1966, Shubert Th.
463 performances.
Book by Bock & Harnick, additional material by Jerome Coopersmith.
Produced by Stuart Ostrow; directed by Mike Nichols; dances by Lee Theodore & Herbert Ross.
Cast included: Barbara Harris, Alan Alda, Larry Blyden, Carmen Alvarez, Marc Jordan, Robert Klein.
Principal songs: What Makes Me Love Him?; The Apple Tree; Go to Sleep, Whatever You Are; I've Got What You Want; Eve; Beautiful, Beautiful World; Oh to Be a Movie Star.
Recorded Version
Columbia KOS 3020 (O.C.).

Barbara Harris shines in this collection of bright musical pieces culled from separate one-act musicals.

THE ROTHSCHILDS
Opened: Oct. 19, 1970, Lunt-Fontanne.
507 performances.
Book by Sherman Yellen.
Produced by Lester Osterman & Hillard Elkins; directed by Michael Kidd.
Cast included: Hal Linden, Paul Hecht, Leila Martin, Keene Curtis, Jill Clayburgh, Leo Leyden, Timothy Jerome, Chris Sarandon.
Principal songs: He Tossed a Coin; Sons; Everything; Rothschild & Sons; I'm in Love! I'm in Love!; In My Own Lifetime.
Recorded Version
Columbia S 30337 (O.C.).

A dramatic, tightly integrated score.

REX
(*See* Richard Rodgers).

THE UMBRELLAS OF CHERBOURG
Opened: Feb. 1, 1979, Public Th.
36 performances.
Book & lyrics by Jacques Demy, translated by Harnick with Charles Burr; music by Michel Legrand.
Produced by N.Y. Shakespeare Festival (Joseph Papp); directed by Andrei Serban.
Cast included: Stefanianne Christopherson, Dean Pitchford, Judith Roberts, Laurence Guittard, Maureen Silliman, Lizabeth Pritchett.

Chapter Twenty-Five
CHARLES STROUSE
Composer

LEE ADAMS
Lyricist

All lyrics by Mr. Adams unless otherwise noted.

BYE BYE BIRDIE
Opened: Apr. 14, 1960, Martin Beck Th.
607 *performances.*
Book by Michael Stewart.
Produced by Edward Padula; directed by Gower Champion.
Cast included: Chita Rivera, Dick Van Dyke, Kay Medford, Paul Lynde, Dick Gautier, Michael J. Pollard, Susan Watson, Marijane Maricle, Jerry Dodge, Kenny Burrell, Charles Nelson Reilly.
Principal songs: One Last Kiss; One Boy; An English Teacher; Baby, Talk to Me; A Lot of Livin' to Do; Rosie; Put on a Happy Face; Kids.
Recorded Versions
Columbia COS 2025 (O.C.).
RCA LSO 1081 (F.V.) (1963)
   The early rockish score is better served by the Broadway cast than by the Hollywood group headed by Ann-Margret, Janet Leigh, & Van Dyke.

ALL AMERICAN
Opened: Mar. 19, 1962, Winter Garden
80 *performances.*
Book by Mel Brooks.
Produced by Edward Padula; directed by Joshua Logan; dances by Danny Daniels.
Cast included: Ray Bolger, Eileen Herlie, Ron Husmann, Anita Gillette, Fritz Weaver, Bernie West, Betty Oakes, Mort Marshall, Will B. Able.
Principal songs: We Speak the Same Language; Once Upon a Time; The Real Me; What a Country!; Nightlife; I've Just Seen Her.
Recorded Version
Columbia AKOS 2160 (O.C.).
   Not one of the team's better efforts.

GOLDEN BOY
Opened: Oct. 20, 1964, Majestic Th.
569 *performances.*
Book by Clifford Odets & William Gibson.
Produced by Hillard Elkins; directed by Arthur Penn; dances by Donald McKayle.
Cast included: Sammy Davis, Billy Daniels, Paula Wayne, Kenneth Tobey, Ted Beniades, Roy Glenn, Jeanette DuBois, Johnny Brown, Jaime Rogers, Louis Gossett, Lola Falana.
Principal songs: Night Song; Gimme Some; Don't Forget 127th Street; Lorna's Here; This Is the Life; Golden Boy; While the City Sleeps; I Want to Be With You.
Recorded Version
Capitol STAO 11605 (O.C.).
   A lively pulsating reincarnation of the Odets play.

IT'S A BIRD IT'S A PLANE IT'S SUPERMAN
Opened: Mar. 29, 1966, Alvin Th.
129 *performances.*
Book by David Newman & Robert Benton.
Produced & directed by Harold Prince; dances by Ernest Flatt.
Cast included: Jack Cassidy, Michael O'Sullivan, Patricia Marand, Bob Holiday, Don Chastain, Linda Lavin.
Principal songs: It's Superman; We Don't Matter at All; The Woman for the Man; You've Got Possibilities; What I've Always Wanted; Ooh, Do You Love You!; You've Got What I Need.
Recorded Version
Columbia AKOS 2970 (O.C.).
   Broadway's first excursion into the "camp" camp, abetted by songs that ably reflect the innocence of the terrain.

APPLAUSE
Opened: March 30, 1970, Palace Th.
896 *performances.*
Book by Betty Comden & Adolph Green.
Produced by Joseph Kipness & Lawrence Kasha; directed by Ron Field.
Cast included: Lauren Bacall, Penny Fuller, Len Cariou, Robert Mandan, Ann Williams, Brandon Maggart, Lee Roy Reams, Bonnie Franklin.
Principal songs: Think How It's Gonna Be; But Alive; Who's that Girl?; Applause; Fasten Your Seat Belts; Welcome to the Theatre; One of a Kind; Something Greater.
Recorded Version
ABC 11 (O.C.).
   The backstage world of the theatre illuminated by the glowing presence of Lauren Bacall.

SIX
Opened: Apr. 12, 1971, Cricket Th.
8 *performances.*
Book & lyrics by Strouse.
Produced by Slade Brown; directed by Peter Coe.
Cast included: Lee Beery, Hal Watters, Gilbert Price, Alvin Ing.
Principal songs: The Garden; Love Song; Six; The Dream.

ANNIE
Opened: Apr. 21, 1977, Alvin Th.
2,377 *performances.*
Book by Thomas Meehan; lyrics by Martin Charnin.
Produced by Mike Nichols, Irwin Meyer, Stephen Friedman, Lewis Allen; directed by Charnin; dances by Peter Gennaro.
Cast included: Reid Shelton, Andrea McArdle, Dorothy Loudon, Sandy Faison, Robert Fitch.
Principal songs: It's the Hard-knock Life; Tomorrow; We'd Like to Thank You; Little Girls; N.Y.C.; Easy Street; You're Never Fully Dressed without a Smile; Something Was Missing; Annie; A New Deal for Christmas.
Recorded Version
Columbia PS 34712 (O.C.).
   An affectionate, comic-strip look at the Thirties.

A BROADWAY MUSICAL
Opened: December 21, 1978.
1 *performance.*
Book by William F. Brown.
Produced by Norman Kean and Garth H. Drabinsky; directed by Gower Champion.
Cast included: Warren Berlinger, Larry Marshall, Patti Karr, Gwyda Donhowe, Anne Francine, Tiger Haynes, Irving Allen Lee.
Principal songs: Smoke and Fire; Let Me Sing My Song; The 1934 Hot Chocolate Jazz Babies Revue; You Gotta Have Dancing.

Chapter Twenty-Six
CY COLEMAN
Composer

WILDCAT
Opened: Dec. 16, 1960, Alvin Th.
171 *performances.*
Book by N. Richard Nash; lyrics by Carolyn Leigh.
Produced by Michael Kidd & Nash; directed by Kidd.
Cast included: Lucille Ball, Keith Andes, Paula Stewart, Edith King, Don Tomkins, Charles Braswell, Swen Swenson, Valerie Harper.
Principal songs: Hey, Look Me Over; You've Come Home; What Takes My Fancy; One Day We Dance; Give a Little Whistle; El Sombrero; Corduroy Road.
Recorded Version
RCA LSO 1060 (O.C.).
   The "Hey, Look Me Over" score has a few other goodies, too.

LITTLE ME
Opened: Nov. 17, 1962, Lunt-Fontanne Th.
257 *performances.*
Book by Neil Simon; lyrics by Carolyn Leigh.
Produced by Cy Feuer & Ernest Martin; directed by Feuer & Bob Fosse.
Cast included: Sid Caesar, Virginia Martin, Nancy Andrews, Mort Marshall, Joey Faye, Swen Swenson, Nancy Cushman, Peter Turgeon, Mickey Deems, Gretchen Cryer.
Principal songs: The Other Side of the Tracks; Deep Down Inside; Boom-Boom; I've Got Your Number; I Love You; Real Live Girl; Here's to Us.
Recorded Version
RCA LSO 1078 (O.C.).
   Much far-out hilarity, abetted by the wit of Miss Leigh's lyrics & the rhythmic freshness of Coleman's music.

SWEET CHARITY
Opened: Jan. 30, 1966, Palace Th.
608 *performances.*
Book by Neil Simon; lyrics by Dorothy Fields.
Produced by Fryer, Carr & Harris; directed by Bob Fosse.
Cast included: Gwen Verdon, John McMartin, Helen Gallagher, Thelma Oliver, James Luisi, Arnold Soboloff, Ruth Buzzi.
Principal songs: Big Spender; If My Friends Could See Me Now; Too Many Tomorrows; There's Gotta Be Something Better than This; Baby, Dream Your Dream; Sweet Charity; Where Am I Going?; I'm a Brass Band.
Recorded Versions
Columbia KOS 2900 (O.C.).
Decca DL 71502 (F.V.) (1968).
   The contents of the 2 albums are basically the same, with the major soundtrack addition being Shirley MacLaine singing "My Personal Property."

SEESAW
Opened: March 18, 1973, Uris Th.
296 *performances.*
Book by Michael Bennett &Neil Simon (uncredited); lyrics by Dorothy Fields.
Produced by Joseph Kipness & Lawrence Kasha; directed by Michael Bennett.
Cast included: Michele Lee, Ken Howard, Tommy Tune, Giancarlo Esposito, Judy McCauley, Anita Morris.
Principal songs: Seesaw; Nobody Does It Like Me; In Tune; Spanglish; Welcome to Holiday Inn; We've Got It; Poor Everybody Else; It's Not Where You Start; I'm Way Ahead.
Recorded Version
Columbia X 15563 (O.C.).
   Another sweetly charitable view of New York.

I LOVE MY WIFE
Opened: April 17, 1977, Ethel Barrymore Th.
857 *performances.*
Book & lyrics by Michael Stewart.
Produced by Terry Allen Kramer & Harry Rigby; directed by Gene Saks; dances by Onna White.
Cast included: Ilene Graff, Lenny Baker, Joanna Gleason, James Naughton.
Principal songs: By Three's; Love Revolution; Someone Wonderful I Missed; Sexually Free; Hey There, Good Times; Lovers on Christmas Eve; Everybody Today Is Turning On; I Love My Wife.
Recorded Version
Atlantic 19107 (O.C.).
   Mate-swapping made breezy.

ON THE TWENTIETH CENTURY
Opened: Feb. 19, 1978, St. James Th.
449 *performances.*
Book & lyrics by Betty Comden & Adolph Green.
Produced by Robert Fryer, Mary Lea Johnson, James Cresson, Martin Richards; directed by Harold Prince; dances by Larry Fuller.
Cast included: John Cullum, Madeline Kahn, Imogene Coca, Kevin Kline, Dean Dittman, George Coe, Judy Kaye.
Principal songs: I Ride Again; Together; Never; Our Private World; Repent; On the Twentieth Century; She's a Nut; The Legacy.
Recorded Version

Columbia JS 35330 (O.C.).
> Almost always on the right track.

BARNUM
Opened: Apr. 30, 1980, St. James Th.
854 *performances*.
Book by Mark Bramble; lyrics by Michael Stewart.
Produced by Judy Gordon, Cy Coleman, Maurice & Lois Rosenfield; directed by Joe Layton.
Cast included: Jim Dale, Glenn Close, Terri White, Marianne Tatum, Leonard John Crofoot.
Principal songs: There's a Sucker Born Ev'ry Minute; The Colors of My Life; One Brick at a Time; Bigger Isn't Better; Come follow the Band; Black and White; Join the Circus.
Recorded Version
Columbia JS 36576 (O.C.)
> Atmospheric, brassy tribute.

CAROLYN LEIGH
Lyricist

PETER PAN
Opened: Oct. 20, 1954, Winter Garden.
152 *performances*.
Play by James M. Barrie; Leigh music by Mark Charlap; music & lyrics also by Jule Styne, Betty Comden & Adolph Green.
Produced by Richard Halliday; directed by Jerome Robbins.
Cast included: Mary Martin, Cyril Ritchard, Margalo Gilmore, Kathy Nolan, Heller Halliday, Sondra Lee, Norman Shelly, Joe E. Marks.
Principal Leigh-Charlap songs: Tender Shepherd; I've Gotta Crow; I'm Flying; I Won't Grow Up.
Recorded Version
RCA LSO 1019 (O.C.).
> The songs for this charming album were divided about evenly between the 2 teams.

WILDCAT
(*See* Cy Coleman).

LITTLE ME
(*See* Cy Coleman).

HOW NOW, DOW JONES
Opened: Dec. 7, 1967, Lunt-Fontanne Th.
213 *performances*.
Book by Max Shulman; music by Elmer Bernstein.
Produced by David Merrick; directed by George Abbott; dances by Gillian Lynne.
Cast included: Anthony Roberts, Marlyn Mason, Brenda Vaccaro, Hiram Sherman, James Congdon, Sammy Smith, Charlotte Jones, Rex Everhart, Tommy Tune, Barnard Hughes.
Principal songs: Live a Little; Walk Away; He's Here!; Step to the Rear.
Recorded Version
RCA LSO 1142 (O.C.).
> The averages are off.

Chapter Twenty-Seven
JERRY HERMAN
Composer-lyricist

I FEEL WONDERFUL
Opened: Oct. 18, 1954, Theatre de Lys.
48 *performances*.
Sketches by Barry Alan Grael.
Produced by Sidney S. Oshrin; directed by Herman; dances by Frank Wagner.
Cast included: Nina Dova, Albie Gaye, Janie Janvier, John Bartis, Phyllis Newman, Richard Tone, Barry Alan Grael.
Principal songs: I Feel Wonderful; When I Love Again; It's Christmas Today; Lonesome in New York.

PARADE
Opened: Jan. 20, 1960, Players Th.
95 *performances*.
Produced by Lawrence Kasha; directed by Herman; dances by Richard Tone.
Cast included: Dody Goodman, Richard Tone, Fia Karin, Charles Nelson Reilly, Lester James.
Principal songs: There's No Tune Like a Show Tune; Your Hand in My Hand; Your Good Morning; Another Candle; Jolly Theatrical Season.
Recorded Version
Kapp 7005(S) (O.C.).
> A bright, engaging introduction to the talents of Jerry Herman.

MILK AND HONEY
Opened: Oct. 10, 1961, Martin Beck Th.
543 *performances*.
Book by Don Appell.
Produced by Gerard Oestreicher; directed by Albert Marre; dances by Donald Saddler.
Cast included: Robert Weede, Mimi Benzell, Molly Picon, Tommy Rall, Thelma Pelish, Lanna Saunders, Juki Arkin, Ellen Madison, Ronald Holgate.
Principal songs: Shalom; Milk and Honey; There's No Reason in the World; That Was Yesterday; I Will Follow You; Hymn to Hymie; It's as Simple as That; Like a Young Man.
Recorded Version
RCA LSO 1065 (O.C.).
> An appealing score full of atmosphere & warmth.

MADAME APHRODITE
Opened: Dec. 29, 1961, Orpheum Th.
13 *performances*.
Book by Tad Mosel.
Produced by Howard Barker, Cynthia Baer, Robert Chambers; directed by Robert Turoff.
Cast included: Nancy Andrews, Cherry Davis, Jack Drummond, Mona Paulee, Rod Colbin.
Principal songs: Beat the World; You I Like; The Girls who Sit and Wait.

HELLO, DOLLY!
Opened: Jan. 16, 1964, St. James Th.

2,844 *performances.*
Book by Michael Stewart.
Produced by David Merrick; directed by
Gower Champion.
Cast included: Carol Channing, David Burns,
Eileen Brennan, Sondra Lee, Charles Nelson
Reilly, Jerry Dodge, Gordon Connell, Igors
Gavon, Alice Playten, David Hartman.
Principal songs; It Takes a Woman; Put on
Your Sunday Clothes; Ribbons Down My
Back; Before the Parade Passes By; Elegance;
Dancing; Motherhood; Hello Dolly!; It Only
Takes a Moment; So Long, Dearie.
Recorded Versions
RCA LSOD 1087 (O.C.).
RCA LSOD 2007 (London O.C.) (1965).
Columbia OS 3110 (German O.C.).
RCA ANL1 2849 (O.C.) (1967).
20th Century-Fox 102 (F.V.) (1969).

Herman's exuberant score gets a much
better workout from the New York company
than from its somewhat pale London carbon—
even with Mary Martin. The German version
seems excessively Teutonic. The 3rd RCA is
the spirited Negro company headed by Pearl
Bailey & Cab Calloway. For the Barbra
Streisand-Walter Matthau film version, 2
songs were cut & 2 were added.

MAME

Opened: May 24, 1966, Winter Garden
1,508 *performances.*
Book by Jerome Lawrence & Robert E. Lee.
Produced by Fryer, Carr & Harris; directed
by Gene Saks; dances by Onna White.
Cast included: Angela Lansbury, Beatrice
Arthur, Jane Connell, Willard Waterman,
Frankie Michaels, Charles Braswell, Jerry
Lanning, Margaret Hall.
Principal songs: It's Today; Open a New
Window; My Best Girl; We Need a Little
Christmas; Mame; Bosom Buddies; If He
Walked into My Life.
Recorded Versions
Columbia KOS 3000 (O.C.).
Warner Bros. 2773 (F.V.) (1974).

The commercial Broadway musical at its
highly polished best. The soundtrack, with one
song cut and one added, stars a miscast Lucille
Ball.

DEAR WORLD

Opened: Feb. 6, 1969, Hellinger Th.
132 *performances.*
Book by Jerome Lawrence & Robert E. Lee.
Produced by Alexander H. Cohen; directed by
Joe Layton.
Cast included: Angela Lansbury, Milo
O'Shea, Jane Connell, Carmen Mathews,
Kurt Peterson, Pamela Hall, John Taliaferro,
Joe Masiell.
Principal songs: The Spring of Next Year;
Each Tomorrow Morning; I Don't Want to
Know; I've Never Said I Love You; Dear
World; Kiss Her Now; The Tea Party; And I
Was Beautiful; One Person.

Recorded Version
Columbia ABOS 3260 (O.C.).

Herman's blend of Gallic charm & fantasy
contains many pleasures.

MACK & MABEL

Opened: Oct. 6, 1974, Majestic Th.
65 *performances.*
Book by Michael Stewart.
Produced by David Merrick; directed by
Gower Champion.
Cast included: Robert Preston, Bernadette
Peters, Lisa Kirk, Jerry Dodge, James
Mitchell.
Principal songs: Movies Were Movies; Big
Time; I Won't Send Roses; I Wanna Make the
World Laugh; Hundreds of Girls; When
Mabel Comes in the Room; Time Heals
Everything; Tap Your Troubles Away; I
Promise You a Happy Ending.
Recorded Version
ABC H 830 (O.C.).

What a crackling good score this is & what
a pity that it remains so unappreciated.

THE GRAND TOUR

Opened: January 11, 1979, Palace Th.
61 *performances.*
Book by Michael Stewart & Mark Bramble.
Produced by James Nederlander, Diana
Shumlin, Jack Schlissel; directed by Gerald
Freedman; dances by Donald Saddler.
Cast included: Joel Grey, Ronald Holgate,
Florence Lacey, Stephen Vinovich, Travis
Hudson, Chevi Colton.
Principal songs: I'll Be Here Tomorrow; Two
Possibilities; For Poland; Marianne; One
Extraordinary Thing; You I Like; I Belong
Here.
Recorded Version
Columbia JS 35761 (O.C.).

Unpretentious, unaffected and grand.

Chapter Twenty-Eight
JOHN KANDER
Composer

FRED EBB
Lyricist

*All music by Mr. Kander & lyrics by Mr. Ebb
unless otherwise noted.*

FROM A TO Z

Opened: Apr. 20, 1960, Plymouth Th.
21 *performances.*
Sketches by Woody Allen, Herbert Farjeon,
Nina Warner Hook; Ebb music by Paul Klein
& Norman Martin; music & lyrics also by
Jerry Herman, Jay Thompson, Dickson
Hughes & Everett Sloane, Jack Holmes,
William Dyer & Don Parks, Mary Rodgers &
Marshall Barer, Charles Zwar & Alan
Melville.
Produced by Carroll & Harris Masterson;

directed by Christopher Hewett; dances by Ray Harrison.
Cast included: Hermione Gingold, Elliott Reid, Alvin Epstein, Louise Hoff, Stuart Damon, Bob Dishy, Nora Kovach, Kelly Brown, Paula Stewart, Beryl Towbin, Virginia Vestoff.
Principal Ebb songs: I Said to Love (Klein); Charlie (Martin); Time Step (Klein).

A FAMILY AFFAIR
Opened: Jan. 27, 1962, Billy Rose Th.
65 *performances.*
Book & lyrics by James Goldman & William Goldman.
Produced by Andrew Siff; directed by Harold Prince; dances by John Butler.
Cast included: Shelly Berman, Eileen Heckart, Morris Carnovsky, Larry Kert, Rita Gardner, Bibi Osterwald, Lulu Bates, Jack DeLon, Paula Trueman, Beryl Towbin, Linda Lavin, Cathryn Damon.
Principal songs: Anything for You; My Son, the Lawyer; Every Girl Wants to Get Married; There's a Room in My House; Harmony; Revenge.
Recorded Version
United Artists AS 5099 (O.C.).
    "Promising" is as good a word as any.

PUT IT IN WRITING
Opened: May 13, 1963, Theatre de Lys.
24 *performances.*
Sketches by David Panich, Steven Vinaver, Jay Thompson; Ebb music by Norman Martin; music & lyrics also by Bud McCreery, G. Wood, Jay Thompson, Robert Kessler & Martin Charnin, Alan Kohan.
Produced by Lucille Lortel & Arthur Cantor; directed by Bill Penn; dances by Joyce Trisler.
Cast included: Jane Connell, Buzz Halliday, Bill Hinnant, Jack Blackton, Will Mackenzie.
Principal Ebb-Martin songs: I Hope You're Happy; What's Cooking?; Emmy Lou; Stock Report.

MORNING SUN
Opened: Oct. 6, 1963, Phoenix Th.
9 *performances.*
Book by Ebb; music by Paul Klein.
Produced by T. Edward Hambleton & Martin Tahse; directed by Daniel Petrie; dances by Donald Saddler.
Cast included: Patricia Neway, Bert Convy, Will Mackenzie, Danny Lockin, Carole Demas, David Thomas.
Principal songs: Morning Sun; Tell Me Goodbye; Good as Anybody; Seventeen Summers.

FLORA, THE RED MENACE
Opened: May 11, 1965, Alvin Th.
87 *performances.*
Book by George Abbott & Robert Russell.
Produced by Harold Prince; directed by Abbott; dances by Lee Theodore.
Cast included: Liza Minnelli, Bob Dishy,

Cathryn Damon, Mary Louise Wilson, Daniel P. Hannafin, Danny Carroll, Joe E. Marks.
Principal songs: A Quiet Thing; Hello Waves; Dear Love; Knock Knock; Sing Happy; You Are You.
Recorded Version
RCA CBL1 2760 (O.C.).
    A deftly constructed score that shows off the talents of Liza Minnelli in her first Broadway role.

CABARET
Opened: Nov. 20, 1966, Broadhurst Th.
1,165 *performances.*
Book by Joe Masteroff.
Produced & directed by Harold Prince; dances by Ronald Field.
Cast included: Jill Haworth, Jack Gilford, Bert Convy, Lotte Lenya, Joel Grey, Peg Murray, Edward Winter.
Principal songs: Willkommen; Don't Tell Mama; Perfectly Marvelous; It Couldn't Please Me More; Tomorrow Belongs to Me; Why Should I Wake Up?; Married; Meeskite; Cabaret.
Recorded Versions
Columbia KOS 3040 (O.C.).
ABC DS 752 (F.V.) (1972).
    Of the 15 songs in this chillingly atmospheric score, 6 were retained for the film version, with 5 new ones added—including Liza Minnelli's dazzling "Maybe This Time."

THE HAPPY TIME
Opened: Jan. 18, 1968, Broadway Th.
286 *performances.*
Book by N. Richard Nash.
Produced by David Merrick; directed by Gower Champion.
Cast included: Robert Goulet, David Wayne, Julie Gregg, Mike Rupert, George S. Irving.
Principal songs: The Happy Time; Tomorrow Morning; Please Stay; I Don't Remember You; The Life of the Party; Seeing Things; A Certain Girl.
Recorded Version
RCA LSO 1144 (O.C.)
    Gentle, evocative pieces that wear well.

ZORBA
Opened: Nov. 17, 1968, Imperial Th.
305 *performances.*
Book by Joseph Stein.
Produced & directed by Harold Prince; dances by Ronald Field.
Cast included: Herschel Bernardi, Maria Karnilova, John Cunningham, Carmen Alvarez, Lorraine Serabian.
Principal songs: Life Is; The First Time; The Top of the Hill; No Boom Boom; The Butterfly; Only Love; Y'Assou; Happy Birthday; I Am Free.
Recorded Version
Capitol SO 118 (O.C.).
    Broadway & bouzouki in a skillful blend.

70, GIRLS, 70
Opened: April 15, 1971, Broadhurst Th.
36 *performances.*
Book by Ebb & Norman L. Martin.
Produced by Arthur Whitelaw; directed by
Paul Aaron & Stanley Prager; dances by
Onna White.
Cast included: Mildred Natwick, Hans
Conried, Lillian Roth, Gil Lamb, Lucie
Lancaster, Henrietta Jacobson, Jay Velie,
Beau Tilden, Joey Faye, Lillian Hayman.
Principal Songs: Old Folks; Coffee in a
Cardboard Cup; Go Visit; Broadway My
Street; You and I, Love.
Recorded Version
Columbia S 30589 (O.C.).
 An occasionally diverting collection of
vaudeville-flavored songs.

CHICAGO
Opened: June 1, 1975, 46th St. Th.
923 *performances.*
Book by Ebb & Bob Fosse.
Produced by Robert Fryer & James Cresson;
directed by Fosse.
Cast included: Gwen Verdon, Chita Rivera,
Jerry Orbach, Barney Martin, Mary
McCarty, M. O'Haughey.
Principal songs: All that Jazz; Funny Honey;
When You're Good to Mama; All I Care
About; A Little Bit of Good; Roxie; My Own
Best Friend; Mr. Cellophane; Razzle Dazzle;
Nowadays.
Recorded Version
Arista 9005 (O.C.).
 A Windy City Cabaret.

THE ACT
Opened: Oct. 29, 1977, Majestic Th.
233 *performances.*
Book by George Furth.
Produced by the Shubert Organization, Cy
Feuer & Ernest Martin; directed by Martin
Scorsese, Gower Champion (uncredited);
dances by Ron Lewis.
Cast included: Liza Minnelli, Barry Nelson,
Arnold Soboloff, Gayle Crofoot, Roger
Minami, Wayne Cilento.
Principal songs: Shine It On; It's the Strangest
Thing; Bobo's; Arthur in the Afternoon; The
Money Tree; City Lights; My Own Space;
Walking Papers.
Recorded Version
DRG 6101 (O.C.).
 Liza in Las Vegas.

Chapter Twenty-Nine
TOM JONES
Lyricist

HARVEY SCHMIDT
Composer

All books by Mr. Jones unless otherwise noted.

THE FANTASTICKS
*Opened:*May 3, 1960, Sullivan St. Playhouse.
Produced by Lore Noto; directed by Word
Baker.
Cast included: Jerry Orbach, Rita Gardner,
Kenneth Nelson, Richard Stauffer, Thomas
Bruce (Tom Jones).
Principal songs: Try to Remember; It Depends
on What You Pay; Much More; Soon It's
Gonna Rain; Round and Round; Plant a
Radish; They Were You.
Recorded Version
MGM S 3872 (O.C.).
 A score rich in imagery and lyrical appeal.

110 IN THE SHADE
Opened: Oct. 24, 1963, Broadhurst Th.
330 *performances.*
Book by N. Richard Nash.
Produced by David Merrick; directed by
Joseph Anthony; dances by Agnes de Mille.
Cast included: Robert Horton, Inga Swensen,
Stephen Douglass, Will Geer, Steve Roland,
Scooter (Anthony) Teague, Lesley Ann
Warren, George Church, Jerry Dodge,
Gretchen Cryer.
Principal songs: Another Hot Day; Love,
Don't Turn Away; The Rain Song; A Man
and a Woman; Old Maid; Everything
Beautiful Happens at Night; Melisande;
Simple Little Things; Is It Really Me?;
Wonderful Music.
Recorded Version
RCA LSO 1085 (O.C.).
 A dramatic flavorful—though strangely
unappreciated—score.

I DO! I DO!
Opened: Dec. 5, 1966, 46th St. Th.
584 *performances.*
Produced by David Merrick; directed by
Gower Champion.
Cast: Mary Martin, Robert Preston.
Principal songs: I Love My Wife; My Cup
Runneth Over; Nobody's Perfect; A Well
Known Fact; The Honeymoon Is Over; Where
Are the Snows; When the Kids Get Married;
What Is a Woman?
Recorded Version
RCA LSO 1128 (O.C.).
 For the Sweete Shoppe crowd.

CELEBRATION
Opened: Jan. 22, 1969, Ambassador Th.
110 *performances.*
Produced by Cheryl Crawford & Richard
Chandler; directed by Jones; dances by Vernon
Lusby.
Cast included: Keith Charles, Michael Glenn-
Smith, Susan Watson, Ted Thurston.
Principal songs: Celebration; Somebody;
Where Did It Go?; I'm Glad to See You've
Got What You Want; Under the Tree; Winter
and Summer.
Recorded Version
Capitol SW 198 (O.C.).

Light & lovely in a *Fantasticks* sort of way.

PHILEMON
Opened: April 8, 1975, Portfolio Studio.
48 *performances.*
Produced by Portfolio Productions (Schmidt & Jones); directed by Lester Collins.
Cast included: Michael Glenn-Smith, Dick Latessa, Leila Martin, Kathrin King Segal.
Principal songs: The Streets of Antioch; Don't Kiki Me; He's Coming; My Secret Dream; I Love His Face; Love Suffers Everything.
Recorded Version
Gallery OC 1 (O.C.).
   Imaginative, stylish & a bit cold.

MITCH LEIGH
Composer

JOE DARION
Lyricist

All music by Mr. Leigh & lyrics by Mr. Darion unless otherwise noted.

SHINBONE ALLEY
Opened: Apr. 13, 1957, Broadway Th.
49 *performances.*
Book by Darion & Mel Brooks; music by George Kleinsinger.
Produced by Peter Lawrence; director uncredited; dances by Rod Alexander.
Cast included: Eartha Kitt, Eddie Bracken, Erik Rhodes, Ross Martin, Jacques d'Amboise, Allegra Kent, Gwen Harmon, George S. Irving, Reri Grist, Lillian Hayman, Cathryn Damon.
Principal songs: Toujours gai; A Woman Wouldn't Be a Woman; Flotsam and Jetsam; Cheerio My Deario.
Recorded Version
Columbia AOL 4963 (S.C.).
   Titled *archie and mehitabel*, this imaginative aural version preceded the stage adaptation. Carol Channing, Eddie Bracken & David Wayne were featured.

MAN OF LA MANCHA
Opened: Nov. 22, 1965, ANTA Washington Square Th.
2,328 *performances.*
Book by Dale Wasserman.
Produced by Albert W. Selden & Hal James; directed by Albert Marre; dances by Jack Cole.
Cast included: Richard Kiley, Irving Jacobson, Ray Middleton, Robert Rounseville, Joan Diener, Jon Cypher, Gerrianne Raphael.
Principal songs: Man of La Mancha (I, Don Quixote); It's All the Same; Dulcinea; I Really Like Him; Little Bird, Little Bird; To Each His Dulcinea; The Quest (The Impossible Dream); Golden Helmet.
Recorded Versions
MCA 2018 (O.C.).

MCA 10010 (London O.C.) (1968).
United Artists 9906 (F.V.) (1972).
Columbia S 31237 (S.C.).
   This affecting work is well preserved in both MCA albums (the London version, starring Keith Michell, is on 2 records). The soundtrack has Simon Gilbert singing for Peter O'Toole; the Columbia features Jim Nabors & Marilyn Horne.

ILLYA DARLING
Opened: Apr. 11, 1967, Mark Hellinger Th.
319 *performances.*
Book by Jules Dassin; music by Manos Hadjidakis.
Produced by Kermit Bloomgarden; directed by Dassin; dances by Onna White.
Cast included: Melina Mercouri, Orson Bean, Titos Vandis, Nikos Kourkoulos, Despo, Rudy Bond, Hal Linden, Harold Gary, Joe E. Marks.
Principal songs: Piraeus, My Love; Illya Darling; Never on Sunday; Love, Love, Love; After Love.
Recorded Version
United Artists 9901 (O.C.).
   A spirited, bouzouki-flavored score, abetted by the exuberant Miss Mercouri.

CRY FOR US ALL
Opened: April 8, 1970, Broadhurst Th.
9 *performances.*
Book by William Alfred & Albert Marre; lyrics by Alfred & Phyllis Robinson.
Produced by Leigh; directed by Marre; dances by Todd Bolender.
Cast included: Robert Weede, Joan Diener, Steve Arlen, Tommy Rall, Helen Gallagher, Paul Ukena, Edwin Steffe, Scott Jacoby.
Principal songs: The Mayor's Chair; The Verandah Waltz; Who to Love; Cry for Us All; Aggie, Oh Aggie; Swing Your Bag; The Leg of the Duck; This Cornucopian Land.
Recorded Version
Project 3 TS 1000 (O.C.).
   This ill-fated musical lives on through its richly evocative score.

HOME SWEET HOMER
Opened: Jan. 4, 1976, Palace Th.
1 *performance.*
Book by Roland Kibbee & Albert Marre; lyrics by Charles Burr, Forman Brown.
Produced by the John F. Kennedy Center for Performing Arts; directed by Marre.
Cast included: Yul Brynner, Joan Diener, Russ Thacker, Diana Davila.
Principal songs: The Tales; Home Sweet Homer; How Could I Dare to Dream?; He Will Come Home Again; He Sang Songs.

SARAVÁ
Opened: Feb. 23, 1979, Hellinger Th.
177 *performances.*
Book & lyrics by N. Richard Nash.
Produced by Eugene V. Wolsk & Leigh;

directed by Rick Atwell.
Cast included: Tovah Feldshuh, P.J. Benjamin, Michael Ingram, Carol Jean Lewis.
Principal songs: Saravá; Nothing's Missing; Vadinho Is Gone; A Simple Man; You Do.

GALT MacDERMOT

Composer

HAIR
Book & lyrics by Gerome Ragni & James Rado.
Opened: Oct. 29, 1967, Public Th.
94 *performances.*
Produced by N.Y. Shakespeare Festival (Joseph Papp); directed by Gerald Freedman.
Cast included: Walker Daniels, Gerome Ragni, Jill O'Hara, Jonelle Allen, Sally Eaton, Shelley Plimpton, Arnold Wilkerson, Steve Dean.
Opened: April 29, 1968, Biltmore Th.
1,742 *performances.*
Produced by Michael Butler; directed by Tom O'Horgan; dances by Julie Arenal.
Cast included: James Rado, Gerome Ragni, Lynn Kellogg, Melba Moore, Sally Eaton, Shelley Plimpton, Lamont Washington, Steve Curry, Diane Keaton.
Principal songs: Aquarius; Ain't Got No; I Got Life; Air; Hair; Easy to Be Hard; Frank Mills; Hare Krishna; Where Do I Go?; Good Morning, Starshine; Let the Sunshine In.
Recorded Versions
RCA ANL1 0986 (O.C.) (1967).
RCA LSO 1150 (O.C.) (1968).
RCA LSO 1170 (Japanese O.C.) (1971).
RCA CBL 2-3274 (F.V.) (1979).
    Enough difference between the 2 NY hirsute albums to make them both recommended. Besides the Japanese version, another offbeat item is *Disin-Hair-ited* (RCA LSO 1163), made up of discarded material. The soundtrack covers 2 records.

TWO GENTLEMEN OF VERONA
Opened: Dec. 1, 1971, St. James Th.
613 *performances.*
Book by John Guare & Mel Shapiro; lyrics by Guare.
Produced by N.Y. Shakespeare Festival (Joseph Papp); directed by Shapiro; dances by Jean Erdman.
Cast included: Raul Julia, Clifton Davis, Jonelle Allen, Diana Davila, Stockard Channing.
Principal songs: I Love My Father; That's a Very Interesting Question; Two Gentlemen of Verona; Follow the Rainbow; Bring All the Boys Back Home; Night Letter; Who Is Silvia? (lyric, Shakespeare); Eglamour; Calla Lily Lady.
Recorded Version
ABC 1001 (O.C.).
    MacDermot's almost consistently appealing

score has been preserved in a 2-record album.

DUDE
Opened: Oct. 9, 1972, Broadway Th.
16 *performances.*
Book & lyrics by Gerome Ragni.
Produced by Adela & Peter Holzer; directed by Tom O'Horgan.
Cast included: William Redfield, Salome Bey, Rae Allen, Dale Soules, Ralph Carter, Nell Carter.
Principal songs: The Highway Life; So Long, Dude; The Days of This Life; I Am who I Am; Weeping.
Recorded Versions
Kilmarnock 72007 (O.C.).
Kilmarnock 72003 (O.C.).
    The first album (called *The Highway Life*) offers most of the cast members; the second, with different songs, spotlights Salome Bey.

VIA GALECTICA
Opened: Nov. 28, 1972, Uris Th.
7 *performances.*
Book by Christopher Gore & Judith Ross; lyrics by Gore.
Produced by George W. George & Barnard Strauss, with Nat Shapiro; directed by Peter Hall.
Cast included: Raul Julia, Virginia Vestoff, Keene Curtis, Mark Baker, Ralph Carter.
Principal songs: Via Galectica; The Other Side of the Sky; The Lady Isn't Looking; New Jerusalem; Children of the Sun.

THE KARL MARX PLAY
Opened: March 16, 1973, American Place Th.
32 *performances.*
Play & lyrics by Rochelle Owens.
Produced by the American Place Theatre (Wynn Handman); directed by Mel Shapiro.
Cast included: Leonard Jackson, Katherine Helmond, Randy Kim, Norman Matlock, Ralph Carter.
Principal songs: Hello, Hello; Jenny von Westphalen; Dying Child; Red Leather Wrist Watch; We Doubt You, Papa.
Recorded Version
Kilmarnock 72010 (O.C.).
    This eclectic, appealing score was recorded by members of both its NY & touring companies.

BURT BACHARACH

Composer

HAL DAVID

Lyricist

PROMISES, PROMISES
Opened: Dec. 1, 1968, Shubert Th.
1,281 *performances.*
Book by Neil Simon.
Produced by David Merrick; directed by Robert Moore; dances by Michael Bennett.

Cast included: Jerry Orbach, Jill O'Hara, Edward Winter, Marian Mercer, A. Larry Haines, Norman Shelly, Ken Howard, Paul Reed, Donna McKechnie, Carole (Kelly) Bishop, Margo Sappington.
Principal songs: Upstairs; You'll Think of Someone; Our Little Secret; She Likes Basketball; Knowing When to Leave; Wanting Things; A Fact Can Be a Beautiful Thing; Whoever You Are; A Young Pretty Girl Like You; I'll Never Fall in Love Again; Promises, Promises.
Recorded Version
United Artists 9902 (O.C.).
Promises kept in a driving, infectious score.

Chapter Thirty
SHERMAN EDWARDS
Composer-lyricist

1776
Opened: March 16, 1969, 46th St. Th.
1,217 performances.
Book by Peter Stone.
Produced by Stuart Ostrow; directed by Peter Hunt; dances by Onna White.
Cast included: William Daniels, Paul Hecht, Clifford David, Roy Poole, Howard DaSilva, David Ford, Ken Howard, Virginia Vestoff, Ronald Holgate.
Principal songs: Sit Down, John; Piddle, Twiddle and Resolve; Till Then; The Lees of Old Virginia; But, Mr. Adams; Yours, Yours, Yours; He Plays the Violin; Cool, Cool, Considerate Men; Momma Look Sharp; The Egg; Molasses to Rum; Is Anybody There?
Recorded Versions
Columbia BOS 3310 (O.C.).
Columbia S 31741 (F.V.) (1972).
A fitting musical celebration of a momentous event. The soundtrack album—with virtually the same cast—has an unnatural hollow sound.

NANCY FORD
Composer

GRETCHEN CRYER
Lyricist
All books by Miss Cryer.

NOW IS THE TIME FOR ALL GOOD MEN
Opened: Sept. 26, 1967, Theatre de Lys.
111 performances.
Produced by David Cryer & Albert Poland; directed by Word Baker.
Cast included: David Cryer, Sally Niven (Gretchen Cryer), Anne Kaye, David Sabin, Steve Skiles.
Principal songs: Tea in the Rain; Halloween

Hayride; See Everything New; All Alone; Stuck Up; On My Own.
Recorded Version
Columbia OS 3130 (O.C.).
A promising start.

THE LAST SWEET DAYS OF ISAAC
Opened: Jan. 26, 1970, Eastside Playhouse.
485 performances.
Produced by Haila Stoddard, Mark Wright, Duane Wilder; directed by Word Baker.
Cast included: Austin Pendleton, Fredricka Weber, C. David Colson, The Zeitgeist.
Principal songs: The Last Sweet Days of Isaac; My Most Important Moments Go By; Love You Came to Me; I Want to Walk to San Francisco; Touching Your Hand Is Like Touching Your Mind.
Recorded Version
RCA LSO 1169 (O.C.).
Rock has seldom been used to better theatrical advantage.

SHELTER
Opened: Feb. 6, 1973, Golden Th.
31 performances.
Produced by Richard Fields & Peter Flood; directed by Austin Pendleton.
Cast included: Marcia Rodd, Terry Kiser, Susan Browning, Joanna Merlin, Tony Wells.
Principal songs: Welcome to a New World; It's Hard to Care; Don't Tell Me It's Forever; Run, Little Girl; Woke Up Today.

I'M GETTING MY ACT TOGETHER AND TAKING IT ON THE ROAD
Opened: June 14, 1978, Public Th.
1,165 performances.
Produced by N.Y. Shakespeare Festival (Joseph Papp); directed by Word Baker.
Cast included: Gretchen Cryer, Betty Aberlin, Joel Fabiani, Don Scardino, Margot Rose.
Principal songs: Natural High; Miss America; Dear Tom; Old Friend; Strong Woman Number; In a Simple Way I Love You; Happy Birthday.
Recorded Version
Columbia X 14885 (O.C.).
An excitingly personal cry of independence.

GARY GELD
Composer

PETER UDELL
Lyricist

PURLIE
Opened: March 15, 1970, Broadway Th.
688 performances.
Book by Ossie Davis, Philip Rose, Peter Udell.
Produced & directed by Rose; dances by Louis Johnson.
Cast included: Cleavon Little, Melba Moore, John Heffernan, Sherman Hemsley, Novella Nelson, Linda Hopkins, George Faison.
Principal songs: Walk Him Up the Stairs;

New-Fangled Preacher Man; Purlie; I Got
Love; First Thing Monday Mornin'; Down
Home; The World Is Comin' to a Start.
Recorded Version
Ampex 40101 (O.C.).

Though things slide a bit after the rousing
opener, Miss Moore shines brightly with "I
Got Love."

SHENANDOAH
Opened: Jan. 7, 1975, Alvin Th.
1,050 *performances.*
Book by James Lee Barrett, Philip Rose, Peter
Udell.
Produced by Peter Rose, Gloria & Louis Sher;
directed by Rose; dances by Robert Tucker.
Cast included: John Cullum, Penelope
Milford, Donna Theodore, Joel Higgins, Ted
Agress, David Russell, Chip Ford.
Principal songs: Raise the Flag of Dixie; I've
Heard It All Before; Why Am I Me?;
Meditation; We Make a Beautiful Pair;
Violets and Silverbells; Freedom; The Only
Home I Know.
Recorded Version
RCA ARL1 1019 (O.C.).

A flavorsome, well-sung collection.

ANGEL
Opened: May 10, 1978, Minskoff Th.
5 *performances.*
Book by Ketti Frings & Udell.
Produced by Philip Rose & Ellen Madison;
directed by Rose; dances by Robert Tucker.
Cast included: Frances Sternhagen, Fred
Gwynne, Don Scardino, Joel Higgins, Leslie
Ann Ray, Patricia Englund, Grace Carney.
Principal songs: Make a Little Sunshine; I
Got a Dream to Sleep On; Feelin' Loved;
How Do You Say Goodbye?; Tomorrow I'm
Gonna Be Old.

STEPHEN SCHWARTZ

Composer-lyricist

GODSPELL
Opened: May 17, 1971, Cherry Lane Th.
2,124 *performances.*
Opened: June 22, 1976, Broadhurst Th.
527 *performances.*
Book by John-Michael Tebelak.
Produced by Edgar Lansbury, Stuart Duncan,
Joseph Beruh; directed by Tebelak.
Cast included: Stephen Nathan, David
Haskell, Lamar Alford, Peggy Gordon.
Principal songs: Prepare Ye the Way of the
Lord; Save the People; Day by Day (lyric, St.
Richard of Chichester); Learn Your Lessons
Well; All for the Best; Light of the World;
Turn Back, O Man; We Beseech Thee.
Recorded Versions
Arista 4001 (O.C.).
Arista 4005 (F.V.). (1973).

The Gospel according to St. Matthew & St.
Schwartz.

PIPPIN
Opened: Oct. 23, 1972, Imperial Th.
1,944 *performances.*
Book by Roger O. Hirson, Bob Fosse
(uncredited).
Produced by Stuart Ostrow; directed by Fosse.
Cast included: Eric Berry, Jill Clayburgh,
Leland Palmer, Irene Ryan, Ben Vereen, John
Rubinstein, Ann Reinking.
Principal songs: Magic to Do; Corner of the
Sky; Simple Joys; No Time at All; Morning
Glow; On the Right Track; Extraordinary;
Love Song.
Recorded Version
Motown M760L (O.C.).

Schwartz has created a bright, infectious
score for this *Candide*-inspired saga.

THE MAGIC SHOW
Opened: May 28, 1974, Cort Th.
1,920 *performances.*
Book by Bob Randall.
Produced by Edgar Lansbury, Joseph Beruh,
Ivan Reitman; directed by Grover Dale.
Cast included: Doug Henning, Dale Soules,
Anita Morris, David Ogden Stiers.
Principal songs: Up to His Old Tricks; Lion
Tamer; West End Avenue; Before Your Very
Eyes; Style.
Recorded Version
Arista 9003 (O.C.).

An empty bag of tricks.

WORKING
Opened: May 14, 1978, 46th St. Th.
25 *performances.*
Book by Schwartz; music & lyrics also by
Craig Carnelia, Mary Rodgers, Susan
Birkenhead, James Taylor.
Produced by Stephen R. Friedman & Irwin
Meyer, with Joseph Harris; directed by
Schwartz; dances by Onna White.
Cast included: Susan Bigelow, Rex Everhart,
Arny Freeman, Robin Lamont, Bobo Lewis,
Patti LuPone, Lenora Nemetz.
Principal Schwartz songs: Neat to Be a
Newsboy; Fathers and Sons; It's an Art.
Recorded Version
Columbia JS 35411 (O.C.).

Studs Terkel's love of labor set to music.

Chapter Thirty-One
JIM JACOBS
Composer-lyricist

WARREN CASEY
Composer-lyricist

GREASE
Opened: Feb. 14, 1972, Eden Th.
3,388 *performances.*
Book by Jacobs & Casey.
Produced by Kenneth Waissman & Maxine
Fox; directed by Tom Moore; dances by
Patricia Birch.

Cast included: Barry Bostwick, Carole Demas, Adrienne Barbeau, Garn Stephens, Timothy Meyers, Don Billett.
Principal songs: Freddy, My Love; Greased Lightnin'; Look at Me, I'm Sandra Dee; We Go Together; It's Raining on Prom Night; Beauty School Dropout; Alone at a Drive-In Movie; Rock 'n Roll Party Queen.
Recorded Versions
MGM 1SE 34 (O.C.).
RSO 2-4002 (F.V.) (1978).
   The 2-record soundtrack retains all but 3 of the original songs & adds 9 others, both old & new.

CHARLIE SMALLS

Composer-lyricist

THE WIZ
Opened: Jan. 5, 1975, Majestic Th.
1,672 *performances.*
Book by William F. Brown, Sam Bobrick (uncredited).
Produced by Ken Harper; directed by Geoffrey Holder, Gilbert Moses (uncredited); dances by George Faison.
Cast included: Stephanie Mills, Hinton Battle, Ted Ross, Tiger Haynes, André DeShields; DeeDee Bridgewater, Mabel King.
Principal songs: He's the Wizard; Soon as I Go Home; Ease on Down the Road; Slide Some Oil to Me; Be a Lion; Don't Nobody Bring Me No Bad News; If You Believe; Home.
Recorded Versions
Atlantic SD 18137 (O.C.).
MCA 2-14000 (F.V.) (1978).
   The 2-record soundtrack—with Diana Ross, Nipsy Russell & Lena Horne—adds little of value to the galvanic original.

MARVIN HAMLISCH

Composer

A CHORUS LINE
Opened: April 15, 1975, Public Th.
101 *performances.*
Opened: July 25, 1975, Shubert Th.
Book by James Kirkwood & Nicholas Dante; lyrics by Edward Kleban.
Produced by N.Y. Shakespeare Festival (Joseph Papp); directed by Michael Bennett.
Cast included: Donna McKechnie, Carole (Kelly) Bishop, Patricia Lopez, Robert LuPone, Sammy Williams, Pamela Blair, Wayne Cilento, Patricia Garland.
Principal songs: I Hope I Get It; At the Ballet; Sing!; Nothing; The Music and the Mirror; One; What I Did for Love.
Recorded Version
Columbia PS 33581 (O.C.).
   Ably conveys the proper showbiz flavor.

THEY'RE PLAYING OUR SONG
Opened: Feb. 11, 1979, Imperial Th.

1,082 *performances.*
Book by Neil Simon; lyrics by Carole Bayer Sager.
Produced by Emanuel Azenberg; directed by Robert Moore; dances by Patricia Birch.
Cast: Robert Klein, Lucie Arnaz.
Principal songs: Fallin'; If He Really Knew Me; They're Playing Our Song; Just for Tonight; When You're in My Arms; Fill in the Words; Right.
Recorded Version
Casablanca NBLP 7141 (O.C.).
   Top of the charts on Broadway.

ELIZABETH SWADOS

Composer-lyricist

All lyrics by Miss Swados unless otherwise noted.

NIGHTCLUB CANTATA
Opened: Jan. 9, 1977, Top of the Gate.
145 *performances.*
Produced by Charles Hollerith Jr. & Rosita Sarnoff; directed by Miss Swados.
Cast included: Shelley Plimpton, Karen Evans, Rocky Greenberg, David Schechter, Mark Zagaeski, Elizabeth Swados.
Principal songs: Things I Didn't Know I Loved (words by Nazim Hikmet); Bird Lament; Ventriloquist and Dummy (words with Judith Fleisher); The Applicant (words by Sylvia Plath); Indecision; Dibarti (words by David Avidan); Are You With Me?; Waiting.

RUNAWAYS
Opened: Feb. 21, 1978, Public Th.
80 *performances.*
Opened: May 13, 1978, Plymouth Th.
267 *performances.*
Produced by N.Y. Shakespeare Festival (Joseph Papp); directed by Miss Swados.
Cast included: Trini Alverado, Jossie DeGuzman, Diane Lane, David Schechter, Evan Miranda, Nan-Lynn Nelson, Carlo Imperato, Bruce Hlibok, Karen Evans.
Principal songs: Every Now and Then; Find Me a Hero; No Lullabies for Luis; We Are Not Strangers; The Basketball Song; Revenge Song; Lullaby from Baby to Baby; Let Me Be a Kid; Enterprise.
Recorded Version
Columbia JS 35410 (O.C.).
   Grim, touching revelations of the homeless.

DISPATCHES
Opened: April 18, 1979, Public Th.
63 *performances.*
Words by Michael Herr.
Produced by N.Y. Shakespeare Festival (Joseph Papp); directed by Miss Swados.
Cast included: William Parry, Karen Evans, Paul McCrane, David Schechter, Rodney Hudson, Gedde Watanabe.
Principal songs: These Were the Faces;

Helicopter, Helicopter; Stoned in Saigon;
Tiger Lady; Take the Glamour Out of War;
This War Gets Old; Back in the World Now.

CAROL HALL

Composer-lyricist

THE BEST LITTLE WHOREHOUSE IN TEXAS

Opened: Apr. 17, 1978, Entermedia Th.
85 *performances.*
Opened: June 19, 1978, 46th St. Th.
1,584 *performances.*
Book by Larry L. King & Peter Masterson.
Produced by Universal Pictures (Stevie
Phillips); directed by Masterson & Tommy
Tune; dances by Tune.
Cast included: Carlin Glynn, Henderson
Forsythe, Delores Hall, Pamela Blair, Jay
Garner, Clinton Allmon.
Principal songs: Twenty Fans; A Li'l Ole Bitty
Pissant Country Place; Twenty-Four Hours of
Lovin'; Girl, You're a Woman; Texas Has a
Whorehouse in It; The Aggie Song; Bus from
Amarillo; Good Old Girl; Hard-Candy
Christmas.
Recorded Version
MCA 3049 (O.C.).
   Raunchy doings on the ranch.

INDEX

465